# By Peaceful Means

"David" by Ray Caron, 2018

# By Peaceful Means

*International Adjudication and Arbitration - Essays in Honour of David D. Caron*

*Edited by*

CHARLES N BROWER

JOAN E DONOGHUE

CIAN C MURPHY

CYMIE R PAYNE

ESMÉ R SHIRLOW

OXFORD
UNIVERSITY PRESS

# OXFORD
### UNIVERSITY PRESS

Great Clarendon Street, Oxford, OX2 6DP,
United Kingdom

Oxford University Press is a department of the University of Oxford.
It furthers the University's objective of excellence in research, scholarship,
and education by publishing worldwide. Oxford is a registered trade mark of
Oxford University Press in the UK and in certain other countries

Published in the United States of America by Oxford University Press
198 Madison Avenue, New York, NY 10016, United States of America

British Library Cataloguing in Publication Data
Data available

Library of Congress Control Number: 2023944466

ISBN 978–0–19–284808–6

DOI: 10.1093/oso/9780192848086.001.0001

Printed and bound by
CPI Group (UK) Ltd, Croydon, CR0 4YY

# Contents

## PART V.  LOOKING TO THE FUTURE

# Table of Cases

## INTERNATIONAL COURTS AND TRIBUNALS

## African Commission On European And Peoples Rights (ACmHPR)

## African Court On European And Peoples Rights (ACtHPR)

## East African Court Of Justice (EACJ)

## Economic Community Of West African States Court Of Justice (ECOWAS)

## United Nations Human Rights Committee (HRCttee)

## United Nations Human Rights Council (HRC)

## Inter-American Commission Of Human Rights (IACommHR)

## Inter-American Court Of Human Rights (IACtHR)

## International Centre For Settlement Of Investment Disputes (ICSID)

## International Chamber Of Commerce

## International Court Of Justice (ICJ)

## International Criminal Court

## International Criminal Tribunal For Rwanda (ICTR)

## International Criminal Tribunal For The Former Yugoslavia (ICTY)

## International Residual Mechanism For Criminal Tribunals (IRMCT)

## International Tribunal For The Law Of The Sea (ITLOS)

## Southern African Development Community (SADC)

## Permanent Court Of Arbitration (PCA)

## Permanent Court Of International Justice (PCIJ)

## United Nations Commission For International Trade Law (UNCITRAL)

# Table of Legislation

## NATIONAL INSTRUMENTS

# List of Abbreviations

| | |
|---|---|
| AAA | American Arbitration Association |
| ACDEG | African Charter on Democracy, Elections and Governance |
| ACEE | accessibility, credibility, effectiveness, and efficiency |
| ACHPR | African Charter on Human Rights and Peoples' Rights |
| ACHR | American Convention on Human Rights |
| ACICA | Australian Centre for International Commercial Arbitration |
| ACmHPR | African Commission on Human and Peoples' Rights |
| ADB | Asian Development Bank |
| ADR | alternative dispute resolution |
| AF | Additional Facility |
| AF AFR | Additional Facility Administrative and Financial Regulations |
| AF AR | Additional Facility Arbitration Rules |
| AF CR | Additional Facility Conciliation Rules |
| ALI | American Law Institute |
| AOSIS | Alliance of Small Island Developing States |
| ASIL | American Society of International Law |
| AU | African Union |
| BBNJ | biodiversity beyond national jurisdiction |
| BIT | bilateral investment treaty |
| BNFL | British Nuclear Fuels Limited |
| CCJ | Community Court of Justice |
| CCJE | Consultative Council of European Judges |
| CCS | Convention on the Continental Shelf |
| CEMAC | Central African Economic and Monetary Community |
| CEPEJ | European Commission for the Efficiency of Justice |
| CESCR | Committee of Economic Social and Cultural Rights Covenant |
| CETA | Comprehensive Economic and Trade Agreement |
| CHM | Common Heritage of Mankind |
| CIL | customary international law |
| CITES | Convention on International Trade in Endangered Species of Wild Fauna and Flora |
| CJEU | Court of Justice of the European Union |
| CLCS | Commission on the Limits of the Continental Shelf |
| CLS | Critical Legal Studies |
| cm | centimetres |
| CMATS | Certain Maritime Arrangements in the Timor Sea |
| CNSP | *Conseil National du Salut de Peuple* |
| COMESA | Common Market for Eastern and Southern Africa |
| CPC | Civil Procedure Code |
| CPPTP | Comprehensive and Progressive Agreement for Trans-Pacific Partnership |
| DDR | disarmament, demobilization, and reintegration |

| | |
|---|---|
| DRC | Democratic Republic of Congo |
| DR-CAFTA | Dominican Republic-Central America FTA |
| DSU | Dispute Settlement Understanding |
| EAC | East African Community |
| EACJ | East African Court of Justice |
| EALA | East African Legislative Assembly |
| ECOSOC | Economic and Social Council |
| ECHR | European Convention on Human Rights and Fundamental Freedoms |
| ECOWAS | Economic Community of West African States |
| ECT | Energy Charter Treaty |
| ECtHR | European Court of Human Rights |
| EECC | Ethiopia-Eritrea Claims Commission |
| EESRSP | Emergency Economic and Social Reunification Support Project |
| EEZ | exclusive economic zone |
| EFTA | European Free Trade Area |
| EIA | Environmental Impact Assessment |
| ERBD | European Bank for Reconstruction and Development |
| FAA | Foreign Arbitral Award |
| FAO | Food and Agriculture Organization of the UN |
| FCN | Friendship, Commerce, and Navigation |
| FET | fair and equitable treatment |
| FFR | fact-finding rules |
| FIDIC | International Federation of Consulting Engineers |
| FSIA | Foreign Sovereign Immunities Act |
| FTA | Free Trade Agreement |
| GAL-TAN | Green-Alternative-Libertarian and Traditional-Authoritarian-Nationalist |
| GATT | General Agreement on Tariffs and Trade |
| HIPC | heavily indebted poor country |
| HKIAC | Hong Kong International Arbitration Centre |
| HRCttee | Human Rights Committee |
| IACommHR | Inter-American Commission on Human Rights |
| IACtHR | Inter-American Court of Human Rights |
| IAM | independent accountability mechanism |
| IBRD | International Bank for Reconstruction and Development |
| ICC | International Criminal Court |
| ICCA | International Council for Commercial Arbitration |
| ICCPR | International Covenant on Civil and Political Rights |
| ICJ | International Court of Justice |
| ICs | international courts |
| ICSID | International Centre for Settlement of Investment Disputes |
| ICTR | International Criminal Tribunal for Rwanda |
| ICTY | International Criminal Tribunal for the former Yugoslavia |
| IDA | International Development Association |
| IDB | Inter-American Development Bank |
| IFC | International Finance Corporation |
| IIA | international investment agreement |
| ILA | International Law Association |
| ILC | International Law Commission |

| | |
|---|---|
| ILO | International Labour Organization |
| ILOAT | International Labour Organization Administrative Tribunal |
| IOIA | International Organizations Immunities Act |
| IPCC | Intergovernmental Panel on Climate Change |
| ISA | International Seabed Authority |
| ISDS | investor–state dispute settlement |
| ITLOS | International Tribunal for the Law of the Sea |
| IUSCT | Iran-US Claims Tribunal |
| IWC | International Whaling Commission |
| JPDA | Joint Petroleum Development Agency |
| LCIA | London Court of International Arbitration |
| LNG | liquid natural gas |
| LOSC | Convention on the Law of the Sea |
| masl | metres above sea level |
| MDBs | multilateral development banks |
| MFN | most favoured nation |
| MIDS | Masters in International Dispute Settlement |
| MIGA | Multilateral Investment Guarantee Agency |
| MOX | mixed-oxide fuel |
| MPEPIL | *Max Planck Encyclopedia of Public International Law* |
| MPIL | *Max Planck Encyclopedia of International Law* |
| MUTP | Mumbai Urban Transport Project |
| NACEC | North American Commission for Environmental Cooperation |
| NAFTA | North American Free Trade Agreement |
| NGO | non-governmental organizations |
| nm | nautical miles |
| OAU | Organization of African Unity |
| OCS | outer continental shelf |
| OSPAR | Convention for the Protection of the Marine Environment of the North-East Atlantic |
| OTP | Office of the Prosecutor |
| PAD | Project Appraisal Document |
| PCA | Permanent Court of Arbitration |
| PCIJ | Permanent Court of International Justice |
| PIF | Pacific Islands Forum |
| PIPA | Phoenix Islands Protected Area |
| PPM | Project-affected People's Mechanism |
| PSC | Peace and Security Council |
| REC | regional economic community |
| REIO | regional economic integration organization |
| RETF | Recipient Executed Trust Fund |
| SADC | Southern African Development Community |
| SAR | Special Administrative Region |
| SATRC | South African Truth and Reconciliation Commission |
| SBT | Southern Bluefin Tuna |
| SIAC | Singapore International Arbitration Centre |
| SIMC | Singapore International Mediation Centre |
| SROC | Special Report on the Ocean and Cryosphere in a Changing Climate |

| | |
|---|---|
| TAC | total allowable catch |
| TPA | Trade Promotion Agreement |
| TSC | Convention on the Territorial Sea and the Contiguous Zone |
| TSERO | Transitional Support for Economic Recovery Grant |
| UKEA | United Kingdom Environment Agency |
| UN | United Nations |
| UNCC | United Nations Compensation Commission |
| UNCITRAL | United Nations Commission for International Trade Law |
| UNCLOS | United Nations Convention on the Law of the Sea |
| UNECE | United Nations Economic Commission for Europe |
| UNGA | United Nations General Assembly |
| UN HRC | UN Human Rights Council |
| UNTAET | United Nations Transitional Authority in East Timor |
| UNTS | United Nations Treaty Series |
| USMCA | United States-Mexico-Canada Agreement |
| VCCR | Vienna Convention on Consular Relations |
| VCLOT | Vienna Convention on the Law of Treaties |
| WP | Working Paper |
| WTO | World Trade Organization |

# List of Authors

**Karen J Alter** is Professor of Law at Northwestern University, Illinois, USA, and iCourts, University of Copenhagen, Denmark.

**Mahnoush H Arsanjani** is President of the World Bank Administrative Tribunal and previously served for thirty-two years in the United Nations Legal Office.

**Bogdan Aurescu** is Professor of International Law, University of Bucharest, Romania; Member of the International Law Commission; and a former Foreign Minister of Romania.

**Randi Ayman** is Senior Research Fellow (PhD), at Max Planck Institute for International Procedural Law, Luxembourg; and a former ICSID Legal Counsel.

**George A Bermann** is the Jean Monnet Professor of European Union Law; and Walter Gelhorn Professor of Law at Columbia University, New York, USA.

**Catalina Turriago Bettancourt** is Legal Contract Manager at Nakisa in Montreal, Canada.

**Andrea K Bjorklund** is Full Professor and L Yves Fortier Chair in International Arbitration and International Commercial Law, McGill University, Canada.

**Morgan Brock-Smith** is an Associate at White & Case LLP, New York, USA.

**Edith Brown Weiss** is University Professor Emerita at Georgetown University, Washington DC, USA, and former Chairperson, Inspection Panel, World Bank.

**Lee M Caplan** is a partner at Arent Fox LLP, USA; and was previously attorney-adviser in the Office of the Legal Adviser at the US Department of State.

**Kathleen Claussen** is a Professor of Law at Georgetown Law, and former Legal Counsel, Permanent Court of Arbitration.

**John R Crook** is Professorial Lecturer in Law at George Washington University, Washington DC, USA.

**Donald Francis Donovan** is an Independent Arbitrator and Member, Arbitration Chambers; and previously Co-Chair of the International Dispute Resolution and Public International Law Groups, Debevoise & Plimpton LLP.

**Malgosia Fitzmaurice** is Professor of Public International Law at Queen Mary, University of London, United Kingdom.

**Hannah R Garry** is Clinical Professor of Law and Founding Director of the International Human Rights Clinic, at the University of Southern California, USA.

**Tom Ginsburg** is the Leo Spitz Distinguished Service Professor of International Law and Professor of Political Science at the University of Chicago, USA.

**O Thomas Johnson** is a member of the Iran-United States Claims Tribunal; and Adjunct Professor of Law at Columbia University, New York, USA.

**Meg Kinnear** is Vice President of the World Bank Group and Secretary General of ICSID.

**Anna Kirk**, PhD, is a barrister at Bankside Chambers at Auckland, New Zealand, and Singapore.

**Nicholas Maisel** is a juris doctorate candidate, University of Southern California Gould School of Law, USA.

**Donald McRae** is Professor Emeritus, University of Ottawa, Canada.

**Natalie Y Morris-Sharma** is Government Legal Counsel in the Attorney General's Chambers of Singapore.

**Sean D Murphy** is the Manatt/Ahn Professor of International Law, George Washington University, Washington DC, USA; and was a Member of the International Law Commission (2012–2022).

**Nilufer Oral** is Director, Centre for International Law, National University of Singapore; and Member of the International Law Commission, Istanbul Bilgi University, Turkey.

**Federico Ortino** is Professor of Law at King's College London, United Kingdom.

**Bernard H Oxman** is the Richard A. Hausler Professor of Law, at the University of Miami, USA.

**Mikael Rask Madsen** is Professor of European Law and Integration, and Director of iCourts, University of Copenhagen, Denmark.

**Lucy Reed** is an Independent Arbitrator and Member, Arbitration Chambers.

**W Michael Reisman** is the Myers S McDougal Professor of International Law, Yale University, Connecticut, USA.

**Yuval Shany** is the Hersch Lauterpacht Chair in Public International Law, Hebrew University of Jerusalem, Israel; and previously served as member of the UN Human Rights Committee (2013–2020).

**Jeremy K Sharpe** is an international arbitrator and Lecturer in Law and Senior Fellow at the International Claims and Reparations Project (ICRP) of the Columbia Law School, New York, USA.

**Elizabeth Sheargold** is Senior Lecturer, Monash University, Australia.

**Philippa Webb** is Professor of Public International Law at King's College London, United Kingdom, and a barrister at 20 Essex Chambers.

**Sir David AR Williams** KNZM, KC is a barrister at Bankside Chambers, Auckland, New Zealand, and Singapore.

**Abdulqawi A Yusuf** is Judge, International Court of Justice; and previously President of the Court (2018–2021).

# 1

# A Multitude, in Celebration of David D Caron

"to bring about by peaceful means, and in conformity with the principles of justice and international law, adjustment or settlement of international disputes or situations which might lead to a breach of the peace ...".

Charter of the United Nations
Article 1, Purposes of the United Nations

## 1. Introduction

David Caron was a scholar, an attorney and barrister, and a professor, judge, and arbitrator. For each of the Editors, and most of the authors of this volume, he was also a very dear friend. For all, he was an inspiration and an example. The purpose of this volume is to celebrate him and to reflect on his work, and on the fields of law in which he laboured.[1] Caron had a wide range of intellectual interests within the law. Environmental law and the law of the sea captured his interest and laid an early claim to his heart, particularly following his training at the Coast Guard Academy and service as a Coast Guard officer, including as a Navigation and Diving Officer on an icebreaker in the Arctic. His formative work in the law, however, was in dispute settlement, and international dispute settlement in particular. It is on this field that this volume centres.

Walt Whitman's *Song of Myself* contains the exclamation "I am large, I contain multitudes".[2] It was a claim that David Caron himself could have made, were it not for his tendency to self-deprecate rather than self-exalt. A consequence of that vastness is that no single volume can adequately capture all his interests or offer a home to all those who might join in celebration.

Nevertheless, in what follows, there is legal work that is doctrinal, sociolegal, theoretical, historical, and often personal. Given that the volume is related to international adjudication and arbitration, and honours a scholar whose roots are in environmental law and the law of the sea, our contributors' examples naturally return to those fields more often than others.[3] Nevertheless, encompassed within this volume are chapters

---

[1] For the most complete professional biography, see "In Memoriam David D. Caron (1952–2018)" (2018) 112 (3) American Journal of International Law 452–59.

[2] Walt Whitman 'Song of Myself', in *Leaves of Grass*, Penguin Classics Edition (London 2017).

[3] Insofar as it is a guide to anything, aside from the typical celebrations of family, friends, and colleagues, David Caron's brief Twitter feed returned most often to climate change and the sea. There were also nuggets of wisdom, including the sadly prescient quotation from *Good Omens* to mark the passing of author Terry Pratchett: "Don't think of it as dying, said Death. Just think of it as leaving early to avoid the rush."

*A Multitude, in Celebration of David D Caron* In: *By Peaceful Means*. Edited by: Charles N Brower, Joan E Donoghue, Cian C Murphy, Cymie R Payne and Esmé R Shirlow, Oxford University Press. © Several Contributors 2024.
DOI: 10.1093/oso/9780192848086.003.0001

that engage a diversity of topics spanning several of Caron's many fields of research, teaching, and practice.

The purpose of this introduction is twofold. First, it aims to highlight the depth and breadth of the chapters that constitute this volume, including to draw out their interconnections and relationship to the theme of international dispute settlement by peaceful means. Second, the introduction places the chapters into a conversation with Caron's own work on these and other themes. In doing so, it continues conversations that Caron started through his research and in discussions with many of the scholars and practitioners contributing to this volume, which has been penned in celebration of his life and work.

## 2. Lessons from the History of Dispute Settlement

As Caron himself noted, "To go forward, it is often wise, and sometimes necessary, to go back."[4] Several of this volume's contributors take up this challenge to explore the history of international dispute settlement in order to identify cross-cutting themes and lessons for its future.

John Crook's exploration of the Bering Straits arbitration engages an early example of international environmental law at work. Arbitration procedures may be particularly valued by disputing parties in such claims, in light of parties' capacity to adapt the powers of the tribunal to fit the unique features of their dispute. The Bering Straits tribunal was, for instance, empowered to develop regulations for the protection of seals which it could recommend to the parties for adoption and application. In its exercise of this power, the tribunal nevertheless provides a useful historical example of something Caron often spoke of: the tension that may arise between a tribunal's jurisdiction and its wider social function, which the tribunal may be procedurally or constitutionally incapable of meeting.[5] As Crook notes, "experience quickly demonstrated the weakness of the Tribunal's regime", which had not been based upon sound scientific evidence regarding the reasons for the declining seal population. Ultimately, this meant that, as Crook explores in detail in his chapter, "[a]bout the best that can be said for the Paris Award is that it was a victory for arbitration and the pacific settlement of disputes—not for the seals".[6]

Caron highlighted similar tensions when analysing the function and performance of the International Whaling Commission (IWC) in relation to the protection of whales. While for some states the IWC's legitimacy rested on its capacity to provide

---

[4] David D Caron, "War and International Adjudication: Reflections on the 1899 Peace Conference" (2000) 94 (1) American Journal of International Law 4–30, 5.

[5] See, for instance, Caron's analysis of whether an international claims process in relation to Iraq's actions in Kuwait could "provide some relief to the victims of this invasion" whilst also "bring[ing] significant additional pressure to bear on President Saddam Hussein": David D Caron, "Iraq and the Force of Law: Why Give a Shield of Immunity? (1991) 85 (1) American Journal of International Law 89–92, 89.

[6] Bailey, *A Diplomatic History of the American People* (Pearson College 1980) 413.

"expert scientific resource management" of whale stocks,[7] for others its role derived from ideological goals related to the protection of the "sanctity" of whales as a species.[8] With such illustrative examples, both Caron and Crook's analyses highlight that the factual scenarios from which international organizations and tribunals emerge can be marked by sharp divisions of interests. The framing of their functions, mandates, and activities—as well as the role of science and politics therein—can significantly impact their effectiveness and also perceptions of their legitimacy by key stakeholders. At the same time, such analysis highlights the danger of unreflective acceptance of appeals to science and conservation-related goals by participants in such regimes.[9] Collectively, they demonstrate the necessity of equipping international organizations and tribunals with the necessary mandates, procedural powers, and institutional flexibilities to react to new scientific consensus and political priorities as they emerge over the lifetime of the relevant body.

Kathleen Claussen continues this historical theme in her chapter, which focuses on how the 1899 Hague Peace Conference and the Permanent Court of Arbitration were portrayed in contemporaneous press reports in the United States (US). As Claussen argues, the prominent and positive coverage of these international developments in US newspapers facilitated a diffusion within civil society of popular support for international institutions. Drawing lessons for contemporary international law, Claussen highlights how today's international institutions face a sustained need for similar public engagement similar to these very first global institutions, whilst at the same time acknowledging the different context within which this information is communicated, transmitted, and absorbed.

Public engagement and transparency in the activities of international institutions, as Caron recognized in his work, cut two ways. On the one hand, and as illustrated in Claussen's chapter, such engagement and transparency may assist local populations to grasp the importance of international law and institutions and to identify more closely with their activities. On the other hand, there are also important benefits for the establishment and work of international institutions themselves.[10] Indeed, "[t]he relationship of the force of public opinion to the statute of the institution holds true for all courts, but it is particularly true for international courts, which lack the coercive force of municipal tribunals and at times need the force of public opinion to be effective".[11]

---

[7] David D Caron, "The International Whaling Commission and the North Atlantic Marine Mammal Commission: The Institutional Risks of Coercion in Consensual Structures" (1995) 89 (1) American Journal of International Law 89 (1), 154–74, 155.

[8] ibid 155.

[9] As Caron and his co-author Stephen Minas explore in relation to marine protected areas, for instance, states may be accused of deploying such "objective" rhetoric in order to serve hidden agendas: David D Caron and Stephen Minas, "Conservation or Claim? The Motivations for Recent Marine Protected Areas" in Harry N Scheiber, Nilufer Oral, and Moon-Sang Kwon (eds), Ocean Law Debates (Brill 2018) 529–52.

[10] See, for example, Caron, "War and International Adjudication" (n 4) 16 ("Although the delegates for the most part viewed 'organized public opinion' as a distraction from the work at hand, they invoked that opinion in support of the need for action by the conference and particularly in rebuttal to Germany's opposition to arbitration. Both White and William Hull credit the popular demand for an arbitration court as playing a significant role in persuading Germany to back down from its opposition to the idea.")

[11] Caron, "War and International Adjudication" (n 4) 25.

Different forms of transparency will be required to achieve these diverse functions.[12] As Claussen's chapter illustrates, and as Shirlow and Caron highlight, for instance, increases in public understanding of international bodies—and support for their activities—may depend upon the creation and release of different types of information about their activities than would be required if the goals of transparency are to permit disputing parties to hold adjudicators accountable for their decisions, or to understand the legal basis for those decisions in advance of preparing for future disputes. Thus, transparency as a multifaceted concept demands the release of different types of information and the engagement of diverse audiences and stakeholders.[13]

The task of communicating information about the activities of international courts and tribunals domestically was one taken seriously by Caron in his role as an adjudicator. Many of the investment awards in which Caron was involved as arbitrator, for instance, include concisely crafted "executive summaries" designed to acquaint government officials and even lay readers with the substance of the award. Such summaries show Caron's awareness that there may be audiences for arbitral awards which lack familiarity with the technical details of the law being applied. This sense of mission was also central to his work at the American Society of International Law (ASIL). As ASIL President, Caron was keen to broaden and deepen the Society's engagement with US lawyers. While the Society's Annual Meeting takes place in Washington DC each Spring, it was Caron's innovation that led to the Mid-Year Meeting bringing the Society together in law schools across the country.[14]

Hannah Garry, with Morgan Brock-Smith and Nicholas Maisel, carry forward some of these threads. In their chapter, the Ethiopia-Eritrea Claims Commission (EECC), a body which Caron appeared before as an advocate, is seen through the lens of transitional justice. They acknowledge a "thickening"[15] of the field in the decades since its coalescence into existence. What, then, can a single tribunal do in the face of the broad demands made of transitional justice? In the case of the EECC the results were mixed. Individuals, in particular, had limited involvement with the Commission—a perhaps inevitable consequence of its institutional design and legal procedures. The authors conclude that

> it is questionable whether the EECC played much of a role in helping to achieve peace and non-recurrence in the region, particularly given that the process failed to re-establish socio-economic rights and development for the affected Tigrayan populations on both sides of the border in the aftermath of the conflict.

---

[12] Esmé Shirlow and David D Caron, "The Multiple Forms of Transparency in International Investment Arbitration: Their Implications, and their Limits" in Thomas Schultz and Federico Ortino, *The Oxford Handbook of International Arbitration* (Oxford University Press 2020).

[13] ibid 488.

[14] Fittingly, it was to this part of the Society's work that the Fund set up in his name was dedicated. See <http://www.asil.org/dcf>. Please note: throughout this book, all websites were last accessed on 28 February 2023.

[15] Kieran McEvoy, "Beyond Legalism: Towards a Thicker Understanding of Transitional Justice" (2007) 34 Journal of Law & Society 411

This demonstrates the weight of expectations that can burden the shoulders of those who sit within the hearing room.

These questions, related to whether claims commissions are capable of achieving broader goals, including by providing justice to individuals affected by armed conflict, also animated much of Caron's own writing. His considerations included the compensatory functions of such commissions, their role in precluding overlapping claims in multiple fora, their function in furthering international law, as well as broader social and political functions associated with the attainment of peace and broader notions of justice.[16]

Caron brought a deep understanding to his analysis from his clerkships with Judges Richard Mosk and Charles Brower at the Iran-US Claims Tribunal (IUSCT)[17] and his subsequent roles as advisor on the creation of the United Nations Compensation Commission (UNCC) and UNCC Commissioner for the "precedent panel". In a 2002 article in the *European Journal of International Law*, for instance, Caron and co-author Brian Morris explored the functions of the UNCC as a "mechanism established to provide a measure of practical justice to those who suffered damage as a direct result of Iraq's invasion and occupation of Kuwait".[18] In a subsequent book chapter, Caron appraised the various phases of the UNCC's work, observing that its resolution of humanitarian claims meant that "[j]ust about every person seriously hurt by the conflict in the region received some assistance in getting back on his or her feet".[19] Picking up similar themes to those explored by Claussen in her chapter, Caron noted that "[a]rguably, the UN missed an important opportunity to heighten global appreciation ... by not making this success [of the UNCC] more widely known".[20]

Caron—as was characteristic in much of his writing—nevertheless viewed the success of the UNCC in a nuanced way. He noted, for instance, that its "major failing" was to omit environmental claims from the "urgent and humanitarian side of the docket" despite their ongoing nature, to address them instead in a second phase of the proceedings.[21] Yet despite such failings, Caron derived lessons from the UNCC for future environmental disputes. Caron characterized the UNCC's approach as recognizing the general international community's interest in the environment, "a simply astounding

---

[16] See, for example, David D Caron, "International Claims and Compensation Bodies" in Cesare Romano, Karen Alter, and Yuval Shany (eds), *Oxford Handbook of International Adjudication* (Oxford University Press 2013); David D Caron, "Fifth Annual Charles N. Brower Lecture on International Dispute Resolution: The Multiple Functions of International Courts and the Singular Task of the Adjudicator" (2017) 111 *Proceedings of the ASIL Annual Meeting* 231-240.

[17] David D Caron and John R Crook (eds), *The Iran-United States Claims Tribunal and the Process of International Claims Resolution* (Transnational Publishers 2000).

[18] David D Caron and Brian Morris, "The UN Compensation Commission: Practical Justice, Not Retribution" (2002) 13(1) European Journal of International Law 183–99, 185.

[19] David D Caron, "The United Nations Compensation Commission: Understanding an Institution and the Three Phases of its Work" in Christopher S Gibson , Trevor M Rajah, and Timothy J Feighery (eds), *War, Reparation and the UN Compensation Commission: Designing Compensation After Conflict* (Oxford University Press 2015) xxxii. See, also, David D Caron, The United Nations Compensation Commission for Claims Arising out of the 1991 Gulf War: The "Arising Prior to" Decision (2005) 14(2) Journal of Transnational Law & Policy 217

[20] Caron, "The United Nations Compensation Commission" (n 19) xxxii.

[21] Caron, "The United Nations Compensation Commission for Claims Arising out of the 1991 Gulf War" (n 19) 228.

achievement," which "requires a point of perspective shift from the classic interstate viewpoint to one where the interest of relevant communities in the health and sustainability of a damaged environment is the focus".[22] As he concluded, the work of the UNCC highlighted that:

> Compensation can be not only about money, but also the reconstruction of an area. Through both innovation and rigor, the UNCC facilitated the environmental reconstruction of entire region. Institutionally, the UNCC has opened a new era of claims resolution process in the areas of the environment and public health.[23]

As Caron elaborated, claims processes concerning the environment face special difficulties—particularly where they concern environmental degradation as a result of armed conflict.[24] Even in such circumstances, however, international courts and tribunals may have a vital role to play, and their procedures and substantive findings a key contribution to make, towards environmental remediation and reconstruction efforts.[25]

## 3. Institutions and Institutional Actors

The theme of institutions and institutional actors pervaded much of Caron's academic research. As he wrote:

> International courts and tribunals, like all courts and tribunals, are institutions. And although legal scholars appropriately may isolate courts from the surrounding political context as they study the jurisprudence of a court or tribunal, it is quite artificial to examine the court as an organic institution without reference to the functions it serves and political context of which it is an integral part.[26]

The early spark for this work was Caron's realization, as he set off for The Hague and the IUSCT immediately after law school, that there was no book to which he could turn to explore how the Tribunal did what it did. After his initial discovery of this gap in the literature, Caron frequently returned in his work to consider connections between the design of adjudicative institutions, the actors that work in them, and their functions

---

[22] David D Caron, "The Profound Significance of the UNCC for the Environment" in Cymie R Payne and Peter H Sand (eds), *Gulf War Reparations and the UN Compensation Commission: Environmental Liability* (Oxford University Press 2011) 268, 275.

[23] David D Caron, "Finding Out what the Oceans Claim: The 1991 Gulf War, the Marine Environment and the United Nations Compensation Commission" in David D Caron and Harry N Scheiber, *Bringing New Law to Ocean Waters* (Brill 2004) 393–415, 415.

[24] See, especially, ibid 393–415.

[25] See, for an illustration of the determination of such issues in more recent international proceedings: *Certain Activities Carried Out by Nicaragua in the Border Area (Costa Rica v Nicaragua)*, Compensation, Judgment, ICJ Reports 2018, 15 (referencing the awards of the United Nations Compensation Commission).

[26] David D Caron, "Towards a Political Theory of International Courts and Tribunals" (2007) 24 Berkeley Journal of International Law 401, 421.

and impacts. In writing about the IUSCT, for instance, Caron observed that "a simple inquiry into the legal 'nature' of an international arbitral process is too undefined because any one of several aspects could be emphasized".[27]

In an attempt to add nuance to such enquiries, Caron's writings provide several useful frameworks for categorizing the implications of different design choices for the work of international adjudicative bodies, and the functions that they serve within the international legal system. He explored, for instance, the impact of design choices related to whether a body is a "community" or "party-" originated institution,[28] or one with a retrospective or prospective mandate.[29] He also explored the role of dynamism in the life of such institutions, noting the necessity of capturing the reality "that initial design is a consequence of politics, and that that political contest can continue in further rounds both within the space created and in efforts to redraw the bounds of the space".[30]

Yuval Shany's chapter in this book engages with this nexus between law and politics to consider the criticisms of politicization that have been levelled against many international institutions in recent years. As Shany explores, the connections between law and politics mean that international institutions cannot remain entirely insulated from the actors, environments, and broader political objectives that they are set up to support and/or serve. Shany's chapter illuminates various goals for international courts and various criteria for evaluating their operations. He suggests that international courts may be able to take into account political considerations in a way that does not undermine their legitimacy and effectiveness, including to highlight the flexibilities inherent within international law and adjudication that may assist international courts and tribunals to balance competing demands.

Caron's work addressed similar concerns related to how the disparate goals for international institutions come to impact appraisals of their legitimacy and effectiveness. He focused on various examples—from the Security Council[31] to specific international dispute settlement bodies[32]—to highlight how such appraisals inevitably focus not

[27] David D Caron, "The Nature of the Iran-United States Claims Tribunal and the Evolving Structure of International Dispute Resolution" (1990) 84 American Journal of International Law 104, 106.

[28] As Caron highlighted, for instance, there are various implications of a court or tribunal being created by a community as opposed to the disputing parties that will appear before it: "Most importantly, the institution exists for the ends of the community, not the ends of the parties. This ownership difference shifts control of the institution's work away from the parties. This shift can be seen, for example, in terms of the question for who does the judge or arbitrator believes themselves to be working? Members of a party-originated tribunal believe themselves to be working for the parties, while judges within a community-originated institution believe themselves to be working for that community. This perspective is reflected in the system of ethics applicable to, and oaths taken by, the members of the tribunal or court." Caron, "Towards a Political Theory of International Courts and Tribunals" (n 26) 404.

[29] Caron highlighted, for example, the potential for retrospective institutions to be particularly path dependent in their approach to both procedural and substantive issues, as compared to a prospective institution which may be "more concerned with ... applying norms of justice as they evolve over time": ibid 404.

[30] ibid 411.

[31] David D Caron, "The Legitimacy of the Collective Authority of the Security Council" (1993) 87 (4) The American Journal of International Law 552.

[32] See, especially, Caron, "Towards a Political Theory of International Courts and Tribunals" (n 26) 401; David D Caron, "Investor State Arbitration: Strategic and Tactical Perspectives on Legitimacy" (2008) 32 Suffolk Transnational Law Review 513.

only on "how well a given institution serves its constituted ends, but also how well it serves the unstated purposes".[33] While an institution's reputation may thus appear to stem from "rather intangible factors",[34] this opacity can at least be partially addressed by bringing such diverse purposes to light, designing institutions to ensure that they are adapted to meet those purposes, and appraising the performance of institutions in respect of those (attainable) purposes on an ongoing basis. Such analysis is necessary to ensure that the design, criticism, and reform of international law and institutions targets institutional, procedural, and substantive laws and frameworks towards achieving the desired goals of relevant stakeholders.[35]

In engaging the institutional features of international dispute settlement, Caron also frequently highlighted the role of key personnel involved in the settlement of international disputes.[36] Two chapters in this volume develop this theme, with their focus upon the adjudicators and tribunal secretaries engaged in the settlement of international disputes.

Lucy Reed's chapter considers how adjudicators and arbitrators go about their work as professionals and, in particular, further develops the David Caron Rule of X.[37] Reed notes that Caron was alive to the "singular task" of such professionals: the "judicial task" of resolving disputes.[38] However, many of them have several singular tasks, insofar as they may have multiple appointments. The David Caron Rule of X is a rule of self-discipline, to be imposed (if at all) by an individual on themselves, taking into account their own circumstances. Reed's chapter broadens consideration of possible applications of the Rule of X (eg to Judges ad hoc at the International Court of Justice (ICJ)) and explores potential intellectual roots in classical literature. Reed's chapter supports and reinforces a view that changes in how particular individuals approach appointments may themselves produce broader, systemic, impacts. As Caron himself observed, application of the Rule of X may "reinforce a virtuous circle: less cases in the hands of a few, and a few cases in the hands of many, with new arbitrators rising from more diverse backgrounds".[39]

David Williams and Anna Kirk consider a different, albeit related, role: that of tribunal secretaries. A common appointee in dispute settlement, in particular in complex cases, a "secretary" or "assistant" to a tribunal is usually a more junior lawyer whose task is akin to that of a judicial clerk. Williams and Kirk address a debate that flared most brightly when Russia sought to challenge the outcome of the *Yukos* arbitration, in part on the basis that the tribunal secretary had effectively been a fourth arbitrator.

---

[33] Caron, "Towards a Political Theory of International Courts and Tribunals" (n 26) 410.

[34] David D Caron, "Reputation and Reality in the ICSID Annulment Process: Understanding the Distinction between Annulment and Appeal" (2014) 7 (1) ICSID Review 21, 21.

[35] David D Caron and Esmé Shirlow, "Dissecting Backlash: The Unarticulated Causes of Backlash" in Andreas Føllesdal and Geir Ulfstein (eds), *The Judicialization of International Law: A Mixed Blessing?* (Oxford University Press 2018)

[36] See, especially, David D Caron and others (eds), *Practising Virtue: Inside International Arbitration* (Oxford University Press 2015) 379–97.

[37] David D Caron, "Arbitration and the Rule of X" Opening Lecture to the 2017–2018 MIDS Academic Year, 28 September 2017 (Geneva).

[38] See, further, Caron, "Fifth Annual Charles N. Brower Lecture on International Dispute Resolution" (n 16).

[39] Caron, "Arbitration and the Rule of X" (n 37).

In their consideration of the role of tribunal secretaries and assistants, Williams and Kirk's analysis also points to a recurring theme in this volume: the parts played by party consent and transparency for the legitimization of arbitral decisions and international dispute settlement more generally.

David Caron's work and practice paid significant attention to both themes.[40] In relation to transparency, for example, Caron's entry into the fray gave expression to a tendency that might appear contrarian but was instead intellectual and discursive. On occasion, when a debate on the law or practice seemed to him to coalesce, or perhaps stagnate, around an easy consensus, Caron would seek to stir some life back into it with a view that would problematize that consensus and lay bare deeper complexity. In "Regulating Opacity: Shaping How Institutions Think" Caron set out to interrogate the debate on transparency through the lens of its antithesis: opacity.[41] As Caron highlighted, opacity in the deliberations of arbitral tribunals is necessary to allow them to discharge their function of deciding disputes in accordance with international law. Such an impulse nevertheless contrasts with attempts to open more of international arbitration to outside view. However, as Caron highlighted, "when a measure of opacity is functionally required, there are regulatory devices other than transparency available to mitigate the possible dangers of such opacity".[42] These include procedural rules that regulate who is permitted to participate in a tribunal's deliberations, what may serve as the basis for the tribunal's decision and the law to be applied in that decision, the requirement that the tribunal provide written reasons to support its decision, and rules around voting in deliberations and individual and dissenting opinions. In this sense, procedures in international dispute settlement may be seen as interconnected. Diverse procedures can be deployed collectively (or in the alternative) to support institutions and tribunals to achieve diverse goals associated with international dispute settlement.

Meg Kinnear and Randi Ayman's chapter picks up on the necessity of balancing diverse objectives through a matrix of procedural innovations, by reference to the newly adopted Additional Facility Rules of the International Centre for Settlement of Investment Disputes (ICSID). Their chapter provides a snapshot of the structure of these Rules, noting the recent ICSID amendment process that has expanded access to the Rules and modified and aligned approaches under the Rules to key procedures in ICSID conciliation and arbitration proceedings. As Kinnear and Ayman note, the amendment process has also resulted in the creation of standalone Fact-Finding and Mediation Rules, outside ICSID's Additional Facility framework. The authors highlight how these amended and new procedural frameworks interact with the goals of the ongoing ISDS reform agenda, whilst also positioning ICSID to deliver tailored dispute settlement services into the future.

---

[40] See, for example, on the role of consent in the interpretation of most-favoured-nation clauses in investment treaties: David D Caron and Esmé Shirlow, "Most Favoured Nation Treatment—Substantive Protection" in M Kinnear and others (eds), *Building International Investment Law: The First 50 Years of ICSID* (Wolters Kluwer 2015).

[41] Caron and Shirlow, "The Multiple Forms of Transparency in International Investment Arbitration" (n 12).

[42] David D Caron, "Regulating Opacity: Shaping How Tribunals Think" in Caron and others (eds), *Practising Virtue* (n 36) 379–97.

In her chapter, Natalie Y Morris-Sharma engages with another recent key development in the landscape of international dispute settlement: the drafting, conclusion, and entry into force of the United Nations Convention on International Settlement Agreements Resulting from Mediation (Singapore Convention). As Morris-Sharma details, this treaty offers an enforcement framework for mediation that is comparable to what the New York Convention offers for arbitration. In this vein, Morris-Sharma explores the similarities and differences between the two treaties and the interactions between them, before exploring the Singapore Convention's own significance for the promotion of mediation as a distinct form of international dispute settlement.

Judge Abdulqawi Yusuf's chapter offers a regional perspective on this theme, examining the development, growth, and role of judicial institutions for the peaceful settlement of inter-state disputes in Africa. The chapter brings into focus a range of such bodies, including five courts and tribunals established by regional African economic communities and the judicial institutions connected to the African Union. In addition to discussing their development and the cases brought before them to date, the chapter also notes the common challenges encountered by these institutions and the efforts that have been taken to overcome those challenges. As Judge Yusuf notes, the key challenges encountered by these arbitral and judicial institutions are twofold, stemming from (i) their underutilization by the states parties to them, and (ii) their need to resist pressures from member states, including by issuing "assertive" and "bold" judgments particularly in the interpretation of the scope of their jurisdiction under their founding treaties. Such challenges are not region-specific, and apply to varying degrees to other international courts and tribunals. In this sense, Judge Yusuf's chapter holds broad resonance and lessons for international dispute settlement in other settings.

Sean Murphy's chapter considers the role of creativity in dispute resolution related to the international law of the sea. Murphy canvasses the promise for such creativity under the UN Convention on the Law of the Sea (UNCLOS), including in relation to the modes of dispute resolution and scope of issues subject to dispute resolution under the Convention. He also highlights the importance of the room left for creativity under the Convention to deal with emerging and pressing issues, including sea level rise as a result of climate change. In appraising these elements of creativity in the design of the UNCLOS dispute settlement framework, Murphy also cautions against too much creativity, particularly insofar as it may provide a basis for potential overreach by those empowered to settle disputes under the terms of the Convention. As Murphy concludes, creativity is necessary and, where it is integrated appropriately into the design of international dispute settlement mechanisms, can also be beneficial to the system as a whole.

In her chapter, Edith Brown Weiss examines the mechanisms that have been created to hold international organizations themselves accountable for their activities. Brown Weiss focusses in particular on the Independent Accountability Mechanisms created by all except two of the multilateral development banks, using the Inspection Panel of the World Bank to illustrate the role and impact of such mechanisms in practice. Her chapter examines the policies and procedures under which such mechanisms operate, and the criteria by which their performance may be appraised. As Brown Weiss notes, ultimately, if such "independent accountability mechanisms are to flourish, a culture of accountability needs to be fostered" amongst concerned stakeholders. The legitimacy and effectiveness of such bodies thus requires independence, impartiality, and integrity which, in turn, can contribute to the legitimacy and effectiveness of the institutions whose actions they are empowered to examine.

Mikael Rask Madsen's chapter brings this theme of institutions and institutional actors to a conclusion with an introduction to what sociology can offer for the study of international courts. Madsen notes that "Caron's writings reflect fundamental questions of the societal embeddedness of law". However, Caron was not a sociologist. Moreover, while the study of international courts and tribunals is a growing field (Madsen notes, amongst others, the work of our contributor, Karen Alter), sociology of law has historically focused on national courts. Madsen's chapter demonstrates how the application of sociological theory to international law can enrich our understanding of both international adjudication and global governance. These are themes central also in Caron's work, which engaged both sociological and political theories to examine various aspects of international courts and tribunals.[43] As Caron's scholarship and the chapters in this part of the volume illustrate, such theories can shed light on the contexts from which international courts and tribunals emerge; their functions, goals, and responsibilities; their processes and relationships to the persons, procedures, and social contexts that constitute them; and appraisals of their effectiveness and legitimacy.

## 4.  Procedures

These themes are continued and developed in the next part of the book, which features chapters focused on the procedures applied by international courts and tribunals, and on procedural guarantees by reference to which international courts and tribunals might appraise domestic measures. These chapters highlight several fundamental cross-cutting procedural features in international dispute settlement. They expand on the relationship between procedure and legitimacy, effectiveness, and capacity for international courts and tribunals to achieve their stated goals and functions.

Andrea Bjorklund and Catalina Turriago Bettancourt address the normative foundations of arbitral due process. The authors examine the contours of arbitral due process in international commercial arbitration, highlighting its role in shaping arbitral decisions, and its interaction with fundamental principles of arbitral procedure including party autonomy and efficiency. The chapter further highlights the links between due process and the rule of law, including "thick" and "thin" conceptions.

Philippa Webb's chapter also explores facets of due process, examining the concept of procedural fairness by reference to the requirement under some investment treaties for host states to accord investors "effective means" of asserting claims or enforcing

---

[43] See, especially, Caron, "Towards a Political Theory of International Courts and Tribunals" (n 26).

rights with respect to their investments. As Webb notes, such clauses may give expression to the notion of procedural fairness in investment treaties insofar as they require host states to avoid undue delay in domestic court proceedings or encompass consideration of the principle of equality of arms. Webb's chapter illuminates these facets of effective means clauses by reference to Caron's "masterful" Expert Opinion in *Chevron Corporation and Texaco Petroleum Company v The Republic of Ecuador*, analysing the scope of an effective means clause in the bilateral investment treaty between the United States and Ecuador.

O. Thomas Johnson and Elizabeth Sheargold address an important procedural innovation in investor–state arbitration, by which tribunals have been empowered to dismiss claims at a preliminary phase of the proceeding where such claims manifestly lack legal merit. As Johnson and Sheargold note, this procedural mechanism was initially designed to improve the efficiency and legitimacy of investor–state arbitration. The chapter explores the procedures established for early dismissal under both treaties and key arbitration rules as well as practice under such procedures to date in order to highlight how such procedures have functioned in fact. Johnson and Sheargold note key reforms that could be adopted in order to ensure that such procedures are able to achieve their twofold goals of contributing to the efficiency and legitimacy of investor–state arbitration.

W Michael Reisman and Mahnoush H Arsanjani note that parallel dispute settlement proceedings are likely to become increasingly prevalent due to the fragmenting and decentralized structure of international law. They illustrate the challenges associated with parallel proceedings by reference to several such proceedings in diverse fields, including by reference to disputes concerning environment and conservation law, human rights law, investment law, and international peace and security law. In light of the nature of the international legal system, Reisman and Arsanjani conclude that there is no one single response to the challenges presented by parallel proceedings under international law. This notwithstanding, they draw from their analysis and survey of such proceedings in practice several recommendations to decision-makers.

Donald Francis Donovan's chapter similarly tackles a common procedural mechanism in international dispute settlement: the capacity for international courts and tribunals to award provisional measures. As Donovan notes, orders of provisional measures engage core components of the adjudicatory function, necessitating care, discipline, and restraint on the part of the court or tribunal ordering them. Such measures are an inherent function of the adjudicatory function yet precede the court or tribunal's final determination of the issues of law and fact implicated in the dispute, and also entail the capacity for the court or tribunal to order measures potentially restraining of core facets of sovereign authority. Donovan demonstrates how these features have informed the development of criteria applicable to granting provisional measures. Donovan highlights the gaps and ambiguities that remain, cautioning that such criteria must be developed in view of the function of provisional measures orders and indeed the function of the international courts and tribunals ordering them.

Such themes complement those reflected in Caron's own scholarship on interim measures of protection before the IUSCT.[44] As Caron himself concluded in 1986, "[n]o matter how detailed the jurisprudence of interim measures becomes, one can be certain that new questions will continue to arise".[45] In his work, Caron acknowledged that there could be several guiding principles for the resolution of such new questions, and highlighted as a thread running through the IUSCT's interim measures decisions "a tension between the desire to protect a party quickly from a prejudicial act and the danger of rushing to a decision that in fact prejudices the other party or the arbitration itself".[46] Donovan's chapter illustrates how such principles and tensions continue to inform the practice of international courts and tribunals to provisional measures requests, and how such challenges might best be overcome into the future.

Collectively, the chapters in this part highlight the important role played by both procedural principles and mechanisms in international dispute settlement. Such procedures perform an integral function in positioning international courts and tribunals to achieve the peaceful settlement of disputes in ways that are fair, effective, efficient, and legitimate. As Caron noted, one key measure of effectiveness for international courts and tribunals is their capacity to perform their judicial task with "speed, accuracy and procedural fairness".[47] The contributors in this part of the volume elaborate upon this theme, to highlight how such goals may best be balanced and the procedural mechanisms needed to achieve them.

## 5. Substantive Law and Legal Principles

Caron's work often returns to how substantive law and legal principles shape the functions of international courts and tribunals, their limits, and their capacity to achieve their institutional goals and expectations of key stakeholders. The chapters in this part of the book pick up this theme to engage with several fundamental substantive rules and principles of international law. Some such rules and principles manifest in specific regimes of international law, whereas others are applied in some form in several regimes. Some of the contributions in this part of the book also address what Caron termed "trans-substantive" rules or principles of international law; that is, rules or principles which "apply regardless of the specific norm (primary rule) allegedly breached".[48] Collectively, these chapters highlight the limits of international adjudication as well as

---

[44] David D Caron, "Interim Measures of Protection: Theory and Practice in Light of the Iran United States Claims Tribunal" (1986) 46 Zeitschrift für Ausländisches Öffenliches Recht und Völkerrecht 465.

[45] ibid 516.

[46] ibid 518.

[47] Caron, "Fifth Annual Charles N. Brower Lecture on International Dispute Resolution" (n 16).

[48] David D Caron, "The Basis of Responsibility: Attribution and Other Transubstantive Rules of State Responsibility" in Richard B Lillich and Daniel B Magraw (eds), *The Iran United States Claims Tribunal: Its Contribution to the Law of State Responsibility* (1998), 109–84, 110. See, also, David D Caron, "The ILC Articles on State Responsibility: The Paradoxical Relationship between Form and Authority" (2002) 96 American Journal of International Law 857, 858.

the capacity for key doctrines of international law to adapt to address emerging and future challenges.

Lee Caplan's chapter engages with a core requirement that is applicable to the justiciability of cases before many international courts and tribunals: the requirement that there be a "dispute". As Caplan notes, the concept of "dispute" has a "long and well-known pedigree" since it first emerged as a core legal concept in the jurisprudence of the Permanent Court of International Justice (PCIJ). Despite its longevity, this concept continues to be subject to contestation and refinement, reflecting perhaps its core role in regulating the types of matters that may be referred to international courts and tribunals. These were issues with which David Caron also engaged in his work as Judge ad hoc at the ICJ. As Caron highlighted in a Dissenting Opinion in *Sovereign Rights and Maritime Spaces*, in particular, the requirement that there be a "dispute" is a complex but necessary requirement to enliven international adjudicative jurisdiction. Caplan focuses specifically on the debates about the concept that were raised in the case between Ecuador and the United States filed under the US-Ecuador bilateral investment treaty. With this case as context, Caplan argues that the present understanding of the concept of "dispute" in international law provides insufficient guidance vis-à-vis the justiciability of "abstract controversies" and would benefit from a "correctness requirement".

Donald McRae also deals in his chapter with a cross-cutting question related to disputes concerning maritime boundary delimitations: the notion of "relevant circumstances". As McRae notes, this concept is core to maritime boundary delimitation but subject to confusion and a lack of systematization. McRae questions whether third-party adjudication of maritime boundary disputes has in some way contributed to such confusion or limited the potential role for the concept. The chapter thereafter looks to alternatives, to examine whether other forms of dispute settlement—like conciliation— might provide a different method and process through which the notion of "relevant circumstances" can be better developed and articulated.

Federico Ortino's chapter considers the role of the "public interest" in analysis of an investor's legitimate expectations under the fair and equitable treatment obligation in international investment law. Ortino notes an "apparent anomaly", arising from the lack of weight given to the public interest in the analysis of legitimate expectations by investment tribunals, as compared to the comparatively greater role given to the public interest in similar analyses under English and European Union (EU) law. As Ortino notes, in the former two systems, "[a] common feature … is that a legitimate expectation will not be afforded protection (that is, it can lawfully be frustrated) if there exists a public interest that justifies overriding the expectation". Concerned that the relative unimportance afforded to the public interest in international investment law analyses of legitimate expectations may undermine the legitimacy of that regime, Ortino seeks to derive insights into the potential role for, and scope of, such considerations from these other bodies of law.

Bernard Oxman's chapter brings into view the central role of third-party dispute settlement procedures for securing compliance by states with the international law relevant to the conservation and management of the living resources of the sea. As

Oxman notes, "[a]rbitration and adjudication are now firmly implanted within the international system for conservation and management of marine living resources as well as the protection and preservation of the marine environment more generally". This dispute settlement framework ensures access to justice, the peaceful settlement of disputes, and authoritative interpretations of international law in circumstances where the facts to which that law applies are constantly evolving.

This challenge of applying law to evolving facts and global circumstances is picked up in the subsequent two chapters in this volume.

Nilufer Oral and Bogdan Aurescu, both members of the International Law Commission, analyse the possible impacts of sea level rise on maritime boundaries, including the implications of adopting ambulatory or fixed baselines in such analyses. Oral and Aurescu highlight the ambiguities in UNCLOS vis-à-vis establishing baselines from which states' ocean entitlements are measured and the uncertain requirements related to the physical existence of islands which, as Oral and Aurescu note, risk "devolving legally into a rock" as a consequence of sea level rise. Caron recognized these challenges as early as 1990, when international attention was only beginning to focus on the threat of global warming and he made significant contributions to the International Law Association study on the topic.[49]

As he observed, "a rising sea level will create uncertainties as to the outer boundaries of the zones of valuable ocean territory and rights possessed by coastal states", yet at the same time, there are "avenues, both normative and institutional whereby this uncertainty and conflict may be avoided or mitigated".[50] Indeed, "inasmuch as nature declines to negotiate, it is we and our laws which must adapt".[51] Several such avenues are highlighted by Oral and Aurescu in their chapter, which brings into focus the role of international courts and tribunals in offering stability and certainty for maritime boundaries in a world impacted by climate change. This includes, in particular, a role for international courts and tribunals to exercise their advisory functions to issue opinions relevant to responding to the lack of clarity and gaps present in existing law in order to equip states and other stakeholders to better deal with the pressures produced by climate change and associated sea level rises.

Malgosia Fitzmaurice's chapter similarly engages a rapidly developing area of substantive international law, in this case the human right to a clean, healthy, and sustainable environment. The development of this right, which has recently been recognized as such by the United Nations General Assembly, is a story featuring a key role for international courts and tribunals which, as Fitzmaurice notes, have played an important role in developing its content. Fitzmaurice traces the fragmented jurisprudence

---

[49] See, especially, International Law Association, Committee on International Law and Sea Level Rise, Conference Report, Sydney (2018).

[50] David D Caron, "Climate Change, Sea Level Rise and the Coming Uncertainty in Oceanic Boundaries: A Proposal to Avoid Conflict" in Seoung-Yong Hong and Jon M Van Dyke (eds), *Maritime Boundary Disputes, Settlement Processes, and the Law of the Sea* (Brill 2009) 1.

[51] Caron, "Climate Change, Sea Level Rise and the Coming Uncertainty in Oceanic Boundaries" (n 50) 17. See, similarly, David D Caron, "When Law Makes Climate Change Worse: Rethinking the Law of Baselines in Light of a Rising Sea Level" (1990) 17 Ecology Law Quarterly 621.

emerging from regional human rights bodies to identify the procedural and substantive dimensions of such a right. While this process of evolution is not yet complete, Fitzmaurice's analysis highlights the key role for international courts and tribunals to identify the contours and limits of rights relevant to responding to—and protecting individuals in the face of—some of the world's most pressing contemporary problems.

Fitzmaurice's analysis illustrates that there is an increasing emphasis on, and place for, environmental considerations in international dispute settlement. The picture painted through her chapter might be contrasted, then, with Caron's own analysis of the space accorded to such considerations in the work of bodies like the UNCC. Writing in 2010, Caron observed, for example, that "[a]n assessment of current institutions ... reveals a quite weak position accorded to the environment".[52] This notwithstanding, throughout his work Caron also drew attention to the importance of these emerging and evolving fields of international law, noting in relation to environmental law in particular that "the waterways of this law have many ... branches ... and many of those branches may be shifting.... In time, there will be more detailed and accurate charts".[53]

Caron would no doubt have read with interest the chart offered by Fitzmaurice in relation to the development of a human right to a healthy environment. Such developments also bear out other themes running through Caron's publications, including his concern that certain areas of international law may develop slowly, haphazardly, and in a fragmented manner to the extent that their content comes to be tied to state reactions to isolated events or case-driven developments.[54] The attention given to the human right to a healthy environment—among other important substantive norms—by states, international organizations, and international courts and tribunals may thus increasingly assist to counter its, to-date, patchy and ad hoc development.

Turning from substantive law to examine the constitution of adjudicative bodies, Jeremy Sharpe's chapter examines the authority delegated to international investment tribunals to interpret and apply investment treaties. As Sharpe notes, this is a field in which arbitral interpretations of treaties have attained a considerable significance in giving shape to open-textured and often vague treaty provisions. Yet increasingly, states are seeking to regain some of this authority for themselves in order to achieve various objectives, including enhanced coherence and consistency amongst arbitral decisions. To do so, as Sharpe outlines in his chapter, they have engaged in various treaty practices including the negotiation of more specific provisions in reformed investment treaties and the use of interpretive statements to clarify their expectations as to the interpretation and application of these provisions. Sharpe argues that such practices illustrate

---

[52] David D Caron, "The Place of the Environment in International Tribunals" in Jay E Austin and Carl E Bruch (eds), *The Environmental Consequences of War* (Cambridge University Press 2010) 253.

[53] David D Caron, "The Law of the Environment: A Symbolic Step of Modest Value" (1989) 14 Yale Journal of International Law 528, 541.

[54] As Caron noted in relation to the rules of international law relevant to catastrophes, for instance: "Driven today by one disaster, tomorrow by another, the *ad hoc* incoherence of legal and institutional response mirrors the fortuity of the catastrophes humanity encounters": David D Caron, "Addressing Catastrophes: Conflicting Images of Solidarity and Separateness" in David D Caron and Charles Leben (eds), *The International Aspects of Natural and Industrial Catastrophes* (Martinus Nijhoff 2001) 3–4.

a move from "delegation" of interpretive authority to investment tribunals towards a more "prescriptive" model.

George A Bermann also engages the idea of delegation, to analyse the juncture between arbitral and judicial authority with particular emphasis on the capacity for US courts to determine the enforceability of agreements to arbitrate. As Bermann highlights, US courts have distinguished between "gateway" and "non-gateway" issues in determining their capacity to determine issues of enforceability if requested by a party to do so. They have further placed particular emphasis on the role of *kompetenz-kompetenz* clauses in agreements to arbitrate (and incorporated procedural rules) in doing so. In view of US case law and practice on these issues, Bermann cautions that the current approach to assessing arbitrability under US law threatens the very legitimacy of arbitration itself. As he concludes, the presumption in favour of arbitrability has been "for all practical purposes" reversed through US cases in which "the mere presence of what has become standard boiler-plate language suffices to establish clear and unmistakable evidence of a delegation".

## 6. Looking to the Future

In the final part of the book the contributors' gaze turns more clearly to the future—looking at the emergence of new institutions and new challenges for international courts and tribunals.

Tom Ginsburg tackles one of Caron's claims head-on, to argue that "in many adjudicative contexts, the argument that courts should limit themselves to their core task of dispute resolution would produce a jurisprudence that is ultimately ineffective and self-undermining". Caron's approach, he suggests, is one of "minimalism". Ginsburg takes Caron's Brower Lecture as a jumping-off point, and recalls (as others do), the distinction between the functions of courts and the task of adjudicators. He notes that David Caron's life in inter-state dispute resolution began and ended at the IUSCT (though it traversed other courts and tribunals as both observer and participant). For Ginsburg, this was (and, presumably, is) "a body for which the task and the function were fairly aligned". He considers that, in other areas such as human rights law, Caron's minimalism would restrict the role that institutions have to play. The focus of Ginsburg's analysis is democracy—a perhaps unlikely subject for international courts and tribunals given that the idea of democracy as a right, proposed in the 1990s, was "generally rejected".[55] Nevertheless, he tracks commitments to democracy across different international organizations to bear out that there is "now a thick set of norms at the regional and subregional level for much of the world that articulate democratic governance as a norm".

---

[55] See, for example, Thomas M Franck, "The Emerging Right to Democratic Governance" (1992) 86 American Journal of International Law 46, and Susan Marks, "What Has Become of the Emerging Right to Democratic Governance?" (2011) 22(2) European Journal of International Law 507.

Karen J Alter's chapter also picks up on the theme of democracy, to examine whether the rise of populism and backlash against globalization and global institutions might precipitate a move away from international adjudication in the future. As Caron and Shirlow have observed, "[t]he term 'backlash' indicates the presence of something more than scrutiny, critique or even crisis", "[w]hereas critique of a system might lead to suggestions for reform, 'backlash' implies actions taken in opposition to the system itself".[56] Numerous authors suggest that international law and institutions have faced a sustained "backlash" in recent decades.[57] Against this context, Alter examines the factors that have produced the significant number of international courts and tribunals in existence today, as well as the significant challenges they are facing vis-à-vis their efficacy and legitimacy. Alter argues that, despite these challenges, *de facto* rather than formal dejudicialization may mark international dispute settlement in the future. As Alter notes, such *de facto* dejudicialization may be produced through a reduction in the number of cases referred to international adjudicatory bodies, a reduced importance being placed upon their rulings, or even a "decay" and erosion of substantive norms through backlash and sustained contestation. Nevertheless, Alter concludes following her analysis of the challenges faced by international adjudicative bodies that we are yet to reach the "high-water mark of international judicialization".

These chapters demonstrate that, even in a time of sustained evolution and contestation, international adjudication is finding ways to adapt in order to retain relevance. This reminds us that the functions of international courts and tribunals, their audiences, and the very law applied by them is neither static nor necessarily enduring. Caron's work highlights the connections between different international institutions, as well as their disparate and overlapping goals. As Caron recalls, "[t]o be effective, international governance must be concentrated in some body other than the whole".[58] His work repeatedly reminds us of the role to be played by a network of international governance and dispute settlement institutions in collectively positioning states and other actors to achieve their disparate objectives and, ultimately, to serve the mission of achieving the settlement of international disputes through peaceful means.

As Caron reminds us, just as with the Hague Conferences establishing the earliest international adjudicative bodies, very often developments on the international plane might be best seen as "a process rather than as events".[59] Yet, as Caron also ably demonstrated, such processes themselves may become "the solution" and as such have the potential to shape and change events on the world stage.[60]

---

[56] Shirlow and Caron (n 35).

[57] See, for example, Mikael Rask Madsen, Pola Cebulak, and Micha Wiebusch, "Backlash against International Courts: Explaining the Forms and Patterns of Resistance to International Courts" (2018) 14 (2) International Journal of Law in Context 197–220; Karen J Alter, James T Gathii, and Laurence R. Helfer, "Backlash against International Courts in West, East and Southern Africa: Causes and Consequences" (2016) 27 (2) European Journal of International Law 293–328.

[58] Caron, "The Legitimacy of the Collective Authority of the Security Council" (n 31) 588.

[59] Caron, "War and International Adjudication" (n 4) 22.

[60] David D Caron, "Protection of the Stratospheric Ozone Layer and the Structure of International Environmental Lawmaking" (1991) 14 Hastings International & Comparative Law Review 755, 773 (referring to "the process as the solution" in the context of environmental law).

From environmental degradation[61] and climate change[62] to populism and associated "backlashes" against international law,[63] Caron's work illuminated the role and limitations of international law in anticipating and responding to many of the pressing challenges that are likely to confront not just international lawyers but humanity at large in the coming years. Caron's work took seriously the role of international law and international institutions in responding to those challenges. Yet, it was also marked by a critical and realistic appraisal of their limits and future capacities. As he reminds us:

> The world may change in ways that were never contemplated when particular legal choices were made, and therefore the law ideally should change accordingly, it should continue to grow and adapt. But given the slow pace of legal evolution, there is inevitably a period of time when the law has not yet changed to reflect modern realities and in that period it often fails to promote either wise policy or just outcomes.[64]

Just as in Caron's work, the contributors in this volume seek to identify such contingencies, to anticipate future legal innovations, and to reflect upon how international law and its institutions may be designed so that they are capable of responding flexibly, effectively and legitimately to as-yet uncontemplated future developments.

## 7. Conclusion

This book has come about at a time of great uncertainty. In concluding his examination of the 1899 Peace Conference, Caron took note:

> If the realist tends to see only the constraints of the present, then the idealist tends to see only the possibilities of tomorrow. Both strains of thought inform great leaders and in turn can often be found in the law.

---

[61] Reflecting on international law related to the environment, for instance, Caron observed that "[i]nternational environmental lawmaking is different from international lawmaking in general in at least three respects. First, environmental lawmaking must be conducted amidst great uncertainty about the reality, cause, and extent of the problem. Second, because the nature of environmental problems such as ozone depletion requires concerted action, it is necessary that at least the major contributors to the problem, present and future, be parties to the regime. Third, because it is difficult to separate environmental problems from one another and from development concerns generally, environmental lawmaking runs the risk of either being unmanageable or not system-oriented." Caron, "Protection of the Stratospheric Ozone Layer and the Structure of International Environmental Lawmaking" (n 60) 773.

[62] "Climate change often presents a set of challenges informed by principles of law, but that in several respects go far beyond existing approaches and will require substantial and innovative law-making": David D Caron, "Climate Change and the Oceans" in Harry N Scheiber and Jin-Hyun Paik (eds), *Regions, Institutions and the Law of the Sea: Studies in Ocean Governance* (Brill 2013) 515–37. See, also, David D Caron, "Negotiating Our Future with the Oceans" in Pierre Jacquet, Rajendra K Pachauri, and Laurence Tubiana (eds), *A Planet For Life 2011—The Oceans: The New Frontier* (TERI Press 2011) 25–34.

[63] Shirlow and Caron (n 35).

[64] David D Caron, "Time and the Public Trust Doctrine: Law's Knowledge of Climate Change" (2013) 35 University of Hawaii Law Review 441–58.

Caron's early passing left much work unfinished,[65] but the nature of his insights and the topics he addressed mean that much of his work retains relevance for analysing, understanding, and tackling the world's current and future challenges. Several authors in this volume pick up unfinished strands in his scholarship, and the Editors hope that the volume may inspire others to do likewise in the future to continue these important conversations. We are grateful to those authors for their contributions. We are grateful, too, to those others who would have been included, had the global COVID-19 pandemic, and a myriad of other impositions, not come to bear.[66]

We thank all those whose assistance brought this book into being—especially the patience and perseverance of everyone at Oxford University Press. We thank Susan Spencer, and David's family, for entrusting us with the project.

And most of all, we thank David, for everything.

The Editors
1 December 2022

---

[65] Some unfinished work, in a very literal sense, includes the now-complete Shirlow and Caron contribution to *The Oxford Handbook of International Arbitration* (Oxford University Press 2020), and Caron's still-unpublished Hague Academy Lectures.

[66] One intended contributor, a good friend and colleague of David Caron, Judge and Professor James Crawford, sadly fell ill and passed away during the making of the book.

# PART I

# LESSONS FROM THE HISTORY OF DISPUTE SETTLEMENT

# 2

# The Bering Sea[1] Fur Seal Arbitration—The Lawyers Try, But Fail, to Save the Seals

*John R Crook*

## 1. Introduction

David Caron, lawyer, judge, legal scholar, and friend, was a man of many interests. His scholarship and practice ranged widely, including international environmental law, the law of the sea, the protection of marine resources and the marine environment, and the theory, practice, and history of international adjudication. Caron was also proud of his service in the US Coast Guard, including a distinguished record at the US Coast Guard Academy. As a young officer, he trained as a "hard hat" diver and served as navigator and diving officer on a Coast Guard icebreaker in the Arctic.

Many of Caron's interests—and his pride in the Coast Guard—intersected in the events that led to the historic, but ultimately unsuccessful, 1893 fur seal arbitration between the United States and Great Britain. Throughout these events, the fur seal was the "special ward" of the US Revenue Cutter Service, the predecessor of the US Coast Guard.[2]

In the closing decades of the nineteenth century, pelagic sealing by Canadian sealers—killing of fur seals at sea in waters beyond the territorial sea—provoked bitter disputes, and even the risk of military confrontation, between the United States and Great Britain. The United States, determined to protect the seal population and reinforced by the need to appear firm in a contest with Great Britain, committed itself to an untested and ultimately unsuccessful claim of jurisdiction to arrest Canadian sealers on the high seas. The British government disputed the US claim, although it sometimes appeared to recognize the need for measures to protect the seal population. However, British manoeuvring room was also limited, largely by pressure from the young Dominion of Canada, which demanded protection—by the Royal Navy if necessary—of Canadian sealers.

---

[1] The modern spelling of the ocean area involved is "the Bering Sea." In the nineteenth century, the area was often referred to as "the Behring Sea." This earlier spelling has been retained where it appears in quotations from documents from the period.

[2] Stephen H Evans, *The United States Coast Guard 1790–1915* (US Naval Institute 1949) 106.

---

John R Crook, *The Bering Sea Fur Seal Arbitration—The Lawyers Try, But Fail, to Save the Seals* In: *By Peaceful Means*. Edited by: Charles N Brower, Joan E Donoghue, Cian C Murphy, Cymie R Payne and Esmé R Shirlow, Oxford University Press. © John R Crook 2024. DOI: 10.1093/oso/9780192848086.003.0002

Through an often-contentious diplomatic process, the United States and Great Britain ultimately agreed in 1892 to arbitrate their dispute. The arbitrators' 1893 award[3] resoundingly rejected US claims to jurisdiction, but an unusual feature of the agreement creating the tribunal empowered it to devise regulations intended to protect the seal herds. The arbitrators' regime was a failure. Continued heavy pelagic sealing, increased by the entry of Japanese sealers around 1900, cast the ultimate survival of the Bering Sea fur seal population into doubt. Years of debate and diplomacy, and the threatened collapse of the seal population, finally led to the North Pacific Fur Seal Convention of 1911,[4] which led to stabilization and recovery of the seal population and is today seen as a significant landmark in the development of international environmental regimes.[5]

## 2. The Seals, the Russians, and the Americans

"As a troublemaker, the Fur Seal has shown that it has no equal among animals. It has proven its ability to provoke international antagonisms."[6] The northern fur seal, *Callorhinus Ursinus*, spends most of its life at sea, but each year, the species carries out an enormous annual migration. The main part of the population migrates from the central California coast to the Bering Sea, where 80 per cent of the species breeds on eight miles of rocky beaches on the three small US-owned Pribilof Islands.[7] The three islands, St Paul, St George, and Otter Island, are all of volcanic origin.[8]

For the first two-thirds of the nineteenth century, the Pribilofs were part of the Russian Empire along with the rest of present-day Alaska. As Russia awakened to the resources of its far eastern and northern territories late in the eighteenth century, Russian hunters began to harvest marine mammals for their furs, seeking the skins of sea otters and fur seals primarily for the Chinese market. In 1789, an imperial ukase of Russian Emperor Paul 1 granted the "Russian-American Company" exclusive rights to hunt and fish in the north-eastern seas and along Alaska's coast. In 1821, Tsar Alexander II issued an imperial ukase reserving fishing and hunting rights in the Bering Sea and large areas of the North Pacific exclusively for the company and Russian nationals. The terms of the 1821 ukase barred foreign vessels from approaching within 100 "Italian miles" of Russian coasts and islands. Following declines in the seal herd due to excessive killing,

---

[3] Award between the United States and the United Kingdom relating to the rights of jurisdiction of United States in the Bering's sea and the preservation of fur seals, 15 August 1893, XXVIII RIAA 263-276 (hereafter Tribunal Award).

[4] Convention for the Preservation and Protection of Fur Seals (signed 7 July 1911, entered into force 15 December 1911), 37 Stat 1542, TS 564, Charles I Bevans, *Treaties and Other International Agreements of the United States*, Vol. 1 (US Dept of State 1968) 804.

[5] Scott Barrett, "The North Pacific Fur Seal Treaty and the Theory of International Cooperation" in Scott Barrett (ed), *Environment and Statecraft: The Strategy of Environmental Treaty-Making* (Oxford University Press 2003) 32 .

[6] Gerald O Williams, *The Bering Sea Fur Seal Dispute 1885–1911* (Alaska Maritime Publications 1984) ii.

[7] The Pribilofs were named for Gerasim Pribiloff, a Russian mariner who in the summer of 1786 followed the migrating fur seals to their breeding grounds. HW Blodgett, "Fur Seal Arbitration" (1895) 3 North Western Law Review 74.

[8] ibid 74–75; Briton Cooper Busch, *The War against the Seals. A History of the North American Seal Fishery* (McGill-Queen's University Press 1985) 95–96.

in 1835, Russia began to impose conservation measures on fur seals in Alaskan waters. These led to a substantial restoration of the herd, which was estimated to number about two or three million by 1867.[9]

As the century progressed, Russia's hold on its North American possessions weakened in the face of growing British and US pressure. Russia was sensitive to its vulnerability to British power revealed by British attacks on Russian bases in eastern Siberia during the Crimean War, to the expansion of the Hudson's Bay Company in Canada's northern territories, and to growing numbers of US traders and whalers in the region.[10] Although the US Civil War delayed negotiations, future American expansion to Alaskan waters appeared likely. "Despite some reluctance to sell in Russia, authorities in St. Peterburg realized that if the colony were not sold it might be seized."[11] By a March 1867 treaty, the United States acquired Alaska from Russia for $7,200,000 in gold.[12] In Article 1 of the Treaty, the Czar ceded "all the territory and dominion now possessed by his said majesty" within a described area. The area's eastern limit was the demarcation line between Russian and British possessions in North America established by an 1825 bilateral convention between those powers. The western limit was a line in the sea "running southwesterly from Bering Strait so as to include in the cession all of the Aleutian Islands as well as the Pribilof Islands with their valuable fur seal industry".[13]

The US government had few means to exercise authority over its vast new territories and their indigenous populations and resources. The principal manifestation of US authority in northern Alaska was the vessels of the US Revenue Cutter Service, the US Coast Guard's venerable predecessor dating to the time of George Washington and his energetic Secretary of the Treasury, Alexander Hamilton.[14] The Service began to dispatch one or more of its ocean-going cutters to cruise in northern waters every summer. These annual cruises carried out multiple missions, including exploration, law enforcement, bringing supplies to remote villages and mines, and rescuing stranded whale ships and seamen.[15] In remote and thinly settled coastal regions, these ships often were the only visible sign of US authority.[16]

[9] Gordon Ireland, "The North Pacific Fisheries" (1942) 36 American Journal of International Law 400; Williams, *Fur Seal Dispute* (n 6) 6; Busch (n 8) 100.

[10] Ken Ross, "Fur Seal's Friend: Henry W. Elliot" in Ken Ross (ed), *Pioneering Conservation in Alaska* (University Press of Colorado 2006) 31; Thomas A Bailey, *A Diplomatic History of the American People* (7th edn, Appleton-Century Crofts 1964) 365; Busch (n 8) 102–03.

[11] ibid 103.

[12] Treaty concerning the Cession of the Russian Possessions in North America by his Majesty the Emperor of all the Russias to the United States of America (concluded 30 March 1867, entered into force 20 June 1867) 15 Stat 539, TS 301.

[13] William Williams, "Reminiscences of the Bering Sea Arbitration" (1943) 37 American Journal of International Law 562. Williams, a junior counsel on the US legal team, was team's sole surviving member when he recorded his reminiscences a half century later.

[14] Evans (n 2) 5.

[15] ibid 108–39.

[16] ibid 108–09.

### 3. Bad News for the Seals

Russia's departure from the Pribilof Islands "signaled a free-for-all scramble by fur traders to get all the skins they could while the getting was good",[17] leading to "ruthless slaughter" of seals.[18] During the summer of 1868, "the rookeries were raided by poachers, mainly from the Pacific ports of the United States and British Columbia, and an indiscriminate slaughter of the seals ... was perpetrated during the entire season".[19] A Revenue Service officer found "four or five companies killing seals as fast as they could hire Aleuts' to do the work", paying the Aleuts in liquor, which wrought havoc on their health and culture.[20] During the next two years, 1869 and 1870, the United States maintained guards and a Revenue Service cutter, which repelled most raids.[21]

Publicity about the extensive killing and the interests of potential investors prompted the US Congress to respond. An 1868 act made Alaska a US customs territory and barred the killing of fur seals and other fur bearing animals "within the limits of said territory or the waters thereof". The next year, Congress declared the St Paul and St Georges Islands to be "a special reservation for government purposes". However, in the statutes adopted in this period, "no definition is attempted of the extent of the waters to which their provisions apply".[22] In 1870, Congress approved "[a]n Act to prevent the extermination of fur-bearing animals in Alaska", authorizing the Secretary of the Treasury conclude twenty-year leases allowing the taking of no more than 100,000 seals a year on land and imposing other restrictions.[23] That same year, the Treasury Department leased exclusive rights to on-shore sealing on the Pribilofs for twenty years to a US entity, the Alaska Commercial Company, subject to limits on the numbers of seals to be killed and restricting killing to males taken on land.[24] A subsequent twenty-year lease extending through 1909 on similar terms was later granted to a different company.[25] The two lease holders came to be important actors in promoting strong US opposition to pelagic sealing in order to protect the value of their rights to take seals on land.

US Government officials initially did not take consistent positions regarding US authority to regulate takings at sea. In 1872, the Secretary of the Treasury told the San Francisco Collector of Customs that "I do not see that the United States would have the jurisdiction or power to drive off" foreign sealers beyond a league from US shores.[26]

---

[17] ibid 111.
[18] Alton Y Roppel, *Management of Northern Fur Seals on the Pribilof Islands, Alaska, 1786–1981* (National Oceanic and Atmospheric Administration, US Dept. of Commerce 1984) 6; Ross (n 10) 32.
[19] Blodgett (n 2) 79.
[20] Evans (n 2) 111.
[21] Blodgett (n 7) 79.
[22] John Bassett Moore, *History and Digest of the International Arbitrations to Which the United States Has Been a Party, Together with Appendices Containing the Treaties Relating to Such Arbitrations and Historical and Legal Notes on Other International Arbitrations Ancient and Modern, and on the Domestic Commissions of the United States for the Adjustment of International Claims* (US Gov't Printing Office 1898) 764.
[23] ibid 764.
[24] ibid 767.
[25] Roppel (n 18) 6.
[26] Moore (n 22) 768.

Nine years later, the Acting Secretary of the Treasury in 1881 took a different view, writing that all of the waters east of the Russian cession line were "comprised within the waters of Alaska Territory" and subject to US statutes barring killing of seals.[27]

Meanwhile, events combined to raise seals' economic importance. Fashion trends in Europe and North America came to favor sealskin apparel, and a "de-hairing machine" and improved dying methods made pelts more profitable.[28] As prices for seal skins increased, Canadian pelagic sealers appeared in increasing numbers; "the great majority of upwards of 100 schooners made Victoria BC their home port".[29] The timing of their arrival was disputed in the 1893 arbitration, but the evidence regarding their usual methods was not disputed. Operating from small boats launched from a sailing schooner, pelagic sealers killed primarily pregnant or nursing females feeding at sea far from the breeding grounds. They typically shot seals sleeping on the surface using a shotgun.[30] "[T]he death of a female usually meant the death also of an unborn pup or one on land. Only about half the seals killed at sea were ever recovered, so for every female killed and recovered at sea, up to four seals may have died."[31] A visitor to the rookeries in 1896 counted 16,000 starving pups.[32]

## 4. The United States Responds—But the British Protest

In 1886, the US administration of Democratic President Grover Cleveland was of mixed minds about how to address the rapid increase in pelagic sealing. Secretary of State Bayard had reservations regarding the strength of the US legal position.[33] Nevertheless, President Cleveland and his cabinet opted for action. In March 1886, the Secretary of the Treasury sent a copy of Treasury's 1881 letter to the Collector of Customs in San Francisco, directing that it be made public. The next month, the Treasury Department ordered the Revenue Cutter Service, then part of the Treasury, to act against pelagic sealers. An agreed statement of facts in the 1893 Tribunal Award included an April 1886 directive[34] from the Acting Secretary of the Treasury to Captain M.A. Healy and the Revenue Cutter *Bear*. By this order, Healy was "hereby clothed with full power to enforce the law contained in the provisions of Section 1956 of the United States' Revised Statutes, and directed to seize all vessels and arrest and deliver to the proper authorities any or all persons whom you may detect violating the law referred to".[35] Healy and the

---

[27] ibid 769.

[28] Williams, *Fur Seal Dispute* (n 5) 8; Bailey (n 9) 410; US Dept of the Interior, "International Fur Seal Treaty Negotiated 50 Years Ago, 2 July 1961" <https://www.fws.gov/sites/default/files/documents/historic-news-releases/1961/19610702.pdf> 2. ("Until 1913 all raw seal skins were shipped to London for processing, for that art was known only to a small group of skilled English workers.")

[29] Williams, *Fur Seal Dispute* (n 6) 10.

[30] Blodgett (n 7) 80.

[31] John M Raymond and Barbara J Fischholz, "Lawyers Who Established International Law in the United States, 1776–1914" (1982) 76 American Journal of International Law 802, 813.

[32] Ross (n 10) 42.

[33] Williams, *Fur Seal Dispute* (n 6) 12, 16, n 20, n 30.

[34] As reproduced in RIAA, this order to Captain Healy in the Tribunal Award (n 3) 273 is dated April 21, 1896. This must be a typographical error; the Acting Secretary's order was issued a decade earlier.

[35] Tribunal Award (n 3) 273.

*Bear*, a wooden-hulled former North Atlantic sealer, were for many years prominent symbols of US government authority in Alaska, both acquiring near legendary status.[36]

Acting on the Treasury Department's instructions, in September 1886, the Revenue Service cutter *Corwin* arrested three Canadian sealing schooners more than sixty miles from land in the Bering Sea east of the 1867 treaty line. The schooners were taken to Sitka, Alaska, where they were ordered forfeited and sold and their officers imprisoned and fined for violating Section 1956, the provision barring killing of fur-bearing animals.[37] The Alaskan territorial judge's charge to the jury set out in an official and public way, apparently for the first time, a theory of the US legal justification for arresting and prosecuting the Canadians. The judge instructed the jury to the effect that Russia had claimed and exercised exclusive jurisdiction across the Bering Sea; other powers had acquiesced in that claim; and Russia's rights to exclusive jurisdiction had passed to the United States in 1867. US legislation barring killing of seals therefore applied to the Canadian sealing vessels seized beyond the territorial sea.[38] This charge in a remote territorial court room became "a decisive act in the controversy because it defined the issue that finally led to arbitration".[39]

The US Department of State in Washington DC seems not to have known of the seizure of the Canadian sealers or of the ensuing court proceedings in Sitka until the British Minister in Washington lodged a protest. Pleading its need for information, the Department did not respond to repeated British communications over the following months seeking clarification and assurances against repetition. (The Department did not receive a partial copy of the 1886 court proceedings in Alaska until April 1887).[40] However, Secretary of State Bayard had doubts about the strength of the US legal position,[41] and in February 1887 told the British Minister that President Cleveland had ordered the release of the seized vessels and persons under arrest.[42] However, the ships and crew were not in fact released as promised. The US marshal in Sitka thought the order to release them was a hoax, and they were not released until the marshal received a second order many months later.[43]

The British came away from the 1886 diplomatic exchanges believing that the United States had agreed not to seize more Canadian sealers, a view disputed by Secretary of State Bayard.[44] In August 1887, the British Minister informed the Department that three more Canadian vessels had been seized and that the vessels seized in 1886 had not been released.[45] In fact, twelve sealers were seized in 1887, equally divided between US and Canadian vessels. The Revenue Service cutters had too few personnel to provide

[36] Irving H King, *The Coast Guard Expands 1865–1915* (Naval Institute Press 1996) 37–46, 82–94; Evans (n 2) 121–25, 129–34. In 1894, the New York *Sun* described Healy as "a good deal more distinguished person in the waters of the far Northwest than any president of the United States or any potentate of Europe". ibid 121.

[37] Ireland (n 9) 401; Blodgett (n 7) 80–81; Williams, "Reminiscences" (n 13) 563; Tribunal Award (n 3) 273.

[38] Moore (n 22) 774 n 1; Williams, *Fur Seal Dispute* (n 6) 13.

[39] ibid 13.

[40] Moore (n 22) 770–73.

[41] Williams, "Reminiscences" (n 13) 563.

[42] Moore (n 22) 772–73.

[43] ibid 775.

[44] ibid 774.

[45] ibid 774.

prize crews, so the seized vessels were ordered to sail to Sitka and turn themselves in. These orders were often ignored.[46] In October 1887, the territorial judge in Sitka filed an elaborate opinion reaffirming his earlier opinion, and expressing elaborate thanks to the lawyer for the Alaska Commercial company—the current holder of the Pribilof's sealing lease—for a brief supporting a claim of *mare clausum*.[47]

Seeking to stave off further controversy, in August 1887, Secretary Bayard invited France, Great Britain, Germany, Japan, Russia, and Sweden and Norway to join in co-operative measures to protect Bering Sea seals. France, Russia, and Great Britain all concurred; in February 1888 the British Foreign Secretary Lord Salisbury endorsed an arrangement to bar takings in a broad area of the Bering Sea between 15 April and 1 November.[48] Negotiations with Russia and the British on a regime progressed well until the British brought them to a screeching halt after the Canadian government objected in May 1888.[49] Canada's objections reflected the views of the Pacific Sealers Association, a loose confederation of Canadian sealing captains and owners that "exercised a considerable economic and political leverage in both the B.C. Provincial and Dominion Parliaments in support of the Canadians sealers".[50]

## 5.  James G Blaine Takes the Case

There were no seizures in 1888, the last full year of President Cleveland's first term,[51] but the newly elected Republican administration of President Benjamin Harrison resumed them in 1889, when five Canadian and a larger number of US sealing vessels were seized.[52] With the change of administrations, Secretary of State Bayard was replaced as Secretary of State by the formidable James G Blaine.[53] Blaine abandoned Secretary Bayard's cautious approach and adopted a full-throated defence of US rights. A vigorous and sometimes heated diplomatic dialogue ensued between the United States and Great Britain.[54] A politician and not a lawyer, Blaine emphasized arguments that were compelling on policy grounds but were not necessarily well anchored in the international law of the late nineteenth century or a full understanding of the facts. Writing half a century later, William Williams, a junior counsel on the US legal team, delicately recalled that some key issues "were not fully understood by our government

[46] Williams, *Fur Seal Dispute* (n 6) 14.
[47] Moore (n 22) 775.
[48] ibid 780.
[49] ibid 782–83; Ireland (n 9) 401; Blodgett (n 7) 81.
[50] Williams, *Fur Seal Dispute* (n 6) 3.
[51] ibid 14; Moore (n 22) 784.
[52] Williams, *Fur Seal Dispute* (n 6) 14.
[53] Blaine twice served as US Secretary of State, was Speaker of the US House of Representatives 1869–1875, and later served as US Senator from Maine. He unsuccessfully sought the US presidency several times. Office of the Historian, US Department of State, "Biographies of the Secretaries of State: James Gillespie Blaine (1830–1893)" <http://www.history.state.gov>. Blaine is sometimes remembered for the taunt hurled by Grover Cleveland's supporters during Blaine's unsuccessful 1884 presidential campaign: "Blaine, Blaine, James G. Blaine: The continental liar from the State of Maine." "1884 Presidential Campaign Slogans" <http://www.PresidentsUSA.net>.
[54] Bailey (n 9) 412; John W Foster, "Results of the Bering Sea Arbitration" (1895) 161 North American Review 693, 695–96.

at the time",[55] and that "Mr. Blaine's brilliantly expressed contentions as to the measures adopted by Russia ... lacked the support of specific instances showing actual exercise of control".[56]

Blaine maintained that "the pursuit and killing of fur seals in Bering Sea was, from the point of view of international morality, an offense *contra bonos mores*".[57] The British government, in the correspondingly formidable personage of Lord Salisbury, countered that "it was not so until there had been some special international arrangement to forbid it, as fur seals were indisputably *ferae naturae* and *res nullius* until caught". Thus, pelagic sealers were engaged in a lawful activity on the high seas, over which the United States had no jurisdiction under international law. While conservation measures might be in order, these required the consent of the States of the affected vessels.[58] The continued diplomatic exchanges "showed the two governments in hopeless disagreement".[59]

In the United States, some had little sympathy for efforts to protect the seal herd, and there was concern about allowing the issue to become a source of confrontation and even to risk war with Great Britain. Writing in 1895, following the collapse of the US arbitration case, the US Agent (and former Secretary of State) John Foster observed that "a prevailing opinion in a large part of the press and with public men [was] that the attitude of the government was legally unsound, and that the interests involved [did] not ... justify the hazard of a great war".[60] A sceptical 1888 *North American Review* article recalled the origins and wide acceptance of the three-mile territorial sea, pointing out that the United States joined other States in opposing Russia's claims to jurisdiction beyond three miles.[61] However, the seals also had supporters. A December 1892 article in the *American Law Register and Review* attacked the British for insisting that "[t]o destroy the last and most valuable seal fishery in the world is to violate no right and transgress no law".[62]

In the United States, the issue took on a partisan hue. In his 1895 article, Foster (a Republican) tried to pin the tail on the Democratic donkey, claiming that the disputed arrests of Canadian sealers "were the act of the administration of President Cleveland and had the indorsement of the executive, politico-judicial and legislative departments of that administration" but were opposed by leading Congressional Republicans.[63] (Foster's argument rings hollow, given the enthusiastic defence of US rights to seize Canadian sealers by the Republican administration of President Harrison and his Secretary of State James Blaine.) Attempts in Congress in 1886 and 1889 to amend US law to make it expressly "include and apply to" all waters east of the Alaska cession line[64]

---

[55] Williams, "Reminiscences" (n 13) 563.
[56] ibid 566.
[57] Ireland (n 9) 401.
[58] Blodgett (n 7) 81.
[59] Foster (n 54) 696.
[60] ibid 697.
[61] Frederick Schwatka, "The Fur-Seal Fishery Dispute" (1888) 146 North America Review 390, 396.
[62] Stephen B Stanton, "The American Side of the Behring Sea Controversy" (1892) American Law Register and Review 809.
[63] Foster (n 54) 695.
[64] Moore (n 22) 764–65.

produced an ambiguous result. An amendment to section 1956 of the Revised Statutes (prohibiting unauthorized taking of seals) declared it to "include and apply to all the dominion of the United States in the waters of the Behring Sea", whatever that meant.[65]

In any case, pelagic sealing created political and practical problems for both the United States and Great Britain. The killing of large numbers of mostly female seals at sea and the ship seizures were facts, as were the complaints of Canadian sealers and the ensuing British diplomatic protests. Neither Democratic President Cleveland nor Republican President Harrison could comfortably appear to back down in the face of British protests. For its part, the British government was perhaps less than fully sympathetic to the pelagic sealers' trade; the British indeed came close to accepting a vigorous regulatory regime before the 1888 season, but Canadian objections brought the effort to a halt. Neither party enjoyed substantial manoeuvring room.

Matters were further complicated by sharp disagreements regarding the reasons for the seal population's decline. The British government pressed Canadian arguments discounting the significance of pelagic sealing and claiming that the greatest injury to the seal populations resulted from indiscriminate slaughter of seals on land under US authority.[66] In April 1890, the British Minister in Washington DC tabled a multi-part proposal to address this factual dispute as part of an overall effort at settlement. The British proposed a short-term closed season on takings on both land and at sea in the spring and fall; a mixed commission of experts to assess the adequacy of US measures on the breeding islands and whether further measures at sea might be required; and providing for the possibility of arbitration should the experts not agree.[67]

President Harrison's cabinet rejected the April 1890 proposal, leading to British threats of "the most serious consequences" in case of further seizures, a not-very-veiled reference to the Royal Navy's battleship and six cruisers in Esquimalt, BC, a force that far outgunned all US vessels then in the North Pacific.[68] The Secretary of the Treasury ordered the Revenue cutters to make no seizures in 1890.[69] This avoided new incidents, but exposed the Republican Harrison Administration to potential accusations of having yielded under British pressure, in contrast to the more robust measures of the previous Democratic Cleveland administration.

## 6.  Why Don't We Arbitrate?

As diplomatic exchanges continued, the parties took steps to reframe the dispute. While Secretary Blaine was not prepared to submit the legality of the seizures to arbitration, he was prepared to arbitrate questions related to what he saw as Russia's historic rights

[65] ibid 766; Williams, "Reminiscences" (n 13) 563.
[66] Moore (n 22) 787.
[67] ibid 788; Williams, *Fur Seal Dispute* (n 6) 16. The British proposal allowed unrestricted pelagic sealing in the high summer months when female seals fed at sea, significantly reducing its benefits to the seal population and its appeal to the US side.
[68] Williams, *Fur Seal Dispute* (n 6) 16-17.
[69] ibid 17.

in the Bering Sea.[70] It was then ultimately agreed that the dispute should be referred to arbitration, largely on the basis of questions formulated by Secretary Blaine. The parties also agreed to create a joint scientific commission to investigate and seek to agree on the facts. Finally, Blaine proposed that while the scientific investigation was underway, the parties should conclude a treaty establishing a *modus vivendi* restricting pelagic sealing enforced by public vessels of both parties.[71] Because of Canadian objections, the treaty establishing the *modus vivendi* remained unsigned as the 1891 season approached. President Harrison overcame the deadlock by agreeing to prohibit commercial sealing on land, leading the British to disregard further Canadian objections. The *modus vivendi* treaty was initialled and quickly brought into force for 1891.[72]

The 1891 *modus vivendi* established a total suspension of pelagic sealing for a year. The United States agreed to prohibit killing of seals by US citizens, except for 7,500 seals for native subsistence. Great Britain agreed to prohibit killing by British subjects for a year, with the Royal Navy assuming a role "to help protect the seals against British poachers".[73] Although the *modus vivendi* "still provoked a storm of protest in British Columbia",[74] a joint US-British Bering Sea patrol of US revenue cutters and both US and British naval vessels stopped forty one of forty-nine pelagic sealing vessels entering the Bering Sea from Victoria.[75]

Renewal of the *modus vivendi* in 1892 was fraught. Sensitive to Canadian opposition, the British initially refused to extend it. This triggered an angry response by President Harrison, then facing a difficult Fall election campaign and acting as his own Secretary of State due to Secretary Blaine's illness. Harrison's heated note became public, stimulating animated public reactions on both sides of the Atlantic.[76] Despite popular pressure in London and Canada, the British Government concluded that the game was not worth the candle, and in April 1892 agreed to extend the *modus vivendi* until the end of the arbitration.[77]

## 7. Organizing the Proceedings

The Treaty of Washington authorizing arbitration of the Bering Sea fur seal dispute was signed on Leap Year Day, 29 February 1892.[78] The US Senate promptly consented to ratification, and the treaty entered into force in May 1892. In addition to questions

---

[70] ibid 24.

[71] ibid 17-18.

[72] Fur Seals Fisheries in Bering Sea (United States - United Kingdom) (15 June 1891), 27 Stat. 980, TS 140; Williams, *Fur Seal Dispute* (n 6) 18.

[73] Evans (n 2) 112; Ireland (n 9) 401.

[74] Williams, *Fur Seal Dispute* (n 6) 20.

[75] Ross (n 10) 42.

[76] Williams, *Fur Seal Dispute* (n 6) 25.

[77] ibid 27; Ireland (n 9) 401–02.

[78] Bering Sea Arbitration Convention (United States—Great Britain) (signed at Washington, 29 February 1892, entered into force 7 May 1892) 27 Stat. 947, TS 140-1, Charles I Bevans, *Treaties and Other International Agreements of the United States of America 1776–1949*, Vol. 12 (US Dep't of State Publication 8761, 1974) 220 (hereafter Arbitration Convention).

addressing the parties' legal claims, the treaty included an unusual article empowering the future arbitration panel, should it rule against the US claim to jurisdiction, to itself devise regulations for the protection of the seals to be adopted and applied by the parties.

Article VI of treaty set out five questions framed along the lines sought by Secretary of State Blaine, directing that the Arbitrators' award was to "embrace a distinct decision upon each". The first four related to US contentions that, through its acquisition of Alaska from Russia, the United States had acquired rights to regulate takings of the seals in Bering Sea waters beyond the territorial sea. The fifth related to a separate line of argument that became the most important part of the US case. However, as will be seen, the US case on all five questions failed.

The tribunal was asked to rule on five specific questions:

1. What exclusive jurisdiction in the sea now known as the Behring's Sea, and what exclusive rights in the seal fisheries therein, did Russia assert and exercise prior and up to the time of the cession of Alaska to the United States?
2. How far were these claims of jurisdiction as to the seal fisheries recognized and conceded by Great Britain?
3. Was the body of water now known as the Behring's Sea included in the phrase Pacific Ocean, as used in the Treaty of 1825 between Great Britain and Russia; and what rights, if any, in the Behring's Sea were held and exclusively exercised by Russia after said Treaty?
4. Did not all the rights of Russia as to jurisdiction and as to the seal fisheries in Behring's Sea east of the water boundary, in the Treaty between the United States and Russia of the 30th of March 1867, pass unimpaired to the United States under that Treaty?
5. Has the United States any right, and if so, what right of protection or property in the fur seals frequenting the islands of the United States in Behring Sea when such seals are found outside the ordinary three-mile limit?

The treaty also included Article VII, which gave the tribunal a role that Professor Ralston rightly found "unusual".[79] Article VII authorized the tribunal to itself devise a solution to the dispute. It directed that, should British concurrence be found necessary to protect the fur seals, the Arbitrators should establish regulations to this end, which the parties committed themselves to implement:

If the determination of the foregoing questions as to the exclusive jurisdiction of the United States shall leave the subject in such position that the concurrence of Great Britain is necessary to the establishment of Regulations for the proper protection and preservation of the fur-seal in, or habitually resorting to, the Behring Sea, the Arbitrators shall then determine what concurrent Regulations, outside the

---

[79] Jackson H Ralston, *International Arbitration from Athens to Locarno* (Stanford University Press 1929). 201.

jurisdictional limits of the respective Governments, are necessary, and over what waters such Regulations should extend;

The High Contracting Parties furthermore agree to cooperate in securing the adhesion of other Powers to such Regulations ....

The treaty called for a seven-member tribunal. The United States and Great Britain each appointed two members. The other three were appointed by the President of the French Republic, the King of Italy, and the King of Sweden and Norway.

US President Benjamin Harrison, a Republican who would later that year be defeated by Grover Cleveland in the 1892 Fall election, appointed US Supreme Court Justice John M Harlan. Harlan is today remembered as the "great dissenter"[80] for his dissenting opinions in cases involving civil liberties, notably in *Plessy v Ferguson*,[81] an ill-reputed 1896 decision affirming Louisiana's legally mandated racial segregation on railroad passenger cars and the principle of "separate but equal". Justice Harlan was joined on the Tribunal by Alabama Senator John T Morgan, the Democratic Chairman of the US Senate Foreign Relations Committee. John Foster described Senator Morgan as "the recognized leader on all international questions in the Senate of the party whose officials had originated the subject matter of the arbitration".[82] Senator Morgan seemed a safe choice; in 1889 Senate debates on the extent of US jurisdiction, he endorsed a US right to protect seals "in seas that do not belong strictly to the *mare clausum* principle".[83] Senator Morgan was also a former slave holder and Confederate brigadier general, an ardent expansionist, and a vehement racist.[84] His conception of his role as a party-appointed arbitrator is perhaps reflected in the "object description" accompanying his portrait on the US Senate's website. This records Morgan's appointment "to a commission representing American interests before the Bering Sea Tribunal, then meeting in Paris".[85]

The British Government named Lord Hannen, a distinguished judge in English Equity and Admiralty Courts,[86] and Sir John Thompson, a Canadian lawyer and political leader who at the time was concurrently Canada's Minister of Justice, Attorney General, and fourth Prime Minister.[87] (Thompson served only two years as Prime Minister, dying of a heart attack at age forty-nine the year after the fur seal arbitration.)

The other members of the panel were jurists with wide diplomatic and legal experience. The President of the French Republic named Baron de Courcel, a member of the French Senate and French Ambassador to London. His 1895 *Vanity Fair* caricature

---

[80] "John Marshall Harlan" <https://en.wikipedia.org/wiki/John_Marshall_Harlan>.

[81] 163 US 537 (1896). Harlan's dissent urged that legally sanctioned segregation violated the 14th Amendment to the US Constitution.

[82] Foster (n 54) 698–99.

[83] Moore (n 22) 766.

[84] "As one of the most outspoken white supremacists of the early Jim Crow era, he vigorously championed the racist policies of black disfranchisement and racial segregation. Morgan advocated the removal of the black population of the South to foreign shores...." "John Tyler Morgan" <http://www.Encyclopedia of Alabama.org>.

[85] "John Tyler Morgan" <https://www.senate.gov/art-artifacts/fine-art/paintings/32_00024.htm>.

[86] Among his many accomplishments, Lord Hannen was in private life Vice President of the London Vegetarian Society. "James Hannen, Baron Hannen" <http://www.en.wikipedia.org>.

[87] "The Right Hon. Sir John Sparrow David Thompson, P.C., Q.C., K.C.M.G., M.P." <http://www.lop.parl.ca>.

THE US CASE    35

in the collection of London's National Portrait Gallery depicts a substantial and well-tailored gentleman, formidably moustached, and peering out with a curious and open expression.[88] The King of Italy named Marquis Emilio Visconti Venosta, a seasoned diplomat and politician who served as Foreign Minister in multiple Italian governments.[89] Minister of State Gregers Gram was named by the King of Sweden and Norway. Gram, a promoter of arbitration to resolve international disputes, sat in several important inter-state cases and was a member of the Institut de droit international.[90] He was one of the first persons appointed to the Permanent Court of Arbitration and remained on the Permanent. Court until his death.

The Tribunal convened in Paris on 23 March 1893 in the Ministry of Foreign Affairs on the Quai d'Orsay, beginning proceedings that stretched until 15 August, nearly five months. Sittings were generally four days a week from 11 a.m. until 4 p.m.[91] Contemporary arbitration practitioners facing tribunals' demanding time restrictions may feel some jealousy for the generous time allotments given to counsel in the fur seal case.

## 8. The US Case

The US legal team for the arbitration seems to have been selected with an eye to both legal acumen and to managing fallout in case of a bad outcome. The Agent was John W Foster, a prominent advocate of international arbitration in inter-state relations, Secretary of State in Harrison's Administration, father-in-law of future Secretary of State Robert Lansing, and grandfather of future Secretary of State John Foster Dulles.[92] He was joined by legal luminaries who included three described as "political friends of Mr. Cleveland": EJ Phelps, previously Cleveland's Minister in London, James C Carter,[93] and Frederic R Coudert.[94] Phelps, Carter, and Coudert were joined by Judge HW Blodgett, a Republican.[95]

The US case developed two broad lines of argument. The first, addressing the first four questions to the Tribunal, was essentially that prior to 1867, Russia asserted exclusive jurisdiction over fishing and hunting in the Bering Sea; that its claim was accepted by other States; and that Russia's rights passed to the United States through the 1867 cession.[96] In commentary on both sides of the Atlantic in the runup to the arbitration,

---

[88] "Alphonse Chodron de Courcel, 1st Baron de Courcel ('Men of the Day. No. 611.')" <http://www.npg.org.uk>.

[89] "Emilio, marquis Visconti-Venosta" *Encyclopedia Britannica*, <https://www.britannica.com/biography/Emilio-Marchese-Visconti-Venosta>.

[90] "Gregers Gram. Prime Minister in Stockholm 1889–1891, 1893–1895 and 1895–1898", <https://www.regjeringen.no/en/the-government/previous-governments/historiske-artikler/offices/norwegian-prime-minister-in-stockholm-18/gregers-winther-wulfsberg-gram/id440574/>.

[91] Williams, "Reminiscences" (n 13) 570.

[92] "Biographies of the Secretaries of State: John Watson Foster (1836–1917)" <http://www.history.state.gov>.

[93] Carter was a leading New York lawyer; the firm he helped found in 1854 endures today as Carter Ledyard & Milburn. He is remembered, *inter alia*, for his role in successfully suing William "Boss" Tween for corruption and graft. "A Brief History of Carter Ledyard & Milburn" <https://www.clm.com/firm/a-brief-history/>.

[94] "Frederic René Coudert Sr." <https://en.wikipedia.org/wiki/Frederic_René_Coudert_Sr.>.

[95] Foster (n 54) 699.

[96] Ireland (n 9) 402.

this part of the US position was sometimes understood to be that the Bering Sea was wholly within US jurisdiction—a *mare clausum*. The US position in the arbitration, however, was more limited and nuanced. As described by a member of the US team, the United States argued that:

> Russia had always protected the seals in Bering Sea by the consent and acquiescence of all other civilized nations, to such an extent that it had ripened into a right, and we had succeeded to all the rights of Russia, including the alleged right to prohibit sealing in Bering Sea ... [*Mare clausum*] was not the position taken—Mr. Blaine insisting that Russia had always, by common consent, protected the seals there, but denying emphatically that he relied on the closed sea position.[97]

However, as Secretary of States Bayard had feared in the early days of the dispute, and as the British team made clear, factual support for the US claim that Russia had acquired recognized rights of exclusive jurisdiction to protect fur seals at sea was thin. After the arbitration, John W Foster observed acidly that when the US case "came to be prepared and the Russian archives were examined, what had been assumed in the legal proceedings to be historical facts could scarcely be substantiated by a single official document".[98] The US case was further embarrassed by US reliance on inaccurate translations of documents from the files of the pre-1867 Russian-American Company. The translations, prepared by a freelance Russian-language translator who seems to have been the only one available, were incorrect and indeed deliberately false in important respects.[99] The US team subsequently provided corrected translations, but "[t]hrough such amendment our position on historical and jurisdictional questions was necessarily weakened".[100]

Accordingly, the United States did not primarily rely on its first line of argument and seems not to have been too surprised by its rejection by the Tribunal.[101] Instead, US arguments emphasized the fifth question, reflecting themes developed by Secretary of State Blaine in his exchanges with Lord Salisbury.[102] The United States in effect argued for the Tribunal to innovate to address the unusual challenges of pelagic sealing. As a contemporary writer put it, "[t]he able representatives of the United States took the position that the Tribunal was bound by no precedents and possessed, by virtue of its origin, a creative as well as a judicial function".[103]

This portion of the case opened with lead US counsel James Carter's discussion of the principles of international law said to apply. In Carter's submission, these included fundamental principles common to international and municipal law, including principles

---

[97] Blodgett (n 7) 82.

[98] Foster (n 54) 698.

[99] Williams, "Reminiscences" (n 13) 566–67.

[100] ibid 567.

[101] Blodgett (n 7) 89.

[102] Foster (n 54) 698.

[103] J Stanley Brown, "Fur Seals and the Bering Sea Arbitration" (1894) 26 Journal of the American Geographical Society of New York 326, 361.

related to property. Carter examined these at length, concluding that "under the law of nature, all property was held in trust for mankind" and that, with certain exceptions, "only its usufruct was available for consumption".[104] Not all on the US team were enthusiastic about Mr Carter's theoretical discourse on the foundations of property. Writing long after, William Williams thought Carter "was unwise in choosing this tribunal as a forum for the discussion of the foregoing propositions because they had but a remote bearing on the issues, tended to divert the attention of the arbitrators ... and furnished our clever opponents with several targets at which they did some successful shooting".[105]

Proceeding from Carter's basic principles, the United States argued that because the fur seals always returned to the Pribilofs to breed, the fur seal was an *anumus revertendi*. The animals' annual return to rookeries owned by the United States and managed under its direction gave the United States an ownership right in the seals themselves, an exclusive right that could be exercised when the animals were at sea.[106] The habits of the seals taken with the US actions to manage and protect the breeding herds thus gave the United States a property interest in the seals and a related right to protect its property beyond the three-mile territorial limit.

Building from these arguments, the United States emphasized the need for management and protection of the seal herd to assure its survival. The United States submitted extensive evidence said to show both the destructive character of pelagic sealing and the reduction in the size of the herd. This included a showing that pelagic sealers mainly killed pregnant or nursing females at sea, with the harm to the population compounded by failure to recover more than half of the killed or injured seals.[107] The US evidence was reinforced by descriptions at the hearing—including by a Canadian lawyer on the British team—graphicly describing conditions on the decks of sealing schooners as gravid and nursing females were skinned, leading Mr. Phelps of the US team to characterize pelagic sealing as "barbarous, inhuman and shocking in its revolting details".[108] HW Blodgett of the US legal team summed up this part of the US argument.

> From this proof we argued that protection of the seals when in the water is absolutely necessary for the preservation of the race for commercial purposes. That as the conceded owner of the territory where the seals have their land homes, where they are begotten and born and spend nearly half of each year of their lives, the United States has such a property right in them that it can lawfully protect them from destruction when in the open sea, and outside our three mile territorial limit from the shore. That the necessity for protection being shown some one must protect them, and that there was no controlling international reason which should prevent the nation most interested in their preservation from so protecting them.[109]

---

104 Williams, "Reminiscences" (n 13) 570.
105 ibid.
106 Williams, *Fur Seal Dispute* (n 6) 2; Williams "Reminiscences" (n 13) 571.
107 Blodgett (n 7) 84–85; Williams, "Reminiscences" (n 13) 575.
108 ibid 581.
109 Blodgett (n 7) 85.

## 9. The British Reply

Charles Russell, Attorney General of Great Britain, led for the British. Russell, a renowned advocate, was Lord Chief Justice of England from 1894 until his death in 1900. His eleven-day speech to the Tribunal in 1893 was rewarded by the British Government with the award of a KCMG "in recognition of services rendered in connection with the recent Behring Sea Arbitration" that year.[110]

Russell "dealt somewhat harshly with Mr. Carter's views on international law and its adaptability to new situations",[111] insisting that the Tribunal had no law-making function. Instead, "the advocates of Great Britain and Canada held that the Tribunal possessed but one function—that its duty was to declare the law and not make it ... it was not vested with the power to make international law, but must keep to the straight and narrow way of settling a contention between two nations".[112] The British accordingly emphasized that the Bering Sea was not a *mare clausum*, a closed sea, but was an open sea providing a highway to Great Britain's northern possessions in the Yukon region and on the McKenzie River[113] The British accepted that whatever rights Russia may have held were transferred to the United States by the 1867 treaty, but denied that Russia had any recognized right in relation to pelagic sealing on the high seas. Instead, as HW Blodgett summarized the British argument:

> [T]he question as to the right of Russia, to protect the seals in the open sea had never arisen during Russia's ownership. That no such pursuit or occupation, as pelagic sealing by white men with modern appliances was known before the cession of Alaska to the United States; wherefore no rule applicable to the question, now before the Tribunal could be deduced from the mode in which Russia had dealt with the territory and the seals, while she controlled the territory.[114]

Russell highlighted that when the Czar sought in 1821 to prohibit non-Russian ships from approaching within 100 miles of the coasts where the Russian-American Company held a sealing monopoly, the United States and Great Britain both protested.[115] These protests were recognized in subsequent treaties in 1824 and 1825 in which Russia agreed that US and British citizens or subjects would not be disturbed or restrained in navigation or fishing except where there were Russian establishments.[116]

In the British view, international law thus did not support any claim of property or of US jurisdiction beyond the territorial sea. The US claim of rights of property and

---

[110] "Charles Russell, Baron Russell of Killowen" <https://en.wikipedia.org/wiki/Charles_Russell,_Baron_Russell_of_Killowen>.
[111] Williams, "Reminiscences" (n 13) 576.
[112] Brown (n 103) 362–63.
[113] Ireland (n 9) 402.
[114] Blodgett (n 7) 86.
[115] Moore (n 22) 756–60.
[116] ibid 760–63; Blodgett (n 7) 86–87; Ireland (n 9) 400.

protection in the seals was dismissed as unprecedented and as inconsistent with US claims in other settings. Seals found beyond the three-mile limit "were like fish, whales, or any other free-swimming animal, the common property of all people, and subject to pursuit and capture by any one who chooses to embark on the business".[117]

## 10. The Tribunal's Award

The Tribunal deliberated in private for almost a month, beginning on 19 July 1893 and handing down its award on 15 August. The Tribunal rejected both the core US arguments.

The award first addressed the treaty's four questions going to US arguments that Russia had rights of protection or property in fur seals throughout the Bering Sea prior to 1867 that were recognized by other States and that passed to the United States. The Tribunal was not impressed. Justice Harlan joined with five arbitrators in rejecting the key US arguments, although Senator Morgan resolutely voted for the US position throughout. Thus, as to the first four points:

> Point 1: A 6--1 majority decided that in negotiations leading to its treaties with the United States in 1824 and Great Britain in 1825, Russia admitted that her jurisdiction "should be restricted to the reach of cannon shot from shore," and that thereafter, "Russia never asserted in fact or exercised any exclusive jurisdiction in Behring's Sea or any exclusive rights in the seal fisheries therein" beyond territorial waters.[118]
>
> Point 2: By 6–1, the Tribunal again decided that "Great Britain did not recognize or concede any claim, upon the part of Russia, to exclusive jurisdiction as to the seal fisheries in the Behring Sea, outside of ordinary territorial waters."[119]
>
> Point 3: This involved both undisputed and contentious issues. The panel found unanimously that the term "Pacific Ocean" in the 1825 British-Russian treaty included "the body of water now known as the Behring Sea." However, the Tribunal also found 6–1 that Russia had "no exclusive rights of jurisdiction in Behring Sea and no exclusive rights as to the seal fisheries therein ... outside of ordinary territorial waters."[120]
>
> Point 4: The panel decided unanimously that "all the rights of Russia as to jurisdiction and as to the seal fisheries in Behring Sea, east of the water boundary ... did pass unimpaired to the United States."[121]

The panel was thus unanimous that whatever rights Russia had to own, manage, or protect fur seals passed to the United States under the 1867 treaty. However, it also

---

[117] Blodgett (n 7) 87.
[118] Tribunal Award (n 3) 269.
[119] ibid.
[120] ibid.
[121] ibid.

determined—with Justice Harlan concurring on key points—that those rights ended where cannon balls fired from shore fell into the sea. Russia did not transfer any internationally recognized right to own or protect fur seals beyond the territorial sea.

The collapse of this part of their case likely did not surprise the US lawyers, given past US advocacy of freedom of the seas, Russia's 1824 and 1825 treaties with the United States and Great Britain (which the Tribunal cited and clearly thought significant), and the thin evidence supporting the US historical claims. In this regard John Foster's *ex post* defence of the Harrison Administration's decision to go to arbitration rather gracelessly sidestepped the role of Secretary of State Blaine in defining the US position, attributing shortcoming in the US case to the Cleveland administration: "whatever fallacies exist ... are chargeable to the previous administration which had occasioned the controversy and marked out the lines of defense".[122]

The US lawyers hoped for more from the Tribunal on the fifth question, which asked the Tribunal in broad terms to determine whether the United States had rights of property or protection in fur seals beyond three miles. However, this part of the case also collapsed, with the Tribunal rejecting the US invitation to make new international law. Instead, it decided by a vote of five to two, with both US-appointed arbitrators in the minority,[123] that the United States did not have the rights it claimed.[124] In his postmortem of the case, HW Blodgett acknowledged the novelty of the US argument, but bemoaned its rejection.

[T]he reasons for a decision in our favor, growing out of the special facts which we proved, seemed so cogent and conclusive that we may be said to have expected that the Tribunal would take an advanced step in international law and hold that, as it was for the obvious interest of the commercial world that the seals should be protected and as our nation was the most deeply and directly interested in their protection, we might protect them by our laws and force.[125]

But, lamented Blodgett:

The neutral arbitrators were all able jurists but doubtless highly conservative, as all good jurists generally are, and they probably thought the seals could be protected and preserved by regulations and thereby enable the Tribunal to avoid any innovation upon the well settled rules of international law ....[126]

---

[122] Foster (n 54) 696.
[123] Justice Harlan wrote a dissent to the majority decision, concurred in by Senator Morgan. Williams, "Reminiscences" (n 13) 583. The dissent is not included with the award in RIAA.
[124] Tribunal Award (n 3) 269.
[125] Blodgett (n 7) 89–80.
[126] ibid 90; Brown (n 103) 364.

## 11. The Tribunal's Regulations

Having rejected the claimed US rights to protect the seals without British concurrence, the Tribunal turned to the unusual task assigned to it by the arbitration treaty: to establish "[r]egulations for the proper protection and preservation of the fur-seal in or habitually resorting to the Behring Sea ... outside the ordinary three-mile limit".

At the end of their presentations to the Tribunal, each party presented its proposed regulations. The United States essentially proposed banning all pelagic sealing throughout the North Pacific. The British argued that a twenty-mile closed zone around the Pribilofs would suffice.[127] In the manner sometimes seen as characteristic of interstate arbitration, the Tribunal appears to have devised a compromise it hoped would be "acceptable to both nations", conceiving (incorrectly) that its regulations "while appearing to concede something to the pelagic sealer, made the conditions just sufficiently hard to prevent him from engaging in the enterprise".[128]

Unfortunately, in crafting its attempt at compromise, the Tribunal did not have sound agreed scientific guidance regarding the reasons for the decline of the seal population. The binational scientific investigation of the state of the herd that was supposed to inform the Tribunal was a failure. "All participants quickly accepted that there was too much killing, but no one was willing to accept the blame", with the result that the 1892 joint commission "broke up when the Canadians argued the evidence was inconclusive".[129] The Canadian investigators claimed the decline was due to US mismanagement of the herds on land at the rookeries and disputed the significance of pelagic sealing; the US participants urged the opposite.[130] Accordingly, the Tribunal did not have a clear and agreed factual foundation, notably on female seals' summertime feeding habits, upon which to base its regime.[131] The result turned out to be disastrous for the seals.

With the concurrence of four members (not including Sir John Thompson of Canada or the two members appointed by the United States), the Tribunal by majority set out a regime to be brought into effect by the British and US Governments. *Inter alia*, the Tribunal's regime provided for the two Governments to:

—Forbid their "citizens and subjects" to "kill, capture or pursue at any time and in any manner whatever" fur seals "within a zone of sixty miles around the Pribilov Islands;"

—Forbid sealing by the citizens and subjects from 1 May until 31 July each year in a broad area of the Pacific Ocean that included the Bering Sea; and

—Limit fur sealing to licensed sailing vessels carrying a distinguishing flag.[132]

---

[127] Williams, *Fur Seal Dispute* (n 6) 43.
[128] Brown (n 103) 368.
[129] Kirk Dorsey, "Scientists, Citizens, and Statesmen: U.S.-Canadian Wildlife Protection Treaties in the Progressive Era" (1995) 19 Diplomatic History 407, 418.
[130] ibid 418; Williams, "Reminiscences" (n 13) 573–75.
[131] Williams, *Fur Seal Dispute* (n 6) 43.
[132] Tribunal Award (n 3) 270.

The Tribunal's regulations also required logging and reporting of sealing operations, "measures to control the fitness of the men authorized to engaged in fur seal fishing," and authorized limited sealing by "Indians dwelling on the coasts" of US or British territory conducted "in canoes or undecked boats ... in the way hitherto practiced by the Indians".[133]

Initial reactions to the Tribunal's Award were mixed. Some critics blamed Secretary of State Blaine for a defeat; in the view of the *New York Nation* the Tribunal found Blaine's history "to be fiction, his geography pure fancy and his international law a mere whim".[134] On the other hand, US Agent John Foster hailed the Tribunal's regulations as more restrictive than the two sets of regulations previously proposed by the United States but rejected by Great Britain.[135] Other US observers were "cautiously optimistic". Canada was less pleased, with some feeling that the outcome sacrificed Canadian interests.[136]

Looking back, Williams contended that the Tribunal wrongly subordinated protection of the seal population to the interests of the pelagic sealers, contrary to the treaty.[137] Writing before the regulations were implemented, Blodgett warned that "[t]he sixty-mile zone within which sealing is prohibited will be of but little service ... as the large schools of fish are usually much farther than that distance away from the islands, and where the fish are the seals will be".[138] His warning was correct.

Following British delays and some posturing and diplomatic melodrama,[139] the United States and Great Britain each adopted legislation in April 1894 to implement the Tribunal regime. "The Bering Sea Patrol Force, composed of four or five [US Revenue Service] cutters under a force commander, was inaugurated in the middle 'nineties and thereafter patrolled the Bering Sea and the Aleutian chain from April to November every year."[140] In 1897, the United States adopted legislation prohibiting US citizens and vessels from pelagic sealing in the Bering sea or the Pacific Ocean north of the thirty-fifth parallel.

Despite such measures, experience quickly demonstrated the weakness of the Tribunal's regime. Sealers of several nationalities waited for feeding seals at the edge of the 60-mile exclusion zone in August and "continued to exact a high toll ... In the 1893 and 1894 seasons, according to London records, pelagic sealers from the northeast Pacific turned in the pelts of nearly 194,000 fur seals."[141] The 1894 season, the first

---

[133] ibid 270–71. The Tribunal's award also incorporated a statement of facts submitted by the British side and agreed by the US Agent and Counsel listing the names and locations of twenty British sealing vessels seized or warned by US Revenue Service cutters between 1886 and 1890. Although the Tribunal did not rule on the issue of damages, the Secretary of State and the British Ambassador subsequently agreed on a settlement of $425,000 for Britain's claims for the vessel seizures. Following Congressional opposition to the required appropriations, some led by Senator Morgan, the claims were ultimately settled and paid in 1898. Williams, *Fur Seal Dispute* (n 6) 51, 58.

[134] NEW YORK NATION, LVII, 113 (17 August 1893 ), in Bailey (n 10) 413.

[135] Foster (n 54) 700.

[136] Williams, *Fur Seal Dispute* (n 6) 47.

[137] Williams, "Reminiscences" (n 13) 583.

[138] Blodgett (n 7) 90.

[139] Williams, *Fur Seal Dispute* (n 6) 49–50.

[140] Evans (n 2) 109.

[141] Ross (n 10) 42.

under the Tribunal's regime, turned out to be the "high rolling year" for the sealers.[142] The US Department of the Interior recorded that pelagic sealing reached a peak that year, recording 61,800 seals taken at sea, a number that did not reflect the much larger number actually killed.[143]

As a result, the seal herd "was rapidly approaching the vanishing point" as the century ended.[144] The 1897 conclusions of a joint scientific investigation, endorsed by British, Canadian, and US representatives, found that the number of seals killed on land in the Pribilofs in 1896 and 1897 was from one-third to one-fifth of the numbers killed previously.[145] In 1907, the inaugural issue of the *American Journal of International Law* noted the US view that "the award regulations are wholly inadequate to protect and preserve the seal herd, and that pelagic sealing, if permitted at all, must inevitably result in the extermination of the herd for commercial purposes".[146] Indeed, destruction of the herd continued to the extent that President Theodore Roosevelt's Annual Message to Congress in December 1906 posed an extraordinary question: whether, if pelagic sealing could not be controlled, "it is not better to end the practise [sic] by exterminating the herd ourselves in the most humane way possible", thereby securing the commercial advantages of taking the remaining skins while saving the expense of the Revenue Cutter Service's Bering Sea patrol.[147]

## 12. The Road to the Fur Seal Convention

Faced with the precipitous decline of the herd, the United States made recurring efforts to secure international cooperation to limit sealing. In 1897, the United States signed a treaty with Russia and Japan barring killing of fur seals in the North Pacific beyond the territorial sea for a year, but the treaty could not enter into force unless Great Britain adhered as well. It declined to do so.[148] The *American Journal of International Law*'s first issue quotes Britain's explanation: that "Her Majesty's Government cannot recognize that Russia and Japan have any interest in the seal fisheries on the American side of the North Pacific".[149] Meanwhile, in an ironic turn of events, beginning in 1888, Russian cruisers began seizing US and Canadian sealers operating in Russia's coastal waters beyond the territorial sea.[150]

Renewed US efforts to secure international cooperation, especially in 1898 and 1903, also failed. However, the continued decline of the seal population, together with the increased activities of Japanese pelagic sealers in the North Pacific, created a new

---

[142] Williams, *Fur Seal Dispute* (n 6) 49.
[143] 1961 Interior Release (n 28) 3.
[144] Evans (n 2) 114.
[145] David Starr Jordan, *Second Preliminary Report of the Bering Fur Seal Investigations, 1897* (US Gov't Printing Office 1898) 45.
[146] "The Fur Seal Question" [1907] 1 American Journal of International Law 727, 746.
[147] ibid 747; Ross (n 10) 46.
[148] Ireland (n 9) 404.
[149] "The Fur Seal Question" (n 146) 745.
[150] Ireland (n 9) 403.

situation. By one estimate, the seal population had by 1911 been reduced to 132,000 from an estimate of five million in 1867.[151] And, Japanese, and not Canadian sealers, "were more prevalent in [the] Bering Sea after the turn of the century".[152]

In January 1909, the United States again invited Great Britain, Russia, and Japan to meet to address the seals' precipitous decline. Russia and Japan, which recently had been at war, accepted. The British did not, insisting on a bilateral settlement to protect Canada's economic interests as a precondition to four-party negotiations.[153] Following two years of negotiations, in February 1911 the two countries signed a bilateral treaty prohibiting pelagic sealing by their citizens and subjects in a broad expanse of the North Pacific and Bering Sea. As compensation for Canadian sealers' losses, the United States agreed to deliver to a Canadian agent each year one-fifth of the value of the sealskins taken on the Pribilof Islands. This agreement was to go into effect when an agreement should enter into force among the United States, Great Britain, Japan, and Russia.[154]

With Canada's sustained objections to limits on pelagic sealing overcome by a promised share of the proceeds of US takings on land,[155] the way was cleared for negotiation of an effective multilateral regime for protection of the seals. A diplomatic conference of the four North Pacific powers—Great Britain, Japan, Russia, and the United States—convened at Washington on 11 May 1911.[156] The turmoil and political and economic trade-offs involved in the ensuing two-month negotiation are beyond the scope of this chapter. However, the four powers ultimately closed a deal, and the Convention between the United States and Other Powers Providing for the Preservation and Protection of Fur Seals, was signed on 7 July 1911 and entered into force on 15 December 1911.[157]

The Convention is widely credited with saving the seals from extinction.[158] Through its provisions

> the Americans and Russians finally put an end to legal pelagic sealing, and the treaty contained provisions for dealing with the illegal kind. Both nations were free to set their own quotas for the killing of bachelor seals.[159] Most importantly, they both received international recognition of their proprietary rights to seals born on their territory. On the other side, the Japanese and Canadians received lucrative cash settlements. Each nation was to get a $200,000 advance and 15% from the Russian and American seal harvests.[160]

---

[151] Williams, *Fur Seal Dispute* (n 6) 5.
[152] ibid.
[153] "Editorial Comment—The North Pacific Sealing Convention" (1911) 5 American Journal of International Law 1025, 1031.
[154] Ireland (n 9) 404.
[155] Kurk Dorsey, "Putting a Ceiling on Sealing: Conservation and Cooperation in the International Arena" (1991) 15 Environmental History Review 27, 38.
[156] AJIL, "Editorial Comment" (n 153) 1031.
[157] Fur Seal Convention (n 4).
[158] Dorsey, "Putting a Ceiling on Sealing" (n 155) 43.
[159] The United States authorized killing of male seals on land on the Pribilofs.
[160] Dorsey, "Putting a Ceiling on Sealing" (n 155) 40. Ireland (n 9) 404. A contemporary official summary of the Convention is reproduced at (1911) 5 American Journal of International Law 1032.

The Convention was hailed at the time as a significant success. The *American Journal of International Law* deemed it

> a conservation measure of the highest importance providing as it does for the equitable adjustment of the conflicting interests of the Powers concerned, and making it to their advantage in the future to protect the seal herds in the North Pacific from the wasteful destruction involved in seal killing at sea, and assuring scientific treatment of the seals upon their breeding grounds to the end that the value of these herds may be increased for the purposes of commerce and the benefit of mankind.[161]

In practice, the Convention was extremely successful. By 1917, the Pribilof herd had more than tripled, and by 1940, North Pacific seals again exceeded two million.[162] The US National Oceanic and Atmospheric Service hails it as a landmark and "a major victory for the conservation of natural resources, a signal triumph of diplomacy ... and a landmark in the history of international cooperation".[163] Nevertheless, the seal population today remains under threat, now from new threats of climate change, food shortages, and historic predators.[164]

## 13.  Conclusion

International arbitration has sometimes served as an escape valve for states facing irritating and persistent issues that cannot otherwise be made to go away at politically acceptable cost. Decisions to go to arbitration can also be shaped by untested or unrealistic assumptions about the merits of a case, by shifting domestic political winds, and by the force of powerful personalities.

All of these factors had a role in the US decision to proceed with the fur seal arbitration. In the end, the case resulted in a resounding defeat for the US legal claims. The defeat was compounded because an unusual feature of the arbitration agreement—tasking the Tribunal to devise a protective regulatory regime, but without having an agreed foundation of sound scientific advice—turned out to be a disaster for the seals it was intended to protect. "About the best that can be said for the Paris Award is that it was a victory for arbitration and the pacific settlement of disputes—not for the seals."[165]

---

[161] AJIL, "Editorial Comment" (n 153) 1025–26.
[162] Barrett (n 5) 32.
[163] National Oceanic and Atmospheric Administration, "North Pacific Fur Seal Treaty of 1911" <https://celebrating200years.noaa.gov/events/fursealtreaty/welcome.html>.
[164] Michael Bhargava, "Of Otters and Orcas: Marine Mammals and Legal Regimes in the North Pacific" (2005) 32 Ecology Law Quarterly 939.
[165] Bailey (n 10) 413.

# 3

# Full Court Press

## International Legal Institutions and US Newspapers at the Turn of the Twentieth Century

*Kathleen Claussen*

## 1. Introduction

Writing in 2000 in the *American Journal of International Law* for which he served on the Board of Editors, David Caron explained how the linkages between the peace movement and advocates for international adjudication resulted in the success of the 1899 Hague Peace Conference and the creation of the Permanent Court of Arbitration (PCA).[1] In that essay, Caron "renew(ed) our sense of the 1899 Conference in terms both of what happened then and of how those events, beliefs, and objectives manifest themselves today".[2] This chapter expands upon Caron's work to tell the broader public-facing story that complements his account.

The 1899 Conference, including the establishment of the PCA, was one of the first international legal developments resulting in a lasting intergovernmental organization captured in widespread media. Advances in print publishing enabled newspapers to share real-time information with the public of the efforts towards creating the first permanent adjudicatory body for international disputes. That those newspapers chose to make the legal details of the Conference and its resulting organizational construction front-page news facilitated the popular diffusion of ideas regarding international law's potential to overcome war.

In public and intellectual life, leaders and civil society actors built support for an international arbitration secretariat, and particularly a court, in the late nineteenth and early twentieth centuries. This bottom-up attention to this lasting international organizations can be seen best not in academic publications or governmental statements as has been done in prior work but rather through the reporting on the events of the time in the media. Interestingly, the intimate legal details of the proposals towards an international arbitration court were presented throughout the United States (US) in local and regional newspapers and magazines. This chapter offers the untold story of the emergence of this first international court in the US public consciousness.

---

[1] David Caron, "War and International Adjudication: Reflections on the 1899 Peace Conference" (2000) 94 American Journal of International Law 4.
[2] ibid 5.

Kathleen Claussen, *Full Court Press* In: *By Peaceful Means.* Edited by: Charles N Brower, Joan E Donoghue, Cian C Murphy, Cymie R Payne and Esmé R Shirlow, Oxford University Press. © Kathleen Claussen 2024. DOI: 10.1093/oso/9780192848086.003.0003

Three features emerge from this glimpse into the popular history of a permanent arbitral body for international disputes: first is the importance of its institutionalization and its structural features. Second is the nationwide coverage of the permanent court and the efforts towards its conclusion. Finally, third is the contrast with the modern day and the coverage of international institutions across the United States in the 2000s.

This chapter takes up these features in each of the subsequent sections. Section 2 contextualizes the reporting about the debates surrounding a permanent arbitral court among social movements at the time. Section 3 demonstrates, through review of a new data set of newspaper articles, that news about the Hague Peace Conferences permeated the United States, and not just as a matter of reporting on the fact that the Conference was taking place. Rather, the press coverage, which reached far corners of the United States, provided significant detail on the procedural and structural proposals advanced by each delegation at the Conferences. Section 4 considers implications of the involvement of the press in the making of the first world court. Taken together, the chapter highlights how today's international institutions face a different reckoning, but the need for public engagement is no fainter than was the case in 1899.

## 2.  All Hands on Deck in Law and Journalism

A good deal of ink has been spilled on the geopolitical events leading up to the Hague Conferences and the major actors on the international stage responsible for their convention. Likewise, scholarship has canvassed well the social movements and international law thinkers that laid the groundwork for an international arbitral body. But little is known about whether these efforts were those of a minority acting in a utopic bubble that would later take hold or something broader. In fact, as this study reveals, daily updates thick with legal detail reached the average US reader from Biloxi to Boise. This section reflects on the many different actors engaged in the push for a permanent arbitration institution: advocates for arbitration, peace activists, world leaders, intellectuals, and international law practitioners and scholars. I take up these multiple fronts before turning to advances in the press that then readily enabled the public to receive information regarding their work.

### 2.1  The Cross-Cutting Support for a Permanent Court

Most histories of the PCA focus on the role of Czar Nicholas II in convening the powers of the world for a conference in The Hague, the home of his cousin, Queen Wilhelmina.[3] The story is one in which the czar was concerned about a growing arms race and instead proposed a conference in furtherance of peace and a peaceful means of

---

[3] See, eg, Arthur Eyffinger, *The 1899 Hague Peace Conference: "The Parliament of Man, the Federation of the World"* (Kluwer Law International 1999).

settlement. Despite some hesitation on the part of certain world powers, the conference took place from 18 May to 29 July 1899. Historians and legal scholars have characterized the meeting with different emphases. For example, Caron stressed the importance of the conference as a way of avoiding war. Others have written about dispute resolution as a top agenda item.[4] Regardless of the order of prioritization, the conference reflected the convergence of two major movements at the time: civil society activists pushing for peace and international law advocates stressing the potential for a permanent arbitral system among states.

As Caron wrote, one cannot understand the pressure for and interest in international adjudication without understanding the horrors of the nineteenth century and its wars. He described the groundswell of energy for a permanent court, what he called a "popular movement".[5] It was made more popular with its dual premises: peace and arbitration. On the peace side, strong non-governmental organization (NGO) advocacy for pacifism as a policy matter intensified after the US Civil War left a wake of destruction in its trail across the United States.[6] In the United States, as elsewhere in the world, the spectre of warfare continued to loom large. Efforts to avoid that eventuality were, literally and figuratively, front-page news.

Around the same time, interest in arbitration had grown as an institution for resolving inter-state disputes.[7] The nineteenth century saw a proliferation of arbitral tribunals but none would serve a lasting role. First, the well-known *Alabama Claims* arbitration between the United States and Great Britain regarding the latter's support of the Confederacy in the US Civil War demonstrated that agreements to arbitrate could avert war between nations.[8] In the decades that followed the *Alabama* decision, dozens of cases among international actors were submitted to arbitration, creating widespread support for the practice.[9]

Early discussion concentrated on the possible establishment of a tribunal for adjudication between Great Britain and the United States to resolve any future differences between them. All the newspaper articles reviewed for this chapter put special emphasis on a *permanent* arbitration court as was the proposal at the time. For one, the *London Times* reported on a meeting held in January 1896 for "those interested in the

---

[4] See, eg, Shabtai Rosenne, *The Hague Peace Conferences of 1899 and 1907 and International Arbitration: Reports and Documents* (Springer 2001). Some vaguely contemporary accounts referring also to the Lake Mohonk conference described herein were published "to present to the public the present phases of the subject of arbitration". John W Foster, *Arbitration and the Hague Court* (Houghton, Mifflin 1904).

[5] See Caron (n 1) 4 ("During the nineteenth century, however, parts of the world developed a confidence in progress and a hope that progress might extend to the abolition of war. Most importantly for this essay, a popular belief circulated at the end of the century that the establishment of a permanent international court would be an important step toward a world free of war. Ad hoc arbitration, as distinct from adjudication by such a permanent court, was not the same and, by itself, not enough. The 1899 Peace Conference was a point of inflection, a turn in the river, in the effort to move beyond ad hoc international arbitration to adjudication by a permanent international court as a means to avoid war and preserve international peace and security.").

[6] See Steve Charnovitz, "Two Centuries of Participation: NGOs and International Governance" (1997) 18 Michigan Journal of International Law 183.

[7] Mary Ellen O'Connell and Lenore VanderZee, "The History of International Adjudication" in Cesare PR Romano, Karen J Alter and Yuval Shany (eds), *The Oxford Handbook of International Adjudication* (Oxford 2013).

[8] ibid.

[9] Frederic L Kirgis, "The Formative Years of the American Society of International Law" (1996) 90 American Journal of International Law 559, 577.

establishment of a permanent court of arbitration for the settlement of disputes".[10] The meeting, detailed in the article, concluded with a recommendation to the British government to form a committee for examining the prospect. But the conversation then turned to a standing tribunal for additional states parties, not just Great Britain and the United States, to be on the ready in case of dispute, including through more organized intergovernmental groups like the Inter-Parliamentary Conference.[11]

The intersection of the peace movement together with this newfound advocacy for arbitration in the form of a permanent tribunal crystallized in the Lake Mohonk conferences beginning in 1895.[12] The energy surrounding the Lake Mohonk gathering with its major benefactors galvanized these grassroots efforts to entice governments to adopt international arbitration as a means to promote world peace.

Alongside the growing promotion of the peaceful settlement of international disputes was a significant push for professionalization in international law. International lawyers founded societies of international law to promote the profession and concentrate its resources. The American Society of International Law,[13] for example, was created in 1906 and was immediately active in supporting international institutions and the Hague Conference.[14] These societies played an important role in bringing the peaceful settlement of disputes onto the government and public agenda.[15] They helped to craft the international instruments in detail, not just in concept.

Outside of international law organizations and budding societies, intellectual leaders made political statements to support the converging movements. The faculty of Dartmouth College issued a statement in 1896 that was printed in *The New York Times*. The statement "express[ed] hearty approval at the effort now being made to secure such action by our Government as shall result in the establishment of a permanent court of arbitration ... between the U.S. and Great Britain".[16] In spring of the same year, the topic of a permanent arbitral tribunal was the topic of the heralded annual Yale-Harvard debate.[17] The principal points of the interlocutors were printed in the *Boston Post*. One side made the case for having arbitral machinery ready, arguing that having a system in place would cause "a lessening of irritation between [the United States and Great Britain], but also a saving of the material loss now produced by the mere apprehension of hostilities". Another defender advocated that "the usage of nations does not make sense in a true sense a law of nations". The debaters set out the terms of what such

---

[10] *The Times*, 15 January 1896, 6.

[11] Bob Reinalda, *Routledge History of International Organizations: From 1815 to the Present Day* (Taylor & Francis Group 2009) 63.

[12] See generally "The Lake Mohonk Conference on International Arbitration" (1914) 8 American Journal of International Law 608.

[13] Caron served as president from 2010 to 2012.

[14] Monroe Leigh and Cristian DeFrancia, "International Law Societies and the Development of International Law" (2001) 41 Virginia Journal of International Law 941, 943–45; John M Raymond and Barbara Frischholtz, "Lawyers Who Established International Law in the United States, 1776–1914" (1982) 76 American Journal of International Law 802, 824–25; Kirgis (n 9) 577.

[15] See O'Connell & VanderZee (n 7).

[16] *The New York Times*, 29 February 1896.

[17] *Boston Post*, 2 May 1896 (noting that the subject of the debate was "that a permanent court of arbitration should be established between the United States and Great Britain").

a court would entail: jurisdiction, duration, and composition, among them. Although the Yale team arguing against such a system was pronounced the winner, it was the full airing of the pros and cons of such a programme that was most valuable. Further, lectures were delivered at "leading universities"[18] and academics would write about the outpouring of these ideas, their rise in popularity, and their merits.[19]

## 2.2  Advances in Newspaper Machinery

While the seeds in support of an international arbitral institution were being sewn, cultivated, and grown among these ideological proponents, the timing was right for tracking international news and conveying it not just to the metropolitan areas of the east coast of the United States but throughout the country. Two factors contributed to such efforts: first was advances in technology and second was the increasing commercialization of newspapers. Both these developments enabled news of the Hague Conferences to reach Americans across the nation in 1899 and again in 1907.

Technology has, for much of history, determined the trajectory and targeted receipt of information by individuals in our societies. In the thirty years before the Civil War, the US newspaper business underwent a massive change owing to the transportation revolution: "Newspapers came to be read widely, both in places of publication and, thanks to the railroads, farther away."[20] The laying of undersea cables in the middle of the nineteenth century made it possible for news from the European continent to reach the United States in time for the post-Civil War developments. International news became US news overnight. Likewise, the growth in the appearance of the telegraph across the country facilitated the movement of information from coast to coast around the same period. The dissemination of reporting from distant places could suddenly be printed with stunning speed.

This was also the era of the rise of the newspaper owing to the creation of the linotype, which allowed newspapers to become longer. Not only could they accommodate more content, they required it. The newspaper as a medium grew in scope, length, and content: "Americans became a nation addicted to newspapers, and in the era before broadcast journalism, newspapers were a considerable force in public life."[21] Specialty journals, dailies, and weeklies flourished. Reporting became a trade as the news was more objective and even-handed, separating opinion from fact.[22] This shift

---

[18] Raymond and Frischholtz (n 14) 825.

[19] James L Tryon, Proposals for an International Court (1914) 23 Yale Law Journal 415, 428–31. This is the first of a series of seven articles by the same author on "subjects of present interest in International Law". See also James L Tryon, A World Treaty of Arbitration (1911) 20 Yale Law Journal 163, 175; James L Tryon, The Hague Conferences (1911) 20 Yale Law Journal 470, 477.

[20] Lorman A Ratner and Dwight L Teeter, *Fanatics and Fire-Eaters: Newspapers and the Coming of the Civil War* (University of Illinois Press 2003) 8.

[21] Aurora Wallace, *Newspapers and the Making of Modern America: A History* (Greenwood Press 2005).

[22] Ratner and Teeter (n 20) note 52. Undoubtedly, some newspapers were affiliated with a particular political party or known for their political bias; as noted further later in this chapter, the articles surveyed here crossed the political spectrum to some degree.

was representative of a broader cultural development as changes in literacy and the demands of industrialization influenced the press and its content.[23]

The press established a new vision about the role of journalism in an increasingly complex American society.[24] This vision was critical in carrying to the masses communications regarding the creation of the first modern international adjudication system—a feat of immense proportions for international lawyers, but which would have otherwise likely been unnoticed in the towns across the by-then massive land. In the decades before the Hague Conference, "foreign news" comprised about 13 per cent of all news topics in US newspapers,[25] which put it roughly fifth out of about a dozen major topics. After the US Civil War, however, much more was possible and indeed achieved, as Section 3 shows.

## 3. Reporting on International Institutions Across the Nation

Journalism scholars and sociologists have described how newspapers shaped public opinion in the nineteenth century, serving as the primary source of information about the developments in policy and culture.[26] Editors had incredible power: selecting what would reach (and not reach) readers, in what configuration, according to what perspective, and on what timeline. Still today, the media selectively filter and define the events they cover, forming a critical function in not just cultural trends but also in the international legal process.[27] Likewise, the absence of media can convey messages of unimportance to the public.[28]

The coverage of the creation of the PCA was one of the first instantiations of this role for newspapers in the United States. Those editorial choices likely shaped readers' outlook by reinforcing or redirecting their values, enhancing notions of the legitimacy of international institutions, and creating a conversation about international law and its potential. Printing accounts of the ideas debated at the Hague Conference may have influenced the average reader's understanding of those ideas and their importance in shaping international relations and possibly, the law. For this reason, the NGOs involved in the movements in support of the Conference put special emphasis on communicating with the general population. The Lake Mohonk conference platform,

---

[23] Gerald Baldasty, *The Commercialization of News in the Nineteenth Century* (University of Wisconsin Press 1992).

[24] ibid.

[25] Donald Lewis Shaw, "News About Slavery from 1820–1860 in Newspapers of South, North and West" (1984) 61 (3) Journalism Quarterly 483.

[26] See, eg, Ratner and Teeter (n 20); Shaw (n 25); Baldasty (n 23).

[27] Monica Hakimi, "The Media as Participant in the International Legal Process" (2006) 16 Duke Journal of Comparative and International Law 1, 1. See also Anne van Aaken and Jose M Reis, "Framing Preferences in International Trade Law" (manuscript on file with the author).

[28] See, eg, Tara J Melish, "From Paradox to Subsidiarity: The United States and Human Rights Treaty Bodies" (2009) 34 Yale Journal of International Law 389, 404 (describing how US media scarcely report on US engagement in human rights bodies). See also Jacob Katz Cogan, Competition and Control in International Adjudication (2008) 48 Virginia Journal of International Law 411, 429 (commenting that the media report only selectively on international adjudicatory developments today).

for example, urged that "public attention should be concentrated [on the Hague Conference]". There is even some suggestion that NGOs were acting as couriers to news outlets of the events and comments at the Hague Conference.[29] It is not possible to know the extent of this relationship as by-lines were not yet common. Some papers would note the source of the news but no author, using instead references like "By Cable to the Times" or "By Leased Wire to the Times".[30]

To examine the proliferation of the permanent arbitral institution idea, I have selected for this study several newspapers published in different parts of the United States. The newspapers represent different political positions; some are urban, some are rural; most were widely circulated, often in weekly editions. The notion of a permanent inter-state court was an aspiration that inched closer to reality—and the dispatches to these papers indicate this notion had quotidian significance. Through the pages of the newspapers they read, Americans had daily or weekly encounters with this international development. In the late 1890s, these reports from abroad signalled that the creation of an international institution was within reach.[31]

## 3.1 National Reach

Unlike some foreign policy decisions taken from the top without public consultation or wide airing, the efforts to create an international arbitration system was a matter that was widely reported in US newspapers. Not only did elites and national-level papers engage in this debate, but also local-level papers including in rural environments far from Washington, DC. Before massive telecommunication developments and the globalization of commerce of the twentieth century, the matter of a permanent international body for adjudicating disputes was a major news topic. More than 1,000 articles may be found in US newspapers from 1890 through 1910 on the topic of a permanent court of arbitration. As early as 1896, the *Los Angeles Herald*, reporting on the negotiations with Great Britain, noted that the possibility of a permanent court of arbitration was near.[32]

The articles increase in frequency and appearance around the height of the negotiations in The Hague. For example, the *Grand Forks Daily Herald* (Grand Forks, North Dakota) carried a story on 4 July 1899, entitled "The Second Reading of Pauncefote's Scheme for a Permanent Court of Arbitration" which covered and compared the details of the proposals of the delegates such as Lord Julian Pauncefote of Great Britain. The same story ran in the Birmingham, Alabama *Age-Herald*, the *Philadelphia Inquirer*, the

---

[29] Reinalda (n 11) 66–67; Charnovitz (n 6) 197.

[30] See, eg, the *Raleigh Times*.

[31] To be sure, the PCA was not the first international organization of the period. The International Committee of the Red Cross of 1863 among other social movements and governmental efforts precipitated the creation of transnational institutions already during that period.

[32] "English Talk is Friendly Favoring a Permanent Court of Arbitration", 11 January, 1896.

*New York Tribune*, the Cleveland, Ohio *Plain Dealer*, and the *Idaho Statesman* of Boise, Idaho.[33]

Other stories from around the same time period take on similar comparisons, reporting on the individual suggestions of participants on the structure and composition of such a permanent court. The *Miami Record-Herald* of Miami, Oklahoma, for one, ran a story on "A Permanent Court of Arbitration" also in July 1899. The *Duluth News-Tribune* of Duluth, Minnesota, likewise reported on "Sir Pauncefote's Project to Institute a Permanent Court of Arbitration". The *Minneapolis Journal* carried an exposé on the German Kaiser's view in opposition to a permanent arbitral tribunal.[34] The *Arkansas Gazette* of Little Rock, Arkansas announced the conference results in an article on 26 July 1899 saying that it would begin a "new epoch".

The same sorts of stories can be found from the late 1890s through 1907. In the intervening years, these papers announced the publication of a roster of panellists, for instance.[35] Reporting continued during the 1907 Convention in big city papers and in small town papers like the *Raleigh Times*. The story in the *Raleigh Times* quoted the US delegate regarding the selection of judges for the permanent arbitral court and reported that that proposal was defeated in favour of a different selection process advanced by the British delegate.[36] The *Daily Herald* of Biloxi, Mississippi announced the accomplishments of the conference on 3 December 1907. Papers from the *Omaha World-Herald* to the *Anaconda Standard* of Anaconda, Montana, featured the details of the conference—not just its occurrence but also its legal developments to which Section 3.2 turns.

## 3.2  Detailed and Prominent Content

Two additional qualities make these stories notable apart from their general topic and far reach to papers around the country. First is the prominence given by editors and publishers to these developments. Many of the stories mentioned above appeared on page one of those papers and nearly all appeared among the first few pages. As the coverage continued into the early part of the twentieth century, the work towards international dispute settlement was consistently covered—even if the coverage was set back farther, such as on pages five and eight of the papers by 1907. (This development may in part be due to the fact that newspapers increased in average length in those intervening years.) While it is impossible to know precisely why these reports were given top billing, one might consider that these depictions of the Hague Conference suggest a level of commitment to international law. As Caron wrote, there was great public pressure to

---

[33] Even where stories were reprinted "via the wire" or via the same publisher, their extensive cross-country reach, made possible by the proliferation of papers, was critical to the widespread sharing of information about these overseas events to at least those who were able to read and have access to them.

[34] 13 June 1899.

[35] "Roster Announced of the Permanent Court of Arbitration", *Grand Forks Daily Herald*, 2 February 1901.

[36] 19 September 1907.

avoid additional warfare. Seeing a permanent arbitral tribunal as a means of achieving that goal was an important development that was captured so well from these several newspapers. There was an educational aspect to them and, apparently, it sold.

Second, the content of these articles was not limited to the announcement of any major breakthrough in the conclusion of the negotiations. What makes these articles especially interesting is not their purported attention to the peace conference generally but rather the detail contained in these reports of the proposed institution. The idea of the court often appears in its own separate article apart from the discussions of the peace conference which also appeared. These accounts were not the product of any press release or statement from a US government actor, issuing a comment of relevance to Americans. Rather, these articles provide detailed information about the legal positions advanced by different delegates at the negotiating table. Some articles review specific features of the proposals as if to speak to an expert audience. For example, certain stories describe a logjam over structural choices for a tribunal such as the number of members and their selection process. Many offer a sort of sport-like blow-by-blow of the negotiations with nuanced legal arguments. They highlight the position of the American delegate as compared to other delegates as if narrating a geopolitical chess match. They describe revisions to original proposals and their reception by the participants. These details which today may be of interest to institutionalists would be considered too heavily in the weeds for a public conversation. Generally, by comparison to modern expectations, the content of the articles was quite technical.

The fact that so many papers *chose* to make prominent these tales of international legal development is telling of their relative importance. Given the commercialization of the newspaper, if these developments were not successful in selling papers they surely would have been omitted. But it was not just that these papers covered the legal developments in The Hague for such a wide audience—it is also important how they did so: conspicuously and in detail. Those accounts were also objective rather than editorial. Few critiques of the development of an international arbitral institution made their way to the mainline newspapers as far as one can tell with the evidence available today. This absence lends further support for the notion's widespread acceptance at the time. What is striking is simply the transparency and centrality of the establishment of a permanent court for everyday readers across the nation and the importance of international legal institutionalization that these stories reveal to the populace. This was among the leading stories of the day.

In sum, by representing to the American people these early-stage developments and their procedural components, these articles laid the foundation for international legal institutions in the public consciousness.

## 3.3 The Peoples' Court

We know far less about how the news was received. Were the readers hopeful? Sceptical? Were they discussing the legal choices made by the delegates in their bars, schools, and homes? In his American Journal of International Law (AJIL) essay, Caron discussed the "spirit" around the movement for peace and arbitration. To be sure, the workings of international arbitration rarely have had a major constituency at least in recent memory. But through newspaper reporting, the "spirit" to which Caron referred may have reached far beyond the advocates at Lake Mohonk or in the east coast universities. As these ideas seeped into the public consciousness through the newspapers, teaching the reader about the possibilities for international law to resolve the horrors of war, the PCA from its earliest days was considered "morally authoritative".[37]

In later decades, a commentator writing in the AJIL remarked on the importance of the "popularization" of international law, referring to The New Yorker's coverage of two developments of international law at the time. The Journal's editor wrote:

> Students of international law should rejoice over this phenomenon .... The body of readers of The New Yorker probably occupy a more strategic position in the formation of current opinion than those of the so-called learned journals. Students of international law and politics also should stand ready to aid in such wise "popularization" of their discipline.[38]

In 1899, such thinking was at best nascent.

Nevertheless, while much of the literature tends to focus on the broad social movements among NGOs, the articles surveyed here suggest a level of underestimated popularization and education among the populace. Our overemphasis on organized movements can detract from the media influence that may have played a critical role in shaping public opinion on the significance and legitimacy of an international dispute settlement body.[39] These accounts demonstrate *how* the news was captured and conveyed: in detail, with particularized notes among the structural options presented by delegates. Ironically, the public had an inside view as governments sought to take their geopolitical discussions off the public stage and relegate them to private arbitral proceedings—a view that would be rare today as governments tend to favour increased protection of their positions and these types of proceedings.

In contemporary academic discussions about accountability, government reports are seen as critical to transparency. Before government reports became so prevalent, however, the press filled some of the gap. This type of reporting may have helped direct public opinion to the zone of law rather than the unfettered fate of war or reliance on policy experts. Thus, the consequences of this type of detailed reporting may have been to support the triumph of legalism and to help Americans imagine the institutionalization of international legal principles. Legalists pervade the conversation with a court as

---

[37] Eyffinger (n 3) 55. This chapter refers to a privileged idea of the "public" that would have been limited to those with means to learn to read and those with access to newspapers; several demographic groups are therefore left out of this shorthand reference given the discrimination they faced in access to education and means.

[38] P.B.P., Popularization of International Law (1944) 38 American Journal of International Law 472.

[39] Without rehearsing its nuance, I draw here on the exposition of "legitimacy" in international legal institutions—in social and political terms—as set out by Caron in his 1993 article. David Caron, "The Legitimacy of the Collective Authority of the Security Council" (1993) 87 American Journal of International Law 552, 556–57.

the mode for addressing future disputes. In short, newspapers may have played a heretofore unseen part in promoting legalism.

This characteristic makes international law special among ideological trends of the day and very exceptional if viewed through a twenty-first century lens. The experience of the average reader vis-à-vis a permanent court stands in stark contrast with those of the abolitionists (and to some degree the peace movement) and suffragettes that created an alternative press to promote their causes in the hopes of counteracting the journalistic hegemony believed to have blocked their progress.[40]

While it is difficult to fully evaluate the trends noted here,[41] at the least we can conclude that some of these journalistic choices shaped the future direction of the law, the constitution of an international legal community, and the promotion of an international rule of law by affirming the authority of the Hague Peace Conference and legitimizing to some degree the process underway there. They undoubtedly contributed to the development of an international dispute resolution psyche that extended beyond the major actors on which historical accounts focus: civil society actors, peace movement, learned societies, bar associations.[42] Those experts advocated for an international legal solution and that is what was conveyed to the public in nearly real-time: a significant shift from preceding years in international legal history.

This overview also serves to supplement the prior accounts that saw the Hague Conferences as the intersection of the peace and arbitral movements. The way the issues are framed in these newspaper articles suggests a dialogue and a language of international legal institutions. Although not a grassroots social movement, the rise of international legal institutions began and was enhanced through these conversations which distinctly separated politics from law. The popularization of this news mutually reinforced the advancement of international law as a collection of positive norms.

## 4.  "To Go Forward, It Is Often Wise . . . To Go Back"

Today, such negotiated nuances as reported in the newspapers at the turn of the century are typically the subject of specialist blog posts and Twitter debates.[43] This shift is the product of many forces beyond the scope of this chapter and I do not intend to question their contours here. In 2022, it is easy to look at the myriad international institutions

---

[40] Rodger Streitmatter, *Mightier than the Sword: How the News Media Have Shaped American History* (Westview Press 2011) 33.

[41] To be sure, this discrete study does not examine larger longitudinal trends that may indicate a level of continuity in the style or nature of reporting on world events.

[42] See, eg, WE Butler, "The Hague Permanent Court of Arbitration" in MW Janis (ed), *International Courts for the Twenty-First Century* (Martinus Nijhoff 1992); ME O'Connell, "Arbitration and the Avoidance of War: The Nineteenth-Century American Vision" in C Romano (ed), *The United States and International Courts and Tribunals* (Cambridge University Press 2009); J Allain, *A Century of International Adjudication: The Rule of Law and its Limits* (T.M.C. Asser Press 2000).

[43] See, eg, Julian Arato, "ISDS Reform: From the Forest to the Trees of an Appellate Mechanism" (*International Economic Law and Policy* Blog, 15 February 2021) <https://ielp.worldtradelaw.net/2021/02/isds-reform-from-the-forest-to-the-trees-of-an-appellate-mechanism.html> (summarizing the negotiations among states seeking to develop new constructs in international investment law and dispute settlement).

dotting our multilateral and plurilateral landscapes and to take them for granted. And it is hard to imagine that debates over the structure and individual proposals of participants in an international negotiation of that sort would have such popular attraction.[44] At the end of the nineteenth century, neither the relative international peace nor the prospect of international organizations could be assumed. Neither ought international law enthusiasts do so when looking towards the future in our present moment.

How should we consider the role of the media in the furtherance of international law today? What does it facilitate amid the public imagination for the future of international institutions in 2023? The proliferation of social media and the changes in the place of newspapers in that evolving landscape present a very different speech backdrop for the dissemination of international legal information in the twenty-first century. A meaningful comparison of any value is difficult, but that difficulty is in itself telling. The over-provision of sources of information has made it both possible for individuals not just in the far reaches of the United States but across the far reaches of the world to follow such developments. Though, no doubt then and now, marginalized populations remain cut off from easy access, the news is largely accessible. But what makes "the news" may have changed.

While some foreign policy decisions are surfaced for public debate, most of the institutional choices such as those occurring at the Hague Conference would in the modern day not reach the masses. Structural decisions and multilateral negotiations are held closely. Governments today explain why negotiating positions cannot be revealed to the public and proceed with considerable secrecy in certain international negotiations. Apart from the occasional general negotiating position, this type of reporting, particularly in these local papers—many of which, it should be noted, have now closed—is rare either because it is superseded by local or national reporting, or for other reasons. That is not to say that international legal arguments do not reach the public sphere. In separate work, I have looked at the significant international law arguments made on the floor of the US Congress as they relate to trade.[45] Recently, US Senator Josh Hawley of Missouri received considerable press for his stance on the World Trade Organization. But few of those comments, even as they reached Senator Hawley's home base through the press, were premised on the detailed workings of the legal institution.

Moreover, the accomplishment of creating an organization equivalent to the PCA or the International Court of Justice, both the result of concerns over world wars and constructed with the aspiration that they would help put an end to conflict, would be difficult to match at the present political moment. Contrast this today with not only the PCA's limited role in the US public sphere, but also that of other international institutions. Indeed, prospects for multilateralism tend to be met with pessimism and despondence even if international arbitration is very much alive and, although those institutions have not been able to stop war entirely, they may have helped and continue

---

[44] Discussions about the World Trade Organization's Appellate Body may come close but they rarely garner front-page attention.

[45] Kathleen Claussen, "Arguing about Trade Law Beyond the Courtroom" in Ian Johnstone and Steven Ratner (eds), *Talking International Law: Legal Argumentation Outside the Courtroom* (Oxford University Press 2021) 298.

to help diffuse conflicts that might have otherwise intensified. Where governments now engage in development of international legal institutions, those stories are rarely the equivalent of "front-page" news except perhaps among experts. Where we *have* seen some prominent headlines, however, has been with respect to the *end* of institutions. Those stories are far less about legal uncertainty, textual debate, or conceptual framing. They are, rather, stories about the political weight with which some governments have sought to abandon certain institutions. The political has risen in importance while the legal has receded.[46]

It may also be relevant to tracing the place of the press in international legal development just how much the current US president promotes international law and public input on matters of relevance to international legal development. US views on international law shift with political tides but at least some administrations have put significant priority on the views of the public. A former official of the Trump Administration expressed this sentiment in a recent interview. Speaking of US foreign policy and specifically trade policy, he said: "it has to be made by U.S. elected officials, because they're the only ones who are really responsible to the voters and it really is their job to sort out like what kind of a country we want to be".[47] To be sure, there is a significant difference between popularization and popularity. Nothing about the reporting trends seen here can accurately capture the latter, nor is that the focus. But in the case of the creation of the PCA, the tools and the timing were right for public engagement with international law.

Finally, although prior analyses of the Hague Conferences have omitted observations on the influence and importance of the contemporaneous media elaboration, that media ought not be underestimated. More work is needed now to trace subsequent developments. After the First World War, before and after the Second World War, and in more recent decades, what has been the role of the media in codification or in socializing international law? Monica Hakimi has taken on the general question, noting the critical importance of the media in multiple respects.[48] More longitudinal work would help us capture better this evolution and evaluate its trajectory.[49] International lawyers would also benefit from taking a wider look at media actors in the propagation of international law over the last century in particular to understand the power of the press bringing international legal argumentation out of the halls of diplomats, out of the courtroom and into people's homes from Montana to Oklahoma.

If nothing else, this short tale of press engagement on matters of international law reminds us of the potential role of the media in communication of international legal

---

[46] For other depictions of similar trends, see Harlan Grant Cohen, "Multilateralism's Life Cycle" (2018) 112 American Journal of International Law 47.

[47] *TradeTalks Podcast*, Episode 111, 4.

[48] Hakimi (n 27) 1.

[49] As this book was going to press, important new work on this subject was being released. See, eg, Daniel Joyce, *Informed Publics, Media and International Law* (Bloomsbury 2022); Madelaine Chiam, *International Law in Public Debate* (Cambridge University Press 2021); Johnstone and Ratner (n 47); Luke Nottage, International Arbitration and Society at Large, in Stefan Kröll, Andrew K Bjorklund, and Franco Ferrari (eds), *Cambridge Compendium of International Commercial and Investment Arbitration* (CUP 2023), 389–423.

ideas and in normative development. These stories contributed to the building of a movement and to the legalization of that movement. Although there was not yet at that time the public input opportunities that we have come to expect such as a process for public comment in regulatory affairs,[50] there was nonetheless an educational campaign underway through the newspaper business.

Query whether the newspapers of today—or their many proxies on the Internet— could serve a similar role as was the case in the late nineteenth and early twentieth centuries. As Hakimi has noted, the media help establish parameters for our international law, disperse intelligence about it, and allocate communal values.[51] These process-oriented functions mean that the press in direct and indirect ways influence the codification and application of international law. Precisely how they do so with respect to modern initiatives such as the reform of the World Trade Organization, the success of the UN Convention on the Law of the Sea and its reception in the United States, the Obama and Trump Administration's engagement with the Paris Climate Change Agreement or the Transpacific Partnership Agreement requires further examination so that international lawyers may harness the energy that these sources provide. Although these institutional arrangements are not centred on peace, they purport nevertheless to enhance it by avoiding conflict over economics or natural resources. The stakes remain high.

## 5. Conclusion

In 2000, Caron commented that the 1899 Conference set in motion an evolution that "circles constantly around a tension between party autonomy and community interest, between consent to appear and obligatory jurisdiction, and between caution as to the integrity of the process and faith in the value of peaceful settlement".[52] These themes continue to resonate today as states re-configure international institutions and revisit the value of inter-state adjudication. Still today, writes Caron, "great innovation will be required to devise a system … that is both sufficiently fixed to secure the expectations of participating states and sufficiently adaptable to grow with the community it seeks to serve".[53] That community engages with the law in immensely different ways than when the PCA was first conceived. May that innovation extend also to its presentation and embeddedness into the public sphere.

---

[50] To be sure, that avenue remains heavily limited in the shaping of foreign policy.
[51] Hakimi (n 28) 8.
[52] Caron, "War and International Adjudication" (n 1) 30.
[53] ibid.

## Acknowledgement

My thanks to the editors for the invitation to participate in this volume in honour of David. He was always a generous mentor to me, welcoming me into the work of the American Society of International Law when I was a student and very junior lawyer and encouraging me to pursue my academic interests. David's leadership inspired many of us to dedicate much of our professional time to the Society and to find our way in international law.

# 4

# The Eritrea Ethiopia Claims Commission

## At the Intersection of International Dispute Resolution and Transitional Justice for Atrocity Crimes?

*Hannah R Garry with Morgan Brock-Smith and Nicholas Maisel*

## 1. Introduction

With the turn of the twenty-first century, the new millennium brought two seemingly unrelated events, one marking a beginning and the other an end. The beginning was the birth of a new, distinct field of scholarship and practice for pursuing holistic justice for systematic, large-scale human rights abuses, often rising to the level of an international or "atrocity" crime,[1] referred to as transitional justice. The end was the laying down of arms after a bitter border dispute between two African countries, Eritrea and Ethiopia, with the signing of the Algiers Agreement of 12 December 2000 (hereinafter Algiers Agreement or the Agreement). In reaching peace, both countries agreed to the establishment of an international dispute resolution mechanism, specifically an ad hoc mixed claims commission, the Eritrea Ethiopia Claims Commission (hereinafter EECC or the Commission), for purposes of resolving their claims stemming from the war. While at first glance the only similarity that the EECC and the field of modern transitional justice seem to share is their appearance in time, what is less known about the EECC is that its mandate included awarding of compensation for harm perpetrated against tens of thousands of individuals, namely civilians and prisoners of war, who suffered greatly during the conflict as a result of serious violations of international humanitarian law, which amounted to war crimes. Consequently, while much has been written about the EECC as established in the line of historic "mixed commissions" for purposes of settling inter-state claims through international legal rules on state responsibility, less attention has been paid to the Commission's role as a mechanism also established for redress for victims of mass atrocities devastating whole communities.

This chapter seeks to address the imbalance. By examining the EECC and its efficacy through a transitional justice lens, it explores the potential for such international

---

[1] For purposes of this chapter, "atrocity crime" is narrowly defined as the core international crimes that have been prosecuted under treaty or customary international law by international, hybrid and national criminal courts and tribunals since the International Military Tribunal at Nuremberg, namely, war crimes, crimes against humanity, and genocide. This term reflects a certain magnitude and character of serious or grave human rights abuse to which individual criminal responsibility attaches under international law when perpetrated. See, eg, David Scheffer, "Genocide and Atrocity Crimes" (2006) 1 (3) Genocide Studies and Prevention 229, 229–50.

Hannah R Garry with Morgan Brock-Smith and Nicholas Maisel, *The Eritrea Ethiopia Claims Commission* In: *By Peaceful Means.* Edited by: Charles N Brower, Joan E Donoghue, Cian C Murphy, Cymie R Payne and Esmé R Shirlow, Oxford University Press.
© Hannah R Garry, Morgan Brock-Smith and Nicholas Maisel 2024. DOI: 10.1093/oso/9780192848086.003.0004

dispute resolution mechanisms to achieve accountability, peace, and reconciliation in the aftermath of armed conflict and mass atrocity situations. As such, this chapter first addresses what is meant by a transitional justice mechanism and the purported goals to be achieved by such processes. Second, in outlining the origins and structure of the EECC, this chapter queries whether the Commission may be considered a transitional justice mechanism as traditionally understood. Finally, this chapter concludes with an examination of whether the EECC experiment might be instructive as a model for future ad hoc mixed claims commissions established at least in part to achieve transitional justice for atrocity crime situations.

## 2. Transitional Justice: Overview

### 2.1 Historical Roots and Modern Definition

While not undisputed, most scholars would agree that "transitional justice" as currently understood began to evolve as a discrete term and area of human rights scholarship in the late 1980s and 1990s that sought to define and describe concrete responses by governments and human rights activists to address political dilemmas and human rights abuses inherent in a number of societies in transition at the time.[2] That said, while the field of modern transitional justice scholarship and practice emerged around the turn of the twenty-first century, it is arguably rooted much further back in time. Some scholars posit that transitional justice is actually a timeless label encompassing a number of pre-modern justice mechanisms dating back to ancient Greece that arguably fit the current definition.[3] Still others point to the end of the Second World War and the establishment of the International Military Tribunals for Nuremberg and Tokyo as a significant starting point for our modern understanding of transitional justice which "inaugurated international processes of criminal accountability for massive violations

---

[2] Marcos Zunino, *Justice Framed: A Genealogy of Transitional Justice* (Cambridge University Press 2019) 12. Paige Arthur, for example, discusses the importance of the 1988 Aspen Institute Conference for launching a conversation among academics concerning the new field of transitional justice, and leading to such seminal works as Diane Orentlicher, "Settling Accounts: The Duty to Prosecute Human Rights Violations of a Previous Regime" (1991) 100 Yale Law Journal 2537, and Paige Arthur, "How 'Transitions' Reshaped Human Rights: A Conceptual History of Transitional Justice" (2009) 31 Human Rights Quarterly 321. See also Padraig McAuliffe, "From Molehills to Mountains (and Myths): A Critical History of Transitional Justice Advocacy" (2011) 22 Finnish Yearbook of International Law 85. McAuliffe similarly charts the development of transitional justice as a distinct field beginning in the 1980s, dissecting the progression of the field into four stages.

[3] Zunino (n 2) 9. For example, Jon Elster traces the first instance of "transitional justice" in history to ancient Athens, which transitioned from an oligarchy to a democracy twice between 411BC and 403 BC. Jon Elster, *Closing the Books: Transitional Justice in Historical Perspective* (Cambridge University Press 2009) 3–23. For other authors who treat transitional justice as a timeless label, see Adriaan Lanni, "Transitional Justice in Ancient Athens: A Case Study" (2010) 32 University of Pennsylvania Journal of International Law 551; Gary Jonathan Bass, *Stay the Hand of Vengeance: The Politics of War Crimes Tribunals* (Princeton University Press 2000) 37–57 (detailing instances of transitional justice after the Napoleonic wars); Robert Meister, "Forgiving and Forgetting: Lincoln and the Politics of National Recovery" in Carla Hesse and Robert Post (eds), *Human Rights in Political Transitions: Gettysburg to Bosnia* (MIT Press 1999) 135–76 (discussing transitional justice after the US Civil War); Ronen Steinberg, "Transitional Justice in the Age of the French Revolution" (2013) 7 International Journal of Transitional Justice 267, 267–85 (discussing transitional justice after the French Revolution).

of human rights"[4] and cemented the idea of justice as a necessary pre-requisite for transitional societies to realize peace.[5] However, with the end of the Cold War period following the Second World War, the wave of transitions to democracy in Latin America, Europe, and South Africa, precipitated in part by the dissolution of the Soviet Union, rekindled conversations on how best to seek justice for past human rights violations that has been ongoing ever since.[6]

For example, in Latin America, while Argentina initially established a truth commission and then criminally prosecuted junta, military, and guerrilla leaders, other countries in Latin America focused on amnesties, truth commissions,[7] and reparations measures.[8] The transitions in Eastern Europe were different from those in Latin America in that they involved widespread economic along with political reform as countries left behind communism for market-driven democracies.[9] Some criminal prosecutions were attempted, and truth commissions, the novel mechanism to emerge from Latin American transitions, were also less favoured amongst post-communist States.[10] Instead, the main mechanism that Eastern European States came to rely on was lustration, which was pioneered in Czechoslovakia through a law passed in 1991 banning former agents or informers of the security apparatus from taking positions in government, armed forces, parliament, courts, academia, and the media.[11] As a result, lustration was incorporated into the range of possible transitional justice responses along with criminal prosecutions, truth commissions, and reparations.[12]

---

[4] Zunino (n 2) 11. While Ruti Teitel states that the origins of modern transitional justice began after the First World War, "transitional justice becomes understood as both extraordinary and international in the postwar period after 1945". Ruti Teitel, "Transitional Justice Genealogy" (2003) 16 Harvard Human Rights Journal 69, 70. See also Dustin N Sharp, "Interrogating the Peripheries: The Preoccupations of Fourth Generation Transitional Justice" (2013) 26 Harvard Human Rights Journal 149, 149–78.

[5] Ruti Teitel, *Globalizing Transitional Justice: Contemporary Essays* (New York University Press 2014) 30–31.

[6] Zunino (n 2) 13.

[7] Truth commissions were established in Bolivia (1982), Uruguay (1985), Chile (1990), El Salvador (1991), and Guatemala (1997). ibid 66.

[8] Reparations measures were implemented in Uruguay, Chile, El Salvador, Paraguay, Guatemala, and Brazil. ibid.

[9] ibid 78.

[10] Some of the trials failed to reach verdicts, or did not focus on human rights violations. ibid 84–86.

[11] ibid 87.

[12] ibid 89–91. While amnesties have been used historically and continue to be used by societies in transition, scholars do not agree as to whether amnesties are compatible with modern transitional justice goals, and many would argue that while they may be used in conjunction with transitional justice mechanisms such as truth and reconciliation commissions, or they may be "qualified amnesties", which do not apply to international crimes, they may not be a considered a proper transitional justice mechanism in and of themselves because they allow for impunity and preclude truth-seeking and the victim's perspective. See, eg, David Tolbert and Marcela Prieto Rudolphy, "Transitional Justice in the 21st Century: History, Effectiveness, and Challenges" in Barbora Hola, Hollie Nyseth Brehm, and Maartje Weerdesteijn (eds), *Oxford Handbook of Atrocity Crimes* (Oxford University Press 2020) <https://law.wm.edu/academics/intellectuallife/researchcenters/postconflictjustice/guest-speakers/tj-symposium/perspectives/ch27_tolbert_prietorudolphy_transitional-justice-in-the-21st-century-mw-002-1dtclean.pdf>; David Tolbert, "Transitional Justice: What it Is & Why it Matters" (Remarks at the William & Mary Law School Symposium: No Transition, No Justice: How the Absence of Transitional Justice Following the Civil War Has Led to Ongoing Racial Injustice in the United States on 18 September 2020) https://www.wm.edu/offices/revescenter/news/2020/william-and-mary-law-school-hosts-symposium-on-transitional-and-racial-justice.php. See also Orentlicher (n 2); Naomi Roht-Arriaza, *Impunity and Human Rights in International Law and Practice* (Oxford University Press 1995); Lisa J Laplante, "Outlawing Amnesty: The Return of Criminal Justice in Transitional Justice Schemes" (2009) 49 Virginia Journal of International Law 916. But see Kieran McEvoy and Louise Mallinder, "Amnesties in Transition: Punishment, Restoration, and the Governance of Mercy" (2012) 39

Simultaneously, the creation of the International Criminal Tribunal for the former Yugoslavia (ICTY) in 1993, the International Criminal Tribunal for Rwanda (ICTR) in 1994, and the South African Truth and Reconciliation Commission (SATRC) in 1995 accelerated the development of transitional justice as a distinct concept and area of scholarship.[13] International criminal justice was solidified as a viable option for societies in transition, which eventually led to the creation of a number of hybrid courts, along with the permanent International Criminal Court (ICC).[14] With a renewed interest by states in international criminal justice came a paradigm shift, whereby "non-impunity was acknowledged as an essential part of any transition" even if the exact form of accountability was left to the transition process.[15]

These historical roots inform our current understanding of transitional justice, which was cemented around 2000 as a distinct field, reflected by the United Nations' adoption of the term, later formalized in Secretary-General Kofi Annan's 2004 report dedicated to the topic.[16] Currently, the understanding of transitional justice has broadened in a number of different ways to cover a much wider terrain of societies in transition from a legacy of large-scale abuse. First, it is applicable to more than liberal political transitions to democracy,[17] including other types of societies, "most notably those attempting negotiated settlement in protracted social conflicts".[18] Second, transitional justice is now contemplated in situations where large-scale abuses are ongoing, or where they have ended but there has been no clear political transition.[19] Further, it is considered applicable beyond just post-conflict situations.[20] Thus, transitional justice has been divorced from its attachment to an extraordinary, clear moment in time, putting into question when transitional justice begins, and when it ends.[21] Third, modern transitional justice has moved away from solely addressing abuses committed within the territory of a state, given that large-scale violence and human-rights abuse often involve a cross-border aspect, and the "the regional dimensions of many conflicts

---

British Journal of Law & Society 410, 410; Tricia Olsen and others, "The Justice Balance: When Transitional Justice Improves Human Rights and Democracy" (2010) 32 Human Rights Quarterly 980, 1005.

[13] Zunino (n 2) 13–14.

[14] ibid 97–101.

[15] McAuliffe (n 2) 111–12.

[16] Report of the Secretary-General, "The Rule of Law and Transitional Justice in Conflict and Post-Conflict Societies" (2004) UN Doc S/2004/616.

[17] Thomas Obel Hansen, "The Time and Space of Transitional Justice" in Cheryl Lawther and others (eds), *Research Handbook on Transitional Justice* (Edward Elgar 2017) 34–35; Dustin N Sharp, "Emancipating Transitional Justice from the Bonds of the Paradigmatic Transition" (2015) 9 International Journal of Transitional Justice 150, 150–51.

[18] Christine Bell, "Transitional Justice, Interdisciplinarity and the State of the 'Field' or 'Non-Field' " (2009) 3 International Journal of Transitional Justice 5, 8.

[19] Hansen (n 17) 34–35.

[20] Ruti G Teitel, *Transitional Justice* (Oxford University Press 2000) 89–90. Eric Posner has argued that transitional justice should be perceived as ordinary as opposed to extraordinary justice in that regime changes are but large-scale transitions amongst a range of transitions that regularly occur in consolidated democracies, and that may raise the same dilemmas as regime change. Because transitional justice is continuous with ordinary justice, Posner posits that "there is no reason to treat transitional justice measures as presumptively suspect on either moral or institutional grounds". Eric A Posner and Adrian Vermeule, "Transitional Justice as Ordinary Justice" (2004) 117 Harvard Law Review 761, 762–65.

[21] Hansen (n 17) 34–35.

contribute to a complex web ... in which combatants, refugees, resources and weapons cross borders".[22] Relatedly, fourth, the question has arisen as to how transitional justice can respond to a wider range of large-scale abuses, including "inter-ethnic violence, cross-border conflict, systematic repression of minorities and injustices committed by established democracies".[23] Fifth, the assumption that transitional justice policies or processes are state-driven has now also come into question. Contemporary discourse imagines the state as only one among several actors with the power to shape and implement transitional justice as it has globalized.[24] Indeed, civil society, as well as regional and international organizations, regularly step in and play an important role in advancing transitional justice objectives.[25] Finally, the field has moved beyond the dualist peace versus justice, and truth versus justice, debates of the past to recognize that no single transitional justice mechanism could ever suffice to respond adequately to all situations of large-scale abuse. There has been a recognition in recent years that transitional justice requires a holistic approach tailored to each specific instance of transition, and the "competing" restorative versus retributive justice focus inherent in some responses as compared to others need not be mutually exclusive, but may even be interdependent.[26] As a result, there has been an increasing willingness in the field to consider a widening range of goals and mechanisms as complementary and mutually reinforcing rather than mutually exclusive.[27]

Consequently, according to the UN Secretary-General, modern transitional justice has evolved and expanded to encompass "the full range of processes and mechanisms associated with a society's attempts to come to terms with a legacy of large-scale past abuses, in order to ensure accountability, serve justice and achieve reconciliation".[28] Similarly, it has been defined holistically by Pablo de Greiff, former UN Special Rapporteur on the Promotion of Truth, Justice, Reparation and Guarantees of Non-Recurrence, as "a *comprehensive* policy implemented to cope with the legacies of massive and systemic violations and abuses, and to restore or establish anew the currency of human rights".[29]

---

[22] Amy Ross and Chandra Lekha Sriram, "Closing Impunity Gaps: Regional Transitional Justice Processes?" (2013) 1 Transitional Justice Review 3, 5.

[23] Hansen (n 17) 35–36. See, eg, an increasing trend of using transitional justice to respond to human rights violations against indigenous communities. Courtney Jung, "Canada and the Legacy of the Indian Residential Schools: Transitional Justice for Indigenous People in a Nontransitional Society" in Paige Arthur (ed), *Identities in Transition: Challenges for Transitional Justice in Divided Societies* (Cambridge University Press 2010) 217–50 (addressing the complexities involved in processing indigenous demands for justice through a transitional justice framework).

[24] Hansen (n 17) 47.

[25] ibid 35.

[26] Wendy Lambourne, "Transitional Justice and Peacebuilding after Mass Violence" (2009) 3 International Journal of Transitional Justice 28, 31.

[27] McAuliffe (n 2) 130–31.

[28] UN Secretary-General, "Guidance Note of the Secretary-General: United Nations Approach to Transitional Justice" (10 March 2010) UN Doc ST/SG(09)/A652.

[29] Pablo de Greiff, "The Future of the Past: Reflections on the Present State and Prospects of Transitional Justice" (2020) 14 International Journal of Transitional Justice 251, fn 2. See also Rachel Kerr and Eirin Mobekk, *Peace and Justice: Seeking Accountability After War* (Polity Press 2007) 3. For a good overview of the range of definitions for modern transitional justice, see Rosemary Nagy, "Transitional Justice as Global Project: Critical Reflections" (2008) 29 Third World Quarterly 275, 275–89.

## 2.2  Goals and Mechanisms

Given the evolution of the modern definition of transitional justice just outlined, Pablo de Greiff and former Special Adviser Adama Dieng have emphasized that there are four constitutive goals which any transitional justice process should seek: truth, justice, reparation, and non-recurrence.[30] Specifically, transitional justice should aim for: (i) disassociation from committed atrocities by, for example, acknowledging victims' suffering, establishing a historical record, and punishing perpetrators; (ii) deterrence of future conflicts by establishing conditions conducive to peace and stability; and (iii) creation and stabilization of a legitimate political order, preferably democratic,[31] which affirms respect for human rights, secures the protection of vulnerable groups, and promotes rule of law.[32]

In order to achieve these goals, central to the transitional justice process are various mechanisms designed to assist societies in moving forward, by addressing the past, present, or future.[33] As noted in this chapter's historical overview, transitional justice mechanisms may take a number of forms, including criminal prosecutions, nationally[34] or internationally[35]; fact-finding by truth

---

[30] HRC, "Joint Study on the Contribution of Transitional Justice to the Prevention of Gross Violations and Abuses of Human Rights and Serious Violations of International Humanitarian Law, Including Genocide, War Crimes, Ethnic Cleansing and Crimes Against Humanity, and Their Recurrence: Report of the Special Rapporteur on the Promotion of Truth, Justice, Reparation and Guarantees of Non-Recurrence and the Special Adviser to the Secretary-General on the Prevention of Genocide" (6 June 2018) UN Doc A/HRC/37/65 para 12; Pablo de Greiff, "Report of the Special Rapporteur on the Promotion of Truth, Justice, Reparation and Guarantees of Non-Recurrence" (12 October 2017) UN Doc A/72/523.

[31] But see Chandra Sriram, "Justice as Peace? Liberal Peacebuilding and Strategies of Transitional Justice" (2007) 21 Global Society 579, 579; Sharp, "Emancipating Transitional Justice" (n 17) 155–59. Current thinking on transitional justice problematizes the notion that marketisation and democratization are in and of themselves guarantors of peace; indeed, each may be destabilizing, and may contribute to a return to conflict. In his presentation, "Transitional Justice: What it Is & Why it Matters" at the William & Mary Law School Symposium "No Transition, No Justice" on 18 September 2020, David Tolbert noted that while many transitional justice scholars focused on democracy as the end goal for transition, now, the initial focus is increasingly on dealing with the past and changing the direction of a society with less focus on a clear transition to democracy as was seen thirty years ago. Tolbert (n 12).

[32] Lavinia Stan and Nadya Nadelsky (eds), *Encyclopedia of Transitional Justice: Volume 1* (Cambridge University Press 2013) 5–6. Pablo de Greiff has helpfully reconceptualized these common goals as a series of steps each transitional justice process aims to meet. The immediate aims of transitional justice are to provide recognition to victims who have experienced harm during the conflict (and reaffirm their equal rights as citizens) as well as to promote civic trust by taking concrete steps to reckon with the past. The final aims of transitional justice are to promote reconciliation (such that citizens may trust one another as citizens again) and democratization. Pablo de Greiff, "Theorizing Transitional Justice" in Melissa S Williams and others (eds), *Transitional Justice* (New York University Press 2012) 41–58.

[33] Lilian A Barria and Steven D Roper, "Mechanisms of Transitional Justice" in Lilian A Barria and Steven D Roper eds, *The Development of Institutions of Human Rights: A Comparative Study* (Palgrave Macmillan US 2010) 4.

[34] National prosecutions may take place in the established criminal justice system or in ad hoc special courts; further, they may apply local customary norms in addition to national legislation to prosecutions such as in the gacaca courts in Rwanda, or Timor-Leste's Community Reconciliation Process. Stan and Nadelsky (n 32) 41; Jaya Ramji-Nogales, "Designing Bespoke Transitional Justice: A Pluralist Process Approach" (2010) 32 Michigan Journal of International Law 1, 54–59.

[35] See, eg, international criminal tribunals noted previously in this chapter such as the ICTY, ICTR, and ICC. Further, criminal prosecutions for serious human rights abuses have taken place before hybrid tribunals which allow for a mix of domestic and international law procedures, such as the Special Court for Sierra Leone or the Extraordinary Chambers in the Courts of Cambodia.

commissions;[36] reparations programmes;[37] memorialization or other forms of social repair; and institutional[38] reform.[39] These mechanisms may be judicial or non-judicial, and range across a spectrum depending on the types of justice or goals that are prioritized.[40]

Within the context of this wide and flexible range of transitional justice mechanisms, there have been a number of critiques with respect to those established thus far. For example, it has been noted that transitional justice has more narrowly focused on accountability and redress for violations of civil and political rights, as opposed to seeking systemic change through upholding social, economic, and cultural rights,[41] and promoting peace-building and development[42] in the interests of non-recurrence.[43] As such, there have been calls for transitional justice to be informed by a holistic human rights approach.[44] Relatedly, some academics and practitioners have advocated for a

[36] Broadly defined, truth commissions are temporary, national, mixed, or international non-judicial bodies which investigate and document large-scale human rights abuses over a set period of time. They aim to establish an inclusive historical narrative focused on patterns of abuse which can restore the dignity of victims and foreclose repetition. By publicly acknowledging past bad acts through reports recommending appropriate remedies and institutional reform, these commissions help to facilitate dialogue and reconciliation between perpetrators and victims. Stan and Nadelsky (n 32) 98–101.

[37] Current understandings of reparations are that they are victim-focused and may be material or symbolic, individual, or collective. These programmes can take a variety of forms: as an actual return of confiscated property, a symbolic monetary payment, or a public apology. Pablo de Greiff, "Justice and Reparations" in Pablo de Greiff (ed), *The Handbook of Reparations* (Oxford University Press 2008) 453. Individual symbolic reparations may take the form of apology letters or copies of truth commission reports, while collective symbolic measures may include the creation of museums and memorials, days of commemoration, etc. Material reparations may be individualized payments, or service packages (such as access to healthcare). Stan and Nadelsky (n 32) 85–86. For a robust discussion of various reparations policies throughout history, see Peter Malcontent, *Facing the Past: Amending Historical Injustices through Instruments of Transitional Justice* (Intersentia Ltd 2016) 208–13.

[38] Forms of institutional reform may include vetting (eliminating or sanctioning abusive officials such as with lustration), restructuring of institutions to promote integrity and legitimacy, creating oversight bodies, reforming or creating new legal frameworks, disbanding and reintegrating ex-militants into society (otherwise known as DDR, disarmament, demobilization, and reintegration), and education. See, eg, "Institutional Reform" (ICTJ) <https://www.ictj.org/our-work/transitional-justice-issues/institutional-reform>.

[39] Anja Seibert-Fohr, "Transitional Justice in Post-Conflict Situations" (*Max Planck Encyclopedia of International Law*, May 2019) <https://opil.ouplaw.com/view/10.1093/law:epil/9780199231690/law-978019 9231690-e419#:~:text=Anja%20Seibert%2DFohr&text=1%20Transitional%20justice%20describes%20a,transit ion%20to%20peace%20and%20democracy>.

[40] See, eg, Lisa J Laplante, "The Plural Justice Aims of Reparations" in Susanne Buckley-Zistel and others (eds), *Transitional Justice Theories* (Routledge 2014) 68 (presenting the idea of a continuum of justice with respect to administrative reparations programmes specifically based upon the justice needs felt by victims of human rights violations including reparative, restorative, civic, and socio-economic justice and can include both pecuniary and non-pecuniary measures).

[41] Makau Mutua, "What is the Future of Transitional Justice?" (2015) 9 International Journal of Transitional Justice 1, 1–9.

[42] Joanna R Quinn, "The Development of Transitional Justice" in Cheryl Lawther and others (eds), *Research Handbook on Transitional Justice* (Edward Elgar 2017) 31–32. See, eg, Lisa J Laplante, "Transitional Justice and Peace Building: Diagnosing and Addressing the Socioeconomic Roots of Violence through a Human Rights Framework" (2008) 2 International Journal of Transitional Justice 331–34; Sharp, "Emancipating Transitional Justice" (n 17) 150–52; Par Engstrom, "Transitional Justice and Ongoing Conflict" in Chandra Lekha Sriram and others (eds), *Transitional Justice and Peacebuilding on the Ground: Victims and Ex-Combatants* (Routledge 2013); Tolbert (n 12).

[43] HRC, "Joint Study on the Contribution of Transitional Justice to the Prevention of Gross Violations and Abuses of Human Rights and Serious Violations of International Humanitarian Law" (n 30), para 12, 15. In a separate statement, Pablo de Greiff posited that "more than a dearth of knowledge and expertise, what hampers better results in the area of prevention is, first, the relative weakness of commitments and the consequent paucity of investments in this area and, second, the great disaggregation of knowledge and resources". de Greiff, "Report of the Special Rapporteur" (n 30) para 20.

[44] Laplante, "Transitional Justice and Peace Building" (n 42) 332. Not all scholars agree that such a broadening of the goals of transitional justice is wise, cautioning that "broadening the scope of what we mean by transitional

pluralist approach to transitional justice that rejects universal application of criminal prosecutions wherever atrocity crimes are concerned.[45] Under this view, mechanisms can and should be tailored as context-specific, based on a wide range of factors including the nature of the conflict, the needs and interests of the societies involved in the conflict, and the human and economic resources available, among others.[46] Further, it is accepted that there may need to be a combination of different mechanisms in order to achieve actual justice in a specific context, and these may complement one another.[47]

Finally, another critique relates to the choice, design, and implementation of transitional justice mechanisms thus far, which often do not adequately include the voices of affected communities. This critique calls for a "transformative justice" frame which

> radically reform[s] its politics, locus and priorities. Transformative justice entails a shift in focus from the legal to the social and political, and from the state and institutions to communities and everyday concerns. Transformative justice is not the result of a top-down imposition of external legal frameworks or institutional templates, but of a more bottom-up understanding and analysis of the lives and needs of populations.[48]

Thus, transitional justice must include the participation of victims as an empowering process that "sees the marginalized challenge, access and shape institutions and structures from which they were previously excluded"[49] and shifts "the focus of rights talk from the metropolis and official spaces to the communities where violations occur".[50] In this way, a "thicker", more effective justice process will result.[51]

---

justice to encompass the building of a just as well as peaceful society may make the effort so broad as to become meaningless". Naomi Roht-Arriaza and Javier Mariezcurrena (eds), *Transitional Justice in the Twenty-First Century* (Cambridge University Press 2010) 2. See also Rama Mani, "Dilemmas of Expanding Transitional Justice, or Forging the Nexus between Transitional Justice and Development" (2008) 2 International Journal of Transitional Justice 253, 253–65 (noting that the patterns of social injustice are so wide and systemic and the victims and consequences so many that it is difficult to envisage how to encompass them within the finite range of current mechanisms for achieving transitional justice).

[45] Seibert-Fohr (n 39); Miriam J Auckerman, "Extraordinary Evil, Ordinary Crime: A Framework for Understanding Transitional Justice" (2002) 15 Harvard Human Rights Journal 39, 40–44. For proponents of a pluralist system, see generally Donald L Hafner and Elizabeth BL King, "Beyond Traditional Notions of Transitional Justice: How Trials, Truth Commissions, and Other Tools for Accountability Can and Should Work Together" (2007) 30 British Columbia International & Comparative Law Review 91; Rachel Lopez, "Post-Conflict Pluralism" (2018) 39 University of Pennsylvania Journal of International Law 749.

[46] Ramji-Nogales (n 34) 4; Richard L Goldstone, "Transitional Justice in Practice: The Importance of Context in Confronting Legacies of Mass Abuse" (2019) 11 Drexel Law Review 835, 843.

[47] Lopez (n 45) 750.

[48] Paul Gready and Simon Robins, "From Transitional to Transformative Justice: A New Agenda for Practice" (2014) 8 International Journal of Transitional Justice 339, 340. See also Mani (n 44) 253–65.

[49] Gready and Robins (n 48) 355–58.

[50] ibid, 358.

[51] For a discussion on the legalistic aspects of transitional justice, see generally Kieran McEvoy, "Beyond Legalism: Towards a Thicker Understanding of Transitional Justice" (2007) 34 Journal of the Law Society 411. See also Tolbert (n 12).

## 3. The EECC: A Transitional Justice Mechanism?

### 3.1 Origins

Turning to the question of whether the EECC may be considered a transitional justice mechanism as currently understood, it is important to note that it was established by Eritrea and Ethiopia as part of their transition from an international armed conflict from May 1998 to December 2000 along their shared border. As such, the EECC was modelled after historic mixed commissions,[52] utilized in the eighteenth to the twentieth centuries primarily for inter-state dispute resolution under international law.[53] At the same time, as a "mixed claims commission", it had broader jurisdiction over individuals' claims, not just state claims.[54]

While the causes of the conflict are too varied and complex to cover fully in this chapter, when Eritrea gained independence from Ethiopia in 1991, Ethiopian militias were left occupying territory that Eritrea considered to be part of the former Italian colony.[55] This aspect is generally recognized as playing a significant role in Eritrea's invasion of Tigray and other border regions in 1998.[56] The larger Ethiopian military responded with a full-scale counterattack. In the course of the armed conflict, an estimated 50,000–100,000 people were killed and close to 1 million forcibly displaced, many of whom were civilians.[57] Further, many individuals were detained, tortured, and expelled as prisoners of war on the battlefield as well as from their homes as enemy aliens. There was also widespread damage to civilian buildings and property

---

[52] Laurence Boisson de Chazournes and Danio Campanelli, "Mixed Commissions" (*Max Planck Encyclopedia of International Law*, December 2006) <https://opil.ouplaw.com/view/10.1093/law:epil/9780199231690/law-978019 9231690-e65> ("Mixed commission (commission mixte) was a commonly used expression in the period between the end of the 18th and the beginning of the 20th centuries for designating mainly (but not exclusively) bilateral inter-State ad hoc dispute settlement institutions" with decision-makers appointed by the states appearing before them) (internal quotations omitted).

[53] Sean D Murphy, Won Kidane, and Thomas R Snider, *Litigating War: Mass Civil Injury and the Eritrea-Ethiopia Claims Commission* (Oxford University Press 2013) xv.

[54] "Mixed claims commissions are bodies founded ad hoc on the basis of international agreements usually consisting of a majority of nationals of the States Parties to the agreements and established with the purpose of settling claims which have arisen between citizens of different States, between citizens of one State and the other State, or between the States themselves in formal and final proceedings." Rudolph Dolzer, "Mixed Claims Commissions" (*Max Planck Encyclopedia of International Law*, May 2011) <https://opil.ouplaw.com/view/10.1093/law:epil/9780199231690/law-9780199231690-e64>. The first mixed claims commissions date back to the late 1700s. See generally Richard B Lillich, "The Jay Treaty Commissions" (1963) 37 St John's Law Review 260.

[55] Murphy, Kidane, and Snider (n 53) 10 ("[M]any farming communities and towns that were on the Eritrean side of colonial boundaries came under the political administration of authorities responsive to Addis Ababa, while those on the Ethiopian side came under the administrative control of Asmara. Consequently, during the 1990s, occasional small-scale disputes erupted along the frontier .... Reviewing the situation on the eve of the conflict, Harold Marcus opined: 'The point that emerges from even a factual recounting of the situation is the lack of clarity in the frontier claims.' ").

[56] ibid 15 ("[T]he use of force against Ethiopia might have served internal domestic purposes for the Eritrean government in galvanizing nationalist support to turn attention away from Eritrea's internal political and economic difficulties.... Using military force along the border would not necessarily mean sparking a lengthy and costly interstate war; possibly the Eritrean leadership doubted that Ethiopia would respond forcefully, or, if it did respond, would be a match for Eritrean fighters who had outwitted the Dergue.").

[57] Ted Dagne, "The Ethiopia-Eritrea Conflict" (CRS Report for Congress 6 July 2000) <https://www.everycrsrep ort.com/files/20000706_RL30598_a2314e387812900135db63fcdf1bb335bba5a082.pdf>.

along the border.[58] By May 2000, Ethiopia had regained all of the disputed territory, destroyed key aspects of Eritrea's infrastructure, and seemed poised to capture the Eritrean capital. However, Ethiopia declared a ceasefire and withdrew to the same positions it had occupied prior to 1998. Shortly thereafter, representatives of both countries signed the Algiers Agreement, a peace treaty through which the EECC was established.

## 3.2  Legal Basis and Structure

When signing the Agreement, the Prime Minister of Ethiopia and President of Eritrea were witnessed by representatives from Algeria, the United States, the United Nations (UN), the Organization of African Unity (OAU) and the European Union. In the preamble, both countries welcomed the commitment of the UN and the OAU to facilitate implementation of the Agreement by working "closely with the international community to mobilize resources for the resettlement of displaced persons, as well as rehabilitation and peacebuilding in both countries".[59] Three institutions and processes were established through the Agreement for achievement of these aims, namely an investigation and report by an independent, impartial body appointed by the Secretary General of the OAU into "the incidents of 6 May 1998 and any other incident ... which could have contributed to the misunderstanding between the parties regarding their common border";[60] a "neutral Boundary Commission" to "delimit and demarcate the colonial treaty border based on pertinent colonial treaties ... and applicable international law";[61] and a "neutral Claims Commission", the EECC, to

> decide through binding arbitration all claims for loss, damage or injury by one Government against the other, and by nationals (including both natural and juridical persons) of one party against the Government of the other party or entities owned or controlled by the other party that are (a) related to the conflict ... or (b) result from violations of international humanitarian law... or other violations of international law.[62]

In terms of its operation, the EECC was an ad hoc body, with Eritrea and Ethiopia having the right to appoint two arbitrators each, who were not nationals or permanent residents of the party making the appointment, with the president of the Commission being selected by the party-appointed arbitrators.[63] The seat of the Commission was at

---

[58] Murphy, Kidane, and Snider (n 53) 1.

[59] UN General Assembly and UN Security Council, "Identical Letters Dated 12 December 2000 from the Permanent Representative of Algeria to the United Nations addressed to the Secretary-General and the President of the Security Council, Annex: Agreement Between the Government of the State of Eritrea and the Government of the Federal Democratic Republic of Ethiopia" (12 December 2000) UN Doc A/55/686-S/2000/1183, 2.

[60] ibid 3.

[61] ibid 4.

[62] ibid 7.

[63] ibid. Where an arbitrator was not selected per the terms of the Agreement, the Secretary-General of the United Nations had authority to make an appointment. ibid.

the Permanent Court of Arbitration (PCA) in The Hague, although the Commissioners had discretion to hold hearings or conduct investigations in Eritrea, Ethiopia, or any other location deemed expedient.[64] In terms of procedure, the Commission was allowed to adopt its own rules based upon the 1992 Permanent Court of Arbitration Optional Rules for Arbitrating Disputes between Two States, and each state was responsible for submitting claims for itself and on behalf of its nationals within one year from the effective date of the Agreement.[65] For purposes of processing potentially large numbers of individual claims, the Commission was authorized to adopt appropriate methods for efficient case management and mass claims processing. In deciding claims by majority vote, the applicable law was international law.[66] Awards of the EECC were to be made, if at all possible, within three years from the deadline for filing of claims, and were deemed final and binding. By signing the Agreement, each state agreed to honour all the decisions and pay any monetary awards promptly. Finally, the expenses for the EECC were to be shared equally between Eritrea and Ethiopia.[67]

## 3.3  Transitional Justice Features

In light of the current understanding that transitional justice broadly consists of "the full range of processes and mechanisms associated with a society's attempts to come to terms with a legacy of large-scale past abuses", in order to achieve one or more goals including accountability, reconciliation,[68] truth, reparation, or non-recurrence,[69] there are a number of aspects of the EECC's establishment that, at first blush, weigh in favour of classifying it as a transitional justice mechanism. First, from the outset, some of the express purposes for the EECC under the terms of the Algiers Agreement were to serve the interests of transitional justice. For example, the Commission, coupled with the OAU investigation and Boundary Commission, was intended to be part of a broader effort to reconcile the two countries and, in so doing, restore peace and security to the region. Further, in resolving claims and awarding reparations, the Commission was specifically meant to address violations of international law and human rights holistically, being called upon for rehabilitation of "the negative socio-economic impact of the crisis on the civilian population, including the impact on those persons who have been deported".[70]

---

[64]  ibid 8.
[65]  ibid. Each state was also allowed to file claims on behalf of persons of Eritrean or Ethiopian origin who may not have been their nationals. ibid 9.
[66]  ibid. Commissioners were not authorized to make decisions *ex aequo et bono* "according to the right and good" or what is fair and equitable, thereby dispensing with strict application of the law. ibid.
[67]  ibid.
[68]  UNSG, "Guidance Note on Transitional Justice" (n 28) 3.
[69]  HRC, "Joint Study on the Contribution of Transitional Justice to the Prevention of Gross Violations and Abuses of Human Rights and Serious Violations of International Humanitarian Law" (n 30), para 12; de Greiff, "Report of the Special Rapporteur" (n 30).
[70]  Algiers Agreement (n 59) 7.

Second, the EECC was given jurisdiction to consider claims not just by each state but also by individual victims who suffered loss, damage, or injury in the armed conflict. Third, allowance was made for the EECC to hold hearings close to the victims and affected communities if the Commissioners considered it appropriate. Fourth, in deciding specific claims for state responsibility during this conflict, the Commission would engage in a form of truth-telling as they established facts for determining whether obligations under international law were breached. Fifth, when finding either Eritrea or Ethiopia in violation of international law and ordering monetary awards through binding decisions, measures of accountability and reparation would be achieved.

Finally, various structural features of the EECC would allow for a legitimate process, which is important from a transitional justice perspective. Not only was their international oversight and facilitation by other countries as well as the UN and OAU in establishing the EECC but the appointed Commissioners were required to serve as impartial neutrals. Further, notable procedural flexibility was allowed the Commissioners for the conduct of the proceedings, with reference to potential adoption of measures that would allow for justice through mass claims processing, in light of the tens of thousands of victims of the war. In addition, emphasis was placed on making the EECC an expeditious process with clear deadlines both with respect to filing of claims and rendering of decisions potentially leading to timely satisfaction for victims.

On the other hand, betraying its origins as a form of mixed commission in international law, the EECC's establishment was top down, between states and intergovernmental organizations, without the involvement of individual victims from impacted communities. Further, while the Commission had power to hold hearings close to the victims, its seat was placed far from them in The Hague. Similarly, while provision was made for individual claims from civilians and prisoners of war, these would be presented by Eritrea or Ethiopia on their behalf, and wide procedural discretion was afforded to the EECC for efficient processing of the claims, such as through mass claims processing. As such, the established procedure would potentially exclude natural persons from having direct access or a voice in the justice process. In addition, factual findings on specific claims relating only to state responsibility would serve as a form of truth-telling that would be piecemeal at best with regard to the entirety of the conflict. Finally, while explicit deadlines were given for filing of claims and rendering of binding decision by the Commission, there was no specific timeline for payment of claims in the Agreement.

Nevertheless, on balance, it seems clear that there is room for inclusion of ad hoc mixed claims commissions such as the EECC in the wide range of transitional justice mechanisms that have evolved over the years, where transitional justice goals are an important part of the process. As recognized in the literature, it is impossible for any single mechanism to fully achieve all of the aspirations in the field—often there is need for a combination of measures for societies to fully move on from situations of large-scale and systematic violence.

## 4. Conclusion: Is the EECC a Model for Mixed Claims Commissions and Transitional Justice?

Having considered the EECC's classification as a transitional justice mechanism in light of the scholarship and practice in the field, the question remains: might the Commission serve as a model for future mixed claims commissions established to achieve, at least in part, transitional justice goals? Here, the actual practice and outcome of the EECC's work are pertinent to the question in addition to the structural features of the Commission already highlighted.

In this respect, the case is less clear. From the outset, the Commission attempted to embrace and build upon innovations of modern mixed claims commissions that seem to promote transitional justice goals. For example, when crafting its Rules of Procedure, the Commission envisioned two processes through which individuals could receive compensation: (i) "individual claims" would require a showing of specific injury, established by individualized evidence, and compensated based on a quantification of that specific injury; or (ii) claims for widespread harm, by contrast, would proceed establishing a claimant as a member of a group subjected to that harm, and result in compensation at fixed-sum levels per individual.[71] This latter mass-claims process had potential to allow for efficient award of reparations to large numbers of victims.[72] Further, the Commission considered award of reparations to individuals holistically for personal injury, not just property damage, relating to violations of international humanitarian law, human rights norms, and customary international law[73] such as "suffering associated with forced displacement" and "deaths and injuries caused by landmines."[74]

In other respects, however, the Commission functioned in a more traditional way that perhaps did not serve the interests of transitional justice, particularly with respect to actually achieving justice and award of reparations for individual victims. Because of its design as an ad hoc arbitral commission, the procedures for hearings, the presentation of evidence, and examination of witnesses, for instance, were modelled closely on inter-state or investor–state dispute resolution models with court-like procedures.[75] This approach proved challenging in several respects. Both Eritrea and Ethiopia, for example, presented witnesses to the Commission (such as former prisoners of war, and civilian victims of war crimes). However, due to the sheer number of individual claims, and the impracticality and expense of calling numerous witnesses to The Hague to testify, both countries submitted instead "claim forms" which were "forms for collecting evidence … filled in by [for example] a former POW … responding at varying length to detailed questions regarding conditions and experiences … in POW camps".[76]

[71] Murphy, Kidane, and Snider (n 53) 60–61.
[72] Ariel Colonomos and Andrea Armstrong, "German Reparations to Jews after World War II" in de Greiff (ed), *The Handbook of Reparations* (n 37); see John Authers, "Making Good Again: German Compensation for Forced and Slave Laborers" ibid.
[73] Murphy, Kidane, and Snider (n 53) 62–68, 70.
[74] ibid 101–02.
[75] See generally ibid 83–93.
[76] ibid 89.

The Commission subsequently deemed these to be of "uncertain probative value".[77] Consequently, in the end, only five individualized claims from Eritrean nationals were addressed by the Commission.[78] Similarly, the mass claims process envisioned by the Commission at its outset was never put into practice because "neither party made use of [those] procedures".[79] Rather, both parties, in effect, embraced claim espousal.[80] Thus, "rather than Ethiopia filing, for example, 3,000 … claims by named individuals injured along the Central Front … Ethiopia filed a single claim on behalf of the government itself alleging harm to its unnamed individuals. Virtually all of Eritrea's claims were also filed as government claims".[81] This development directly impacted how damages were awarded at the end of the proceedings. Rather than ordering the respective parties to pay individual claimants directly, the Commission's judgments provided for lump sum payments to be paid out by the respective states: Eritrea was awarded a total of "$161,455,000 for sixteen different findings of liability. It was also awarded a total of $2,065,865 for the five individual Eritrean Claimants."[82] Ethiopia received "compensation in the amount of $174,036,520" for Eritrea's violations of international humanitarian law and for having initiated the conflict in the first place.[83]

Further, in light of the numbers of claims, the breadth and depth of the claims' subject matter, and the arbitral procedural process, the Commission was unable to conclude its work within the three years envisioned in the Algiers Agreement. Following the filing by Ethiopia and Eritrea of their claims in December 2001 addressing matters on the conduct of military operations in the front zones such as treatment of prisoners of war, treatment of civilians and their property, diplomatic immunities, and the economic impact of government activities during the conflict, the Commission delivered fifteen partial and final awards on liability and damages, concluding its work in August 2009.

As a result, the record of the EECC in facilitating an effective transitional justice process is mixed. On the one hand, the Commission clearly played a role in Eritrea and Ethiopia addressing large-scale death, abuse, and destruction that occurred as a result of their armed conflict from 1998 to 2000. Both states were found, through a fair, detailed procedural process resulting in binding decisions, to be in breach of international humanitarian and human rights law norms. As such, a measure of accountability was achieved. Further, the process sent a clear message of the importance of upholding the rule of law. In addition, there was arguably some establishment of the historical record and truth-telling important for both countries and their populations, even if it was incomplete being based solely on the claims that were brought by each country.

---

[77] Eritrea-Ethiopia Claims Commission, "Partial Award, Prisoners of War, Ethiopia's Claim 4" (2003) 42 International Legal Materials 1056, 1063.

[78] Murphy, Kidane, and Snider (n 53) 61 ("[A]ll of Ethiopia's claims were filed as government claims. Virtually all of Eritrea's claims were also filed as government claims, but a handful of individual claims of Eritrean nationals were also submitted to the commission, and the commission ultimately issued findings in favour of four named individuals for amounts ranging from $21,250 to $1,500,000.").

[79] ibid 61.

[80] ibid 68–69.

[81] ibid 61.

[82] ibid 93–94.

[83] ibid 94.

However, for individual victims, the process was largely inaccessible as they had no voice in the process other than the few who served as witnesses. Not only were individuals barred from presenting their claims directly to the Commission but in the end, single claims were largely filed by each government on behalf of itself and unnamed individuals, with the exception that Eritrea presented five individual claims. Further, while several hearings took place from July 2001 to August 2009, these were based in The Hague, far from the affected populations. In addition, for individual victims, there is the perception that while a measure of justice was achieved, it was neither actual nor swift, with the final awards on damages rendered nearly a decade after initiation of the process. Further, there was no stipulated process for direct payment to individual victims by the governments of Eritrea and Ethiopia given the lump sum nature of the awards, and damages have never been paid out. This could have been anticipated with a commission set up for payment of compensation by two impoverished countries in the aftermath of a devastating war. As such, reparation has not been achieved through this process and justice for individuals was largely symbolic. Also, from the perspective of the victim communities, the money spent by their governments on an expensive arbitral process for nearly a decade might better have been used for reconstruction and development for their devastated communities. Finally, with the conclusion of the EECC's work in 2009, full peace and reconciliation between the two was not achieved until a decade later in July 2018, when both countries finally agreed to fully implement the Algiers Agreement after Ethiopia accepted the ruling of the Boundary Commission on borders rendered in 2003.[84] As such, it is questionable whether the EECC played much of a role in helping to achieve peace and non-recurrence in the region, particularly given that the process failed to re-establish socio-economic rights and development for the affected Tigrayan populations on both sides of the border in the aftermath of the conflict. Indeed, at the writing of this chapter, conflict has flared up once again in the region, wherein Tigrayans in both countries seek self-determination and flee persecution.[85]

Moving forward, as a mixed claims commission, the EECC is an imperfect, albeit important model to consider both with respect to its design and execution for future transitional justice contexts. Where mixed claims commissions are established with clearly articulated transitional justice objectives in their founding documents, they have potential to serve as important complimentary mechanisms alongside other processes for addressing atrocity crimes. For example, the EECC experiment demonstrates that mixed claims commissions may, with their focus on assigning state responsibility through legally binding decisions, be an important tool for closing the impunity gap for atrocity situations with respect to other actors outside of individual perpetrators,

[84] Susan Stigant and Payton Knopf, "Ethiopia-Eritrea Peace Deal Brings Hope to Horn of Africa" (United States Institute of Peace, 2 August 2018) <https://www.usip.org/index.php/publications/2018/08/ethiopia-eritrea-peace-deal-brings-hope-horn-africa>.

[85] "Eritrean Refugees Cut Off from Aid, Threatened by Ethiopia's Continuing Conflict" (The New Humanitarian, 30 November 2020) <https://www.thenewhumanitarian.org/news-feature/2020/11/30/Ethiopia-Eritrea-refugee-camps-tigray-cut-off?utm_source=The+New+Humanitarian&utm_campaign=3882f4ec41-EMAIL_CAMPAIGN_11_30_2020_DAILY&utm_medium=email&utm_term=0_d842d98289-3882f4ec41-15684725>.

which is the sole focus in international criminal trials. Further, mixed claims commissions may provide a more reparative, restorative justice approach to atrocity contexts with their focus on award of compensation to potentially large numbers of individual victims, through procedures such as mass claims processes. Similarly, the EECC demonstrates that mixed claims commissions may provide a more holistic human rights approach to transitional justice where they emphasize remedying abuse of socio-economic rights and promotion of peace and development for affected communities as equally important to addressing violations of civil and political rights that result in grave physical injury to victims. Finally, in light of the considerable flexibility available in the establishment of ad hoc mixed claims commission, they have potential to bring a more pluralist transitional justice approach to atrocity situations that is appropriately tailored to address a specific context rooted in shared history.

On the other hand, the EECC also demonstrates that the potential for mixed claims commissions as transitional justice mechanisms is seriously undermined where there is mere lip service to centring individual victims in the process without the political will or resources necessary for doing so. In the first place, creation of mixed claims commissions should avoid being purely top-down, or a state-driven process only. Rather, means should be found for inclusion of a bottom-up approach to both design and execution that effects "transformative justice" wherein commissions are informed and shaped by consultation with marginalized victim communities to better understand and address their needs. Further, individual victim claimants should have access to the process as much as possible. This is better realized where the seat of a mixed claims commission is located within or close to the affected communities and they are regularly informed of the process; individuals have the ability bring their claims directly on their own behalf; payment of damages is ordered to be directly paid to individual claimants under specified procedures and deadlines that are enforceable; and expenses for the operation of a mixed claims commission do not prevent eventual payment of claims to individual victims when all is said and done. In this regard, outside states and international organizations may have a role to play in provision, not only of expertise and oversight for purposes of legitimacy as was done with the EECC but also in making available resources for payment of reparations. Only by cantering victims in the mixed claims commission process will the transitional justice goals of reparation, reconciliation and non-recurrence be achieved. Otherwise, from the perspective of victim communities, the process is at risk of becoming one of symbolic justice only, akin to no justice at all.

## Dedication by Hannah R Garry:

This chapter is dedicated to two experts in the field of international dispute resolution, David Caron and Lucy Reed, both of whom participated in the Eritrea Ethiopia Claims Commission—Lucy as Commissioner and David as Counsel for Ethiopia. While an associate at Freshfields, Bruckhaus, Deringer LLP, I had the privilege of assisting Lucy when she was Commissioner and of observing David, my former professor at Berkeley Law, press eloquent arguments before the Commission while Lucy skilfully probed counsel during hearings in The Hague. Both are cherished mentors who taught me much about the theory and practice of international law and opened up opportunities along the way. I am deeply grateful to them both, and continue to mourn David, whose brilliant life ended far too soon.

# PART II

# INSTITUTIONS AND INSTITUTIONAL ACTORS

# 5

# International Courts in a Politicized World

*Yuval Shany*

## 1. Introduction

One of the harshest forms of criticisms directed at international institutions generally, and international courts specifically, is that they are political or politicized.[1] Such a criticism appears to presume (i) that law and politics, in general, and international adjudication and international politics, in particular, can be divorced from one another; and (ii) that the values and interests advanced through international adjudication would be better served by insulating international courts from the vicissitudes of world politics.

This chapter is written in honour of Professor David Caron, from whose work I have learned a lot, and whom I had the pleasure and privilege of cooperating with when we were both involved as law deans in the Center for Transnational Legal Studies, London. It seeks to question the feasibility and desirability of fully separating international adjudication from international politics. The main claim I make in this chapter is that, although it is vital to separate between law and politics, there are unavoidable points of contact between the two domains. Furthermore, I maintain that international courts should take cognizance of certain political considerations. While international courts do not serve as a direct extension of international politics, they do interact with their political environment, and depend in meaningful ways on the support of political actors. As a result, international courts cannot afford to completely ignore their political context, yet they must also strive to maintain a distinction between law and politics. This tension between "can't do with" and "can't do without" is at the heart of the present chapter.

As a point of departure, Section 2 of the chapter discusses the goals of international courts, and Section 3 introduces two key perspectives for evaluating their operations—legitimacy and effectiveness. Section 4 describes several dominant points of contact

---

[1] See eg US State Department, Secretary Michael R. Pompeo's Remarks to the Press, 17 March 2020, <https://www.state.gov/secretary-michael-r-pompeo-remarks-to-the-press-6/> ("Turning to the ICC, a so-called court which is revealing itself to be a nakedly political body: As I said the last time I stood before you, we oppose any effort by the ICC to exercise jurisdiction over U.S. personnel. We will not tolerate its inappropriate and unjust attempts to investigate or prosecute Americans. When our personnel are accused of a crime, they face justice in our country"); Roberta Rampton, Lesley Wroughton, and Stephanie van den Berg, "U.S. withdraws from international accords, says U.N. world court 'politicized'", *Reuters,* 3 October 2018; Isaac B Kardon, "China Can Say 'No': Analyzing China's Rejection of the South China Sea Arbitration—Toward a New Era of International Law With Chinese Characteristics" (2018)13 (1) University of Pennsylvania Asian Law Review 29; Alexai Trochev, "The Russian Constitutional Court and the Strasbourg Court: Judicial Pragmatism in a Dual State" in Laurie Mälksoo and Wolfgang Benedek (eds), *Russia and the European Court of Human Rights: The Strasbourg Effect* (Cambridge University Press 2018) 145.

Yuval Shany, *International Courts in a Politicized World* In: *By Peaceful Means.* Edited by: Charles N Brower, Joan E Donoghue, Cian C Murphy, Cymie R Payne and Esmé R Shirlow, Oxford University Press. © Yuval Shany 2024. DOI: 10.1093/oso/9780192848086.003.0005

between international adjudication and the political world—acceptance of jurisdiction, support of judicial operations, and enforcement of judgments—and Section 5 discusses some of normative and practical implications of juxtaposing judicial goals and the political context against which they should be realized. Specifically, I ask there whether and how courts can take cognizance of political considerations without undermining their legitimacy and effectiveness, and propose that legal notions and doctrines, such as accommodating legitimate or reasonable expectations, avoiding imposing on international actors impossible or unreasonable burdens when interpreting and applying legal norms, affording states a margin of appreciation and developing flexible remedies, may play a useful role in this regard. Section 6 concludes.

## 2. The Goals of International Courts and Tribunals

International courts and tribunals comprise a diverse set of independent judicial institutions possessing the power to adjudicate questions of fact and international law, often arising under, or in connection with, specific treaties or international regimes.[2] The judicial services provided by international adjudicative bodies to international actors participating in these treaties or regimes vary broadly. Still, what is common to all international judicial bodies is that they were established by political actors—typically, the state parties to their constitutive instrument—as non-political bodies: they are composed of independent judges, who decide cases on the basis of legal considerations, leading to the application of legal norms to facts pursuant to a fixed legal procedure.

As further explained later in the chapter, the distinction between political and judicial bodies is not a sharp one, in the sense that judicial bodies are not always oblivious to political considerations of power and interest, and political bodies do not ignore legal considerations and operate under conditions of legally constrained power and authority.[3] Moreover, there are many international decision-making institutions which are neither exclusively judicial or political in nature, such as expert legal bodies that only have the power to issue non-binding recommendations for political bodies to consider,[4] and independent institutions with decision-making authority that operate on

---

[2] For a definition of international courts and tribunals, see Christian Tomuschat, "International Courts and Tribunals", *Max Planck Encyclopedia of International Law* (May 2019) (MPIL) ("international courts and tribunals ('ICTs') are permanent judicial bodies made up of independent judges who are entrusted with adjudicating international disputes on the basis of international law according to a pre-determined set of rules of procedure and rendering decisions which are binding on the parties").

[3] See Robert E Goodin, "The State of the Discipline, The Discipline of the State" in Robert E Good (ed). *The Oxford Handbook of Political Science* (Oxford University Press 2009) 5 ("politics is the constrained use of social power"). See also Mark A Graber, "Constitutional Law and American Politics" in Gregory A Caldeira and others (eds), *The Oxford Handbook of Law and Politics* (Oxford University Press 2008) 300, 314; Brian L Porto, "May It Please the Court: Judicial Processes and Politics in America" (Routledge 2009) 257–58; Ran Hirschl, "The Judicialization of Politics" in Good (ed), *The Oxford Handbook of Political Science* 253, 254–55.

[4] For example, see the World Bank Inspection Panel. Yvonne Wong, "Inspection Panel: World Bank", *Max Planck Encyclopedia of Public International Law (MPEPIL)* (online version; last updated in 2019).

the basis of non-legal criteria.[5] While I am not generally claiming in this chapter that, as a normative matter, judicial decision-making is superior to political decision-making (or vice versa), I do suggest that international judges and arbitrators aspire to conform, or at least to present themselves as conforming, to an "ideal type" judicial decision-making model,[6] involving a commitment to resolve legal questions exclusively on the basis of legal criteria.

The institutions on which such judges and arbitrators sit range from permanent global institutions, like the International Court of Justice (ICJ) or the International Criminal Court (ICC) in The Hague, through standing regional bodies, such as the Court of Justice of the EU (CJEU) or the European or Inter-American Court for Human Rights (ECtHR and IACtHR, respectively), to permanent arbitration bodies, such as the panels operating under the WTO or arbitrations under the World Bank's International Centre for Settlement of Investment Disputes (ICSID). Beyond the twenty or so institutions that qualify as full-fledged courts or permanent arbitration bodies,[7] one can also mention dozens of other mechanisms with quasi-judicial powers,[8] which resemble international courts in many respects, such the Human Rights Committee (HRCttee) that reviews individual communications alleging violations of the International Covenant on Civil and Political Rights (ICCPR).[9] Notwithstanding the similar decision-making methodologies applied by them, distinct judicial and quasi-judicial institutions have different constituencies, jurisdictional structures, rules of procedure, and fields of expertise. They are also expected to achieve different goals—that is, they are subject to different sets of stakeholder expectations relating to their performance.[10]

The first international courts grew out of the institution of international arbitration as part of an evolution which started with a transition from ad hoc arbitration to permanent arbitration bodies.[11] Like arbitration bodies, international courts were designed to decide, on the basis of international law, inter-state disputes and, in certain cases, disputes between states and private persons adversely affected by their conduct.[12] Still, over time, other judicial functions assumed by international courts have become more and more prominent and integral to the expectations of their constituencies.

---

[5] See for example, the exercise of independent decision-making by international monetary institutions, such as the World Bank. See eg Benedict Kingsbury, "Global Administrative Law in the Institutional Practice of Global Regulatory Governance" (2012) 3 (3) *The World Bank Legal Review* 13.

[6] See Eileen Braman, *Law, Politics and Perception: How Policy Preferences Influence Legal Reasoning* (University of Virginia Press 2009) 25. cf Martin Shapiro, *Courts: A Comparative and Politics Analysis* (University of Chicago Press 1981)194.

[7] See Tomuschat (n 2).

[8] For example, the UN human rights treaty bodies exercise non-binding quasi-judicial authority pursuant to individual complaints mechanisms. See eg Wouter Vandenhole, *The Procedures Before the UN Human Rights Treaty Bodies: Divergence or Convergence* (Intersentia 2004) 29–30.

[9] International Covenant on Civil and Political Rights and Optional Protocol to International Covenant on Civil and Political Rights, 16 Dec. 1966, 999 UNTS 171.

[10] For a discussion of what are the goals–of international courts, see Yuval Shany, *Assessing the Effectiveness of International Courts* (2014) 17–20.

[11] See eg Karen J Alter, "The Evolution of International Law and Courts" in Orfeo Fioretos, Tulia G Falleti, and Adam Shengate (eds), *The Oxford Handbook of Historical Institutionalism* (Oxford University Press 2016)

[12] See eg Statute of the International Court of Justice, 26 June 1945, art 38(1), 33 UNTS 993 ("The Court, whose function is to decide in accordance with international law such disputes as are submitted to it, shall apply …").

Resolution of disputes on the basis of international law necessarily entails a process of law interpretation, and through assuming this interpretative function, international courts have significantly contributed to the gradual development of international law in general, and to the development of specific areas of law in particular.[13] In the absence of a permanent international legislature, the law-interpreting function exercised by international courts has come to represent a distinct judicial goal, which assumes great importance in international life since it facilitates the incremental adjustment of international law to new situations and challenges.[14]

The application of international law by international courts also plays an important role in promoting the goals of the international regimes under which they operate. For example, an international court enforcing international human rights or investment law norms increases the costs associated with violation of these norms, potentially resulting in improved long-term compliance.[15] Law enforcement is, actually, the main function of international criminal courts, which were created in order to bring to justice those bearing the greatest responsibility for serious international crimes, with a view to ending impunity.[16] Furthermore, law interpretation and law application by international courts typically contribute to the normative agenda of the legal regime to which they belong. For example, it has been claimed that the pro-trade liberalization agenda of the World Trade Organization (WTO) dispute settlement mechanism, contributes towards increasing international trade volumes—for example, through the combination of narrowly construing trade exceptions and exercising compulsory jurisdiction over disruptive trade disputes.[17]

Finally, by exercising some degree of supervision over international organizations and by allowing those affected by the exercise of government power to challenge such power on the international sphere, international courts confer a degree of legitimacy on the project of international governance and on the governments and institutions whose conduct they review. For example, the judicial review services provided by the CJEU on EU regulations serve as an important safeguard against abuse of authority by the EU Council,[18] and the participation of members states of the Council of Europe

---

[13] See eg Rüdiger Wolfrum, "Sources of International Law", *MPEPIL* (n 4) para 46.

[14] See eg Christian J Tams, "The ICJ as a 'Law-Formative Agency': Summary and Synthesis" in Christian J Tams and James Sloan (eds), *The Development of International Law by the International Court of Justice* (Oxford University Press 2013) 377, 377–88.

[15] See egArmin von Bogdandy and Ingo Venzke, "In Whose Name? An Investigation of International Courts' Public Authority and Its Democratic Justification" (2012) 23 (7) European Journal of International Law 17–18.

[16] Rome Statute of the International Criminal Court, 17 July 1998, preamble, 2187 UNTS 3 ("Determined to put an end to impunity for the perpetrators of these crimes and thus to contribute to the prevention of such crimes").

[17] See eg Wonkyu Shin and Dukgeun Ahn, "Trade Gains from Legal Rulings in the WTO Dispute Settlement System" (2019) 18 (1) World Trade Review 30–31. Kati Kulovesi, *The WTO Dispute Settlement System: Challenges of the Environment, Legitimacy and Fragmentation* (Wolters Kluwer 2011) 21–22. But see Gabriele Gagliani, "The Interpretation of General Exceptions in International Trade and Investment Law: Is a Sustainable Development Interpretive Approach Possible?" (2015) 43 Denver Journal of International Law & Policy 559, 570–73 (describing a gradual expansion in the interpretation of trade exceptions by WTO dispute settlement bodies).

[18] See eg Shai Dothan, "International Courts Improve Public Deliberation" (2018) 39 Michigan Journal of International Law 217, 230–31; Wolfgang Wessels, "The European Council" in Robert Shütze and Takis Tridimas (eds), *Oxford Principles of European Union Law: The European Union Legal Order* (Oxford University Press 2018) 490, 511–12.

in the ECtHR allows these states to project to the rest of the world an image of human rights-respecting countries or at least of aspirants for such a status.[19]

## 3. Legitimacy and Effectiveness

Two key notions in legal theory and political science—legitimacy and effectiveness— offer a comprehensive framework for evaluating the authority of international courts and their success in achieving their goals. When examining international courts through the prism of legitimacy, the perspective is mostly external and the evaluative criteria applied are either sociological or normative in nature. Do outside constituencies accept the authority of an international court? And should they accept its authority?[20] Examination of effectiveness, on the other hand, focuses on the actual performance of international courts—primarily, did they attain the specific goals they were expected to.[21] A particularly important set of goals, which often dominates effectiveness assessments, is the goals of the mandate providers of international courts (ie the States and international institutions that concluded the constitutive instruments establishing and governing the operations of international courts).[22] Such goals are intertwined with the source legitimacy of international courts (since their legal powers originate from the legal mandate granted to them by the mandate providers) and are likely to exert considerable influence on their actual operations (since the mandate providers can provide or withhold support for them).

The two notions—legitimacy and effectiveness—are, however, interdependent in the sense that a more effective court is likely to be viewed as more legitimate and a more legitimate court is likely to be more effective.[23] For example, if one of the goals of creating international courts is to confer legitimacy on the exercise of governmental power at the international level, an international court can only do this effectively if it is itself perceived to be legitimate in nature. At the same time, an international court that is not effective—for example, a court that is unable to resolve conflicts because states refuse to comply with its decisions or refrain from submitting cases to it—would not be perceived as authoritative in the eyes of outside observers, and would also lose, sooner or later, its legitimacy in the eyes of relevant constituencies.

Another key insight in this regard is that every international court possesses some initial "legitimacy capital", comprising source legitimacy which includes, *inter alia*, legitimacy that derives from the binding authority of the legal instrument that led to its

---

[19] See eg Daniel C Tomas, *The Helsinki Effect: International Norms, Human Rights, and the Demise of Communism* (Princeton University Press 2001) 16.
[20] See eg Nienke Grossman, "The Normative Legitimacy of International Courts" (2013) 86 Temple Law Review 61, 80; Allen Buchanan and Robert O. Keohane, "The Legitimacy of Global Governance Institutions" (2006) 20 Ethics & International Affairs 405, 405; Shany, *Assessing the Effectiveness of International Courts* (n 10) 138–40.
[21] ibid 6–8.
[22] ibid.
[23] See eg Yuval Shany, "Stronger Together? Legitimacy and effectiveness of International Courts as Mutually Reinforcing or Undermining Notions" in Nienke Grossman and others (eds), *Legitimacy and International Courts* (Cambridge University Press 2018) 354, 363–64.

creation (eg an international treaty concluded by sovereign states or a resolution by the Security Council) and the process legitimacy that is attendant to decision-making processes based on fair judicial procedures and objective legal criteria.[24] Such initial legitimacy capital is expected to be particularly high for certain international courts due to the positive symbolism associated with them being designated as "courts of justice" or "courts of human rights", and the "halo effect" related to their involvement in solving weighty international problems, such as ending impunity.[25] The legitimacy capital of international courts fluctuates over time, however, and the "balance" in the capital "account" may be affected by structural factors, such as the quality or independence of the judges, the extent of acceptance of jurisdiction by states and their actual propensity to invoke the court's jurisdiction. It may also be affected by the perceived quality and fairness of the process before the international court in question.[26]

Significantly, one may also identify fluctuations in legitimacy tied to judicial outcomes: Arguably, a chronic or serious gap between judicial outcomes and constituency preferences could result in the delegitimization of the international court in question. This dynamic can be explained through two complementary explanations. First, decisions that sharply contrast with important interests of parties to litigation are less likely to be complied with, since judgment compliance appears to be partly correlated to a cost-benefit analysis conducted by the losing party that considers the impact of the judgment on its national interests.[27] Yet, even isolated instances of interest-driven non-compliance with judicial decisions may have ripple effects. If some unsatisfied litigants are able to "get away" with non-compliance, then litigants in other cases, equally unhappy with judicial decisions issued against them, might follow suit, and the international court might find itself enmeshed in a vicious circle of ineffectiveness.[28] After compliance rates fall below a critical threshold, the court in question might be regarded as failing to attain its goals (eg resolving disputes), and would not be deemed worthy of the support and resources necessary for its continued operation by the constituencies that it is intended to serve.

Second, rulings that go directly against important political interests of the parties to litigation are also likely to generate challenges on their part to the legitimacy of the

---

[24] ibid 358. See also Mia Swat, "Judicial Independence at the Regional and Sub-regional African Courts" (2014) 29 Southern Africa Public Law 388 389.

[25] See eg Theresa Squatrito, "International Courts and the Politics of Legitimation and De-Legitimation" (2019) 33 Temple International Comparative Law Review 298, 302–03.

[26] For example, some believe that the International Criminal Tribunal for Yugoslavia (ICTY) went out of its way to gain more legitimacy throughout the Western Balkans by attempting to bring to justice individuals from almost all of the nationalities involved in the Yugoslav wars, demonstrating thereby an even-handed approach to the application of international criminal law. See eg Margaret M deGuzman, "Choosing to Prosecute: Expressive Selection at the International Criminal Court" (2012) 33 Michigan Journal of International Law 265, 279; James Meernik, "Victor's Justice or the Law? Judging and Punishing at the International Criminal Tribunal for the Former Yugoslavia" (2003) 47 Journal of Conflict Resolution 140, 147.

[27] See eg Courtney Hillebrecht, *Domestic Politics and International Human Rights Tribunals: The Problem of Compliance* (Cambridge University Press 2014) 114; Diana Kapiszewski and Matthew M Taylor, "Compliance, Conceptualizing, Measuring and Explaining Adherence to Judicial Rulings" (2013) 38 Law & Social Inquiry 803, 819. cf Andrew Guzman, "A Compliance-Based Theory of International Law" (2002) 90 California Law Review 1823, 1883–84.

[28] See Shai Dothan, *Reputation and Judicial Tactics: A Theory of National and International Courts* (Cambridge University Press 2016) 89.

international courts which issued these rulings. This is because perceptions of justice are often intertwined with self-interest,[29] and a judgment clashing with an important self-interest could motivate the aggrieved party to openly criticize what it considers to be an act of injustice.[30] One example of such interplay can be seen in the harsh reactions to actual or potential ICC proceedings by countries in respect of which the ICC already started an investigation or is actively contemplating commencing one (including, *inter alia*, the United States, Russia, Israel, Kenya, and Burundi). Such countries have not only criticized the legal approach taken by the Court but also called into question its legitimacy—in particular, the fairness and propriety of exercising jurisdiction over nationals of non-parties, as well as the allegedly selective, baseless or politicized manner of the Court's operations.[31] Significantly, some of the countries critical of the ICC opposed the Court from its very creation,[32] but others have grown sour on it only after it had zoomed in on them and generated decisions which run contrary to what they consider to be critical national interests.

It stands to reason that the interplay between outcome legitimacy and effectiveness has not eluded those working in international courts, yet it is deemed inappropriate for judges and other senior officials working in international courts to admit that they are taking cognizance of the anticipated reaction of their constituencies. This is because acknowledging it might suggest that considerations other than the legal merits of the case are improperly influencing the court's decisions. The tendency to disavow the relevance of the political context against which judicial decisions are issued renders *Madame Prosecutor*—the memoires of Carla Del Ponte about her term as Chief Prosecutor in the International Criminal Tribunal for Yugoslavia (ICTY) and International Criminal Tribunal for Rwanda (ICTR)—an exceptional text, which offers

---

[29] See Melvin J Lerner and Susan Clayton, "Justice and Self-Interest: Two Fundamental Motives" (2001) 63. cf Paul R Williams and Michael P Scharf, *Peace with Justice? War Crimes and Accountability in the Former Yugoslavia* (Rowman & Littlefield Publishers 2002) 235.

[30] See eg Chandra Lekha Sriram, "International Rule of Law? Ethics and Impartiality of Legal Professionals in International Criminal Tribunals" in Vesselin Popovski (ed), *International Rule of Law and Professional Ethics* (Routledge 2014) 171, 174. cf Michael Byers, *Custom, Power and the Power of Rules: International Relations and Customary International Law* (Cambridge University Press 1999) 120.

[31] See eg Secretary Michael R Pompeo's Remarks to the Press, 17 March 2020, <https://www.state.gov/secretary-michael-r-pompeo-remarks-to-the-press-6/> ("Turning to the ICC, a so-called court which is revealing itself to be a nakedly political body: As I said the last time I stood before you, we oppose any effort by the ICC to exercise jurisdiction over U.S. personnel. We will not tolerate its inappropriate and unjust attempts to investigate or prosecute Americans"); Ketrin Jochecová, Russia blasts back at ICC over Putin arrest warrant, Politico, 20 March 2023, < https://www.politico.eu/article/putin-russia-icc-criminal-case-moscow-ukraine-war/>; State of Israel Office of the Attorney General, The International Criminal Court's Lack of Jurisdiction Over the So-called "Situation in Palestine", 20 December 2019, 1, <https://mfa.gov.il/MFA/PressRoom/2019/Documents/ICCs%20lack%20of%20jurisdiction%20over%20so-called%20%E2%80%9Csituation%20in%20Palestine%E2%80%9D%20-%20AG.pdf>

(The Palestinian attempts to draw the ICC into core political aspects of the Israeli-Palestinian conflict have brought into a sharp focus precisely the risk that the Court might be exploited for illegitimate political gain); Stephen A Lamony, "Kenya Following Sudan Tactics to Undermine ICC", *African Arguments*, 3 April 2013; Laurel Hart, "The International Criminal Court: Biased or Simply Misunderstood?", *UNA-UK Magazine*, 28 October 2018.

[32] See eg Georg Nolte, "The United States and the International Criminal Court" in David M Malone and Yuen Foong Kong (eds), *Unilateralism and U.S. Foreign Policy: International Perspectives* (Lynne Rienner Publishers 2003) 71, 71.

students of international courts a rare peek into the mindset of a senior court official confronting the possibility of a serious political fallout.[33]

One key decision that Del Ponte had to take shortly after assuming office was on requests to open an investigation into crimes allegedly committed by NATO forces during the 1999 Kosovo air campaign. While she defended the decision not to investigate on legal grounds (lack of evidence against specific perpetrators),[34] she also acknowledged that opening such an investigation would have "collided with the edge of the political universe in which the tribunal was allowed to function".[35] Arguably, a decision by the Office of the Prosecutor (OTP) to investigate NATO service members would have rendered it unlikely that NATO forces in the Balkans would continue to cooperate with the Tribunal in arresting war crime suspects. It might also have jeopardized political support by NATO members in UN bodies for the continued mandate of the Tribunal and for allocation of the funding necessary for its operations.

The Del Ponte *memoire* suggests that court officials sometimes do take cognizance of the link between the manner in which they exercise their authority on the one hand, and the risk of alienating a key constituency on the other hand. In other words, they are sometimes aware of the link between perceived legitimacy and effectiveness. The next sections explain why international courts should—as a normative matter—take cognizance of certain aspects of the relationship between judicial decisions and the political environment, and how they can do so, in certain cases, in a transparent and proper manner.

## 4. The Political Environment

The presence of politics in the life of international courts manifests itself through several contact points, including acceptance of jurisdiction, political support for judicial operations and enforcement of judgments. Still, international courts tend to publicly ignore or downplay their interaction with the political world in order to protect their legitimacy, which hinges on them being perceived as operating on the basis of legal, and not political, considerations. Indeed, international courts have perfectly good reasons to distance themselves from the vicissitudes of international politics, since engaging in politics may not only harm their reputation, but also introduce political tensions and conflicts into their day-to-day operations.[36] I maintain, however, that international courts cannot afford to completely ignore all aspects of the political context in which they operate, since doing so might result in adverse consequences for their legitimacy and effectiveness.

---

[33] Carla Del Ponte, *Madame Prosecutor: Confrontations with Humanity's Worst Criminals and the Culture of Impunity* (Other Press 2009).
[34] ibid 60.
[35] ibid.
[36] See eg Marko Milanovic, "Danish Judge Blasts ICTY President [Updated]", *EJIL Talk!*, 13 June 2013.

## 4.1 Accepting Jurisdiction as a Political Decision

My first claim in this regard is that the very decision by states to establish an international court and to invest it with jurisdiction either over a specific case or a set of policy problems is a political decision; so is the decision to actually invoke a pre-existing jurisdictional clause and refer a specific dispute to an international court.

Decisions to opt for judicial settlement of international disputes have second-order implications, as they imply a preference for depoliticizing policy problems by removing decision-making power and a significant degree of control over the disposition of a specific international problem from politicians to independent judges.[37] This not only entails a change in the identity of the decision-makers but also in the decision-making methodology and the type of considerations employed: Politicians tend to be driven by a cost-benefit analysis that often privileges, due to election cycles, short-term interests over long-term benefits. They also tend to prioritize electorate wishes and expectations over all other considerations. Judges, by contrast, decide cases in accordance with general legal principles that tend to prioritize the long-term interests of "repeat players" and which, at times, conflict with the specific policy preferences of some of the parties to litigation and are unpopular with domestic public opinion.[38]

In light of the differences in the configuration of the decision-making process relevant to conflict resolution, one can understand the decision to channel policy problems to international adjudication through *ex ante* acceptance of jurisdiction as a political decision,[39] which reflects in itself a cost-benefit calculus. Accepting in advance the jurisdiction of international courts suggests a commitment to the rule of law in certain areas of international relations—a decision that may generate for the international actor concerned positive reputational dividends.[40] It also provides some legal guarantee for states participating in close cooperation arrangements, such as the WTO or the EU,

---

[37] See eg Brian McGarry and Josef Ostřanský, "Before the Law: The Process and Impact of Judicial Screening Bodies" in Freya Baetens (ed), *Legitimacy of Unseen Actors in International Adjudication* (Cambridge University Press 2019) 207. But see Martins Paparinskis, "Limits of Depoliticization in Contemporary Investor-State Arbitration" (2012) 3 Select Proceedings of the European Society of International Law 271, 273; Tim Stephens, "International Environmental Disputes: To Sue or Not to Sue?" in Nathalie Klein (ed), *Litigating International Disputes: Weighing the Options* ( Cambridge University Press 2014) 284, 291

[38] See Rosalyn Higgins, "Policy Considerations and the International Judicial Process" (1968) 17 International Comparative Law Quarterly 58, 74. cf Wayne Batchis, "Constitutional Nihilism: Political Science and the Deconstruction of the Judiciary" (2008) 6 Rutgers Journal of Law & Public Policy 1, 17–20; Christopher J Peters and Neal Devins, "Alexander Bickel and the New Judicial Minimalism" in Kenneth D Ward and Cecilia R Castillo (eds), *The Judiciary and American Democracy: Alexander Bickel, the Countermajoritarian Difficulty and Contemporary Constitutional Theory* (State University of New York Press 2005) 45, 59.

[39] See eg Elihu Lauterpacht, "The Waning of the Requirement of Consent" (1991) 85 Proceedings of the American Society of International Law 38, 38; Shabtai Rosenne, "Poor Drafting and Imperfect Organization: Flaws to Overcome in the Rome Statute" (2000) 41 Virginia Journal of International Law 164, 175; Susan W Tiefenbrun, "The Role of the World Court in Settling International Disputes: A Recent Assessment" (1997) 20 Loyola of Los Angeles International & Comparative Law Journal 1, 23.

[40] See eg Dothan, *Reputation and Judicial Tactics* (n 28) 93–94, 144; Gary L Scott and Craig L Carr, "The ICJ and Compulsory Jurisdiction: The Case for Closing the Clause" (1987) 81 American Journal of International Law 57, 59; Rachel M Fleig-Goldstein, "The Russian Constitutional Court versus the European Court of Human Rights: How the Strasbourg Court Should Respond to Russia's Refusal to Execute ECtHR Judgments" (2017) 56 Columbia Journal of Transnational Law 172, 198.

that they would be able to reap the promised economic or political dividends of membership therein. Furthermore, the availability of a competent judicial venue provides international actors with a clear path to problem-solving, which circumvents the cumbersome, unpredictable, and sometimes deadlocked political decision-making process, facilitating thereby the advancement of the policy agenda underlying the international regime in question.[41] At a higher level of abstraction, one can regard the decision to promote a specific policy agenda through the introduction of an efficient and accessible international adjudication mechanism as a political decision in the sense that it reflects a choice to give "right of way" to implementation through judicial enforcement of certain values or interests at the expense of other values or interests implemented through other means.[42]

What's more, acceptance of the jurisdiction of an international court and issuance by the latter of a decision disposing of an international dispute occur at two separate moments in time.[43] For politicians, especially those operating within relatively short election cycles, this may represent an opportunity for capitalizing immediately on the benefits of cooperation facilitated by acceptance of jurisdiction, while deferring to an uncertain point in the future the potential costs associated with losing in adjudication. The gap between costs and benefits is even more pronounced when, at the time of acceptance of jurisdiction, there is significant uncertainty about how, if at all, an international court would decide a case relating to the state in question (ie whether or not there will be negative consequences to acceptance of jurisdiction).[44] Such uncertainty, when combined with an "optimism bias" about future judicial outcomes,[45] allows politicians to present the decision to accept the jurisdiction of an international court or to refer a specific case to it as entailing concrete political benefits without any tangible costs. And even when international courts occasionally rule against the preferences of a domestic constituency, the politicians that put in place the legal edifice which authorized the court to do so can try to deflect the blame for the decision from themselves to the court (which might be accused of politicization, power grab, bias etc).[46]

However, if it turns out that the political calculus underlying acceptance of jurisdiction by states was fundamentally flawed—for example, if judicial outcomes are generating serious political costs for governments that outweigh the benefits of acceptance of jurisdiction—then political support for accepting the jurisdiction of an

---

[41] See eg Markus W Gehring, "Litigating the Way out of Deadlock" in Amrita Narlika (ed), *Deadlocks in Multilateral Negotiations: Causes and Solutions* (Cambridge University Press 2010) 96, 98.

[42] See eg Yuval Shany, *Questions of Jurisdiction and Admissibility before International Courts* (Cambridge University Press 2015) 8. There is a significant body of literature expressing concern, for instance, about the utilization of the WTO dispute settlements in order to implement trade interests at the expense of other societal interests. See eg Andrew Lang, *World Trade Law after Neoliberalism: Reimagining the Global Economic Order* (Oxford University Press 2011) 132–33; Armin von Bogdandy and Ingo Venzke, *In Whose Name?: A Public Law Theory of International Adjudication* (Oxford University Press 2014) 87–90.

[43] cf Oona Hathway, "International Delegation and State Sovereignty" (2008) 71 Law and Contemporary Problems 115, 127–33.

[44] cf ibid 133–37.

[45] For a general discussion of optimism bias, see Christine Jolls, "Behavioral Law and Economics" in Peter Diamond and Hannu Vartiainen (eds), *Behavioral Economics and Its Applications* (Princeton University Press 2007) 123.

[46] See eg Dothan, *Reputation and Judicial Tactics* (n 28) 300.

international court could turn into outright political hostility or backlash.[47] The case of the indictments of serving heads of state by the ICC is a case in point in which frustrated expectations about the costs and benefits of membership in the Rome Statute have led to renunciations of the Statute and attempts to orchestrate a mass withdrawal of African states from the ICC.[48] Another example of what appears to be a case of a "buyer's remorse" can be seen in the chain of events leading to the collapse of the Southern African Development Community (SADC) Court.[49] The Court, an economic integration court loosely modelled after the CJEU, has issued in 2008 a major decision labelling Zimbabwe's expropriation of White farmers' lands as a human rights violation.[50] This decision has changed, however, the political calculus for some of the state parties to the Court's constitutive instrument, since they accepted the Court's ability to hear individual complaints on the basis of the expectation that it would focus only on regional economic issues. Consequently, they withdrew their support for the Court—a blow from which it has never recovered.

Frustrated political expectations or a renewed cost-benefit analysis can also follow a domestic power transition, which invites a new assessment of a past decision to accept the jurisdiction of an international court. This is especially the case when the new government is confronting adverse decisions rendered against it. Examples for decisions to backtrack on past acceptance of jurisdiction following adverse judicial rulings can be found in the withdrawal of the Reagan administration from the ICJ optional clause after the 1984 *Nicaragua* judgment,[51] and the renunciations by the George W Bush and Trump administrations of compromissory clauses under the Vienna Diplomatic and Consular Relations treaties in response to the *Avena*[52] and the *Jerusalem Embassy*[53] proceedings before the ICJ.[54] Another example is the withdrawal of the current regimes in Venezuela and Russia from the IACtHR and ECtHR, respectively, following a number of adverse rulings rendered against them in politically sensitive cases.[55]

Ultimately, the political decision by international actors to accept or reject the jurisdiction of an international court has significant implications for its legitimacy and

---

[47] For a discussion of backlash against international courts, see David Caron and Esmé Shirlow, "Dissecting Backlash: The Unarticulated Causes of Backlash" in Andreas Føllesdal and Geir Ulfstein (eds), *The Judicialization of International Law: A Mixed Blessing?* (Oxford University Press 2018) 159.

[48] For a discussion, see Peter Brett and Line Engbo Gissel, *Africa and the Backlash Against International Courts* (Bloomsbury 2020) 47–53.

[49] For a discussion, see Karen J Alter, James T Gathii, and Laurence R Helfer, "Backlash against International Courts in West, East and Southern Africa: Causes and Consequences" (2016) 27 American Journal of International Law 293, 306–14.

[50] SADC (T) Case No 2/2007, *Campbell v Zimbabwe*, SADC Court judgment of 28 November 2008.

[51] *Military and Paramilitary Activities in and against Nicaragua* (Nicaragua v USA), 1984 ICJ 392.

[52] *Avena* (Mexico v United States of America), 2004 ICJ 12.

[53] *Relocation of the United States Embassy to Jerusalem* (Palestine v USA), Order of 15 November 2018, 2018 ICJ 708.

[54] See eg Mark Feldman, The United States as an International Litigant, in Klein (ed) (n 37) 106, 118–20; Jean Galbraith (ed), "Trump Administration Announces Withdrawal from Four International Agreements" (2019) 113 American Journal of International Law 131.

[55] See Timothy Gill, "Venezuela says 'adios' to the Inter-American Court of Human Rights", *The Christian Science Monitor*, 11 September 2013; "Russian MPs vote to quit European Court of Human Rights", *Al Jazeera*, 7 June 2022. Although the Al Jazeera story cites opposition to decisions by the Court, the Russian withdrawal is also related, no doubt, to the expulsion of Russia from the Council of Europe following its invasion of Ukraine.

effectiveness. This is because acceptance of jurisdiction is the principal legal method for accepting the authority of courts and is an important marker of political support for it. In practice, the ability of international courts to effectively realize their mandates without a sizeable jurisdictional title remains very limited.

## 4.2  Political Support for International Courts

A second sphere of interface between international adjudication and the outside political world, already alluded to in Section 2, is the critical support lent by international actors to the ongoing operations of international courts: They pay for their budgets, they elect their judges, and they cooperate with their specific pre- and post-judgment procedures, including the transfer of suspects to international criminal courts and the enforcement of international court judgments. The dependency of international courts on such political support might incentivize international courts to try not to alienate the key international constituencies that support them, out of fear that clashing with them might derail their operations. In fact, a real concern exists that international courts might be illegitimately pressured—even blackmailed—to approximate their operations to strong preferences held by key actors in the political universe in which they operate.[56]

I have already mentioned above the difficult decision by Del Ponte not to start a criminal investigation into NATO military operations against Serbia, and her observation that such an investigation would have generated a strong collision with political actors on whose support the ICTY depended.[57] Interestingly enough, both the ICJ and ECtHR have also refused, citing rather controversial legal reasons, to find that they have jurisdiction to review some aspects of the same military operation.[58] The problematic nature of the legal reasoning employed in the three cases and the overwhelming political interests implicated in these cases has given rise to suspicions that extra-legal considerations might have influenced the outcomes in a manner that remains unacknowledged.[59]

---

[56] cf Rod Rastan, "Comment on Victor's Justice & the Viability of Ex Ante Standards" (2010) 43 John Marshall Law Review 569, 600–01. A current example of what appears to be illegitimate and extreme form of pressure on an international court is the refusal by the US to nominate members for the WTO Appellate Body, citing concerns about the Body's jurisprudence. Tom Miles, "U.S. Blocks WTO Judge Reappointment as Dispute Settlement Crisis Looms", *Reuters* 27 August 2018.

[57] Del Ponte (n 33) 60.

[58] *Legality of Use of Force* (Serbia and Montenegro v Belgium), 2004 ICJ 279 (holding that Serbia and Montenegro was not a party to the ICJ Statute when initiating proceedings); *Legality of Use of Force* (Serbia and Montenegro v Belgium), 199 ICJ 124 (refusing to issue provisional measures to stop the bombing operation due to the fact that the operation began before the period for which the Court had jurisdiction); *Bankovic v Belgium,* App No 52207/99, decision of the ECtHR of 12 December 2001 (holding that the bombing of Belgrade did not fall within the geographical scope of application of the ECHR).

[59] See eg Andreas Laursen, "NATO, The War over Kosovo, and the ICTY Investigation" (2002) 17 American University International Law Review 765, 774; Dominic McGoldrick, "The Interface between Public Emergency Powers and International Law" (2004) 2 I.CON 380, 403; Simon Olleson, " 'Killing Three Birds with One Stone'? The Preliminary Objections Judgment of the International Court of Justice in the *Legality of the Use of Force* Cases" (2005) 18 Leiden Journal of International Law 237, 253–54 (explaining that the decision of the majority in the 2004 *NATO* case appears to have been driven less by legal analysis and more by strategic considerations relating to other pending cases before the Court).

Another example underscoring the very real dependency of international courts on support of their political environment involves the famous *Barayagwiza* case before the ICTR. In 1999, the ICTR Appeals Chamber decided to release Jean Bosco Barayagwiza, one of three individuals accused of inciting to genocide through radio broadcasts, because his due process rights as a detainee were seriously violated.[60] In response, the Rwandan government not only expressed outrage with the decision, it also announced a suspension of its cooperation with the Tribunal.[61] Needless to say, this was a massive blow to the ICTR, since most witnesses and physical evidence for the cases it prosecuted were located in Rwanda and it relied on governmental cooperation completely for access to them. The legitimacy of the Tribunal in the eyes of the Rwandan victims of the genocide also suffered greatly as a result of the decision to release Barayagwiza. In light of this impending catastrophe, which would have seriously derailed the work of the Tribunal, the OTP sought and obtained a review hearing at the Appeals Chamber, which reversed in 2000 its 1999 decision.[62] Interestingly enough, one of the individual opinions appended to the 2000 decision noted the Prosecutor's position that the reality confronting the Tribunal is that retaining the *Barayagwiza* release decision implies the end of prosecution and investigation activities,[63] but denied being influenced by pressures and threats of this nature.[64] Despite this assurance, the 2000 decision was subject to academic criticism, which questioned the propriety and the sincerity of the Appeals Chamber's approach, speculating that it did in fact reverse course in response to Rwandan pressure.[65]

At a more general level, international courts are expected to try to maintain the trust and support of key international actors in order to rely on their backing in international fora and to avoid the backlash that would emanate from them being perceived as hostile to important constituency values and interests. Arguably, some ICJ decisions, which have been criticized in the literature as overly timid in their legal approach, may be understood as reflective of an effort not to alienate powerful groupings of states in matters involving high-stage political issues. These include the advisory opinions on questions relating to the legality of nuclear weapons and the unilateral declarations of independence of Kosovo.[66] In the first case, the refusal by the Court to conclude whether the use of nuclear weapons in the face of an existential security threat would be unlawful averted a clash between the Court and the permanent members of the Security Council.[67] In the second case, the Court narrowly interpreted the question of

[60] Case ICTR-99-52, *Barayagwiza v Prosecutor*, ICTR decision of 3 November 1999,.

[61] "Kigali protest against UN tribunal", *BBC News*, 15 November 1999.

[62] Case ICTR-99-52, *Barayagwiza v Prosecutor*, ICTR decision of 31 March 2000, <http://www.worldcourts.com/ictr/eng/decisions/2000.03.31_Barayagwiza_v_Prosecutor.pdf>.

[63] ibid, Declaration of Judge Nieto-Navia, para 2

[64] ibid para 7.

[65] See eg Willian Schabas, "Barayagwiza v. Prosecutor" (2000) 94 American Journal of International Law 563, 566–67; Jacob Cogan Katz, "International Criminal Courts and Fair Trials: Difficulties and Prospects" (2002) 27 Yale Journal of International Law 111, 135; Jenia Iontcheva Turner, "Defense Perspectives on Law and Politics in International Criminal Trials" (2008) 48 Virginia Journal of International Law 529, 591.

[66] *Legality of the Threat or Use of Nuclear Weapons*, 1996 ICJ 226; *Accordance with International Law of the Unilateral Declaration of Independence in Respect of Kosovo*, 2010 ICJ 403.

[67] See eg Robert F Turner, "Nuclear Weapons and the World Court: The ICJ's Advisory Opinion and its Significance for U.S. Strategic Doctrine" (1998) 72 International Law Studies 309, 310; David Kennedy, "The

the legality of Kosovo's declaration of independence (focusing instead on the legality of the declaration itself), thus avoiding the need to clash with political camps supporting or opposing Kosovo's bid for statehood (and more generally, the camps supporting the doctrines of self-determination by secession and state sovereignty that underlie it).[68]

Even decisions which have alienated permanent members of the Security Council, such as the judgment on admissibility in *Military and Paramilitary Activities in Nicaragua*[69] or the *Chagos* advisory opinion,[70] might be explained as attempts by the Court to win the support of a critical constituency—developing countries—even at the expense of a superpower. According to this possible explanation, the Court's liberal approach in the 1984 judgment vis-à-vis the validity of Nicaragua's optional clause declaration was intended to offset the criticism of excessive formalism in jurisdictional matters in the service of geopolitical interests of Western countries, which was directed against the Court following its 1966 *South West Africa* advisory opinion.[71] In the same vein, the broad and deep unpopularity of the British position in relation to Chagos can explain the strong legal stance taken by the Court against the less-than-full decolonization of Mauritius by the United Kingdom.[72]

A similar dilemma to that which allegedly confronted the ICJ in the *Military and Paramilitary Activities in Nicaragua* and *Chagos* cases, entailing a choice between different constituency expectations, confronts other tribunals as well. For example, some commentators have linked the turn from the initial jurisprudence of the WTO Appellate Body in environmental matters, which was criticized as reflective of an exaggerated pro-trade liberalization agenda on the part of the Organization, towards a more environmental-friendly approach to the 1999 Seattle protests and the need to redeem the credibility of the WTO in the eyes of the general public.[73]

---

*Nuclear Weapons* Case" in Laurence Boisson de Chazournes and Philippe Sands (eds), *International Law, the International Court of Justice and Nuclear Weapons* (Cambridge University Press 1999) 462, 471–72.

[68] See eg Alain Pellet, "Kosovo—The Questions Not Asked: Self-Determination, Secession, and Recognition" in Marko Milanovic and Michael Wood (eds), *The Law and Politics of the Kosovo Advisory Opinion* (Oxford University Press 2015) 268, 271; Alexandros XM Ntovas, "The Paradox of Kosovo's Parallel Legal Orders in the Reasoning of the Court's Advisory Opinion" in Duncan French (ed), *Statehood and Self-Determination: Reconciling Tradition and Modernity in International Law* (Cambridge University Press 2013) 139–40.

[69] *Case Concerning Military and Paramilitary Activities in and Against Nicaragua (Nicaragua v United States of America), Jurisdiction and Admissibility, Judgment*, ICJ Reports 1984, 392.

[70] *Legal Consequences of the Separation of the Chagos Archipelago from Mauritius in 1965*, 2019 ICJ 95.

[71] See eg Antonios Tzanakopoulos and Anna Ventouratou, "Nicaragua in the International Court of Justice and the Law of Treaties" in Edgardo Sobenes Obregon and Benjamin Samson eds), *Nicaragua Before the International Court of Justice: Impacts on International Law* (Springer 2018) 215, 216; Eric A Posner, *The Perils of Global Legalism* (University of Chicago Press 2009) 147–48; Lori Fisler Damrosch, "The Impact of the *Nicaragua* Case on the Court and Its Role: Harmful, Helpful, or In Between?" (2012) 25 Leiden Journal of International Law 135, 141.

[72] For a discussion of the political background to the *Chagos* case, see Philippe Sands, *The Last Colony: A Tale of Exile, Justice and Britain's Colonial Legacy* (Orion 2022) 135–39.

[73] See eg Robert Howse, "The World Trade Organization 20 Years On: Global Governance by Judiciary" (2016) 27 European Journal of International Law 9, 36–43; Elaine Hartwick and Richard Peet, "Neoliberalism and Nature: The Case of the WTO" (2003) 590 Annals of the American Academy of Political and Social Science 188, 202.

## 4.3 Enforcement of Judgments

Since international courts typically have weak enforcement mechanisms, their ability to generate compliance with their decisions depends to a large extent on the political acceptability of their decisions. A decision which represents a total political anathema to the losing state or to the dominant political *milieu* therein would most likely not be complied with,[74] and chronic non-compliance may threaten the long-term legitimacy and effectiveness of the international court in question.[75] The ECtHR's well documented clash with the United Kingdom over prisoner voting, following judgments in the *Hirst* and *Greens* cases,[76] illustrates that even an international court with a strong record of compliance, such as the ECtHR, may generate at times decisions which, due to political reasons, cannot be fully complied with.[77]

Arguably, an international court can afford to confront such situations on an exceptional basis, but it cannot allow them to become the rule (especially when non-compliance emanates from what are, otherwise, rule of law-respecting states).[78] The concern about chronic non-compliance may explain why a court like the ECtHR provides states with a margin of appreciation in interpreting and applying the ECHR in cases involving questions on which there is no European consensus (such as balancing between privacy and freedom of expression), issues in relation to which deep moral convictions are held by the public (eg abortion), and delicate security matters (such as whether or not a state of emergency exists).[79] I will return to the use of margin of appreciation by international courts in Section 5.

Furthermore, one can perhaps understand the tendency of the ICJ to resort to what Georges Abi-Saab referred to as "transactional justice"—judgments that leave all parties to the case partly satisfied[80]—as aimed at ensuring a good level of compliance with its decisions. The *Genocide* case may illustrate this point. In its 2007 judgment on the merits, the Court accepted the Bosnian claim that a genocide had been committed in

---

[74] See eg Heather L Jones, "Why Comply? An Analysis of Trends in Compliance with Judgments of the International Court of Justice since Nicaragua" (2012) XII Chicago-Kent Journal of International & Comparative Law 57, 84; Aloysius P Llamzon, "Jurisdiction and Compliance in Recent Decisions of the International Court of Justice" (2007) 18 European Journal of International Law 815, 836.

[75] See eg Squatrito (n 25) 310–11; Karen J Alter, "Agents or Trustees? International Courts in their Political Context" (2008) 14 European Journal of International Relations 33, 46.

[76] *Hirst v UK*, App. No. 74025/01, ECtHR judgment of 6 October 2005; *Greens v UK*, App No 60041/98, ECtHR judgment of 23 November 2010.

[77] For a discussion of the clash over prisoner voting, see eg Ed Bates, "Analysing the Prisoner Voting Saga and the British Challenge to Strasbourg" (2014) 14 Human Rights Law Review 503; David Davis, "Britain Must Defy the European Court of Human Rights on Prisoner Voting as Strasbourg is Exceeding its Authority" in Spyridon Flogaitis, Tom Zwart, and Julie Fraser (eds), *The European Court of Human Rights and its Discontents: Turning Criticism into Strength* (Edward Elgar 2013) 65.

[78] See eg Dothan, *Reputation and Judicial Tactics* (n 28) 142.

[79] For a review of margin of appreciation under the ECHR, see eg Andrew Legg, *Margin of Appreciation in International Human Rights Law: Deference and Proportionality* (Oxford University Press 2012) 83–86, 182–88; Janneke Gerards, *General Principles of the European Convention on Human Rights* (Cambridge University Press 2019) 168, 185, 243–44.

[80] Georges Abi-Saab, "Fragmentation or Unification: Some Concluding Remarks" (1999) 31 New York University Journal of International Law & Policy 919, 930 at note 8.

Bosnia and Herzegovina, but limited its findings to events in and around Srebrenica, and held that Serbia did not incur direct responsibility for the genocide. In addition, it ruled that the government of Serbia did incur international responsibility for failing to prevent the genocide, but that it does need to pay any compensation.[81] Arguably, the "hedged" nature of the judgment, as well as the issuance of relatively low-demanding remedies—cooperation with the ICTY, measures of satisfaction and guarantees of non-repetition[82]—increased the chances of compliance with the judgment. Indeed, in the aftermath of the judgment, Serbia did arrest and transfer to the ICTY high-profile fugitives[83] and has issued an apology to the victims of the Srebrenica genocide,[84] suggesting that the remedies decreed by the Court were indeed politically acceptable.

## 5. Can International Courts Take Cognizance of Politics Considerations?

Previous sections of this chapter posed the following dilemma: international courts operate within a political context and might be impacted by the political fallout resulting from their decisions. Their effectiveness depends, to a considerable extent, on the continued support and cooperation from their political constituencies, including the international actors that created them and which accepted their jurisdiction. The legitimacy of international courts is also tied to their effectiveness in the sense that they are expected to cause change in the conduct of a good part, if not all, of the international actors to whom their legal decisions are addressed, and a feckless international court would attract limited respect for its authority. At the same time, the legitimacy of international courts heavily depends on their non-politicized decision-making process (process legitimacy)—that is, on their independent and impartial mode of operation, which involves deciding cases on the basis of legal, not political, considerations. Although the objective nature of legal discretion can be viewed as somewhat of a myth, it is a useful myth,[85] and exposing it as such by explicitly introducing political considerations into judicial decision-making would have adverse implications for the legitimacy of international courts. And again, since legitimacy and effectiveness are inter-dependent, once legitimacy is seriously compromised, so is the ability of international courts to realize the expectations of their relevant constituencies.

---

[81] *Application of the Convention on the Prevention and Punishment of the Crime of Genocide* (Bosnia and Herzegovina v Serbia and Montenegro), 2007 ICJ 43.

[82] ibid 238–39.

[83] See eg "Serbia Extradites War Crimes Suspect to Hague", *Al Jazeera*, 22 May 2011. But see Marija Ristic, Hague Tribunal Slams Serbia Again for Non-Cooperation", *BIRN*, 15 September 2016.

[84] See eg "Serbian Parliament Apologizes for Srebrenica Massacre", *CNN*, 31 March 2010; "Serbian President Apologises for Srebrenica 'Crime'", *BBC*, 25 April 2013. But see Denic Džidić, "War Crimes: Why 'Sorry' is Never Enough", *BRIN*, 22 May 2015.

[85] cf Wesley G Skogan, "Judicial Myth and Reality" [1971] Washington University Law Review 309, 314–21; Jerome Franck, *Courts on Trial: Myth and Reality in American Justice* (Princeton University Press 1973) (originally published in 1949) 204.

So how can the circle be squared? How can the gap between "can't do with" and "can't do without" taking cognizance of politics be bridged by international courts? I suggest in this section that courts may utilize certain legal notions that reflect *legitimate* political considerations, and that addressing such notions in ways which are doctrinally sound and transparent may assist courts in avoiding unnecessary clashes with their political environment, while preserving their credibility. Such an approach is, I believe, preferable to weighing political considerations in a clandestine manner, as might have been done in some of the cases discussed in Section 4. To be clear, none of the solutions proposed in this section is a panacea to the tensions between law and politics in international adjudication; they should rather be regarded as potential tension-mitigating measures. Neither does the list of possible measures discussed here purport to be exhaustive in nature.[86]

## 5.1  Legitimate or Reasonable Expectations

One notion that has been used by international courts as an interpretative tool, and which may assist in avoiding a political backlash, is the need to protect the legitimate or reasonable expectations of parties to litigation when construing legal instruments. Although the major canons of interpretation of international treaty law focus on text, context and object and purpose,[87] the legitimate or reasonable expectations of the parties to a legal instrument may play a role as well in the interpretative process. Such expectations may determine the specific meaning of terms used in a treaty,[88] influence the subsequent practice of the parties,[89] reveal themselves in the *travuax préparatoires*,[90] and assist in identifying absurd or unreasonable outcomes.[91] They can also aid in identifying bad faith practices that generate unacceptable results for some of the parties to legal transactions. It is within this interpretative framework that factoring in the legitimate or reasonable expectations of the parties is likely to reduce the prospects of issuing decisions completely at odds with critical political interests, which could lead to non-compliance and other manifestations of backlash.

Although the ICJ rejected in its 2018 *Access to the Pacific Ocean* judgment the general applicability in international law of the doctrine of legitimate expectations (outside the context of international investment law, where it is a well-recognized doctrine),[92] there is some support in the literature that, within narrow confines, it does operate as

---

[86] Other measures not discussed here, which may avert unnecessary clashes between courts and their constituencies, include discretion in scheduling hearings and publishing decisions, use of harsh versus moderate language when formulating the decision, deciding not to decide certain aspects of a case which would not significantly change the final outcome, and the choice of legal references with which to support the decision.

[87] Vienna Convention on the Law of Treaties, art 31(1).

[88] ibid art 31(4).

[89] ibid art 31(3)(b).

[90] ibid art 32.

[91] ibid art 32(b).

[92] *Obligation to Negotiate Access to the Pacific Ocean* (Bolivia v Chile), 2018 ICJ 507, 559. See also India—*Patent Protection for Pharmaceutical and Agricultural Chemical Products* (US), WTO Doc. WT/DS50/AB/R, (1997), at para 45 ("The legitimate expectations of the parties to a treaty are reflected in the language of the treaty itself").

a general principle of law.[93] Indeed, the Court itself implicitly relied on party expect-ations in some cases, including the *Fisheries Jurisdiction* case, where it narrowly con-strued a Canadian reservation to its jurisdiction on the basis of its specific intentions when submitting it,[94] and the *Certain Properties* case, where it found that there was no common understanding between the parties to the case on which it could rely, con-cerning the application of the German-Czech Settlement Convention to Liechtenstein Property.[95] The reference to "intent" and "understanding" in the two cases can be re-garded also as an implicit reference to the legitimate or reasonable expectations of the parties. In earlier cases, the Court developed the notion that states may rely on repre-sentations by other states[96] and on the proposition that a well-understood established practice can generate a specific right (or local custom)[97]—both ideas closely related to protecting legitimate or reasonable expectations. In fact, one can construe, at a high level of abstraction, the theory of customary international law to be premised on the need to protect legitimate or reasonable expectations generated by state practice and *opinio juris*.[98]

Other international courts also resort implicitly to notions of legitimate or reason-able expectations when identifying international law norms, interpreting and applying them to specific circumstances. For example, the International Tribunal for the Law of the Sea (ITLOS) has recognized in a number of cases the doctrine of estoppel (which was tied at least in one case explicitly by one of the parties to protecting its legitimate expectations).[99] In the field of human rights law, one may note that the ECtHR has re-jected claims brought before it involving a failure to investigate crimes occurring before the ratification of the ECHR on the basis of the position that, beyond a certain point in time, states cannot be reasonably expected to elucidate past crimes.[100] In another ECtHR case, relating to interpretation and application of provisions of the ECHR to overseas military operations by state parties, the Court construed their consistent prac-tice of not derogating from the provisions of the European Convention governing such circumstances as indicative of an implied agreement to reinterpret or modify relevant provisions of the Convention and to adjust them to the situation.[101] In other words,

---

[93] Eirik Bjorge, "Public Law Sources and Analogies of International Law" (2018) 49 Victoria University Wellington Law Review 533, 559; Chester Brown, "The Protection of Legitimate Expectations as a 'General Principle of Law': Some Preliminary Thoughts" (March 2009) 6(1) Transnational Dispute Management. See also Case T-115/94, *Opel Austria GmbH v Council of the European Union* [1997] ECR II-39, at paras 78, 93 (alluding to the principle of good faith in international law as a manifestation of the principle of legitimate expectations) .

[94] *Fisheries Jurisdiction* (Spain v Canada), 1998 ICJ 432, 454 ("since a declaration under Article 36, paragraph 2, of the Statute, is a unilaterally drafted instrument, the Court has not hesitated to place a certain emphasis on the intention of the depositing State").

[95] *Certain Property* (Liechtenstein v Germany), 2005 ICJ 6, 25–26.

[96] *Temple of Preah Vihear* (Cambodia v Thailand) 1962 ICJ 6, 32.

[97] *Right of Passage over Indian Territory* (Portugal v India), 1960 ICJ 6, 43.

[98] Jack L Goldsmith and Eric A Posner, "A Theory of Customary International Law" (1999) 66 University of Chicago Law Review 1113, 1138; Maurice H Mendelson, "The Formation of Customary International Law" (1998) 272 Recueil des Cours 155, 184–85, 290–92.

[99] Case No 25, *The M/V "Norstar"* (Panama v Italy), ITLOS judgment of 4 November 2016, at paras 299, 306–307; Case No 16, *Delimitation of the Maritime Boundary Between Bangladesh and Myanmar in The Bay of Bengal* (Bangladesh/Myanmar), ITLOS judgment of 12 March. 2012, paras 119–125.

[100] See eg *Šilih v Slovenia*, App No 71463/01, ECtHR judgment of 9 April 2009, at para 157.

[101] See *Hassan v UK*, App No 29750/09, ECtHR judgment of 30 August 2011, at para 101.

since the state parties did not expect the Convention to apply "as is" to overseas military operations, the Court could resort to reinterpretation of the relevant provisions to accommodate such expectations.

## 5.2 Impossible or Disproportionate Burden

Another legal notion related to reasonable expectations, which one can associate with accommodating political interests through legal interpretation and application, is the notion of avoiding the imposition on international actors of impossible or disproportionate burdens.[102] A key area in which the notion of impossible or disproportionate burdens is particularly relevant is the delineation of due diligence obligations, involving the expectation that states (and other international duty-holder) must undertake reasonable efforts to attain a certain outcome or to protect or advance certain legal interests.[103] Due diligence obligations can be found in the caselaw of international human rights bodies, for example, with respect to procedural duties to investigate alleged human rights violations, and it was held in this context that such duties should not result in the imposition of impossible or disproportionate burden on the state in question.[104] Comparable obligations can be found in respect of measures of protection afforded in order to prevent human rights abuses committed by third persons.[105] Related notions of reasonable and proportional legal requirements also permeate the work of international criminal courts applying norms of international humanitarian law.[106]

The ICJ has implicitly alluded to the notion of impossible or disproportionate burdens in connection with decisions on remedies. For example, it has stated that compensation should be resorted when restitution entails "materially impossible or unduly burdensome".[107] It has even been claimed in this regard that undue burdens that clash with important state interests may be invoked in certain exceptional circumstances as grounds for releasing states from their obligations under international law.[108]

---

[102] The need to avoid imposing impossible or disproportionate burdens is, in turn, associated with the principle of reasonableness in international law. See Olivier Corten, "Reasonableness in International Law", *MPEPIL* (n 4) paras 1–3.

[103] See eg Timo Koivurova, "Due Diligence", *MPEPIL* (n 4) para 1; Samantha Besson, La *due diligence* en droit international (2021) 149–151.

[104] See eg *Brecknell v UK*, App No 32457/04, ECtHR Judgment of 27 February 2008 para 62.

[105] See eg *Sawhoyamaxa Indigenous Community v Paraguay*, Judgment of the I/A CHR of 29 March 2006, para 155; Human Rights Committee, General Comment 36: The Right to Life, UN Doc CCPR/C/GC/36 (2018), para 21.

[106] See generally, Rogier Bartels, "Dealing with the Principle of Proportionality in Armed Conflict in Retrospect: The Application of the Principle in International Criminal Trials" (2013) 46 Israel Law Review 271. See also Final Report to the Prosecutor by the Committee Established to Review the NATO Bombing Campaign Against the Federal Republic of Yugoslavia, (2000) 39 ILM 257 paras 50–51.

[107] See eg *Certain Activities Carried Out by Nicaragua in the Border Area* (Costa Rica v Nicaragua), 2018 ICJ 15, 26. See also Attila Tanzi, "Restitution", *MPEPIL* (n 4) para 10.

[108] See eg Wolff Heintschel von Heinegg, "Treaties, Fundamental Change of Circumstances", *MPEPIL* (n 4) para. 1.

## 5.3 Margin of Appreciation

Another doctrine which allows international courts to take cognizance of important political interests, which was already mentioned above, is the margin of appreciation doctrine that has been developed in the caselaw of the ECtHR but also has potential application in other fields of international law.[109] At the core of the doctrine lies the proposition that national authorities are better placed than international courts to apply international law norms in certain concrete circumstances,[110] and that the breadth of the margin afforded to states may be influenced, *inter alia*, by the significance or sensitivity of the national interests or values implicated.[111] Furthermore, the doctrine, as applied by the ECtHR, encourages the incremental development of human rights law (through a gradual narrowing of the margin afforded to states), in correlation with the development and consolidation of European consensus on contested legal and societal issues.[112] This too helps the Court to deflect political resistance and to ensure that it is not distancing itself excessively through its decisions from the interests and values of the political environment in which it is embedded. Note that even human rights bodies that do not adhere to the margin of appreciate doctrine, such as the HRCttee, tend to defer to domestic courts in matters of facts or interpretation of domestic law, including with regard to risk assessment or the finding of guilt or innocence in criminal proceedings.[113]

The delegation of decision-making power from international courts (and quasi-courts) to national institutions minimizes clashes between the outcomes of international adjudication and the political preferences of states (which domestic institutions typically capture better than international institutions). Furthermore, the ability of states to invoke the authority of domestic institutions affords them with some guarantee that interests important to them will be given proper weight in the decision-making process before international courts. It is not surprising therefore that states have called, on a number of occasions, on international courts to afford them with more deference or a broader margin of appreciation.[114]

---

[109] See generally, Yuval Shany, "Toward a General Margin of Appreciation Doctrine in International Law?" (2005) 16 European Journal of International Law 907; Jean-Pierre Cot, "Margin of Appreciation", *MPEPIL* (n 4); Yuval Shany, "Margin of Appreciation" in Christina Bunder and others (eds), *Elgar Encyclopedia of Human Rights Law* (Edward Elgar 2022) (Online version).

[110] See eg *Handyside v UK*, App No 5493/72, ECtHR Judgment of 7 December 1976, para 48.

[111] See eg *A, B and C v Ireland*, App No 25579/05, ECtHR Judgment of 16 December 2010, para. 232; *Leander v Sweden*, App No 9248/81, ECtHR Judgment of 26 March 1987, para 59.

[112] See eg *Evans v UK*, App No 6339/05, Judgment of 10 April 2007, para 77. See also generally, Nikos Vogiatzis, "The Relationship Between European Consensus, the Margin of Appreciation and the Legitimacy of the Strasbourg Court" (2019) 25 European Public Law 445.

[113] See eg Comm No 2728/2016, *Teitiota v New Zealand*, Views of the HRCttee of 24 October 2019, para 9.12; Comm No 891/1999, *Tamihere v New Zealand*, Views of the HRCttee of 18 April 2000, para 4.4.

[114] See eg High Level Conference on the Future of the European Court of Human Rights Brighton Declaration (19–20 April 2012), para 12; United States Trade Representative, 2018 Trade Policy Agenda and 2017 Annual Report (2018) 27–28.

## 5.4  Remedies

Finally, it may be mentioned that international courts retain considerable flexibility in designating remedies after a violation of international law had been established. Such flexibility may appertain, *inter alia*, to the timeline for compliance, the means and manner of compliance, what specific remedies to order, how to calculate compensation, and what role to afford the parties to litigation in implementing the judgment. Arguably, such flexibility enables international courts to consider and mitigate, if necessary, the political ramifications of their judgments.

For example, it can be speculated that the ICJ tailored a flexible remedy in the 2004 *Avena* case ("review and reconsideration" of convictions in capital cases)[115] with a view to avoid a political clash with the United States that would have ensued from the stricter remedies requested by Mexico (eg ordering automatic retrials in all the impugned cases). Other examples of flexibility, allowing for the accommodation of important political interests in the context of decision on remedies, are the *de facto* choices afforded by the WTO Dispute Settlement Understanding (DSU) to litigating parties between complying with Panel or Adjudicating Body reports and suffering retaliatory trade measures that would restore the trade equilibrium,[116] the notion of "just satisfaction" under the ECHR, which creates a broad space for the Committee of Ministers (the judgment enforcement body of the Council of Europe that supports the operations of the Court) to accept limited measures taken by the losing state as a sufficient form of compliance,[117] and discretion on ways of calculating compensation sums decreed by arbitral bodies reviewing investment disputes, so as to avoid issuing economically debilitating awards.[118] The HRCttee has also resorted in some sensitive cases, where requiring full reparation might be deemed as unwarranted due to the particular circumstances of the case, to a merely declarative remedy.[119]

The upshot of these and similar legal doctrines and the decision-making spaces they open for international courts is that the expectations, choices, and capabilities of the parties to litigation, which often reflect the political interests appertaining to a legal

---

[115] *Avena and Other Mexican Nationals* (Mexico v USA), 2004 ICJ 12, 60.

[116] See eg Sivan Shlomo Agon, *International Adjudication on Trial: The Effectiveness of the WTO Dispute Settlement System* (Oxford University Press 2019) 66; Sherzod Shadikhodjaev, *Retaliation in the WTO Dispute Settlement System* (Wolters Kluwer 2009) 29.

[117] See eg the compromise by which the United Kingdom expanded voting to prisoners on Temporary License. Neil Johnson, Prisoners' Voting Rights: Developments since May 2015 (UK Parliament Research Briefing, 2020), <https://commonslibrary.parliament.uk/research-briefings/cbp-7461/>. See also Octavian Ichim, *Just Satisfaction under the European Convention on Human Rights* (Cambridge University Press 2014) 78; Alexia Solomou, "The Contribution of the European Court of Human Rights and the Inter-American Court of Human Rights to the Emergence of a Customary International Rule of Just Satisfaction and the Creative Expansion of its Scope" (2014) 14 *Revista do Instituto Brasileiro de Direitos Humanos* 11, 23–24.

[118] See eg Kathryn Khamsi, "Compensation for Non-expropriatory Investment Treaty Breaches in the Argentine Gas Sector Cases: Issues and Implications" in Michael Waibel and others (eds), *The Backlash Against Investment Arbitration: Perceptions and Reality* ( Wolters Kluwer 2010) 165, 176; Vivian Kube and Ernst-Ulrich Petersmann, "Human Rights Law in International Investment Arbitration" (2016) 11 Asian Journal of WTO & International Health Law & Policy 65, 103.

[119] See eg Comm No 2005/2010, *Hicks v Australia*, Views of the HRCttee of 5 November 2015, para 6.

transaction or to the underlying legal relationship find ways to influence the contents of the law, as interpreted and applied by international courts. The introduction of flexible discretion in doctrinal contexts that allow the weighing of extra-legal interests enable international courts, in turn, to bridge some of the gap between law and politics—that is, to apply international law in a credible manner without excessively alienating their political environment, and without crossing the dividing line between a political body and a legal body.[120] Rejecting the use of such tension-mitigating doctrines could perhaps strengthen the image of international courts as speaking law to power, but it might also facilitate the emergence of powerful enemies for international courts, which could actively work to weaken their powers or maintain them understaffed, overworked, and with limited legal powers.

Finally, it is important to note that political interests are not stagnant and that they may change over time in different places. International courts can play an important role in this regard by signalling what is, and what is not, an acceptable position for an international actor to embrace. In that sense too, international courts play a political role and can influence the political dynamic within states and international organizations. A critical evaluation of the engagement of international courts with their political environment should therefore reflect not merely whether international courts navigate international politics in ways that enable them to legitimately and effectively perform their function but also whether they have a positive influence on national and international politics.

## 6.  Conclusion

I have argued in this chapter that international courts have no choice but to take cognizance of their political environment, since political interests influence their legitimacy and effectiveness. This requires, as a practical matter, international courts to uphold legal norms, while keeping an open eye on the political context in which they operate. Developing legal doctrines taking cognizance of party expectations and burdens imposed on them, affording them a certain margin of deference and applying flexible remedies, are among some of the ways that allow international courts to square the circles in which they travel in a transparent and doctrinally acceptable manner, although there is hardly a one-size-fits-all formula for all cases of legal-political clashes.

Still, being transparent about the considerations resorted to by international courts within the aforementioned legal doctrines is generally useful, and it is better, in my opinion, than engaging in what has been sometimes described by observers of judicial practice as distorted interpretation and application of international law for hidden political or strategic reasons. Still, one has to accept that full transparency in judicial

---

[120]  Rastan (n 56) 592 ("If we adjust legal criteria to accommodate political considerations, where should it stop? How does a judicial body avoid the risk of engaging in politics? If we reject the relevance of political impact on prosecutorial discretion how should a court respond to legitimate expectations for universal redress?").

decision-making may be unattainable, and that there may be circumstances in which openly acknowledging the weighing of political considerations in the exercise of judicial discretion (eg relating to remedy design) might undermine the useful myth of separation of law from political considerations.

Ultimately, it may be worth recalling that working with and around political constraints is not uniquely the challenge of international courts. Domestic courts, too, often confront many similar pressures.[121] Yet, international courts—dealing directly with international actors over high-stake issues, and having weaker enforcement and administrative capacities—are arguably more vulnerable to political pressure and more dependent on political power.[122] Hence, they have a greater need than their domestic counterparts to take cognizance of the interplay between judicial action and the political environment.

---

[121] See eg Ran Hirschl, "The Judicialization of Politics" in Robert E Goodin (ed), *The Oxford Handbook of Political Science* (Oxford University Press 2011).

[122] See eg Tom Ginsburg, "Political Constraints on International Courts" in Cesara PR Romano, Karen Alter, and Yuval Shany (eds), *The Oxford Handbook of International Adjudication* (Oxford University Press 2013) 483, 486–87.

# 6

# The David Caron "Rule of X":
# A Call for Arbitrator Self-Discipline

*Lucy Reed*

## 1. Introduction

In September 2018, I was extended the honour of delivering a keynote speech at the Conference in Commemoration of Professor David D Caron 1983 at the University of California, Berkeley, entitled "The Elegance of International Law". I wanted to address something that he was actively working on when we lost him so prematurely. I knew that he had begun focusing research on the role of the adjudicator in international dispute resolution, having heard him deliver the Fifth Annual Charles N Brower Lecture at the Annual Meeting of the American Society of International Law in April 2017. Caron opened his Brower Lecture, entitled "The Multiple Functions of International Courts and Tribunals and the Singular Task of the Adjudicator" with the following thoughts:

> The work regarding international courts often comes around to the functions they serve and how the academy might—given such functions—assess effectiveness. But curiously, the relationship between the many functions of courts and tribunals and what adjudicators do is not explored. On the one hand, so much is asked, hoped, and perhaps even expected of international courts and tribunals, and, on the other hand, the adjudicator is given a singular task. That relationship presents difficulties because those functions and the singular task do not necessarily align with one another. These misalignments, sometimes openly and sometimes insidiously, pose difficulties for how adjudicators deliberate with one another and for academic assessments of both adjudicators and international courts.[1]

In following this trail on SSRN, I had the good fortune of finding the text—"as delivered" and not finalized for publication—of the Opening Lecture he had given in September 2017 to the then-entering class of the prestigious Masters in International Dispute Settlement programme at the Graduate Institute in Geneva (MIDS).[2]

---

[1] David D Caron, "Fifth Annual Charles N. Brower Lecture on International Dispute Resolution: The Multiple Functions of International Courts and the Singular Task of the Adjudicator", downloaded from <https://www.cambridge.org/core>, American Society of International Law (footnotes omitted).

[2] David D Caron, "Arbitration and the Rule of X", King's College London Dickson Poon School of Law Legal Studies Research Paper No 2017–41 (28 September 2017), <https://ssrn.com/abstract-3062537.

Lucy Reed, *The David Caron "Rule of X": A Call for Arbitrator Self-Discipline* In: *By Peaceful Means*. Edited by: Charles N Brower, Joan E Donoghue, Cian C Murphy, Cymie R Payne and Esmé R Shirlow, Oxford University Press. © Lucy Reed 2024.
DOI: 10.1093/oso/9780192848086.003.0006

The title was mysterious—"Arbitrators and the Rule of X"—but the content was not. I found that he had begun approaching difficult issues of arbitrator ethics from the perspective of self-discipline rather than external codes of conduct. Caron introduced his MIDS lecture topic as focused on "the far-flung array of individuals who serve as international adjudicators, arbitrators, commissioners and judges", whom he found to be "the most difficult group in international courts to predict, to give a logic to".[3] He stated at the outset that "this discussion is only starting and in [his] view presents a much deeper agenda than currently set out".[4]

I delivered my short keynote at Berkeley, "Arbitration and the Rule of X".[5] In closing, I committed to deepen the agenda by "raising the 'David Caron Rule of X', in terms, with colleagues" and "develop[ing] his concept of the 'Rule of X' in international law and perhaps more ambitiously". I have done my best to do so. I run the risk of being labelled evangelical in promoting the Rule of X in international arbitration circles and, as a full-time international arbitrator, try my best to practise what I preach. In October 2019, when invited to deliver (remotely) the 25th Goff Lecture at the City University of Hong Kong, I deepened Caron's agenda with research into classical Greek and Roman ethical constructs to speak on "Arbitrator 'Temperance': David Caron's Rule of X".[6]

This chapter is the latest iteration and expansion of the Rule of X. Following a description of Caron's original Rule of X for international arbitrators, the chapter reprises the classical ethics underpinning of the Rule, addresses the tension between self-discipline and external codes of arbitrator conduct, and then offers brief commentary on the applicability of a Rule of X to International Court of Justice (ICJ) ad hoc judges and international mediators.

## 2. The David Caron Rule of X: For International Arbitrators

### 2.1 The Rule of X Itself

Caron did not accept that international arbitrators constitute a mafia or club or cartel, comprising members who appoint and reappoint each other each other regardless of proven merit. He chose to research and explore the contrary proposition that leading international arbitrators serve and strive for reappointment "by virtue of their reputation".[7]

Obvious risks to reputation are the delay and disruption posed by arbitrator overcommitment, which Caron identified as the cause of the rising level of criticism of

---

[3] ibid 3.
[4] ibid 3.
[5] Reed, "The David Caron Rule of X" (2019) 37 Berkeley Journal of International Law 163; (2019) 46 Ecology Law Quarterly 9.
[6] Video available in the AV Library of the Hong Kong International Arbitration Centre, <http://www.hkiac.org>.
[7] Caron, "Arbitration and the Rule of X" (n 1) 3.

international arbitrators and international arbitration. It is arbitrator overcommitment that can lead a three-member tribunal (or even a sole arbitrator) to schedule a hearing date more than two years out from the preliminary conference. It is arbitrator overcommitment that can cause a tribunal to arrive on the first day of a hearing unprepared and depart on the last day without having deliberated. And it is arbitrator overcommitment that can leave private and state parties waiting years for final awards.

Unlike other critics who equate overcommitment with too large a case load, Caron observed that the problem is "more nuanced and widespread" than the particularly packed schedules of particularly busy arbitrators:

> It includes the practitioner who has only two arbitrations he or she sits on but which are difficult to mix with the unrelenting demands of clients. It likewise includes the academic who has only one or two arbitrations he or she sits on but which are difficult to accommodate within teaching schedules.[8]

Caron acknowledged external efforts to control the risks of overcommitment. The main international arbitration institutions no longer accept a cursory statement from an arbitrator candidate that she or he "has capacity" to take on a new appointment. The International Chamber of Commerce International Court of Arbitration (the ICC) and the World Bank's International Centre for Settlement of Investment Disputes (ICSID) and other institutions now require prospective arbitrators to document their anticipated availability and capacity in advance of appointment. For example, the ICC requires arbitrator candidates to disclose the number of cases on which they are sitting as chair and co-arbitrator, and to black out existing hearing dates and other commitments on calendars three years out.

In Caron's view, such external requirements, however laudatory, serve only to provide a minimum of information to the appointing parties. These requirements are not "what arbitrators professionally should demand of themselves and each other".[9] What is needed, in addition and in parallel, is an internal system of control.

To this end, Caron created a rule of arbitrator self-discipline, the "Rule of X".

> Arbitrators need to reflect on the amount of appointments they are reasonably able to handle. For the issue posed by over commitment, the needed internal commitment is gained by what I call the Rule of X.[10]

The heart of the Rule of X is that international arbitrators should "set a number—X—as the upper limit of cases that he or she is capable of responsibly sitting on at the same time".[11] The purpose of the Rule of X is to build and protect a reputation for excellence,

---

[8] ibid 10.
[9] ibid 3.
[10] ibid 11.
[11] ibid 11.

which in turn promotes re-appointment and (I expect Caron would agree) is a good in and of itself.

Again unlike critics who equate overcommitment with caseload size, Caron emphasized that there cannot be a universal fixed number X. Given that "the individual circumstances and capacities of arbitrators vary tremendously",[12] the factor X—to be useful—must also vary with individual circumstances and capacities. Obvious factors are experience, age, full-time versus part-time arbitrator status, academic versus law practice schedule, legal culture, and reliance on tribunal secretaries. The factor X should vary over time and over a career. As discussed in this chapter, the factor X should also rise and fall with the mix of different international adjudicator roles an arbitrator plays.

Caron identified one critical variable of X to be the number of presiding arbitrator appointments, which can exponentially increase the work required. In my talk at Berkeley, I added this:

> If [Caron] had had more time, no doubt he would have expressly elaborated on more variables: treaty vs. commercial cases, complex vs. modest cases, personal factors like family-life balance, intellectual challenge, the sheer fun that can come with sitting with certain other arbitrators and hearing certain counsel.[13]

Caron, it seems, had begun to practice the self-discipline of calculating his personal Rule of X and applying it to his arbitrator work. He observed that this forced him to evaluate prospective appointment more critically:

> I began to think very seriously about the characteristics of the arbitrations I most seek to be part of—is a state or government agency a party, who are the other arbitrators, the counsel, what is the issue?[14]

He reflected that following a personal Rule of X created "a clear strong incentive to more promptly finish some of the X arbitrations"[15] and promoted service with "a more robust conception" of the arbitrator role, and thereby improve the quality of personal work and international arbitration in general.[16] Caron connected this to the true cost of overcommitment, namely that "over commitment in the number of arbitrations is under commitment to any particular arbitration".[17]

Caron also predicted, or at least hoped for, a deeper and broader impact of the Rule of X. When arbitrators—especially the most well-established and busy ones—are at their personal factor X, or close to X, they will turn down arbitrations that are either relatively small or unchallenging for them, and those appointments may go to younger

---

[12]  ibid 11.
[13]  Reed, "The David Caron Rule of X", (n 5) 166; (n 5) 12.
[14]  Caron, "Arbitration and the Rule of X" (n 1) 12.
[15]  ibid 13.
[16]  ibid 13.
[17]  ibid 13.

and more diverse arbitrators.[18] He concluded his lecture in Geneva with a description of the virtuous circle that could be unleashed in international arbitration with the Rule of X: "[fewer] cases in the hands of a few, and a few cases in the hands of many, with new arbitrators rising from more diverse backgrounds".[19]

## 2.2 The Foundation of the Rule of X: Self-Discipline

Just as intriguing as the possible future impact of the Rule of X is the foundation of the Rule. As noted, the Rule of X is a rule of self-discipline for arbitrators. It is the discipline of honest self-assessment in responsibly managing a case load, ideally in balance with life outside arbitration.

Although Caron did not publish any of the thinking or research that led him to the Rule of X concept, he was no doubt aware that self-discipline is often overlooked and undervalued in our commercial market. Perhaps he was motivated by classical moral and ethical philosophy. I followed this line of thinking in drafting the 2020 Goff Lecture.

In brief, the main ancient Greek philosophers—Socrates, Plato, and Aristotle—did not write of self-discipline per se but questioned what it meant to be "good" and how to reach *eudaimonia* (εὐδαιμονία), roughly translated as "happiness" or "well-being". This comes through examination of virtues such as justice, moderation, and courage. *Eudaimonia* is different than the modern definition of "happiness" in that it is related to purpose and correctness rather than emotion. To have *eudaimonia*, one is fulfilling his or her life in the correct way in accordance with nature.

The Greek philosophers focused on virtue as a means to *eudaimonia*. In Aristotle's *Nicomachean Ethics*, written circa 350 BCE, one of the main points is that virtue is essential in and of itself, as opposed to a means to an end. So, "honor, pleasure, intelligence, and excellence in its various forms" are chosen not only for their own sakes but for the sake of securing *eudaimonia*, or well-being.[20]

Stoic philosophy, founded by Zeno around the third century BCE, goes further. The central tenet of Stoicism—different than the modern definition of the term—is that the only thing necessary for goodness and happiness is moral virtue. Stoics believed that *eudaimonia* could be achieved through adherence to the virtues only, whereas Plato and Aristotle believed that external things, such as health and wealth, also contribute to happiness.

Plato, Aristotle, and Zeno all considered self-control a central virtue. Much of Hellenistic moral and ethical philosophy is concerned with the concept of *sophrosyne* (σωφροσύνη), roughly translated as "temperance"—in Latin, *temperantia*. Sophrosyne

---

[18] ibid 13.

[19] ibid 13, citing Susan D Franck and others, "The Diversity Challenge: Exploring the 'Invisible College' of International Arbitration" (2015) 53 Columbia Journal of Transactional Law 429; and Chiara Giorgetti, "Who Decides Who Decides in International Investment Arbitration" (2014) 35 University of Pennsylvania Journal of International Law 431.

[20] Aristotle, *Nicomachean Ethics* (H. Rackham tr, Harvard University Press 1934) 19.1097b3–6.

means temperance in the sense of inner balance or moderation, and control over the self, not measured against outside responsibilities or compliance with external laws or codes. Plato's *Republic*, written circa 375 BCE, is a series of didactic dialogues between Socrates and various Athenians about how to form an ideal city-state. In Plato's *Republic*, *sophrosyne* is translated as "sobriety", a "kind of beautiful order" linked to self-control.

In speaking of temperance in this context, it is worth remembering that lawyers and arbitrators are members of a learned profession. The legitimacy of a profession, and what distinguishes it from a trade or craft, is that professionals, as individuals, bear a sense of responsibility to the greater public, above and beyond material incentives. It is not surprising that George Beaton of Melbourne Law School, in an article on the relevance of professionalism, refers back to the Greeks: "Professionalism as set forth in the early Dialogues of Plato holds that the true professional not only possesses the practical skills and knowledge of his or her trade but is also disciplined in moral excellence."[21] How might the philosophical concepts of *eudaimonia*, as well-being, and *sophrosyne*, as temperance, inform Caron's Rule of X for international arbitrators? Recalling that Caron was addressing the disruptive practice of over-commitment, these concepts underscore the personal responsibility of an arbitrator not to take on more cases than he or she is able to manage diligently. When an arbitrator identifies "the upper limit of cases that he or she is capable of responsibly sitting on at the same time", it is an act of self-discipline.[22] The Rule of X can serve as a tool to assist arbitrators in fulfilling their ethical and professional and responsibilities in general, and the norm of expediency in particular.

## 2.3  Calculating and Implementing the Rule of X

Caron made a start on addressing how international arbitrators might implement the Rule of X, by asking the basic question of why an X factor is useful. If overcommitment risks an arbitrator's reputation, why is it that he takes on too many cases? One answer, Caron ventured, is paranoia: with or without justification, an arbitrator is reluctant to turn down a new appointment, for fear of not being asked again. Another answer, rooted in human nature, is an arbitrator's reluctance to disappoint by saying "no" to an appointment.

These possible reasons for overcommitment indicate that two stages of self-discipline are necessary. An arbitrator must first thoughtfully set her factor X, and then she must rigorously apply it. At each stage, an arbitrator has to be deliberative and unflinchingly realistic. This means, for example, accounting for uncertainty and avoiding the "planning fallacy" heuristic: the human tendency to underestimate how long a task will

---

[21] George Beaton, "Why Professionalism is Still Relevant" (2010) Melbourne Law School Legal Studies Research Paper No 445, 2.
[22] Caron, "Arbitration and the Rule of X" (n 1) 11.

take.[23] There is always a possibility that a new arbitration, supposedly not requiring substantial attention for many months, may open with a barrage of emergency interim measures applications.

One way to do this, which Caron might well have addressed with more time, could be to draw up a checklist. Atul Gawande of Harvard Medical School, in *The Checklist Manifesto: How To Get Things Right*,[24] builds on the two reasons for human fallibility identified by philosophers: ignorance and ineptitude, the latter being instances in which "the knowledge exists, yet we fail to apply it correctly".[25] In Gawande's words:

> Avoidable failures are common and persistent, not to mention demoralizing and frustrating across many fields ... We need a different strategy for overcoming failure, one that builds on experience and takes advantage of the knowledge people have but somehow also makes up for our inevitable human inadequacies. And there is such a strategy—though it will seem almost ridiculous in its simplicity, maybe even crazy to those of us who have spent years developing ever more advanced skills and technologies. It is a checklist.[26]

Checklists, Gawande writes, seem to provide protection against failure, because they "remind us of the minimum necessary steps and make them explicit".[27] Good checklists are precise, to the point, and easy to use under time pressures. In focusing attention on necessary issues for consideration, good checklists instil self-discipline—returning to the classical ethical concept, temperance.

In my Goff Lecture, as an exercise building on Caron's early thinking, I presented two illustrative checklists. The first is for calculating a personal factor X (Figure 6.1), and the second for applying that factor (Figure 6.2).

There no doubt are many other relevant factors. That is the point. As Caron underscored: "Admittedly, coming to a value for 'X' is an entirely subjective exercise."[28]

Ultimately, adherence to the Rule of X will require, for some, accepting fewer rather than more appointments. This involves the practice of essentialism, described by the author Greg McKeown as the pursuit of less-but-better, undertaken in a disciplined way:

> By definition, applying highly selective criteria is a trade-off; sometimes you will have to turn down a seemingly very good option and have faith that the perfect option will soon come along ... Like any Essentialist skill, it forces you to make decisions by design, rather than default.[29]

[23] The social scientist Daniel Kahneman, together with Amos Tversky, coined the phrase "planning fallacy" in 1979: Daniel Kahneman and Amos Tversky, "Intuitive Prediction: Biases and Corrective Procedures" (1979) 12 TIMS Studies in Management Science 313–27.
[24] Atul Gawande, *The Checklist Manifesto: How to Get Things Right* (Metropolitan Books 2009).
[25] ibid 5.
[26] Gawande (n 24) 6 (emphasis added).
[27] ibid 11.
[28] Caron, "Arbitration and the Rule of X" (n 1) 12.
[29] Greg McKeown, *Essentialism: The Disciplined Pursuit of Less* (Crown Business 2014) 97.

| | CHECKLIST 1:  FACTORS IN CALCULATING X |
|---|---|
| 1 | Overall time frame:  3 years? 5 years? Retirement? |
| 2 | Financial needs and wants |
| 3 | Overall amount of time available for arbitrator work |
| 4 | Anticipated family and/or other personal commitments |
| 5 | Desired balance of presiding and co-arbitrator roles |
| 6 | Desired intellectual challenge? Commercial vs treaty cases? |
| 7 | Desired travel – How much?  Where? |
| 8 | Risk tolerance – Parties and geography |
| 9 | Existing backlog |
| 10 | Other |

**Figure 6.1**  Checklist for Calculation of a Personal Factor X[a]
Reed, 25th Goff Lecture (n 6).

| | CHECKLIST 2:  FACTORS IN EVALUATING NEW APPOINTMENTS, AGAINST X |
|---|---|
| 1 | Presiding or co-arbitrator appointment? |
| 2 | Identity of co-arbitrators, including reputation? |
| 3 | Identity of counsel?  Experts? |
| 4 | Commercial or treaty case? |
| 5 | Apparent complexity? |
| 6 | Amount in dispute, as proxy for complexity? |
| 7 | Compensation factors? |
| 8 | Intellectual challenge:  apparently new or repeat issues? |
| 9 | Anticipated calendar? |
| 10 | Likelihood of applications for provisional measures? |
| 11 | Anticipated level of contentiousness? |
| 12 | Drafting backlog? |
| 13 | Risk:  Legal seat? Likely hearing venue? |
| 14 | Overall:  Will the case add interest or fun? |
| 15 | Other |

**Figure 6.2**  Factors in Evaluating New Appointments, Against X[a]
ibid.

Or, in Caron's words:

> I believe that if an arbitrator has mentally settled on an upper limit of appointments, then it is probable that he or she will at least be hesitant to accept any appointment that puts her or him above X, at X+1, or X+2. Importantly, arbitrators that benchmark themselves will be less likely to take on an irresponsible number of appointments, far beyond what they are able to handle, from which they must then dig themselves out.[30]

This focus on self-discipline and self-initiation naturally gives rise to the question of the comparative role of external codes of conduct in regulating arbitrator behaviour.

## 2.4  External Codes of Conduct

Since Caron's MIDS lecture, due largely to controversy around investor–state dispute settlement (ISDS), there has been increasing scrutiny and criticism of international arbitrator conduct. The attention goes far beyond the questions of arbitrator availability and timeliness underlying Caron's research and concerns. The focus is not only on the familiar panoply of issues of arbitrator independence and impartiality, whether conflicts of interest or substantive issue conflict, but also on repeat party appointments by both states and investors, so-called double-hatting (where one individual serves as arbitrator, counsel and/or expert in different cases at the same time); the impact of lack of gender diversity and other forms of diversity; and civility in behaviour.

It is not surprising that, in the wake of now-common soft codes of conduct for party representatives in international arbitration,[31] efforts have accelerated to craft targeted international arbitrator codes of conduct.[32] The most advanced and most visible is the "Draft Code of Conduct for Adjudicators in Investor-State Dispute Settlement", prepared jointly by the Secretariats of ICSID and UNCITRAL and issued on 1 May 2020 (ICSID-UNCITRAL Draft Code of Conduct),[33] on which ICSID and UNCITRAL encouraged public comment.[34]

Draft Article 8—entitled "Availability, Diligence, Civility and Efficiency"—is directed in part to the issues motivating the Rule of X. Draft Article 8.2 raises the possibility—the

---

[30] Caron, "Arbitration and the Rule of X" (n 1) 12.

[31] For example, the IBA Guidelines on Party Representation in International Arbitration (25 May 2013); Singapore Institute of Arbitrators Guidelines on Party-Representative Ethics (26 April 2018).

[32] For example, the IBA. In his 2007 Goff Lecture, Judge Charles Brower noted the recurring theme in the Goff Lectures of the "ineluctable trend towards a uniformity of rules and laws governing international commercial arbitration". Charles N Brower, "W(h)ither International Commercial Arbitration" (2008) 24 Arbitration International 181, 182–183.

[33] United Nations Commission On International Trade Law and the International Centre for Settlement of Investment Disputes, "Draft Code of Conduct for Adjudicators in Investor-State Dispute Settlement", <https://icsid.worldbank.org/sites/default/files/Draft_Code_Conduct_Adjudicators_ISDS.pdf  and  https://uncitral.un.org/en/codeofconduct>.

[34] United Nations Commission On International Trade Law and the International Centre for Settlement of Investment Disputes, "ICSID and UNCITRAL Release Draft Code of Conduct for Adjudicators", Press Release, 1 May 2020.

full text is purposefully bracketed, for overall comment—of limiting an ISDS arbitrator to a fixed number of arbitrations, designated (for the avoidance of doubt, with no connection to the David Caron Arbitrator Rule of X) as "[X]", explicitly for the purpose of expediting tribunal decisions: "[Adjudicators shall refrain from serving in more than [X] pending ISDS proceedings at the same time so as to issue timely decisions]."[35]

ICSID and UNCITRAL received substantial public comments on the Draft Code of Conduct, through to 18 December 2020. The public comments submitted on draft Article 8(2) were predominantly against including any absolute number [X] for arbitrator ISDS appointments in the Code of Conduct, with several commentators expressing a preference instead for robust pre-appointment disclosure by arbitrator candidates of their caseloads.[36]

As an example, the ICCA Watch Group on Investor-State Dispute Settlement (the ICCA Watch Group) submitted the following observations:

> The Watch Group points out the difficulty of regulating availability in the manner Article 8(2) proposes. Even for adjudicators whose adjudication activity is their sole profession, a raw number will not take account of complexity, time demands, and stage of the proceedings of different cases. For those whose adjudication activity is not their sole profession, that number will provide an even less reliable indication of their availability. Finally, the number of cases does not take account of an individual's capacity for and pace of work.
>
> ...
>
> The Watch Group would propose simply that the Code provide that a party may request a reasonable report of an adjudicator's professional commitments and a general description of her or her adjudication caseload before the appointment may be confirmed. A calendar like the one used by the ICC International Court of Arbitration is one means by which availability might be assessed, although perhaps with more guidance that what is meant by "unavailable" is unable to conduct a hearing or devote substantial time to the matter.[37]

Interestingly, in relation to Caron's professed aspiration that the Rule of X could promote diversity, the United Kingdom made the follow observations on draft Article 8(2):

> The UK welcomes the commitments made in Article 8 on the availability, diligence, civility and efficiency of arbitrators, however the UK believes that there should not be an absolute limit on the number of cases an arbitrator can handle at any given time as per the suggested drafting in Paragraph 2. This could again create a barrier of entry to

---

[35] Draft ISDS Code (n 35) Article 8.2.

[36] Comments by State/Commenter as of 14 January 2021, <https://icsid.worldbank.org/resources/code-of-conduct> 142–48.

[37] ibid 111. The ICCA Watch Group noted in their comments, dated 30 November 2020, that the observations were not considered by the ICCA Governing Body or ICCA as a whole, and do not necessarily represent the view of each member of the Watch Group. In the interests of full transparency, the author is a member of the Watch Group.

newer, less experienced arbitrators who may need multiple cases to make arbitration a full-time role. Instead, other commitments around availability or efficiency, for example, will require that an arbitrator has the capacity to properly service all their cases and can be held accountable to those commitments.[38]

In roughly the same time period, the Queen Mary University of London School of International Arbitration and the Corporate Counsel International Arbitration Group conducted an empirical study of investors' views to "identify which reforms, from their perspective, may best improve the resolution of investment disputes between states and investors and encourage foreign investment". The survey was conducted in November–December 2019, leading to publication of the "QMUL-CCIAG Survey: Investors' Perceptions of ISDS" in May 2020.[39]

One subject of the survey was the possible introduction of a universal code of conduct for ISDS arbitrators. The general reaction was favourable. In response to the question "Would a code of conduct for arbitrators improve ISDS?" 27 per cent of respondents selected the answer "Greatly Improve"; 37 per cent, "Somewhat Improve"; 29 per cent, "Neither Improve Nor Undermine"; and 7 per cent, "Somewhat Undermine".[40]

When asked about the impact of restrictions on the activity of arbitrators, the greatest concern of the respondents—at 63 per cent—was the availability of arbitrators.[41] When asked specifically about a possible cap on the number of appointments per ISDS arbitrator, the respondents offered a very different view than the commentators on the ICSID-UNCITRAL Draft Code of Conduct.

> With the caveat that the response rate for this question was lower than 50%, those who did respond overwhelmingly felt that arbitrators should disclose the number of their ongoing ISDS appointments as part of the appointment process (80%). They also felt (82.5%) that there should be a maximum number of ISDS appointments an arbitrator should be involved in at any one time. There was a clear preference from respondents to cap the number of ISDS appointments at 5 (57%), with the second most popular response being no more than 10 ongoing ISDS appointments (31%).[42]

It is yet again easy to predict that Caron would firmly oppose a case number cap on ISDS arbitrator service, whether it be five or ten or more cases. It bears repeating that the algebra of the David Caron Rule of X is individual and subjective, as recognized by commentators on the ICSID-UNCITRAL Draft Code of Conduct.

---

[38] ibid 65.

[39] Queen Mary University School of International Arbitration-Corporate Counsel International Arbitration Group Survey: Investors' Perceptions of ISDS (May 2020), <http://www.arbitration.qmul.ac.uk>. The QMUL-CCIAG Survey was limited to investors, not counsel and arbitrators; the sponsors received eighty-six responses from corporate counsel and corporations.

[40] ibid Chart 9, 14.

[41] ibid Chart 10, 15. In comparison, 54 per cent flagged concerns about diversity of arbitrators; 43 per cent about quality of decisions; 42 per cent about expertise; and 33 per cent about correctness of decisions.

[42] ibid 15 (emphasis added).

To offer a surprising example (albeit outside the investor–state arena), X for the late and legendary Professor Pierre Lalive was five or six cases.[43] There are ISDS arbitrators known to carry more than twenty cases, who master their cases and stay current on awards. As Caron warned in his MIDS lecture, a practitioner or academic arbitrator with a single ISDS case might well cause as much delay in tribunal progress as a colleague with many more appointments. What would have been most important, for Caron, is that the important field of investment treaty arbitration could lose a great deal of expertise by arbitrarily limiting arbitrators to five or ten or any fixed number of ISDS cases, without necessarily opening the door to additional qualified arbitrators.

It is fair to say that codes of conduct for international arbitrators in both commercial and ISDS arbitrations have their place and are perhaps overdue. Both hard and soft rules can and should be complementary to the self-policing of a Rule of X. However, as Caron foresaw with his MIDS lecture, a code of conduct rule setting a universal maximum [X] case number per arbitrator is too blunt a tool to correct the recognized disruption caused by arbitrator over-commitment. Far more effective would be arbitrator self-discipline—sophrosyne or temperance—to manage individual caseloads and to achieve the norm of expedient decision-making.

As I observed in my Goff Lecture, this does not mean a return to that "golden age" of pure self-regulation in international arbitration, when mostly older White European men developed and practised modern international commercial arbitration. They had a near monopoly on the practice, understandable given the time and circumstances. We are told that they followed the unwritten code of upstanding arbitrator conduct, including by ensuring availability and attention to the cases they accepted, because each trusted the others to do the same.

That golden age is not the province of Caron's Rule of X. The overall international arbitration community likely benefits if arbitrators follow the Rule of X, but it is at heart an individual regime.


## 3. The David Caron Rule of X: ICJ Judges Ad Hoc

To recall, Caron stated at the outset of his MIDS lecture in Geneva that his topic was not solely international arbitrators but "the far-flung array of individuals who serve as international adjudicators, arbitrators, commissioners and judges", whom he found to be "the most difficult group in international courts to predict, to give a logic to".[44] At the close of the lecture, he mentioned his service as a Judge ad hoc with the International Court of Justice—a role that brought him great pride—and promised that he had "recommendations there as well, but that awaits another lecture".[45]

---

[43] "Q&A with Professor Pierre Lalive" (November 2008) 5 Global Arbitration Review 3 <https://globalarbitrationreview.com/article/1027734/q-a-with-professor-pierre-lalive>.

[44] Caron, "Arbitration and the Rule of X" (n 1) 3.

[45] ibid 14. Under Article 31, paragraphs 2 and 3, of the Statute of the Court, a state party to a case which does not have a judge of its nationality on the Bench may choose a person to sit as judge ad hoc in that specific case under the conditions laid down in Articles 35–37 of the Rules of Court.

Another lecture was not to come and so there is no way to know with certainty what Caron's recommendations for ICJ Judges ad hoc would have been. It is likely that he would not have recommended a separate self-imposed Rule of X—or perhaps Rule of Y—for ICJ Judge ad hoc appointments, as they are far too rare to warrant a separate numerical factor.[46] Caron might have recommended that an individual fortunate enough to be appointed as Judge ad hoc in an ICJ case, most often as an academic, prioritize her ICJ role and limit other international adjudicator positions, including by lowering the X number in her existing Rule of X for new arbitrator appointments. Caron might have recommended that an international arbitrator with at or near a full X case load, however regretfully, should not accept an ICJ Judge ad hoc appointment because of the strict requirement that ICJ Judges be always available for ICJ proceedings, including for requests for the urgent indication of provisional measures, which could disrupt the procedural calendars and thereby prejudice the parties in his pending arbitrations.[47]

The Rule of X algebra for ICJ Judge ad hoc appointments could be challenging, as ICJ cases tend to last longer and require less sustained active involvement than international arbitrations but carry a higher level of importance for international adjudicators. In this context, it is intriguing to think that Caron perhaps would have equated one ICJ Judge ad hoc appointment with, say, three international commercial arbitrations or two investment treaty arbitrations, leading an adjudicator, upon receiving an ICJ appointment, to lower her Arbitrator X to X minus 3 or X minus 2.

Consistent with the reflection and research that led Caron to the Arbitrator Rule of X, Caron perhaps would have utilized his next Rule of X lecture to identify possible factors for the internal ethical calculus to be done by a nominee before accepting an ICJ Judge ad hoc appointment, and then regularly reviewed during the tenure of that appointment. Whatever variables might be involved with that calculus, it is safe to predict that Caron would not have been in favour of an external rule setting a fixed number of ICJ Judge ad hoc appointments one person could accept at one time or limiting the number of other arbitrations a Judge ad hoc could retain or accept during her or his ICJ position.

Given Caron's faith in the dedication of ICJ Court judges, I am confident that he would not have agreed with the need for the ICJ rule prohibiting Court Members

---

[46] According to the Court's website <http://www.icj-cij.org>, as of January 2021, there were twenty-one Judges ad hoc sitting in thirteen pending Court cases, four of whom had multiple appointments as Judge ad hoc.

[47] The Rules of Court (1978), Adopted on 14 April 1978 and Entered into Force on 1 July 1978 are available on the Court website, <http://www.icj-cij.org>.

Article 20 of the Rules of Court provides in relevant part:
  2. The obligation of Members of the Court under Article 23, paragraph 3, of the Statute, to hold themselves permanently at the disposal of the Court, entails attendance at all such meetings, unless they are prevented from attending by illness or for other serious reasons duly explained to the President, who shall inform the Court.
  3. Judges ad hoc are likewise bound to hold themselves at the disposal of the Court and to attend all meetings held in the case in which they are participating. . . .
Article 74 of the Rules of Court provides in relevant part:
  1. A request for the indication of provisional measures shall have priority over all other cases.
  2. The Court, if it is not sitting when the request is made, shall be convened forthwith for the purpose of proceeding to a decision on the request as a matter of urgency.

serving on international arbitration tribunals which post-dates his premature passing. The then President of the Court, His Excellency Mr Abdulqawi A Yusuf, announced the new restrictions on the occasion of his address to the Seventy-Third Session of the United Nations General Assembly on 25 October 2018. At the close of his address, President Yusuf stated:

> I would now like to take the opportunity, in the spirit of transparency, to touch upon the question of extrajudicial activities that Members of the Court occasionally undertake, in particular in the field of international arbitration. The Court is cognizant of the fact that, while the judicial settlement of disputes offered by the Court is enshrined in the Charter, States may, for several reasons, be interested in settling their disputes by arbitration. In such instances, Members of the Court have sometimes been called upon by States to sit on the arbitral tribunals in question dealing in some cases with inter-State disputes while in others with investor-State disputes—a testament, of course, to the high esteem in which the Court's Judges are held by the international community.
>
> Over the years, the Court has taken the view that, in certain circumstances, its Members may participate in arbitration proceedings. However, in light of its ever-increasing workload, the Court decided a few months ago to review this practice and to set out clearly defined rules regulating such activities. As a result, Members of the Court have come to the decision, last month, that they will not normally accept to participate in international arbitration. In particular, they will not participate in investor-State arbitration or in commercial arbitration. However, in the event that they are called upon, exceptionally, by one or more States that would prefer to resort to arbitration, instead of judicial settlement, the Court has decided that, in order to render service to those States, it will, if the circumstances so warrant, authorize its Members to participate in inter-State arbitration cases. Even in such exceptional cases, a Member of the Court will only participate, if authorized, in one arbitration procedure at a time. Prior authorization must have been granted for that purpose, in accordance with the mechanism put in place by the Court. Members of the Court will, however, decline to be appointed by a State that is a party in a case pending before the Court, even if there is no substantial interference between that case and the case submitted to arbitration. This is essential to place beyond reproach the impartiality and independence of Judges in the exercise of their judicial functions. Finally, I cannot stress enough that any participation of Members of the Court in such inter-State arbitrations is subject to the strict condition that their judicial activities take absolute precedence.[48]

The bottom line is that, as of late 2018, an ICJ Court Member may serve on only one international arbitration tribunal at a time, and that only in an inter-state arbitration with prior authorization.

---

[48] <https://www.icj-cij.org/public/files/press-releases/0/000-20181025-PRE-02-00-EN.pdf>, 11–12 See Callum Musto, "New Restrictions on Arbitral Appointments for Sitting ICJ Judges", *EJIL: Talk!* (5 November 2018), <http://www.ejiltalk.org/new-restrictions-on-arbitral-appointments-for-for-sitting-icj-judges/>.

Here, knowing Caron's great respect for the Court and for the exceptional obligation of Court Members to give "absolute precedence" to Court activities, it is again a safe prediction that he would fully endorse the Court's imposition, in effect, of a Rule of 1.

## 4. The David Caron Rule of X: International Mediators

Although international mediators and conciliators are, by definition, not international adjudicators, Caron might well have included them in his research going forward. Like ICJ Judges ad hoc, the field of public international law conciliators is small and it would not be realistic to assign a separate Rule of X to the field.

However, to the extent an international arbitrator takes on treaty conciliation appointments, any such appointments should be factored into her Rule of X. Conducted properly, a treaty conciliation will be extremely demanding and time-consuming. The lead example is the successful Conciliation Between the Democratic Republic of Timor-Leste and the Commonwealth of Australia, the one mandatory conciliation to date under Articles 74 and 83 of the United National Convention on the Law of the Sea. After Timor-Leste initiated the proceedings in April 2016, the five-member Conciliation Commission issued its reasoned Decision on Australia's Objections to Competence only five months later in September 2016.[49] The Commission thereafter worked closely with the representatives of Timor-Leste and Australia as they negotiated a new boundary agreement in March 2018, after which the Commission issued its exhaustive final Report in May 2018.[50] The five Conciliators—and especially the Chairman HE Ambassador Peter Taksøe-Jensen—dedicated themselves fully to their task over these two years.[51]

An international adjudicator invited to take on a similar high-level treaty conciliation task in future would, of necessity, have to give serious consideration to whether the appointment would fit comfortably within his existing X number of cases, and be prepared to lower the X factor over the expected life of the conciliation.

## 5. Conclusion

In reflecting upon and attempting to deepen the agenda of Caron's MIDS lecture, it is not my goal to see the Rule of X become an international arbitrator norm of practice and certainly not to be included in any arbitrator code of conduct. That would be

---

[49] Conciliation Between the Democratic Public of Timor-Leste and the Commonwealth of Australia, Decision on Competence (19 September 2016) PCA 2016-10, <https://pcacases.com/web/sendAttach/1921>.

[50] Conciliation Between the Democratic Public of Timor-Leste and the Commonwealth of Australia, Report and Recommendations of the Compulsory Conciliation Commission Between Timor-Leste and Australia on the Timor Sea (9 May 2018) PCA 2016-10, <https://pcacases.com/web/sendAttach/2327>.

[51] Hao Duy Phan, Tara Davenport, Robert Beckman (eds), *The Timor-Leste/Australia Conciliation: A Victory for UNCLOS and Peaceful Settlement of Disputes* (World Scientific Publishing Co. Pte. Ltd, 2019) Chapter 3.

unrealistic and presumptuous, and indeed inconsistent with the very nature of the Rule of X as a personal compass.[52]

Borrowing from the title of Caron's 2017 Brower lecture, the "singular task" of the international adjudicator is to resolve disputes. International adjudicators bring with them different legal training, different approaches to adjudication, different perspectives and, no doubt, different unconscious biases. But all should also bring with them the same foundational ethical rules for international adjudication. Cast in the title of Caron's 2017 MIDS lecture, these should include the self-disciplinary Rule of X.

---

[52] As stated at the close of my talk at Berkeley, my goal instead is "to honor David's intentions, expressed in his MIDS lecture, to develop his concept of the 'Rule of X' in international arbitration". Reed, "The David Caron Rule of X" (n 5) 169; title of article (n 5) 15.

# 7

# The "Fourth Arbitrator" Laid to Rest—The End of the Controversy over Tribunal Secretaries

*Sir David AR Williams KNZM, KC and Anna Kirk*

## 1. Introduction

Since Constantine Partasides published his well-known article "The Fourth Arbitrator? The Role of Secretaries to Tribunal in International Arbitration"[1] in 2002, there has been a continuous debate over the proper role of the tribunal secretary to an arbitral tribunal. That debate reached its peak following the 2015 Russian challenge to the *Yukos* awards,[2] which was based in part on the alleged improper utilization of the tribunal secretary. In this chapter, we suggest that this debate has had its day, with significant clarity having now been achieved through judicial analysis and institutional guidance as to the proper role of the tribunal secretary.

Courts in several jurisdictions have made it clear that they will give arbitral tribunals considerable latitude in how to use a secretary effectively, provided that the tribunal does not delegate its crucial decision-making task. As a result, any tenable challenge to an award or to an arbitrator based on the activities of the tribunal secretary will need to demonstrate improper delegation of this essential task. This strict approach should neutralize fears that dissatisfied parties may try to use the role of the secretary as a makeshift vehicle for challenging awards, simply because they do not like an unfavourable outcome.[3] However, parties to international arbitrations should now be reassured by helpful judicial guidance on best practice and by the fact that the courts will not allow an arbitral tribunal to neglect its fundamental duty to itself to decide the dispute. The guidance provided by arbitral institutions in recent years aligns with this approach and encourages best practice in the appointment process for tribunal secretaries.

The balance struck by the courts and arbitral institutions preserves the efficiencies of the tribunal secretary role, while protecting the integrity of the arbitration by clearly delimiting tasks that an arbitral tribunal cannot delegate to any third party.

---

[1] Constantine Partasides "The Fourth Arbitrator? The Role of Secretaries to Tribunal in International Arbitration" (2002) 18 Journal of International Arbitration 147.
[2] See discussion of the *Yukos* challenge in this chapter.
[3] Chloe Carswell and Laura Winnington-Ingram "Awards: Challenges Based on Misuse of Tribunal Secretaries" in J William Rowley QC (ed), *The Guide to Challenging and Enforcing Arbitration Awards* (2nd edn, Global Arbitration Review 2021) 84.

Sir David AR Williams and Anna Kirk, *The "Fourth Arbitrator" Laid to Rest—The End of the Controversy over Tribunal Secretaries*
In: *By Peaceful Means*. Edited by: Charles N Brower, Joan E Donoghue, Cian C Murphy, Cymie R Payne and Esmé R Shirlow, Oxford University Press. © Sir David AR Williams and Anna Kirk 2024. DOI: 10.1093/oso/9780192848086.003.0007

## 2. The Purpose of a Tribunal Secretary

The purpose of a tribunal secretary is to enhance the efficiency and quality of the arbitral proceeding by decreasing cost, delay, and the administrative burden on parties and tribunals. In most cases "tribunal secretaries add quality and speed to the arbitral process, which is in the best interest of all stakeholders involved".[4] They should, in theory, make international arbitration more attractive and increase party satisfaction with the process.[5] This is particularly so as cost, lack of efficiency, and lack of speed—all issues that tribunal secretaries should ameliorate—were rated in the top four "worst characteristics" of international arbitration in 2015.[6] Unsurprisingly, 71 per cent of respondents to the same survey considered tribunal secretaries to be useful and only 9 per cent thought secretaries were not useful.[7] This suggests that tribunal secretaries are in fact doing the job they were designed to do.

Secretaries are not a new concept, with Swiss legislation having recognized the utility of the tribunal secretary role since 1969.[8] Tribunal secretaries are usually (younger) lawyers who assist a tribunal with a range of tasks from file management and logistical/administrative matters to drafting communications, procedural orders, and possibly elements of the award. Most of these tasks are not controversial.[9]

Tribunal secretaries are used primarily in complex cases, particularly those involving three-member tribunals.[10] Many senior arbitrators use tribunal secretaries on at least some of their cases. Indeed, for arbitrators in high demand, the use of a secretary can be crucial to ensuring the smooth running of their busy practices. In addition, the International Centre for Settlement of Investment Disputes (ICSID), and sometimes the Permanent Court of Arbitration (PCA), have long assigned tribunal secretaries to arbitrations they administer.

The role of a tribunal secretary is often compared to a judge's assistant or clerk, whose presence is common in many jurisdictions.[11] Judge's clerks are a well-accepted position

---

[4] J Ole Jensen, "Aligning Arbitrator Assistance with the Parties' Legitimate Expectations: Proposal of a 'Traffic Light' Scale of Permissible Tribunal Secretary Tasks" (2020) 38 (2) ASA Bulletin, 375, 376,

[5] ibid 377.

[6] "2015 International Arbitration Survey: Improvements and Innovations in International Arbitration", Queen Mary University of London, 7.

[7] ibid 42.

[8] Swiss Intercantonal Arbitration Convention, 27 March 1969, art 15 (see also art 7).

[9] The 2012 Queen Mary Survey found that tasks considered highly controversial by both arbitrators and parties were drafting substantive parts of the award and discussing the merits of the case with the tribunal. For the most part party expectations aligned closely with tasks actually carried out by tribunal secretaries. "2012 International Arbitration Survey: Current and Preferred Practices in the Arbitral Process", Queen Mary University and White & Case, 12 (see also 2015 Queen Mary Survey (n 6) 43) <https://arbitration.qmul.ac.uk/media/arbitration/docs/2012_International_Arbitration_Survey.pdf>. For a more in-depth discussion of potential tasks see J Ole Jensen *Tribunal Secretaries in International Arbitration* (Oxford University Press 2019) Chapter 5.

[10] The 2012 Queen Mary Survey found that tribunal secretaries were used in 35 per cent of international arbitrations (2012 Queen Mary Survey (n 9) 11), but by 2015 53 per cent of respondents said that they had been involved in an arbitration where a tribunal secretary had been appointed (2015 Queen Mary Survey (n 6) 42).

[11] In *A v B*, First Civil Law Court of the Swiss Federal Tribunal, Decision 4A_709/2014, 21 May 2015, the Court held at para 3.2.2: "The role of the legal secretary is comparable to a clerk in state proceedings: to organize the exchange of briefs, to prepare the hearings, to keep the minutes, to prepare the statements of costs, etc. They do not exclude some assistance in drafting the award under the control of and in accordance with the directives from the arbitral tribunal, or if it is not unanimous, from the majority arbitrators, which presupposes that the secretary

and there is little by way of controversy as to the function they perform. The rationale for judge's assistants is also efficiency. It is considered that having an assistant to help with research, preparation, and drafting tasks frees up the judge to concentrate on decision-making.[12] This form of assistance is uncontroversial in judicial circles,[13] but ironically is the very type of assistance that fuels suspicion of tribunal secretaries. In the context of arbitration, as such activities are seen by some as a delegation of the decision-making mandate provided to the arbitrator rather than freeing up time for the arbitrator to concentrate on making the decision.

## 3. The Controversy: The Spectre of the Fourth Arbitrator

Despite a general acceptance of the perceived efficiencies of tribunal secretaries, over the past couple of decades there is evidence of increasing unease amongst users of international arbitration as to the proper role of the tribunal secretary. This unease has stemmed in part from a lack of visibility as to the tasks actually being undertaken by a secretary in any given case and (previously) a lack of clear guidance as to the limits of the role. This is despite the fact that expectations of both tribunals and parties as to the tasks to be performed by tribunal secretaries generally align. The 2012 Queen Mary Survey stated, "the concerns which are often raised regarding tribunal secretaries are generally unjustified: only 10% of arbitrators said that tribunal secretaries appointed in their cases prepared drafts of substantive parts of awards, and only 4% said tribunal secretaries discussed the merits of the dispute with them".[14]

Scrutiny of the role of the tribunal secretary intensified significantly following Russia's challenge to the validity of the *Yukos* awards in the Dutch courts, which included a challenge to the role of the tribunal secretary. The claimants in that case, former shareholders in OAO Yukos Oil Company, were successful in their expropriation claims against Russia under the Energy Charter Treaty. They were awarded over US$50 billion in compensation in July 2014.[15]

In January 2015, the Russian Federation sought to set aside the *Yukos* awards in The Hague District Court. One of the grounds for challenge was that the arbitrators did not

---

participates in the hearings and the deliberations of the arbitral tribunal. However, but for an agreement of the parties to the contrary, the secretary is forbidden from carrying out any function of a judicial nature, which must remain the prerogative of the arbitrators only."

[12] See Consultative Council of European Judges (CCJE), Summary of the responses to the questionnaire for the preparation of the CCJE Opinion No 22 (2019) on "The role of court clerks and legal assistants within the courts and their relationships with judges", Working Document, 13 August 2019 (The International Council for Commercial Arbitration 2015).

[13] Young ICCA Guide on Tribunal Secretaries, 28.

[14] 2012 Queen Mary Survey (n 9) 12.

[15] There were three awards rendered in the arbitration: *Hulley Enterprises Limited (Cyprus) v The Russian Federation*, UNCITRAL, PCA Case No AA 226, Final Award, 18 July 2014; *Yukos Universal Limited (Isle of Man) v The Russian Federation*, UNCITRAL, PCA Case No AA 227, Final Award, 18 July 2014; *Veteran Petroleum Limited (Cyprus) v The Russian Federation*, UNCITRAL, PCA Case No AA 228, Final Award, 18 July 2014 (together the "*Yukos* awards").

personally fulfil their mandate due to the disproportionate participation of the Assistant to the Tribunal in deliberations, analysing evidence and submissions, and drafting the awards.[16] Russia expressly argued that he had fulfilled the role of a "fourth arbitrator" on the tribunal. This argument was made primarily on the basis of the hours invoiced by him but also (famously) on the basis of analysis of the awards by two linguistic experts who considered it likely that he had written large portions of the awards.[17] Russia submitted that this drafting contribution was tantamount to the "outright scrapping of the *intuitu personae* principle or the delegation prohibition applicable to arbitrators".[18]

Russia did not raise any concern about the hours spent on the case by the tribunal secretary and assistant secretary appointed by the PCA.[19] The combined hours of those two individuals significantly exceeded those of the secretary appointed by the tribunal (although Russia did argue that, given the hours spent by the PCA secretaries, the secretary appointed by the tribunal should have had even fewer tasks to perform than usual). Quite rightly, parties do not generally appear to take issue with the role performed by institutional tribunal secretaries.

In 2016, the District Court of the Hague set aside the *Yukos* awards on jurisdictional grounds. The Court did not address the role of the tribunal secretary. In February 2020, the Court of Appeal of The Hague reversed the District Court's decision and reinstated the awards. The Court of Appeal expressly dismissed the allegations relating to the tribunal secretary.[20] However, the case fuelled significant discussion (and suspicion) of the role played by tribunal secretaries behind closed doors.

In 2017, the English High Court considered a challenge against an arbitral tribunal on a similar basis.[21] The complainant in that case also said that, while it had agreed to the appointment of the tribunal secretary, the secretary had spent a disproportionate number of hours on particular tasks compared to other members of the tribunal. Interestingly, this was not a challenge to an award (no substantive award had been issued) but a request to remove the arbitrators.[22] The allegations were based primarily on three procedural rulings.[23]

The Court in both the *Yukos* and English High Court cases dismissed the challenges in strident terms. The decisions are discussed below, but of concern is that such

---

[16] Mr Martin Valasek had the official title of "Assistant to the Tribunal", given that the PCA, as the institution administering the arbitration, itself had appointed a tribunal secretary and also an assistant secretary, but effectively he functioned as secretary to the Yukos Tribunal and hereafter will be referred to as its secretary. The Tribunal did not consult the parties prior to engaging Mr Valasek, but no objection was raised by any party when they were informed of his appointment.

[17] See *Veteran Petroleum Limited et al. v The Russian Federation*, Judgment of the Court of Appeal of The Hague, Civil Law Section, Case No 200.197.079/01, 18 February 2020, at [6.6.2].

[18] *Veteran Petroleum Limited et al. v The Russian Federation* (n 17) [6.6.10] referring to Defence on Appeal no 994.

[19] Mr Brooks Daly was the PCA-appointed tribunal secretary and Ms Judith Levine was the PCA-appointed assistant tribunal secretary. Both were full-time employees of the PCA.

[20] See full discussion in Section 4 of this chapter.

[21] *P v Q and ors* [2017] EWHC 194 (Comm).

[22] The challenge in the High Court involved the two co-arbitrators only, as the presiding arbitrator had been removed by the LCIA on unrelated grounds.

[23] Seventy-five per cent of respondents to the 2015 Queen Mary survey considered that preparing drafts of procedural orders was an appropriate task for a tribunal secretary. (2015 Queen Mary Survey (n 6) 43).

challenges may needlessly reinforce a suspicion of tribunal secretaries, even when they are dismissed by the Court. Nonetheless, it should be recalled that, while colourful controversies such as those described above may fuel concerns about tribunal secretaries, cases in which controversy arises due to tribunal secretary activity are relatively few. In at least some of those situations, a challenge to the tribunal secretary may have been seen as a useful strategy to try to overcome an unfavourable decision. Of course, most cases proceed without any issue as to the secretary's role arising and, as noted above, most parties consider that a tribunal secretary contributes to the efficiency of an arbitration.

## 4. The Prevailing Consensus: Guidance from Arbitral Institutions and the Judiciary

There is a prevailing consensus in the literature and jurisprudence that a tribunal secretary can undertake a wide range of tasks, certainly beyond those considered purely administrative. Indeed, if it were not so, many of the benefits and efficiencies offered by tribunal secretaries would be lost and there would no need to use secretaries with legal training.

In recent years, consensus has also emerged as to the outer limit of a tribunal secretary's tasks. It is now unequivocally accepted that first, a tribunal cannot delegate its decision-making powers to a tribunal secretary and secondly, the tribunal secretary must operate under the supervision and direction of the tribunal. Provided such limits are respected, and there is no agreement of the parties to the contrary, secretaries may assist in intellectual tasks such as research and preparation of drafts directed by the tribunal, as well as providing more mundane assistance such as logistical support and note taking.

### 4.1 Institutional Guidance

In 2014, a seminal piece of work was undertaken by 'Young ICCA'—the youth branch of the International Council for Commercial Arbitration (ICCA). Young ICCA surveyed international arbitration practitioners in 2012 and 2013 and, based on this information, produced a "Guide on Arbitral Secretaries". The survey results clearly showed that there was general support for the role of the tribunal secretary (provided that parties had been consulted on the appointment),[24] but that there was also a need for best practice guidelines.[25]

---

[24] Whether that be through providing consent or being given an opportunity to object (see Young ICCA Guide (n 8) 72–74). Almost 75 per cent of those responding said that an arbitral tribunal should not be able to use a tribunal secretary without formally appointing them and without telling the parties (ibid 75).

[25] Ninety-six per cent of those responding approved of the use of tribunal secretaries and 78 per cent of them supported the development of best practice guidelines (ibid 43, 50–51).

The Young ICCA Guide delineates purely administrative and organizational tasks tribunal secretaries regularly perform, such as logistical support for meetings and hearings and organizing the file.[26] It also specifically states that "[w]ith appropriate direction and supervision by the arbitral tribunal an arbitral secretary's role may legitimately go beyond the purely administrative".[27] Examples of non-administrative tasks that secretaries may perform include research, drafting procedural orders and similar documents, reviewing and summarizing submissions and evidence, and drafting appropriate parts of the award.[28]

In relation to the most controversial task—drafting parts of the substantive award—the commentary in the Guide observes:[29]

> On the question of the drafting of awards (a practice that is long-standing in other fora, including notably the role played by clerks to justices in drafting judicial opinions for US courts), it is surely for the individual arbitrator to determine whether he or she can delegate part or all of the drafting function to an arbitral secretary without jeopardizing decision-making control. On this sensitive subject, dogmatism is unhelpful. For some, the act of drafting is indeed the ultimate safeguard of intellectual control. For others, the same level of control can be achieved in other ways. Ultimately, this surely must be a question for the arbitrator's judgment. And if your arbitrator gets such a significant decision wrong, then the problem is not with the institution of secretaries, it is with the choice of arbitrator.

As will be seen shortly, this is the approach that has been adopted by the courts when considering the appropriate role of tribunal secretaries.

The Young ICCA Guide has been very well-received and is often referred to by tribunals, suggesting that tribunals' practices and users' expectations regarding tribunal secretaries are, in reality, closely aligned. Over the past few years, many arbitral institutions have followed the Young ICCA lead and incorporated specific guidance on the role of tribunal secretaries into their rules or guidance notes. Some arbitral institutions also provide panels of tribunal secretaries for those wishing to engage the services of a secretary, and there are specific training courses available for secretaries wishing to hone their skills.[30]

A brief survey of the guidance provided by arbitral institutions as to the role of the secretary confirms the emergence of the consensus indicated above. Some specific points to note:

---

[26] ibid art 3(2)(a)–(d).

[27] ibid art 3(1).

[28] Article 3(2)(g) and (j). The Guide notes that using secretaries to help draft some parts of the award (including legal reasoning and the operative decisions) is controversial, but the Guide does not specifically exclude assistance in drafting such sections (ibid Commentary to Article 3(2)(j)).

[29] ibid 28.

[30] For example, the Hong Kong International Arbitration Centre and the Australian Centre for International Commercial Arbitration offer panels of tribunal secretaries.

*Consent*: Most arbitral institutions require the parties to consent to the appointment of a secretary or, at least, to have the opportunity to object to the appointment (ie implied consent through lack of objection).

*Definition of role*: Most institutions provide a non-exhaustive list of the tasks that may be performed by a tribunal secretary. Discretion is usually given to the tribunal and the parties to agree an exact list of tasks, but the default list assists in setting expectations as to appropriate tasks.

*Supervision*: An express requirement for tribunal supervision of secretaries is now becoming more common in institutional guidance, reflecting recent jurisprudence that appropriate supervision and direction from arbitrators minimises the risk that a tribunal secretary may encroach on decision-making tasks.

*Impartiality*: Most institutions require the tribunal secretary to remain impartial and independent of the parties at all times and disclose any circumstances likely to give rise to justifiable doubts as to his or her impartiality or independence. This is so, even though the secretary performs no decision-making functions.

It is worth considering a few examples of the guidance provided by arbitral institutions to illustrate the consensus.

### 4.1.1  International Chamber of Commerce (ICC)

The ICC's Note to the parties and to the arbitral tribunals on the conduct of the Arbitration according to the ICC Arbitration Rules was updated in 2021. Secretaries may be appointed where the tribunal considers it appropriate for the particular circumstances of the arbitration, provided that the tribunal has informed the parties and provided them with the proposed secretary's curriculum vitae, a statement of independence and undertakings from the secretary and the tribunal that the secretary will act in accordance with the ICC's Note.[31] The secretary may not be appointed if a party objects.

Once appointed, the secretary must act under the tribunal's strict and continuous supervision. The tribunal cannot delegate its decision-making function or its "essential duties". Any task performed by the secretary does not release the tribunal from its duty to review the file "and/or draft itself any arbitral tribunal's decision".[32] A non-exhaustive list of tasks that a secretary may perform is provided in the Note, including drafting correspondence, preparing factual parts of the award, research, attending and taking notes at meetings, and drafting procedural orders. A secretary must be remunerated by the arbitral tribunal out of the fees paid to the tribunal for the arbitration.[33]

---

[31] ICC Note to the parties and to the arbitral tribunals on the conduct of the Arbitration according to the ICC Arbitration Rules, paras 218–221.

[32] ibid para 223. For an interpretation of this phrase, see the discussion on *European Commission v Emek İnşaat Şti and WTE Wassertechnik* Jugement du Tribunal de première instance francophone de Bruxelles, Section Civile, Jugement 4ème chambre affaire civiles, 17 June 2021 (unofficial English translation) in this chapter.

[33] ibid para 230.

### 4.1.2  London Court of International Arbitration (LCIA)

Article 14A of the LCIA Rules provides guidance on tribunal secretaries. Recent changes to these rules emphasise that the guiding principle is that "under no circumstances may an Arbitral Tribunal delegate its decision-making function to a tribunal secretary" and that supervision by the tribunal is required at all times.[34] Prospective secretaries must sign a declaration that they are impartial and independent and have the capacity to devote sufficient time to the arbitration. Parties' approval is required for the appointment, but this may be implied through a lack of objection within a reasonable time.[35] When seeking parties' consent, the tribunal must agree with the parties the tasks that may be carried out by the secretary and the hourly rate (if any) to be charged.

Somewhat controversially, the LCIA is the only institution that allows parties to directly challenge a tribunal secretary. Challenges will be determined by the LCIA Court in the same way that challenges to arbitrators are determined. The authors are not aware of any challenges that have been made to secretaries using this provision.[36]

The LCIA also provides guidance to tribunals on the use of secretaries.[37] The LCIA's Note to Arbitrators gives examples of the tasks that a tribunal secretary may perform with agreement from the parties.[38] These tasks range from the administrative (including communicating on behalf of the tribunal, organizing documents and procedural matters, proofreading, and invoicing) to more substantive tasks (summarising submissions, reviewing authorities, and preparing drafts of awards (or parts thereof) and procedural orders).

### 4.1.3  Hong Kong Court of International Arbitration (HKIAC)

The HKIAC provides a renowned training course for tribunal secretaries and also offers the services of its staff as secretaries to tribunals. As with the institutions discussed earlier, the HKIAC's Guidelines on tribunal secretaries emphasize the need for secretaries to act under the tribunal's strict instruction and supervision.[39] As expected, arbitral tribunals are prohibited from delegating any decision-making functions or "essential duties" to the secretary.[40] The tribunal must consult the parties before appointing the secretary, and the secretary must provide similar declarations to those required by the ICC and LCIA.

The HKIAC's non-exhaustive list of permitted tasks includes administrative functions, as well as undertaking legal research, preparing summaries of the submissions and evidence, and preparing drafts of the non-substantive parts of awards and decisions.[41] The HKIAC Guidelines appear narrower in the scope of the permitted tasks as

---

[34] LCIA Rules (2021) art 14.8.

[35] ibid art 14.12. Implied approval is a recent change to the Rules, so as to prevent a party from unnecessarily delaying proceedings by not expressly providing its approval.

[36] The LCIA publishes a challenge digest which is available on its website and provides anonymised summaries and extracts from challenge decisions. Currently decisions between 2010 and 2017 are available.

[37] LCIA Notes for Arbitrators (2014 Rules). The LCIA is in the process of updating this Note for the 2020 Rules.

[38] LCIA Notes for Arbitrators, para 71.

[39] HKIAC Guidelines on the Use of a Secretary to the Arbitral Tribunal (1 June 2014), para 3.1.

[40] ibid para 3.2.

[41] ibid para 3.4.

they expressly state that a tribunal is not released from its duty personally to draft substantive parts of the award or of any decision.[42]

## 4.2  Judicial Decisions on the Role of the Tribunal Secretary

The courts have also provided clear guidance regarding the limits to the role of the tribunal secretary. It is evident that the courts generally will not intervene in cases alleging procedural misconduct in relation to a tribunal secretary, except in the most egregious of cases. It is useful to briefly outline the relevant jurisprudence in this area.

### 4.2.1  Total Support Management v Diversified Health Systems

Total Support Management (Pty) Ltd v Diversified Health Systems (SA) (Pty) Ltd is a 2002 case in the South African Supreme Court of Appeal.[43] The appellant challenged the award on the basis of procedural irregularity due to the extent of the role played by the tribunal secretary. The appellant said it had been unaware, when it agreed to the appointment of the secretary, that his role would be so extensive and claimed the award was essentially the decision of the secretary. The case was based primarily on the hours invoiced by the secretary.[44]

The Court accepted that the secretary's role was undefined but did not find it credible that the appellant would have assumed that the secretary would play only "a formal or secretarial role in the arbitration".[45] All parties accepted that the secretary had in fact assisted with a range of tasks including research and preparing the first draft of the award. In addition, the arbitrator said that he had discussed the merits of the arbitration with the secretary.

The Court held that an arbitrator must personally determine the dispute and that this function cannot be delegated. The Court found nothing objectionable about the secretary being closely involved in the arbitration, provided decision-making was not abdicated. The Court said "ultimately the question to be asked, and answered, is whether the arbitrator exercised his own judgment in deciding the issues. This will depend upon the facts of each particular case."[46] The Court answered this question by saying that the arbitrator had provided proper instructions to the secretary prior to the draft award being prepared and had thoroughly reviewed and revised the draft thereafter. Consequently, there was no evidence that the arbitrator had been influenced (consciously or unconsciously) by the secretary in making his decision.[47] The challenge was dismissed.

---

[42] ibid para 3.6.
[43] *Total Support Management (Pty) Ltd v Diversified Health Systems (SA) (Pty) Ltd* [2002] ZASCA 14.
[44] ibid [37].
[45] ibid [42].
[46] ibid [41].
[47] ibid [46].

### 4.2.2 *Sonatrach v Statoil*

In 2014, Sonatrach applied to set aside an ICC award under section 68 of the English Arbitration Act 1996 on the grounds that the Tribunal had (i) overlooked or mischaracterized crucial evidence and (ii) misused the administrative secretary.[48]

The Tribunal had informed both parties of its intention to use a tribunal secretary to help prepare notes for the deliberations. The Tribunal invited the parties to confirm by a specified date whether they had any objection to the appointment. No objection was raised. Sonatrach suggested that the tribunal secretary had exceeded her remit by impermissibly participating in the Tribunal's deliberations. In the end, no specific submissions were made on this point but it was not formally withdrawn.

Mr Justice Flaux of the English High Court said that it was standard practice for tribunal secretaries to produce notes to assist the tribunal (as occurred in this case) but that this did not mean that a secretary had participated in deliberations.[49] The Court showed little tolerance for arguments concerning the role of the tribunal secretary made without a solid evidential foundation. Flaux J rebuked Sonatrach for attempting to have the award set aside on this ground without proper evidence. He dismissed the allegation of participation in the decision-making process saying, in no uncertain terms, that it was "a very serious allegation which [was] completely without merit and which should never have been made".[50]

### 4.2.3 *P v Q*

In *P v Q*,[51] the respondent in an LCIA arbitration challenged the Tribunal for failing to properly supervise the tribunal secretary (with reference to three procedural decisions) and for improper delegation of tasks to the secretary. This latter allegation was partly based on an email from the presiding arbitrator to the secretary asking for his reaction to a certain piece of correspondence. The email had accidently been sent to the respondent.

The LCIA Court removed the presiding arbitrator for unrelated reasons, but the LCIA Court dismissed the allegations relating to the role of the tribunal secretary. The Respondent took its case against the remaining two co-arbitrators to the English High Court.

In his judgment, Popplewell J gave useful guidance on the role of the tribunal secretary. He was clear that the line of impropriety is only crossed when an arbitrator delegates his or her decision-making power to another person, such as a tribunal secretary. Any work done by a tribunal secretary on behalf of the tribunal must be undertaken on instruction from the tribunal and must be properly supervised.[52] He said that decision-making meant independent judgment and noted that a tribunal was not prohibited

---

[48] *La Societe pour La Recherche, La Production, Le Transport, La Transformation, et La Commercialisation des Hydrocarbures SPA ("Sonatrach") v Statoil Natural Gas LLC* [2014] EWHC 875 (Comm).
[49] ibid [48].
[50] [46].
[51] *P v Q* (n 21) 21.
[52] ibid [65].

from seeking the views of others, including the tribunal secretary, although he did caution the need for care in doing so.[53]

In its challenge, the respondent partly relied on the hours spent by the co-arbitrators reviewing three procedural decisions, compared to the hours spent by the presiding arbitrator and secretary. Popplewell J held that the time spent by the co-arbitrators reviewing the draft procedural decisions was sufficient, given the nature of the decisions, and that it was common practice for the presiding arbitrator to prepare initial drafts for the co-arbitrators' review.[54] The presiding arbitrator was required to supervise the tribunal secretary properly when doing so, but the co-arbitrators had no duty to supervise president's interactions with the secretary.[55]

Having reviewed a range of guidelines on the subject of tribunal secretaries, Popplewell J concluded that:[56]

> [w]hatever the divergence of views amongst practitioners and commentators as to best practice, the critical yardstick for the purposes of section 24 of the 1996 Act is that the use of a tribunal secretary must not involve any member of the tribunal abrogating or impairing his non-delegable and personal decision-making function. That function requires each member of the tribunal to bring his own personal and independent judgment to bear on the decision in question, taking account of the rival submissions of the parties; and to exercise reasonable diligence in going about discharging that function. What is required in practice will vary infinitely with the nature of the decision and the circumstances of each case.

Popplewell J did note that the parties had not agreed any limits to the tribunal secretary's role in this case. Had the parties done so, the Tribunal would have been obliged to respect those limits. Finally, on a separate note, the Court was critical of the respondent for changes made to certain allegations against the co-arbitrators, which echoed criticism in *Sonatrach*. Popplewell J said:[57]

> This changing pattern of allegations is entirely inappropriate on an application under section 24(1)(d) of the 1996 Act. An allegation against an arbitrator that he has failed properly to conduct the reference so as to cause substantial injustice is a serious allegation. It should only be made after careful consideration. It should be formulated with precision.

### 4.2.4 *Yukos*

As discussed above, the District Court of The Hague initially set aside the *Yukos* awards on jurisdictional grounds. This decision was reversed by The Hague Court of Appeal.

---

[53] ibid [67].
[54] ibid [33].
[55] ibid [45] and [76].
[56] ibid [65].
[57] ibid [30].

As a result of reversing the jurisdictional decision, the Court of Appeal decided to consider the other arguments advanced by Russia for annulment—including the role played by the tribunal secretary.

Russia had challenged his role based primarily on the number of hours undertaken by him compared to the tribunal members and (remarkably) a linguistic analysis of the text of the award. The Court rejected Russia's submission that the tribunal had delegated inappropriately to the tribunal secretary, finding no proof of over-delegation. The Court found the studies of Russia's linguistic experts to be "problematic", but said that it would nonetheless assume that the tribunal secretary had drafted significant contributions to the award that may have been incorporated in whole or in part by the arbitrators.[58]

The Court did not consider such drafting to be evidence that the tribunal secretary was involved in the decision-making process because the simple act of drafting did not: (i) establish that the secretary had advised on the merits of the parties' arguments; (ii) that the tribunal had delegated any decision to the secretary; (iii) that the drafting took place before the tribunal had made its decisions; or (iv) that the drafts influenced the decision-making of the tribunal in any way.[59]

The Court held that, even if substantive sections of the award are drafted by a secretary under instruction, it is up to the arbitrators to check the text for correctness and completeness. It considered that secretaries were permitted to draft parts of the award, including substantive findings, provided that the arbitrators "assume responsibility for the draft versions of [the secretary's text]" and do not simply accept it without "a second thought".[60] In the Court's view, the mandate given to the tribunal would only be violated if the secretary had had final responsibility for certain parts of the award. For this reason, the drafting of any section in an award by a tribunal secretary does not imply that the secretary independently made decisions.[61]

An exception would be where the parties had expressly agreed that such tasks were prohibited.[62] There had been no such agreement in the *Yukos* case. However, the Court did acknowledge Russia's contention that the Tribunal failed to fully inform the parties in advance of the secretary's role, only introducing the secretary as "an assistant and contact person". Assuming this was true, the Court concluded that "the Tribunal failed to fully inform the parties on this point of the nature of [the secretary's] work. However, under the circumstances, this does not constitute such a serious violation of the mandate that it should lead to the setting aside of the arbitral awards."[63]

The Hague Court of Appeal's decision has now been referred to the Dutch Supreme Court. In the Supreme Court, Russia alleges that the Court of Appeal's findings on the tribunal secretary were wrong on six grounds, including that the Court of Appeal failed

---

[58] *Veteran Petroleum Limited et al. v Russia*, (n 17) [6.6.5].
[59] ibid [6.6.6].
[60] ibid [6.6.10].
[61] ibid [6.6.10].
[62] ibid [6.6.14].
[63] ibid [6.6.14.2].

to recognise an (unwritten) rule that a secretary cannot write substantive parts of an arbitral award without express permission from the parties, and that the Court was wrong to find that the Tribunal's failure to fully inform the parties of the nature of the secretary's tasks was not a "serious" violation of its mandate.[64]

At the time of writing, the decision of the Dutch Supreme Court was pending, but was widely expected to confirm the Court of Appeal decision. In December 2020, the Supreme Court refused an application by Russia to suspend the enforcement of the awards while the Supreme Court determines the appeal. The Supreme Court said that, in its provisional assessment, the probability of Russia's complaints succeeding (including the complaint regarding the role of the tribunal secretary) was not such that it would justify suspension of enforcement.[65]

In addition, in a non-binding opinion, the Advocate-General of the Supreme Court, Mr Paul Vlas, has recommended that the Supreme Court reject Russia's appeal and follow the decision in the Court of Appeal.[66] In Mr Vlas' view, the findings of the Court of Appeal were correct and comprehensible and Russia's appeal should fail.[67] He stated that there was no generally accepted rule or practice that a secretary is not allowed to write substantive parts of an arbitral award, which is why some arbitral rules explicitly address the matter. If the applicable rules do not address the issue, a tribunal has discretion to delegate certain tasks to the secretary, as long as they fulfil their own duties.[68]

### 4.2.5 *European Commission v Emek İnşaat Şti and WTE Wassertechnikrussels*

At the time of writing, the most recent judicial pronouncement on the role of tribunal secretaries was from the Brussels Court of First Instance.[69]

This case involved a dispute between the European Commission and two contractors Emek İnşaat Şti and WTE Wassertechnikrussels. The parties had entered into a contract for the construction of sewers, water pipes, and sewage pump stations in Cyprus and an issue had arisen has to which party was responsible for alleged defects in the system. An FIDIC (International Federation of Consulting Engineers) adjudicator initially ruled in favour of the contractors, but the Commission commenced an ICC arbitration seated in Belgium in 2017. The arbitral tribunal issued a partial award on liability in favour of the European Commission.[70]

The contractors challenged the partial award in a Belgian Court on several grounds, including that the tribunal secretary had assisted with tasks that should have been undertaken by the tribunal itself. These tasks included drawing up a set of questions asked by the President of the Tribunal to the experts during the hearing and drafting all

---

[64] Opinion of the Advocate General of the Supreme Court of The Netherlands, No 20/01595, 23 April 2021, [3.193]–[3.195].

[65] *Russia v Hulley Enterprises Limited et al.*, Judgment of the Supreme Court of The Netherlands, Civil Law Division, Case Number 20/01892, 4 December 2020.

[66] Opinion (n 64).

[67] ibid [3.192]–[3.201].

[68] ibid [3.186].

[69] *European Commission v Emek İnşaat Şti and WTE Wassertechnik* (n 32).

[70] Partial Award on Liability, 11 February 2020 (Tribunal: Andreas Reiner (President), Vera Van Houtte and Jean-Marie Vulliemin).

or part of the decision-making section of the award, including the reasoning for the decision. The contractors submitted that these acts constituted an "excess of power" by the tribunal secretary and that this over-delegation vitiated both the constitution of the tribunal and the arbitral procedure itself.[71] The contactors argued that the award should be set aside under the Belgian Civil Code.

On 17 June 2021, the Brussels Court of First Instance dismissed the application. Importantly the Court held that allowing a tribunal secretary to write all or part of an award was permissible under the ICC Rules.[72] The Court based this ruling on the wording on paragraph 187 of the ICC's "Note to Parties and Arbitral Tribunals on the Conduct of the Arbitration" (2019), which the Court considered implicitly (but certainly) authorizes a tribunal secretary to write drafts of the award, provided that the tribunal reviews and amends the draft, following its own examination of the evidence and submissions.[73] Paragraph 187 of the 2019 ICC Note states:

> A request by an arbitral tribunal to an administrative secretary to prepare written notes or memoranda shall in no circumstances release the arbitral tribunal from its duty personally to review the file and/or to draft any decision of the arbitral tribunal.

The Court held that this paragraph authorises a tribunal to rely on its secretary to draft parts of an arbitral award or even the entire award, as long as the tribunal reviews and corrects the draft according to its own views. The Court said that, had the ICC intended to exclude this possibility, it would not have used the words "and/or" in this paragraph.[74]

The key, according to the Court, was that the tribunal must not delegate its "power to judge".[75] The Court said that, allowing a tribunal secretary to draft all of part of any award was not "in itself, sufficient to demonstrate a delegation of the decision-making power of the arbitrators".[76]

Similarly, the Court held that there was no evidence that the tribunal president was not properly prepared for the hearing. The President of the Tribunal confirmed that the secretary had prepared a list of questions for the expert that he had reviewed in advance of the hearing. He also confirmed that the secretary had attended discussions among the tribunal members but did not participate in them. Finally, the President said that the secretary had assisted in drafting some parts of the award, but there was "not a single sentence in the award and not a single footnote that has not at least been reviewed, verified and if necessary, corrected by me in the light of my point of view

---

[71] *European Commission v Emek İnşaat Şti* (n 32) [66].
[72] ibid [77].
[73] ibid [77]. Note that the 2021 version of the Note to Parties and Arbitral Tribunals differs slightly. The provisions relating to the tribunal secretary can be found at paragraphs 216–230. Paragraph 223 contains similar wording to paragraph 187 of the 2019 Note.
[74] ibid [78].
[75] ibid [73].
[76] ibid [81].

THE DEATH OF THE "FOURTH ARBITRATOR"    137

and the deliberations of the Arbitral Tribunal".[77] The co-arbitrators confirmed that the award was the product of the Tribunal's joint intellectual endeavours.

The Court accepted this evidence and dismissed the allegation of improper delegation by the Tribunal.

## 5. The Death of the "Fourth Arbitrator"

The use of tribunal secretaries is widespread and, for the most part, parties consider tribunal secretaries to be helpful. The issue it seems is not tribunal secretaries themselves but concerns about transparency and regulation. With the clarity now brought to the role of tribunal secretaries by courts and arbitral institutions, much of this concern should dissipate. In our view, the jurisprudence emphasizes two key principles that are at the heart of allaying concerns about the function of the tribunal secretary: the personal mandate of the tribunal to decide the dispute and the consent of the parties to the appointment of a secretary and the scope of his or her role.

### 5.1 Personal Mandate

In most arbitrations, the parties choose the members of the arbitral tribunal.[78] In accepting the appointment, the arbitrator undertakes personally to decide the dispute before the tribunal. This personal mandate was recognized long before any controversy over tribunal secretaries arose. In 1989, the Italian Supreme Court said that arbitrators who had no legal training had breached their mandate by appointing a lawyer as an expert to draft the award for them.[79] Legal decision-making was a task which could not be delegated.[80] The Supreme Court noted that "[d]ue to the arbitrators' professed incapacity to decide issues other than technical construction problems, it amounted to delegating a third person to formulate the final decision, which the arbitrators were not able to conceive and which they could not critically examine once it had been drafted".[81]

This personal mandate to decide the dispute is not inconsistent, however, with receiving help from a junior lawyer in delivering an efficient and effective service. As noted in *P v Q*, exercising independent judgment by arbitrators is key.[82] If an arbitrator makes his or her decision having analysed the evidence and then instructs an assistant to prepare the initial draft of certain parts of the award based on that arbitrator's instructions, that mandate is fulfilled, provided the draft is thoroughly reviewed and

---

[77] ibid [41].
[78] Standard practice is for each party to nominate an arbitrator and then for the two nominated arbitrators to select a presiding arbitrator after consultation with the parties.
[79] *Sacheri v Robotto*, 7 June 1989 ("Decision", excerpt available in Yearbook Commercial Arbitration (1991) 16 156–57).
[80] ibid paras 3 and 4.
[81] ibid para 1.
[82] *P v Q* (n 21) [67].

adopted by the arbitrator. Such a process reflects the way that many judges operate and has been endorsed by the courts.

There is no doubt that this process requires arbitrators to know and understand the submissions and evidence in the case before them. An arbitrator cannot make an informed decision on any issue without having properly reviewed the materials.

In our view, however, the mandate does not *require* the tribunal members to summarise the materials themselves (for the purpose of the award) or to draft memoranda, notes, or even sections of the award without assistance. The courts recognize that the process of decision-making varies among arbitrators and they give proper and deserved deference to arbitrators in respect of this process. It is trite to say arbitrators will all have their own way of ensuring the intellectual integrity of the award they sign. For some arbitrators the writing process will be an integral part of the way in which they make their decision. For those arbitrators, delegating the writing of substantive parts of the award would be inappropriate. For others, decisions are made through reviewing and reflecting on the submissions and evidence, and through discussion with their fellow arbitrators. If a tribunal comes to a decision through this method and provides appropriate instructions to an assistant to draft the decision, which is then carefully reviewed and amended by the tribunal, it is difficult to see how this process could involve any improper delegation of decision-making. The key is that the tribunal provides the initial instruction, supervises the assistant properly, and takes ownership of the final product. In this way, the tribunal adopts the drafting for itself.

In practice, this is no different to the way most awards by three-member tribunals are prepared. It is well-accepted that three-member arbitral tribunals do not draft awards "by committee". This does not mean that those arbitrators who did not draft an award (or sections of it) somehow relinquished their decision-making power. If this were so, on every three-member tribunal there would always be two members who had breached their mandate in some respects. Therefore, it cannot be said that an award must be personally written by an arbitrator in order for that arbitrator to have made the decision. Popplewell J confirmed as much in *P v Q*. An arbitrator who has reviewed, refined, and adopted draft text prepared by someone else (including by a fellow arbitrator) still fulfils his or her mandate to make their own decision.

Ultimately, it is a question of the integrity and professional conscience of the arbitrators to ensure that they fulfil the personal mandate they have been given. Arbitrators who fail to do so are unlikely to be reappointed. Of course, transparency assists parties in having confidence that this mandate is being fulfilled. For this reason, consent of the parties is important to the legitimacy of the tribunal secretary role.

## 5.2  Consent

The deference given by the courts to arbitral tribunals in their use of tribunal secretaries is limited by any agreement of the parties on the tasks to be performed by the secretary. The institutional guidance reviewed above confirms this position.

If the parties have expressly limited the role of the tribunal secretary to certain tasks, then this must be respected by the tribunal. Any breach of this agreement is a procedural issue that may be sufficiently serious to endanger the award (whether it is sufficiently serious will be matter for the court to determine in any given case).

Consent aids transparency and ensures that parties have an opportunity to help shape the secretary's role and define its scope. This, in turn, should give the parties confidence that the tribunal secretary is undertaking appropriate tasks. Through seeking party consent, arbitrators are better able to determine which (if any) elements of the tribunal secretary's role the parties may have concerns about, and respond accordingly. Once parties are made fully aware of the pertinent aspects of the tribunal secretary's role, the risk of challenges or other issues arising is greatly reduced.

There are differing practices between institutions as to whether express consent to the appointment of a tribunal secretary is required. Some institutions require such express consent, while others simply require the tribunal to consult with the parties and provide an opportunity for objections to be raised. In either case, an opportunity for a party to be heard is the primary factor. It is doubtful, based on the cases to date, that a failure to gain consent (express or implied) to the appointment of a secretary would be sufficient to have an award set aside. It is nonetheless clear that the courts expect tribunals to do so. In *Yukos*, the Court of Appeal said that the failure to inform the parties properly of the role being undertaken by the secretary was a procedural breach, though not so serious as to warrant setting aside the awards.[83]

In our view, it is unlikely that a tribunal appointing a secretary these days would do so without appropriate discussion with the parties, especially if acting under institutional rules. This is a welcome innovation and should be applied by tribunals, regardless of whether it is required by an institution. Communication is key to allaying fears and suspicions (even unfounded ones) of tribunal secretaries.

In seeking consent, tribunals routinely explain and clarify to the parties the tasks that will be performed by the secretary. This need not be an exhaustive list, but may simply refer to a set of guidelines or rules or define the limits of the role. A clear appointment process, culminating in formal terms of appointment, is likely to increase transparency and confidence in the tribunal secretary's role.[84] Formal appointment terms also allow a tribunal secretary to confirm lack of conflicts and agree to be bound by confidentiality obligations.[85] The immunity of the secretary should also be confirmed by the parties.[86] This provides protection for the tribunal secretary in line with that given to most arbitrators under statute, arbitral rules or terms of appointment.

---

[83] See also *A v B* (n 11) para 3.2.2.

[84] Jensen, "Aligning Arbitrator Assistance with the Parties' Legitimate Expectations (n 4).

[85] IBA Guidelines on Conflict of Interest in International Arbitration 2014 (IBA Guidelines) provide that both "secretaries and assistants to the Arbitral Tribunal are bound by the same duty of independence and impartiality (including the duty of disclosure) as arbitrators" (IBA Guidelines, General Standard 5(b)).

[86] The HKIAC Guidelines (para 3.8) grant immunity to the secretary (except for dishonest acts), but this may not be automatic under other institutional rules or where no such rules apply.

## 6.  Conclusion

The plethora of institutional guidance now available and the recent decisions from a range of courts across several jurisdictions have brought much clarity to the proper role of the tribunal secretary. While there are still some differences in approach, the fundamental limits of the role have now been properly defined.

It is well accepted that the tasks routinely performed by tribunal secretaries go beyond purely administrative tasks. This is recognized in almost all arbitral rules and judicial pronouncements. There is nothing wrong or surprising about this and such assistance does not mean that the tribunal has abdicated its decision-making responsibilities. Provided that the tribunal communicates clearly with the parties when appointing the secretary, the parties should feel confident as to the scope of the role being performed by the secretary and, of course, in the integrity of their appointed arbitrators to properly perform their role and supervise the secretary.

The cases discussed in this chapter show that challenges to awards or tribunals on the basis of the role of the tribunal secretary should not be made lightly. The authors are not aware of any successful challenges to awards or arbitrators, based on the use (or misuse) of tribunal secretaries. Any party wishing to succeed on such a challenge will need to provide clear proof that the role has been exceeded and that the arbitrators have failed to perform their core functions. Basing such a challenge on circumstantial evidence (such as the number of hours undertaken by a secretary) is not sufficient to substantiate an allegation that a tribunal has delegated decision-making powers. Now that the guidance is clear, and to avoid the tribunal secretary's role being used as a vehicle for unmeritorious challenges to unfavourable awards, courts should generally consider awarding costs on an increased basis against any party mounting an untenable challenge.

The role of the tribunal secretary, when properly utilized, undoubtedly increases the efficiency and quality of the arbitral process. If tribunals clearly communicate with the parties at the appointment stage, the benefits brought to the arbitration by the secretary are obvious. It is unhelpful, in the wake of the clear guidelines that now exist, to keep the spectre of the fourth arbitrator alive . . . may it rest in peace.

# 8

# The Past and Future of ICSID Additional Facility Dispute Settlement

*Meg Kinnear and Randi Ayman*

## 1. Introduction

In 1978, almost twelve years after the founding of the International Centre for Settlement of Investment Disputes (ICSID or the Centre), the Administrative Council of ICSID established the ICSID Additional Facility (AF 1978). The AF 1978 offered arbitration and conciliation in investor–state disputes (ISDS) that were unable to rely on the ICSID Convention rules due to an absence of jurisdiction under the Convention.[1] This situation arose most frequently in arbitration and conciliation of investment disputes between parties, one of which was not an ICSID Contracting State or a national of an ICSID Contracting State. It might also arise in arbitration and conciliation of investment disputes that did not arise "directly" out of an investment, even if at least one of the parties was an ICSID Contracting State or national of a Contracting State.[2] The AF 1978 also offered fact-finding in ISDS disputes.[3] The AF was thus an "additional" mechanism, as suggested by its name, and not an alternative or competitor to proceedings under the ICSID Convention.[4] Indeed, when the AF was first proposed, some delegates were concerned that the availability of the AF might disincentivize new ICSID membership and so it was initially launched for a five-year trial period.[5] These concerns turned out to be unwarranted, and the Administrative Council permanently adopted the AF 1978 in 1984.[6]

By 30 October 2022, 72 AF arbitrations and two AF conciliations had been commenced.[7] The majority of these AF proceedings were initiated based on consent in

---

[1] The Convention on the Settlement of Investment Disputes between States and Nationals of Other States (the Washington Convention or the ICSID Convention) (signed on 18 March 1965, entered into force on 14 October 1966). The requirements for jurisdiction under the ICSID Convention as set out in Article 25 are: (i) The existence of a legal dispute that directly arises out of an investment; (ii) Between an ICSID Member State and a national of another ICSID Member State; (iii) To which the parties to the dispute consent in writing to submit to the Centre.

[2] ICSID Additional Facility Rules, 2006, Booklet, Introduction; Additional Facility Rules, art 2(a) and (b).

[3] Additional Facility Rules, art 2(c).

[4] ICSID Additional Facility Rules, 1979, Booklet, Article 4, Comment (i), 5.

[5] Resolution of the Administrative Council, AC (12)/RES/38, adopted by the Administrative Council of the Centre at its Twelfth Annual Meeting on 27 September 1978, ICSID Annual Report 1978/1979, 33.

[6] For the evolution of the AF Rules, see Aron Broches, "The 'Additional Facility' of the International Centre for Settlement of Investment Disputes (ICSID)" (1979) IV Yearbook of Commercial Arbitration 373; and Antonio Parra, *The History of ICSID* (2nd edn, Oxford University Press 2017) 134–35, 193–94, 223–37.

[7] See ICSID Case Database, <https://icsid.worldbank.org/cases/case-database>.

Meg Kinnear and Randi Ayman, *The Past and Future of ICSID Additional Facility Dispute Settlement* In: *By Peaceful Means*. Edited by: Charles N Brower, Joan E Donoghue, Cian C Murphy, Cymie R Payne and Esmé R Shirlow, Oxford University Press.

an international investment treaty, in particular the North American Free Trade Agreement (NAFTA) before Canada and Mexico joined ICSID,[8] and Venezuelan bilateral investment treaties (BITs) after its withdrawal from ICSID membership.[9] A handful of AF cases have invoked a domestic investment law as the instrument of consent, and one AF case relied on contractual consent.[10]

Since its adoption in 1978, the AF has undergone three rounds of amendment.[11] First, in 2003 the AF rules were amended to make them more consistent with the Convention Rules, thus eliminating unnecessary differences between the two sets of rules.[12] Further revisions were introduced in 2006, in particular aligning the AF rules with the amendments to the Convention arbitration and conciliation rules of 2006.[13] The most substantial amendment of the AF and its rules occurred in 2022, with the comprehensive rules amendment process undertaken by ICSID from 2016 to 2022, and adopted by Member States effective 1 July 2022.

This chapter will focus on the 2022 version of the AF Rules (AF 2022). The 2022 revisions of the AF Rules can be grouped into four categories. First, the availability of AF conciliation and arbitration was expanded with the adoption of new ICSID AF Rules.[14] These make AF arbitration and conciliation available in cases where neither disputing party is affiliated with a Contracting State, where only one disputing party is a Contracting State or national of a Contracting State, or if a regional economic integration organization (REIO) is a disputing party (Section 2). Second, the procedural rules for AF arbitration[15] and conciliation[16] were modified and, in most cases, have been further aligned with their counterparts in ICSID Convention arbitration and conciliation. In addition, a set of AF Administrative and Financial Regulations was adopted for AF cases (Section 3).[17] Third, the Fact-Finding Rules became a stand-alone feature and have been significantly updated (Section 4).[18] Fourth, new Mediation Rules have been adopted as a stand-alone ruleset and are available by consent of the parties in cases which might also be the subject of AF arbitration or conciliation (Section 5).[19]

---

[8] Nineteen AF cases have been based on NAFTA Chapter 11.

[9] Sixteen AF cases have been based on Venezuelan investment treaties.

[10] See the ICSID Case Database at <https://icsid.worldbank.org/cases/case-database>.

[11] See overview of amendments at: <https://icsid.worldbank.org/news-and-events/speeches-articles/brief-history-amendment-icsid-rules-and-regulations>.

[12] Parra (n 6) 221–24.

[13] ibid 221–30. For a detailed discussion of the operation of the AF under the 2006 rules and relevant jurisprudence, see Aurélia Antonietti and Randi Ayman, "Additional Facility Arbitration Rules (2006): International Centre for Settlement of Investment Disputes (ICSID)" in Hélène Ruiz Fabri (ed), *Max Planck Encyclopedia of International Procedural Law* (Oxford University Press March 2020).

[14] <https://icsid.worldbank.org/sites/default/files/documents/ICSID_Additional_Facility.pdf>.

[15] <https://icsid.worldbank.org/sites/default/files/Additional_Facility_Arbitration_Rules.pdf>.

[16] <https://icsid.worldbank.org/sites/default/files/Additional_Facility_Conciliation_Rules.pdf>.

[17] <https://icsid.worldbank.org/sites/default/files/Additional_Facility_Administrative_Financial_Regulations.pdf>.

[18] <https://icsid.worldbank.org/sites/default/files/documents/ICSID_Fact-Finding.pdf>.

[19] <https://icsid.worldbank.org/sites/default/files/documents/ICSID_Mediation.pdf>.

## 2.  Expanded Scope of the AF Rules

The AF Rules of 2022 authorize the Centre to administer AF proceedings concerning investment disputes where the nationality of the disputing parties, the subject matter of the dispute, or the type of proceeding is not covered by the ICSID Convention. Effectively, this means that ICSID Rules are available in all investment disputes, either under the Convention or under the Additional Facility. The new AF Rules both expand access to the AF and simplify the provisions outlining its scope.

The AF Rules establish the scope of application of the AF in four short articles, addressing definitions (Article 1), AF jurisdiction (Article 2), the relationship of the AF to the ICSID Convention (Article 3), and the rules applicable to AF proceedings (Article 4). The AF Rules are followed by three sets of procedural rules: the Additional Facility Arbitration Rules (AF AR), the Additional Facility Conciliation Rules (AF CR), and the Additional Facility Administrative and Financial Regulations (AF AFR).

### 2.1  Definitions

Article 1 contains definitions necessary to understand the scope of the 2022 AF Rules. The provision maintains the definitions of "Secretariat", "Centre", and "Convention" found in the 2006 AF Rules and deletes the definition of "Secretary-General". This deletion reflects the fact that there is no longer a specific role for the Secretary-General in initiation of an AF case as the approval of access requirement has been abolished.

Several new definitions have been added in Article 1 to reflect the expanded scope of the AF Rules. Article 1(4) defines a Regional Economic Integration Organization as "an organization constituted by States to which they have transferred competence in respect of matters governed by these [AF] Rules, including the authority to make decisions binding on them in respect of such matters". This definition is required because the amended AF is available for cases commenced by or against an REIO (assuming this is offered by the instrument of consent). It reflects the fact that increasingly investment obligations are undertaken by REIOs in their own name.[20] The definition of REIO in the AF is based on the definition of REIO in numerous international instruments, including the Energy Charter Treaty, the Food and Agriculture Organization Constitution, and the World Health Organization Framework Convention on Tobacco Control.[21]

Article 1(5) defines national of another state. In contrast with the previous rules which referred simply to a person who did not have the nationality of the host state,[22]

---

[20] See eg Comprehensive Economic and Trade Agreement between the European Union and Canada Article 8.23.7(b); European Union and Vietnam Investment Protection Agreement, Article 3.33.2(b); European Union and Singapore Investment Protection Agreement, Article 3.6.1(b).

[21] See ICSID Rules Amendment Working Paper (WP) # 1, paras 930–934 and WP # 4, para 197.

[22] Article 1(6) of the 2006 AF Rules.

this definition now refers to natural or juridical persons who are nationals of a state other than the state party to the dispute or other than any constituent state of an REIO party to the dispute. Using the phrase "other than the State party to the dispute" in the new AF Rules (instead of "not a national of the State party to the dispute") allows states to determine in their instrument of consent whether dual nationals holding host state nationality could commence proceedings.[23] In addition, Article 1(5)(b) includes juridical persons that are nationals of one of the disputing parties but which the parties have agreed not to treat as a national for the purposes of the AF Rules. Article 1(5) also clarifies that nationality is to be assessed "on the date of consent to the proceeding", a point which was not express in the previous AF Rules.

These definitions diverge from the ICSID Convention with respect to the nationality requirement in three ways. First, the nationality of a natural person under the 2022 AF Rules is assessed only on the date of consent, whereas the Convention looks at the date of consent and the date of the request for arbitration or conciliation. In practice, the date of consent and the date of the request often coincide, given that most cases are based on a treaty or a law and in such circumstances, the investor usually provides their consent in the request for arbitration or conciliation. However, it may be especially useful in the context of cases based on contract, where consent is likely to be included in the contract as of the date of the contract, but the request for arbitration or conciliation might be made subsequently. Second, the definition of a juridical person under the Convention specifically refers to foreign control, whereas foreign control is not expressly included in the AF. This provides the disputing parties with greater flexibility to tailor the relevant requirements through their treaty, contract, or law. Third, the AF definition gives parties greater flexibility by adding the "unless otherwise agreed" clause in the chapeau of Article 1(5). Indeed, most AF tribunals considering whether an investor qualified as a national of a state under the former rules looked to the criteria in the underlying instrument of consent.[24] Only a few tribunals in prior AF arbitrations applied the criteria developed by ICSID Convention jurisprudence.[25]

## 2.2  Jurisdiction

Article 2, titled "Additional Facility Proceedings", is the key provision conferring jurisdiction under the 2022 AF Rules. Article 2(1) authorizes AF arbitration or conciliation to settle legal disputes arising out of an investment between a state or REIO and a national of another state which the parties consent in writing to submit to the Centre if:

---

[23] WP # 2, paras 565–566.

[24] See eg *Metalclad Corporation v Mexico*, ICSID Case No ARB(AF)/97/1, Award (30 August 2000) para 8, fn 1; *Gold Reserve Inc v Venezuela*, ICSID Case No ARB(AF)/09/1, Award (22 September 2014) para 252 et seq; and *Strabag SE v Libya* ICSID Case No ARB(AF)/15/1, Award (29 June 2020) paras 114–120.

[25] See eg *Vincent J. Ryan, Schooner Capital LLC, and Atlantic Investment Partners LLC v Republic of Poland*, ICSID Case No. ARB(AF)/11/3, Award (17 November 2015), paras 200–208.

- none of the parties to the dispute is an ICSID Contracting State or a national of a Contracting State (Article 2(1)(a));
- one (but not both) of the disputing parties is an ICSID Contracting State or a national of a Contracting State (Article 2(1)(b)); or
- an REIO is a party to the dispute (Article 2(1)(c)).

These provisions make several notable changes from the previous AF scheme. First, with respect to nationality, the administration of arbitration and conciliation is extended *ratione personae* to disputes where neither the host state nor the investor's home state is an ICSID Contracting State. Second, they extend AF proceedings to disputes in which an REIO is a disputing party. Third, they further delink the AF from the Convention in that the definition of disputes in AF Article 2(1) is not stated by reference to the ICSID Convention.[26] This reinforces the stand-alone nature of the revised AF, with jurisdiction based on the AF and the relevant instrument of consent, and not by negative reference to the ICSID Convention. Fourth, the Centre's services are also extended *ratione materiae* to legal disputes that do *not* arise "directly" out of an investment. This includes those disputes encompassed by former Article 2(b), without making it a specific category.[27] In practice, Article 2(b) had never been used,[28] and the deletion of the directness requirement further simplifies resort to the AF by avoiding debate over whether a dispute arises directly or indirectly from an investment.[29]

Revised Rule 2 of the 2022 AF Rules also marks the delinking of the AF from the Convention with respect to the notion of investment. Questions as to the relationship between the ICSID Convention and the AF Rules have inevitably arisen in past cases when assessing the existence of an investment.[30] Like the ICSID Convention, the AF does not expressly define "investment".[31] Some tribunals under the previous AF Rules noted the express reference to Article 25 of the ICSID Convention in Article 4 of

---

[26] Compare to Article 2(a) of the ICSID 2006 AF Rules: "The Secretariat of the Centre is hereby authorized to administer, subject to and in accordance with these Rules, proceedings between a State (or a constituent subdivision or agency of a State) and a national of another State, falling within the following categories: (a) conciliation and arbitration proceedings for the settlement of legal disputes arising directly out of an investment which are not within the jurisdiction of the Centre because either the State party to the dispute or the State whose national is a party to the dispute is not a Contracting State . . . ."

[27] Article 2(b) of the ICSID 2006 AF Rules allowed the Centre to administer: "(b) conciliation and arbitration proceedings for the settlement of legal disputes which are not within the jurisdiction of the Centre because they do not arise directly out of an investment, provided that either the State party to the dispute or the State whose national is a party to the dispute is a Contracting State".

[28] Article 2(b) was only raised once as an alternative basis for jurisdiction under the AF in *Nova Scotia. v Venezuela* where the Tribunal found that the Claimant had not made any investment within the meaning of the BIT or the ICSID Convention. Considering the claims based on Article 2(b) as an alternative ground, the Tribunal concluded that if there was no investment under the BIT, there could not be an "investor", and hence there was no basis for jurisdiction under Article 2(b) of the AF: *Nova Scotia Power Incorporated v Bolivarian Republic of Venezuela*, ICSID Case No. ARB(AF)/11/1, Award (30 April 2014), para 146.

[29] See WP # 1, paras 916–979; WP # 2, para 567; WP # 3, paras 218–219; and WP # 4, paras 195–197.

[30] *MNSS B.V. and Recupero Credito Acciaio N.V. v Montenegro*, ICSID Case No ARB(AF)/12/8, Award (4 May 2016), paras 184 et seq. See also, with respect to consent, *Oded Besserglik v Republic of Mozambique*, ICSID Case No ARB(AF)/14/2, Award (28 October 2019) para 317.

[31] ICSID Additional Facility Rules, 1979, Booklet, Article 4, Comment (iv), 6. *Sistem Mühendislik İnşaat Sanayi ve Ticaret A.Ş. v Kyrgyz Republic*, ICSID Case No ARB(AF)/06/1, Decision on Jurisdiction (13 September 2007) paras 68–69.

the 2006 AF Rules.[32] On the other hand, many awards rejected the application of any provision of the ICSID Convention, including Article 25.[33] Such tribunals relied on Article 3 of the AF Rules expressly stating that "none of the provisions of the [ICSID] Convention shall be applicable" in AF proceedings.[34] Similar text is retained in current Article 3 of the AF Rules.[35]

The removal of the nexus of the AF with the Convention is thus consistent with current practice. In fact, an analysis of awards under the previous AF shows that the focus of tribunals was not on the existence of an investment under the AF Rules.[36] Rather, the majority of tribunals determined whether the claimant made an investment based on the wording of the instrument of consent invoked (most usually a treaty), which typically contained a definition of investment (ie the subjective definition of investment).[37] For example, in *Vannessa Ventures v Venezuela*, the Tribunal noted that, "[t]he question whether there was an 'investment' within the meaning of the BIT was a question to be answered by reference in the first place to the BIT".[38] In *David Minnotte v Poland*, the Tribunal found that the claimants had made an investment for the purpose of the underlying BIT.[39] Hence, the so-called double keyhole approach (ie examining both subjective and objective[40] criteria for investment) adopted in Convention cases is not relevant in an AF case, although it had been applied by some AF tribunals.[41]

Article 2(2) confirms that a constituent subdivision or agency of a State or an REIO can be a disputing party in AF proceedings if the state or REIO concerned approves their consent or notifies the Centre that no such approval is needed. In this regard, the Article mirrors the corresponding provision in Article 25(3) of the ICSID Convention.[42] A constituent subdivision or agency of a state already had access to the

---

[32] See for example, *MNSS v Montenegro*, paras 184 et seq; *Oded Besserglik v Mozambique*, para 317.

[33] *Strabag SE v Libya*, para 109.

[34] The Tribunal in *Strabag SE v Libya* underlined that "pursuant to Article 3 of the Additional Facility Rules, none of the Convention provisions, including its Article 25, are applicable to Additional Facility arbitrations." *Strabag SE v Libya*, para 109.

[35] Article 3 provides that "[t]he provisions of the Convention do not apply to the conduct of ICSID Additional Facility proceedings".

[36] See for example, *Abengoa S.A. y COFIDES S.A. v United Mexican States*, ICSID Case No ARB(AF)/09/2, Award (18 April 2013); *ADF Group Inc. v United States of America*, ICSID Case No ARB(AF)/00/1, Award (9 January 2003); *Apotex Holdings Inc. and Apotex Inc. v United States of America*, ICSID Case No ARB(AF)/12/1, Award (25 August 2014); *Bayview Irrigation District and others v United Mexican States*, ICSID Case No ARB(AF)/05/1, Award (19 June 2007); *Crystallex International Corporation v Bolivarian Republic of Venezuela*, ICSID Case No ARB(AF)/11/2, Award (4 April 2016); and *Lion Mexico Consolidated L.P. v United Mexican States*, ICSID Case No ARB(AF)/15/2, Decision on Jurisdiction (30 July 2018).

[37] See for example, *Bayview v Mexico*, paras 90 et seq; and *Gold Reserve v Venezuela*, paras 257 et seq.

[38] *Vannessa Ventures Ltd. v Bolivarian Republic of Venezuela*, ICSID Case No ARB(AF)04/6, Award (16 January 2013), para 118.

[39] *David Minnotte & Robert Lewis v Republic of Poland*, ICSID Case No ARB (AF)/10/1, Award (16 May 2014), para 150(a).

[40] Objective criteria traditionally include contribution, duration, and risk. See eg *Nova Scotia v Venezuela*, para 84; *Vincent J. Ryan et al v Poland*, para 197; *Grupo Francisco Hernando Contreras v Republic of Equatorial Guinea*, ICSID Case No ARB(AF)/12/2, Award (4 December 2015), paras 138–140; and *MNSS v Montenegro*, para 189.

[41] See eg *Grupo Francisco v Equatorial Guinea*, paras 138–140; *MNSS v Montenegro*, paras 184–202. Note that this approach has also been followed in some UNCITRAL arbitration cases, see eg *Romak S.A. (Switzerland) v The Republic of Uzbekistan*, UNCITRAL, PCA Case No AA280, Award (26 November 2009) para 189 et seq.

[42] Article 25(3) provides that "(3) Consent by a constituent subdivision or agency of a Contracting State shall require the approval of that State unless that State notifies the Centre that no such approval is required".

AF under the previous Rules, but the new AF Rules removes any ambiguity as to the requirements of approval of consent and notification.

Article 2(3) states that an arbitration or conciliation proceeding under the AF is conducted according to the relevant AF arbitration or conciliation rules and the AF Administrative and Financial Regulations, the latter now fully incorporated in the AF.

## 2.3 Deletion of the Approval of Access

A further simplification in the AF Rules 2022 is the deletion of the approval of access requirement in Article 4 of the 2006 AF Rules. This two-step process—that is, the application for approval of access and the institution of proceedings—was originally intended to prevent the AF from becoming a means to circumvent the jurisdiction of the Centre under the ICSID Convention.[43] It was also seen as a filter for unnecessary jurisdictional objections and resultant delay and cost. The idea was to have the underlying arbitration clause vetted by the Centre in advance to ensure that it did not have obvious flaws.[44] Pursuant to this step, the Secretary-General approved access to the AF if satisfied that all requirements under Article 25 of the ICSID Convention, but for the *ratione personae* or *ratione materiae* requirements, were met at the time of the application for access. Article 4 also required the disputing parties to provide their consent *in lieu*. This meant that the disputing parties must consent to apply the ICSID Convention should all necessary jurisdictional requirements be met by the time the proceeding was instituted. As such, Article 4 was primarily a safeguard against any overlap or circumvention of an eligible recourse to the Centre's jurisdiction under the ICSID Convention. The purpose of the two-step approval had become less evident over time, and it seemed an unnecessary requirement by 2022.[45]

## 2.4 The Applicable Rules

The last provision in the AF Rules is Article 4 which specifies that, unlike proceedings under the ICSID Convention, the applicable Rules under the AF are those in force on the date of the filing of the request for arbitration or conciliation. This point was not expressly set out in the previous versions. The disputing parties remain free to agree otherwise under the 2022 AF Rules.

---

[43] ICSID Additional Facility Rules, 1979, Booklet, Article 4, Comment (i), 5.
[44] ibid.
[45] WP # 1 paras 983–990.

## 3. Amendments to AF Arbitration, Conciliation, and Financial Rules

The AF 2022 includes AF AR, AF CR, and AF AFR. These largely mirror their Convention equivalents, except where a distinction is required to reflect the fact that the Convention is not applicable or where a distinction is available in the non-Convention context.[46]

### 3.1 Additional Facility Arbitration Rules

Additional Facility arbitrations incorporate the procedural innovations found in the amended ICSID Convention Arbitration Rules. Thus, for example, the AF AR include provisions concerning reduction of the time and costs of proceedings (eg AF AR 11, 19, 20, 69); the requirement to file a notice of third-party funding (AF AR 23); case management conferences (AF AR 40); disputes arising from a request for production of documents (AF AR 47); tribunal-appointed experts (AF AR 49); bifurcation of a proceeding (AF AR 52, 54); consolidation and coordination of like proceedings (AF AR 56); security for costs (AF AR 63); enhanced transparency (AF AR 73–78); and expedited arbitration (AF AR 79–88).

AF AR 1 states that the AF AR apply to an arbitration conducted pursuant to the AF Rules, hence incorporating the broader availability of these rules under the 2022 amendments. The applicable procedural rules are those in force on the date of filing the request unless the parties agree otherwise (AF AR 1(4)). This preserves the ability of parties to apply the 2022 rules to AF cases originally filed under the 2006 rules. It differs from the Convention Arbitration Rules, which apply the rules in force on the date of consent to arbitration by virtue of Article 44 of the Convention.[47]

AF AR 2–9 address institution of proceedings and are similar to the Institution Rules applicable to ICSID Convention arbitration. As the requirement to obtain access to the Additional Facility has been eliminated in the 2022 amendments, a party will commence their AF arbitration by electronic filing of a request for arbitration (AF AR 2, 5). The request contains the usual required information (AF AR 3) but also recommends that a requesting party include information as to the number and method of appointment of arbitrators; the proposed seat of arbitration; the law applicable to the dispute; the potential use of expedited arbitration; and the names of persons or entities owning or controlling the requesting party. The Secretary-General is required to register the request if, based on the information provided, it appears that the claim is not manifestly outside the scope of Article 2(1) of the Additional Facility Rules. This threshold

---

[46] ibid para 1406.
[47] ibid vol 3, para 1502.

is similar to Article 36(3) of the Convention.[48] AF AR 1–9 cannot be modified by party agreement (AF AR 1(2)).

A number of the AF AR reflect the fact that the Convention is not applicable in AF proceedings and provide the requisite direction. For example, AF AR 41 states that the parties shall agree on the seat of arbitration, failing which, the seat shall be determined by the tribunal having regard to the circumstances of the case.[49] As AF arbitration is not delocalized and relies on domestic legal systems for recognition and enforcement of Awards, the AF AR must address establishment of a seat of arbitration. Compared to the prior AF rules, AF AR 41 no longer limits the seat to a New York Convention jurisdiction, and it allows the parties to agree on a seat. The parties may also agree to hold a hearing at any place and are not limited to holding hearings at the seat of arbitration (AF AR 42(2)).

The AF AR have made several changes to the rules regarding appointment and disqualification of arbitrators. The Secretary-General is now the default appointing authority if the tribunal has not been constituted within ninety days after the date of registration (AF AR 26). The Secretary-General is also available at any time to assist the parties in appointing a President of the tribunal or a sole arbitrator (AF AR 25). AF AR 22 has slightly modified the language on disqualification, requiring the arbitrator to be "impartial and independent", as opposed to the prior wording requiring an arbitrator "who may be relied upon to exercise independent judgment". This brings the language in line with generally accepted standards and the prevailing interpretation of the standard.[50] AF AR 30(1)(b) has replaced the prior threshold of "a manifest lack of the qualities required" by a determination that "circumstances exist that give rise to justifiable doubts as to the qualities of the arbitrator". This is consistent with the change in AR AF 22.[51] AF AR 30(3) also adds that the non-challenging party can consent to a challenge, in which instance the challenged arbitrator must resign. AF AR 31 gives the Secretary-General authority to decide the challenge, replacing the previous rule which gave authority to decide challenges to the non-challenged arbitrators or the Chair of the ICSID Administrative Council. Finally, AF AR 33 allows an arbitrator to resign simply by notifying the Secretary-General and the other members of the tribunal. It deletes the prior requirement that the tribunal must consent to a resignation.

The AF AR on provisional measures has been revised in two important respects. First, AF AR 57 allows a tribunal to "order" provisional measures on its own initiative, whereas prior AF AR 46 referred only to "a recommendation" for provisional measures made on the tribunal's own initiative. Such orders will be enforceable as procedural orders if permitted by the law of the place of arbitration.[52] Second, AF AR 57(7) reformulates prior AF AR 46(4). It allows parties to avail themselves of judicial or other interim measures in local courts.[53]

[48] ibid vol 3, paras 1517–1519.
[49] ibid vol 3, paras 1541–1548.
[50] ibid vol 3, para 1566.
[51] ibid vol 3, paras 1579–1581.
[52] ibid vol 3, para. 1620.
[53] ibid vol 3, para. 1621.

The AF AR rules on transparency are similar to those in the Convention arbitration context, with one exception. Under the Additional Facility, awards are made public in the same way as decisions or orders: they are published within sixty days of their issuance with redactions agreed to by the parties, and the tribunal is available to address disputed redactions (AF AR 73). This is different from the ICSID Convention AR, which are bound by Article 48(5) of the Convention requiring party consent to publication of an Award.

## 3.2  Additional Facility Conciliation Rules

The AF CR have been very substantially revised, in the same manner as the Convention Conciliation Rules. The goal of these revisions was to create a more modern, flexible, and widely available conciliation process. Additional Facility conciliation is available in accordance with the scope provisions in the Additional Facility Rules (AF Rules Article 2), and hence broadly available where one or both parties are not affiliated with an ICSID member State or where an REIO is a party to the conciliation (AF CR 1). AF CR 2–9 govern institution of an AF conciliation, through a request for conciliation. Like the AF AR, an AF conciliation will be registered if it appears based on the information provided that "the Request is not manifestly outside the scope" of AFR 2(1). Unless the parties decide otherwise, the costs of the conciliation commission and of the Centre are borne equally by the parties (AF CR 16).

The AF CR address confidentiality of the process in a manner similar to the Mediation Rules. All information relating to or generated in the conciliation is confidential unless the parties agree otherwise; the information is required to be published by ICSID; the information is available independently of the conciliation; or disclosure is required by law (AF CR 17). Parties may not rely on information generated in the conciliation, such as offers of settlement, admissions, or the conciliation report, unless the parties decide otherwise (AF CR 18). These provisions are intended to encourage use of conciliation.

The parties may agree to a sole conciliator or any uneven number of conciliators. However, in default of agreement there will be a sole conciliator (AF CR 19). Conciliators must be persons of high moral character and recognized competence. As in the AF AR, they must also be "impartial and independent" (AF CR 20), replacing the former language requiring a person "who may be relied upon to exercise independent judgment". The Secretary-General (not the Chair of the Administrative Council) is available to assist parties with appointment of conciliators at any time and is the default appointing authority under these rules (AF CR 23).

The basic function of the Conciliation Commission remains as before, to clarify the issues in dispute and assist the parties in reaching a mutually acceptable resolution of all or part of the dispute (AF CR 32(1)). However, the AF CR (and the CR) expand the ways in which this may be achieved. For example, the conciliator may make recommendations orally or in writing, and may communicate or meet with the parties jointly or separately (AF CR 32, 40). The conciliation process is intended to be expeditious, with parties filing a brief initial statement of the case within thirty days of the Commission's constitution and holding a first session within sixty days of the constitution of the Commission (AF CR 33, 38, 39).

## 3.3  Additional Facility Administrative and Financial Regulations

The AF Rules and Regulations include Administrative and Financial Regulations. These are similar to the administrative and financial regulations for Convention arbitration and conciliation. They provide for an ICSID tribunal or commission secretary to be assigned to the proceeding, address the Centre's depositary function, provide for payment of fees of tribunal and commission members, and outline the consequences of default in payment and lodging fees (AF AFR 2–10). As the immunities of the ICSID Convention do not apply in AF proceedings, AF AFR 13 provides that a commission or tribunal member shall not give testimony concerning the arbitration or conciliation in a judicial, arbitral, or similar process, and will not be liable for any act or omission in connection with the exercise of their functions unless there is fraudulent or wilful misconduct (AF AFR 13).

## 4.  Stand-Alone Fact-Finding Rules

The original Additional Facility included a specific set of rules for fact-finding.[54] While these were available at any time, they were particularly intended to provide parties with a preventive mechanism at the pre-dispute stage. Fact-finding offered an impartial assessment of facts, which, if accepted by the parties, would prevent differences from escalating into a formal legal dispute.

The fact-finding rules in AF 1978 have never been used by parties, and so there is no case law or experience with this process. As a result, there was some consideration as to whether they should be retained in the 2022 amendments. Ultimately, it was decided to retain fact-finding rules (FFR) as they have the potential to be useful to disputing parties, but to considerably modernize their content.

The 2022 amendments removed the fact-finding provisions from the AF and made them into a set of stand-alone rules.[55] As a result, they are available in the context of a Convention or AF case, and indeed can be commenced as a stand-alone process or ancillary to arbitration, conciliation or mediation under the Convention or Additional Facility.

---

[54] See, Schedule A, Fact-Finding (Additional Facility) Rules, <https://icsid.worldbank.org/sites/default/files/AFR_2006%20English-final.pdf>.

[55] For development of the Fact-Finding Rules, see WP # 1, paras 1250–1315; WP # 2, paras 715–746; WP # 3, paras 312–333; WP # 4, paras 204–219; WP # 5, paras 157–170; WP # 6, para 40.

The 2022 FFR[56] are available for proceedings related to an investment involving a state or an REIO, and which the parties consent in writing to submit to the Centre. The parties need not be ICSID member states or nationals of such states to use the FFR, and the primary requisite to invoke these rules is consent. The process is initiated by a request for fact-finding filed with the Secretary-General. The request provides a summary of the dispute and a description of the parties, affirms that the parties consent to fact-finding, and includes any proposals or agreements on the identification of the fact-finders or the process to be followed. Once registered, a fact-finding committee is struck, consisting of a sole or uneven number of members. The committee meets with the parties and determines a protocol for its work. Fact-finding proceedings are confidential, and the parties can decide whether the results of the committee will be binding or advisory (FFR 20). The FFR are accompanied by administrative and financial provisions (the FF AFR), similar to the administrative and financial provisions for arbitration, conciliation, and mediation.

## 5.  Application of Stand-Alone Mediation Rules

The amendments of 2022 also created a stand-alone set of Mediation Rules with dedicated Administrative and Financial Rules for Mediation.[57] Mediation proceedings are available in disputes related to an investment involving a state or REIO, and which the parties consent in writing to submit to the Centre.[58] As a result, parties involved in an arbitration or conciliation under the AF could agree to pursue a mediated resolution at any time during the process, or indeed before a formal proceeding has been commenced.

## 6.  Conclusion

The AF Rules 2022 significantly expand the availability of ICSID administration to a wide range of proceedings that previously were beyond its jurisdiction. At the same time, they include the innovations of the 2022 rules amendment process, and so they offer the most up to date set of ISDS rules.

---

[56] <https://icsid.worldbank.org/rules-regulations/fact-finding#:~:text=In%202022%2C%20ICSID%20relea sed%20an,in%20the%20pre%2Ddispute%20phase>.
[57] <https://icsid.worldbank.org/sites/default/files/documents/ICSID_Mediation.pdf>.
[58] Mediation Rule 2.

# 9

# The Singapore Convention on Mediation:
## *Per Aspera Ad Astra*

*Natalie Y Morris-Sharma*

## 1. Introduction

The United Nations Convention on International Settlement Agreements Resulting from Mediation, also known as the Singapore Convention on Mediation, is the first treaty on international mediation. The Singapore Convention opened for signature on 7 August 2019, and entered into force just over a year later, on 12 September 2020. There were fifty-three signatories to the Convention at the time of writing, of which forty-six signed the Convention on the day it opened for signature.[1] This take up rate of the Convention has been said to be "one of the highest number of first day signatories for any United Nations trade convention".[2] By comparison, the Convention on the Recognition and Enforcement of Foreign Arbitral Awards, more commonly referred to as the New York Convention, which had 166 Parties at the time of writing, was signed by ten countries on the day it opened for signature.[3]

The Singapore Convention is the product of a multilateral negotiations process at the United Nations Commission for International Trade Law (UNCITRAL).[4] It was the culmination of many years of effort. At many points, it seemed unlikely that a multilateral treaty would emerge from the negotiations.

UNCITRAL had made a previous attempt to harmonize laws on the enforcement of the settlement outcomes of mediation or conciliation, as part of its work on the 2002 UNCITRAL Model Law on International Commercial Conciliation.[5] The product of

---

[1] By the time of publication, the number of signatories to the Singapore Convention had increased to 55, and the number of Parties to the Singapore Convention had increased from six to eleven. See UNCITRAL, "Status: United Nations Convention on International Settlement Agreements Resulting from Mediation", <https://uncitral.un.org/en/texts/mediation/conventions/international_settlement_agreements/status>.

[2] Digital Event to Commemorate the Entry into Force of the Singapore Convention on Mediation, video available online at <https://www.singaporeconvention.org/events/scm2020>, at 00min 25sec.

[3] There were 172 Parties by the time of publication. See UNCITRAL, "Status: Convention on the Recognition and Enforcement of Foreign Arbitral Awards (New York, 1958) (the 'New York Convention')", <https://uncitral.un.org/en/texts/arbitration/conventions/foreign_arbitral_awards/status2>.

[4] For a description of the multilateral negotiations process, see, for example, Hal Abramson, "The New Singapore Mediation Convention: The Process and Key Choices" in Hal Abramson, *Beyond the Courtroom: Resolving Disputes Through Agreement* (Touro University Press 2020).

[5] For an account of UNCITRAL's previous attempt, see, generally, Natalie Y Morris-Sharma, "The Changing Landscape of Arbitration: UNCITRAL's Work on the Enforcement of Conciliated Settlement Agreements" (2018) Austrian Yearbook on International Arbitration 123.

Natalie Y Morris-Sharma, *The Singapore Convention on Mediation:* Per Aspera Ad Astra In: *By Peaceful Means.* Edited by: Charles N Brower, Joan E Donoghue, Cian C Murphy, Cymie R Payne and Esmé R Shirlow, Oxford University Press.
© Natalie Y Morris-Sharma 2024. DOI: 10.1093/oso/9780192848086.003.0009

this attempt was a placeholder in the Model Law on Conciliation, that "the enacting State may insert a description of the method of enforcing settlement agreements or refer to provisions governing such enforcement". This placeholder represented "the smallest common denominator between the various legal systems",[6] considering that legislative approaches to the enforceability of conciliated settlement agreements "differ[ed] widely".[7]

Twelve years later, in 2014, the delegation of the United States put the issue of the cross-border enforcement of mediated settlement agreements back on the table with their proposal that UNCITRAL develop a convention for mediated settlement agreements akin to what the New York Convention is for arbitral awards.[8] During our negotiations process, we saw that the discussions and difficulties identified in the earlier UNCITRAL discussions leading up to 2002 did not disappear when the work was taken up again and began in earnest in 2015. From 2015 to 2017, in the course of our negotiations, we worked to narrow down the issues.

We concluded the negotiations in 2018, with the adoption of the Singapore Convention by the UNCITRAL Commission in July 2018. Later that year, in December, the General Assembly adopted the Convention by consensus. Additionally, alongside the Singapore Convention, we also took the step—unprecedented for UNCITRAL—of developing, in parallel, amendments to the Model Law on Mediation. This was done in a spirit of compromise, to accommodate jurisdictions with less experience with international mediation. A benefit from the parallel development of the model law alongside the Convention, however, is that we now have a ready model, should countries need a reference point when crafting their domestic implementing legislation.

And so it is, that with lots of hard work and creative thinking by the many who were involved in the process, and a little bit of luck, we pushed through to deliver a treaty that has since not only been compared to the New York Convention but also termed as a game-changer.[9] This chapter introduces the Singapore Convention by drawing out five key similarities and five key differences between the Singapore Convention and the New York Convention. It then examines some of the likely impacts of the Singapore Convention on the dispute resolution landscape before offering concluding remarks.

---

[6] UNCITRAL, Report of the Working Group on Arbitration on the work of its thirty-fifth session (Vienna, 19–30 November 2001), UN Doc A/CN.9/506 (21 December 2001), 37. Also see UNCITRAL, Draft Guide to Enactment and Use of the UNCITRAL Model Law on International Commercial Conciliation, UN Doc A/CN.9/514 (27 May 2002), 26.

[7] UNCITRAL, Report of the Secretary-General, Settlement of commercial disputes—Possible uniform rules on certain issues concerning settlement of commercial disputes: written form for arbitration agreement, interim measures of protection, conciliation, UN Doc A/CN.9/WG.II/WP.110 (22 September 2000), 38.

[8] UNCITRAL, Note by the Secretariat, Planned and possible future work—Part III, Proposal by the Government of the United States of America: Future work for Working Group II, UN Doc A/CN.9/822 (2 June 2014). Mr Timothy Schnabel, head of the US delegation, also played a pivotal role in shaping the Singapore Convention and enabling it to come into fruition.

[9] See eg Baldev Bhinder, "The Singapore Convention Can Change the Game", *The Business Times*, 8 August 2019, referring to how "[t]his week broadsheets and Web sites have been filled with sweeping enthusiasm for the Singapore Convention. Most point to the cross-border enforcement of mediated settlements facilitated by the Singapore Convention as being a game changer." Also see Craig Carter, "Singapore Convention 2018: Reshaping Alternative Dispute Resolution and Enforcement", *LSJ Online*, 1 September 2018, highlighting that "[l]ike the *New York Convention* before it, this document also has the potential to reshape alternate dispute resolution and enforcement throughout the world".

## 2. The Singapore Convention: The New York
## Convention for Mediation

The Singapore Convention provides an efficient and harmonized framework for cross-border reliance on mediated settlement agreements. With the Convention, an international mediated settlement agreement need not be transformed into another enforceable instrument, such as a court judgment or an arbitral award, before it can be relied upon before a court.

The Singapore Convention applies to international settlement agreements that result from mediation and resolve a commercial dispute.[10] Mediation is defined in the Convention as a process "whereby parties attempt to reach a settlement of their dispute with the assistance of a third person or persons ('the mediator') lacking the authority to impose a solution upon the parties to the dispute".[11] The Convention may apply so long as the settlement agreement is in writing, signed by the parties to the agreement, and there is evidence that the settlement agreement resulted from mediation.[12] There are limited grounds for refusing to grant relief under the Convention. These may either be raised by a party to the settlement agreement against whom relief is being sought, or *sua sponte* by the competent authority of a Party to the Convention where relief is sought.[13]

The Singapore Convention has often been referred to as the New York Convention for mediation.[14] Noting that the New York Convention has been described as "[t]he mortar in the edifice of international commercial arbitration", this speaks to the ambition that some have for the Singapore Convention.[15] Apart from ambitions for the future, that there have been comparisons between the two international treaties is not surprising. When it was proposed in 2014 that UNCITRAL develop a multilateral convention on the enforceability of international commercial settlement agreements reached through mediation, the articulated goal of the initiative was to encourage

---

[10] Article 1(1) of the Singapore Convention on Mediation.

[11] Article 2(3) of the Singapore Convention on Mediation. The term "mediation" is used with the intention that it be understood the same way as the term "conciliation", as used in the context of UNCITRAL's earlier work on conciliation. To address concerns over an inadvertent substantive change in meaning resulting from the use of the term "mediation" in lieu of "conciliation", it was agreed that the text accompanying the Convention would explain the historical developments of the terminology in the UNCITRAL texts and emphasize that the term "mediation" is "intended to cover a broad range of activities that would fall under the definition as provided in article 1(3) of the Model Law regardless of the expressions used". See UNCITRAL, Report of Working Group II (Dispute Settlement) on the work of its sixty-seventh session (Vienna, 2–6 October 2017), UN Doc A/CN.9/929 (11 October 2017) (hereinafter, "UNCITRAL WG II October 2017 Report"), 16; UNCITRAL, Report of Working Group II (Arbitration and Conciliation) on the work of its sixty-fourth session (New York, 1–5 February 2016), U.N. Doc. A/CN.9/867 (10 February 2016) (hereinafter, "UNCITRAL WG II February 2016 Report"), 19.

[12] Article 4(1) of the Singapore Convention on Mediation.

[13] Article 5 of the Singapore Convention on Mediation.

[14] For example, see Laila El Shentenawi, "A New York Convention for Mediation may be Coming Soon", <https://www.tamimi.com/law-update-articles/a-new-york-convention-for-mediation-may-be-coming-soon/>.

[15] Richard Graving, "Status of the New York Arbitration Convention: Some Gaps in Coverage but New Acceptances Confirm its Vitality" (1995) 10 ICSID Review 1.

mediation in the same way that the New York Convention had facilitated the growth of arbitration.[16]

The comparisons are also appropriate. Both instruments establish international frameworks for the enforcement of outcomes of international dispute resolution. When the Singapore Convention opened for signature in Singapore on 7 August 2019, the Prime Minister of Singapore, Mr Lee Hsien Loong, referred to the Singapore Convention as "the missing third piece in the international dispute resolution enforcement framework",[17] joining other international treaties on the recognition and enforcement of court judgments and arbitral awards.[18] Furthermore, the New York Convention was a key reference point when the Singapore Convention was negotiated and drafted.[19]

The New York Convention thus provides us with a useful prism through which to view, and understand, the Singapore Convention.

## 2.1 Five Key Similarities between the Singapore Convention and the New York Convention

There are similarities in terms of the nature of the regimes that the New York Convention and the Singapore Convention, respectively, establish.

First, both Conventions address the recognition and enforcement of outcomes of international dispute resolution processes. The Singapore Convention does not use the language of "recognition and enforcement", which is a term familiar to us from its use in treaties such as the New York Convention. However, the intended legal effect of settlement agreements that are relied upon under the Singapore Convention's rubric is the same. Specifically, such a settlement agreement would not only be capable of being relied upon as a "sword", and enforced. It could also be utilized as a "shield", and invoked as a defence if a dispute arises concerning a matter that a party claims was already resolved by the settlement agreement.[20]

---

[16] UNCITRAL, Note by the Secretariat, Planned and possible future work—Part III, Proposal by the Government of the United States of America: Future work for Working Group II, UN Doc A/CN.9/822 (2 June 2014).

[17] Singapore Prime Minister Lee Hsien Loong, "Speech at Singapore Convention Signing Ceremony and Conference", 7 August 2019, <https://www.pmo.gov.sg/Newsroom/PM-Lee-Hsien-Loong-at-Singapore-Convention-Signing-Ceremony-and-Conference>.

[18] Referring to the international treaties that apply to arbitral awards and judgments, including the Convention of 30 June 2005 on Choice of Court Agreements; the Convention of 2 July 2019 on the Recognition and Enforcement of Foreign Judgments in Civil or Commercial Matters; and the Convention on the Recognition and Enforcement of Foreign Arbitral Awards.

[19] For instance, when the grounds for refusal in the Singapore Convention were negotiated, frequent reference was made to the New York Convention. See eg UNCITRAL, Report of Working Group II (Arbitration and Conciliation) on the work of its sixty-third session (Vienna, 7–11 September 2015), UN Doc A/CN.9/861 (17 September 2015) (hereinafter, "UNCITRAL WG II September 2015 Report"), 17; UNCITRAL WG II February 2016 Report, 25, on deliberations over the phrase "null and void, inoperative or incapable of being performed" (in Article 5(1)(b)(i) of the Singapore Convention on Mediation), which is also found in Article II(3) of the New York Convention; UNCITRAL WG II October 2017 Report, 14, on deliberations over the terms "binding" and "final" (in Article 5(1)(b)(ii) of the Singapore Convention on Mediation), in view of what is found in Article V(1)(e) of the New York Convention.

[20] Article 3 of the Singapore Convention on Mediation. This functional approach to the concept of "recognition and enforcement" has been elsewhere described as a "creative masterstroke". See Natalie Y Morris-Sharma, "Constructing the Convention on Mediation: The Chairperson's Perspective" (2019) 31 (Special Issue) Singapore Academy of Law Journal 487, 503.

Second, both Conventions establish a framework for cross-border enforcement of dispute settlement outcomes, while leaving Parties to apply the relevant rules of procedure. In respect of the Singapore Convention, this is expressly set out in Article 3 of the Convention.

Third, the New York Convention and the Singapore Convention are both pro-enforcement. Through their design—such as the burdens of proof and exhaustive grounds of refusal—both Conventions establish a "meaningful presumption" in favour of recognition and enforcement.[21] In addition, the Conventions establish a "ceiling" for the level of control that Contracting Parties may exercise over each Convention's subject instruments, or a "floor" for the level of generosity that the subject instruments may be afforded, thereby facilitating the cross-border enforcement of foreign arbitral awards and international mediated settlement agreements, respectively, to the greatest extent possible. In Article III of the New York Convention, Contracting States are given the discretion to determine the applicable rules for recognition and enforcement so long as, in doing so, they do not impose "substantially more onerous conditions". In Article VII of the New York Convention, it is provided that the New York Convention "shall not deprive any interested party of any right he may have to avail himself of an arbitral award". A similar provision is found in Article 7 of the Singapore Convention. Accordingly, a Party to the Singapore Convention may apply more favourable treatment to a settlement agreement.[22]

Fourth, both Conventions have also been designed so that they do not freeze the development of the law, either of arbitration or of mediation. Article VII of the New York Convention has been proclaimed as a "genius" element of the Convention in this regard.[23] In referring to "any right" in "the law or the treaties", the point of reference is a "living" and dynamic one. Article VII of the New York Convention finds its equivalent in Article 7 of the Singapore Convention.

Fifth, and finally, both treaties are applicable to outcomes of investor–state dispute settlement. This is of especial significance because of the ongoing efforts to reform the investor–state dispute settlement system.[24] Awards rendered in the context of an investment treaty arbitration have been treated as falling within the scope of the New York Convention, even when states have entered a reservation declaring that it will apply the Convention only to "commercial" matters.[25] In respect of the Singapore

---

[21] George Bermann, *International Arbitration and Private International Law* (Brill-Nijhoff 2017) 555.
[22] See UNCITRAL, Report of Working Group II (Dispute Settlement) on the work of its sixty-fifth session (Vienna, 12–23 September 2016), UN Doc A/CN.9/896 (30 September 2016) (hereinafter, "UNCITRAL WG II September 2016 Report"), 36; UNCITRAL, Report of Working Group II (Dispute Settlement) on the work of its sixty-sixth session (New York, 6–10 February 2017), UN Doc A/CN.9/901 (16 February 2017) (hereinafter, "UNCITRAL WG II February 2017 Report"), 13–14.
[23] Emmanuel Gaillard, "The Urgency of Not Revising the New York Convention" in Albert Jan van den Berg (ed), *50 Years of the New York Convention: ICCA International Arbitration Conference* (Vol 14, Kluwer Law International 2009) 689, 692.
[24] In 2017, UNCITRAL Working Group III was entrusted with a broad mandate to work on the possible reform of investor-State dispute settlement. See United Nations, Report of the United Nations Commission on International Trade Law: Fiftieth session (3–21 July 2017), UN Doc A/72/17 (2017), 43–47.
[25] For example, see *United Mexican States v Metalclad*, Canada, Supreme Court of British Columbia, 2.5.2001, [2001] BCSC 664, para 44. Also see Marc Bungenberg and August Reinisch, *From Bilateral Arbitral Tribunals and Investment Courts to a Multilateral Investment Court* (2nd edn), European Yearbook of International Economic Law (Special Issue) (Springer 2020), 170–71.

Convention, the text of the Convention provides that it applies to international settle-ment agreements that result from mediation and resolve a commercial dispute.[26] The intention was for the term "commercial" in the Singapore Convention to be understood broadly.[27] Furthermore, during the negotiations for the Singapore Convention, it was understood that "commercial" settlement agreements included agreements involving government entities. This was in recognition of the fact that government entities do engage in commercial activities and may seek to use mediation to resolve disputes in the context of such activities.[28] Unless a reservation or declaration is made under Article 8(1)(a) in relation to settlement agreements to which a Party to the Singapore Convention, or its governmental agencies or agents, is party, the Convention would apply to such agreements.[29]

## 2.2  Five Key Differences between the Singapore Convention and the New York Convention

There are a number of differences between the Singapore Convention and the New York Convention, an examination of which serves to illuminate some of the key facets of the Singapore Convention.

First, the subject instruments of the treaties differ. While the New York Convention is concerned with the recognition and enforcement of foreign arbitral awards, the Singapore Convention is concerned with international mediated settlement agree-ments. The Singapore Convention recognizes international mediated settlement agree-ments as a *sui generis* category of legal agreements that can be enforced in their own right instead of being treated as mere contracts. This was not an uncontroversial point during the negotiations, when it was noted that the enforcement procedure "would fa-vour settlement agreements over ordinary contracts".[30]

One basis for the distinction between mediated settlement agreements and ordinary contracts is the involvement of a third-party neutral in a process that the parties have agreed to, and where the parties retain control over the outcome. This is because, unlike in an arbitration or court litigation, the third-party neutral would lack the authority to impose a solution upon the parties to the dispute.[31] It has been observed that mediators

---

[26] Article 1(1) of the Singapore Convention on Mediation.

[27] Model Law on International Commercial Mediation and International Settlement Agreements Resulting from Mediation of the United Nations Commission on International Trade Law, GA Res 73/199, adopted at the 73rd Session (20 December 2018), footnote 1.

[28] UNCITRAL WG II September 2015 Report, 9–10; and UNCITRAL WG II September 2016 Report, 12. Also see UNCITRAL WG II February 2016 Report at 18; and UNCITRAL, Report of Working Group II (Dispute Settlement) on the work of its sixty-eighth session (New York, 5–9 February 2018), UN Doc A/CN.9/934 (19 February 2018) (hereinafter, "UNCITRAL WG II February 2018 Report") 13.

[29] At the time of writing, Belarus, Iran, and Saudi Arabia, had entered reservations pursuant to Article 8(1)(a) of the Singapore Convention on Mediation. See UNCITRAL, "Status: United Nations Convention on International Settlement Agreements Resulting from Mediation", <https://uncitral.un.org/en/texts/mediation/conventions/international_settlement_agreements/status>. By the time of publication, Georgia and Kazakhstan had also rati-fied the Singapore Convention and entered a reservation pursuant to Article 8(1)(a).

[30] UNCITRAL WG II September 2015 Report, 5.

[31] See the definition of "mediation" in Article 2(3) of the Singapore Convention on Mediation.

may "facilitate information exchange, communication, deliberation and decision-making" as they are able to assist the disputing parties in diagnosing the cause of their dispute, and overcoming "strategic and cognitive barriers".[32] Other bases for the distinction that have been suggested are the facts that parties to a mediated settlement agreement have "likely already given up contractual rights in settling their dispute, and have spent time and money on the mediation".[33]

Furthermore, the Singapore Convention addresses itself only to mediated settlement agreements and not to agreements to mediate. This is in recognition of the fact that mediations may be commenced through different procedures, and not necessarily on the basis of agreements to mediate. There might therefore not be an agreement to mediate concluded by the parties.[34] In any event, enforcement of agreements to mediate would be a matter to be determined under the domestic law of the state in which enforcement is sought. By comparison, the New York Convention applies to both arbitral awards as well as agreements to arbitrate.[35]

Second, the basis of determining a "foreign" or "international" instrument under the treaties differ. The New York Convention refers to "foreign" and "non-domestic" arbitral awards.[36] In contrast, the Singapore Convention refers to "international" settlement agreements. Under the Singapore Convention, the internationality of a settlement agreement is determined by reference to the places of business of the parties to the agreement, at the time of the conclusion of the settlement agreement.[37] The distinction between international and domestic mediation processes is not drawn, taking into account that many jurisdictions do not differentiate between international and domestic international processes.[38]

During the negotiations for the Singapore Convention, there was consideration of the suggestion to adopt the approach in the New York Convention, of referring to "foreign" arbitral awards. The attendant opportunity to draw on the relevant practice under the New York Convention held the potential promise of "simplifying" the implementation of the Singapore Convention.[39] Nevertheless, this suggestion was not taken up

---

[32] Bobette Wolski, "Enforcing Mediated Settlement Agreements (MSAs): Critical Questions and Directions for Future Research" (2014) 7 Contemporary Asia Arbitration Journal 87, 103. Also see Tobi Dress, "International Commercial Mediation and Conciliation" (1988) 10 Loyola Los Angeles International and Comparative Law Journal 569, examining why direct negotiations fail (at 571–72) and the primary role of a mediator (at 573).

[33] Timothy Schnabel, "The Singapore Convention on Mediation: A Framework for the Cross-border Recognition and Enforcement of Mediated Settlements" (2019) 19 Pepperdine Dispute Resolution Law Journal 1, 11.

[34] UNCITRAL WG II September 2015 Report, 6 and 13; UNCITRAL WG II October 2017 Report, 7. There is also the question of whether or not enforcing agreements to mediate would contradict the voluntary nature of mediation. See eg Carlos Esplugues, "General Report: New Developments in Civil and Commercial Mediation—Global Comparative Perspectives" in Carlos Esplugues and Louis Marquis (eds), *New Developments in Civil and Commercial Mediation: Global Comparative Perspectives* (Springer 2015) 589, in the affirmative; and Peter Tochtermann, "Agreements to Negotiate in the Transnational Context—Issues of Contract Law and Effective Dispute Resolution" (2008) 13 Uniform Law Review 685, 712, providing a view in the negative. In any event, there have been calls to clarify the enforceability of agreements to mediate. See eg Maryam Salehijam, "A Call for a Harmonized Approach to Agreements to Mediate" (2019) 6 (1) Yearbook of International Arbitration 199.

[35] Article I(1) of the New York Convention.

[36] ibid.

[37] Article 1(1) of the Singapore Convention on Mediation.

[38] UNCITRAL WG II September 2015 Report 7.

[39] ibid 7–8.

as settlement agreements typically do not have a legal seat in the same way that arbitral awards do.[40] Amongst other implications, this means that there is no requirement for the mediation or the mediated settlement to comply with the domestic legal requirements of any particular state of origin, and no one state has the ability to set aside a settlement agreement in a manner that would be binding on other jurisdictions.[41]

Third, the lists of grounds for refusal of recognition and enforcement (or enforcement and invocation) in the New York Convention and the Singapore Convention, while exhaustive, differ in terms of their content. The differences in the grounds for refusal stem from an acknowledgment that, while the New York Convention "may provide an enforcement mechanism, ... its application to the amicable process of mediation creates an imperfect fit".[42]

Some of the grounds for refusal in the Singapore Convention were inspired by those in the New York Convention. These include where there was incapacity of a party to the settlement agreement (inspired by Article V(1)(a) of the New York Convention);[43] if the settlement agreement was null and void, inoperative, or incapable of being performed (inspired by Article II(3) of the New York Convention);[44] or if the settlement agreement was not binding (drawing from Article V(1)(e) of the New York Convention).[45] Like Article V(2) of the New York Convention, enforcement can be refused on grounds of public policy or if the subject matter was not capable of settlement by mediation, and these grounds can be raised *sua sponte* by a court before which relief is sought.[46]

That being said, there are a number of grounds for refusal in the New York Convention that are not found in the Singapore Convention. As it has been noted, "mediation recommends, arbitration decides".[47] Owing to the different natures of arbitration and mediation, there are no provisions in the Singapore Convention that are equivalent to Article V(1)(b), Article V(1)(c), and Article V(1)(d) of the New York Convention.[48]

Article V(1)(b) and Article V(1)(d) of the New York Convention seek to address procedural irregularities in arbitral proceedings. When a party to an arbitration was not given proper notice of the appointment of the arbitrator or of the arbitration proceedings, or was otherwise unable to present his case, the recognition and enforcement of the arbitral award may be refused under Article V(1)(b). When the composition of the arbitral authority or the arbitral procedure was not in accordance with the agreement of the parties, or else the law of the country where the arbitration took place, the recognition and enforcement of the arbitral award may be refused under Article V(1)(d). Such

---

[40] ibid 8.

[41] Schnabel (n 33) 22.

[42] Brette Steele, "Enforcing International Commercial Mediation Agreements as Arbitral Awards under the New York Convention" (2007) 54 UCLA Law Review 1385, 1387.

[43] Article 5(1)(a), Singapore Convention on Mediation.

[44] Article 5(1)(b)(i), Singapore Convention on Mediation. Also see UNCITRAL WG II September 2016 Report, 18.

[45] Article 5(1)(b)(ii), Singapore Convention on Mediation.

[46] Article 5(2), Singapore Convention on Mediation.

[47] Quoted by Aron Broches in Note by the General Counsel transmitted to the Executive Directors, II-1 *History of the ICSID Convention* 7.

[48] See UNCITRAL WG II February 2016 Report, 27–28. Also see Morris-Sharma, "The Changing Landscape of Arbitration" (n 5) 136–37; Wolski, "Enforcing Mediated Settlement Agreements (MSAs)" (n 32) 98.

due process concerns do not manifest in the context of a mediation. In a mediation, the mediator does not have the authority to impose a settlement on the parties, who may withdraw from the mediation process at any time.[49] Moreover, if these grounds for refusal were to be applied to the mediation context, the "restrictions on contracting, convening, and caucusing stand to strip mediation of some of its benefits".[50]

Article V(1)(c) of the New York Convention concerns arbitral awards which contain decisions on matters "beyond the scope of the submission to arbitration". Apart from the fact that the Singapore Convention does not deal with agreements to mediate, a similar ground for refusal in the Singapore Convention, as applied to a mediated settlement agreement and focussing on the scope of matters referred to the mediation, would be contrary to the spirit of mediation. In a mediation, the parties are encouraged to "expand the pie" and create value so that the outcome of the mediation is beneficial to both sides. This could mean going beyond the initial issues identified at the time the dispute crystallized or at the commencement of the mediation process.

By the same token, some of the grounds for refusal in the Singapore Convention are specific to mediation, and therefore do not have counterpart provisions in the New York Convention. These concern the impact of the mediation process, and conduct of the mediators, on the enforcement procedure.

The Singapore Convention provides that relief may be refused where there was a "serious breach" by the mediator of standards applicable to the mediator or the mediation, without which breach that party would not have entered into the settlement agreement.[51] The Convention also provides that relief may be refused where there was a failure of the mediator to disclose to the parties to the settlement agreement circumstances that raise "justifiable doubts" as to the mediator's impartiality or independence, and such failure to disclose had a "material impact or undue influence" on a party, without which failure that party would not have entered into the settlement agreement.[52]

These grounds for refusal in the Singapore Convention were included as part of a five-issue packaged deal in the negotiations. One of the reasons given for their inclusion was to highlight the importance of the ethics and conduct of mediators, and "contribute to ensuring" that the mediation process that led to the settlement agreement was "conducted in an appropriate manner".[53] Importantly, in respect of Article 5(1)(e), a serious breach must have had a direct impact on the settlement agreement. Similarly, for Article 5(1)(f), there had to have been a causal link between a failure to disclose and the decision of a party to enter into the settlement agreement.[54]

---

[49] UNCITRAL WG II February 2016 Report, 27–28; UNCITRAL WG II September 2016 Report, 19 and 33.

[50] Steele, "Enforcing International Commercial Mediation Agreements as Arbitral Awards under the New York Convention" (n 42) 1412. Also see Dress, "International Commercial Mediation and Conciliation" (n 32) 576–77, describing the process of caucusing; Klaus Peter Berger, "Integration of Mediation Elements into Arbitration: 'Hybrid' Procedures and 'Intuitive' Mediation by International Arbitrators" (2003) 19(3) Arbitration International 387, 392, identifying caucusing as a "distinctive feature" of commercial mediation.

[51] Article 5(1)(e) of the Singapore Convention on Mediation.

[52] Article 5(1)(f) of the Singapore Convention on Mediation.

[53] UNCITRAL WG II February 2017 Report, 8–9.

[54] UNCITRAL WG II September 2016 Report, 33–34.

There are also grounds for refusal for when the settlement agreement has been sub-sequently modified,[55] to ensure that only the latest version of the settlement agreement concluded by the parties is enforced;[56] or the obligations in the settlement agreement have been performed, which was included to provide greater certainty to a few dele-gations in the negotiations; and when the obligations in the settlement agreement are not clear or comprehensible, to cater to situations where a settlement agreement is "so confusing or ill-defined";[57] or where relief would be contrary to the terms of the settle-ment agreement,[58] to give effect to the principle of party autonomy.[59] While such elem-ents of the grounds for refusal may strike as being "too obvious to need to be stated",[60] and while certain of the grounds for refusal set out in Article 5(1) potentially overlap,[61] the structure and content of Article 5(1) reflect the accommodation of the concerns expressed during the negotiations, from the perspective of different domestic legal systems.

Fourth, the reservations in the two instruments differ. There are only two permis-sible reservations in each of the New York Convention and the Singapore Convention. The reservations enable a Party to either Convention to exclude or modify the legal effect of certain provisions of the treaty in their application to the Party making the reservation.[62]

The New York Convention has a reciprocity reservation and a commercial reserva-tion. The reciprocity reservation provides that states may declare that they will apply the Convention only to awards made in the territory of another Contracting State. The commercial reservation provides that states may declare that it will apply the Convention only to differences arising out of legal relationships that are commercial. At the time of writing, out of 166 Parties, 79 had entered a reciprocity reservation, and 55 had entered a commercial reservation.[63]

The Singapore Convention does not have these reservations. The reciprocity res-ervation in the New York Convention would not have meaning in the context of the Singapore Convention, which does not require that a place where the mediated settle-ment agreement is "made" be identified. As for the commercial reservation in the New York Convention, it was included following a suggestion by the delegate from the

[55] Article 5(1)(b) of the Singapore Convention on Mediation.
[56] UNCITRAL WG II October 2017 Report, 14.
[57] Article 5(1)(c)(i) and Article 5(1)(c)(ii) of the Singapore Convention on Mediation. Also see Schnabel (n 33) 47–48.
[58] Article 5(1)(d) of the Singapore Convention on Mediation.
[59] Article 5(1)(d) of the Singapore Convention on Mediation. Also see UNCITRAL WG II September 2016 Report, 17.
[60] Schnabel (n 33) 47.
[61] UNCITRAL WG II February 2018 Report, 11. That there might be overlap amongst the grounds of refusal provided for in Article 5(1) was acknowledged by the negotiators. The intention is for the competent authorities to take this into account when interpreting the various grounds.
[62] See Article 2(1)(d) of the Vienna Convention on the Law of Treaties, 1155 UNTS 331 (23 May 1969), stating the definition of a reservation.
[63] See UNCITRAL, "Status: Convention on the Recognition and Enforcement of Foreign Arbitral Awards (New York, 1958) (the 'New York Convention')", <https://uncitral.un.org/en/texts/arbitration/conventions/foreign_arbitral_awards/status2>. By the time of publication, there were 172 Parties to the New York Convention and, of these, 83 had entered a reciprocity reservation, and 59 had entered a commercial reservation.

Netherlands. The delegate argued that such a reservation would make it easier for countries that would otherwise have difficulties because their commercial law was distinct from civil law. This argument was not raised during the Singapore Convention negotiations.[64] Instead, as noted in this chapter, the text of the Singapore Convention already provides that it applies to international mediated settlement agreements that resolve a commercial dispute.[65] The intention was for the term "commercial" to be understood broadly, but subject to the exclusions stated in the Convention, for settlement agreements concluded to resolve a consumer dispute, or relating to family, inheritance or employment law.[66]

The Singapore Convention has a governmental agencies reservation and a parties' opt-in reservation.[67]

The governmental agencies reservation provides for the possibility of Parties to the Convention to enter a reservation to the effect that they will not, to the extent specified in their reservation, apply the Convention to settlement agreements to which they, or any of their governmental agencies or agents, are parties.[68] Without such a reservation being entered by a Party to the Convention, the Singapore Convention would apply to settlement agreements involving government entities. This reservation was included to give flexibility to states, making it possible for more states to consider becoming a Party to the Singapore Convention.[69] This is because, in some jurisdictions, government entities are not authorized to conclude settlement agreements. At the same time, a blanket exclusion of settlement agreements involving government entities was assessed by the negotiators to not be desirable, since such entities do engage in commercial activities.[70]

The parties' opt-in reservation gives Parties to the Singapore Convention the option of entering a declaration to require that the parties to a settlement agreement agree, or opt-in, to the application of the enforcement mechanism under the Convention.[71]

---

[64] United Nations Conference on International Commercial Arbitration, Summary Record of the Twenty-third Meeting, E/CONF.26/SR.23, 7, 12.

[65] Article 1(1) of the Singapore Convention on Mediation.

[66] Article 1(2) of the Singapore Convention on Mediation. Reference can be made to the illustrative list retained in footnote 1 in the UNCITRAL Model Law on International Commercial Mediation. See Model Law on International Commercial Mediation and International Settlement Agreements Resulting from Mediation of the United Nations Commission on International Trade Law, GA Res 73/199, adopted at the 73rd Session (20 December 2018), footnote 1.

[67] At the time of writing, Belarus, Iran, and Saudi Arabia, had entered the governmental agencies reservation, and only Iran had entered the parties' opt-in reservation. See UNCITRAL, "Status: United Nations Convention on International Settlement Agreements Resulting from Mediation", <https://uncitral.un.org/en/texts/mediation/conventions/international_settlement_agreements/status>. By the time of publication, Georgia and Kazakhstan had also entered both the governmental agencies reservation and the parties' opt-in reservation, when ratifying the Singapore Convention.

[68] Article 8(1)(a) of the Singapore Convention on Mediation.

[69] UNCITRAL WG II February 2018 Report, 12.

[70] UNCITRAL WG II September 2015 Report, 9.

[71] Article 8(1)(b) of the Singapore Convention on Mediation. At the time of writing, out of the fifty-three signatories to the Singapore Convention, only Iran had made a declaration upon signature, requiring that parties to a settlement agreement opt-in for the Singapore Convention to apply. None of the six ratifying countries have made this declaration. See UNCITRAL, "Status: United Nations Convention on International Settlement Agreements Resulting from Mediation", <https://uncitral.un.org/en/texts/mediation/conventions/international_settlement_agreements/status>. By the time of publication, there were fifty-five signatories and eleven Parties to the Singapore Convention. Georgia and Kazakhstan, which ratified the Singapore Convention, entered a reservation pursuant to Article 8(1)(b).

Without such a reservation being entered by a Party to the Convention, parties to an international settlement agreement need not confirm their consent to enforce their obligations in the settlement agreement in order for the Singapore Convention to apply. This reservation was included, like the grounds for refusal specific to mediation, as a compromise and as part of the five-issue packaged deal in the negotiations.[72] Its inclusion was seen as facilitative of maximal participation in the Singapore Convention while preserving its object and purpose.[73] It is a declaration that gave comfort to some delegations that saw express consent as a natural follow-through of the consensual nature of mediation and party autonomy.[74] It is a declaration that some have said, if made, will probably be withdrawn over time, with the growth in familiarity with international mediation, and understanding that it would be in line with the expectations of the disputing parties that the mediated settlement agreement that they reach would be enforceable.[75] Nevertheless, in practical terms, parties to a settlement agreement should consider where their agreement is likely to be relied upon or invoked. If in a Party to the Singapore Convention that has made a declaration under Article 8(1)(b), it could be prudent to agree on a clause opting-in to the application of the Convention, irrespective of the every intention of the parties to the settlement agreement that the obligations therein will be performed.

Fifth, whereas the New York Convention applies on a reciprocal basis, the Singapore Convention does not. Article XIV of the New York Convention states that "[a] Contracting State shall not be entitled to avail itself of the … Convention against other Contracting States except to the extent that it is itself bound to apply the Convention". This general reciprocity clause has rarely been invoked, and available case law suggests that the enforcement of an arbitral award has never been denied on the basis of Article XIV.[76] It could be because the interpretation of Article XIV has not been settled. At the time when the New York Convention was adopted, there were already concerns about the confusion that Article XIV might cause, and the view was expressed that Article XIV should not serve as a precedent for any other conventions.[77]

In contrast, under the Singapore Convention, a mediated settlement agreement may be enforced or invoked in any Party, without a requirement to consider its reciprocal application in another jurisdiction. One may ask then what benefit there is in a state

---

[72] For a pithy summary of the drafting history and discussion that led to Article 8(1)(b), see, for example, Itai Apter and Coral Henig Muchnik, "Reservations in the Singapore Convention—Helping to Make the 'New York Dream' Come True" (2019) 20 Cardozo Journal of Conflict Resolution 1267, 1276–79.

[73] This idea was first mooted at the 64th session. See UNCITRAL WG II February 2016 Report, 23.

[74] UNCITRAL WG II September 2015 Report, 12; UNCITRAL WG II February 2016 Report, 22–23. Also see UNCITRAL WG II February 2016 Report, 29; UNCITRAL WG II September 2016 Report, 22–23; UNCITRAL WG II February 2017 Report, 8.

[75] UNCITRAL WG II September 2015 Report, 12; UNCITRAL WG II February 2016 Report, 23; UNCITRAL WG II September 2016 Report, 23; UNCITRAL WG II February 2017 Report, 7.

[76] UNCITRAL, UNCITRAL Secretariat Guide on the Convention on the Recognition and Enforcement of Foreign Arbitral Awards (United Nations 2016) 328–29.

[77] Young-Joon Mok, "The Principle of Reciprocity in the United Nations Convention on the Recognition and Enforcement of Foreign Arbitral Awards of 1958" (1989) 21 Case Western Reserve Journal of International Law 123, 139 and 141–46, citing the negotiation history of the New York Convention, and the different opinions regarding the interpretation of Article XIV of the New York Convention.

(or a regional economic integration organization)[78] becoming a Party to the Singapore Convention, since individuals or businesses from a non-Party to the Convention could still seek to enforce or invoke a mediated settlement agreement by applying to the competent authority of a Party. For that matter, such an individual or business could similarly have a mediated settlement agreement enforced or invoked against them. In response to this, it can be highlighted that there is value in becoming a Party to the Singapore Convention to demonstrate support for the multilateral trading system as well as the principles that the Convention promotes, such as access to justice and the rule of law.[79] There are also efficiencies to be reaped from a state's competent authority being able to deal with an application for reliance on a mediated settlement agreement, using the expedited enforcement framework of the Singapore Convention.[80]

## 3. The Singapore Convention: Its Own Significance

Beyond comparisons with the New York Convention, the Singapore Convention, in establishing a framework for international enforcement of the outcomes of mediation, is likely to impact the dispute resolution landscape. That is not to say that the success of the Singapore Convention should be measured against how often it is invoked. The nature of mediation is such that, having invested in a decision to settle and the terms of resolution, parties to a settlement agreement are more likely to seek a legally binding agreement to reflect their settlement, and to implement the agreement, than they would be in the case of an externally imposed outcome.[81] Instead, three areas of impact are examined in this section: the promotion of the use of mediation, with its flexibilities; interaction with other modes of dispute settlement; and influence on efforts to reform the investor–state dispute settlement regime.

---

[78] See Article 12 of the Singapore Convention on Mediation.

[79] For example, see Sundaresh Menon, "Mediation and the Rule of Law", Keynote Address at The Law Society Mediation Forum (10 March 2017), text available online at <https://www.supremecourt.gov.sg/Data/Editor/Documents/Keynote%20Address%20-%20-Mediation%20and%20the%20Rule%20of%20Law%20(Final%20edition%20after%20delivery%20-%2020090317).pdf>. Note that access to justice and the rule of law are principles reflected, in particular, in the United Nations Sustainable Development Goal 16 on peace, justice, and strong institutions.

[80] This builds on findings that, more generally, mediation saves government court administration costs. For example, see Giuseppe de Palo and others, "Quantifying the Cost of Not Using Mediation—A Data Analysis", Note by European Parliament Policy Department C: Citizens' Rights and Constitutional Affairs (April 2011), <http://www.europarl.europa.eu/document/activities/cont/2011/05/20110518ATT19592/20110518ATT19592EN.pdf>; Transformation Management Services, "Court-Annexed Mediation—Broadmeadows Pilot evaluation" (October 2008), <http://www.transformation.com.au/docs/Broadmeadows%20Evaluation%20REPORTDFNov.pdf>; Teresa G Campbell and Sharon L Pizzuti, "The Effectiveness of Case Evaluation and Mediation in Michigan Circuit Courts", Report to the State Court Administrative Office, Michigan Supreme Court (31 October 2011), <http://courts.mi.gov/Administration/SCAO/Resources/Documents/Publications/Reports/The%20Effectiveness%20of%20Case%20Evaluation%20and%20Mediation%20in%20MI%20Circuit%20Courts.pdf>.

[81] Eileen Carroll QC and Karl Mackie CBE, *International Mediation: Breaking Business Deadlock* (Bloomsbury Professional Ltd 2016) 103. Also see generally Craig McEwen and Richard Maiman, "Mediation in Small Claims Court: Achieving Compliance Through Consent" (1984) 18 Law and Society Review 11.

## 3.1 Promotion of the Use of Mediation, with its Flexibilities

Already, the last few decades have seen the emergence of mediation internationally, marked for instance by the development of institutional capacity by existing international commercial arbitration institutions as well as by new international commercial mediation institutions.[82] Against the backdrop of initiatives such as the One Belt One Road and Great Mekong Subregion, the interest in mediation has continued to flourish. This is because large infrastructure projects, in particular, are complex and have long runways. This has generated interest in dispute resolution mechanisms that are not only time- and cost-effective but can also preserve the business relationship and take into account wider operational considerations. Mediation counts as foremost amongst these. Amongst other of its features mediation places focus on the interests of the parties. This is unlike arbitration, which emphasizes the legal rights and positions of disputing parties.[83]

The Singapore Convention, by providing a framework for cross-border enforcement of international mediated settlement agreements, is expected to promote the use of mediation further. For one, the "diversity" of enforcement mechanisms of such settlement agreements had been identified as "a major obstacle to the development of global mediation practice".[84] By harmonizing the enforcement of mediated settlement agreements, predictability in the outcomes of mediation is enhanced, increasing the attractiveness of mediation as a method of dispute resolution.

The enforceability of dispute resolution outcomes is a key factor influencing choices of dispute resolution processes. For example, in a survey conducted on the perceived advantages of arbitration for continental European and United States lawyers, the existence of an enforcement mechanism was praised and rated as one of arbitration's strong advantages.[85] Specific to cross-border mediation, a survey conducted in October and

---

[82] Nadja Alexander, "Ten Trends in International Commercial Mediation" (2019) 31 (Special Issue) Singapore Academy of Law Journal 405, 407–08.

[83] Berger (n 50) 391, providing a list of essential differences between arbitration and mediation. Also see William Ury's distinction between power-based, rights-based, and interest-based approaches to dispute resolution, in William Ury and others, *Getting Disputes Resolved: Designing Systems to Cut the Costs of Conflict* (Jossey-Bass 1988).

[84] Nadja Alexander, "Nudging Users Towards Cross-Border Mediation: Is it Really about Harmonised Enforcement Regulation?" (2014) 7 Contemporary Asia Arbitration Journal 405, 408–09. Also see Chang-Fa Lo, "Desirability of a New International Legal Framework for Cross-Border Enforcement of Certain Mediated Settlement Agreements" (2014) 7 Contemporary Asia Arbitration Journal 119, 121; Wolski, "Enforcing Mediated Settlement Agreements (MSAs)" (n 32) 89; Edna Sussman, "The New York Convention through a Mediation Prism" (2009) 15 (4) Dispute Resolution Magazine 10, 11. Though by no means the only obstacle. Other reasons for the low uptake of international commercial mediation include a lack of sensitivity to legal and cultural differences and the lack of a track record for businesses to trust. In this regard, see Lucy Reed, "Ultima Thule: Prospects for International Commercial Mediation", Keynote Address at the Inaugural Schiefelbein Global Dispute Resolution Conference (18 January 2019), video available online at: <https://www.indisputably.org/?p=13752> and associated paper available at: <https://cil.nus.edu.sg/activities/18-january-2019-director-lucy-reed-delivers-keyn ote-address-at-inaugural-schiefelbein-global-dispute-resolution-conference-at-sandra-day-oconnor-school-of-law-at-arizona-state-university/>.

[85] Christian Buhring-Uhle and others, "The Arbitrator as Mediator: Some Recent Empirical Insights" (2003) 20 Journal of International Arbitration 81. Also see Christian Buhring-Uhle and others, *Arbitration and Mediation in International Business* (2nd edn, Wolters Kluwer Law & Business 2006) 108–09.

November 2014 by the International Mediation Institute found that 90.5 per cent of those surveyed were of the opinion that the absence of any kind of international enforcement mechanism for mediated settlements either presented a major impediment or was one deterring factor to the growth of mediation as a mechanism for resolving cross-border disputes.[86] In another survey, 74 per cent of respondents indicated that they thought an international convention concerning the enforcement of settlement agreements would encourage mediation and conciliation.[87] It has been suggested that the desire for enforceability of a mediated settlement agreement may be "particularly high" in the commercial context, as "businesses often worry about worst-case scenarios, however unlikely, and want legal assurances as opposed to merely precatory language".[88]

Furthermore, the Singapore Convention will raise the profile of mediation as a means of cross-border dispute settlement. In fact, one may suggest that it has already done so. There are a few aspects to how this could promote the use of mediation. First, the mere awareness of mediation will increase its chance of being considered, and possibly utilized, in the event of a dispute. Second, with an international framework for the enforcement of mediation outcomes, particularly one developed under the auspices of the United Nations, mediation's legitimacy will be bolstered, making it more attractive to users of dispute resolution.[89] As it has been observed, "[o]ne could even go as far as to say that the Convention will give international mediation the patina that international arbitration has under the New York Convention".[90] Third, the Singapore Convention is likely to lead to a strengthening of the supporting structures for mediation. This could be in respect of the support that local legal systems and legal institutions lend to mediation and mediated settlement agreements.[91] Internationally, we may

[86] International Mediation Institute, IMI survey results overview: How Users View the Proposal for a UN Convention on the Enforcement of Mediated Settlements (2014), <https://imimediation.org/2017/01/16/users-view-propopsal-un-convention-enforcement-mediated-settlements/>. The UNCITRAL Working Group that negotiated the Singapore Convention was informed of this survey in UNCITRAL, Note by the Secretariat, Settlement of commercial disputes: enforceability of settlement agreements resulting from international commercial conciliation/mediation, UN Doc A/CN.9/WG.II/WP.187 (27 November 2014) (hereinafter, "UNCITRAL WP 187"), 6.

[87] Stacey Strong, "Use and Perception of International Commercial Mediation and Conciliation: A Preliminary Report on Issues Relating to the Proposed UNCITRAL Convention on International Commercial Mediation and Conciliation" (2014) University of Missouri School of Law Legal Studies Research Paper No 2014-28, 45. The UNCITRAL Working Group that negotiated the Singapore Convention was similarly informed of this survey in UNCITRAL WP 187, 6.

[88] Stacey Strong, "Beyond International Commercial Arbitration? The Promise of International Commercial Mediation" (2014) 45 Washington University Journal of International Law and Policy 11, 35.

[89] Albeit not writing about mediation in the commercial context, Lauterpacht has observed that "unless there is in the background a court endowed with compulsory jurisdiction, little respect is paid to the conciliator". See Hersch Lauterpacht, *The Function of Law in the International Community* (The Lawbook Exchange 2008), 276. The same observation has been made in respect of arbitration. See eg Thomas Carbonneau, "At the Crossroads of Legitimacy and Arbitral Autonomy" (2005) 16 The American Review of International Arbitration 213, 215–16 ("The right of judicial supervision must be exercised to maintain arbitration's effectiveness and to safeguard its legitimacy by correcting fundamental abuses"); Julian Lew, "Does National Court Involvement Undermine the International Arbitration Process?" (2009) 24 American University International Law Review 489, 492–93 ("Without prejudice to autonomy, international arbitration does regularly interact with national jurisdiction for its existence to be legitimate and for support, help, and effectiveness").

[90] Reed, "Ultima Thule" (n 84).

[91] In one study, it has been suggested that the development of private international law treaties and frameworks, as well as model laws, enable countries to strengthen their local legal systems and legal institutions. Such treaties, frameworks, and model laws provide the means for reform and development, and enable the internalization of rules, norms, and practices. See Catherine Rogers and Christopher Drahozal, "Does International Arbitration

also see a reinvigoration of efforts to grow the mediation ecosystem, through training, accreditation, and the establishment of international standards, or a code of conduct, for mediators.[92]

Importantly, in the growth that mediation is expected to experience, the flexibilities of mediation practice, and the diversity in mediation practice models, will be preserved. When the Singapore Convention was negotiated, it was important to the negotiators that the introduction of an enforcement mechanism for settlement agreements would not "blur the distinction that currently existed between arbitration and conciliation by adding more formal requirements to conciliation".[93]

The definition of mediation in the Singapore Convention respects the different processes by which mediations can be carried out.[94] It focuses on the involvement of a neutral third person who does not have the authority to impose a solution on the disputing parties. There is no requirement for the mediation process to be "structured".[95] Mediations may include those administered by, or undertaken under, the auspices of an institution.[96] In addition, the definition accommodates the flexible nature of settlement agreements. It does not limit the types of remedies that can be reflected in a settlement agreement. In particular, the negotiators decided against limiting enforcement only to the pecuniary obligations in a settlement agreement,[97] preferring instead for there to be no limitation on the nature of the remedies or contractual obligations that the settlement agreements to be enforced may contain.[98] This shows appreciation for how parties to a mediation can design a settlement that responds to their needs, such a settlement often extending beyond pure monetary relief.[99]

As a further illustration, the form requirements that a settlement agreement must meet in order for it to be enforceable under the Singapore Convention are simple and not overly prescriptive.[100] As noted earlier in this chapter, the Convention may apply

---

Enfeeble or Enhance Local Legal Institutions" in Daniel Behn and others (eds), *The Legitimacy of Investment Arbitration: Empirical Perspectives* (Cambridge University Press 2019), <https://ssrn.com/abstract=3404615>. Also see Carrie Shu Shang and Ziyi Huang, "The Singapore Convention in Light of China's Changing Mediation Scene" (2020) 2 Asian Pacific Mediation Journal 63, for the anticipated impacts of the Singapore Convention on the mediation scene in China.

[92] During the negotiations for the Singapore Convention, the standards applicable to the mediator and the mediation process were discussed. It was recognized that they take different forms, ranging from domestic legislation on mediation to codes of conduct developed by professional associations. The UNCITRAL Secretariat was requested to include, in the explanatory material accompanying the Singapore Convention, an illustrative list of examples of such standards. See UNCITRAL WG II February 2017 Report, 16; UNCITRAL WG II October 2017 Report, 15–16.

[93] UNCITRAL, Report of Working Group II (Arbitration and Conciliation) on the work of its sixty-second session (New York, 2–6 February 2015), UN Doc A/CN.9/832 (11 February 2015) (hereinafter, "UNCITRAL WG II February 2015 Report"), 7.

[94] See eg UNCITRAL WG II February 2016 Report, note 5, 18–19. For an elaboration of the different models of and variations in mediation, see Laurence Boulle, "International Enforceability of Mediated Settlement Agreements: Developing the Conceptual Framework" (2014) 7 Contemporary Asia Arbitration Journal 35, 48–56.

[95] UNCITRAL WG II February 2016 Report, –18-19; UNCITRAL WG II September 2016 Report, 8–9 and 28–29.

[96] UNCITRAL WG II February 2016 Report, 19.

[97] UNCITRAL WG II September 2015 Report, 10.

[98] UNCITRAL WG II September 2016 Report, 4.

[99] See discussion in UNCITRAL WG II February 2015 Report, 9; UNCITRAL WG II September 2015 Report, 10; UNCITRAL WG II September 2016 Report, 4.

[100] UNCITRAL WG II February 2016 Report, 21.

so long as the settlement agreement is in writing, signed by the parties to the agreement, and there is evidence that the settlement agreement resulted from mediation.[101]
Notably, the "in writing" and signature requirements can be met by an electronic communication.[102] This caters for situations such as online mediation, or where the parties
to a settlement agreement are not physically in the same location when the agreement
is drafted.[103]

When deciding on the form requirements, the negotiators considered but did not
incorporate a requirement for a mediated settlement agreement to be encapsulated
in a "single document", as distinct from an exchange of communication between the
parties, or other contract formulation practices such as incorporation by reference.[104]
While it was suggested that a "single document" requirement would make it easier for
an enforcing authority to determine the terms of the settlement and therefore expedite
enforcement, there were doubts that it would necessarily be aligned with current practices in the conclusion of mediated settlement agreements, and could therefore place an
additional burden on parties.[105]

Regarding evidence that the settlement agreement resulted from mediation, the
Singapore Convention provides an open, illustrative list as to what such evidence might
be.[106] The illustrative list provides guidance for a party relying on a settlement agreement, while preserving flexibility, as to what evidence may be supplied. In this way, different mediation practices in different jurisdictions are respected.

## 3.2   Interaction with Other Methods of Dispute Resolution

A number of dispute resolution institutions have promulgated arbitration rules that
allow tribunals to render an award on agreed terms, if the disputing parties settle their
dispute during arbitral proceedings.[107] These provisions were first introduced in order
to encourage the settlement of disputes. However, they have also been utilized strategically as a means of enforcing mediated settlement agreements under the umbrella
of the New York Convention, leveraging on the New York Convention's broad network
of Contracting States.[108]

---

[101] Article 4(1) of the Singapore Convention on Mediation.
[102] Article 2(1) and Article 4(2) of the Singapore Convention on Mediation.
[103] Allan Stitt, "The Singapore Convention: When has a Mediation Taken Place (Article 4)?" (2019) 20 Cardozo
Journal of Conflict Resolution 1173, 1175.
[104] UNCITRAL WG II February 2016 Report, 21.
[105] UNCITRAL WG II September 2016 Report, 13 and 30–31.
[106] Article 4(1)(b) of the Singapore Convention on Mediation.
[107] For example, see Article 47.10 of the China International Economic and Trade Arbitration Commission
Arbitration Rules (2015); Rule 32.10 of the Singapore International Arbitration Centre Rules 2016; Article 45(1)
of the Stockholm Chamber of Commerce Arbitration Rules (2017); Article 37(1) of the Vienna International
Arbitration Centre Rules of Arbitration and Mediation (2018). The UNCITRAL Model Law on International
Commercial Arbitration, in Article 30, also provides for the ability of tribunals to render awards on agreed terms,
with the same status and effect as any other award on the merits of the case.
[108] Wolski, "Enforcing Mediated Settlement Agreements (MSAs)" (n 32) 96. This is also observable in the context of investor-State dispute settlement. For example, see *Joseph Charles Lemire v Ukraine I*, Case No ARB(AF)/98/
1, Award (Embodying Settlement Agreement), 18 September 2000; *Miminco LLC, John Dormer Tyson and Ilunga
Jean Mukendi v Democratic Republic of the Congo*, ICSID Case No ARB/03/14, Award (Embodying Settlement

Additionally, institutions have introduced hybrid processes, such as arb-med, med-arb and arb-med-arb. The mixing of arbitration and mediation is "a process which occurs naturally some of the time" through, for instance, the use of "mediation windows" in arbitration.[109] The "formalization" of hybrid processes seeks to further encourage disputing parties to settle their agreements.[110] In some cases, such processes have been introduced with the intention of enabling mediated settlement agreements to be enforced using the New York Convention.[111]

In med-arb, the disputing parties commence with a mediation. After reaching a settlement, the outcome of their mediation is submitted to an arbitral tribunal for a consent award to be rendered. In arb-med-arb, the disputing parties commence an arbitration with the intention of entering into mediation thereafter. If a settlement is reached, the outcome of the mediation is recorded as a consent award by the arbitration tribunal. If a settlement is not reached, the arbitration process resumes and the tribunal will render a decision that is binding on the disputing parties.

The use of consent awards and hybrid processes for the enforcement of mediated settlement agreements has attracted critique.

First, the question arises as to whether the New York Convention necessarily applies. A consent award is but a "trick of legal fiction", a "sleight of hand" by which a settlement agreement becomes an arbitral award.[112] Accordingly, it was been queried whether a consent award is, in fact, an arbitral award, or "something definitionally distinct to be given the same status and effect as an arbitral award".[113] Both consent awards and hybrid processes may not always satisfy the requirement in the New York Convention for there to have been "differences" between the parties, as jurisdictions may require that a dispute must subsist when the arbitration agreement is entered into and when the arbitrator is appointed.[114]

---

Agreement), 19 November 2007; *Trans-Global Petroleum, Inc. v Hashemite Kingdom of Jordan*, ICSID Case No ARB/07/25, Consent Award, 8 April 2009; *TCW Group, Inc & Dominion Energy Holdings, L.P. v Dominican Republic*, PCA Case No 2008-06, Consent Award, 16 July 2009; *EVN AG v Macedonia, former Yugoslav Republic of Macedonia*, ICSID Case No ARB/09/10, Award (Embodying Settlement Agreement), 2 September 2011; *Mobil Investments Canada Inc. v Canada*, ICSID Case No ARB/15/6, Consent Award, 4 February 2020, for which the respective settlements were recorded in the form of an award on agreed terms.

[109] Bobette Wolski, "Arb-Med-Arb (and MSAs): A Whole Which is Less Than, Not Greater Than, the Sum of its Parts?" (2013) 6 Contemporary Asia Arbitration Journal 249, 268.

[110] ibid 268.

[111] For example, see the website of the Singapore International Mediation Centre (SIMC), where arb-med-arb is introduced as "a flexible and efficient form of alternative dispute resolution, which combines the advantages of confidentiality and neutrality with enforceability and finality", <https://simc.com.sg/dispute-resolution/arb-med-arb/>. The SIMC, together with the Singapore International Arbitration Centre (SIAC), are behind the SIAC-SIMC Arb-Med-Arb Protocol, which was launched on 5 November 2014. The Protocol enables an SIAC arbitration to be stayed while the dispute is submitted for mediation at the SIMC, and thereafter for any settlement reached in the course of the mediation to be recorded by the arbitral tribunal as a consent award. If the dispute is not settled by mediation, arbitral proceedings are resumed.

[112] Steele, "Enforcing International Commercial Mediation Agreements as Arbitral Awards under the New York Convention" (n 42) 1397.

[113] ibid 1397.

[114] Laurence Boulle and Jay Qin, "Globalising Mediated Settlement Agreements" (2016) 3 Journal of International and Comparative Law 33, 41; Wolski, "Enforcing Mediated Settlement Agreements (MSAs)" (n 32) 97; Sussman, "The New York Convention through a Mediation Prism" (n 84) 12. Also see Christopher Newmark and Richard Hill, "Can A Mediated Settlement become an Enforceable Arbitration Award?" (2000) 16 Arbitration International 81.

Second, while the New York Convention may provide a mechanism for enforcement, its application to mediation, an amicable form of dispute resolution, results in an "imperfect fit".[115] Some of the "arbitration-based" grounds for refusal in the New York Convention, for instance, do not transfer well to the mediation context.[116] As discussed in this chapter, the procedural irregularities that are the subject of Article V(1)(b) and Article V(1)(d) of the New York Convention do not manifest in the context of a mediation, and applying these grounds to the mediation context could strip mediation of some of its benefits.

One of the purposes behind the Singapore Convention was to "address the enforceability of settlement agreements directly, rather than [rely] on the legal fiction of deeming them to be arbitral awards".[117] The question may thus be asked as to the likely impact of the Singapore Convention on arbitration, specifically whether mediation will grow at the expense of arbitration, or whether consent awards and mixed mode of dispute resolution might be rendered obsolete.

The short answer to the question is no: there will not be any such growth where mediation gains at the expense of arbitration, nor consequential obsolescence of consent awards or hybrid processes.

Mediation will not grow at the expense of arbitration. For one, the dispute resolution pie is expanding. With more cross-border commercial relations, there will be more international disputes. Further, it has been observed that the profile of cross-border disputants is also changing, with "all sorts of people ... finding themselves engaged in cross-border disputes".[118] This is likely to translate into a demand for different types of dispute resolution processes. In addition, different types of disputes are suited to different types of dispute resolution processes; some disputes are suited to arbitration, and some to mediation.

Depending on the subject matter of the dispute, the urgency of the situation, the relationship between the parties and other factors, disputing parties may choose litigation, arbitration, mediation, or some combination of these, to resolve their dispute.[119] Similarly, consent awards and hybrid processes will continue to be relevant and helpful to some users of dispute resolution, depending on the circumstances of their dispute. In respect of hybrid processes, the flexibility to move between mediation and arbitration could be useful to disputing parties. For instance, mediation could be utilized to

---

[115] Steele, "Enforcing International Commercial Mediation Agreements as Arbitral Awards under the New York Convention" (n 42) 1387.

[116] ibid 1412.

[117] UNCITRAL, Note by the Secretariat, Planned and possible future work – Part III, Proposal by the Government of the United States of America: Future work for Working Group II, UN Doc A/CN.9/822 (2 June 2014), 4.

[118] Alexander, "Ten Trends in International Commercial Mediation" (n 82) 407. Alexander observes that "[i]ncreasing the diversity in the characteristics and needs of disputants in cross-border disputes has enhanced the appeal of mediation".

[119] In a similar vein, it has been observed that mediation is "no magic wand for every dispute". Some cases may be more suited to litigation because of the opportunity to thereby obtain an authoritative precedent. Also, the potential for a successfully resolved dispute in the context of a mediation sometimes requires the seizing of "narrow windows of opportunity". See Thomas Walde, "Efficient Management of Transnational Disputes: Mutual Gain by Mediation or Joint Loss in Litigation" (2006) 22 Arbitration International 205, 216–17.

crystallize the issues in a dispute, or resolve part of the dispute, leaving arbitration to tackle what remains and which may benefit from adjudication.[120] The association between mediation and arbitration could also serve to enhance the use of mediation in dispute settlement.[121]

The Singapore Convention broadens the suite of options available to users of dispute resolution. It does so not just by making mediation more meaningful, effective, and viable for the resolution of international commercial disputes; the Convention preserves other vehicles for enforcement.

The Singapore Convention does this by excluding from its scope of application settlement agreements that have been approved by a court or concluded in the course of proceedings before a court, and that are possible of being enforced as a judgment in the state of that court. It also does not apply to settlement agreements that have been recorded and are possible of being enforced as an arbitral award.[122] These exclusions were incorporated to address concerns over not only gaps, but also overlap, in the enforcement regimes of judgments, arbitral awards, and mediated settlement agreements. Specifically, the purpose was to avoid overlaps or gaps between the Singapore Convention, on the one hand, and the Hague Conventions on court judgments as well as the New York Convention, on the other hand.[123]

The Singapore Convention also acknowledges the practice of combined dispute resolution processes. In the definition of mediation in the Convention, the phrase "at the time of mediation" does not appear as it was seen as unnecessary. Nevertheless, the understanding is that the lack of authority to impose a solution is specific to the time of the mediation. In this way, the Singapore Convention accommodates hybrid processes, such as med-arb.[124]

The Singapore Convention simply seeks to "[level] the playing field ... with respect to enforceability" between the outcomes of different forms of dispute resolution.[125] If disputing parties choose mediation, they may not always pay attention to the details of enforcement of their eventual settlement agreement. The need to provide for enforcement may only become significant or may only become apparent later, when one party does not live up to its part of the deal, or when there is a need to demonstrate that the matter has been resolved. Alternatively, disputing parties may not wish to address the issues of enforcement at the time when they are seeking to achieve an amicable resolution, for fear of derailing that process.

What the Singapore Convention offers is a real choice between the different forms of dispute resolution and certainty in the form of follow-on effects from that choice,

---

[120] For example, see Berger (n 50) 395.

[121] Jeswald Salacuse, "Is There a Better Way? Alternative Methods of Treaty-Based, Investor–State Dispute Resolution" (2007) 31 Fordham International Law Journal 138, 182–83, although writing of investor–state disputes.

[122] Article 1(3) of the Singapore Convention on Mediation.

[123] Also see UNCITRAL WG II September 2016 Report, 35–36.

[124] UNCITRAL WG II February 2018 Report, 6.

[125] Stacey Strong, "Beyond International Commercial Arbitration? The Promise of International Commercial Mediation" (2014) 45 Washington University Journal of International Law and Policy 11, 28.

knowing that there will be certainty in the recognition and enforcement of the outcomes of the method of dispute resolution that is pursued, including mediation. The significance of such certainty cannot be overstated. This has been brought to bear particularly in view of the world's experience with the COVID-19 pandemic, which has presented and will continue to present new uncertainties and challenges, and which has led to greater encouragement to consider mediation.[126]

## 3.3 Influence on Efforts to Reform the Investor–State Dispute Settlement Regime

The Singapore Convention will play into ongoing efforts to reform the investor–state dispute settlement regime, particularly by making investor–state mediation more attractive on account of the international enforceability of its outcomes.

In response to calls for reform of the investor–state dispute settlement regime, most recently, the effort has been taken up by UNCITRAL. In the discussions at UNCITRAL, amicable methods of dispute resolution other than arbitration, such as mediation, have been raised as a means of improving the efficiency of ISDS.[127] There was a generally shared view amongst the UNCITRAL delegations that such alternative dispute resolution methods could prevent disputes from being "escalated" to arbitration and also assuage concerns about the costs and duration of arbitration.[128]

---

[126] See eg British Institute of International and Comparative Law, "BIICL publishes a Concept Note on the effects of the pandemic on commercial contracts and legal consideration in mitigating mass defaults", Media Release (27 April 2020), <https://www.biicl.org/documents/10302_concept_note_270420.pdf>, quoting Lord Phillips, former President of the UK Supreme Court, that "parties should consider mediation, and conciliation should be encouraged at an early stage of legal proceedings". Also see British Institute of International and Comparative Law, "Breathing Space: A Concept Note on the effect of the pandemic on commercial contracts", <https://www.biicl.org/breathing-space>, a series of three concept notes on the effect of the 2020 pandemic on commercial contracts, including the proposal of a set of practical guidelines to encourage a more conciliatory approach to contractual disputes; Jonathan Lux, "Dispute Resolution and Mediation during the Covid-19 Disruption—Maritime and Transport Law Committee, July 2020" (International Bar Association Maritime and Transport Law Committee Publications 16 July 2020), <https://ibanet.org/Article/NewDetail.aspx?ArticleUid=CEB54377-412E-40F2-8328-533902295BD8>; Ivana Nincic, "The Impact and Lessons of the COVID-19 Crisis as Regards the Efficiency of Justice and the Functioning of the Judiciary—A View from the Mediator's Lens", International Mediation Institute website (11 June 2020), <https://imimediation.org/2020/06/11/the-impact-and-lessons-of-the-covid-19-crisis-as-regards-the-efficiency-of-justice-and-the-functioning-of-the-judiciary-a-view-from-the-mediators-lens/>; Kohe Hasan and Teh Joo Lin, "Firms Should Consider Mediation to Settle Rows amid Covid-19 Disruption", The Straits Times (updated 23 May 2020), <https://www.straitstimes.com/opinion/firms-should-consider-mediation-to-settle-rows-amid-covid-19-disruption>. Also see European Commission for the Efficiency of Justice (CEPEJ), CEPEJ Declaration on "Lessons learnt and challenges faced by the judiciary during and after the COVID-19 pandemic", CEPEJ (2020)8rev (10 June 2020), <https://rm.coe.int/declaration-en/16809ea1e2>, in which "access to justice" and "forward looking justice" were highlighted as important principles that would be helped by greater consultation and necessary dialogue with all justice professionals, including mediators.

[127] UNCITRAL, Report of Working Group III (Investor-State Dispute Settlement Reform) on the work of its thirty-sixth session (Vienna, 29 October–2 November 2018), UN Doc A/CN.9/964 (6 November 2018), 17. Also, interventions of the International Law Association at the thirty-seventh session (01/04/2019 15:00:00–01/04/2019 18:00:00); and of Turkey at the thirty-eighth session (15/10/2019 15:00:00 – 15/10/2019 18:00:00), audio recordings available online at <http://uncitral.un.org/en/audio>.

[128] UNCITRAL, Report of Working Group III (Investor-State Dispute Settlement Reform) on the work of its thirty-fourth session (Vienna, 27 November-1 December 2017) – Part II, UN Doc A/CN.9/930/Add.1/Rev.1 (26 February 2018), 17.

Investor–state disputes have specific characteristics and contexts that render mediation well placed to respond. For one, such disputes involve the challenge by investors of acts and measures of the state. These often involve public policy issues which means that, apart from potential implications for a state's right to regulate, other stakeholders such as interested members of the public may have views. Typically, the disputants have an "intended" long-term engagement or investment relationship that sometimes amounts to "a state of interdependence" between the investor and host state.[129] The amounts of money at stake are also often high.[130]

Against this backdrop, mediation commends itself because of the high degree of flexibility and autonomy that it offers to disputing parties, enabling parties to agree on a solution to their dispute that could extend beyond what initially triggered the dispute and beyond the mere payment of financial compensation. In contrast to an arbitral decision, disputants in a mediation retain control over the outcome of their dispute, an important factor for states vis-à-vis their policy and regulatory functions.[131] Furthermore, unlike arbitration which is "primarily means to liquidate an economic relationship", a mediated outcome could be helpful to preserving, perhaps even improving, the long-term relationship between the investor and the host state.[132]

The role of mediation in investor–state dispute settlement has been recognized by arbitral tribunals. In the *Achmea* arbitration, for instance, the tribunal in the final award had noted that "a settlement in this case would be a good thing ... and that the black and white solution of a legal decision in which one side wins and the other side loses is not the optimum outcome in this case".[133] In the *Perenco v Ecuador* arbitration's Interim Decision on the Environmental Counterclaim, the tribunal encouraged the disputing parties to consider "embarking on a mediation process or some other consensual

[129] Salacuse (n 121) 140–43.

[130] For example, see generally Diana Rosert, "The Stakes Are High: A Review of the Financial Costs of Investment Treaty Arbitration", International Institute for Sustainable Development (July 2014), <https://www.iisd.org/system/files/publications/stakes-are-high-review-financial-costs-investment-treaty-arbitration.pdf>, noting that "[t]he average claim in [treaty-based] investor-state arbitrations ... is about US$492 million ... Recent billion-dollar awards—such as the US$50 billion award against Russia in relation to the dissolved Yukos oil company and a US$1.77 billion award for Occidental in a dispute with Ecuador—highlight just how large the stakes can get."

[131] At the same time, there have been suggestions that investor–state mediation, as a collaborative exercise between the disputing parties, could draw suspicion for reducing the accountability of host states, and that the issue of transparency in the context of investor-State mediation may need to be addressed. For example, see Michael Reisman, "International Investment Arbitration and ADR: Married but Best Living Apart" in Susan Franck and Anna Joubin-Bret (eds), *Investor–State Disputes: Prevention and Alternatives to Arbitration II* (United Nations 2011) 22, 26; UNCITRAL, Report of Working Group III (Investor–State Dispute Settlement Reform) on the work of its thirty-ninth session (Vienna, 5–9 October 2020), UN Doc A/CN.9/1044 (10 November 2020) (hereinafter, "UNCITRAL WG III October 2020 Report"), 8.

In this regard, the Guide on Investment Mediation endorsed by the Energy Charter Conference suggests that a state party may wish to "define an internal monitoring mechanism that requires the state's representative in the mediation regularly to report to a group of officials with full access to the file about the progress of the discussions and any proposal that may have been made by the mediator". The Guide also suggests that "parties could agree to disclose the fact that the mediation is taking place and the main aspects of the settlement". See International Energy Charter, "Guide on Investment Mediation", 15–16, <https://www.energycharter.org/fileadmin/DocumentsMedia/CCDECS/2016/CCDEC201612.pdf>.

[132] Salacuse (n 121) 155. Also see UNCITRAL WG III October 2020 Report, 7.

[133] *Achmea B.V. v The Slovak Republic*, UNCITRAL PCA Case No 2008-13, Final Award, 7 December 2012, para 60.

procedure to assist in arriving at a mutually acceptable figure" for a suitable amount of compensation.[134]

There has also been favourable reception on the part of investors of the prospect of mediation in the investor–state context. For instance, 64 per cent of respondents to a survey in 2020 on investors' perceptions of investor–state dispute settlement would strongly or somewhat favour introducing mandatory mediation before arbitration proceedings can be commenced.[135]

More generally, interest in mediation as a form of alternative dispute resolution in the investor–state context has increased. Rules that can be applied to investor–state dispute settlement have been drafted by the International Bar Association and the International Chamber of Commerce.[136] In addition, the Energy Charter Conference endorsed a Guide on Investment Mediation in 2016.[137] On the part of governments, this can be gleaned from the general interest at the UNCITRAL Working Group on investor–state dispute settlement reform, in having further work done on the question of mediation and other forms of alternative dispute resolution, "with a view to ensure that ADR [alternative dispute resolution] could be more effectively used".[138] This includes capacity-building, and training of potential mediators and other stakeholders.[139]

As things stand, mediation is either not explicitly referred to in the majority of existing investment treaties (though this may not mean that the use of mediation is prevented in such cases) or referenced but without elaboration of how a mediation should proceed. That being said, recent treaties have signalled possible new trends through the introduction of frameworks such as annexes dedicated to mediation as a complement to the option of investor–state arbitration and the possibility for a respondent state to request mandatory mediation as a prerequisite of arbitration.[140] The international

---

[134] *Perenco Ecuador Limited v Republic of Ecuador*, ICSID Case No ARB/08/6, Interim Decision on the Environmental Counterclaim, 11 August 2015, paras 593–594.

[135] Though respondents also acknowledged that mediation may not be appropriate for all investment disputes, and may lead to an increase in costs and duration in investor–state dispute settlement. See Queen Mary University of London, "2020 QMUL-CCIAG Survey: Investors' Perceptions of ISDS (May 2020)", <http://www.arbitration.qmul.ac.uk/media/arbitration/docs/QM-CCIAG-Survey-ISDS-2020.pdf>.

[136] The International Bar Association's Rules on Investor-State Mediation, adopted by a resolution of the International Bar Association Council on 4 October 2012, <https://www.ibanet.org/Document/Default.aspx?DocumentUid=8120e11-F3C8-4A66-BE81-77CB3FDB9E9F>. The International Chamber of Commerce (ICC) Mediation Rules, dated 1 January 2014, <https://iccwbo.org/dispute-resolution-services/mediation/mediation-rules>.

[137] The Guide on Investment Mediation was endorsed by the Energy Charter Conference on 19 July 2016. <https://www.energycharter.org/fileadmin/DocumentsMedia/CCDECS/2016/CCDEC201612.pdf>. The Guide was prepared with the support of the International Mediation Institute, the International Centre for Settlement of Investment Disputes, the Arbitration Institute of the Stockholm Chamber of Commerce, the International Court of Arbitration of the ICC, UNCITRAL, and the Permanent Court of Arbitration.

[138] UNCITRAL WG III October 2020 Report, 9.

[139] UNCITRAL WG III October 2020 Report, 9.

[140] See Article 3.4 (Mediation and Alternative Dispute Resolution) and Annexes 6 (Mediation Mechanism for Disputes between Investors and Parties) and 7 (Code of Conduct for Members of the Tribunal, the Appeal Tribunal and Mediators) of the EU-Singapore Investment Protection Agreement of 2018; Article 3.31 (Mediation) and Annexes 10 (Mediation Mechanism for Disputes between Investors and Parties) and 11 (Code of Conduct for Members of the Tribunal, Members of the Appeal Tribunal and Mediators) of the EU-Vietnam Investment Protection Agreement of 2019. Also see the treaty survey examining the mediation clauses contained in existing international investment agreements, including model bilateral investment treaties, in Kun Fan, "Mediation of Investor–State Disputes: A Treaty Survey" (2020) 2 Journal of Dispute Resolution 327.

Mandatory mediation is provided for in Article 14.23 (Conciliation) of the Indonesia-Australia Comprehensive Economic Partnership of 2019.

framework for mediation is also being further developed. At the time of writing, work is underway at the International Centre for Settlement of Investment Disputes (ICSID) on a new set of mediation rules.[141]

Yet the UNCITRAL Working Group has noted that, in spite of increasing efforts to promote forms of dispute settlement other than arbitration, such as mediation, these forms remain underused in investor–state dispute settlement.[142] There are a number of reasons for the underuse of mediation in investor–state dispute settlement. A 2016 report by National University of Singapore's Centre for International Law found that states are more reluctant to settle disputes than investors and that the main reason for their reluctance is a preference to defer responsibility for deciding disputes to third-party adjudicators. Fear of allegations or prosecution for corruption, fear of public criticism, and fear of setting a settlement precedent that might encourage other in-vestors to make claims, hold states back from mediating disputes with investors.[143] The 2020 Singapore International Dispute Resolution Academy International Dispute Resolution Survey Final Report found that, in respect of investor–state disputes, arbi-tration was the top choice for users of the international dispute resolution system from civil and common law jurisdictions. One of the main reasons cited for this was the en-forceability of arbitral awards.[144]

The Singapore Convention is not a panacea for all of the obstacles to the use of me-diation in investor–state dispute settlement, and not all disputes are suited to being mediated. However, the Convention will directly address the issue of enforceability of mediated investor–state settlement agreements.

The Singapore Convention, which adopts a broad understanding of "commercial" international mediated settlement agreements, by default applies to settlement agree-ments in the investor–state dispute settlement context. Already, the Convention has been taken into consideration by various mediation rules, such as ICSID's new me-diation rules.[145] In addition, during discussions at the UNCITRAL Working Group

---

[141] The latest draft at the time of writing is available online via <https://icsid.worldbank.org/services-arbitrat ion-investor-state-mediation>. At the time of publication, ICSID's new mediation rules were approved by member states. The rules came into effect on 1 July 2022. ICSID's mediation rules are "the first institutional mediation rules designed specifically for investment disputes".

[142] See UNCITRAL WG III October 2020 Report, 9. Note that concrete information on the use of mediation in investor–state disputes is difficult to find. See Catherine Kessedjian and others, "Mediation in Future Investor-State Dispute Settlement", Academic Forum on ISDS Concept Paper 2020/16 (5 March 2020), <http://www.jus.uio. no/pluricourts/english/projects/leginvest/academic-forum/> 8–10. Also see Walde (n 119) 217.

[143] Seraphina Chew and others, "Report: Survey on Obstacles to Settlement of Investor–State Disputes", NUS-Centre for International Law Working Paper 18/01 (September 2018), <https://cil.nus.edu.sg/publications>. Also see Stephen Schwebel, "Is Mediation of Foreign Investment Disputes Plausible?" (2007) 22 ICSID Review—Foreign Investment Law Journal 237, concluding that "[i]t may be in the nature of bureaucracies, governmental and corporate, to prefer to shift rather than assume responsibility". Though see the reflections of Metalclad's former CEO, Grant Kesler, regarding his experience with NAFTA Chapter Eleven, "that the arbitral mechanism he ex-perienced was do dissatisfying that he wished he had merely entrusted his company's fate to informal mechan-isms". As described in Jack Coe, Jr, "Toward a Complementary Use of Conciliation in Investor–State Disputes—A Preliminary Sketch" (2005) 12 University of California Davis Journal of International Law and Policy 7, 8–13.

[144] Singapore International Dispute Resolution Academy, "SIDRA International Dispute Resolution Survey: 2020 Final Report", <https://sidra.smu.edu.sg/sites/sidra.smu.edu.sg/files/survey/index/html>.

[145] As part of its work to amend its rules, ICSID proposed in August 2018 to expand the scope of its Additional Facility to encompass a new set of mediation rules for investor–state disputes, citing as part of the introduction to the proposal, the new Singapore Convention. Amendments were also proposed to the conciliation rules to fa-cilitate the enforcement of any settlement agreement reached as a result of the conciliation, under the Singapore

session in October 2020, which was the most recent session at the time of writing, "[i]t was said that policies as well as the legal framework for encouraging mediation would be necessary. In that context, it was highlighted that [the Singapore Convention] provided for a useful instrument also in the context of [investor–state dispute settlement]."[146]

There is the possibility of State Parties to the Singapore Convention entering a governmental agencies reservation. If the obstacles to states mediating can be tackled, this reservation could be less commonly made. There are a number of ways of going about this. Apart from capacity-building and the sharing of best practices, treaty dispute settlement mechanisms could be designed to give more room for mediation, including stipulating when mediation should or could take place (such as during the "cooling-off period", ie the time frame during which disputing parties were required to attempt amicable settlement before arbitration), and how mediation could interrelate with other forms of dispute resolution such as an ongoing or subsequent arbitration.[147] Government structures could also be designed to give room for mediation, including structures to improve coordination among the relevant government agencies when negotiating an amicable settlement to a dispute, and to ensure that there is the appropriate authorization and accountability on the part of state representatives to utilize mediation.[148]

## 4.  Conclusion

As Judge Schwebel noted in the context of the New York Convention, "[t]reaty-making is a laborious and difficult process, which governments undertake with a view not toward violating but toward implementing the resultant treaty rights and obligations to their mutual benefit".[149]

Aside from the likely impacts of the Singapore Convention on the dispute resolution landscape that have been explored in this chapter, the Convention stands as a testament to the survival of multilateralism, having been born out of a multilateral negotiations process at the United Nations. In addition, the Singapore Convention

---

Convention. See ICSID, Proposals for Amendment of the ICSID Rules—Working Paper (2 August 2018), <https://icsid.worldbank.org/resources/rules-and-regulations/icsid-rules-and-regulations-amendment-working-papers>, 409 and 748.

[146] UNCITRAL WG III October 2020 Report, 8.
[147] Aspects of investment treaty dispute settlement mechanism design are the subject of ongoing work at UNCITRAL, which is at its early stages. At the thirty-ninth session of Working Group III (Investor–State Dispute Settlement Reform) in October 2020, which was the most recent meeting at the time of writing, the UNCITRAL Secretariat was requested to prepare guidelines and best practices for participants in investor–state mediation. In addition, the Secretariat was requested to develop rules for investor–state mediation, as well as clauses that could be used in investment treaties. See UNCITRAL WG III October 2020 Report, 9. In respect of "cooling-off" provisions in investment treaties, a study by the Academic Forum estimates that 71 per cent of existing investment treaties contain such provisions. See Kessedjian and others (n 142) 5–6.
[148] For example, see UNCITRAL WG III October 2020 Report, 8.
[149] Stephen Schwebel, "A Celebration of the United Nations New York Convention on the Recognition and Enforcement of Foreign Arbitral Awards" in Stephen Schwebel, *Justice in International Law: Further Selected Writings* (Cambridge University Press 2011) 276, 277.

can be, and has been, celebrated as a treaty that contributes to the multilateral rules-based global economy. During the event commemorating the entry into force of the Singapore Convention, Honourable Aiyaz Sayed-Khaiyum, Attorney-General and Minister for Economy, Civil Service and Communications, Republic of Fiji spoke of the Convention's contribution towards "a rules-based economic system for the benefit of businesses across our borders".[150] In the remarks of the Kingdom of Saudi Arabia's Minister of Commerce, HE Dr Majid Al-Kassabi, the minister spoke of the Singapore Convention's contribution towards a "predictable and frictionless trade system".[151]

It has been heartening to see the support that has been expressed for the Singapore Convention, not least in the form of early signatories and ratifications. This support could not have been anticipated when we were contending with an uncertain start and the challenges of finding consensus.

As we continue to reach for the stars, there are a few elements that are directly relevant to the Convention, which we still need to look out for to stay the course. Amongst these, two stand out. First, the consistent interpretation and application of the Convention by legislatures and competent authorities, so that the effort at harmonization is not undermined by divergent approaches to the implementation of the Convention. Second, increasing the number of signatories to the Convention including, as permitted by Article 12 of the Convention, regional economic integration organizations, so that the reach of the enforcement framework will be extended.[152]

In short, the work is not yet done and these are not easy tasks by any measure. But, as they say, *per aspera ad astra*. The striving will be worth the while, for the pursuit of the rule of law and access to justice, by peaceful means.

## Author's Note

This chapter is informed by the author's involvement as the chairperson of the negotiations for the Singapore Convention on Mediation, and as the rapporteur for the United Nations Commission for International Trade Law (UNCITRAL) Working Group on investor–State dispute settlement reform. The views expressed herein are the views of the author and do not necessarily represent the views of the Government of Singapore.

---

[150] Remarks of Honourable Aiyaz Sayed-Khaiyum, Attorney-General and Minister for Economy, Civil Service and Communications, Republic of Fiji, at the Digital Event to Commemorate the Entry into Force of the Singapore Convention on Mediation, video available online at <https://www.singaporeconvention.org/events/scm2020> at 11min 45sec.

[151] Remarks of HE Dr Majid Al-Kassabi, Minister of Commerce, Kingdom of Saudi Arabia, at the Digital Event to Commemorate the Entry into Force of the Singapore Convention on Mediation, video available online at <https://www.singaporeconvention.org/events/scm2020> at 15min 41sec.

[152] The European Union participated actively in the negotiations for the Singapore Convention. For an overview of the European Union's views during the deliberations when developing the Singapore Convention, see Alan Anderson and others, "The United Nations Convention on International Settlement Agreements Resulting from Mediation: Its Genesis, Negotiation and Future" in Christian Campbell (ed), *The Comparative Law Yearbook of International Business* (Wolters Kluwer 2020), describing how "the EU approached the project with skepticism and frequent opposition", but also suggesting that "the EU's purported concerns regarding conflicts between the Singapore Convention and other international instruments should not be an impediment".

# 10

# The Growth of Regional Courts and the Judicial Settlement of Inter-State Disputes in Africa

*Abdulqawi A Yusuf*

## 1. Introduction

When the Charter of the first continental organization in Africa, the Organization of African Unity (OAU), was adopted by the newly independent African states in 1963, it did not contain any reference to judicial settlement of disputes between the member states of the organization. One of the principles to which member states declared their adherence, under Article III of the Charter, was the "peaceful settlement of disputes by negotiation, mediation, conciliation or arbitration", and, to that end, a Commission on Mediation, Conciliation and Arbitration was created by the OAU through a protocol adopted in 1964.[1] However, there was no mention anywhere of the possibility for OAU member states to settle their disputes by judicial means.

This situation changed due to two developments in the late 1990s and early 2000s. First, the establishment of regional economic integration schemes, the first of which was the Common Market for Eastern and Southern Africa (COMESA) created in 1998; and secondly, the adoption on 11 July 2000 of the Constitutive Act of the African Union (AU) which replaced the Charter of the OAU and created a new continental organization. Both the COMESA treaty and the AU Constitutive Act provided for the establishment of courts of justice for the settlement of disputes among states in their respective areas of competence.[2]

The treaties establishing other regional economic communities (RECs), such as the Economic and Monetary Community of Central African States (CEMAC) in 2000,[3] the East African Community (EAC) in 2001,[4] the Economic Community of West African States (ECOWAS) in 2002,[5] and the Southern African Development Community

---

[1] Charter of the Organization of African Unity (adopted 25 May 1963, entered into force 13 September 1963) 479 UNTS 39, art III(4).
[2] Treaty Establishing the Common Market for Eastern and Southern Africa (adopted 5 November 1993, entered into force 8 December 1994) 2314 UNTS 265 (hereafter COMESA Treaty); Constitutive Act of the African Union (adopted 11 July 2000, entered into force 26 May 2001) 2158 UNTS 3.
[3] Traité instituant la Communauté économique et monétaire de l'Afrique centrale (adopted 16 March 1994, entered into force June 1999) arts 2, 5.
[4] Treaty for the Establishment of the East African Community (adopted 30 November 1999, entered into force 7 July 2000, amended 14 December 2006 and 20 August 2007) 2144 UNTS 255 (hereafter EAC Treaty).
[5] Revised Treaty of the Economic Community of West African States (adopted 24 July 1993, entered into force 23 August 1995) 2373 UNTS 233 (hereafter ECOWAS Treaty).

Abdulqawi A Yusuf, *The Growth of Regional Courts and the Judicial Settlement of Inter-State Disputes in Africa* In: *By Peaceful Means.* Edited by: Charles N Brower, Joan E Donoghue, Cian C Murphy, Cymie R Payne and Esmé R Shirlow, Oxford University Press. © Abdulqawi A Yusuf 2024. DOI: 10.1093/oso/9780192848086.003.0010

(SADC) in 2005,[6] soon followed suit and created their own courts and tribunals. Consequently, there are at present five courts of justice or tribunals created by RECs in Africa. Meanwhile, a protocol establishing the Court of Justice of the African Union has been adopted by the AU but has never become operational, and subsequent agreements have superseded its founding protocol.[7] Once the relevant AU protocols come into force, the Court of Justice of the African Union will be merged with the African Court of Human and Peoples' Rights to form an African Court of Justice and Human Rights.[8]

The creation of all these courts clearly indicates a shift in attitudes among African states toward the judicial settlement of disputes since the early days of independence. However, it appears that the reluctance to use judicial means of dispute settlement has not been fully overcome even in the context of regional integration schemes. This chapter will first review briefly the role of the regional courts as originally envisaged in their founding treaties. Secondly, it will examine some of the notable cases decided by three of these courts (the East African Court of Justice, the ECOWAS Community Court, and the SADC Tribunal) to ascertain the nature of the cases so far brought before them. Finally, the chapter will appraise the difficulties faced by these courts in carrying out their mandates and their relative underutilization by member states for the settlement of disputes arising from the interpretation or application of the integration treaties.

## 2. The Role of the Courts under the Founding Treaties

### 2.1 The Court of Justice of the Common Market for Eastern and Southern Africa (COMESA)

The COMESA Court of Justice, which was the first regional court to be established in the African continent, became operational in 1998. It has general jurisdiction to deal with all matters which may be referred to it pursuant to the treaty establishing COMESA (COMESA Treaty).[9] This includes reference by a member state alleging that another member state or the Council of COMESA has failed to fulfil an obligation under the COMESA Treaty or has infringed the provisions of the treaty. It also includes references by a member state or by any person who resides in a member state alleging that any act, directive, decision, or regulation is unlawful or infringes any provision of the treaty. However, disputes between member states regarding the COMESA Treaty may only be submitted to the Court under a special agreement between the member states

---

[6] Treaty of the Southern African Development Community (adopted 17 August 1992, entered into force 5 October 1993) (1993) 32 ILM 120.

[7] Protocol of the Court of Justice of the African Union (adopted 1 July 2003, entered into force 11 February 2009).

[8] Protocol on the Statute of the African Court of Justice and Human Rights (adopted 1 July 2008) (2009) 48 ILM 317.

[9] COMESA Treaty (n 2) art 23.

concerned. Meanwhile, reference by individuals is possible only on condition that the person concerned has first exhausted local remedies in the national courts or tribunals of the member state.[10] The COMESA Court of Justice also has the power to arbitrate contractual disputes between a state and a corporation or a state and an individual, provided there is a clause in the contract granting such jurisdiction.[11] Thus, natural and legal persons are granted standing before the Court, which also serves as an administrative tribunal that can hear disputes between the COMESA and its employees.[12]

The COMESA Court of Justice also has competence to issue a preliminary ruling, upon request by national courts, regarding a legal question on the application or interpretation of the COMESA Treaty, or on the validity of a regulation, directive, or decision of the Common Market. However, if the question on which a ruling is to be sought arises in the context of a case pending before a national court against whose judgment there is no judicial remedy under the national law of the member state, that court has an obligation to refer the matter to the COMESA Court of Justice. Finally, the Court may give advisory opinions where it is requested to do so by the COMESA Authority, the Council of Ministers, or a member state on questions of law arising from the provisions of the COMESA Treaty.[13]

## 2.2  The Court of Justice of the Communauté Economique et Monétaire de l'Afrique Centrale (CEMAC)

The CEMAC Court of Justice became operational in 2000 and has a very broad jurisdiction. The Court is organized into two chambers, the Judicial Chamber and the Chamber of Auditors. The Judicial Chamber is a court of first and last resort for disputes between member states related to the treaties or laws of the CEMAC, and in all cases between the CEMAC and its agents. It also has the power to issue advisory opinions, at the request of a member state or an organ of the community, on the conformity to the CEMAC treaties of legal texts proposed by a member state or an organ of the community on matters falling within the scope of these treaties.[14] It acts as the court of last resort with respect to suits for damages against the CEMAC and its agents.[15] Further, it acts as a court of last resort for cases between the Banking Commission of the Central African States and its credit establishments.[16]

---

[10]  ibid arts 24–26, 28.

[11]  ibid art 28.

[12]  ibid art 27.

[13]  ibid arts 30, 32.

[14]  Article 6, Convetion Regissant la Cour de Justice de la CEMAC, Libreville, 5 July 1996.

[15]  Traité révisé de la Communauté économique et monétaire de l'Afrique centrale (adopted 25 June 2008) art 48; Convention régissant la Cour de Justice Communautaire (adopted 30 January 2009) (hereafter Revised Convention on the CEMAC Court of Justice) arts 22–29, 34.

[16]  ibid art 23 (referring to actions against Community Organs which per Article 1 includes the Banking Commission of Central Africa); Convention régissant la Cour de Justice de la CEMAC (adopted 5 July 1996, superseded by Revised Convention on the CEMAC Court of Justice (n 14)) art 4.

The CEMAC Court of Justice's founding statute gives broad standing to claimants, such that disputes can be brought by member states, the Executive Secretary, and organs of the Community, and any natural persons regarding violations of conventions of the Community. Applicants may thus challenge acts of member states and CEMAC organs for violating Community law.[17] Like the COMESA Community Court, the CEMAC Court of Justice can also issue preliminary rulings on questions of law on which a national court seeks its advice with regard to the interpretation of the treaties or other legal instruments of the CEMAC.[18]

## 2.3  The East African Court of Justice (EACJ)

The EACJ became operational in 2001. It has had an appellate division since 2007. Its primary mandate is to interpret the treaty establishing the East African Community (EAC Treaty) and hear claims of violations of the EAC Treaty that can be referred by partner states or by the Secretary General (after he/she has requested the state to provide observations on such a violation).[19] Further, the EACJ can hear matters arising from an arbitration clause that confers such jurisdiction, or disputes between member states regarding the EAC Treaty pursuant to a special agreement.[20]

In addition to the bases of jurisdiction mentioned in this chapter, the EAC Treaty envisages empowering the Court to hear human rights claims in the future, although such an extension of the Court's jurisdiction has not yet occurred.[21] However, this has not prevented the Court from deciding to hear cases involving allegations of human rights violations.[22] In recent years, the EAC has also created a quasi-judicial body dealing specifically with questions arising under its Customs Union, and has given national courts almost exclusive jurisdiction over matters related to the Community Market Protocol, thereby depriving the EACJ of the possibility of exercising its jurisdiction over certain disputes otherwise arising under the rubric of the EAC.[23]

## 2.4  The ECOWAS (Economic Community of West African States) Community Court

The ECOWAS court became operational in 2002. This court also has broad jurisdiction, perhaps the broadest among the regional courts. In addition to its jurisdiction over disputes arising from the interpretation and application of ECOWAS law, it has,

---

[17] Revised Convention on the CEMAC Court of Justice (n 14) art 24.
[18] ibid, ar. 26.
[19] EAC Treaty (n 4) arts 23, 27–29.
[20] ibid art 32(b).
[21] ibid art 27(2).
[22] See Section 3.1.
[23] Protocol on the Establishment of the East African Community Common Market (adopted 20 November 2009), art 54; Protocol on the Establishment of the East African Customs Union (adopted 2 March 2004) art 41.

among others, the power to issue advisory opinions and act as a court of arbitration.[24] Most notable, however, is its clear authority to hear cases arising from allegations of human rights violations that occur in any member state under the 2005 Supplementary Protocol amending the Protocol on the Community Court of Justice (Supplementary Protocol of 2005).[25] This sets it apart from other regional courts where jurisdiction over human rights matters is not as clear under the statutes.

It is equally distinguishable from other regional courts by its broad jurisdiction "over any matter provided for in an agreement where the parties provide that the court shall settle disputes arising from the agreement".[26] This could be either an agreement between states or an agreement between a state and an investor.

The Court also has jurisdiction to hear disputes between the Community and its officials. It has the power to determine the non-contractual liability of the Community, and may order it to pay damages or make reparations for official acts or omissions of any Community institution or official in the performance of official duties or functions.[27]

## 2.5 The SADC (Southern African Development Community) Tribunal

The SADC Tribunal became operational in 2005 but was practically dissolved in 2011 by the member states. The SADC Tribunal's jurisdiction mainly related to the interpretation and application of the treaty establishing the community (SADC Treaty), protocols, and subsidiary instruments adopted within the framework of SADC, and acts of the institutions of the community. It also had appellate jurisdiction over the findings of panels set up by SADC. In addition, subject to the exhaustion of local remedies, natural or legal persons were entitled to bring disputes before the tribunal relating to violations by member states of the SADC Treaty, protocols, and subsidiary instruments.[28]

It is in the context of this jurisdiction that the SADC Tribunal ran into trouble, following its decisions on a string of cases brought soon after its establishment by individuals against Zimbabwe. The SADC Tribunal was placed in a suspended state when the SADC Summit decided in 2010 not to renew the terms of the serving judges and not to appoint new judges, pending a review of the Tribunal's jurisdiction and mandate.[29] At the end of the review process, a new protocol was adopted by the member states in 2014, which explicitly limits the jurisdiction of the Tribunal to disputes between

[24] Supplementary Protocol A/SP.1/01/05 amending Protocol A/P.1/7/91 relating to the Community Court of Justice (adopted 19 January 2005) (ECOWAS Court Supplementary Protocol) art 3; Protocol A/P.1/7/91 on the Community Court of Justice (adopted 6 July 1991) art 10.
[25] ECOWAS Court Supplementary Protocol (n 23) art 4.
[26] ibid art 3.
[27] ibid art 3.
[28] Protocol on the Tribunal and Rules thereof (adopted 7 August 2000) arts 14, 15.
[29] Final Communiqué of the 30th Jubilee Summit of SADC Heads of State and Government, 17 August 2010, [32].

states.[30] The new protocol has not yet received the ratifications necessary for its entry into force. Thus, the Tribunal still remains dormant.

## 3. Notable Cases Decided by the EACJ, ECOWAS Court, and SADC Tribunal

Although the African regional courts differ in their organization and areas of competence, they share a primary statutory mandate: adjudicating disputes between member states or between REC institutions and member states regarding the interpretation of founding treaties. While the jurisdiction of some courts, such as the ECOWAS Community Court, has subsequently been expanded to include human rights, the founding treaties predominantly stress the role of the courts in the interpretation and application of the rules governing sub-regional economic integration. The case law of the EACJ, ECOWAS Court, and SADC Tribunal indicates that member states are still reluctant to refer their disputes to the regional courts. Compared to states, private persons have demonstrated greater interest in turning to the regional courts to enforce their rights under REC law. As a result, the case law of the courts has developed in unexpected ways, sometimes provoking tensions between member states and the courts.

### 3.1 The East African Court of Justice (EACJ)

The EACJ has heard a number of interesting cases in its twenty years of existence and the cases have had a significant impact on the court's jurisdiction. As noted in this chapter, the EAC Treaty designates the EACJ as the arbiter of disputes between member states or between member states and EAC institutions regarding the interpretation of the founding treaty and its application. However, at the time of writing, the Court has yet to hear any inter-state cases. And while cases regarding the powers and operation of EAC institutions comprise a significant share of its docket, the bulk of the EACJ's recent activity has been focused on adjudicating the claims of private persons claiming violations of their rights under the EAC Treaty. The EACJ has thus entertained an increasing number of cases brought by private persons seeking to enforce rights against member states, despite the absence of an explicit grant of jurisdiction to hear human rights claims. The evolution of the EACJ's docket reflects in part its willingness in its early case law to affirm its authority to ensure that EAC institutions and member states operate according to Community law and principles.

In its first case, *Mwatela v East African Community*,[31] applicants challenged certain actions of the EAC Council of Ministers (the Council) and the Secretariat. Four private

---

[30] Protocol on the Tribunal in the Southern African Development Community (adopted 18 August 2014) (Revised Protocol on the SADC Tribunal) art 33.
[31] East African Court of Justice (EACJ) Reference No 1 of 2005 (First Instance Judgment of 10 October 2006).

members' bills were pending before the East African Legislative Assembly (EALA or the Assembly) in 2004. The Council, in its meeting of November 2004, decided that policy-oriented bills that have implications either for the member state's sovereign interests or for the budget of the community should be submitted to the Assembly by the Council rather than by private members. The Council therefore took responsibility for the bills and subsequently decided not to present the bills. Some members of the EALA took the matter to the EACJ.[32] The Court found that any member of the Assembly had the power to introduce a bill and that the right of legislative initiative did not rest with the Council alone. Once in the Assembly, the bills belonged to the Assembly and could not be withdrawn by the Council as had been done in this case. The Court further clarified the relationship between the Council and the Assembly by stating that even with respect to policy decisions, the Council did not have the power to dictate to the Assembly.[33] Finally, it confirmed that the Assembly was an organ of the Community and had competence only with respect to matters conferred to it by the EAC Treaty, and as such could only address matters on which the member states had surrendered sovereignty to the EAC.[34] The Court, however, ultimately declined to determine whether the three bills presented by the Assembly members fell within this category.[35] This case was significant because the Court was able to draw the boundaries between the functions of the various organs of the EAC and showed its readiness to rein in the Council and Attorneys-General of the EAC when they had overstepped their sphere of competence.

In another important case, *Nyong'o v Kenya*,[36] the court was asked to rule on the process of electing Kenya's representatives to the EALA. The court had been petitioned under Article 30 of the EAC Treaty to enjoin the swearing-in of Kenya's nine members of the EALA. The applicants were members of the Kenyan Parliament and contended that the rules of the Kenyan Parliament regarding such elections violated Article 50 of the EAC Treaty, since the representatives were appointed by the Business Committee of the Kenyan Parliament and not elected by the Parliament itself. The Attorney-General of Kenya, in a petition for the respondents, argued that Article 52(1) of the EAC Treaty specifically reserved jurisdiction to the High Court of Kenya. The court, however, disagreed with the Attorney-General, ruling that since an Article 50 election did not take place, the application of Article 52(1) was precluded.[37]

The EACJ held that Article 50 of the EAC Treaty required an election (ie choosing by vote), and, while there were a number of ways in which this could be accomplished (eg secret ballot, acclamation, show of hands), the "bottom line for compliance with Article 50 is that the decision to elect is a decision of and by the National Assembly".[38] The Court thus found that the National Assembly of Kenya did not undertake an election

---

[32] ibid 1–5.
[33] ibid 17–18, 20–21.
[34] *Mwatela v EAC* (n 30) 23–24.
[35] ibid 22–23.
[36] EACJ Reference No 1 of 2006 (First Instance Judgment of 30 March 2007).
[37] ibid 22–34.
[38] ibid 34.

within the meaning of Article 50 when its Business Committee unilaterally appointed (or rejected) individuals from lists of candidates presented to it by the various political parties in the Assembly rather than by putting the candidacies to a vote.

In a third case concerning human rights, *Katabazi v Secretary General of the East African Community*,[39] the EACJ stated that even though it did not have explicit jurisdiction over human rights issues, it would not "abdicate from exercising jurisdiction under Article 27(1) [of the EAC Treaty] merely because the reference includes allegation of human rights violation".[40] In other words, the Court was of the view that it should not refuse to rule on a case where allegations of human rights violations were incidental to the case itself. It then decided the case on the basis of Article 23(1) to ensure adherence to the law on the interpretation and application of the EAC Treaty.

The underlying facts here concerned sixteen persons who were brought before the Ugandan High Court and charged with treason. The High Court granted bail to fourteen of them; they were, however, re-arrested by the Ugandan security forces soon afterwards. The matter was brought to the Constitutional Court of Uganda, which ruled that the intervention by the security forces was unconstitutional. Since the men were not released even after the decision of the Constitutional Court, the EACJ was petitioned to determine the lawfulness of their continued detention.[41] The Secretary-General of the EAC and the Attorney General of Uganda challenged the court's jurisdiction, arguing that Article 27 of the EAC Treaty did not grant the court jurisdiction on human rights matters.[42] The Court, however, determined that although it did not have jurisdiction over human rights issues, Article 23 of the EAC Treaty empowered it to ensure adherence to the rule of law, which meant that where the law—even domestic law—has not been adhered to by a member state, the Court could exercise jurisdiction.[43]

Adherence to the rule of law by a member state, as established in Articles 6(d) and 7(2) of the EAC Treaty, has since become one of the most important grounds invoked by the EACJ for the exercise of its jurisdiction over cases regarding alleged violations by member states of their domestic laws, and, it may be added, for the extension of jurisdiction to human rights cases. Two recent cases further illustrate the jurisprudence of the Court according to which it may enquire into a member states' compliance with its domestic law to determine whether it breached its obligations under the EAC Treaty to observe the rule of law.

One case, *Union Trade Centre (UTC) v Rwanda*,[44] concerned the takeover of a mall owned by UTC, a company incorporated under the laws of Rwanda, by a Rwandan municipal commission charged with managing properties. UTC brought an action against Rwanda in 2013, but the trial division of the EACJ held that it lacked jurisdiction because UTC failed to establish that Rwanda violated due process, the rule of law and

---

[39] EACJ Reference No 1 of 2007 (First Instance Judgment of 1 November 2007).
[40] ibid 16.
[41] ibid 1–3.
[42] ibid 12.
[43] ibid 14–16.
[44] EACJ Reference No 10 of 2013 (First Instance Judgment of 26 November 2020).

human rights guaranteed under Articles 6(d) and 7(2) of the EAC Treaty.[45] However, the appellate division of the EACJ ordered a retrial of the case, since, in its view, the written pleadings of both parties failed to comply with the requirements of the rules of the Court on the presentation of evidence.[46] In the new trial, the trial division of the Court, recalling its jurisprudence on the member states' obligations in respect of adherence to the rule of law, stated that it had the power to enquire whether a member state had complied with its domestic law. It then ruled that Rwanda was responsible for the acts of the municipal commission and that the commission violated the principles of rule of law, good governance, accountability, transparency, and human rights under Articles 6(d), 7(2), and 8. The EACJ also found that Rwanda had violated its duty to promote "private sector confidence in partnerships with the public sector" and "people-centred and market-driven cooperation" in violation of Articles 5(3)(g) and 7(1)(a).[47]

In another recent case, *Malek v South Sudan*,[48] a judge of the Appeals Court of South Sudan brought a case to the EACJ against an order by the President of South Sudan to remove the judge (Malek) from office. South Sudan objected to Malek's claims on two grounds. First, for South Sudan, presidential acts could not be challenged before the Court due to the President's immunity from suit. Second, South Sudan argued that the judge's participation in an illegal strike justified his removal.[49]

The court dismissed South Sudan's objections as inapposite to the claims before it, and proceeded to the determination of whether the presidential order complied with South Sudanese law. The Court ruled that it had the power to determine, under the EAC Treaty, whether the presidential order complied with South Sudanese law on the basis that if a member state contravenes its domestic law "then, ipso facto, that State falls afoul of the rule of law principle in Articles 6*(d)* and 7(2) of the EAC Treaty".[50] The Court concluded that the President could only remove a judge following an investigation, a decision of the Board of Discipline, and a recommendation of the National Judicial Service Council. The presidential order having made no reference to the required recommendation, the Court concluded that the removal order violated the applicable legislation and the principle of the rule of law guaranteed by Articles 6(d) and 7(2) of the EAC Treaty.[51]

The cases examined in this chapter show two important tasks performed by the EACJ. First, there are those cases which showcase the role played by the Court in the interpretation and application of the provisions of the EAC Treaty relating to the functioning of the institutions and organs of the EAC, their respective powers, and their relations with the member states. Secondly, there are other cases which demonstrate that the EACJ has, to a certain extent, become a watchdog of the adherence of member

---

[45] *UTC v Rwanda*, EACJ Reference No 10 of 2013 (First Instance Judgment of 27 November 2014).
[46] *UTC v Rwanda*, EACJ Appeal No 1 of 2015 (Judgment of 20 November 2015).
[47] ibid [136].
[48] EACJ Reference No 9 of 2017 (First Instance Judgment of 24 July 2020).
[49] ibid [25], [26].
[50] ibid [30].
[51] ibid [36].

states to the rule of law in their own countries. This is a role which member states may not have expected the Court to assume, but that the Court itself appears to consider as being based, among other grounds, on Articles 7(2) and 23 of the EAC Treaty. In order to curb what has been viewed by the member states as judicial activism on the part of the Court, particularly with respect to human rights cases, the EAC member states amended the provisions of the EAC Treaty on the composition of the EACJ, its jurisdiction, the removal of judges, and standing before the Court. Notably, the amendments to Article 30 set a maximum limit of two months after the right of action arises for the institution of proceedings by persons against member states or EAC institutions. At the same time, the amendments to Article 26 of the treaty have made it easier for the Summit of Heads of State and Government or for a member state to remove or suspend EACJ judges, signalling a stronger potential for political interference in the Court by the highest organ of the EAC or by individual member states.[52] It is also noteworthy that the EACJ has not so far received any references regarding inter-state disputes on the interpretation or application of the EAC Treaty or on regional integration issues.

## 3.2 The ECOWAS Court

In contrast to the EACJ, the ECOWAS Community Court is empowered by a Supplementary Protocol of 2005 to deal with human rights cases and most of its judgments have so far dealt with human rights issues. This power was granted following a period of time during which the Court was inactive for a number of years. However, it was soon challenged by one of the ECOWAS member states, The Gambia. The Gambia tried to impose hurdles on the Court's jurisdiction with regard to human rights following one of the Court's first judgments in a case brought by a Gambian national (*Manneh v Gambia*).[53] The applicant, a journalist, was allegedly arrested without warrant, denied access to family or legal counsel, and subjected to mistreatment and poor detention conditions. He petitioned the Court, seeking a finding that his treatment violated the African Charter on Human and Peoples' Rights and release and compensation. The respondent did not enter a defence although the applicant had not previously brought any claims in the local courts.[54] The ECOWAS Community Court ruled that the Gambia had violated the applicant's human rights, ordered his release, and ordered compensation of US$100,000.[55] The Gambian government of President Yahya Jammeh subsequently submitted a proposal to the ECOWAS Commission to revise the Supplementary Protocol of 2005 to limit the jurisdiction of the Court on human rights matters. However, the Gambian proposals failed to obtain the endorsement of the ECOWAS Council of Justice Ministers, and were later abandoned by the government.

---

[52] EAC Treaty (n 4) arts 26, 30.
[53] ECOWAS Judgment No ECW/CCJ/JUD/03/08 (5 June 2008).
[54] ibid [1]–[6].
[55] ibid [41], [44].

In another widely publicized case concerning human rights, *Koraou v Niger*,[56] the applicant sued the state of Niger for not doing enough to protect her from slavery. She had allegedly been sold into slavery at the age of twelve, and was forced to serve as a slave and concubine. She remained in this condition for nine years, during which time she had four children by her master. In 1995, her master allegedly decided to "emancipate" her but would not allow her to leave because he claimed she was his wife. The applicant first filed her application with local courts, and in the same period married another man, as a result of which bigamy proceedings were brought against her.[57] Niger raised before the ECOWAS Community Court a preliminary objection, alleging that the applicant had not exhausted local remedies (as the case was still pending in divorce court). The ECOWAS Community Court dismissed the objection and heard the case.[58] In its judgment, the Court found that the applicant was a victim of slavery and that the state of Niger could be held responsible as a result of its inaction. The applicant was awarded compensation by the Court.[59]

In recent years, the Court has dealt with a number of cases dealing with the standing of legal persons to bring claims under human rights instruments, particularly with respect to the right to property. In general, the ECOWAS Court has jurisdiction over investment disputes pursuant to Article 33(7) of the Supplementary Act Adopting Community Rules on Investment and the Modalities for their Implementation with ECOWAS (Supplementary Act).[60] However, it has not yet exercised such jurisdiction. The Supplementary Act's dispute resolution provisions apply only to investors who are nationals of member states or companies organized under the laws of a member state.[61] In addition to the dispute resolution mandate under the Supplementary Act, Article 16 of the Revised Treaty of the Economic Community of West African States provides for the establishment of an Arbitration Tribunal of the Community.[62] This tribunal has yet to be established. In the meantime, the ECOWAS Court has been dealing with some cases concerning investment disputes, brought under its human rights jurisdiction. However, the Court's jurisprudence on these cases has been somewhat inconsistent, and the Court itself has acknowledged this inconsistency in its judgments in *Dexter Oil v Liberia*[63] and *Taakor Tropical Hardwood v Sierra Leone*.[64]

In *Dexter Oil v Liberia*, a company incorporated in Liberia with Nigerian shareholders and directors brought a claim against Liberia for confiscating funds in the company's bank account.[65] The Court ruled that Dexter Oil had standing to bring human rights claims against Liberia under Article 10(d) of the Protocol on the Community Court

---

[56] ECOWAS Judgment NoECW/CCJ/JUD/06/08 (27 October 2008).
[57] ibid [1]–[34].
[58] ibid [35].
[59] ibid [36]–[53].
[60] Supplementary Act AA/SA.3/12/08 Adopting Community Rules on Investment and the Modalities for their Implementation with ECOWAS (adopted 19 December 2008).
[61] ibid art. 35.
[62] ECOWAS Treaty (n 5).
[63] ECOWAS Judgment No ECW/CCJ/JUD/03/19 (6 February 2019).
[64] ECOWAS Judgment No ECW/CCJ/JUD/02/19 (24 January 2019).
[65] *Dexter Oil v Liberia* (n 62) [3], [4].

of Justice, as amended by the Supplementary Protocol of 2005 (Amended Protocol on the ECOWAS Court). The Court acknowledged that its jurisprudence had been somewhat inconsistent on this point. According to the Court, a strict interpretation of the English text of Article 10(d) limited the capacity to institute an action for the violation of a human right to natural persons. The Court nonetheless acknowledged that the French version of the text, which conferred standing upon "*toute personne victime de violations des droits de l'homme*", could be interpreted as encompassing natural and legal persons.[66] Indeed, the Court had interpreted Article 10(d) as conferring standing on legal persons based on its French text in *National Coordinating Group of Departmental Representatives of the Cocoa-Coffee Sector (CNDD) v Côte d'Ivoire*,[67] *Center for Democracy and Development (CDD) v Tandja*,[68] and *Hassan v Governor of Gombe State*.[69]

Despite these judgments, the Court opined that most of its decisions had adopted the strict interpretation based on the English text of Article 10(d). It then reasoned that the explicit reference to individuals and corporate bodies in Article 10(c) supported this strict interpretation of Article 10(d) as excluding legal persons. For the Court, the French text had to be read as limiting standing to persons capable of bearing human rights. The Court thus held that the article conferred standing on human beings with only limited exceptions recognized in international human rights law. The Court described the recognized exceptions as fundamental rights not dependent on human rights, notably the right to a fair hearing, the right to property, and the right to freedom of expression.[70]

In *Taakor Tropical Hardwood v Sierra Leone*, the applicant, a limited liability company registered in the United States and in Sierra Leone, brought an action against Sierra Leone for violating a concession agreement. The Court acknowledged that it had made limited exceptions allowing for corporate standing. However, it determined that none of them applied to Taakor. Referring to its judgment in *Ocean King Nigeria v Senegal*,[71] the Court invoked its inherent jurisdiction to entertain claims of denial of the right to a fair hearing brought by a corporate entity. It also added that the right to a fair hearing was "a fundamental right, open to any party who is affected by a tribunal's decision".[72] However, the Court was of the view that it could not avail itself of the exception relating to a fair hearing because Taakor claimed a violation of its right to work rather than its right to a fair hearing. The Court thus concluded that, as a corporate entity, Taakor lacked standing to bring a suit under Article 10(d) of the Protocol.[73]

The Court has tried hard to explain and overcome the inconsistencies in its jurisprudence arising from the differing interpretation and application of the English and

---

[66] ibid [55]–[72].
[67] ECOWAS CCJ Judgment No ECW/CCJ/JUD/05/09 (17 December 2009) [27]–[30].
[68] ECOWAS CCJ Judgment No ECW/CCJ/JUD/05/11 (9 May 2011) [27].
[69] ECOWAS CCJ Judgment No ECW/CCJ/RUL/07/12 (15 March 2012)
[70] *Dexter Oil v Liberia* (n 62) [55]–[72].
[71] ECOWAS CCJ Judgment No ECW/CCJ/JUD/07/11 (8 July 2011).
[72] *Taakor Tropical Hardwood v Sierra Leone* (n 63) 17–18 (citing *Ocean King Nigeria v Senegal* (n 70) [51]).
[73] ibid.

French texts of Article 10(d) of the Amended Protocol on the ECOWAS Court. It appears to have made some headway in so far as it has now developed a new jurisprudence on the standing of corporate entities to bring claims based on the alleged violation of certain fundamental rights such as the right to a fair hearing or the right to property. Much will therefore depend in the future on the consistent application of this jurisprudence to legal entities which bring human rights claims to the Court independently of the difference in the English and French text of Article 10(d) of the Amended Protocol on the ECOWAS Court.

## 3.3 The SADC Tribunal

The jurisdiction of regional courts to hear human rights claims has proven especially controversial within SADC. The SADC Tribunal has dealt with perhaps one of the best-known cases brought before an African regional court in the recent past, that of *Campbell v Zimbabwe*.[74] Soon after the establishment of the SADC Tribunal, William Michael Campbell and ultimately seventy-seven other individuals brought a case against the state of Zimbabwe before the Tribunal challenging the government's land acquisition policy. The applicants claimed that Zimbabwe's land acquisition policy was unlawful because it was not established that the acquisition was reasonably necessary for resettlement purposes in conformity with the land reform programme. Applicants were allegedly denied access to local courts and also denied compensation for the takeover of their lands. Finally, applicants argued that they had suffered racial discrimination. Zimbabwe challenged the jurisdiction of the court, which in its view was not empowered to hear human rights cases. It also argued, among others, that the acquisitions were not discriminatory because the applicants themselves had acquired the land as a result of circumstances brought about by colonial history with the land reform programme being aimed at correcting colonially inherited land ownership inequities.[75]

The Tribunal first granted a request for provisional measures designed to protect the applicants' interests during the proceedings. The SADC Tribunal found that it had jurisdiction since applicants were not able to have their claims heard in national courts. The Tribunal cited decisions by the European Court of Human Rights and the African Commission on Human and People's Rights to support its finding that applicants had a right to a fair hearing and access to justice. Finally, the Tribunal cited the findings of a number of international and regional organs, including the UN Human Rights Committee, to rule that even though there was no mention of race or ethnicity in the land acquisition law in question, the effects of the law, felt by Zimbabwean White farmers only, constituted indirect discrimination or a substantive inequality.[76]

[74] *Campbell Ltd. v Zimbabwe*, SADC Case No 2/2007 (Judgment of 28 November 2008).
[75] ibid.
[76] ibid.

Zimbabwe responded to the 2007 and 2008 *Campbell* decisions of the Tribunal by challenging the legitimacy of the SADC Tribunal itself, arguing that the Tribunal did not have jurisdiction to hear human rights claims as there was nothing in the SADC Treaty or other instruments that granted such power. It also refused to recognize the decisions, let alone enforce them, claiming that it had not ratified the protocol establishing the SADC Tribunal and was therefore not subject to its jurisdiction. After the Tribunal referred Zimbabwe's failure to comply with its decisions to the Summit of Heads of State and Government (Summit) in 2008,[77] Zimbabwe argued that the Tribunal itself was illegal as it had not been founded in accordance with the requirements of the protocol and that the Summit had not made it fully operational. Additionally, in 2009 Zimbabwe announced that it would withdraw the member appointed by its government (Justice Antonia Guvava) from the Tribunal. In response to these events, and after sustained political efforts by the government of Zimbabwe, the SADC Summit decided in 2012 that a new protocol on the Tribunal should be negotiated and that the Tribunal's mandate should be limited to interpretation of the SADC Treaty and protocols relating to disputes between member states.[78] Consequently, the Summit resolved to do away with the Tribunal's jurisdiction over disputes between legal and natural persons and member states. The new protocol on the Tribunal was adopted by the SADC Summit in 2014.[79] This protocol has not yet entered into force. Thus, the SADC Tribunal remains in a state of suspension.

## 4. The Challenges Faced by the Courts and the Efforts to Overcome Them

The brief survey carried out in this chapter of the mandate and jurisprudence of the recently created African regional courts highlights two issues: (i) their underutilization for the settlement of inter-state disputes arising from the interpretation and application of the treaties establishing the RECs; and (ii) their resistance to pressures from member states with regard to their jurisdiction, and the consequent tensions between the courts and the member states of RECs.

### 4.1  Underutilization

All the regional courts, except the SADC Tribunal, have been functioning normally since they became operational. They have been receiving cases with which they have regularly dealt, building up an interesting jurisprudence along the way. As the discussion in this chapter has demonstrated, however, most of these cases have not related

---

[77] *Campbell v Zimbabwe*, SADC Case No 03/2009 (Ruling of 5 June 2009).
[78] Final Communiqué of the 32nd Summit of SADC Heads of State and Government, 18 August 2012, [24].
[79] Revised Protocol on the SADC Tribunal (n 29).

to the primary purpose for which these courts were created, namely the settlement of disputes between member states of the RECs regarding the interpretation or application of their treaties and related protocols. This does not mean that disputes have never arisen among the member states in relation to these issues. It may rather be attributed to a manifest reluctance by member states to have recourse to these courts with regard to disputes arising amongst them on the interpretation of the treaties or in other areas related to their economic integration. These states appear to prefer direct negotiations or mediation to judicial settlement of such disputes. This underutilization of the courts for the settlement of inter-state disputes is likely to change as the courts gradually build up their image and credibility and acquire the confidence of member states.

There are, nonetheless, other reasons for the general underutilization of regional courts. The regional courts remain underutilized because there are systemic limitations within their mandates. In the case of the EACJ, for example, the need for national courts to refer to the EACJ questions of interpretation of the EAC Treaty for preliminary ruling and their subsequent failure to do so means the Court remains underutilized in this function, particularly in comparison to similar regional courts such as the European Court of Justice which is called upon to interpret treaty provisions with some frequency. This is because under the EAC Treaty, such preliminary rulings need only be requested when necessary to enable the national court to make its decision; it is not an automatic consequence of a question of interpretation of the treaty being brought to a national court. Encouraging the use of preliminary rulings by the EACJ is one way to assist the integration of the EACJ into the broader framework of the EAC and to build the Court's jurisprudence gradually. It is also necessary for the proper implementation of the EAC Treaty.

Finally, the regional courts are underutilized because in many ways they remain beyond the reach of most individuals who may need to petition these courts, either because there is not enough awareness of the rights granted under the regional treaties or because there are insufficient resources to enable meaningful access to the judicial bodies. This can only be remedied by broad educational programmes that increase awareness of the courts and tribunals and their mandate, and of more comprehensive pro bono and legal aid programmes that assist individuals who may not otherwise be able to bring their claims to the regional courts because of economic concerns. Here again much collaboration is required between regional and national courts and among the member states, as well as between the regional courts and local non-governmental organizations that may have a more neutral attitude towards bringing human rights claims against states at the international level.

## 4.2  Resistance to Pressures from Member States

The underutilization of these courts by the states that established them appears to be in part compensated, at least for the time being, by the assertiveness of these courts in terms of the interpretation of their jurisdiction. The bold decisions made by the EACJ, the ECOWAS Community Court, and the SADC Tribunal clearly show the determination of the judges of these courts to assert their judicial independence and to ensure adherence to the law among the member states of the regional integration groupings.

Member states have tried in the past, and may try in the future, to curb this judicial independence, and limit what they perceive as judicial activism on the part of the courts. They managed in the case of the SADC Tribunal to silence a judicial body and effectively dissolve it due to the complaints of a single member state. However, in the case of the EACJ and the ECOWAS court, attempts by member states to limit the jurisdiction of the courts or to restrict the independence of the judges have not fully succeeded so far. Nevertheless, in the case of the EACJ they led to some changes to the structure and composition of the court, as well as amendments to its founding treaty.[80]

## 5.  Conclusion

As the jurisprudence of these courts grows (and it has indeed grown in the past few years), and as it becomes better known and analysed in academia and in the media, there is no doubt that recourse to these jurisdictions will increase not only by individuals but also by states. Disputes on the interpretation and application of the treaties establishing the RECs are also likely to increase as integration advances and as trade in goods and services expands in the various regions of Africa. Thus, despite their current underutilization, it appears that these regional courts have brighter days and a promising future ahead of them in the consolidation of the rule of law in the African continent as well as in the promotion of economic and political integration.

[80] See generally Karen J Alter, James T Gathii, and Laurence R Helfer, "Backlash against International Courts in West, East and Southern Africa: Causes and Consequences" (2016) 27 European Journal of international Law 293.

# 11

# Creativity in Dispute Settlement Relating to the Law of the Sea

*Sean D Murphy*

## 1. Introduction

David Caron was a careful but also creative international lawyer, and his scholarly attention turned towards not just international dispute resolution but also the law of the sea.[1] The focus of this chapter is on creativity in dispute resolution relating to the law of the sea. When the 1982 UN Convention on the Law of the Sea (UNCLOS) was adopted in 1982, its dispute settlement procedures were heralded as highly creative in offering an array of possibilities for states (and even non-state actors).[2] Now that almost three decades have passed since the Convention's entry into force in 1994, can it be said that the promise of such creativity has been fulfilled?

It appears that the answer to that question is largely yes, not just in the modes by which dispute resolution is occurring (negotiation, mediation, conciliation, arbitration, and judicial settlement) but also in the wide-ranging issues being addressed within those modes, and perhaps even in the express and tacit dialogue occurring among the dispute settlers. The system, of course, is not perfect and could be more robust, but we may be amidst a "rising tide" of maritime dispute resolution, one that is strengthening and developing this area of the law. At the same time, a word of caution is in order; some aspects of the creativity found within the decisions of dispute settlers may well be giving at least some states pause as to the procedures they have unleashed.

## 2. 1982 UNCLOS

As is well-known, UNCLOS seeks to regulate comprehensively virtually all aspects of the seas,[3] beginning with rules on the existence of baselines along the coasts of states;

---

[1] See eg David D Caron and Harry N Scheiber (eds), *The Oceans in the Nuclear Age: Legacies and Risks* (Brill 2010).

[2] UN Convention on the Law of the Sea (opened for signature 10 December 1982, entered into force 16 November 1994) 1833 UNTS 3 (UNCLOS).

[3] For general analysis of the contemporary law of the sea, see Jean-Paul Pancracio, *Droit de la mer* (Dalloz 2010); James Harrison, *Making the Law of the Sea: A Study in the Development of International Law* (Cambridge University Press 2011); Harry N Scheiber and Jin-Hyun Paik (eds), *Regions, Institutions, and the Law of the Sea: Studies in Ocean Governance* (Martinus Nijhoff 2013); David Freestone (ed), *The 1982 Law of the Sea*

Sean D Murphy, *Creativity in Dispute Settlement Relating to the Law of the Sea* In: *By Peaceful Means*. Edited by: Charles N Brower, Joan E Donoghue, Cian C Murphy, Cymie R Payne and Esmé R Shirlow, Oxford University Press. © Sean D Murphy 2024. DOI: 10.1093/oso/9780192848086.003.0011

a few rules relating to internal waters that exist on the landward side of the baselines; then rules on the seaward side of the baselines in the territorial sea,[4] the contiguous zone,[5] the exclusive economic zone,[6] the continental shelf,[7] and finally the high seas.[8] Islands are capable of generating their own maritime zones, but much depends on, first, whether it is an "island", and, second, whether the island is a "rock" that cannot sustain human habitation or economic life of its own.[9] Special rules address straits,[10] archipelagos,[11] enclosed or semi-enclosed seas,[12] and even land-locked states.[13] Wide-ranging freedoms are acknowledged for all states on the high seas, including of navigation, overflight, laying of submarine cables and pipelines, construction of artificial installations, fishing, and scientific research;[14] many of these freedoms also operate in the exclusive economic zone subject to the provisions of that zone.[15] Warships benefit from these rules and from some special rules, such as relating to their immunity.[16]

UNCLOS also sets forth rules relating to exploitation of the deep seabed beyond national jurisdiction and, in that regard, creates an international organization—the International Seabed Authority—for decision-making and implementation, consisting principally of an Assembly (with equal representation from States Parties), a Council (with regional and interest group representation of States Parties), and a Secretariat.[17] As is well-known, disagreement over the original scheme for addressing the deep seabed resulted in a 1994 "implementing agreement" that significantly revised the deep seabed provisions.[18] Further, UNCLOS establishes important rules for environmental protection of the seas, which are so extensive that they arguably constitute an environmental treaty embedded within UNCLOS.[19] In addition to discrete parts of UNCLOS addressing marine scientific research[20] and the transfer of marine technology,[21] it sets forth throughout important rules relating to jurisdiction over ocean vessels, which give

---

*Convention at 30: Successes, Challenges, and New Agendas* (Brill 2013); Donald R Rothwell and others (eds), *The Oxford Handbook of the Law of the Sea* (Oxford University Press 2015); Donald R Rothwell and Tim Stephens, *The International Law of the Sea* (2nd edn, Hart 2016); Alexander Proelss (ed), *United Nations Convention on the Law of the Sea: A Commentary* (Beck/Hart/Nomos 2017); Mathias Forteau and Jean-Marc Thouvenin (eds), *Traité de droit international de la mer* (Pedone 2017); Myron H Nordquist and others (eds), *Legal Order in the World's Oceans: UN Convention on the Law of the Sea* (Brill 2018); Philippe Vincent, *Droit de la mer* (2nd edn, Larcier 2020); Robin Churchill, Vaughan Lowe, and Amy Sander, *The Law of the Sea* (4th edn, Manchester 2022); Yoshifumi Tanaka, *The International Law of the Sea* (4th edn, Cambridge University Press 2023).

[4] UNCLOS (n 2) pt II, §§ 1–3.
[5] ibid pt II, § 4.
[6] ibid pt V.
[7] ibid pt VI.
[8] ibid pt VII.
[9] ibid pt VIII.
[10] ibid pt III.
[11] ibid pt IV.
[12] ibid pt IX.
[13] ibid pt X.
[14] ibid art 87.
[15] ibid art 58(1).
[16] See ibid arts 29–33, 95, 102, 107, 110–11, 224, 236.
[17] ibid pt XI.
[18] Agreement Relating to the Implementation of Part XI of the United Nations Convention on the Law of the Sea of 10 December 1982 (adopted 28 July 1994, entered into force 28 July 1996) 1836 UNTS 3.
[19] UNCLOS (n 2) pt XII.
[20] ibid pt XIII.
[21] ibid pt XIV.

primary authority to the flag state, but recognize as well certain roles for coastal, port, and other states.

This brief *tour d'horizon* recalls the broad range and complexity of UNCLOS for the purpose of stressing why dispute settlement was viewed during the negotiations as essential for the Convention to succeed. Though the Convention is highly detailed, the drafters understood that disputes would arise regarding its interpretation and application, and without a means of resolving those disputes, the Convention might not succeed. A prime example in this regard is the rules on delimitation of exclusive economic zones and of continental shelves, which simply provide that such delimitation "shall be effected by agreement on the basis of international law … in order to achieve an equitable solution".[22] If states cannot reach such agreement "within a reasonable period of time", they may resort to UNCLOS dispute settlement procedures,[23] but there is no further guidance in the Convention as to how to resolve such disputes, thus inviting a degree of creativity.[24]

Consequently, UNCLOS Part XV establishes an innovative system for the settlement of disputes.[25] Section 1 of Part XV obliges states to settle their disputes concerning the interpretation or application of the Convention peacefully, and, to that end, to pursue any agreed-upon method of dispute settlement or to consider pursuing conciliation in accordance with the procedures set forth in Annex V. If no settlement is reached under Section 1 methods, then Section 2 provides for compulsory dispute settlement before one of four possible venues: (i) the International Tribunal for the Law of the Sea (ITLOS), which is based in Hamburg; (ii) the International Court of Justice (ICJ), which is based in The Hague; (iii) ad hoc arbitration in accordance with UNCLOS Annex VII; or (iv) a "special arbitral tribunal" constituted in accordance with Annex VIII for certain categories of disputes. When ratifying or acceding to the Convention, or at any time thereafter, a state may make a declaration choosing one or more of these venues; in the absence of a declaration, the state is deemed to have accepted arbitration under

[22] ibid arts 74(1) and 83(1).

[23] ibid arts 74(2) and 83(2). On delimitation, see generally *International Maritime Boundaries* (Martinus Nijhoff 1993–2020) (various editors; eight volumes to date); Rainer Lagoni and Daniel Vignes (eds), *Maritime Delimitation* (Martinus Nijhoff 2006); Yoshifumi Tanaka, *Predictability and Flexibility in the Law of Maritime Delimitation* (Hart 2006); Seoung-Yong Hong and Jon M Van Dyke (eds), *Maritime Boundary Disputes, Settlement Processes, and the Law of the Sea* (Martinus Nijhoff 2009); Bjarni Már Magnusson, *The Continental Shelf Beyond 200 Nautical Miles: Delineation, Delimitation and Dispute Settlement* (Brill 2015); Thomas Cottier, *Equitable Principles of Maritime Boundary Delimitation: The Quest for Distributive Justice in International Law* (Cambridge University Press 2015); Stephen Fietta and Robin Cleverly, *A Practitioner's Guide to Maritime Boundary Delimitation* (Oxford University Press 2016); Alex G Oude Elferink and others (eds), *Maritime Boundary Delimitation: The Case Law—Is it Consistent and Predictable?* (Cambridge University Press 2018); Nicholas A Ioannides, *Maritime Claims and Boundary Delimitation: Tensions and Trends in the Eastern Mediterranean Sea* (Routledge 2020).

[24] ITLOS Vice-President and Judge Tomas Heider remarked on 10 June 2022, as part of Volterra Fietta's 40th Anniversary of UNCLOS Seminar Series, that the "decision of States at the Third Conference to codify only vague provisions on EEZ and continental shelf delimitation—agreeing only that the solution should be equitable—implicitly authorized international courts and tribunals to assert a creative function in developing the delimitation process".

[25] See generally Natalie Klein, *Dispute Settlement in the UN Convention on the Law of the Sea* (Cambridge University Press 2005); Constantinos Yiallourides *Maritime Disputes and International Law: Disputed Waters and Seabed Resources in Asia and Europe* (Routledge 2019); Joanna Mossop, "Dispute Settlement in Areas beyond National Jurisdiction" in Vito De Lucia and others (eds), *International Law and Marine Areas beyond National Jurisdiction* 392 (Brill 2022).

Annex VII. When a dispute arises, if the two states have chosen different venues and cannot agree upon which one to use, then the default is to go to Annex VII arbitration.

While it was believed important to include compulsory jurisdiction in UNCLOS, it was nevertheless viewed as necessary to establish certain automatic limitations and optional exceptions to that jurisdiction, which are contained in Section 3 of Part XV. These carve-outs can be quite important, such as an automatic limitation that precludes compulsory dispute settlement concerning the coastal state's determination of the allowable catch in the exclusive economic zone.[26] The optional exceptions, which may be invoked by a state when it joins UNCLOS, include disputes concerning maritime boundary delimitation, historic bays or titles, or military activities.[27] If one of these carve-outs preclude legally binding dispute settlement, the states nevertheless are obligated to pursue conciliation (a process sometimes referred to as "compulsory conciliation"), though that process does not result in a legally binding decision.

As of 2023, 169 states have become parties to UNCLOS,[28] and 152 of these states have become party to the 1994 Implementing Agreement.[29] Moreover, additional efforts to codify the law of the sea have continued apace. Some further agreements are global in nature, such as the agreement reached in 1995 to handle the vexing problem of fish that migrate between or "straddle" areas under the jurisdiction of two or more states or the high seas.[30] Other agreements are regional in nature, sometimes targeting specific issues, such as management of a particular species of fish.[31] Some agreements tackle unusual issues, such as how to handle ancient shipwrecks discovered on the floor of the ocean.[32] Because UNCLOS States Parties are committed to compulsory dispute resolution with respect to "any dispute concerning the interpretation or application of an international agreement related to the purposes of this Convention, which is submitted ... in accordance with the agreement",[33] there are about a dozen multilateral agreements and a few bilateral agreements in force that provide for resolution of disputes arising under those agreements through UNCLOS procedures.[34] Looking to the future, efforts are underway to ratify a 2023 agreement on biodiversity beyond national

---

[26] UNCLOS (n 2) art 297(3)(a).

[27] ibid art 298. China, for example, has invoked all these optional exceptions. See UN Treaty Collection, "United Nations Convention on the Law of the Sea", <https://perma.cc/7GSH-9ZUH>. On the potential for creative interpretation of the Section 3 carve-outs, with a focus on the South China Sea arbitration, see Natalie Klein, "The Vicissitudes of Dispute Settlement under the Law of the Sea Convention" (2017) 32 International Journal of Marine & Coastal Law 332.

[28] See "United Nations Convention on the Law of the Sea" (n 27).

[29] See UN Treaty Collection, "Agreement relating to the implementation of Part XI of the United Nations Convention on the Law of the Sea of 10 December 1982", <https://perma.cc/HY9H-JCBZ >.

[30] Agreement for the Implementation of the Provisions of the United Nations Convention on the Law of the Sea of 10 December 1982 Relating to the Conservation and Management of Straddling Fish Stocks and Highly Migratory Fish Stocks (adopted 4 August 1995, entered into force 11 December 2001), 2167 UNTS 3.

[31] Convention on the Conservation and Management of Highly Migratory Fish Stocks in the Western and Central Pacific Ocean (opened for signature 5 September 2000, entered into force 19 June 2004), 2275 UNTS 43.

[32] UNESCO Convention on the Protection of the Underwater Cultural Heritage (adopted 2 November 2001, entered into force 2 January 2009), 2562 UNTS 3.

[33] UNCLOS (n 2) art 288(2).

[34] See International Tribunal for the Law of the Sea, "International Agreements Conferring Jurisdiction on the Tribunal", <https://perma.cc/37D7-QN3U>.

jurisdiction (BBNJ).[35] Consequently, the law of the sea today is a complicated series of global, regional, and even bilateral agreements,[36] with a backdrop of well-established customary rules,[37] ensconced in a creative scheme for dispute settlement.

An important driver of many maritime disputes is the deep interest in exploitation of ocean resources, be it fish, energy, oil, gas, or minerals. Such interest has only increased since entry into force of UNCLOS in 1994, fuelled in part by ever-increasing technologies that promote cost-efficient exploitation. The initial excitement in the 1970s about deep seabed mining faded by the 1990s, largely due to a collapse in world metal prices, the development of synthetics in place of some minerals, and the emergence of new sources in developing states. Even so, interest in seabed mining in this century has re-emerged; the International Seabed Authority, set up under UNCLOS, has now approved numerous contracts with private entities for seabed exploration.[38] While not the only source of frictions among states, access to ocean resources underlies many of the disputes in this area of the law, and is likely to be so for some time.

## 3. Negotiation

In light of the detailed rules available under the contemporary law of the sea, the increasing desire to exploit natural resources from the various zones, and the possibility of compulsory dispute settlement, it is perhaps of no surprise that states have been motivated, in the first instance, to negotiate with each other to resolve their disputes.[39] Identifying the existence of such negotiations is not always easy; states will often engage in negotiations quietly. Even so, various studies suggest that negotiations since the entry into force of UNCLOS in 1994 have flourished. For example, Igor Karaman catalogues more than sixty negotiations between states from 1994 to 2012; some of those negotiations succeeded, some have not, and others remain ongoing.[40]

Negotiations that succeeded have resulted in a number of international agreements, such as the 2004 Treaty between Australia and New Zealand establishing certain

---

[35] See Agreement under the United Nations Convention on the Law of the Sea on the Conservation and Sustainable Use of Marine Biological Diversity of Areas Beyond National Jurisdiction, 19 June 2023, UN Doc A/CONF.232/2023/4* (2023); Cymie R Payne (ed), "Symposium on Governing High Seas Biodiversity" (2018) 112 American Journal of International Law Unbound 118.

[36] See eg Treaty Concerning Pacific Salmon (United States–Canada) (adopted 28 January 1985, entered into force 17 March 1985) TIAS 11,091, 1469 UNTS 357 (further amended in June 1999, December 2002, May 2014).

[37] See eg J Ashley Roach, "Today's Customary International Law of the Sea" (2014) 45 Ocean Development & International Law 239.

[38] See Michael W Lodge, "The Deep Seabed" in Rothwell and others (eds) (n 3) 226; Catherine Banet (ed), *The Law of the Seabed: Access, Uses and Protection of Seabed Resources* (Brill Nijhoff 2020). Much of that exploration is focused on copper, zinc, lead, and rare earth deposits formed near hydrothermal vents, where mineral-rich water rises up through the ocean floor. See Yves Fouquet and Denis Lacroix (eds), *Deep Marine Mineral Resources* (Springer 2014); Rahul Sharma (ed), *Deep-Sea Mining: Resource Potential, Technical and Environmental Considerations* (Springer 2017).

[39] See Sarah McLaughlin Mitchell and Andrew P Owsiak, "Judicialization of the Sea: Bargaining in the Shadow of UNCLOS" (2021) 115 American Journal of International Law 579 (for a symposium on this article, see (2021) 115 American Journal of International Law Unbound 368–403).

[40] Igor V Karaman, *Dispute Resolution in the Law of the Sea* (Martinus Nijhoff 2012) 331–36

Exclusive Economic Zone and Continental Shelf Boundaries,[41] the 2008 Agreement between Mauritius and the Seychelles on the Delimitation of their Exclusive Economic Zones,[42] and the 2009 Maritime Boundary Delimitation Treaty between Barbados and France concerning delimitation between Barbados and France's overseas departments of Guadeloupe and Martinique.[43] In some instances, such agreements themselves provide for the possibility of dispute settlement in the event that a disagreement arises with respect to interpretation or application of the agreement.[44]

Creativity is clearly present in the process and substance of such negotiations. With respect to process, UNCLOS is crafted so as not to preclude states from negotiating outcomes *inter se* if there is political will to do so. Certainly, delimitation calls in the first instance for a negotiated outcome,[45] but even in other contexts, UNCLOS reflects an openness to the political will of states, whether it be in sharing the allowable catch in the exclusive economic zone;[46] determining the location of submarine cables or pipelines;[47] sorting out historic rights in archipelagic waters;[48] or addressing navigational, safety, and environmental matters in straits.[49] Even with respect to the resort to dispute settlement, the preference of the two states is paramount, superseding any mandatory dispute settlement.[50]

With respect to the substance of such negotiations, creativity is observable from the fact that states may negotiate outcomes that would not be possible if they left matters to a dispute settler required to follow a strict application of international law. In the context of maritime delimitation, for example, a dispute settler is typically limited to awarding sovereignty or jurisdiction over maritime areas solely to one state or the other.[51] Yet in a negotiated settlement of overlapping claims to maritime resources, states are free to establish joint development arrangements, whereby States largely set aside their legal claims (at least for the time being) and focus instead on practical measures to secure their underlying objectives.[52] Such an approach allows the states to maintain their respective claims regarding the boundary but to proceed on a more functional basis for

---

[41] Treaty between the Government of Australia and the Government of New Zealand establishing certain exclusive economic zone boundaries and continental shelf boundaries (Australia–New Zealand) (adopted 25 July 2004, entered into force 25 January 2006) 2441 UNTS 235.

[42] Agreement between the Government of the Republic of Mauritius and the Government of the Republic of Seychelles on the delimitation of the exclusive economic zone between the two states (Mauritius-Seychelles) (adopted 29 July 2008, entered into force 19 November 2008) 2595 UNTS 225.

[43] Agreement between the Government of the French Republic and the Government of Barbados on the delimitation of the maritime space between France and Barbados (Barbados-France) (adopted 15 October 2009, entered into force 1 January 2010) 2663 UNTS 163.

[44] See Yacouba Cissé and Donald McRae, "The Legal Regime of Maritime Boundary Agreements" in David A Colson and Robert W Smith (eds), *International Maritime Boundaries* (5th edn, Martinus Nijhoff 2005) 3300–03.

[45] UNCLOS (n 2) arts 74(1) and 83(1).

[46] ibid arts 69(3) and 70(3).

[47] ibid art 79.

[48] ibid art 51.

[49] ibid art 43.

[50] ibid art 280 ("Nothing in this Part [XV] impairs the right of any States Parties to agree at any time to settle a dispute between them concerning the interpretation or application of this Convention by any peaceful means of their choice.").

[51] Karaman (n 40) at 186–87 (quoting Shigeru Oda, "Dispute Settlement Prospects in the Law of the Sea" in Shigeru Oda (ed), *Fifty Years of the Law of the Sea: Selected Writings of Shigeru Oda* (Kluwer 2003) 869).

[52] Such arrangements are encouraged by UNCLOS (n 2) arts 74(3) and 83(3).

both managing and exploiting the resources, even in situations where the full extent of those resources are not known.[53] Dozens of joint development zones now exist, scattered across every region of the world.[54]

It is clear that negotiation is, by far, the most preferred method of dispute settlement under the law of the sea, with states turning to other forms of dispute settlement only when negotiations stall. David Anderson—a former legal adviser to the UK Foreign and Commonwealth Office and former ITLOS judge—notes that, when it comes to boundary delimitation, there are certain inherent advantages for states in pursuing negotiation. He writes that "[t]he parties retain control over a series of important issues, such as the precise results of the negotiations and in particular the course of the boundary lines; the way in which the line is defined; the terms and timing of the agreement; and its presentation to public opinion".[55] Indeed, he opines that "litigation always carries risks for the parties".[56]

# 4. Mediation

By contrast, resort by states to mediation or "good offices" has been far more modest, apparently numbering fewer than a dozen since 1994.[57] Examples certainly exist, such as the Organization of American States' effort to mediate the territorial and maritime dispute between Belize and Guatemala,[58] or the UN Secretary-General's mediation of Equatorial Guinea and Gabon's maritime boundary dispute.[59] Mediation allows for the same creativity as is possible for negotiation; neither the mediator nor the disputing states are bound to solutions driven by strict application of the law. Further, this approach need not end at an effort to mediate, as the mediation might result in the states gaining sufficient confidence to pursue more formalized dispute resolution. For example, France's mediation of the Eritrea-Yemen maritime boundary dispute ultimately led the states to reach agreement on resolving the dispute through arbitration.[60]

---

[53] Even though not dictated by rules of international law, arguably such actions may have an influence on the development of international law in this area. See David M Ong, "Joint Development of Common Offshore Oil and Gas Deposits: 'Mere' State Practice or Customary International Law?" (1993) 93 American Journal of International Law 771.

[54] Victor Prescott and Clive Schofield, *The Maritime Political Boundaries of the World* (2nd edn, Martinus Nijhoff 2005) 264.

[55] David Anderson, "Negotiating Maritime Boundary Agreements: A Personal View" in Lagoni and Vignes (n 23) 122–23 (reprinted in David Anderson, *Modern Law of the Sea: Selected Essays* (Brill 2008) 417.

[56] ibid at 123.

[57] Karaman (n 40) 337–38.

[58] See Montserrat Gorina-Ysern, "OAS Mediates in Belize-Guatemala Border Dispute" (2000) 5(20) ASIL Insights, <https://perma.cc/8BDZ-6XKC>.

[59] See Gbenga Oduntan, *International Law and Boundary Disputes in Africa* (Routledge 2015) 168; "Gabon and Equatorial Guinea Set Terms of UN Mediation over Disputed Islands" *UN News Centre*, 20 January 2004, <https://perma.cc/KC8M-P8U4>.

[60] *Award of the Arbitral Tribunal in the First Stage of Proceedings (Territorial Sovereignty and the Scope of the Dispute) (Eritrea v Yemen)*, Decision of 9 October 1998, 22 RIAA 209, para 77 (2006).

## 5. Conciliation

Prior to UNCLOS, conciliation of a dispute relating to the law of the sea was relatively rare, with the notable exception being the conciliation between Iceland and Norway in 1981 concerning the continental shelf between Iceland and the Norwegian island of Jan Mayen.[61] Even so, conciliation as a method of dispute settlement is featured in UNCLOS Part XV, along with an annex devoted to its procedures.[62] As previously noted, one creative aspect of this procedure is the concept of "compulsory conciliation". If one of the automatic limitations or optional exceptions contained in Section 3 of Part XV precludes binding compulsory dispute settlement, the States Parties nevertheless may be *obliged* to pursue conciliation under Annex V, Section 2.[63] For example, if a State Party has exercised its right to opt out of binding compulsory dispute settlement concerning maritime boundary disputes or historic bays or titles, the state nevertheless is bound to accept submission to conciliation of any such dispute that arises after entry into force of UNCLOS.[64] Although compulsory conciliation does not result in a legally binding decision, the States Parties are required to negotiate an agreement on the basis of the commission's report and, if agreement is not reached, "the parties shall, by mutual consent, submit the question" to one of the Part XV, Section 2, compulsory dispute procedures.[65] The words "by mutual consent" suggest that a state may not be compelled to accept any particular binding dispute settlement procedure, though it has been suggested that the word "shall" introduces ambiguity in that regard, which might be tested through a unilateral application.[66]

Notwithstanding the emphasis of UNCLOS on conciliation, to date states still do not seem attracted to this method; the only conciliation under the Convention has been between Timor-Leste and Australia concerning their maritime boundary in the Timor Sea and associated issues. Timor-Leste unilaterally initiated the process, leading to the constitution of a commission in 2016, which thereafter decided in favour of its competence. After several sessions with the parties, the process led in 2018 to the adoption by the two parties of a Treaty on Maritime Boundaries and to the Commission's issuance of a final report and recommendations.[67]

---

[61] *Conciliation Commission on the Continental Shelf Area between Iceland and Jan Mayen*, Report and Recommendations of June 1981, 27 RIAA 1 (2009) ; see Elliot L Richardson, "Jan Mayen in Perspective" (1988) 82 American Journal of International Law 443.

[62] Part XV, Section 1, is designed to promote settlement of disputes without resort to litigation. The conciliation procedure envisaged in Article 284 entails each party choosing two conciliators (of which one may be its national) from a list established by UNCLOS parties. The four conciliators then select a fifth to serve as chairperson. After considering the views of both parties, the panel is to issue a report in which it makes non-binding recommendations. UNCLOS Annex V is devoted to conciliation procedures.

[63] UNCLOS (n 2) Annex V, arts 11–14.

[64] ibid art 298(1)(a)(i).

[65] ibid art 298(1)(a)(ii).

[66] See Robert Beckman, "UNCLOS Part XV and the South China Sea" in S Jayakumar and others (eds), *The South China Sea Disputes and the Law of the Sea* (Edward Elgar 2014) 246.

[67] The Commission's decision on competence and its report/recommendations are at 34 RIAA 206 and 245 (2022) respectively; other documents, decisions, and the treaty may be found at the website of the Permanent Court of Arbitration, <https://pca-cpa.org/en/cases/132/> accessed 14 August 2023.

The best explanation for why conciliation is not attractive to states is probably that once states have decided to give up control over a dispute and to allow for a relatively formal decision by the third-party body, then states are inclined to go all the way by accepting that the ultimate decision should be legally binding, which means selecting arbitration or judicial settlement. Indeed, states may well prefer to lose an arbitration and use the fact of a legally binding obligation to help tamp down political resistance at home, rather than to "lose" a conciliation and have no obligation to comply with the outcome.

## 6.  Arbitration

By contrast, arbitration of law of the sea disputes has proved to be popular since 1994, typically through arbitral tribunals convened under UNCLOS Annex VII. As in all arbitration, there is a fair amount of flexibility (if not creativity) in the procedures of the tribunal, and in their interplay with judicial settlement of disputes.[68] Generally, these tribunals consist of five arbitrators, with each party appointing one arbitrator, and then agreeing upon the remaining three (with the President of ITLOS serving as the appointing authority, if needed). The arbitral tribunal decides upon its own procedures, unless the parties agree otherwise, and hence the process can be more flexible than judicial settlement of disputes. As of 2023, fifteen Annex VII cases have been pursued, all but one administered under the auspices of the Permanent Court of Arbitration.[69] Perhaps creativity is best seen in the wide range of ancillary issues that counsel have managed to place before these tribunals, which may well not have been anticipated

---

[68] On judicial settlement, see section 7 below.

[69] *Southern Bluefish Tuna (New Zealand v Japan, Australia v Japan)*, Award of 4 August 2000, 23 RIAA 1 (2006); *MOX Plant (Ireland v United Kingdom)* (proceedings terminated in June 2008); *Land Reclamation in and around the Straits of Johor (Malaysia v Singapore)*, Award of 1 September 2005, 27 RIAA 133 (2009); *Delimitation of the Exclusive Economic Zone and the Continental Shelf between Barbados and the Republic of Trinidad and Tobago (Barbados v Trinidad and Tobago)*, Award of 11 April 2006, 27 RIAA 147 (2009); *Guyana v Suriname*, Award of 17 September 2007, 30 RIAA 1 (2012); *Delimitation of the Maritime Boundary in the Bay of Bengal (Bangladesh v India)*, Award of 7 July 2014, 32 RIAA 13 (2019); *Chagos Marine Protected Area Arbitration (Mauritius v United Kingdom)*, Award of 18 March 2015, 31 RIAA 365 (2018); *"ARA Libertad" (Argentina v Ghana)* (proceedings terminated in November 2013); *South China Sea Arbitration (Philippines v China)*, Award of 12 July 2016, 33 RIAA 155 (2020); *"Arctic Sunrise" (Netherlands v Russian Federation)*, Award of 10 July 2017, 32 RIAA 317 (2019); *Atlanto-Scandian Herring Arbitration (Kingdom of Denmark in respect of the Faroe Islands v European Union)* (proceedings terminated in September 2014); *Duzgit Integrity Arbitration (Malta v São Tomé and Príncipe)*, Award of 18 December 2019; *The "Enrica Lexie" Incident (Italy v India)*, Award of 21 May 2020; *Dispute Concerning Coastal State Rights in the Black Sea, Sea of Azov, and Kerch Strait (Ukraine v the Russian Federation)*, Award on Preliminary Objections of 21 February 2020 (proceedings still pending); *Dispute Concerning the Detention of Ukrainian Naval Vessels and Servicemen (Ukraine v the Russian Federation)*, Award on Preliminary Objections of 27 June 2022 (proceedings still pending). Six additional cases that started as Annex VII arbitrations were later transferred to ITLOS: *The M/V "Saiga" (No 2) Case (Saint Vincent and the Grenadines/Guinea)*, Judgment of 1 July 2999, ITLOS Reports 1999, 10; *Dispute Concerning Delimitation of the Maritime Boundary in the Bay of Bengal (Bangladesh/Myanmar)*, Judgment of 14 March 2012, ITLOS Reports 2012, 4; *Dispute Concerning Delimitation of the Maritime Boundary between Ghana and Côte d'Ivoire in the Atlantic Ocean (Ghana/Côte d'Ivoire)*, Judgment of 23 September 2017, ITLOS Reports 2017, 4; *The M/T "San Padre Pio" (No 2) Case (Switzerland/Nigeria)*, Order of Discontinuance of 29 December 2021; *Dispute concerning Delimitation of the Maritime Boundary between Mauritius and Maldives in the Indian Ocean (Mauritius/Maldives)*, Judgment of 28 April 2023; *The M/T "Heroic Idun" (No. 2) Case (Marshall Islands/Equatorial Guinea)* (proceedings still pending).

when UNCLOS was crafted (and hence the resolution of which may be disturbing to some states).

## 6.1  Issues of Sovereignty

UNCLOS is not designed to resolve issues of sovereignty and, as such, Annex VII tribunals are not expected to determine whether a land mass is part of the territory of one of the disputing parties. At the same time, it is commonly said that the "land dominates the sea", which means that a state's rights and obligations in areas of the sea often turn upon sovereignty over adjacent land masses. This issue arose in the *Chagos Marine Protected Area Arbitration*, after the United Kingdom, in April 2010, declared a marine protected area at the Chagos Archipelago, which the United Kingdom administers as the "British Indian Ocean Territory". Mauritius disputes the UK's sovereignty over this territory, believing that the archipelago should have been included as part of the territory of Mauritius when Mauritius emerged from the period of colonization and became an independent state in 1968. Consequently, in December 2010 Mauritius initiated a proceeding under UNCLOS before an Annex VII arbitral tribunal. UNCLOS allows a "coastal state" to establish a marine protected area adjacent to its coast, but one aspect of Mauritius' claims was that the United Kingdom was not the "coastal state" in respect of the Chagos Archipelago for the purposes of the Convention. Alternatively, Mauritius claimed that certain undertakings by the United Kingdom had endowed Mauritius with rights as a "coastal state" in respect of the Archipelago.

The tribunal found in 2015 by a majority of three votes to two that it lacked jurisdiction to consider either of these claims.[70] According to the tribunal, such claims—at their core—concerned the question of sovereignty over the Chagos Archipelago, not disagreements about the meaning of "coastal state" or some other issue relating to the marine protected area. Therefore, according to the tribunal, these claims were not truly a matter concerning the interpretation or application of UNCLOS. The Tribunal, however, did not assert that the issue of sovereignty could never be addressed in UNCLOS proceedings. Rather, the Tribunal said that it did "not categorically exclude that in some instances a minor issue of territorial sovereignty could indeed be ancillary to a dispute concerning the interpretation or application of the Convention".[71] Indeed, it suggested "that an issue of land sovereignty might be within the jurisdiction of a Part XV court or tribunal if it were genuinely ancillary to a dispute over a maritime boundary or a claim of historic title".[72]

---

[70] *Chagos Marine Protected Area Arbitration (Mauritius v United Kingdom)*, Award of 18 March 2015 (n 69) paras 203–221, 228–230, and 547(A)(1). The Tribunal also unanimously found that there was no dispute between the parties with respect to Mauritius' claim concerning submissions to the Commission on the Limits of the Continental Shelf, and therefore that the tribunal was not required to rule on whether it had jurisdiction over the claim. ibid paras 331–350 and 547(A)(2).

[71] ibid para 221.

[72] ibid para 218.

Undaunted, Mauritius thereafter successfully lobbied the UN General Assembly to seek an advisory opinion from the International Court of Justice on whether the separation of the Chagos Archipelago from Mauritius during the process of decolonization was unlawful.[73] The Court advised that it was, stating that, "having regard to international law, the process of decolonization of Mauritius was not lawfully completed when that country acceded to independence in 1968, following the separation of the Chagos Archipelago", and that "the United Kingdom is under an obligation to bring to an end its administration of the Chagos Archipelago as rapidly as possible".[74] With these findings in hand, Mauritius launched an Annex VII arbitration (thereafter placed before ITLOS) on maritime delimitation against the Maldives, which is located to the north of the Chagos Archipelago. The Maldives argued that ITLOS (sitting as a special chamber) lacked jurisdiction, since any delimitation between the Parties would necessarily have to find that Mauritius was (and the United Kingdom was not) sovereign over the Chagos Archipelago, a matter that was in dispute.[75] The Chamber, however, concluded that the matter had been resolved by the ICJ's advisory opinion, finding that "determinations made by the ICJ in an advisory opinion cannot be disregarded simply because the advisory opinion is not binding" and that "[w]hile the process of decolonization has yet to be completed, Mauritius' sovereignty over the Chagos Archipelago can be inferred from the ICJ's determinations".[76]

The issue of sovereignty also hovered in the background of perhaps the most famous of the Annex VII arbitrations to date—that of the Philippines against China, which challenged China's claims to and activities in the South China Sea and the underlying seabed. China had been asserting some kind of claim, perhaps to sovereignty or more likely to "historic rights" or "historic title", over a rather large area of the South China Sea lying within what is known as the "nine-dash line," a line that has appeared on maps produced by China. Further, China claimed sovereignty over several islands or maritime features in the South China Sea. Given such claims, it was unclear whether an UNCLOS case might be brought against China, since addressing issues of sovereignty is problematic. Even so, in 2013, the Philippines instituted arbitral proceedings against China under Annex VII, artfully avoiding in its pleading any request that the tribunal address issues of sovereignty. Rather, the Philippines focused on whether certain maritime features were capable of being islands (if not, then no state could exercise sovereignty over them); for maritime features that were islands, the Philippines focused on resolving rights to maritime entitlements in the South China Sea even if one were to assume Chinese sovereignty over those islands.

---

[73] GA Res. 71/292 (22 June 2017).
[74] *Legal Consequences of the Separation of the Chagos Archipelago from Mauritius in 1965*, Advisory Opinion, ICJ Reports 2019, 95, para 183 (3)–(4).
[75] *Dispute concerning Delimitation of the Maritime Boundary between Mauritius and Maldives in the Indian Ocean (Mauritius v Maldives)*, Annex VII Arbitral Tribunal, Judgment on Preliminary Objections of 28 January 2021, para 101 et seq., <https://perma.cc/G3S3-NW3S>.
[76] ibid paras 205, 246.

Framed in that way, and despite China's decision not to participate in the case, the tribunal found that it had jurisdiction[77] and then issued a final award in 2016.[78] Among other things, the tribunal concluded that, while Chinese navigators and fishermen (and those of other states) had historically made use of the islands in the South China Sea, there was no evidence that China had exercised *exclusive* control over the waters or their resources. Further, even if China previously had historic rights to resources in the waters of the South China Sea, such rights were extinguished to the extent that they were incompatible with the exclusive economic zones provided by UNCLOS to the states surrounding the South China Sea. As such, there was no legal basis for China to claim historic rights to resources of the sea areas within the "nine-dash line". The tribunal's wide-ranging decision addresses a host of other issues as well; particular attention has been paid to its interpretation of what is meant, in UNCLOS Article 121(3), by the phrase "rocks which cannot sustain human habitation or economic life of their own".[79]

Concerns with respect to sovereignty also arose in *Coastal Rights in the Black Sea, Sea of Azov and Kerch Strait*.[80] In that case, Ukraine filed an Annex VII arbitration against Russia alleging that Russia had violated Ukraine's rights as a coastal state, such as to maritime living and hydrocarbon resources. Russia raised as a preliminary objection that the tribunal lacked jurisdiction because the dispute in reality concerned Ukraine's claim to sovereignty over the Crimean peninsula. Ukraine responded by arguing that there was no sovereignty dispute since Russia had acted unlawfully in seizing Crimea from Ukraine in 2014 and, alternatively, that even if there was a sovereignty dispute, it was an ancillary matter.[81] In an award on preliminary objections, the Tribunal unanimously upheld Russia's objection "to the extent that a ruling of the Arbitral Tribunal on the merits of Ukraine's claims necessarily requires it to decide, directly or implicitly, on the sovereignty of either Party over Crimea".[82] According to the Tribunal, the dispute over sovereignty was not ancillary to the interpretation or application of UNCLOS; whether Ukraine was a coastal State was a prerequisite to deciding a number of Ukraine's claims.[83] This outcome was consistent with the Annex VII arbitral award in the *Chagos* case.

## 6.2  Issues on the Use of Force

A different ancillary issue that has arisen concerns the use of force, and especially the difference between permissible maritime law enforcement and impermissible

[77] *South China Sea Arbitration (Philippines v China)*, Award on Jurisdiction and Admissibility of 29 October 2015, 33 RIAA 1, 143–51, paras 397–413 (2020).

[78] *South China Sea Arbitration (Philippines v China)*, Award of 12 July 2016 (n 69).

[79] See eg Yoshifumi Tanaka, "Reflections on the Interpretation and Application of Article 121(3) in the South China Sea Arbitration (Merits)" (2017) 48 Ocean Development & International Law 365; Sean D Murphy, *International Law relating to Islands* (Brill 2017) 88–95.

[80] *Dispute Concerning Coastal State Rights in the Black Sea, Sea of Azov, and Kerch Strait (Ukraine v Russia)*, Annex VII Arbitral Tribunal, Award on Preliminary Objections of 21 February 2020, <https://perma.cc/Z3QL-8CRR>.

[81] ibid para 161.

[82] ibid paras 197, 492(a).

[83] ibid para 195.

violation of the UN Charter. For example, in *Guyana v Suriname*, an Annex VII arbitral tribunal used UNCLOS Article 279 as a hook to address this issue; that article provides that the parties shall settle any dispute between them under UNCLOS "by peaceful means".[84] Seeing that article as allowing it to apply the *jus ad bellum* of the UN Charter and general international law, the tribunal found "that in international law force may be used in law enforcement activities provided that such force is unavoidable, reasonable and necessary".[85] In this instance, Suriname's action of sending a patrol vessel to order an oil rig to leave the contested waters did not meet such a standard and was thus determined to be an unlawful threat of force. That determination turned on the circumstances of the particular incident: the rig was approached at midnight and given twelve hours to leave; the rig was told if it didn't leave "the consequences will be yours"; and the men on the rig perceived that this meant military force would be used if they did not leave.[86]

In the context of using force, the "military activities" exception to UNCLOS dispute settlement may feature.[87] If so, the case law to date is less creative than confusing. Given that China had invoked the exception when adhering to UNCLOS, the *South China Sea* arbitral tribunal found that it had no jurisdiction over a Philippines claim concerning Chinese non-military vessels that had sought to prevent Philippine military vessels from resupplying its military personnel stationed at Second Thomas Schoal.[88] By contrast, the same tribunal found that the exception did not apply to a Philippines claim concerning Chinese military vessels used for land reclamation activities.[89] In the *Coastal Rights* case, Russia was not able to invoke the exception as a basis for excluding jurisdiction over Ukraine's case concerning coastal rights relating to Crimea. Russia's assertion that the dispute related to the 2014 Ukraine-Russia conflict was deemed by the Annex VII arbitral tribunal as insufficient for triggering the exception; to do so, the specific acts at issue in Ukraine's complaints had to constitute military activities.[90] Further, simply alleging that force was used to deny access to resources was not enough; among other things, the tribunal noted that maritime enforcement action and other "non-military" functions may be exercised equally by military and non-military vessels.[91]

At the provisional measures phase of *Detention of Three Ukrainian Naval Vessels*, ITLOS interpreted this exception when ordering Russia to release the Ukrainian naval vessels, as well as their crew, that had been detained in or near the Kerch Strait on 25 November 2018.[92] Although Russia had invoked the military activities exception when adhering to

---

[84] UNCLOS (n 2) art 279.

[85] *Arbitration Regarding the Delimitation of the Maritime Boundary Between Guyana and Suriname (Guyana v Suriname)*, Award of 17 September 2007 (n 69) para 445.

[86] ibid paras 432–439.

[87] UNCLOS (n 2) art 298(1)(b); see note 27 and accompanying text.

[88] *South China Sea Arbitration (Philippines v China)*, Award of 12 July 2016 (n 69), 597, paras 1161–1162.

[89] ibid 554–544, paras 1026–1028.

[90] *Dispute Concerning Coastal State Rights in the Black Sea, Sea of Azov, and Kerch Strait (Ukraine v Russia)*, Award on Preliminary Objections of 21 February 2020 (n 80), para 331.

[91] ibid para 335.

[92] *Detention of Three Ukrainian Naval Vessels (Ukraine v Russia)*, Order on Provisional Measures of 25 May 2019, ITLOS Reports 2019, 283, para 120.

UNCLOS, ITLOS found it *prima facie* was not applicable to a situation where Russian naval vessels forcibly seized Ukrainian naval vessels and crew. According to ITLOS, the underlying dispute concerned the legal status of the Kerch Strait, which was not military in nature.[93] Moreover, the Ukrainian naval vessels had abandoned their effort to pass through the strait when they were nevertheless detained by Russia, which, according to ITLOS, cast the event as in the nature of a law enforcement rather than a military operation.[94] The lone dissenting judge regarded navigational activities at sea of a state's warships to be inherently "military" and regarded this particular incident as involving military activities by both sides.[95] The case then proceeded before an Annex VII arbitral tribunal, which at the jurisdictional phase carved a path between these two positions. On the one hand, the tribunal in found that that the events of 25 November 2018 were, up until a certain point in time, "military activities" excluded from the tribunal's jurisdiction; on the other hand, after that point in time, the arrest of the Ukrainian naval vessels were more in the nature of a law enforcement operation falling within its jurisdiction. The precise point in time when things changed was left for consideration at the merits phase.[96]

## 6.3  Issues on Immunity

Issues concerning immunity, which are not central to the law of the sea, are nevertheless in play in some of these cases. For example, in a 2012 shooting incident at sea during a counter-piracy operation, two Italian marines on board an Italian-flagged commercial oil tanker, the *MV Enrica Lexie*, fired on a small fishing boat and killed two Indian fishermen who were mistaken for pirates. When Indian authorities charged the marines with murder, Italy claimed that they were entitled to functional immunity (immunity *rationae materiae*) for their conduct as members of the Italian armed forces. Thereafter, Italy requested a provisional measures order from ITLOS, asserting that India had infringed upon the immunity applicable to the marines. ITLOS prescribed provisional measures, as did an Annex VII arbitral tribunal established under UNCLOS Annex VII, resulting in a relaxation of bail conditions such that the two marines were allowed to return to Italy.[97] At the merits phase, the arbitral tribunal was confronted with whether it had jurisdiction to decide a claim concerning such immunity, given that none of the UNCLOS articles address such immunity (as opposed to immunity of warships).[98] In essence, the tribunal found that the issue of its entitlement to exercise jurisdiction over the incident could not

---

[93] ibid paras 68–72.

[94] ibid paras 73–76.

[95] ibid Dissenting Opinion of Judge Kolodkin, paras 9–10.

[96] *Dispute Concerning the Detention of Ukrainian Naval Vessels and Servicemen (Ukraine v. Russia)*, Annex VII Arbitral Tribunal, Award on Preliminary Objections of 27 June 2022, para 208(a), (b), and (c), <https://perma.cc/3XKS-ALNC>.

[97] See *The "Enrica Lexie" Incident (Italy v India)*, Decision on Provisional Measures of 24 August 2015, ITLOS Reports 2015, 182; *The "Enrica Lexie" Incident Arbitration (Italy v India)*, Annex VII Arbitral Tribunal, Order on the Request for Prescription of Provisional Measures of 29 April 2016, <https://perma.cc/D2N5-XGCX>.

[98] *The "Enrica Lexie" Incident Arbitration (Italy v India)*, Annex VII Arbitral Tribunal, Award of 21 May 2020, paras 796–799, <https://perma.cc/B8V3-FN6F>.

be satisfactorily answered without first addressing the question of the immunity of the marines.[99] Quoting from the *Case Concerning Certain German Interests* before the PCIJ, the tribunal creatively found that the issue of immunity of the marines "belongs to those 'questions preliminary or incidental to the application' of the Convention".[100]

More squarely present in UNCLOS is the immunity of warships.[101] In *Detention of Three Ukrainian Naval Vessels*, ITLOS found at the provisional measures stage that the rights to immunity claimed by Ukraine for its three vessels (and their military and security crew) were plausible.[102] At the jurisdictional stage before the Annex VII arbitral tribunal, Russia focused its arguments on the lack of any immunity for the Ukrainian vessels within the territorial sea. The Annex VII tribunal, however, decided that the location of the seizure of the vessels was not yet determined, such that Russia's objection could only be addressed at the merits stage.[103]

## 7. Judicial Settlement

Creativity in UNCLOS dispute resolution procedures is readily apparent in the allowance for negotiation and mediation, the emphasis on conciliation, and the openness to Annex VII (and the as-yet unused Annex VIII) arbitration. Yet the creativity arose not just in opening the door to those modes of dispute resolution but also in keeping the door open for judicial settlement, and to do so not just with the existing ICJ, but also through a new international court, ITLOS.[104] Not only have these judicial avenues for dispute resolution been active since 1994, again allowing for a wide range of issues to be resolved pacifically but, as indicated in this chapter, they have set in motion an important interplay or dialogue among arbitral and judicial bodies, whereby jurisprudence may be creatively developed and strengthened.

### 7.1 Contentious Cases

#### 7.1.1 ITLOS
Creativity in relation to judicial settlement began with the creation of an entirely new international court in the form of ITLOS, which is based in Hamburg.[105] ITLOS

---

[99] ibid para 808 ("The Arbitral Tribunal could not provide a complete answer to the question as to which Party may exercise jurisdiction without incidentally examining whether the Marines enjoy immunity.").

[100] ibid (quoting *Case Concerning Certain German Interests in Polish Upper Silesia (Germany v Poland)*, Judgment of 25 August 1925, PCIJ Series A, No 6, 18).

[101] See UNCLOS (n 2) arts 32, 58, 95–96.

[102] *Dispute Concerning the Detention of Ukrainian Naval Vessels and Servicemen (Ukraine v. Russia)*, Award on Preliminary Objections of 27 June 2022 (n 96) paras 97–99.

[103] ibid paras 152–155.

[104] On how a state's domestic legal tradition influences its preferred dispute resolution forum, see Emilia Justyna Powell and Sara McLaughlin Mitchell, "Forum Shopping for the Best Adjudicator: Dispute Settlement in the United Nations Convention on the Law of the Sea" (2022) 9 Journal of Territorial & Maritime Studies 7.

[105] See Gudmundur Eiriksson, *The International Tribunal for the Law of the Sea* (Martinus Nijhoff 2000); P Chandrasekhara Rao and Rahmatullah Khan (eds), *The International Tribunal for the Law of the Sea: Law and*

consists of twenty-one judges elected by the UNCLOS States Parties. Each State Party may nominate up to two candidates, and no two judges may be nationals of the same state. Moreover, to preserve an equitable geographic distribution, there is an agreed distribution of seats among the regional groups. Members are elected for nine years and may be re-elected; the terms of one-third of the members expire every three years.[106]

Though it is common to note the relatively light caseload of ITLOS at any given time, its presence as an institution available to address matters of urgent concern fills an important void that previously existed for the law of the sea. Thus, ITLOS may indicate provisional measures of protection, either for cases filed at ITLOS or for cases filed before an Annex VII tribunal,[107] if ITLOS considers that: (i) *prima facie* the relevant tribunal would have jurisdiction over the dispute, (ii) "the urgency of the situation so requires", and (iii) the measures are appropriate to the circumstances to preserve the rights of the parties pending final decision.[108] With respect to (ii), although not identified as an express requirement in the Convention, the Tribunal's jurisprudence has evolved so as to include an assessment, first, of whether the rights being advanced by an applicant are at least "plausible", and then of whether there is urgency in protecting those rights.[109] If the rights are not plausible, then the extraordinary step of ordering provisional measures should not be taken to protect the asserted rights. The exact contours of the concept of "plausibility" of rights is somewhat elusive, but ITLOS and the ICJ appear to be in a dialogue on this matter; it would seem to require "something more than [a simple] assertion but less than [full] proof".[110]

Moreover, ITLOS has the ability to hear "prompt release" cases so as to address, on an expedited basis, situations where a coastal state has seized a foreign vessel and crew for violation of rules relating to its exclusive economic zone, but has failed to promptly release them, even upon the posting of a reasonable bond.[111] A creative feature in this regard is that natural or juridical persons may appear before ITLOS to seek the prompt

---

Practice (Martinus Nijhoff 2001); P Chandrasekhara Rao and Philippe Gautier (eds), *The Rules of the International Tribunal for the Law of the Sea: A Commentary* (Martinus Nijhoff 2006); Miguel García García-Revillo, *The Contentious and Advisory Jurisdiction of the International Tribunal for the Law of the Sea* (Brill Nijhoff 2015); Bimal N Patel (ed), *Law of the Sea: International Tribunal for the Law of the Sea Jurisprudence: Case Commentary, Case-Law Digest and Reference Guide (1994–2014)* (Eastern Book Company 2015).

[106] UNCLOS (n 2) Annex VI.

[107] ibid art 290(5); ibid Annex VI, art 25; see eg *Case Concerning the Detention of Three Ukrainian Naval Vessels (Ukraine v the Russian Federation)*, Provisional Measures Order of 25 May 2019, (n 92).

[108] UNCLOS (n 2) art 290(1) and (5).

[109] See eg *The "Enrica Lexie" Incident (Italy v India)*, Decision on Provisional Measures of 24 August 2015, ITLOS Reports 2015, 182, paras 83–88.

[110] *Certain Activities Carried out by Nicaragua in the Border Area (Costa Rica v Nicaragua)*, Provisional Measures, Order of 8 March 2011, Declaration of Judge Greenwood, ICJ Reports 2011, 47, para 4; see also *Questions Relating to the Seizure and Detention of Certain Documents (Timor-Leste v Australia)*, Provisional Measures, Order of 3 March 2014, Dissenting Opinion of Judge Greenwood, ICJ Reports 2014, 195, para 4; *Pulp Mills on the River Uruguay (Argentina v Uruguay)*, Provisional Measures, Order of 13 July 2006, Separate Opinion of Judge Abraham, ICJ Reports 2006, 141, para 11.

[111] UNCLOS (n 2) arts 73 and 292. See eg *M/V "Saiga" (Saint Vincent and the Grenadines v Guinea)*, ITLOS Reports 1997, 16.

release of a vessel and its crew when detained by a coastal state, though they only do so "on behalf of" the flag state of the detained vessel (and therefore must first receive authorization from that state).[112]

Rather than ITLOS as a whole deciding a contentious matter, a chamber of the tribunal may instead be convened if desired by the disputing parties.[113] Indeed, ITLOS has established chambers for summary procedure, fisheries disputes, marine environment disputes, and maritime delimitation disputes in an effort to foster such an approach. Further, there exists a Seabed Disputes Chamber, which is set up under UNCLOS Part XI and has jurisdiction over certain disputes concerning the deep seabed.[114] Again, there is some creativity in moving away from exclusively inter-state dispute settlement for seabed disputes. Not only may States Parties (and state enterprises) appear before the Seabed Disputes Chamber to resolve disputes relating to Part XI, but so may two entities created by the Convention— the International Seabed Authority and the Enterprise[115]—as well as, in certain circumstances, natural or juridical persons and prospective contractors who have been sponsored by a state.[116]

Although thirty-two cases have been filed at ITLOS as of 2023, they have mostly related to requests for provisional measures or for prompt release.[117] In recent years, however, ITLOS cases have begun expanding in scope. ITLOS has decided maritime boundaries between Bangladesh and Myanmar in the Bay of Bengal[118] and (by means of a chamber) between Ghana and Côte d'Ivoire in the Atlantic Ocean[119] and between Mauritius and Maldives in the Indian Ocean.[120] Further, looking at the totality of its jurisprudence, ITLOS may be seen as shaping the law of the sea in myriad ways. For example, to understand permissible coastal state regulation of vessels operating on the seas, one might consider not just the text of UNCLOS, but also a series of ITLOS cases that, collectively, shed light on the matter: the *M/V "Norstar"* case indicated that bunkering of leisure vessels on the high seas is part of the freedom of navigation under Convention Article 87;[121] the *M/V "Virginia G"* case maintained that generally the bunkering of fishing vessels in an exclusive economic zone can be regulated and enforced

---

[112] UNCLOS (n 2) art 292(2).

[113] ibid Annex VI, art 15(2).

[114] ibid arts 186–187.

[115] The International Seabed Authority administers the resources of the deep seabed area. The Enterprise will serve as the Authority's mining operator, but as of 2023 has not yet been established. For a discussion of the possibility for investor claims relating to deep seabed mining being pursued under UNCLOS dispute settlement, see Alberto Pecoraro, *UNCLOS and Investor Claims for Deep Seabed Mining in the Area: An Investment Law of the Sea?* GCILS Working Paper Series No. 5 (November 2020), <https://perma.cc/7XYN-FHQL>.

[116] UNCLOS (n 2) art 187.

[117] See ITLOS website <http://www.itlos.org> accessed 14 August 2023.

[118] *Delimitation of the Maritime Boundary in the Bay of Bengal (No 16) (Bangladesh v Myanmar)*, Judgment of 14 March 2012, ITLOS Reports 2012, 4.

[119] *Delimitation of the Maritime Boundary in the Atlantic Ocean (No 23) (Ghana/Côte d'Ivoire)*, Judgment of 23 September 2017, ITLOS Reports 2017, 4.

[120] *Dispute concerning Delimitation of the Maritime Boundary between Mauritius and Maldives in the Indian Ocean (Mauritius/Maldives)*, ITLOS, Judgment of 28 April 2023, <https://perma.cc/GKN7-VUYK>.

[121] *M/V "Norstar" Case (Panama v Italy)*, Judgment of 10 April 2019, ITLOS Reports 2019, 10, para 219.

against by the coastal state;[122] the *M/V "Saiga" (No 2)* case explained that, in such a circumstance, the coastal state cannot apply its customs laws and regulations, though it can do so with respect to artificial islands, installations, and structures;[123] and the *Duzgit Integrity* case supports the general proposition that an archipelagic state may regulate and enforce against ship-to-ship oil transfers in archipelagic waters.[124]

### 7.1.2 ICJ

The ICJ has been very active in settling law of the sea disputes since 1994, continuing a role it has played since its inception. Jurisdiction might be established at the ICJ based on UNCLOS, but to date the Court's jurisdiction has been invoked in other ways, thereby allowing the Court at times to decide not just issues arising under the Convention, but other issues was well, including claims to sovereignty.[125] It is to be noted that David Caron was appointed judge ad hoc of the Court by Colombia in *Alleged Violations of Sovereign Rights and Maritime Spaces in the Caribbean Sea (Nicaragua v Colombia)*, a case on which he sat until his passing.[126]

Keeping the ICJ in play for dispute resolution under UNCLOS was a wise move as the Court's jurisprudence is significantly enriching our understanding of the interpretation and application of the Convention. For example, the methodology used by courts and tribunals for many years to delimit maritime areas varied considerably, and UNCLOS did little to clarify matters. But the ICJ, in its unanimous 2009 *Black Sea* judgment, indicated that, in cases where no agreement has been reached by the two states, usually a three-step approach to delimitation is appropriate. First, the tribunal should establish a provisional equidistance line, meaning a line every point of which is equidistant from the nearest basepoints of the two adjacent or opposite states.[127] Second, the tribunal should "consider whether there are factors calling for the adjustment or shifting of the provisional equidistance line in order to achieve an equitable result".[128] Third, the tribunal should "verify

---

[122] *M/V "Virginia G" Case (Panama v Guinea-Bissau)*, Judgment of 14 April 2014, ITLOS Reports 2014, 4, para 217.

[123] *M/V "Saiga" (No 2) (Saint Vincent and the Grenadines v Guinea)*, Judgment of 1 July 1999, ITLOS Reports 1999, 10, para 127.

[124] *Duzgit Integrity Arbitration (Malta v São Tomé and Príncipe)*, Annex VII Arbitral Tribunal, Award of 5 September 2016, <https://perma.cc/RJ7J-G89A>.

[125] The principal ICJ cases relating to the law of the sea since 1994 have been: *Maritime Delimitation and Territorial Questions between Qatar and Bahrain (Qatar v Bahrain)*, Judgment of 16 March 2001, ICJ Reports 2001, 40; *Land and Maritime Boundary between Cameroon and Nigeria (Cameroon v Nigeria: Equatorial Guinea intervening)*, Judgment of 10 October 2002, ICJ Reports 2002, 303; *Territorial and Maritime Delimitation between Nicaragua and Honduras in the Caribbean Sea (Nicaragua v Honduras)*, Judgment of 8 October 2007, ICJ Reports 2007, 659; *Maritime Delimitation in the Black Sea (Romania v Ukraine)*, Judgment of 3 February 2009, ICJ Reports 2009, 61; *Territorial and Maritime Dispute (Nicaragua v Colombia)*, Judgment of 19 November 2012, ICJ Reports 2012, 624; *Maritime Dispute (Peru v Chile)*, Judgment of 27 January 2014, ICJ Reports 2014, 3; *Maritime Delimitation in the Caribbean Sea and the Pacific Ocean (Costa Rica v Nicaragua)* and *Land Boundary in the Northern Part of Isla Portillos (Costa Rica v Nicaragua)*, Judgment of 2 February 2018, ICJ Reports 2018, 139; *Maritime Delimitation in the Indian Ocean (Somalia v Kenya)*, Judgment of 12 October 2021, ICJ Reports 2021, 206; *Alleged Violations of Sovereign Rights and Maritime Spaces in the Caribbean Sea (Nicaragua v Colombia)*, ICJ, Judgment of 21 April 2022, <https://perma.cc/2YQG-SVYL>; *Question of the Delimitation of the Continental Shelf between Nicaragua and Colombia beyond 200 Nautical Miles from the Nicaraguan Coast (Nicaragua v Colombia)*, ICJ, Judgment of 13 July 2023, <https://perma.cc/N43B-GC4Z>.

[126] He was replaced by Donald McRae. For the Court's final judgment in 2022, see note 125.

[127] *Maritime Delimitation in the Black Sea (Romania v Ukraine)*, Judgment of 3 February 2009, ICJ Reports 2009, 61, para 119.

[128] ibid para 120.

that the [delimitation] line … does not … lead to an inequitable result by reason of any marked disproportion between the ratio of the respective coastal lengths and the ratio between the relevant maritime area of each State by reference to the delimitation line".[129] This approach has now been utilized by Annex VII arbitral tribunals as well, such as in the *Bangladesh v India* maritime delimitation case.[130]

The fact that judicial and arbitral tribunals are in dialogue does not necessarily mean that they are always in agreement. Indeed, with the proliferation of dispute resolution bodies, there arises, quite naturally, a concern with fragmentation of international law. Yet some forms of disagreement can also be a method for creative development of the law, whereby courts and tribunals refine the relevant rules over time through a process of action and reaction. An example might be the types of measures that a state may pursue on a provisional basis in a disputed area of the continental shelf. In the *Aegean Sea Continental Shelf* case, Greece sought a provisional measures order requiring that both Greece and Turkey not engage in exploration activities in the Aegean Sea, arguing that Turkey's activities threatened the exclusivity of Greece's rights with respect to the extent and location of seabed resources. The dispute arose before the adoption of UNCLOS and thus the Court did not apply it; rather, it was applying its own rules and jurisprudence with respect to whether conditions existed meriting provisional measures of protection by the Court, prior to a judgment on matters of jurisdiction or the merits. The Court said that provisional measures are only warranted if necessary to ensure that states do not undertake activities that cause "physical damage to the seabed or subsoil" (as opposed to exploratory activity such as seismic exploration), do not establish installations on the continental shelf (as opposed to activities of a "transitory character"), and do not engage in actual appropriation or other use of natural resources.[131]

For ITLOS, however, whether such invasive activities are occurring within a disputed area of the continental shelf appears not to be the automatic touchstone when determining whether to issue an order on provisional measures of protection. The 2015 *Ghana/Côte d'Ivoire* Special Chamber's order on provisional measures accepted that drilling causes a "significant and permanent modification of the physical character of the area in dispute and … such modification cannot be fully compensated by financial reparations".[132] Yet the Chamber declined to order Ghana to suspend *existing* oil exploration and exploitation activities in the disputed maritime area.[133] Rather, it allowed exploitation of shelf resources to continue even within the disputed area, because suspending such activities would cause prejudice to Ghana (Ghana had been engaged in such exploitation before Côte d'Ivoire claimed that the area was part of its continental shelf) and could cause harm to the marine environment.[134]

[129] ibid para 122.
[130] *Bay of Bengal Maritime Boundary Arbitration (Bangladesh v India)*, Award of 7 July 2014, 32 RIAA 1 (2019).
[131] *Aegean Sea Continental Shelf Case (Greece v Turkey), Interim Protection*, Order of 11 September 1976, ICJ Reports 1976, 3, para 30.
[132] *Delimitation of the Maritime Boundary in the Atlantic Ocean (Ghana/Côte d'Ivoire), Provisional Measures*, Order of 25 April 2015, ITLOS Reports 2015, 146, paras 89–90.
[133] ibid paras 99–100, 108.
[134] ibid.

Conversely, the Chamber found that some non-invasive activities may also merit provisional measures of protection. Thus, the Chamber found that acquisition and subsequent use of geological information concerning the disputed area created a risk of irreversible prejudice.[135] Ultimately, the Special Chamber ordered: (i) Ghana to "take all necessary steps to ensure that no new drilling either by Ghana or [by others] under its control take place in the disputed area"; (ii) Ghana to "take all necessary steps to prevent information resulting from past, ongoing or future exploration activities conducted by Ghana, or with its authorization, in the disputed area that is not already in the public domain from being used in any way whatsoever to the detriment of Côte d'Ivoire"; (iii) Ghana to "carry out strict and continuous monitoring of all activities undertaken by Ghana or with its authorization in the disputed area, with a view to ensuring the prevention of serious harm to the marine environment"; (iv) both parties to "take all necessary steps [in the disputed area] to prevent serious harm to the marine environment, including the continental shelf and in its superjacent waters", and to "cooperate toward that end"; and (v) both parties to "pursue cooperation and refrain from any unilateral action that might lead to aggravating the dispute".[136] This approach reflects a creative development of the law in this area that begins with but goes well beyond the approach taken by the Court in the *Aegean Sea Continental Shelf Case*. In due course, it may help inform the Court's approach to such issues.

## 7.2  Advisory Opinions

Advisory opinions issued either by the ICJ or by ITLOS can also feature in dispute settlement under the law of the sea, and here too creativity may be observed. In addition to resolving contentious disputes, a chamber of ITLOS—known as the Seabed Disputes Chamber—has express authority to "give advisory opinions at the request of the Assembly or the Council on legal questions arising within the scope of their activities".[137] In response to certain questions posed by the Council, the Chamber issued its first advisory opinion in 2011 entitled *Responsibilities and Obligations of States Sponsoring Persons and Entities with Respect to Activities in the Area*.[138] Among other things, the Chamber clarified that a state that sponsors contractors who engage in activities on the deep seabed is responsible for supervising them, including any drilling, dredging, or excavation. Further, states must engage in a precautionary approach with respect to such activities, must use best environmental practices, and must conduct environmental impact assessments.

---

[135] ibid para 95.
[136] ibid para 108(1).
[137] UNCLOS (n 2) art 191.
[138] *Responsibilities and Obligations of States Sponsoring Persons and Entities with Respect to Activities in the Area,* Advisory Opinion of 1 February 2011, ITLOS Reports 2011, 10.

In contrast with the Seabed Disputes Chamber, UNCLOS does not provide any express authority to ITLOS as a whole to issue advisory opinions. Even so, in 2013, the Sub-Regional Fisheries Commission, which is a fisheries commission comprising seven West African nations,[139] requested an advisory opinion from ITLOS. The Commission asked ITLOS four questions about the rights and obligations of flag and coastal states regarding fishing in the exclusive economic zone, such as to what extent a flag state may be held liable for illegal fishing activities conducted by vessels sailing under its flag.[140] Twenty-two UNCLOS States Parties filed written statements with ITLOS on these questions, as did the Commission and six other international organizations.[141] An oral hearing was held in 2014, at which ten States Parties appeared, as well as the Commission and two other international organizations,[142] thereby allowing a robust exchange of views on the issues at hand.

ITLOS's jurisdiction to issue advisory opinions was contested; many States Parties argued that it had no power to do so. Nevertheless, in 2015 ITLOS found that it is capable of providing advisory opinions,[143] hence opening the door to potentially wide-ranging guidance on the interpretation and application of UNCLOS, including on matters that are less susceptible to resolution through contentious cases. ITLOS then went on to provide a broad analysis of the obligations of flag states with respect to sustainable fisheries management, which one hopes will guide those states when regulating their flag vessels in another state's exclusive economic zone, not just off the coast of West Africa but worldwide.[144] In any event, the door now appears open for ITLOS advisory opinions; in 2022, a new advisory opinion was filed on the obligations of States Parties under UNCLOS to prevent pollution of, and protect, the marine environment in relation to climate change.[145]

## 8. Commission on the Continental Shelf

UNCLOS also establishes a Commission on the Limits of the Continental Shelf (CLCS), which consists of twenty-one members who are "experts in the field of geology, geophysics or hydrography, elected by States Parties to this Convention from among their nationals, having due regard to the need to ensure equitable geographical

---

[139] Those States are Cape Verde, Gambia, Guinea, Guinea Bissau, Mauritania, Senegal, and Sierra Leone. The backdrop to this request were allegations by West African states that third state vessels were engaged in illegal, unreported, or unregulated fishing off the coast of West Africa that was imperilling fish stocks.

[140] *Request for an Advisory Opinion Submitted by the Sub-Regional Fisheries Commission*, Advisory Opinion of 2 April 2015, ITLOS Reports 2015, 4, para 2.

[141] ibid para 17. Interestingly, the United States was also permitted to file a written statement even though it is not an UNCLOS party, apparently because it is a party to the 1995 Straddling Fish Stocks Agreement. ibid para 24.

[142] ibid para 29.

[143] ibid paras 37–69.

[144] ibid paras 85–219.

[145] Request [to ITLOS] for an Advisory Opinion submitted by the Commission of Small Island States on Climate Change and International Law, 12 December 2022, <https://perma.cc/8FDM-JB2S>.

representation, who shall serve in their personal capacities".[146] Strictly speaking, the CLCS is not a dispute resolution body. Having said that, it receives submissions from coastal states about their claims to continental shelves extending beyond 200 nautical miles and, after receiving comments from other states, it issues recommendations to the coastal state. If the coastal state establishes the limits to its extended continental shelf in a manner that takes into account these recommendations, then those limits shall be final and binding.[147] Thus, the CLCS is a new institutional mechanism that in the long term may be important in reducing disputes among states regarding the permissibility of extended continental shelves. As of 2023, the CLCS has received ninety-three submissions from states and has issued about thirty-eight recommendations, some with respect to the same submission.[148]

One interesting issue is the interplay of applications to/recommendations by the CLCS and dispute resolution before other fora on delimitation of the outer continental shelf (OCS, meaning the shelf beyond 200 nautical miles). One particular question is whether an international court or tribunal should exercise jurisdiction to delimit the OCS between states with opposite or adjacent coasts if the CLCS has not yet made recommendations as to the existence of those states' respective shelves. The two processes—a CLCS recommendation as to whether/where a state may claim an OCS and an international tribunal's delimitation of the overlapping OCS of two states—are clearly distinct, the former being governed by UNCLOS Article 76 and the latter by UNCLOS Article 83.[149] Even so, it has been argued that until a coastal state actually demonstrates the existence of its claimed OCS by means of the CLCS process, an international court or tribunal should not delimit such a claim vis-à-vis another state. That argument presents a "chicken-and-the-egg situation", however, in that the CLCS by its rules will not proceed with issuance of a recommendation in situations where there is a dispute over the delimitation of the relevant OCS, unless the states concerned so consent.[150] The CLCS is also slow in issuing recommendations and has a considerable backlog of submissions awaiting its examination.

Consequently, so as to avoid an impasse, international courts and tribunals have gingerly but creatively proceeded with such OCS delimitations. In *Bangladesh/Myanmar*, both states had made submissions to the CLCS but had not given consent for the CLCS to issue recommendations on each other's claims. Even so, ITLOS concluded that it had an obligation to delimit the overlapping area of the two OCS claims and proceeded to

---

[146] UNCLOS (n 2) Annex II, art 2.

[147] ibid art 76(8); see Peter J Cook and Chris M Carleton (eds), *Continental Shelf Limits: The Scientific and Legal Interface* (Oxford University Press 2000) 20; Ted L McDorman, "The Role of the Commission on the Limits of the Continental Shelf: A Technical Body in a Political World" (2002) 17 International Journal of Marine & Coastal Law 301; Michael Sheng-ti Gau, "The Commission on the Limits of the Continental Shelf as a Mechanism to Prevent Encroachment upon the Area" (2011) 10 Chinese Journal of International Law 3.

[148] See Commission on the Limits of the Continental Shelf, "Submissions, through the Secretary-General of the United Nations, to the Commission on the Limits of the Continental Shelf, pursuant to article 76, paragraph 8, of the United Nations Convention on the Law of the Sea of 10 December 1982", <https://perma.cc/ER4D-22RZ>.

[149] *Delimitation of the Maritime Boundary in the Bay of Bengal (No 16) (Bangladesh v Myanmar)*, Judgment of 14 March 2012, ITLOS Reports 2012, 4, 99, para 376.

[150] CLCS Rules of Procedure, CLCS/40/Rev.1 (2008), Rule 46 and Annex I, para 5(a).

do so, albeit "without prejudice" to the subsequent establishment of each state's OCS.[151] Interestingly, the *apparent* existence of a OCS for both states based on uncontested scientific evidence influenced the Tribunal; it said that it "would have been hesitant to proceed with the delimitation of the area beyond 200 nautical miles had it concluded that there was significant uncertainty as to the existence of a continental margin in the area in question."[152] In *Ghana/Côte d'Ivoire*, the two states had consented to CLCS examination of each other's submissions, despite overlapping claims, and Ghana had received affirmative recommendations, but no CLCS recommendation had yet been reached on Côte d'Ivoire's submission. Again, ITLOS (by special chamber) proceeded to delimit the overlapping OCS and, once again, did so based on there being "no doubt" that an OCS existed for Côte d'Ivoire.[153]

In *Somalia v Kenya*, the two states had made submissions to the CLCS, neither had received recommendations, and neither questioned that the other had an OCS. Even so, whether one or both states actually possessed an OCS was much less clear than in *Bangladesh/Myanmar* or in *Ghana/Côte d'Ivoire*. The International Court of Justice itself recognized this by noting that its adjusted equidistance line entailed the "possibility" of a "grey area" (an area where Kenya *might* possess sovereign rights to an OCS while Somalia possessed sovereign rights to the exclusive economic zone).[154] Yet, despite this uncertainty, the Court proceeded to delimit the area of the OCS as between the two states, a step that elicited concerns from some of the judges.[155]

## 9. Conclusion

The existence of numerous inter-state maritime disputes today is self-evident, and they no doubt will continue in the years to come. While delimitation disputes obviously come to mind, many other sources of friction might also be mentioned: the resurgence of piracy, recurrent military incidents on the seas, the recovery of cultural or historical objects at sea, access to maritime genetic resources, disputes over islands, and the vexing issue of maritime smuggling of persons.[156] One issue likely to spawn future disputes relates to global climate change, which is causing a rise in sea levels due to the

---

[151] *Delimitation of the Maritime Boundary in the Bay of Bengal (No 16) (Bangladesh v Myanmar)*, Judgment of 14 March 2012, ITLOS Reports 2012, 4, 100, para 379, 103, para 394.

[152] ibid 115, para 443.

[153] *Delimitation of the Maritime Boundary in the Atlantic Ocean (No 23) (Ghana/Côte d'Ivoire)*, Judgment of 23 September 2017, Judgment, ITLOS Reports 2017, 4, 136, para 491 ("the Special Chamber has no doubt that a continental shelf beyond 200 nm exists for Côte d'Ivoire since its geological situation is identical to that of Ghana, for which affirmative recommendations of the CLCS exist").

[154] Maritime Delimitation in the Indian Ocean (*Somalia v Kenya*), Judgment of 12 October 2021, ICJ Reports 2021, para 197.

[155] See ibid Separate Opinion of President Donoghue, para 4 ("the Court has scant evidence regarding the existence, shape, extent and continuity of any outer continental shelf that may appertain to the Parties"); ibid Individual Opinion, Partly Concurring and Partly Dissenting, of Judge Robinson, para 9 ("the Court must have at hand reliable information confirming the existence of a continental margin in the area beyond 200 nautical miles if it is to be in a position to carry out a delimitation in that area. However, ... the Court ignores this requirement.").

[156] See generally Natalie Klein, *Maritime Security and the Law of the Sea* (Oxford University Press 2011); Gemma Andreone (ed), *Jurisdiction and Control at Sea: Some Environmental and Security Issues* (Giannini Editore 2014).

expansion of ocean water and the melting of glaciers and polar ice. That rise in sea levels is causing shifts in coastlines, with the potential for greater uncertainty in the location of baselines and of the seaward maritime zones. As David Caron well-observed, current law here may be misguided, as it calls for ambulatory baselines, rather than allowing states to "freeze" their baselines and maritime zones in place, thereby protecting their rights to maritime spaces.[157]

To resolve such disputes, the creativity of the drafters of UNCLOS will no doubt be put to good use; the Convention's substantive rules will be central, but the robust and varied dispute resolution procedures created by and available to states will also be important. Some creativity may be merited and essential when addressing vague, ambiguous, or undefined terms, or when applying even clear rules and procedures by dispute settlers to unique circumstances that the UNCLOS drafters did not envisage. Yet it is important to keep in mind that, as creative a lawyer as David Caron was, he also worried about the potential overreach of dispute settlers,[158] and in particular that their creativity in resolving a problem might extend beyond the settled law and jurisdiction accorded to them by states. Given the importance of a transparent and well-grounded system of rules for inducing compliance by states and others, creativity in deciding cases relating to the law of the sea may be beneficial in measured doses, but it is perilous if unbounded.

# Acknowledgements

My thanks to John Catalfamo (GW Law '22) for research assistance.

---

[157] David D Caron, "When Law Makes Climate Change Worse: Rethinking the Law of Baselines in Light of a Rising Sea Level" (1990) 17 Ecology Law Quarterly 621.

[158] See eg David D Caron, "The ILC Articles on State Responsibility: The Paradoxical Relationship between Form and Authority" 96 (2002) American Journal of International Law 857, 858 (expressing concern that arbitral panels might rely on the ILC articles without sufficient probing as to whether they reflect settled rules of international law).

# 12

# Independent Accountability Mechanisms in Dispute Settlement

*Edith Brown Weiss*

## 1. Introduction

Within the last three decades, a new form of institution has emerged to give voice to citizens and affected people to enable them to hold multilateral development banks (MDBs) accountable. The body, known as an independent accountability mechanism (IAM), addresses disputes between those affected by an organization's projects or programmes and management and staff of the organization. The form has now spread beyond the multilateral development banks to organizations in the United Nations systems and other international organizations, to national organizations concerned with overseas investments, and to the private sector.[1] The legitimacy of international organizations (and other organizations) depends upon their having measures to hold them accountable for their actions and operations. Giving a voice to people affected by their actions is a very important development.

MDBs, of which there are now eight major ones, are responsible for billions of dollars in loans and grants to developing and emerging market economies every year.[2] The first table provides data for their annual commitments (Table 12.1).

Controversy has often arisen over their projects and programmes. People harmed or potentially harmed by these projects and programmes can bring their dispute to the MDB to try to hold the institution accountable for its work. To address these complaints, all MDBs except the New Development Bank and the Islamic Bank have established an independent accountability forum, known generically as an independent accountability mechanism (IAM).[3] The IAMs consist of either one or two parts: one in which individuals can approach the institution and engage in alternative dispute resolution

---

[1] The national institutions include, among others, the former US Overseas Private Investment Corporation Office of Accountability, Japanese Bank for International Cooperation Examiner for Environmental Guidelines, and Nippon Export and Investment Insurance Objection Procedures on Environmental Guidelines. The European Investment Bank also has a Complaints Mechanism.

[2] The World Bank Group (IBRD, IDA, IFC, MIGA, and RETF), African Development Bank, Asian Development Bank. European Bank for Reconstruction and Development, Inter-American Development Bank, Asian Infrastructure Investment Bank, the Islamic Development Bank, and the New Development Bank based in Shanghai.

[3] For a good overview of the IAMs and their operations, see Kristen Lewis, *Citizen-Driven Accountability for Sustainable Development: Giving Affected People a Greater Voice—20 Years On* (June 2012), Independent Accountability Mechanisms Network <https://www.inspectionpanel.org/sites/www.inspectionpanel.org/files/publications/CitizenDrivenAccountability.pdf>; Owen McIntyre and Suresh Nanwani (eds), *The Practice of Independent Accountability Mechanisms (IAMS)* (Brill/Nijhoff 2020)

Edith Brown Weiss, *Independent Accountability Mechanisms in Dispute Settlement* In: *By Peaceful Means*. Edited by: Charles N Brower, Joan E Donoghue, Cian C Murphy, Cymie R Payne and Esmé R Shirlow, Oxford University Press. © Edith Brown Weiss 2024.
DOI: 10.1093/oso/9780192848086.003.0012

Table 12.1  Annual Commitments by Multilateral Development Bank[a]

| | 2017 | 2018 | 2019 |
|---|---|---|---|
| **World Bank Group** | | | |
| International Bank for Reconstruction and Development (IBRD) | 22.6 | 23.0 | 23.2 |
| International Development Association (IDA) | 19.5 | 24.0 | 22.0 |
| International Finance Corporation (IFC) | 11.9 | 11.6 | 8.9 |
| Recipient Executed Trust Fund (RETF) | 3.0 | 3.0 | 2.7 |
| Multilateral Investment Guarantee Agency (MIGA)[b] | 4.8 | 5.3 | 5.5 |
| Total | 61.8 | 66.9 | 66.3 |
| **African Development Bank Group[c]** | | | |
| *Approvals* | 6.2 | 7.28 | 7.30 |
| *Technical Assistance* | 0.018 | 0.040 | 0.033 |
| **Asian Development Bank (ADB)** | | | |
| *Commitments* | 31.8 | 35.5 | 33.7 |
| *Loans, Grants, & Others* | 19.7 | 21.6 | 21.7 |
| *Technical Assistance* | 2.01 | 2.41 | 2.37 |
| *Co-financing, including Trust Funds* | 11.9 | 13.6 | 11.9 |
| **European Bank for Reconstruction and Development (EBRD)** | | | |
| *Annual Bank Investment* | 9.7 | 9.5 | 10.1 |
| *Annual Mobilized Investment[d]* | 1.1 | 1.5 | 1.3 |
| *Total project value[e]* | 38.4 | 32.6 | 34.5 |
| **Inter-American Development Bank** | | | |
| *Loans and Guarantees Approved* | 13.4 | 14.8 | 13.3 |
| **Asian Infrastructure Investment Bank** | | | |
| *Net Committed (cumulative)* | 4.1 | 7.4 | 8.4 |
| **New Development Bank** | | | |
| *Approved Loans* | 1.9 | 4.6 | 7.2 |
| **Islamic Development Bank** | | | |
| *Net Approvals* | 9.8 | 7.0 | 7.8 |

[a] Table compiled by the author, Edith Brown Weiss. Figures for commitments are taken from the annual financial reports of each MDB for the year in question. Disbursements lag commitments and are generally less than the commitment in the same year. All figures are in hundreds of millions of US Dollars, except those for the African Development Bank Group (hundreds of millions UA); and the EBRD (hundreds of millions of Euros). The figures have been rounded off to the nearest hundred million.

[b] Gross issuance of investment guarantees.

[c] Includes loans, grants, equity investments, emergency operations, and heavily indebted poor country (HIPC) debt.

[d] Annual mobilized investment is the volume of commitments from entities other than the EBRD made available to the client due to the Bank's direct involvement in mobilizing external financing during the year.

[e] Total project value is the total amount of finance provided to a project, including both EBRD and non-EBRD finance, and is reported in the year in which the project first signs. EBRD financing may be committed over more than one year, with Annual Bank Investment reflecting EBRD finance by year of commitment. The amount of finance to be provided by non-EBRD parties is reported in the year the project first signs.

(ADR) methods to resolve their special problems; and a second that responds to complaints of affected people and communities about harm or anticipated harm from projects or Rprograms financed by the MDBs because management and staff have not complied with the MDB's own policies and procedures. The latter is sometimes referred to as compliance review. In a few MDBs, resort to alternative dispute resolution is a prerequisite to requesting a compliance review to address a dispute.

The next table indicates the number of cases that were before the IAMs in 2019 for individual alternative dispute resolution and for reviewing compliance with policies and procedures (Table 12.2).

The third table indicates the subject matter for those cases subject to compliance review (Table 12.3). Many of the latter involve infrastructure projects.

This chapter looks at the IAM as a critically important forum for hearing disputes and providing for accountability. It focuses on disputes about compliance with the MDB's policies and procedures. The IAM operates as an informal dispute settlement body, in contrast to a court or arbitral tribunal. It conducts formal investigations and relies on fact-finding to resolve disputes. It issues a formal report with its findings and analysis to the Board of Executive Directors. By determining whether the MDB has complied with its policies and procedures, the IAM effectively holds it accountable. These IAMs are often characterized as quasi-judicial.

This analysis considers the specific example of the World Bank and its Inspection Panel, which was the first IAM to be established and served as a model for the others. In doing so, the author draws upon her experience as the Chairperson of the World Bank Inspection Panel for four years and as a Panel member in the preceding year. The chapter begins by setting forth a framework for accountability and a proposed principle of accountability in international law, followed by its application to the World Bank and its Inspection Panel and a discussion of operational issues. It continues by suggesting criteria for evaluating IAMs and concludes with reflections on the benefits and limitations of an IAM. This chapter is dedicated to David Caron in recognition of his outstanding contributions to dispute settlement and to many other aspects of public international law. He was a splendid scholar and distinguished arbitrator.

## 2. The Framework of Accountability

The legitimacy of international law rests on adherence to the law. The framework of accountability provides the essential process for ensuring such adherence. There is a norm of mutual accountability that is deeply embedded in diverse cultures and religions.[4] The norm is reflected in the obligation to "do what is right". The norm underlies the emergence of a principle of accountability, which serves to enforce norms, laws, regulations, and other obligations.

---

[4] Edith Brown Weiss, "Establishing Norms in a Kaleidoscopic World" 396 *Recueil des cours*: Collected Courses of the Hague Academy of International Law (Brill/Nijhoff 2018); *Establishing Norms in a Kaleidoscopic World* (Brill/Nijhoff 2020).

**Table 12.2** New and Continuing MDB Cases in ADR and Compliance Review in 2019[a]

| MDB | ADR Cases | Compliance Cases | Compliance Sector |
|---|---|---|---|
| Inter-American Development Bank | New: 4 | New: 0 | |
| | Continuing: 5 | Continuing: 3 | Hydroelectricity (3) |
| Asian Infrastructure Investment Bank[b] | New: 0 | New: 0 | |
| | Continuing: 0 | Continuing: 0 | |
| Asian Development Bank | New: 12 | New: 2 | Road (2) |
| | Continuing: 0 | Continuing: 0 | |
| European Bank for Research and Development | New: 0 | New: 1 | Hydroelectricity<br>Oil |
| | Continuing: 4 | Continuing: 4 | Electricity grid<br>Gas<br>Hydropower |
| African Development Bank | New: 1 | New: 0 | |
| | Continuing: 5 | Continuing: 3 | Coal Plant<br>Agriculture<br>Road |
| World Bank Group CAO | New: 0 | New: 0 | |
| | Continuing: 20 | Continuing: 32 | Port infrastructure and services (3)<br>Manufacturing (6)<br>Coal infrastructure, coal power market (2)<br>Financial markets<br>Hydro infrastructure, market (7)<br>Oil, gas, mining, chemicals (5)<br>Agribusiness (3)<br>Petroleum and coal products<br>Education<br>Agribusiness market and tourism<br>Transmission line advisory services |
| World Bank Group Inspection Panel | New: N/A | New: 13 | Flood response and urban planning<br>Dry port<br>Dry reservoir (flood control dam) (9)<br>Road<br>Land tenure regularization |
| | Continuing: N/A | Continuing: 5 | Road<br>Dam (2)<br>Water treatment plant (2) |

[a] Table complied by the author, Edith Brown Weiss, using data from each multilateral development bank's accountability mechanism's website and annual report for 2019. ADR refers to alternative dispute resolution.

[b] The Asian Infrastructure Investment Bank's complaint-handling mechanism, the Project-affected People's Mechanism (PPM), was established in 2018; there are no reported cases yet. See "Policy on the Project-Affected People's Mechanism" (2018) AIIB <https://www.aiib.org/en/policies-strategies/operational-policies/policy-on-the-project-affected-mechanism.html>.

Table 12.3  Compliance cases for all MDBs in 2019 by subject[a]

| Subject | New | Continuing | Total |
|---|---|---|---|
| **Electric Power** | | | |
| *Hydroelectricity infrastructure & market* | 1 | 13 | 14 |
| *Electricity & transmission lines* | 0 | 2 | 2 |
| SUB-TOTAL | 1 | 15 | 16 |
| **Fossil Fuel Resources** | | | |
| *Oil, gas, mining, chemicals* | 0 | 7 | 7 |
| *Coal plant and coal power markets* | 0 | 4 | 4 |
| *Petroleum and coal products* | 0 | 1 | 1 |
| SUB-TOTAL | 0 | 12 | 12 |
| **Water and Water Resources** | | | |
| *Flood control dams, urban planning* | 10 | 0 | 10 |
| *Water treatment plant* | 0 | 2 | 2 |
| SUB-TOTAL | 10 | 2 | 12 |
| **Transport Infrastructure** | | | |
| *Ports* | 1 | 3 | 4 |
| *Roads* | 3 | 2 | 5 |
| SUB-TOTAL | 4 | 5 | 9 |
| **Agriculture, Agrobusiness** | | | |
| *Agriculture* | 0 | 1 | 1 |
| *Agribusiness* | 0 | 3 | 3 |
| *Agribusiness market & tourism* | 0 | 1 | 1 |
| SUB-TOTAL | 0 | 5 | 5 |
| **Other** | | | |
| *Manufacturing* | 0 | 6 | 6 |
| *Financial markets* | 0 | 1 | 1 |
| *Education* | 0 | 1 | 1 |
| *Land tenure* | 1 | 0 | 1 |
| SUB-TOTAL | 1 | 8 | 9 |
| GRAND TOTAL | 16 | 47 | 63 |

[a] Table complied by the author, Edith Brown Weiss, based on data from each multilateral development bank's accountability mechanism's website and annual report for 2019.

How is accountability defined? *Webster's English Dictionary* defines accountable as "being obliged to account for one's actions, i.e. to give satisfactory reasons".[5] Many legal and political science scholars use the term accountability to mean that there are actors who can hold other actors to certain legal rules or standards, to judge whether they have fulfilled their obligations, and to impose consequences, namely sanctions, if they

---

[5] *Merriam-Webster Online Dictionary*, <http://www.merriam-webster.com/dictionary/accountable>.

have not.[6] Accountability needs to be reconceived as mutual accountability and as a dynamic process, in which learning can take place in response to holding actors accountable. The focus on sanctions as the only consequence for non-fulfilment needs to give way to consideration of other possible consequences that take into account the reason why the actor did not meet the obligation, which is relevant to determining how the actor is to be held to account.

Accountability is generally viewed as a formal, non-dynamic event. For purposes of ensuring accountability for those who have failed to comply with criminal law, this may generally be the case. However, accountability in international law needs to be reconsidered as a dynamic process. Even in the context of international criminal law, accountability can involve a dynamic process.

## 2.1  Phases of Accountability

There are at least four phases in the process of dynamic accountability: identification of the party held to account and the party holding another to account, together with the obligations between them; the implementation of the obligation; the means for holding a party accountable and the range of consequences for failure to perform or for breaching an obligation; and the learning and feedback loops, if appropriate, for both the party held accountable and the party holding another to account. It is especially important to conceive of accountability as a dynamic process when holding MDBs accountable for their actions and when considering the role of accountability mechanisms at the MDBs.

## 2.2  First Phase: Setting the Stage

In economic analysis and in business relations, accountability is often described in terms of principal–agent theory.[7] In this framework, accountability starts with the principal's selection of the agent. If the agent has the intent and capacity to carry out the delegated programmes or to comply with the obligations, then the process of accountability can build upon a relationship of trust between the principal and agent. This has important implications for the measures needed to ensure accountability. For example, an obligation of transparency during implementation of the obligation can build upon or strengthen trust that the agent will carry out the programme and comply with obligations, while intrusive, detailed monitoring and auditing at every step could undermine the trust.[8]

---

[6] See eg R Grant and RO Keohane, "Accountability and Abuses of Power in World Politics" (2005) 99 American Political Science Review 29; J Goldsmith, *Power and Constraint: The Accountable Presidency After 9/11* (W.W. Norton 2012) 237 (accountability as focused on sanctions).

[7] For an extended discussion of principal-agent accountability, see S Gailmard, "Accountability and Principal-Agent Theory" in M Bovens and others (eds), *The Oxford Handbook of Public Accountability* (Oxford University Press 2014). Stewart has described the relationship as an account holder holding an accounter to account. Richard B Stewart, "Remedying Disregard in Global Regulatory Governance: Accountability, Participation, and Responsiveness" (2014) 108 American Journal of International Law 245.

[8] Jane A Mansbridge, "A Contingency Theory of Accountability" in Bovens and others (eds) (n 10) 59.

In a framework of mutual accountability, the agent is not only responsible for carrying out the delegated programme but the principal is accountable to the agent for "doing the right thing", which means being honest about the intent of the assignment and acting with integrity toward the agent. In cases in which a party is responsible for complying with a law or regulations, mutual accountability could arguably reach back to those who promulgated the law or regulation.

## 2.3  Second Phase: Implementing the Obligation

There are several important elements of the process of accountability in implementing an obligation or carrying out a programme. The literature and experience indicate that two elements are essential: transparency in the process of accountability and the existence of a way to hold a party accountable and to seek redress. Other elements may include participation in the decision for which a party is to be held accountable, or the techniques of monitoring, auditing, and evaluation.

## 2.4  Third Phase: Holding to Account

The third phase of dynamic accountability refers to the process by which the party who does not meet the obligation is held to account and the consequences for breach of the obligation or failure to perform. As mentioned, the focus in the literature on accountability is on punitive measures. However, research into compliance with international agreements indicates that the two most importance factors affecting a state's compliance with international agreements are a state's intent and its capacity to comply.[9] These may vary over time and affect the measures that need to be taken to ensure compliance. This argues for broadening the range of consequences available to hold a party to account. They include measures based on sunshine or transparency so that others are aware of what has happened; incentives such as capacity building or financial or technical resources to ensure that the party can fulfil the obligation; and penalties and sanctions to punish the party and to deter such behaviour in the future. [10]

## 2.5  Fourth Phase: Learning through Accountability

Both the party held to account and the party holding another to account can learn from the process of accountability. This can happen either during the ongoing process for ensuring accountability, or at the end of the process when a party has failed

---

[9] Edith Brown Weiss and Harold K Jacobson, *Engaging Countries: Strengthening Compliance with International Environmental Accords* (MIT Press 1998) 535–42.

[10] ibid at 542–52. The possibility of sanctions can serve as an important backdrop to motivate compliance.

to perform or to comply with obligations or even when compliance occurs. Learning can take place through a feedback mechanism. Both the party held to account and the party holding an agent to account can learn. Learning can lead to changes in the way the existing obligations are implemented or even in how the obligations are defined. Accountability can lead to rethinking what needs to be done to accomplish defined goals or foster certain values, a process which is known as transformative learning. This may lead to developing different obligations or actions from the present ones.[11] The element of learning gives dynamism to accountability and gives the accountability process additional value.

## 3.  Accountability at the World Bank

I focus on accountability at the World Bank Group because it is the largest and oldest of the MDBs and the pioneer in IAMs. The World Bank Group provides billions of dollars of assistance to developing and emerging market economies every year.[12] Its commitments in 2019 totalled more than $62 billion, with World Bank loan commitments reaching more than $23 billion, and the International Development Association (IDA) credits and grants totalling close to $22 billion. Before analysing the role of the World Bank's accountability mechanism—the Inspection Panel—in resolving disputes, it is useful to understand how the World Bank operates. Some of the loans are investment project financing for specific purposes, such as infrastructure or forest reform. Some are classified as development policy financing. These provide general budgetary support for broad changes in economic policy and include several lending instruments, including grants. This distinction is relevant to later consideration of the forest reform project and the policy loan in Democratic Republic of Congo (DRC).

In response to public concern in the 1980s and early 1990s about negative impacts of projects and policy reforms, the World Bank adopted "safeguard policies" to address social and environmental impacts of Bank-financed projects and programmes. These safeguard policies covered environmental assessment, natural habitats, forests, pesticides, Indigenous peoples, cultural resources, involuntary resettlement, and safety of dams. They were the subject of Requests to the Inspection Panel in the case studies in this chapter. In 2016, the Board of Executive Directors approved a new Environmental and Social Framework, which applies to all subsequent investment project financing

---

[11] Different types of learning can take place through feedback mechanisms. Single-loop learning is learning how to do the job better as it stands, and double-loop learning improves the underlying values of the job. See K Yang, "Emergent Accountability and Structuration Theory: Implications" in Alnoor Ebrahim and Edward Weisband (eds), *Global Accountabilities: Participation, Pluralism, and Public Ethics* (Cambridge University Press 2007) 278.

[12] The International Bank for Reconstruction and Development (World Bank) was established in 1946 as one of the Bretton Woods Institution. Its primary mission was the reconstruction of countries destroyed or heavily damaged after the Second World War. For historical coverage, see Edward S Mason and Robert E Asher, *The World Bank Since Bretton Woods* (The Brookings Institution 1973); Devesh Kapur and others, *The World Bank: Its First Half Century* (The Brookings Institution 1997).

and focuses on building the capacity of borrowing countries to meet their own safe-guard standards.[13] The Inspection Panel retained its role, as noted later in this chapter.

To understand how a principle of accountability operates in practice at the World Bank, it is important to understand the project cycle. The origin, design, approval, and implementation of Bank-financed projects follows a standard pattern, which is known as the project cycle.[14] Many projects are infrastructure projects, such as construction of dams, roads, and pipelines, which often involve resettlement of people, and raise issues of possible harm to locally affected communities or of failure to provide the project benefits to locally affected people, such as electricity, water, or sewerage access.

In the first phase of accountability for a project—setting the stage—the country borrowing the money identifies the project it wishes the World Bank to finance and is responsible for designing and developing it. In practice, staff at the World Bank generally participate in conceiving and designing the project in a professional collaboration with the country. Once the broad outlines of a project are defined, consultants selected by the borrowing country with the approval of the Bank prepare the project. The operational staff members of the Bank oversee the preparation of the project. Since part of the financing comes from the World Bank, the project is subject to World Bank policies and procedures. Management prepares an appraisal report on the proposed project, called the Project Appraisal Document (PAD), which is sent to the World Bank Board of Executive Directors, who represent member governments, to approve.

Accountability extends to all aspects of the design, development, and appraisal of the project. The Inspection Panel, the independent forum for accountability, has jurisdiction to hear complaints regarding compliance with World Bank policies and procedures in the design, development, appraisal, and implementation of the project.[15]

The second phase of accountability arises after the Board of Executive Directors has approved the project. Management and staff then "supervise" project implementation (though this role has decreased) and file a Project Implementation Report when the project is completed and the loan fully disbursed. It is in this phase that many of the complaints arise about Bank compliance with its policies and procedures. If people are harmed, such as from environmental or health effects from pipeline construction or from resettlement, or were overlooked in the design as a group affected by the project, they can bring a Request for Inspection to the Inspection Panel.

The third phase of accountability arises when the Bank is held to account for following or not following its policies and procedures. The Inspection Panel serves as the

[13] <https://www.worldbank.org/en/projects-operations/environmental-and-social-framework>. The framework was launched in 2018.

[14] Warren C Baum, *The Project Cycle* (IBRD 1982), for authoritative description and analysis. The publication refers to the appraisal report, which is now called the Project Appraisal Document (PAD). Programme financing involves similar phases.

[15] About fifteen years ago, the Bank initiated the country systems strategy, which relies on a country's laws and their equivalence to World Bank policies and procedures. The role of the Inspection Panel remained the same for loans under this strategy. "[T]he Inspection Panel could, with regard to the issues raised, examine management's assessment of the equivalence of the relevant Bank policies and procedures with the country system (and any additional measures agreed upon to achieve equivalence) in materially achieving the objectives of Bank policies and procedures ...." Joint Statement on the Use of Country Systems, Edith Brown Weiss, Chairperson, Inspection Panel and Roberto Danino, General Counsel, IBRD, 2005. <https://www.inspectionpanel.org>.

forum to which those affected by the project can complain. This role is considered in detail later in the chapter. The fourth phase of accountability, learning, happens after the Inspection Panel has issued its report and the findings are translated back into the operations of the Bank. The Panel's series of Emerging Lessons reports contains insights from its findings and reports.

While the focus in this chapter is on accountability through giving a voice to affected people, it is essential to note that the World Bank is accountable foremost to its member governments, which include both donor and recipient countries. Member governments are responsible for adopting the policies and procedures that management and staff are to follow. While in practice management proposes policies and procedures, the Board of Executive Directors must approve them. Governments hold management accountable for ensuring that the projects and programmes actually result in reducing poverty and fostering sustainable growth, within acceptable costs. There is an element of mutual accountability here, in the sense that if governments pressure Bank management and staff to disburse funds as rapidly as possible without regard to quality of preparation or implementation or if they do not provide necessary funding, it is more difficult to hold them accountable for the results.

The World Bank is additionally accountable to the communities and people affected by the World Bank-financed project. These are people who are supposed to benefit from the project or at least not be harmed by it. While the Agreement establishing the World Bank does not explicitly provide for accountability to the people affected by the project, such accountability arises indirectly from a concept of third party accountability. The borrowing government is directly responsible and accountable for the use of the project or programme funds and resources. The World Bank, is however, responsible for ensuring that the policies and procedures adopted by the Board of Executive Directors are followed and that the projects and programmes are carried out as provided in the contractual documents between the World Bank and the borrowing government.

## 4. Inspection Panel of the World Bank

The World Bank Inspection Panel operates as an accountability mechanism. The Panel provides accountability between management and staff, on the one hand, and people affected by the Bank-financed projects or programmes on the other. It holds management and staff accountable for complying with the Bank's policies and procedures. In doing so, it serves as an important forum for resolving disputes between people affected by World Bank operations and the World Bank. The Inspection Panel reflects a basic principle of mutual accountability in the sense that while Bank management and staff are being held to account for complying with Bank policies and procedures, people lodging complaints are accountable for not using the process to pursue political agendas, potentially at the expense of the welfare of locally affected people.

The World Bank Board of Executive Directors created the Inspection Panel in 1993 in response to strong concerns about the Bank's projects and about management and staff compliance with its own policies and procedures.[16] During the late 1980s and early 1990s, the Bank was sharply criticized for some of its projects, especially for its Sardar Sarovar Dam and projects on the Narmada River in India, which involved resettling 120,000 people. In response, then-President Lewis Preston asked Brad Morse, former administrator of the United Nations Development Programme, and Thomas Berger, former Justice of the British Columbia Supreme Court in Canada, to head a commission to review projects financed by the Bank in this area. The Commission's report indicated serious failures by the Bank to comply with its own policies and procedures and documented dire social and environmental consequences associated with Bank projects. [17] At the same time, the Bank established an internal task force to review its projects, which then-Vice President of the World Bank Wapenhans led. The resulting report criticized the Bank's "approval culture" in which staff were incentivized to seek Board of Executive Directors approval for as many projects as possible, without sufficient attention to social and environmental effects and project implementation.[18]

As a result of these reports, the Board of Executive Directors established the Inspection Panel, an independent body separate from management and staff, with the responsibility to hear complaints from affected people who were being harmed or could be harmed by World Bank-financed projects or programmes.[19] In effect, this made the World Bank accountable to the people it was trying to assist, in addition to its existing accountabilities. It gave for the first time a voice to affected people. In 2020 the World Bank Board of Executive Directors adopted an Accountability Mechanism, which incorporates the Inspection Panel.

The Inspection Panel is not a formal judicial body, though its procedures partially resemble those of such a body. The Panel receives a complaint (called a "Request for Inspection") from two or more people affected by a Bank-financed project or programme, which alleges harm. In practice, the complaint usually represents many, sometimes hundreds of people. The Panel determines according to specified criteria whether to register the complaint,[20] which is public, and management has twenty-one business

---

[16] For background on the Inspection Panel, see eg Daniel D Bradlow, "International Organizations and Private Complainants: The Case of the World Bank Inspection Panel" (1994) 34 Virginia Journal of International Law 553.

[17] Morse Commission, Sardar Sarovar: The Report of the Independent Review (1992).

[18] World Bank, Effective Implementation: Key to Development Impact. Report of the Portfolio Management Task Force (1992).

[19] International Bank for Reconstruction and Development, Resolution No IBRD 93-10 and International Development Association, Resolution No IDA 93-6, 22 September 1993. <https://www.inspectionpanel.org>. For early consideration of issues relevant to the Panel, see eg Dana Clark, Jonathan Fox, and Kay Treakle (eds), *Demanding Accountability: Civil-Society Claims and the World Bank Inspection Panel* (2003); David Hunter, "Using the World Bank Inspection Panel to Defend the Interests of Projected-Affected People" (2003) 4 Chinese Journal of International Law 201.

[20] Until recently the Panel was required to "promptly register the Request" if it appeared to contain "sufficient required information" unless "the matter is without doubt manifestly outside the Panel's mandate". "Operating Procedures", adopted by the Panel, August 1994. As of 2014, the Panel Operating Procedures added an additional step before registration. Within fifteen business days of receiving a Request, the Panel determines whether it is admissible and then registers an admissible Request. In practice this has meant that some Requests that would have been promptly registered have not been, because of judgments about the required information, such the link between a Bank violation and the alleged harm. The additional step has been controversial with affected people and with civil society. The Resolution establishing the Inspection Panel excludes decisions relating to procurement from the Panel's mandate.

days to respond. The Panel then has twenty-one business days to decide whether to rec-ommend an investigation, which is subject to Board approval on a non-objection basis.

The investigation is an intensive fact-finding exercise, in which the Panel reviews relevant documents, interviews management and staff, and visits the country to meet with those making the request and other affected people, views relevant sites, inter-views public officials at all levels, meets with civil society, and speaks with the private sector, if relevant. The objective is to determine whether the Bank has complied with its policies and procedures. The report is factually based and does not include recom-mendations. It may, however, include significant observations about important issues and references to best practices for specific problems.

Management must respond to the Panel's investigation report with an Action Plan laying out how it intends to fix problems of non-compliance that have been un-covered. The Board of Executive Directors then considers both the Panel's report and management's response and takes a decision. In my tenure on the Panel, the Board al-ways approved the Panel's report, sometimes requested more action by management to address the problems uncovered, and in several important instances, asked the Panel to continue its fact-finding about management's implementation of its plan responding to the Panel's findings. All the documents are public and available on the Panel's website, and generally through links on the Bank's website.[21]

On 8 September 2020, the Board of Executive Directors adopted a structural change to the Inspection Panel. It approved a new overarching World Bank Accountability Mechanism to house both the Inspection Panel and a new Dispute Resolution Service as an option available to the parties once the Board of Executive Directors approves a Panel recommendation for a Panel investigation. Under this option, the parties can use mediation and other alternative dispute resolution means to address issues approved for Panel investigation; the process is time limited. The Inspection Panel is to retain its independence in the World Bank Accountability Mechanism.[22]

At the same time, the Board approved an updated Resolution for the Inspection Panel, which consolidated the original Resolution and subsequent Clarifications and included some significant changes aimed at enhancing the Panel. [23] These include extending the time limit for bringing complaints to the Panel beyond when 95 per cent of the funds are disbursed, authorizing the Panel to verify implementation of management's action plan responding to Panel findings, giving those who made the complaint access to the Panel's report before the Board of Executive Directors considers it, and formally af-firming the Panel's role in providing lessons learned from its cases.

---

[21] For an authoritative book on the Inspection Panel and the Resolution establishing it, see Ibrahim FI Shihata, *The World Bank Inspection Panel: In Practice* (2nd edn, Oxford University Press 2000).

[22] International Bank for Reconstruction and Development, Resolution No IBRD2020-0005 and International Development Association, Resolution No IDA 2020-0004, 8 September 2020, <https://inspectionpanel.org/files/documents/AccountabilityMechanismResolutoin.pdf>. The Accountability Mechanism should be fully oper-ational by 2022.

[23] International Bank for Reconstruction and Development Resolution No IBRD 2020-0004, and International Development Association Resolution No IDA 2020-0003, 8 September 2020, <https://inspectionpanel.org/files/documents/AccountabilityMechanismResolution.pdf>.

## 5. Inspection Panel Investigations

Three diverse Inspection Panel investigations illuminate the Panel's work: forest reform in DRC;[24] resettlement of people caused by road expansion in Mumbai, India;[25] and design and operation of the Yacyretá hydroelectric dam on the Paraná River between Argentina and Paraguay.[26] A brief summary of each investigation follows. The Panel's work deals with many different issues and is of necessity mired in detail.[27]

### 5.1  Yacyretá Dam

The Yacyretá Dam on the Paraná River between Argentina and Paraguay consists of two 40-metres high, 5 kilometre-long concrete dams and 65 kilometres of embankment dam. In 1973, Argentina and Paraguay concluded a treaty, which set forth the terms of the joint undertaking and created a semi-autonomous binational entity, the Entidad Binacional Yacyretá, to implement the project.[28] The World Bank entered into its first loan agreement for the Project in 1971 and funded a second Project in 1992. Dam construction began in 1983; in 2002, the dam was not yet operating at its full targeted level.

In 2002, a Paraguayan non-governmental organization (NGO), FEDAYIM, submitted a request to the Inspection Panel on behalf of more than 4,000 families in Encarnación and nearby barrios contending that their lives and their environment were being seriously harmed by the design and implementation of the Yacyretá Dam. The complaints were numerous: that the power plant's reservoir level had severe environmental impacts, including constant flooding of urban creeks, a higher water table, and spread of disease; that the proposed wastewater treatment plant would further pollute the environment; that the resettlement and compensation programmes had left hundreds of affected families and businesses with no or inadequate compensation, poor resettlement housing and facilities, and prolonged economic hardship; and that employees of brick and ceramic factories had not been compensated for their loss of income. There were many other related issues.

Four World Bank policies and procedures were relevant: Environmental Assessment, Involuntary Resettlement, Project Supervision, and Monitoring and Evaluation. The

---

[24] World Bank Inspection Panel, Investigation Report: Democratic Republic of Congo: Transitional Support for Economic Recovery Credit (TSERO) and Emergency Economic and Social Reunification Support Project (EESRSP), Report No 40746-ZR (31 Aug. 2007), <https://www.inspectionpanel.org>.

[25] World Bank Inspection Panel, Investigation Report for India: Mumbai Urban Transport Project, Report No 34725 (21 December 2005), <https://www.inspectionpanel.org>.

[26] World Bank Inspection Panel, Investigation Report for Paraguay—Reform Project for the Water and Telecommunications Sector (Loan No 3842-PA), Argentina—SEGBA V Power Distribution Project (Loan 2854-AR), Report No 27995 (24 February 2004), https://www.inspectionpanel.org.

[27] For a review of the Panel's work, see World Bank Inspection Panel, The Inspection Panel: Accountability at the World Bank at 25 Years (2018), <https:www.inspectionpanel.org>.

[28] Argentina and Paraguay, Treaty of Yacyretá (1973), 1380 UNTS 79.

Board of Executive Directors authorized an investigation by the Inspection Panel.[29] For the investigation the Panel hired expert consultants in hydrology, environmental issues, and anthropology, and conducted field trips to the area.

The Panel found that management had followed many aspects of its environmental policies and procedures, but the project did not comply with many requirements related to resettlement and compensation. These included erroneous omission of a significant number of people affected by the project from the census, inadequate grievance procedures, exclusion in practice of compensation for informal workers of the brick and roof-tile industries, and issues related to the resettlement plan, including consideration of alternative sites. One important finding was that the reservoir was frequently operated under conditions that produced a water level in excess of the stated level of 76 masl (metres above sea level) at Encarnación, Paraguay, which was not consistent with the loan agreement and the Third Owners Agreement, as amended. Since the division of moneys between the two countries was based on operating levels, this meant that Paraguay was entitled to additional funds from the higher level of operation of the reservoir. However, the reservoir was not the cause of urban creek flooding, one of the issues raised in the Request.

The Board of Executive Directors approved Management's Action Plan prepared in response to the Panel's findings. It approved additional measures related to the over 2,000 families already relocated and the 6,000 families waiting to be relocated, steps to remedy grievance procedures, and actions related to the operational level of the reservoir. The Board also asked management to report back in three months and the Panel to review management's progress report for the Board. Since the Inter-American Development Bank (IDB) was also funding the project, the Board asked management to collaborate with the IDB on issues identified in the Inspection Panel Report. The Panel returned to Paraguay to meet with those making the Request, discuss the Panel's investigation report with them, and respond to questions and concerns. This was an important step, because it respected their right to be informed about the Panel's findings, and enabled them to discuss with the Panel's Brazilian hydrological expert a problem not attributable to the Bank's failure to comply with policies and procedures.

## 5.2  Resettlement and Mumbai Urban Transport Project

The second example of a Panel investigation is the Mumbai Urban Transport Project (MUTP), which was a large-scale Bank-financed project to expand and improve the rail and road infrastructure in Mumbai, India. It involved the resettlement of an estimated 120,000 people. Four different groups of Requesters, totalling more than a thousand people and including shopkeepers along the roads as well as residents in nearby

---

[29] World Bank Inspection Panel, Investigation Report for Paraguay—Reform Project for the Water and Telecommunications Sector (Loan No 3842-PA), Argentina—SEGBA V Power Distribution Project (Loan No 2854-AR), Report No 27995 (24 February 2004), <https://www.inspectionpanel.org>.

neighbourhoods, brought a number of claims: that for the shopkeepers along the roads the entitlement to 225 square feet in the resettlement areas, regardless of the size of the present structure and nature of the business, made it impossible to continue with their businesses; that the baseline surveys of affected people, access to information, and consultations were inadequate; that the location and conditions at the resettlement sites were unsuitable; and that the project failed to consider income restoration—among other concerns. After the Board of Executive Directors approved an investigation, the Panel followed its customary investigation procedures, which included field visits and hiring a local expert from the University of Mumbai.

In the investigation, the Panel found that the Bank had not complied with its policies and procedures in important respects, particularly with policies on Involuntary Resettlement and certain aspects of Environmental Compliance. [30] When the Bank initially developed the project for resettlement of people as a separate project, it had considered the needs of the shopkeepers displaced by road expansion, as required by Bank policy. However, when the freestanding resettlement project was merged into the road and rail infrastructure project for appraisal and presentation to the Board, the project document that went to the Board overlooked the needs of shopkeepers. The number of people subject to resettlement was given as 80,000 in the appraisal document. No risk assessment was conducted, contrary to Bank policy. The Board approved the project in 2002. By the beginning of 2004, the number of people needing resettlement had risen to 120,000, with 3,000 affected shopkeepers.

In response to the Panel's findings regarding resettlement of displaced people and the relocation of shopkeepers, management proposed an Action Plan to bring the Project into compliance, which included expanded options to the shopkeepers for resettlement sites, improvement in social and environmental services at resettlement sites, such as sanitation and water supply, improved grievance redress measures, and improved databases on affected people. Notably, the Board of Executive Directors in response to the Panel's findings suspended disbursement on the road and resettlement components of the Project, some $US80 million, a drastic step. It lifted the suspension about three months later, after concluding that the state of Maharashtra had by then substantially met the required conditions. The Board again asked the Panel to report back on management's implementation of its Action Plan.

As a result of the Panel investigation, the shopkeepers got more options so that a 2,000 square foot business, such as for textile dyeing or lumber, on a busy commercial road did not have to squeeze into 225 square feet on a road in a resettlement housing development. The water and sewerage pipes at the targeted resettlement site did get connected and became operational, though they continued to have problems. The grievance procedure was made more independent of the implementing agency.

---

[30] World Bank Inspection Panel, Investigation Report for India: Mumbai Urban Transport Project, Report No 34725 (21 December 2005), <https://www.inspectionpanel.org>.

## 5.3  Forest Reform in Democratic Republic of Congo

DRC has great natural resource wealth but is one of the world's lowest-income countries. Forests cover about 60 per cent of the country and are the home and source of livelihood and cultural identity for many people. The World Bank was responsible for two Bank-financed operations involving DRC's forests and forest concessions. One was a project loan and the other a development policy loan in the form of a single tranche disbursement of money in support of a medium-term policy framework.[31] The Bank policies and procedures for a development policy loan are much less extensive than for a project loan.

The Inspection Panel received a Request from a network of Pygmies (forest people) representing local communities in six provinces across DRC. The Pygmies claimed that they had been harmed or would be harmed by the implementation of a new commercial forest concession system that would review existing logging concessions and convert those validated as legal into twenty-five-year titles to engage in industrial logging. The Pygmies had consistently been at the bottom of the social ladder, facing economic, social, and political discrimination.

DRC is about the size of western Europe and contains about 134 million hectares of forest. The forests have world-class biodiversity value and are home to many endangered species of fauna. Many of the leases under review in DRC were acquired during a moratorium on logging, or had been issued as "swaps" for forested areas that had already been logged or cleared, thus essentially providing new leases to log during the moratorium. The Board of Executive Directors approved a Panel investigation. The investigation included field visits with affected people and communities in eastern and western DRC, national government officials in Kinshasa and regional ones in eastern DRC, timber company officials, and NGOs.

The Panel's Investigation Report[32] found that the Bank erred in finding that there were no Indigenous peoples in the forests, which would have meant that management did not need to prepare an Indigenous people's plan to consider their needs and interests. To the contrary, the Panel's expert estimated that there were between 250,000 and 600,000 Pygmies in DRC, including in forested areas covered by the project and by the development policy loan.[33] Management's response to the Panel's investigation revealed the presence of Pygmies across DRC forests.

The Panel also found that management was not in compliance with its policies and procedures in determining that there were no significant environmental or social

---

[31] Transitional Support for Economic Recovery Credit (TSERO) (IDA Grant No H1920-DRC) and Emergency Economic and Social Reunification Support Project (EESRSP) (IDA Credit No 3824-DRC and Grant No H064 DRC).

[32] World Bank Inspection Panel, Investigation Report: Democratic Republic of Congo: Transitional Support for Economic Recovery Credit (TSERO) and Emergency Economic and Social Reunification Support Project (EESRSP), Report No 40746-ZR (31 August 2007), https://www.inspectionpanel.org

[33] ibid xvi, 32.

effects of the forest component in development policy lending and hence no need for an environmental assessment. It further found that there was a lack of meaningful participation by Pygmy peoples and local communities in the concession reform process and in pilot zoning. Most importantly, the Panel noted that when the Bank initially became engaged in DRC and decided to support work in the forest sector, it provided estimates of export revenue from logging concessions that turned out to be much too high. This encouraged a focus on reform of the existing concessions at the expense of pursuing sustainable use of forests and exploring the potential for community forests and conservation. For the most part, foreign companies or local companies controlled by foreigners benefited from this focus. Those whose concessions were to be confirmed in the review process would benefit from new twenty-five-year leases.

After the Panel's report and Management's Response and Action Plan, Pygmy people were for the first time given representation on the national commission reviewing the concessions (though under conditions that made it hard for them to participate effectively); logging concessions that were confirmed were legally obligated to enter into social responsibility contracts with local communities; the Bank developed a "DRC Strategic Framework for the Preparation of a Pygmy Development Plan"; DRC Indigenous peoples communities and local communities received some grant financing for forest management and conservation projects; efforts were made to strengthen monitoring of the forests; and Pygmy representatives were included in an important international conference on forests in Brussels. Pygmies who brought the initial complaint to the Inspection Panel have written a book indicating that the Panel's Investigation Report was very helpful to their peoples and to forest management in DRC.[34]

Management's Action Plan contained further follow-up measures in DRC and the Africa region.[35] The Bank reportedly modified its consideration of whether there were Indigenous people in the Africa region who would be affected by Bank-financed projects and programmes and strengthened efforts to address Indigenous peoples' issues in the Congo Basin. In the forest sector, management committed to ensuring that forest governance, participatory zoning, customary rights, critical natural habitats, law enforcement, and independent monitoring, which had been neglected in the DRC project, were featured in future forest-related operations.

## 6. Fact-finding Bodies to Resolve Disputes

The Inspection Panel operates as a fact-finding body, with detailed investigations. Fact-finding to address disputes has a long history in public international law.

---

[34] Willi Loyombo and Adrien Sinafasi, *Les peoples autochtones de la RDC: Histoire d'un partenariat—The Indigenous Peoples of the DRC: Story of a Partnership* (2017), <https://www.inspectionpanel.org>.

[35] World Bank, Third Progress Report on the Implementation of the Management Action Plan in Response to the Inspection Panel Investigation Report (Report No 40746-ZR) on the Democratic Republic of Congo Transitional Support for Economic Recovery Grant (TSERO) (IDA Grant No H1920-DRC) and Emergency Economic and Social Reunification Support Project (EESRSP) (IDA Credit No 3824-DRC and Grant No H064 DRC, 14 May 2012), <https://www.inpspectionpanel.org>.

Commissions of inquiry, which focused on investigations and fact-finding, date to the Hague Conventions of 1899 and 1907.[36] The commissions investigated wartime incidents between belligerent or neutral States. The 1909 Boundary Waters Agreement between Canada and the United States provided a Reference procedure by which the International Joint Commission could impartially investigate facts, issue a report, and, on the basis of its findings, offer recommendations to the two governments.[37]

After 1919, a number of treaties established permanent commissions of investigation and conciliation. These commissions could impartially investigate and establish facts as the basis for resolving controversies. In the last sixty years, commissions of inquiry have again emerged as important vehicles for fact-finding and for resolving disputes. For example, the 1977 Convention for the Prohibition of Military or Any Other Hostile Use of Environmental Modification Techniques provides for a Consultative Committee of Experts, which would operate as a commission of inquiry.[38] More recently, the 1993 North American Convention on Environmental Cooperation provided for fact-finding by the Secretariat on complaints by a person or NGO, interpreted to include a corporate entity, that one of the three countries was not enforcing its environmental law.[39] The Secretariat issued more than sixty fact-finding reports addressing such complaints, as a vehicle for resolving disputes.[40]

The United Nations has set up thirty commissions of inquiry to investigate an array of difficult issues. These include, for example, the United Nations Security Council authorized Commissions of Inquiry for Darfur (2004)[41] and the Central African Republic (2013).[42] The UN Human Rights Council has established many Commissions of Inquiry to investigate alleged human rights abuses, more recently for Burundi (2016),[43] the 2018 "protests in the occupied Palestinian Territory",[44] and the United States (June 2020).[45] While the Commissions have engaged in fact-finding, they have also been criticized as lacking standard procedures, guidelines, and best practices, as lacking visits to the territory at issue, and as taking on a political role.[46]

---

[36] Convention for the Pacific Settlement of International Disputes (signed 29 July 1899, entered into force 4 September 1900) arts 9–29; Convention for the Pacific Settlement of International Disputes (signed 18 October 1907, entered into force 26 January 1910) arts 9–36.

[37] Treaty between the United States and Great Britain relating to boundary waters and questions arising between the United States and Canada (signed 11 January 1909, entered into force 5 May 1910) art IX. The International Joint Commission has received 58 references since 1912. See International Joint Commission Dockets—Applications & References <https://ijc.org/en/library/dockets?title=&combine=Reference&field_date_value%5Bdate%5D=2020-12-04&field_region_target_id=All>.

[38] Convention on the Prohibition of Military or Any Other Hostile Use of Environmental Modification Technique (signed 10 December 1976, entered into force 5 October 1978) srt V.

[39] North American Convention on Environmental Cooperation (signed 14 September 1993, entered into force 1 January 1994) srts 14, 15.

[40] Commission for Environmental Cooperation Registry of Submissions <http://www.cec.org/submissions-on-enforcement/registry-of-submissions/page/9/>; Commission for Environmental Cooperation SEM Compliance Tracker <http://www.cec.org/submissions-on-enforcement/sem-compliance-tracker/>.

[41] United Nations Security Council Resolution 1564 of 18 September 2004, UN Doc. S/RES/1564.

[42] United Nations Security Council Resolution 2127 of 5 December 2013, UN Doc S/RES/2127.

[43] Human Rights Council Resolution 33/24 of 30 September 2016, UN Doc A/HRC/RES/33/24.

[44] Human Rights Council Resolution S-28/1 of 18 May 2018, UN Doc A/HRC/RES/S-28/1.

[45] Human Rights Council Resolution 43/1 of 19 June 2020, UN Doc A/HRC/RES/43/1.

[46] For analysis, see eg M Cherif Bassiouni, "Appraising UN Justice-Related Fact-Finding Missions" (2001) 5 Washington University Journal of Law & Policy 35; Philip Alston, "Introduction: Commissions of Inquiry as

## 7. The Inspection Panel as a Fact-Finding Body: Practicalities

The Inspection Panel's fact-finding process for an investigation differs sharply from the adversarial common law judicial process, where judges rely upon the information and documents that have been submitted to them as a basis for determining facts and reaching a decision. In fact-finding by an IAM, it is essential to collect information from all relevant participants and stakeholders and to find and review all relevant documents. The process is reminiscent of peeling one or more onions. The details are key. Accountability mechanisms need to establish and follow procedures for fact-finding to ensure that the process is thorough, impartial, objective, and respectful of those who are subject to the process. The issues cannot be prejudged. In the case of the Inspection Panel, it is important to talk with Bank management and staff at all levels. Often the Panel found significant non-compliance with certain policies and procedures and compliance with others within the same project or programme. In my experience, individual staff members were sometimes unhappy with having had to short-circuit certain policies and procedures and were not unhappy to see the Panel investigate and find a failure to comply with required measures.

In some cases, the affected people lodging the complaints requested confidentiality (anonymity) because of the fear of retaliation. The Inspection Panel guaranteed confidentiality in such cases and did not include their names on the registry of Requests for Inspection or in material that was shared with management or the Board of Executive Directors. Since the Panel always had to verify validity of the Requesters' signatures, the Panel had to be very careful to meet the Requesters in a setting in which anonymity would be protected. An NGO might serve as a Requester to protect against identification and retaliation.

Even if those making the request do not ask for confidentiality, retaliation can be a constant threat. The threat of retaliation might come from national or local officials, from private company officials, or from other groups. The Inspection Panel has always had a firm policy against retaliation, which in practice meant conveying this policy to relevant officials and groups wherever the threat arose or could arise. In March 2016, the Inspection Panel adopted Guidelines to Reduce Retaliation Risks and Respond to Retaliation during the Panel Process, which call for assessment of the risk of retaliation for each request, detailed measures to deal with risks, and actions to be taken if retaliation exists.[47]

Human Rights Fact-Finding Tools" (2011) 105 Proceedings Annual Meeting American Society International Law 81; Micaela Frulli, "Fact-Finding or Paving the Road to Criminal Justice: Some Reflections on United Nations Commissions of Inquiry" (2012) 10 Journal of International Criminal Justice 1123; Philip Alston and Sarah Knuckey (eds), *The Transformation of Human Rights Fact-Finding* (Oxford University Press 2015); Ted Piccone, *U.N. Human Rights Commissions of Inquiry and the Quest for Accountability* (Brookings Institution 2017); Christian Henderson (ed), *Commissions of Inquiry: Problems and Prospects* (Hart Publishing 2017).

[47] Text of Guidelines available at <https://www.inspectionpanel.org>.

Field visits are essential to a Panel investigation. They involve meeting with the array of relevant stakeholders: affected people who brought the Request, government officials, local leaders and communities, civil society, NGOs, and frequently the private sector. Field visits reveal what is really happening on the ground, which may differ from what written documents state, what Bank officials say, or what those in charge of implementing the project or the programme on the ground state in briefings or visits. For example, in the Yacyretá investigation regarding the resettlement of thousands of people caused by the construction of the dam, we were informed by local officials and project staff that the resettlement units were in excellent condition and the roads in good condition. When we visited through the entrance to the resettlement site, this appeared to be the case. But when local people making the complaint to the Panel took us to the back of the resettlement site, the houses provided to the people being resettled already showed cracks, the streets were not adequately paved, and sewage water was seeping down the hill to settlements below. In Mumbai, connections to water and the septic system had not been completed, information centres were not easily accessible or informative, and potential options for lower middle-income shopkeepers had not been considered. In DRC, we were informed that there was a moratorium on commercial logging, only to uncover in visits in the east and west that commercial logging had continued. In Cambodia, we were told confidently by the international body monitoring a forest concession project that no illegal logging was occurring, despite the lack of aerial or satellite coverage of part of the sites, only to encounter an illegal logging truck up-country loaded with large logs.[48]

When we engaged in fact-finding in the field, consultations with NGOs were useful. These sources can provide critical contextual background and can identify important sources of factual information. Interviews with the private sector on the ground may be essential. All relevant participants need to be heard, and the facts ascertained as objectively as possible.

The local people who have lodged the complaint are both essential sources of information and protectors of those who are conducting the investigation because they know the local dangers and ways to avoid them. Since many local people do not speak one of the major languages, interpreters are often needed. The challenge is to locate reliable expert interpreters. The Panel hired its own interpreters to try to ensure accurate interpretations and avoid perceptions of bias that would flow from using Bank or official government interpreters. In Mumbai, an expert from the University of Mumbai accompanied us on site visits and served as an effective translator.

Listening to local people in the field can also be a challenge. Local people must feel comfortable in sharing their concerns and providing information. A meeting with a large group may be dominated by a local leader, who may harbour his/her own political agenda, which may influence the course of the meeting. Smaller groups are generally

---

[48] World Bank Inspection Panel, Investigation Report for Cambodia: Forest Concession Management and Control Pilot Project, Report No 3556 (30 March 2006), <https://www.inspectionpanel.org>.

more productive. People need to trust that their remarks will be secure. The accuracy of the information needs to be verified.

Numerous other issues arise in connection with the fact-finding process in accountability mechanisms. One of these is whether the fact-finding report could contain recommendations. This varies among fact-finding bodies in other contexts. The Reference procedure for the US-Canada Joint Commission allows recommendations. The North American Commission for Environmental Cooperation (NACEC) dtd not permit its fact-finding reports to contain recommendations. The instrument establishing the Inspection Panel limits its role to fact-finding and does not permit recommendations. While civil society has criticized this feature, one can argue that a factual report to which management must respond by indicating how it will fix any instances of failure to comply is far more powerful than a report that includes recommendations, which can be dismissed as not reflecting deep experience with the practical problems on the ground. In practice, the report can incorporate observations as to best practices or other effective options to address the problems without offering them as recommendations. The requirement that management must respond to an Inspection Panel investigation with an Action Plan to address the problems identified and take corrective measures is a powerful measure.

Yet another important issue is whether both parties (management/staff and affected people) have the opportunity to review a draft report and comment on it before it is finalized. The purpose of doing so would be to help ensure the accuracy and completeness of the report. Providing a draft report before it is finalized would raise problems. It could invite pressures to change findings and enable either party to gather support for its position before the report is considered by the Board of Directors. The draft report could be leaked to the press by either party, which could politicize the process of finalizing the report and its acceptance. By not sharing the draft report before it is finalized, the accountability mechanism functions more like a judicial body. Draft judicial opinions are not circulated to the parties for review before they are issued. This is to ensure the independence and legitimacy of the judicial body. The same applies to the accountability mechanism.

The Inspection Panel procedures call for management to consult with local people before finalizing its Action Plan. In my experience, this rarely happened. In 2020, the Board of Executive Directors changed the procedure for the Inspection Panel's report. The final Investigation Report now goes to the affected people lodging the complaint at the same time that it goes to management. This gives those bringing the complaint a chance to bring issues and concerns to management's attention as it develops the Bank's response to the investigation. It gives civil society an opportunity for input to members of the Board of Executive Directors before the Board's meeting to consider the Panel's Investigation Report and the Management Response and Action Plan. It responds to the need for transparency and for getting the most effective response. It can strengthen the Action Plan's legitimacy in the view of local people.

Once the Board of Executive Directors has approved an Action Plan and decided upon what additional measures, if any, are to be taken, the question arises as to who verifies that the Action Panel is being implemented so that it does not exist in name only. Management has the responsibility for monitoring its work and for ensuring compliance with its policies and procedures. This cannot and should not be delegated away from management. The issue is whether the accountability mechanism also has a role to play. The resolution establishing the Inspection Panel provided in its 1999 Clarification that the Panel was not authorized to engage in monitoring.[49] However, in some cases, it is essential to have independent verification that the Board approved measures are being implemented.

On several occasions between 2003 and 2007, particularly in the Yacyretá Dam project and the Mumbai Urban Transport Project, the Board of Executive Directors asked the Inspection Panel to follow up on management's implementation and report back to the Board. To do this, the Panel continued its fact-finding function, hired one or two expert local consultants, who were usually associated with the Panel's Investigation Report, to verify facts locally, and issued fact-finding reports to the Board on implementation. In the Mumbai Urban Transport Project, the Panel continued its reports to the Board for more than a year.

The situation of the Inspection Panel on monitoring contrasts with that of accountability mechanisms at other multilateral development banks, which generally have a mandate to monitor compliance.[50] While civil society has generally viewed this as highly favourable, it does raise concerns. To the extent that it shifts the burden for monitoring from management and staff to the accountability mechanism, it diminishes an essential function of the Bank itself. Not all Action Plans need monitoring. As a practical matter, a country may not accept on-the-ground monitoring of an Action Plan by an accountability mechanism, which means any monitoring would be external. Careful and comprehensive monitoring may require significant resources. If monitoring is not careful and complete, it runs the risk of being easily discredited by the Bank or alternatively of being viewed by civil society as a whitewash. This is especially a risk if those who are hired by an accountability mechanism to monitor lack sufficient expertise and experience. Management needs to retain responsibility for monitoring, and the accountability mechanism needs the authority to verify implementation when necessary. This continues the role of the accountability mechanism as a fact-finding body.

In 2020, the Board of Executive Directors approved a new measure to permit the Inspection Panel to do "independent and proportionate risk-based verification, when approved by the Board, of the implementation of Management Actions Plans developed in response to Panel Investigation Reports".[51] This continues the Panel's role in fact-finding. This development is very significant and certainly positive. It would be preferable, though, to let the Inspection Panel determine whether to verify implementation of the Action Plan, perhaps in consultation with the Board, rather than requiring

---

[49] International Bank for Reconstruction and Development, International Development Association, 1999 Clarification of the Board's Second Review of the Inspection Panel, Article 16. <https://www.inspectionpanel.org>.
[50] *Citizen-Driven Accountability for Sustainable Development* (n 4).
[51] The Inspection Panel, <https://www.inspectionpanel.org>.

Board authorization. This approach would be more consistent with other IAM arrangements. In any case, the Board always has the authority to ask the Panel to verify in a specific case, whether or not the Panel would independently decide to do so.

## 8. Evaluating Independent Accountability Mechanisms for Dispute Settlement

Independent accountability mechanisms are increasing in number in multilateral development banks, the United Nations and other international organizations, and other national and private sector institutions. They, too, need to be evaluated, as a way of making them accountable. To do this, criteria are needed. I have identified at least four criteria for evaluating such mechanisms: accessibility, credibility, effectiveness, and efficiency (ACEE).[52] Again, the World Bank Inspection Panel offers a useful example for applying these criteria.

### 8.1  Accessibility

Accessibility refers to whether those who believe they have been harmed or could be harmed can access the Inspection Panel. This depends on whether they know about the Panel. One obvious place to learn about the Panel is during the project preparation phase of the project cycle. Yet, until about 2006, the World Bank did not include a reference to the Inspection Panel in official documents for projects or programmes or on websites providing specific details on a project. In practice, civil society and the Panel have taken the lead in disseminating information about the Panel's availability. The Panel produced two pamphlets: one for affected people in twelve languages and one for staff. It spoke at various non-governmental forums, such as the World Social Forums, organized informational meetings in various countries, and developed further its own website. Most recently the Panel has been holding virtual presentations and discussions on particular subjects, such as biodiversity offsets and gender-based violence.

Accessibility also includes the process for accessing the Panel. If the process is expensive and time-consuming or personally dangerous, complaints will not be made. For the Inspection Panel, a simple letter stating mainly that the affected people are suffering

---

[52] Richard Bissell, a member of the first World Bank Inspection Panel, identifies the core elements of IAMs as public access, access to information, independence from management of the institution, fairness of the compliance review process, and effectiveness of the mechanism. Richard Bissell, (Owen McIntyre and Suresh Nanwani (eds), "The Origin and Evolution of International Accountability Mechanisms" *The Practice of Independent Accountability Mechanisms (IAMS)* (Brill/Nijhoff 2020). David Hunter has identified three components for accountability: (i) quality and nature of normative standards in protecting interests of the benefitting actor; (ii) accessibility, objectivity, and predictability in evaluating the responsible actor's behaviour against the standards; and (iii) frequency, availability, and appropriateness of the consequences of failure to meet the standards. David Hunter, "Contextual Accountability, the World Bank Inspection Panel and the Transformation of International Law in Edith Brown Weiss's Kaleidoscopic World" (2020) 32 Georgetown Environmental Law Review 439, 453–62.

harm from a World Bank financed project or programme suffices. It could be written in any language. However, potential retribution against those who complain often hovers in the wings. Thus, while it is essential to provide information to them about the Panel process, it is important neither to encourage nor to discourage a Request for Inspection.

In some cases, those who file the complaint ask to remain anonymous. In this case, the Panel does not reveal the names of the complainants to anyone. As noted earlier, the need for anonymity poses an especially tricky problem in authenticating the signatures on the complaint. In Cambodia, for example, we met upon arrival with a large group of affected people concerned about forest concessions, which included those who had made the request. We were able to verify the signatures during the course of the larger meeting while protecting the anonymity of the signers. This occurred before the Panel met officially with government ministers and staff and with the timber company.

## 8.2  Credibility

Accountability mechanisms must be credible. This means that Panel members, Panel staff, and consultants must be highly competent and not subject to charges of bias or conflicts of interest. They must have credibility, which means competence, independence, impartiality, and integrity. For the Inspection Panel, the Board appoints three Panel members for a single five-year non-renewable term. The Chairperson is full-time and the other two Panel members part-time. Panel members come from different disciplines and different areas of the world. They cannot have worked for the Bank in any capacity, including as a consultant, during the previous two years, and can never work for the World Bank again after serving on the Inspection Panel. This is to guard against the possibility that a Panel member could pull his/her punches in the process or reach conclusions that were favourable to management in the hopes of securing a subsequent position with the Bank.

The selection process for the Panel members is key. In the past, the Human Relations Department selected a short list from all applicants to be considered by the selection committee, which consisted of two Board members and two senior managers. The committee recommended two applicants; the President interviewed both and decided whom to recommend to the Board of Executive Directors. The Board had the final approval decision. The current process differs slightly in that an outside consulting group selects the applicants for further consideration by the Bank. The selection process is critical, for the Panel's credibility depends upon having highly qualified Panel members who believe in the independence of the Panel. Affected people especially need to trust the Panel to listen to their voices and make competent and impartial findings.

The independence and quality of the Panel's staff and the Panel's budget also affect its credibility. The Executive Secretary of the Panel was originally established as a permanent appointment, which has subsequently been limited to a set term of seven years, renewable once. During my tenure, there were three permanent professional staff positions, several administrative positions, and a few short-term interns. While the human relations department reviewed applicants for consistency with position requirements, the Panel decided whom to hire. The permanence of the professional staff positions is key to the perception of independence and integrity of the Panel, lest staff on short-term contracts be tempted to align their positions with those of management to pre-serve or advance a career in the Bank, or perhaps to retain a valued visa when a contract term position expires. The Panel's budget comes from the Board of Executive Directors, not from management. This is to guard against influence from management on the work of the Panel.

## 8.3 Effectiveness

A third evaluation criterion is whether the Inspection Panel (or any accountability mechanism) is effective. First, this requires identifying "for what" the Panel is to be ef-fective. A key criterion is whether the Panel is effective in addressing the dispute that affected people bring to the Panel. In order to achieve this objective, the Panel needs to be effective in receiving the complaints, listening to the affected people, considering the complaints through impartial fact-finding, and delivering results that can be used by all concerned. In some cases, just the threat of a Panel investigation has produced results that met the Requesters' concerns.[53]

In a number of cases, the Panel has identified people or communities affected by the project who were not included in the initial assessments and whose omission could be effectively addressed. For example, in the forest reform project in DRC, the assessments did not consider the effects upon the several hundred thousand Pygmies living in DRC. Subsequent to the Panel's investigation and report, the Pygmies were considered as relevant stakeholders and participated in meetings for allocating timber concessions. This gave them a voice for the first time to raise their concerns.

A significant limitation on the effectiveness of the process for affected people is that while harm may have occurred that is linked to the project or programme, mon-etary compensation is usually not forthcoming. The focus is on the Bank's compliance with its policies and procedures. In the Yacyretá case, though, the Board of Executive Directors did authorize the Bank to provide additional money to affected people to ad-dress the Bank's failure to comply with some of its policies and procedures.

Another element of effectiveness is whether the IAM provides benefits to the insti-tution that improve the development process for affected people. Benefits occur when

---

[53] In a 2006 Request concerning flooding and road damage from the Mine Closure and Social Mitigation Project in Romania (IBRD Loan No 4509), the Panel delayed sending to the Board of Executive Directors its recommen-dation for an investigation, while the Requesters, Bank management and the Government of Romania reached an agreement resolving the problems. The Requesters sent a "Letter of Contentment" to the Panel and Board of Executive Directors about the agreed actions. The Request, Management's Response, and the Panel's Eligibility Report are available on the Inspection Panel's website, <https://www.inspectionpanel.org>. In one case, the Board approved an investigation, but the parties reached agreement thereafter and forestalled the investigation. Inspection Panel Report and Recommendation on Request for Inspection, Mexico: Indigenous and Community Biodiversity Project (COINBO), GEF Trust Fund Grant No TF24372 (2004), <https://www.inspectionpanel.org>.

244 INDEPENDENT ACCOUNTABILITY MECHANISMS IN DISPUTE SETTLEMENT

institutional learning takes place as a result of Panel actions and investigations, either within a sector or a region, or more broadly in the institution's operations. In the context of the projects or policy loans on forest reform, the Panel's investigations in DRC and in Cambodia led to Bank-wide review and changes in forest sector projects and programmes.[54]

The Inspection Panel has published six reports as part of its Emerging Lessons series that provide insights from Panel investigations and contribute to institutional learning on the part of the Bank: Involuntary Resettlement; Indigenous Peoples; Environmental Assessment; Consultation, Participation and Disclosure of Information; Biodiversity Offsets; and Gender-Based Violence.[55] These reports are targeted to Bank management and staff but are relevant for everyone concerned with development. The ultimate goal is to enhance development effectiveness by ensuring that the people who are supposed to be helped by a project or programme have a voice and that the project or programme benefits them and does not inflict harm. The ultimate test of the effectiveness of an accountability mechanism and its work is whether it makes a positive difference in the development outcome and garners the trust of all the stakeholders in the process.

## 8.4 Efficiency

The fourth evaluation criterion is whether the accountability mechanism is efficient, as measured by the cost of the mechanism and by the amount of time it takes to investigate and to develop the report, in relation to the results. Efficiency involves looking at both benefits and costs. While it is easy to calculate the costs of any single investigation, or of the Panel's operations as a whole, it is more difficult to calculate the benefits. In part this is because the benefits relate not only to the specific project or programme but more broadly to longer term benefits in the specific sector or region or to operations as a whole. It is also difficult to quantify in monetary terms the value to the institution of having an accountability mechanism, the value to the affected people, and the value more broadly to governments and to civil society. Yet unless the broader benefits are identified and considered, the easily quantified monetary costs can be taken to outweigh the benefits.

While it is always important to look for ways to operate efficiently and with timeliness, a report that is quickly prepared with little fact-finding may be inexpensive but its benefits and effectiveness may be paltry at best. Sometimes delays in investigations are caused by events external to the Panel or even to the Bank. For example, in DRC, violence broke out that caused the United Nations to ban travel to the country for some months. The Panel's budgetary needs may vary, depending upon the Requests brought

---

[54] Other cases in which the Panel's Investigation Reports have had significant impacts include Integrated Coastal Zone Management and Clean-Up Project (First Request), Report No 46596 – AL (Albania) (24 November 2008), and China: Western Poverty Reduction Project, Report No INSP/R 2000-4 (28 April 2000), <https://www.inspectionpanel.org>.

[55] The Reports were published from 2016 to 2020, <https://www.inspectionpanel.org>.

to it. In my tenure, the budget for the Panel from the Board of Executive Directors was generally adequate and stayed the same for five years, though the number of Requests increased.

## 9. Conclusion: The Value of the Independent Accountability Mechanisms in MDBs

The World Bank Inspection Panel and all independent accountability mechanisms are essential to an effective development process. The World Bank benefits from being willing to have an independent accountability mechanism review its work in response to concerns from people affected by its projects or programmes.

From the perspective of affected people, the Inspection Panel or other such mechanism gives them a voice with which to try to avoid or to redress harm that has occurred and to ensure that they receive intended benefits of the project or programme. It gives them an independent forum in which to address disputes about actions that they think have harmed or could harm them. It promotes transparency and engagement by local people in the development process. We heard the same plea in many countries and in many languages: "We are poor, and what little we have is about to be taken away from us.... You are our only hope."

For the Board of Executive Directors, the Inspection Panel provides a way to hold management and staff accountable for their work and to ensure a level playing field in the application of the Bank's policies and procedures to its borrowing or grantee countries. It can strengthen the legitimacy of the work of management and staff, and potentially validate their compliance with policies and procedures. Serious problems with a project or programme may exist, but Bank management and staff may not be at fault. The Panel also provides a safety valve when the Bank supports risky projects, because there is a mechanism already in place for the voices of those that could be or are harmed to be heard. To civil society and the private sector, the Panel offers a forum for resolving disputes about the effects of the Bank's work and for ensuring that development assistance helps those who need it.

While the accountability mechanisms in the various MDBs address specific complaints that are brought to them, they have a much broader impact upon the institution. They can cause management and staff to take greater care in preparing and implementing projects so as to avoid resort to the Inspection Panel. They can make innovative projects or programmes that involve significant risks more acceptable, as highlighted earlier. The Panel investigation reports can also lead to changes in policies and procedures, whether in a specific sector such as infrastructure, in a policy such as that for Indigenous peoples, or in its practices.

In the framework for a principle of accountability as set forth at the beginning of this chapter, the Inspection Panel serves not only as the means for providing accountability and for resolving disputes, but also as a means for institutional learning. Learning occurs through such measures as presentations to a given region, presentations and material for training sessions for new employees, and the Emerging Lessons publication series. This role for the Inspection Panel may increase, as the Board of Executive Directors' revisions to the Inspection Panel in 2020 explicitly approved what it termed the advisory function, which refers to the Emerging Lessons series.

At the same time, using the Inspection Panel or other accountability mechanisms to resolve disputes raises issues. The mechanisms need resources. The process requires management and staff time to respond to complaints from Requesters, and, if there is an investigation, to develop an Action Plan to address any findings of non-compliance. Some have contended that the existence of such a mechanism may cause management and staff to "Panel proof" a project so as to make it unlikely to be subject to Panel review.

The value of an IAM depends upon whether the institution supports an independent accountability mechanism or tries to undermine or to co-opt it. It is to the institution's credit that it has an accountability mechanism, a point that needs to be stressed, especially in the field. At the same time, management or staff do not always appreciate having an independent body review their work. They may try to dismiss the role of the Panel or to treat the Panel as if it were more appropriate for it to be part of management and to try to limit its independence. The President of the institution has an essential role in conveying support for the Panel and in ensuring that management and staff respond accordingly. All three World Bank Presidents were supportive of the Panel during my tenure.

In the United States, in light of the recent United States Supreme Court decision in the *Jam* case,[56] it is especially important that MDBs have a robust, independent forum for resolving disputes about their operations. For this, the Inspection Panel, and indeed all accountability mechanisms, need the support of the institution of which they are a part. The Panel, in turn, has the responsibility to be scrupulously careful and accurate in its findings.

If the independent accountability mechanisms are to flourish, a culture of accountability needs to be fostered. Most importantly, the accountability system depends upon trust in the Inspection Panel or other mechanism by all concerned: the affected people and communities, Bank management and staff, the Bank's Board of Executive Directors, civil society, and, as relevant, the private sector. Affected people are generally not used to having a voice and to trusting others. This means that the Panel or other mechanism must be independent and impartial and act with integrity. Generating and maintaining the trust of all concerned is difficult but essential.

---

[56] In *Jam v Int'l Fin. Corp (Jam v. IFC)*, petitioners sued the IFC for harm to air, land, and water in Gujarat stemming from polluting activities of the Coastal Gujarat Power Limited, a coal-fired power plant. *Jam v Int'l Fin. Corp.*, 139 SCt759, 760 (2019). The International Organizations Immunities Act (IOIA) provides that international organizations "shall enjoy the same immunity from suit and every form of judicial process as is enjoyed by foreign governments". The US Supreme Court interpreted this as providing "the same immunity from suit that foreign governments enjoy today under the FSIA." (Foreign Sovereign Immunities Act). ibid 760. On remand, the US district court held the IFC was immune from suit as the commercial activity exception to immunity in the FSIA did not apply in this case. *Jam v Int'l Fin. Corp.*, 442 FSupp3d 162, 179 (DDC 2020). The Court determined that the gravamen of the suit was the IFC's failure to enforce conditions of the loan agreement, which are conduct or inaction in India, not the United States. ibid 177.

Independent accountability mechanisms, such as the Inspection Panel, are a very useful forum for resolving disputes about the effects of development projects on local people. They can investigate, consider all relevant information, engage directly with those bringing the dispute, and offer insights on avoiding practices that cause harm.

More broadly, for the complex and multidisciplinary world today, independent accountability mechanisms offer attractive, less formal means for resolving disputes. They can encompass the many aspects of the dispute, delve deeply into the issues, engage relevant disciplines in the process, and retain flexibility for those who must provide the remedies for responding to the dispute resolution findings. They give voice to those who are harmed or could be harmed by an institution's actions. We should consider them for both public and private sector institutions as a way to resolve disputes and to ensure that those who might be harmed by their actions can be heard—that they have a voice.

## Acknowledgements

The author thanks Olivia Le Menestrel and Sara Zaat, Georgetown Law, for research assistance, especially with Tables.

The research and analysis for this chapter were completed in September 2020.

# 13

# International Courts through a
# Sociological Lens

*Mikael Rask Madsen*

## 1. Introduction

As lawyers, we tend to think about law and legal institutions in normative terms. Our job is to figure out and systematize intra-normative connections between sources of law and come up with compelling arguments for normative results. Yet at the same time, only the most ardent legal positivists would claim that the phenomenon of law as such is a normative one. On the contrary, it is clearly a societal—or sociological—one. Law, national and international, is informed and developed in society—and law helps develop society.[1] Experts on international law and courts, and David Caron was one of the finest among these, are familiar with this slight paradox. Caron's writings reflect fundamental questions of the societal embeddedness of law. Some of his best-known papers concern precisely issues related to authority and legitimacy of international organizations and law, and he even ventured into the thorny question of the political theory of international courts.[2] Among scholars of international courts (international courts), the turn to a more social scientific perspective is not new. The Second President of the Permanent Court of International Justice (PCIJ), Max Huber (1874–1960), was a pioneer in this regard, using sociology in his studies of international law when a professor of law at the University of Zurich before being appointed to the international bench.[3]

It was probably no coincidence that Huber turned to sociology at this moment in time. It coincided with the breakthrough of modern sociology where Max Weber in particular became very central, also for law. Trained as a lawyer, Weber was instrumental in making questions of legitimacy and authority central to sociology and notably his sociology of law. This interest in law and the formation of modern society

---

[1] This chapter repeats the analysis presented in an earlier and longer chapter: Mikael Rask Madsen, "Sociological Approaches to International Courts" in Karen Alter, Cesare PR Romano, and Yuval Shany (eds), *Oxford Handbook of International Adjudication* (Oxford University Press 2014).

[2] See eg David D Caron, "The Legitimacy of the Collective Authority of the Security Council" (1993) 87 (4) The American Journal of International Law<https://doi.org/10.2307/2203616>; "The ILC Articles on State Responsibility: The Paradoxical Relationship between Form and Authority" (2002) 96(4) The American Journal of International Law 401 <https://doi.org/10.2307/3070682>; "Towards a Political Theory of International Courts and Tribunals" (2006) 24 (2) Berkeley Journal of International Law.

[3] Huber's original study, "Beiträge zur Kenntnis der soziologischen Grundlagen des Völkerrechts und der Staatengesellschaft" was published in 1910 in *Jahrbuch des öffentlichen Rechts der Gegenwart*.

Mikael Rask Madsen, *International Courts through a Sociological Lens* In: *By Peaceful Means*. Edited by: Charles N Brower, Joan E Donoghue, Cian C Murphy, Cymie R Payne and Esmé R Shirlow, Oxford University Press. © Mikael Rask Madsen 2024.
DOI: 10.1093/oso/9780192848086.003.0013

notwithstanding, few of the early sociologists demonstrated much interest in international law. Needless to say, international courts were such a novelty that they held little empirical interest for those interested in understanding society. With some exceptions such as Huber,[4] many of the insights of the pioneers of sociology have therefore since been lost to students of international courts. More generally, sociology has been peripheral to the discipline of international law and its sub-fields such as human rights.[5] In this chapter, I will first return to some of these ideas and show how they can enrich our understanding of international courts and international law more generally. Then, I will consider a number of new sociological studies of international courts and global governance which have been carried out in recent years.

## 2. Classic Sociology and the Question of Law and Courts

Sociologists have long studied law and legal institutions in society. This is true for both the classics such as Weber and Durkheim and leading contemporary sociologists, for example Jürgen Habermas,[6] Pierre Bourdieu,[7] Niklas Luhmann,[8] and Bruno Latour.[9] Sociologists however study law and courts using a distinct starting point. If law has as its overarching object of inquiry the normative order of legal norms, and political science's key object is politics and associated institutions and actors, sociology is above all concerned with society, either in the Durkheimian sense, as a pre-existing but evolving social structure within which action takes place, or in the revitalized Tardeian sense, as suggested by contemporary sociologists such as Bruno Latour, as the outcome of networks of actors (and actants).[10] Between these two extremes, one finds a great diversity in approaches that differ most profoundly in their view on respectively structures, agency and materials.

With regard to studying international courts more specifically, sociology typically construes institutions in a broader sense than what is found in both law and political science: either as assemblages of practices within larger social fields or more generally as devices for ordering society. Both perspectives will be introduced in the following subsections in which I focus on what classic sociological theories can contribute to our understanding law and courts. Classic sociology generally had a twin objective, namely both to establish a new discipline and to conduct actual empirical studies of modern

---

[4] Martti Koskenniemi argues that French public international law scholarship in the period 1871–1950 had a distinct sociological dimension. Martti Koskenniemi, *The Gentle Civilizer of Nations: The Rise and Fall of International Law 1870–1960* (Cambridge University Press 2001).

[5] Mikael Rask Madsen and Gert Verschraegen, "Making Human Rights Intelligible: An Introduction to Sociology of Human Rights" in Mikael R. Madsen and Gert Verschraegen (eds), *Making Human Rights Intelligible: Towards a Sociology of Human Rights* (Hart 2013).

[6] Jürgen Habermas, *Faktizität und Geltung: Beiträge zur Diskurstheorie des Rechts und des Demokratischen Rechtsstaats* (Suhrkamp Verlag 1992).

[7] Pierre Bourdieu, "The Force of Law: Toward a Sociology of the Juridical Field" (1987) 38 The Hastings Law Journal 805.

[8] Niklas Luhmann, *Das Recht der Gesellschaft* (Suhrkamp 1993).

[9] Bruno Latour, *La Fabrique du Droit: Une Ethnographie du Conseil D'état* (La Découverte 2002).

[10] Bruno Latour, *Reassembling the Social: An Introduction to Actor-Network Theory* (Oxford University Press 2005).

society. In other words, early sociologists wanted to explain modern society both by theory and empirical study, meanwhile developing the necessary tools for these undertakings. For the same reasons, the theories presented in the following tend to involve both macro-level theorizing of more general societal logics and middle-range empirical exploration of law and courts in society.

## 2.1 Interpretative Sociology

Max Weber's analysis of the evolution of law in terms of a set of different ideal-typical forms of rationality is probably the most cited among the classics. It is also the one that comes closest to contemporary mainstream social science studies of international courts. Generally, Weber provides a set of typologies for describing the rise of modern Western law as an evolution from "formally irrational" and "substantively irrational" to law becoming "formally rational" and "substantively rational".[11] According to Weber, these rationalities generally correspond to different forms of domination: from charismatic to traditional to legal. Importantly, at no point does Weber claim a complete conversion from one domination or rationality to another. Rather, he maintains that elements of each of these ideal-typical representations of law are present in contemporary society, but to varying degrees. They are indeed ideal-typical representations in the sense that they are abstracted models devised to help identify society in a more clear and systematic way in order to allow for comparison. When grounded in empirical studies, they provide a conceptual apparatus for the inevitable task of any social science, namely to make a selection and abstraction from the infinite multitude of social reality. With respect to examining international courts, they basically help turn international courts into tangible empirical objects of research.

As I demonstrated in my examination of the European Court of Human Rights (ECtHR), Weber provides a set of reflexive tools for understanding international courts as evolutionary institutions that develop specific institutional and legal rationalities which are reflective of institutions' embedded rationality—or situated cognition—in their decision-making processes.[12] Contrary to much law and political science scholarship, which tends to view international courts in predetermined categories—for example as transplanted institutions that resemble their national counterparts or other international courts, or on the basis of a abstracted hypothesis of institutional behaviour or institutional design—the Weberian approach has a different focus. Its analytical focal point is the historically founded different rationalities of the institution in question, and how these are reflective of both society at large and the very agents of

---

[11] Max Weber, *Wirtschaft und Gesellschaft. Grundriss der Verstehenden Soziologie* (5th edn, Mohr 1980).

[12] Mikael Rask Madsen, "Legal Diplomacy—Law, Politics and the Genesis of Postwar European Human Rights" in Stefan Ludwig Hoffmann (ed), *Human Rights in the Twentieth Century: A Critical History* (Cambridge University Press 2011); Mikael Rask Madsen, "The Challenging Authority of the European Court of Human Rights: From Cold War Legal Diplomacy to the Brighton Declaration and Backlash" (2016) 79(1) Law & Contemporary Problems 141.

the institution.[13] This particular way of approaching international courts also provides a sociologically informed alternative for understanding questions related to the legitimacy of international courts; that is, legitimacy in this approach is neither tied up to a legalist notion of legitimacy via legality, nor as an abstracted political philosophical notion. Max Weber seeks instead to explain how legitimacy is contingent on different forms of domination—from traditional to charismatic to legally rational—and thereby embedded in society.[14]

According to Weber, at the end of the day what makes a certain practice of power legitimate is the process through which authority justifies its exercise of power and gains social acceptance. Applied to international courts, it follows that their legitimacy does not stem from them being *representative* of society; it stems from them being *reflective* of society.[15] For example a national supreme court is typically not demographically or politically representative of society but it might very well reflect society and, thereby, justify its practices. In other words, the legitimacy of a given international court cannot simply be statistically deduced from the judges' representativeness of society and politics at large. This also means that even the best and most carefully thought-out procedures related to the elections of judges, in the most extreme cases seeking to make courts representative as a sort of quasi-democratic political institution, might ultimately fail if the court's practices are not reflective of society. On the other hand, the profiles of a specific set of judges might very well help them gain legitimacy in specific environments, ranging from law to politics and civil society.[16] Using this framework, it could be argued with respect to the cited example of the genesis of the ECtHR that its institutionalization in a way followed what Weber termed the "routinization of charisma": the initial institutionalization process was a legitimization process around the specific individuals and their practices. Ultimately, the authority of the ECtHR was originally derived from the high status of the bench and the way these judges developed a set of politically fine-tuned legal practices that reflected the social and political conditions under which it operated.[17]

From this brief introduction to Weber, the difference between contemporary law and political science explorations of international courts and the particular empirical and conceptual sensitivity of sociology becomes clear. While mainstream political scientific examinations of international courts typically test rationalized hypotheses against different sets of data, the goal of a Weberian approach is different: it seeks to make law

---

[13] ibid.

[14] Weber (n 11).

[15] The argument is further developed in Mikael Rask Madsen, "Explaining the Power of International Courts in Their Context: From Legitimacy to Legitimization" in Adriana S D de Klor, Miguel P Maduro and Antoine Vauchez (eds), *Courts, Social Change and Judicial Independence* (Euorpean University Institute, 2012) 23.

[16] See also Daniel Terris, Cesare PR Romano, and Leigh Swigart, *The International Judge: An Introduction to the Men and Women Who Decide the World's Cases* (Oxford University Press 2007); Freya Baetens, *Identity and Diversity on the International Bench: Who is the Judge?* (Oxford University Press 2020).

[17] Mikael Rask Madsen, "The Protracted Institutionalisation of the Strasbourg Court: From Legal Diplomacy to Integrationist Jurisprudence" in Mikael Rask Madsen and Jonas Christoffersen (eds), *The European Court of Human Rights between Law and Politics* (Oxford University Press 2011).

and courts intelligible as societal institutions.[18] The aim of this so-called interpretive sociology (*Verstehende Soziologie*) is precisely to link habits and motives to action; that is, to make action intelligible by corresponding action to the agents in terms of a specific form of "methodological individualism".[19] The prime example of this approach is Weber's famous analysis of the role of the Protestant sprit in the making of capitalism. Here the "spirit" of the agents—notably internalized norms of duty and correctness—is the backdrop for explaining the rapid growth of a capitalist economy in Germany. But as just shown, the same could be done on a smaller scale with regard to international courts either by a study of the judges or the normative schemes in society which drive the push for international courts.

Although Weberian sociology might at first glance appear as yet another grand attempt at deducing universal socio-logics, it should be stressed that its actual goal is not to devise a universal theory but to explain society by creating a framework of inquiry that facilitates an exploration of micro and macro levels of society. First of all, Weber is not seeking to get rid of the usual units of middle-range social scientific analysis such as groups, collectives, and institutions, but is instead pointing to the basic observation that only individuals can have intentions. Consequently, individuals provide a key unit of analysis, even if the goal is not to understand individuals' motivations as such but societal development as driven by groups of individuals or, for example, institutions. As demonstrated in the above cited study on the ECtHR, this is directly applicable to analyses of international courts. Yet different from both the traditional legal realist take on legal actors, and many of the subsequent legal realist-inspired studies of judicial behaviour, the focal point of such a Weberian study of international courts is not the individuals as such but the societal and institutional developments which can be made intelligible by exploring the individuals' motivations and its impact on the rationalization of the institutions.[20] Thus Weber provides above all a historical-sociological approach to law with a focus on the transformation of the institutions of society, including courts. From that perspective, international courts are institutions of global society which studied as such using Weberian research tools.

## 2.2  Structural Functionalism and Systems Theory

Weberian insights have also inspired subsequent notions of rational choice which are central to much current scholarship on international courts. Drawing on Weber's notion of "purposive" or "goal rationality" (*Zweckrationalität*),[21] it was Talcott Parsons, a

---

[18] An exception to this trend is some historical institutionalist scholarship. See for example Karen Alter, *Establishing the Supremacy of European Law: The Making of an International Rule of Law in Europe* (Oxford University Press 2001).

[19] For an overview of the notion, see Soma Hewa, "The Genesis of Max Weber's 'Verstehende Soziologie'" (1988) 31(2) Acta Sociologica 143.

[20] cf Madsen, "The Protracted Institutionalisation of the Strasbourg Court" (n 17).

[21] Corresponding to the overall framework, Weber operated with more forms of action rationalities. In addition to the instrumental character of "purposive rationality", his notion of "value-rationality" (*Wertrationalität*) should be mentioned here.

Weber follower himself, who set the scene for some of this later influential scholarship in his seminal book *The Structure of Social Action* (1937) in which he introduced the notion of the "action frame of reference".[22] I will, however, not pursue this connection further but instead outline the other key inspiration to Parsons' work, namely Emile Durkheim, another of the classical sociologists, who made an early contribution to the understanding of law in society. And I will argue that Durkheim has had a monumental impact on studies of international law and courts, even if this impact is rarely acknowledged.

According to Durkheim, law is an index of social solidarity; that is, it represents the evolution of social integration. This is explained in Durkheim's famous evolutionary model, outlining the transformation from primitive to modern society and with that a change in forms of solidarity from mechanical to organic, following a thesis of societal differentiation.[23] Just like Weber, Durkheim links law and its institutions to the emergence of modern society. Durkheim has, however, less to offer with regard to understanding courts specifically. He views them as mainly "deliberating on behalf of society in a manner somewhat similar to that of the legislature".[24] His main interest is instead law as a means of stabilizing and integrating society. Primitive (or traditional) societies are generally kept together by kinship and tribal justice, according to Durkheim. In modern societies interdependences between different specialized areas of work secure the integration of society. In this regard, law has an important function as an instrument of integrating these differentiated social spheres. This is precisely what he means by arguing that courts "deliberate" on behalf of society at large—and with the goal of securing society's coherence against its increased differentiation and specialization.

Durkheim's approach is directly applicable to understanding the role of international courts in contemporary global society. In modern social scientific terms, the question is what function international courts perform with respect to integrating regional or global society, rather than, as it most often is the case in the current literature, the more specific and limited functional aims of individual international courts. The heuristic take-away of posing the question in the broader sociological way proposed by Durkheimian sociology is that it avoids trapping the research in the functional purposes of specific institutions, which have tended to dominate debates on international courts. Instead, it is concerned with a set of broader question, which involves states and international courts and organizations as providers of specialized labour of a crucial kind in contemporary society. The overall aim is to understand society at large—both its specialized components and what ensures coherence notwithstanding specialization. Such a macro-level analysis of international courts and global society is yet to be conducted using post-Durkheimian sociology but the basic social scientific tools are clearly available.[25]

---

[22] Talcott Parsons, *The Structure of Social Action* (McGraw Hill 1937) 43–51.

[23] Émile Durkheim, *De la Division du Travail Social: Étude sur l'organisation des Sociétés Supérieures* (Alcan 1893).

[24] Roger Cotterrell, *Emile Durkheim: Law in a Moral Domain* (Stanford University Press 1999) 172.

[25] Although not focused on international courts, the most explicit attempt at understanding the international legal ordering of society is probably found in Günther Teubner, *Constitutional Fragments: Societal*

The most direct and pervasive influence of Durkheimian sociology is clearly the focus on functions, as well as what later becomes the notion of systems in structural-functionalism and systems theory, which both draw on the Durkheimian differentiation thesis. In fact, considering the vast body of functionalist literature, particularly in political science and law, the impact of this way of perceiving and constructing the social world can hardly be overstated. Armin von Bogdandy and Ingo Venzke go as far as describing functionalism as virtually the orthodoxy of legal research.[26] Another example is the often-cited thesis of the fragmentation of international law which is also based on such a functionalist reading of public international law.[27] In both cases, they build on a very long tradition in international law of perceiving public international law in functionalist terms. Hersch Lauterpacht's *The Function of Law in the International Community* (1933) is not only an important reference to legal scholarship in this regard but also with regard to the application of the Durkheimian idea of precisely linking international law and international community.[28] In political science, one will come across similar claims to those of lawyers with respect to understanding international courts and international law in terms functions and functionalities. Although the bigger societal picture is often missing in the analysis of both lawyers and political scientists, this is nevertheless an important point of convergence between classic sociology and contemporary law and political science explorations of international courts.

Drawing on socio-legal studies of (national) courts and society, Bogdandy and Venzke offer a good summary of how functionalism is also helpful for more specifically theorizing the functions of international courts in international society. According to the authors, these are (i) settling disputes, (ii) stabilizing normative expectations, (iii) making law, and (iv) controlling and legitimating public authority.[29] Although they do not cite Durkheim, these functions clearly echo a Durkheimian way of thinking of courts in society. Similar functionalist claims can be found in a host of sociologies of courts in society in the tradition of structural functionalism and systems theory, starting with Parsons, who argues that courts' main function is to integrate society's different sub-systems by "mitigat[ing] potential elements of conflicts and to oil the machinery of social intercourse".[30] Building on the combined insights of structural functionalism and notions of differentiation and integration, key students of Parsons have provided even more detailed explorations of particularly the "integrative functions" of

*Constitutionalism and Globalization* (Oxford University Press 2012). As concerns the European level, see particularly Chris Thornhill, "The Formation of a European Constitution: An Approach from Historical-Political Sociology" (2012) 8(3) International Journal of Law in Context 354. See also Richard Münch, "Constructing a European Society by Jurisdiction" (2008) 14(5) European Law Journal 519.

[26] Armin von Bogdandy and Ingo Venzke, "On the Functions of International Courts: An Appraisal in Light of Their Burgeoning Public Authority" (2013) 26(1) Leiden Journal of International Law 49.

[27] Martti Koskenniemi and Päivi Leino, "Fragmentation of International Law? Postmodern Anxieties" (2002) 15(3) Leiden Journal of International Law 553.

[28] Hersch Lauterpacht, *The Function of Law in the International Community* (Oxford University Press 1933).

[29] Compare this to the goals defined in Yuval Shany, "Assessing the Effectiveness of International Courts: A Goal-Based Approach" (2012) 106 (2) The American Journal of International Law 243–47.

[30] Talcott Parsons, "The Law and Social Control" in William M Evan (ed), *Law and Sociology: Exploratory Essays* (Free Press 1962).

courts in society as in the case of Harry C Bredemaier[31] and the specific role of law and courts to "stabilize normative expectations" as developed by Niklas Luhmann.[32]

What functionalism offers is a general sociological theory of law and courts in society based on a specific rational reading of courts as being functional to a differentiated society. While it is hard to disagree with the overriding claims of these theories, partly because of the level of abstraction on which they operate, it is plain to see that they also tend, to a considerable extent, to reproduce the very claims of formalist legal scholarship and even law itself. This criticism can also be directed at a great deal of political science literature, using functionalism in a narrow way and establishing a direct causality between an identified problem and its solution via international courts.[33] This critique is also precisely the starting point for what can be labelled "critical studies of international law and courts", which as a common thread seek to go beyond the self-descriptions of institutions and agents with the goal of providing what they believe is a more realistic understanding of law and society. In fact, they seek to study what one well-known sociological functionalist, Robert K Merton, famously termed the "dysfunctions of courts" whereby he himself approached critical studies as well as fundamentally challenged functionalism as a viable sociological paradigm.[34]

## 2.3  Marxism and Critical Theory

As regards sociology, critical studies can generally be said to have their origins in Marxism, which traditionally is described as the third branch of classic sociology. While it shares with the Durkheimian school an interest in social structures, the underlying assumption of coherence of functionalism is explicitly rejected in the Marxist scholarship, for which the overriding driver of societal evolution is conflict and domination.[35] Classic Marxism has mainly an interest in courts and justice as expressions and tools of social domination as exercised by existing dominant classes. Likewise, judges are viewed as agents of a suppressive superstructure mainly put in place to ensure the status quo and, thus, the interests of the ruling elite. If functionalism takes its starting point in a thesis of differentiation, classic Marxism takes it in stratification. There are, however, very important differences between classic (and orthodox) Marxism and its main focus on industrial relations in terms of property owners and labourers, and modern critical studies and its ambition to critique modern society more generally with the goal of liberating the individual from the forms of domination characterizing it.[36]

---

[31]  Harry C Bredemaier, "Law as an Integrative Mechanism" in ibid.

[32]  Luhmann (n 8).

[33]  For example Barbara Koremenos, Charles Lipson, and Duncan Snidal, "The Rational Design of International Institutions" (2001) 55(4) International Organization 761.

[34]  Robert K Merton, *Social Theory and Social Structure* (Simon & Schuster 1949).

[35]  An attempt at devising an explicit Marxist agenda for the study of international law is found in BS Chimni, "Marxism and International Law: A Contemporary Analysis" (1999) 34(6) Economic and Political Weekly 337. See, more recently, Ntina Tzouvala, *Capitalism as Civilisation: A History of International Law* (Cambridge University Press 2020).

[36]  The term critical theory is largely contested and covers in practice a whole range of approaches, ranging from the Frankfurter School to many contemporary post-structural sociologies.

I will not dwell here on the myriad schools of critical studies and their differences and convergences but simply underscore that some important elements of Marxist and critical thinking have made significant impact on contemporary sociological studies of international courts—and often in combination with Weberian readings of institutions and professions. These include, for example, the emphasis on elites as key agents of law, the conceptualization of international law and courts as adversarial social spaces, and the focus on the power of law—both as symbolic power, following the Bourdieusian tradition,[37] and as a structural phenomenon with regard to, for example, notions of empire. Whereas functionalist sociology, as argued above, has significantly influenced both legal and political scientific analysis of international courts, starting in the late 1960s it tended to lose much of its appeal as a sociological paradigm.[38] The actual fate of functionalism is of course debatable, but what is certain is that the combined issues of elites, power, and conflict of the critical camp have increasingly come to define a great deal contemporary sociological scholarship on international courts. In the following, emphasis will therefore be put on this branch of sociology with the goal of accentuating distinct sociological contributions to understanding international courts.

## 3. Sociology of International Courts

I have so far sought to demonstrate how classical sociological theories have provided a series of general studies of law and courts in society with considerable relevance for understanding international courts and society. Sociology has obviously evolved considerable since the Weber, Marx and Durkheim. The more recent specialization of sociology into subdisciplines such as sociology of law and, in the US context, the law and society movement, has further produced more specific yet ambiguous research paths in this regard.[39] Generally, the sociology of law has maintained an overall interest in (national) courts[40]—an interest that has been intensified in the debates on judicialization and the growing role of constitutional courts.[41] Focus in the following is on the subset of studies which have more explicitly engaged with international courts.

### 3.1 Precursors to the Sociology of International Courts

From its very beginnings in the mid-1960s, law and society has been a heterogeneous field of research. Nevertheless, what has kept it together is a collective interest in a critique of both formal law and legal formalism. In some ways, law and society has

---

[37] Pierre Bourdieu, *Language and Symbolic Power* (Harvard University Press 1991).
[38] Notable exceptions to this overall trend is the work of Niklas Luhmann and some contemporary organization theory as explained in this chapter.
[39] A third related path which shall however not be examined here is of course Critical Legal Studies (CLS).
[40] For an overview of this literature, see chapter 7 in Roger Cotterrell, *The Sociology of Law: An Introduction* (Butterworths 1992).
[41] For a good overview of this literature, see Thornhill (n 25) 354–55.

developed as an outgrowth of earlier legal realism, particularly American legal realism with which it also shared its original geographical focus. However, with respect to the subject of this chapter, the anti-formalism and anti-institutionalism of much law and society scholarship has in one important aspect made it take a very different turn than American legal realism which largely was court-centred. Quite on the contrary, and inspired by the *Zeitgeist* of the late 1960s and 1970s, law and society scholarship has developed a distinct focus on the alternatives to courts in terms of alternative dispute resolution and even alternatives to law in terms of informal law.[42] This, combined with its original US focus, has become somewhat of an obstacle to studying international law and institutions.[43] Or, as I will argue in this chapter, it has required a "detour" via less formalized international law and institutions to eventually finding a converging interest in particularly international criminal law over the last decade.

Similar patterns of relative disinterest with regard to law and legal institutions can also be found in mainstream sociology during the same period.[44] The area of human rights, perhaps one of the most salient societal evolutions of the post-Second World War era and thus seemingly of interest to both sociology and law and society, is highly illustrative in this respect. Law and society research, due to its precise object of in-quiry, took an interest in international human rights fairly early on, but mainly as part of the overall critical agenda, and thus opted for studying non-governmental organ-izations (NGOs) in international law and other ways of addressing international law from below. Sociology at large was in fact far more reluctant to address human rights and its corresponding architecture of international law and courts. Human rights, to put it simply, were not considered a genuine sociological object of study.[45] Sociologists generally saw the topic as marred by debates which, as concerns law, was either highly normative or formalist or, in the case of political science, dominated by rationalist the-oretical notions essentially foreign to the core of sociology or entirely driven by stat-istical demonstration based on positivist assumptions. Further alienating sociologists from this specific field has been, on the one hand side, the normative philosophical ex-plorations of the idea and ideal of universal human rights, and, on the other hand side, the parallel debates in anthropology on universalism and relativism of human rights. Many sociologists simply perceived this as an ideological abstraction.[46]

The eventual emergence of what now is undoubtedly a growing sociological schol-arship on international law and international courts was in part driven by studies

[42] cf Bryant G Garth, "Tilting the Justice System: From ADR as Idealistic Movement to a Segmented Market in Dispute Resolution" (2001) 18(4) Georgia State University Law Review 927.

[43] An exception to the US focus was the so-called Law and Development Movement which was led by Law and Society scholars such as Bill Felstiner, Marc Galanter, and David Trubek.

[44] It should perhaps be pointed out that during the same period in IR, as well as political science more generally, that studies of international courts was predominantly the domain of a small, specialized group of researchers. The proliferation of studies of international courts has in practice gone hand in hand with the proliferation of inter-national courts themselves in recent years.

[45] Madsen and Verschraegen (n 5).

[46] There is in a way nothing particularly new about this as Durkheim, Weber, and Marx were all highly sceptical about the possibility of and indeed need for a universalistic and normative basis for human rights. In fact, until recently the sociology of citizenship has in many ways came to function as a kind of substitute for a sociology of human rights. See eg Bryan S Turner, *Vulnerability and Human Rights* (Pennsylvania University Press 2006).

interested in the globalization and trans-nationalization of law and legal professionals. Since at least the early 1980s, a number of sociologists of law started investigating what was increasingly termed "transnational legal phenomena".[47] A seminal book in this regard, as well as with respect to subsequent sociological scholarship on international institutions and courts, is the analysis of international commercial arbitration conducted by Yves Dezalay and Bryant Garth in *Dealing in Virtue*.[48] Using both legal and sociological insights, they demonstrated how the battle over the form and the law of international commercial arbitration could be explained as a battle between not only different forms of expertise (European academic law versus American-style Wall Street law) but also as a clash different global elites. The work is based on two different research traditions which are brought together via a set of broader conceptual frameworks provided by the sociologist Pierre Bourdieu: first, a sociology of professions with a view to analysing how professions increasingly compete with one another in the construction of new transnational markets and arenas;[49] secondly, it builds on a sociology of elites with the aim of exploring how a set of distinct social groups of (legal) agents hold the power to define new areas of legal practice, with consequences not only for the profession at large but also for international politics and society.[50] Drawing on Pierre Bourdieu, they frame these battles as social *fields* in terms of spaces of contestation over defining the law in which different agents occupy positions relative to the portfolio of capitals they can muster and which are "capitalized" according to the logic of the specific field in question.[51]

Dezalay and Garth's work also has a methodological feature which has turned out to be of special interest to understanding international courts. Although legal institutions are clearly important to their studies, they are not taking centre stage in the original study on international commercial arbitration and even less so in their subsequent studies of the role of professional battles in the transformation of states in Latin America[52] and Asia.[53] What they instead provide is a sociological alternative to the assumption of many studies in both law and political science that institutions in themselves can explain the emergence of new transnational legal fields. Much closer to neo-institutionalist scholarship on organizational fields,[54] yet still different, they claim

[47] For example Boaventura de Sousa Santos, *Toward a New Common Sense: Law, Science and Politics in the Paradigmatic Transition* (Routledge 1995).

[48] Yves Dezalay and Bryant G Garth, *Dealing in Virtue. International Commercial Arbitration and the Construction of a Transnational Legal Order* (University of Chicago Press 1996).

[49] Yves Dezalay and David Sugerman (eds), *Professional Competition and Professional Power: Lawyers, Accountants and the Social Construction of Markets* (Routledge 1995).

[50] Yves Dezalay, "Les Courtiers de L'international: Héritiers Cosmopolites, Mercenaires de l'impérialisme et Missionnaires de l'universel" (2004) 4 Actes de la recherche en sciences sociales 151–52.

[51] Bourdieu. See also, Yves Dezalay and Mikael R Madsen, "The Force of Law and Lawyers: Pierre Bourdieu and the Reflexive Sociology of Law" (2012) 8 Annual Review of Law and Social Science 433. Compare Florian Grisel, "Competition and Cooperation in International Commercial Arbitration: The Birth of a Transnational Legal Profession" (2017) Law & Society Review 790.

[52] Yves Dezalay and Bryant Garth, *The Internationalization of Palace Wars: Lawyers, Economists, and the Contest to Transform Latin American States* (University of Chicago Press 2002).

[53] Yves Dezalay and Bryant G. Garth, *Asian Legal Revivals: Lawyers in the Shadow of Empire* (University of Chicago Press 2010).

[54] For example Paul J DiMaggio and Walter W Powell, "The Iron Cage Revisited: Institutional Isomorphism and Collective Rationality in Organizational Fields" (1983) 48(2) American Sociological Review 147.

that individual agents, and particularly the agents' personal and professional trajectories into the fields and institutions in question provide unique data for understanding
how institutions come about and transform. Using a methodology which they term
"collective biographies", a form of prosopography, they map out the social characteristics of the social spaces of institutions in terms of the combined and accumulated
trajectories of the main agents.[55] This is also where they deploy Bourdieusian notions
of capitals—social, educational, political, legal, etc—to explore the specific legal elite
formations of these socio-legal spaces. Dezalay and Garth's identification of legal elites
as an entrance to studying transnational legal fields has had considerable impact on a
series of in-depth empirical studies of international courts, ranging from the areas of
international criminal law to European law, which emerged at about the same time in
the beginning of the 2000s.

## 3.2 The New Sociology of International Courts

The International Criminal Tribunal for the Former Yugoslavia (ICTY) was analysed in
the influential book *Justice in the Balkans* by John Hagan.[56] Coming from criminology
and law and society studies, Hagan very openly states his inspiration from the insights
of Dezalay and Garth on the role of legal agency as particularly developed in *Dealing
in Virtue*.[57] His goal is, however, more institutional than what is found in Dezalay and
Garth, yet he uses precisely the described methodology of examining the trajectories
of the main agents in order to map the institution in question and its transformation.
Hagan more concretely scrutinizes the interplay between investigators, prosecutors,
and witnesses, as well as specific powerful individuals employed by the tribunal (em-
blematically Richard Goldstone, Louise Arbour, and Carla Del Ponte), in a complex
analysis of the making of humanitarian and international criminal law, and how it
eventually gains a force of law with a reference to the Bourdieusian conception of the
legal field.[58] By the latter, what is meant is that to understand the power of law, one has
to study the social conditions making that power possible. And that is precisely what
John Hagan's study does through its in-depth examination of the various players and
emerging institutions producing international justice with a legal force in the Balkans.

From Hagan's original study one can trace a more general sociological interest in
international criminal law and its new set of associated institutions.[59] This scholarship manages very well to combine insights from earlier law and society studies on the

---

[55] Compare this to the more institutionalist version of Bourdieusian sociology of organizations presented in
Mustafa Emirbayer and Victoria Johnson, "Bourdieu and Organizational Analysis" (2008) 37(1) Theory and
Society 1.
[56] John Hagan, *Justice in the Balkans. Prosecuting War Crimes in the Hague Tribunal* (University of Chicago
Press 2003).
[57] Hagan explains the precise usage in chapter 22 of Simon Halliday and Patrick Schmidt, *Conducting Law and
Society Research: Reflections on Methods and Practices* (Cambridge University Press 2009).
[58] See John Hagan and Ron Levi, "Crimes of War and the Force of Law" (2005) 83(4) Social Forces 1499.
[59] A number of these scholars have contributed to two the special issues (nos 173 and 174) in 2008 of *Actes de la
recherche en sciences sociales*.

informal sides of law with the analysis of the less institutionalized practices of inter-national law and institutions. An example is the role of mediation and alternative con-flict resolution in the area of international criminal law and war crimes.[60] Similarly, they combine contemporary criminology with new questions derived from the move-ment towards criminalizing war crimes and its international institutionalization and judicialization. Generally, by defining their object of inquiry in less institutional and legal terms than the mainstream law and political science scholarship in the area, they open up for an analysis of the various social spaces in which the possible—and sometimes failed—push for institutionalization and judicialization are played out.[61] A common thread in this literature is the focus on the agency of international law and institutions, yet its actual place is clearly disputed among the scholars in question.

Another branch of sociology of international courts that has found an inspiration in both the work of Bourdieu and that of Dezalay and Garth is a set of projects related to exploring the emergence of a field of European law with a particular focus on the two European inter- and supranational courts, the ECtHR and the Court of Justice of the European Union (formerly the ECJ). Using these approaches has enabled these authors to examine the interplay between the agency of European supranational courts and the simultaneous transformation of the social structures in which they evolve.[62] Moreover, this novel approach to the double-structuring of European law by the interplay of agency and structural transformation has allowed them to revise the taken-for-granted story of the emergence of European law and the role played by supra- and international courts in this process.[63] By using a distinct power perspective on the making of inter-national (European) law and its relative force, they have highlighted how larger societal and geopolitical currents have had an enduring impact on the evolution of European law and institutions, as well as European integration more generally.[64] Not unlike many of the studies cited above, these inquiries into the deeper socio-logics of European international courts combine insights from theories of professions and professionals with critical approaches to law and its power in society which highlights how law is

---

[60] For example Sanja Kutnjak Ivkovich and John Hagan, "La Politique de Punition et le Siège de Sarajevo: Vers une Application de la Théorie du Conflit à la Perception d'une (in)Justice Internationale" (2008) 3 (173) Actes de la recherche en sciences sociales 62.

[61] An example is Julien Serrousi, "The Cause of Universal Jurisdiction: The Rise and Fall of an International Mobilisation" in Yves Dezalay and Bryant G Garth (eds), Lawyers and the Construction of Transnational Justice (Routledge 2012). See also Pierre-Yves Condé, Des Juges à La Haye. Formation d'une Judiciabilité Universaliste, Des Amis de la Paix à la Lutte Contre l'impunité (École Normale Supérieure de Cachan 2012).

[62] Most explicitly in Madsen, "The Protracted Institutionalisation of the Strasbourg Court" (n 17).

[63] See eg Antoine Vauchez, "The Transnational Politics of Judicialization. Van Gend En Loos and the Making of EU Polity" (2010) 16(1) European Law Journal 1. See also Antonin Cohen, "Constitutionalism without Constitution: Transnational Elites between Political Mobilization and Legal Expertise in the Making of a Constitution for Europe (1940s–1960s)" (2007) 32(1) Law & Social Inquiry 109. On human rights, see Mikael Rask Madsen, La Genèse De L'europe des Droits de l'homme : Enjeux Juridiques et Stratégies d'état (France, Grande-Bretagne et Pays Scandinaves, 1945–1970) (Presses universitaires de Strasbourg 2010).

[64] Antonin Cohen and Mikael Rask Madsen, "Cold War Law: Legal Entrepreneurs and the Emergence of a European Legal Field (1945–1965)" in Volkmar Gessner and David Nelken (eds), European Ways of Law: Towards a European Sociology of Law (Hart Publishing 2007). Mikael Madsen, "Rask From Boom to Backlash? The European Court of Human Rights and the Transformation of Europe", in H Aust and D Esra (eds) The European Court of Human Rights: Current Challenges in Historical and Comparative Perspective (Edward Elgar Publishing 2011) 21–42.

mobilized, in specific cases or as part of broader legal movements.[65] It is exactly because of these combined interests that their analysis tends to find their overriding frameworks in sociological theories in the tradition of, on the one hand, Max Weber and the power and evolution of professions, and, on the other hand, theories of social configurations such as Norbert Elias, Michel Foucault, and Pierre Bourdieu.

Contemporary sociology-based studies of international courts are however not confined to the cited studies, even if they now stand out as the perhaps most distinct sociological contributions to the understanding of international courts.[66] Within the broader camps of sociological institutionalism and, to a slightly lesser extent, historical institutionalism, one finds numerous studies that could be assigned the label sociological. However, as highlighted in Section 2, some currents of sociology are by definition more focused on institutions than others and, thus, more inclined to be interested in international courts as such. While functionalism in this respect has a rather large group of followers in both law and political science, in sociology its role has been be used in either more organizational analysis of international courts or to depict the global structures of society, the latter either in a Luhmannian tradition of global society,[67] in terms of world system theory of Immanuel Wallerstein,[68] or, in more constructivist terms, as "global culture".[69] While organizational studies are focused on deeper institutional logics, neither of the approaches in the second camp are interested in international courts per se, but rather—following broadly speaking the Durkheimian tradition—on how international courts to varying degrees are important institutions in the transformation of the deeper structures of society under contemporary globalization.[70]

It is self-evidently in the field of sociology of organizations that one comes across studies that more specifically address questions directly relevant to understanding the institutional dynamics and problems of international courts. Yet while organizational sociologists have offered sophisticated frameworks and theories for such analysis, it has been predominantly lawyers and political scientists who have done the actual empirical work, importing insights from the sociology of organization for solving puzzles in existing research on international courts. The law professor Yuval Shany's work on the effectiveness of international courts is illuminating in this regard.[71] With regard to the second camp of research, a particularly interesting branch of sociology is the "world culture" literature, which in many ways builds on the earlier Stanford school of

---

[65] For example Vauchez (n 63). See also chapter 4 on jurist advocacy networks in Karen Alter, *The European Court's Political Power. Selected Essays* (Oxford University Press 2009).

[66] These sociological insights of have also been widely used up by historians interested in European law and integration, for example Morten Rasmussen, "The Origins of a Legal Revolution: The Early History of the European Court of Justice" (2008) 14(2) Journal of European Integration History 77.

[67] For example Rudolf Stichweh, *Die Weltgesellschaft: Soziologische Analysen* (Suhrkamp 2000). See also the reference n 24.

[68] For example Immanuel Wallerstein, *The Modern World-System I: Capitalist Agriculture and the Origins of the European World-Economy in the Sixteenth Century* (Academic Press 1974).

[69] Frank J Lechner and John Boli, *World Culture. Origins and Consequences* (Blackwell 2005).

[70] A somewhat similar view, although based on a more historical sociological account of globalization is found in Saskia Sassen, *Territory, Authority, Rights: From Medieval to Global Assemblages* (Princeton University Press 2006).

[71] Shany, "Assessing the Effectiveness of International Courts" (n 29).

"world polity" theory.[72] In this regard, Frank J Lechner and John Boli's analysis of the making of the International Criminal Court (ICC) provides a highly illustrative case of the sociological "world culture" research paradigm.[73] Being precisely interested in the production of world culture by a host of different globalizing practices, they emphasize the ways in which the idea of the ICC and its legal codification triggered the mobilization of more than a hundred states and some 800 NGOs.[74] This mass mobilization around the ICC they perceive as "world culture in action" and, thus, as a distinct indicator of the very existence of a global societal layer in certain fields of practice.[75] Characteristic of this scholarship on the evolving structures of world society, a single court, even one as emblematic as the ICC, is seen as no more than a specific attempt at instituting global culture. It is clearly an important attempt with a long history of fighting war by international law dating back at least a century, but the actual research interest is broader and when it does include international courts, they are seen as particular ways of instituting and articulating global society among many other ways.

## 4. Conclusion

This chapter has provided an outline of sociological approaches to international courts and how the turn to sociology changes the object of inquiry and the focus of the research. We can observe the development of a plethora of approaches ranging from post-structuralism to neo-functionalism which share an interest in making international courts intelligible as social institutions. Although there is currently a certain momentum in this area of research, the study of international courts have yet to fully benefit from this broader sociological toolbox. There is arguably still a lot to be gained, theoretically, methodologically, and ultimately empirically, by using sociological perspectives, either as add-ons to existing research or as a new paradigm for understanding international court. Basic notions of institutions and agency are defined differently in sociology which also impacts the very questions asked about international courts, including the central question of legitimacy and authority. This is however not to claim that sociological perspectives are superior but rather to underline that they give rise to different kinds of questioning which in some cases challenges widespread assumptions of what international courts are in the first place. As all the great scholars, David Caron was driven by curiosity and he was interested in what happened to legal objects of inquiry when they were viewed from other conceptual or theoretical starting points. He was not a sociologist but he was interested in the contextual understanding of law in order to understand the fundamental questions of authority and legitimacy.

---

[72] For example John W Meyer, "World Society, Institutional Theories, and the Actor" (2010) 36 Annual Review of Sociology 1.

[73] Chapter 10 in Lechner and Boli (n 69).

[74] Lechner and Boli (n 69) 221. For a further analysis of the role of NGOs in world culture see John Boli and George M Thomas, "World Culture in the World Polity: A Century of International Non-Governmental Organization" (1997) 62 (2) American Sociological Review 171.

[75] Lechner and Boli (n 69) 230.

# PART III
# PROCEDURES

# 14

# Normative Foundations of Arbitral Due Process

*Andrea K Bjorklund and Catalina Turriago Bettancourt*

## 1. Introduction

When one of us was asked to reflect on the normative foundations of due process in the realm of commercial arbitration as part of the conference launching the comparative study masterminded by Franco Ferrari, Friedrich Rosenfeld, and Dietmar Czernich,[1] that inquiry prompted a train of thought about the normative foundations due process and relatedly the role they play in investment treaty arbitration as well. In the ongoing debates about the future of investor–state dispute settlement (ISDS), the concepts of due process and the rule of law are invoked by proponents and critics alike. The former tend to rely on them to justify and defend the process, whilst the latter point out how ISDS falls short when assessed against certain rule-of-law criteria; due process can be regarded by critics either as an inadequate safeguard against rule-of-law violations or as an independent ground for inadequacy should proceedings fail to provide adequate process.

Lawyers have a lot of confidence in due process. It is not necessarily a belief that the right process will *guarantee* the right result but rather a belief that the right process will *make likely* the right result—and even that it will help to create a *defensible* result—that underpins this allegiance. A decision is certainly more likely to be in line with the rule of law if it has been made in accordance with due process. To put it another way, due process acts as a check on lawless results even if it does not guarantee perfect justice. As Lucy Reed explained in her Freshfields lecture, "due process means that persons are not to be deprived of their property or other rights, without the fair opportunity to defend themselves before neutral judges".[2]

Due process is thus a pillar of arbitration and considered to be a tool to limit arbitrators' discretion.[3] Due process protections are included in domestic arbitral statutes and international instruments such as the New York Convention,[4] the ICSID

---

[1] Franco Ferrari, Friedrich Rosenfeld, and Dietmar Czernich (eds), *Due Process as a Limit to Discretion in International Commercial Arbitration* (Kluwer Law International 2020). Professor Bjorklund gave one of ht eopening speeches at the conference on Due Process in International Arbitration hosted by New York University's Center for Transnational Litigation, Arbitration, and Commercial Law on 18 October 2019.

[2] Lucy Reed, "Ab(use) of Due Process: Sword vs Shield" (2017) 33 (3) Arbitration International 361, 366.

[3] Zoran Jordanoski, "Due Process as Minimal Procedural Safeguard in International Commercial Arbitration" (2017) 8 Iustinianus Primus Law Review 1, 1; Franco Ferrari, Friedrich Rosenfeld, and Dietmar Czernich, "General Report" in Ferrari, Rosenfeld, and Czernich (eds) (n 1) 1.

[4] Convention on the Recognition and Enforcement of Foreign Arbitral Awards, 10 June 1985, 330 UNTS 3 (entered into force 7 June 1959) (New York Convention).

Andrea K Bjorklund and Catalina Turriago Bettancourt, *Normative Foundations of Arbitral Due Process* In: *By Peaceful Means*. Edited by: Charles N Brower, Joan E Donoghue, Cian C Murphy, Cymie R Payne and Esmé R Shirlow, Oxford University Press.
© Andrea K Bjorklund and Catalina Turriago Bettancourt 2024. DOI: 10.1093/oso/9780192848086.003.0014

Convention,[5] and the United Nations Commission on International Trade Law Model Law (the UNCITRAL Model Law).[6] Failure to comply with those procedural guarantees can lead to a refusal of recognition and enforcement of an arbitral award or its vacatur.

Ensuring that disputing parties receive due process is one of the legitimising factors of arbitration. Due process is seen as ensuring that arbitration comports with the state's obligations to protect the rights of the populace and ensure justice consistent with the rule of law. A question that will be explored more deeply below is whether the protections found in the New York Convention, the ICSID Convention, and the UNCITRAL Model Law (or indeed other domestic arbitration laws) are really sufficient to perform that legitimating function, particularly if one conceives of the rule of law in a "thick" sense as ensuring substantive justice as well as procedural fairness.

In the arbitration arena, due process can be in tension with the essential principles of arbitration: party autonomy and efficiency. Due to its ambiguous nature due process is frequently the justification for party demands, triggering in some arbitral tribunals 'due process paranoia'—a reluctance to use their procedural discretion due to a fear that the award will be challenged on due process grounds.[7] Nevertheless, case law has shown that courts tend to display a pro-arbitration approach by giving deference to arbitral decisions, interpreting due process protections narrowly, and establishing a high threshold for procedural issues to amount to due process violations.[8]

Due process thus plays a significant role in international commercial arbitration. However, in this work we show why critics might argue that its role is insufficient to appease the critics of ISDS, who have raised various concerns about legitimacy. Unlike typical international commercial arbitration, ISDS usually involves the "public interest" such that decisions have a larger impact on a larger number of citizens. Therefore, critics might argue that due process guarantees fail to ensure fairness and justice in ISDS and continue to question whether private parties should make decisions related to the public interest.[9] Moreover, due process protections that looks primarily to ensuring that the procedural rights of the parties are protected in an individual case are unlikely to satisfy concerns about the lack of consistency and predictability in ISDS writ large.[10]

This chapter is divided as follows. We address the role that due process plays in international commercial arbitration in Section 2, including some analysis of the tensions between due process and the principles of party autonomy and efficiency. Section 3 then turns to a short exposition on the rule of law, with some attention paid to "thin"

---

[5] Convention on the Settlement of Investment Disputes between States and Nationals of other States, 17 UST 1270, 575 UNTS 159 (1966) (ICSID Convention).

[6] UNCITRAL Model Law on International Commercial Arbitration 1985, with Amendments as Adopted in 2006 (United Nations 2006) (UNCITRAL Model Law).

[7] Queen Mary University of London and White & Case LLP, 2015 International Arbitration Survey: Improvements and Innovations in International Arbitration, Executive Summary, <http://www.whitecase.com/sites/whitecase/files/files/download/publications/qmul-international-arbitration-survey-2015_0.pdf> 10; Reed (n 2) 364, 372.

[8] Ferrari, Rosenfeld, and Czernich (eds) (n 1) 7.

[9] Andrea K Bjorklund, "The Legitimacy of the International Centre for Settlement of Investment Disputes" in Nienke Grossman and others (eds), *Legitimacy and International Courts* (Cambridge University Press 2018) 244.

[10] ibid 245, 250. See also David D Caron, "Towards a Political Theory of International Courts and Tribunals" (2006) 24 Berkeley Journal of International Law 401.

and "thick" conceptions of the concept and how those intersect with due process protections. Section 4 then discusses the reasons why "thin" protections might be unable to appease critics of ISDS. Section 5 concludes.

## 2. Due Process in International Commercial Arbitration

Due process is an essential guarantee in judicial procedures.[11] Due process protections were originally viewed in the context of municipal courts as a constitutional right to protect individuals from overreach by state authorities.[12] However, the concept has evolved to "become one of the core pillars of private justice in arbitral procedures" as well.[13]

### 2.1 Procedural Guarantees

One of the main duties of arbitrators is to issue enforceable awards.[14] To do so, the award must comply with certain minimum procedural standards contained in domestic arbitration statutes and international rules.[15] In other words, due process shapes arbitral tribunals' decisions.

Due process protections have been adopted by the majority of states in their corresponding arbitration statutes as a means to limit arbitral tribunals' discretion.[16] A recent report from 2020, which is the introduction to a book on due process in international commercial arbitration (the Report),[17] presents the procedural guarantees adopted by nineteen states[18] in their internal legislation and interpreted by their courts. Often the municipal arbitration law mirrors the UNCITRAL Model Law. Those jurisdictions that have not adopted the UNCITRAL Model Law tend to have similar grounds for set-aside with a strong focus on procedural protections.[19] For the purposes of this short section, which primarily focuses on due process in international commercial arbitration, we will focus on the grounds for set-aside found in the UNCITRAL Model Law that are also mirrored in the New York Convention on recognition and enforcement of arbitral awards. The same standards are relevant in investment treaty arbitrations

---

[11] Ferrari, Rosenfeld, and Czernich (eds) (n 1) 1.

[12] Matti S Kurkela and Santtu Turunen, *Due Process in International Commercial Arbitration* (2nd edn, Oxford University Press 2010) 1.

[13] Ferrari, Rosenfeld, and Czernich (eds) (n 1) 1.

[14] Kurkela and Turunen (n 12) 1–2. On arbitrators' obligations more generally see Andrea K Bjorklund and Lukas Vanhonnaeker, "The Powers, Duties, and Rights of International Arbitrators" in Stefan Kröll, Andrea K Bjorklund, and Franco Ferrari (eds), *Cambridge Compendium on International Commercial and Investment Arbitration* (CUP 2023) 1012.

[15] Kurkela and Turunen (n 12) 2.

[16] Jordanoski (n 3) 1.

[17] Ferrari, Rosenfeld, and Czernich (eds) (n 1).

[18] The states are Argentina, Brazil, Canada, China, The Republic of Cyprus, France Germany, Hong Kong, India, Italy, Japan, Middle East, the Netherlands, Norway, Russia, Singapore, Switzerland, the United Kingdom, and the United States.

[19] Francesca Ragno, "Country Report: Italy" in Ferrari, Rosenfeld, and Czernich (eds) (n 1) 238.

subject to enforcement under the New York Convention and set-aside in the place of arbitration. The ICSID Convention also permits an application for annulment for violations of due process; the ICSID Convention will be discussed in Section 4.[20]

The grounds for set-aside (aka vacatur or annulment) and to refuse recognition and enforcement found in the UNCITRAL Model Law and the New York Convention concern the minimal due process protections that must be accorded to individuals for the arbitral process to pass muster. While process-related concerns can be discerned in other provisions as well, the primary process protections are in two provisions:

- The party making the application was not given proper notice of the appointment of an arbitrator or of the arbitral proceedings or was otherwise unable to present his case;[21]
- The composition of the arbitral tribunal or the arbitral procedure was not in accordance with the agreement of the parties.[22]

Furthermore, two other grounds found in the UNCITRAL Model Law and the New York Convention, arbitrability and particularly public policy, reassure the state that it can limit the types of disputes that can be sent to arbitration and preserve any core principles of the state that might be compromised in an individual arbitration.[23] Concerns on that front might also be found in the refusal of some states to countenance waivers (at least *ex ante*) of set-aside procedures or the ability to resist recognition and enforcement of awards, at least on due process grounds.[24] In addition, another measure that demonstrates states' commitment to protect the public interest and ensure private justice is the prohibition of waivers based on subject matter found in some jurisdictions. For example, courts in France have stated that waivers related to grounds that protect the public interest, like public policy, might not be permitted.[25]

Although there is agreement regarding the importance of arbitral tribunals' adherence to due process, there is no consensus with respect to its meaning as it varies among legal systems.[26] Instead, due process in arbitration constitutes a capacious concept containing procedural protections for the parties.[27] Canadian courts, for instance, have included the right to notice of a dispute, the right to be heard, and the right to an impartial

---

[20] ICSID Convention (n 5), art 52(1)(d): "that there has been a serious departure from a fundamental rule of procedure".

[21] New York Convention (n 4) art V(1)(b); UNCITRAL Model Law (n 6) art 34(2)(a)(ii).

[22] New York Convention (n 4) art V(1)(d); UNCITRAL Model Law (n 6) art 34(2)(a)(iv).

[23] The ICSID Convention contains no similar provisions.

[24] Quebec, for example, has refused to accept these waivers, though a majority of Canadian jurisdictions accept them. Frédéric Bachand and Fabien Gélinas, "The Implementation and Application of the New York Arbitration Convention in Canada" (2014) 92 Canadian Bar Review 457, 469; Andrea K Bjorklund and Benjamin R Jarvis, "Country Report: Canada" in Ferrari, Rosenfeld, and Czernich (eds) (n 1) 110–11.

[25] Ferrari, Rosenfeld, and Czernich (eds) (n 1) 16.

[26] Fabricio Fortese and Hemmi Lotta, "Procedural Fairness and Efficiency in International Arbitration" (2015) 3 (1) Groningen Journal of International Law 110, 112–113;112–13.

[27] Ferrari, Rosenfeld, and Czernich (eds) (n 1) 2.

decision as due process protections.[28] Some of these procedural guarantees are shared by other states such as Argentina,[29] Brazil,[30] China,[31] and Germany.[32]

Despite the lack of a universally accepted list of due process guarantees, the most common procedural protections include the right to be heard, the right to equal treatment of the parties, the right to proper notice of a dispute, the right of access to justice, the opportunity to present one's case, and the right to an independent and impartial decision-maker.[33]

The observance of due process has been described as one of arbitration's principal legitimizing factors.[34] That is the reason why procedural protections are recognized globally. When parties enter into an arbitral agreement, they are waiving their right to seek justice in court in the event of a dispute.[35] Since access to justice is usually considered a human right, arbitral procedures must comply with certain minimum procedural requirements to compensate for the lack of access to the judiciary.[36]

## 2.2  Due Process, Party Autonomy, and Efficiency

Party autonomy and efficiency are also two essential elements of arbitration. Parties decide to arbitrate their disputes instead of resorting to national courts "with the objective of obtaining fair, neutral procedures which are efficient and tailored to their particular dispute, without reference to the formalities of procedural rules applicable in national courts".[37]

In arbitral procedures, the principles of due process, party autonomy, and efficiency meet and it becomes arbitral tribunals' duty to balance them.[38] In practice, the normative foundations of due process are intimately linked to, and potentially even eclipsed by, other normative foundations of arbitration, including the all-important principles of party autonomy and at least theoretical efficiency.

In order to provide a basis for discussing the interplay between due process, party autonomy, and efficiency, the second two elements will be explored briefly in the next subsections.

---

[28] See *Rusk Renovations Inc v Dunsworth* 2013 NSSC 179, [19]–[32]; *Crystallex International Corporation v Bolivarian Republic of Venezuela* 2016 ONSC 4693; *Grow Biz v DLT Holdings Inc* 2001 PESCTD 27; *CE International Resources Holdings LLC v Yeap Soon Sit* 2013 BCSC 1804; *Assam Company India Limited v Canoro Resources Ltd* 2014 BCSC 370, CanLII; *1552955 Ontario Inc v Lakeside Produce Inc* 2017 ONSC 4933, CanLII; *Corporacion Transnacional de Inversiones, SA de CV v STET International, SpA and others* (1999) 45 OR (3d) 183 [Ontario Superior Court of Justice]; Reed (n 2) 366; Bjorklund and Jarvis (n 24) 93.
[29] Julio César Rivera, "Country Report: Argentina" in Ferrari, Rosenfeld, and Czernich (eds) (n 1) 43.
[30] Rafael Francisco Alves, "Country Report: Brazil" ibid 63.
[31] Tang, "Country Report: China" ibid 116.
[32] Friedrich Rosenfeld, "Country Report: Germany" ibid 177.
[33] ibid 19; Kurkela and Turunen (n 12) 2; Jordanoski (n 3) 7.
[34] Ferrari, Rosenfeld, and Czernich (eds) (n 1) 1.
[35] Kurkela and Turunen (n 12) 2.
[36] ibid 2. For a discussion of the interplay of access to justice as found in Article 6 of the European Convention of Human Rights and arbitration, see *Beg SpA v Italy*, Application No 5312/11, Judgment of 20 May 2021.
[37] Gary B Born, *International Arbitration: Law and Practice* (2nd edn, Kluwer Law International 2005) 156.
[38] Fortese and Lotta (n 26) 122.

### 2.2.1 Party autonomy

One of the most attractive features of arbitration is the principle of party autonomy, a core reason why parties choose to arbitrate their disputes. Indeed, the fact that parties opt for arbitration as a means to resolve their disputes is in itself a key manifestation of party autonomy. Arbitration law, with its associated control mechanisms, seeks to honour that critical choice. Consent to arbitration is also an important standard to ensure the parties have indeed exercised their autonomy to select arbitration. Thus, one does see objections based on consent, and relevant control mechanisms permit a challenge to the authority of arbitral tribunals on the ground that the parties have not consented to arbitration. Should those objections fail, however, due process violations become the most salient likely grounds to challenge an arbitral decision.

Furthermore, the principle of party autonomy means that parties are free within certain boundaries to decide on the rules of procedure that would govern a potential dispute between them.[39] That freedom means the disputing parties are able to select an arbitral institution should they wish to do so or opt for ad hoc arbitration, choose a place of arbitration (which will bring with it the *lex arbitri*), and even to craft a particular set of rules suitable to their particular situation and interests or, more usually, to utilize pre-established rules somewhat tailored for their particular dispute.[40]

It must be noted that party autonomy to agree on the procedure to be followed is broad as it is only limited by narrowly interpreted procedural guarantees, especially the opportunity to be heard and the provision of equal treatment.[41] In other words, the principle of party autonomy is limited by due process.

Even then, however, the significant weight given to party autonomy in arbitration is the ample freedom parties have with respect to waiving their right to resist recognition and enforcement or to apply to set aside an award—*ex post* and even *ex ante* waivers—in some jurisdictions.[42]

### 2.2.2 Efficiency

Another attractive characteristic of arbitration is its efficiency compared to court proceedings. While sometimes overstated in actual practice—and certainly years-long arbitrations exist—for more than three decades the international community has witnessed the multiple developments to promote and protect efficiency of arbitral procedures.

During its 1994 congress in Vienna, the International Council for Commercial Arbitration concluded that arbitration rules should aim to simplify arbitral proceedings instead of increasing their complexity to ensure efficiency.[43] From that time, multiple international arbitration institutions have progressively amended their institutional rules to enhance efficiency, such as by adding innovations including emergency

---

[39] Born (n 37) 156.
[40] Fortese and Hemmi (n 26) 113–14.
[41] Born (n 37) 156.
[42] Bjorklund and Jarvis (n 24) 109.
[43] Fortese and Hemmi (n 26) 117.

arbitrators who can decide urgent matters before a tribunal is constituted, establishing presumptive time limits for arbitral tribunals to honour, and even imposing penalties on arbitrators should they fail to deliver awards within the applicable period.

Similarly, the UNCITRAL Model Law enables arbitral tribunals to conduct arbitration procedures as they deem appropriate when there is no agreement by the parties, which includes the power to "determine the admissibility, relevance, materiality and weight of any evidence".[44] Managing evidentiary requests and sometimes limiting party requests can contribute to efficiency and streamlined proceedings, though such decisions cannot interfere with a party's right to be heard and to present its case.

The promotion of efficiency is not only found in arbitration rules. Courts have also been part of that journey. An example is the US Supreme Court, which held in *Hall Street Associates v Mattel* that the grounds to set-aside an award under the Federal Arbitration Act could not be expanded by the parties as those should be interpreted narrowly in order to ensure an efficient arbitration.[45]

While efficiency of arbitration is understood by some in terms of time and cost only, others have emphasized that efficiency goes beyond those two elements and also relates to the quality of the award and its enforceability.[46] The issue is, however, that "what one party considers efficient, the other often considers a violation of due process".[47] This consideration is not new. In fact, it has been suggested that in arbitration there is a "magic triangle", where parties face the dilemma of choosing only two elements from among the three values of quality of the award, time efficiency, and cost savings.[48]

## 2.3  Tensions Between Due Process and Party Autonomy and Efficiency

As already described in this chapter, party autonomy is used as a theoretical basis for honouring arbitral decisions and deferring to the parties' initial decision to opt for arbitration, and their presumptive decision to opt for everything that comes with arbitration including an exclusion from substantive review by local courts. Additionally, the general assumption that arbitration should be less cumbersome on the evidentiary front also serves as a basis for upholding arbitral decisions that arguably truncated due process.

In practice, then, there is an almost inevitable tension between party autonomy and efficiency on the one hand and due process on the other. Courts are filled with applications to set-aside or resist recognition and enforcement of arbitral awards based on due

---

[44] UNCITRAL Model Law (n 6) art 19 (2).

[45] *Hall St Assocs, LLC v Mattel, Inc,* [2008] 552 US 576; Ina C Popova and Duncan Pickard, "Country Report: United States" in Ferrari, Rosenfeld, and Czernich (eds) (n 1) 446.

[46] Jennifer Kirby, "Efficiency in International Arbitration: Whose Duty Is It?" (2015) 32(6) Journal of International Arbitration 689, 693.

[47] ibid 693.

[48] Joerg Risse, "Ten Drastic Proposals for Saving Time and Costs in Arbitral Proceedings" (2013) 29(3) Arbitration International 453, 454, 455.

process grounds.[49] While challenges to awards that threaten the procedural fairness of arbitration should be encouraged, the *abuse* of challenges based on due process grounds should be discouraged. Lucy Reed, in her Freshfields lecture, pointed out that parties often abuse due process by using it as a sword instead of a shield.[50] Built into the phraseology of due process is a recognition that there are limitations to the process to which a disputing party is entitled—they are entitled to "due" process, not "endless" process. Professor Reed also stated memorably that parties frequently present claims seeking an "endless opportunity to be heard and not merely a 'reasonable opportunity'."[51]

Indeed, the right to receive a decision is itself a part of due process, suggesting that at some point one type of process must give way to another. One need only think of *Jarndyce and Jarndyce*[52] to realize that process must be limited if it is to be linked to the rule of law, even as it is essential to the rule of law.

## 2.4  A Pro-Arbitration Approach

The lack of a single definition of due process has prompted parties to present numerous claims to courts on due process grounds.[53] Nonetheless, case law has shown that, in general, courts have a pro-enforcement approach when facing those types of claims and thus refusing recognition and enforcement or granting applications to set aside arbitral awards is uncommon.

The Report indicates that most of the courts in the nineteen states analysed interpret the grounds to set aside and to refuse recognition and enforcement narrowly.[54] That means that the threshold for a procedural disagreement to be considered a violation of due process is high. In other words, "not every breach justifies a court to set-aside or to refuse recognition and enforcement of an arbitral award".[55]

The threshold to determine whether a breach of due process amounts to a violation serious enough to warrant vacatur varies depending on the jurisdiction. However, there seems to be a consensus that a "qualified" breach is required in order to trigger a violation of due process.[56] The Report identified four categories of "qualified" breaches. The first category refers to the cause-and-effect relationship between the breach and the outcome of the award. Courts falling in this category focus on whether the tribunal's decision would have been different had there been no breach.[57] The second category requires the procedural breach to produce a demonstrable impact on the award or significant prejudice in order to qualify as a breach of due process.[58] Jurisdictions falling in

---

[49] Ferrari, Rosenfeld, and Czernich (eds) (n 1) 2.
[50] Reed (n 2) 364.
[51] ibid 376.
[52] Charles Dickens, *Bleak House* (1853; Bantam Classics 1985).
[53] Ferrari, Rosenfeld, and Czernich (eds) (n 1) 2.
[54] ibid 7.
[55] ibid 10.
[56] ibid 10–12.
[57] ibid 10.
[58] ibid 10–11.

the second category are, for instance, the United States, Singapore, India, Hong Kong, and Lebanon.[59] The third category requires a "relevant" breach.[60] Canadian courts display that trend.[61] Lastly, in the fourth category courts focus on a qualified breach causing a significant impact on an award—examples of that trend are Argentina and the United Kingdom.[62]

Due to these matters—the requirement of a 'qualified' breach and the narrow interpretation by courts with respect to the grounds to refuse recognition and enforcement and set aside awards—granting claims on due process grounds is rare.

With respect to the right to be heard, there is consensus among jurisdictions that this right is neither endless nor absolute. For instance, a decision of the Tokyo High Court in 2018 interpreting Japan's arbitration act (Law No 138 of 2003), which mirrors Article 34(2) of the Model Law, stated that arbitrators were not obliged to provide parties with never-ending opportunities to present their case.[63] More recently, in 2020, the Singapore Court of Appeal decided a set-aside application in *China Machine New Energy Corp. v Jaguar Energy Guatemala LLC*, concluding that the right to be heard based on Article 18 of the Model Law was not limitless but was tempered by reasonableness and fairness.[64]

As far as the right to equal treatment is concerned, differential treatment of parties does not generally constitute a per se breach of due process.[65] To illustrate, in Singapore, a party alleged that the tribunal had not respected his right to equal treatment and that he was not able to present the case because the tribunal did not consider an expert's report and refused to grant time extensions.[66] Nonetheless, the court refused the challenge, highlighting that equal treatment did not mean precisely identical treatment.[67] It must be noted, however, that differential treatment for parties in comparable situations is likely to constitute a violation equal treatment and thus a breach of due process.[68]

Canadian practice is to preserve arbitral autonomy over due process, or to take a slightly more complex view, to honour arbitral discretion to decide contentious procedural points.[69] In fact, the jurisprudential trend in Canada is arguably that procedural irregularities may not lead to a refusal to recognize an award unless the irregularity amounts to a public policy violation under Article V(2)(b)[70] In other words, very few challenges based on due process—either in the set-aside or in the enforcement context—are successful.[71]

[59] ibid 10–11.

[60] ibid 10–11.

[61] Bjorklund and Jarvis (n 24) 99.

[62] Ferrari, Rosenfeld, and Czernich (eds) (n 1) 10.

[63] Koji Takahashi, "Country Report: Japan" in ibid 254–55.

[64] Chiann Bao, "Return to Reason: Reigning in Runaway Due Process Claims" (2021) 38 (1) Journal of International Arbitration 59, 64–65.

[65] Ferrari, Rosenfeld, and Czernich (eds) (n 1) 31.

[66] *China Machine New Energy Copr v Jaguar Energy Guatemala LLC and another* (2018) SGHC 101; Lim (n 66) 365.

[67] China Machine (n. 67 125); Jonathan Lim, "Country Report: Singapore" in Ferrari, Rosenfeld, and Czernich (eds) (n 1) 365.

[68] ibid 31.

[69] Bjorklund and Jarvis (n 24) 93.

[70] See Bachand and Gélinas (n 24) 472.

[71] The few cases where courts decided to refuse recognition and enforcement or set-aside an award are: *Rusk Renovations v Dunsworth* 2013 NSSC 179; Luis Dreyfus SAS c Holding Tusculum BV 2008 QCCS 5903; Actherm

These are only some of the many cases that illustrate the general trend that courts display when conducting judicial review of arbitral awards. Courts give significant deference to arbitral tribunals. This practice underscores the position of many scholars that "it is possible to maintain high standards of due process, while at the same time running arbitration proceedings efficiently".[72]

## 3. The "Rule of Law" and Due Process

The preceding few pages have discussed the theoretical background of due process and the role it plays in international commercial arbitration. In the next section, we will briefly introduce the notion of the "rule of law" and discuss the interplay between it and due process in the arbitral context. The link between due process and the rule of law is undeniable. As Professor Lucy Reed has noted: "Due process is the procedural cornerstone of the 'rule of law.'"[73]

The rule of law is recognized and supported worldwide by states with differing legal systems and political structures.[74] It has been argued that "no other single political ideal has ever achieved global endorsement".[75] In fact, the rule of law is often considered a "legitimating political ideal" in modern societies.[76] However, despite the confidence almost everyone seems to have in the rule of law, an unequivocal, universally accepted definition of the concept does not exist.[77] Instead, the rule of law "continues to remain open-ended, contested as well as burdened with conflicting normative assertions".[78]

Attempts to define the rule of law are neither scarce nor new. In fact they date at least to the time of Aristotle.[79] In the nineteenth century, Dicey emphasized the supremacy of the law, that all individuals are equal before the law and its enforcement by the courts.[80] Since then, the number of definitions of the rule of law has increased. Those definitions often differ as they each contain particular historical and political aspects inherent in different societies and states.[81] A report from the International Law

---

Spol SRO, Re, 16 PPSAC (3d) 136 (ONSC 2010); *Amos Investments Ltd v Minou Enterprises Ltd* 2008 BCSC 332; *Petro-Canada v Alberta Gas Ethylene Co* (1991) 121 AR 199 (QB) reversed on unrelated grounds (1992) 127 AR 128 (ABCA 1992) and Ridley Terminals Inc v Minette Bay Ship Docking Ltd, 63 DLR (4th) 141 (BCSC 1989) affirmed 70 DLR (4th) (BCCA 1990).

[72] Ferrari, Rosenfeld, and Czernich (eds) (n 1) 38.

[73] Reed (n 2) 366.

[74] Brian Tamanaha, *On the Rule of Law: History, Politics, Theory* (Cambridge University Press 2004) 1–3.

[75] ibid 3.

[76] ibid 4.

[77] Committee on International Commercial Arbitration, "Conference Report on the Rule of Law and International Investment Law" in *International Law Association Conference Report Sydney* (Sydney 2018) (International Law Association 2018) 1, 2.

[78] Peer Zumbansen, "The Rule of Law, Legal Pluralism, and Challenges to a Western-centric View: Some Very Preliminary Observations" (2017) King's College London Law School Research Paper No 2017-05, 4 <https://papers.ssrn.com/sol3/papers.cfm?abstract_id=2869190>.

[79] Aristotle, *Politics* (H Rackham tr, Loeb Classical Library 1932). Aristotle famously contrasted the rule of law with the rule of men.

[80] AV Dicey, *Introduction to the Study of the Law and the Constitution* (4th edn, Macmillan 1893) 177-78, 208..

[81] Tamanaha (n 74) 4; ILA Report (n 77) 18.

Association Committee on the Rule of law and International Investment Law (ILA Committee) in 2018 presented notions of the rule of law from fifteen countries or regions and international organizations, offering a basis for analysis of both similarities and differences (ILA Report).[82]

Thus, finding a universal definition of the rule of law is challenging.[83] The ILA Committee attributed that difficulty to the fact that it is subject to cultural context.[84] Nonetheless, while conceptions are diverse,[85] there appears to be some level of agreement on certain core elements: "a government of laws, the supremacy of the law, and equality before the law".[86]

Another instance where there is consensus is on the categorization of the various interpretations of the rule of law into two main categories. These are sometimes called the formalistic and substantive versions,[87] or more colloquially the "thin" and "thick" theories, respectively.[88]

## 3.1  "Thin" and "Thick" Rule of Law

The "thin" rule of law focuses on the procedural and formal elements of the law,[89] whilst the "thick" rule of law takes into account the content of the law and has a moral component.[90] A norm would be deemed to adhere to the "thin" rule of law if it is in conformity with particular pre-established standards.[91] While those pre-determined criteria are not universal,[92] there are some common influential elements identified by scholars such as generality, clarity, publicity, stability, and non-retroactivity of the law, and independence of the judiciary.[93] Critics of the "thin" rule of law have argued, however, that notwithstanding the necessity of those formal elements, those are insufficient to ensure a just legal system.[94]

Thus, substantive conceptions acknowledge the formal criteria of the "thin" rule of law[95] but go further to assess the law in accordance with "standards of fairness and justice".[96] Defenders of the "thick" version link the rule of law with "good law" and social values.[97]

---

[82]  ibid.

[83]  Christopher May, *The Rule of Law: The Common Sense of Global Politics* (Edward Elgar Publishing 2014) 35.

[84]  ILA Report (n 81) 18.

[85]  ibid 2.

[86]  Simone Chesterman, "An International Rule of Law" (2008) 56(2) American Journal of Comparative Law 331, 342.

[87]  Tamanaha (n 74) 91.

[88]  ibid; ILA Report (n 81) 2.

[89]  Tamanaha (n 74) 92.

[90]  ILA Report (n 81) 3.

[91]  Ronald J Daniels and Michael Trebilcock, "The Political Economy of Rule of Law Reform in Developing Countries" (2004) 26(1) Michigan Journal of International Law 99, 105.

[92]  ibid 105.

[93]  Tamanaha (n 74) 93.

[94]  Daniels and Trebilcock (n 91) 107.

[95]  Tamanaha (n 74) 102.

[96]  Daniels and Trebilcock (n 91) 106.

[97]  ILA Report (n 81) 3.

Although there is agreement on the core elements of the "thin" and "thick" rule-of-law conceptions, each theory has been criticized.[98] Critics of the "thin" rule-of-law notion posit that it is insufficient to ensure justice in a legal system because if the rules or laws are inherently flawed or structurally deficient then merely following them will not result in a just decision; on the other hand favouring thin over thick points to the importance of predictability and certainty, the need to constrain judicial decision-making, and the role in society played by law-givers and rule-makers—usually the legislator—as representatives of the electorate.[99] As shown in the ILA Report, there are states that do not relate the notion of the rule of law contained in their legal systems to either the "thin" or "thick" conceptions.[100] Additionally, while some scholars might argue that the two branches are mutually exclusive, others tend to emphasize their interconnectivity. Some have proposed theories that combine "thin" and "thick" approaches and suggested that they are complementary.[101] For example, Tamanaha suggests that the formal and substantive versions of the rule of law each contain sub-concepts that fall in a spectrum from "thinner" to "thicker" considerations.[102]

In short, thin-rule-of-law protections seem indispensable to having just outcomes in individual cases, but if the goal is to have a robust overall system of adjudication, they might not go far enough towards achieving that goal.

## 3.2 "Thin" and "Thick" Rule of Law, Due Process, and Arbitration

The "thin" and "thick" conceptions of the rule of law can both be discerned in the foundational role due process protections are called upon to play in the arbitral context from the viewpoint of the state. In the first instance, due process is the means by which the state assures itself that arbitration is a viable alternative to litigation and one worthy of court support. In that respect it helps the state to defend its decision to support arbitration.

In the second instance, it is the means by which the state fulfils its duty to protect the rights of its citizens—the due process requirements are a way to protect its citizens at least at a minimal level—to ensure that they get the private justice for which they have contracted, and a private justice that warrants the use of the word "justice". Arbitral agreements prevent access to courts but compliance with procedural standards during the arbitral procedure ensure access to justice through a reasoned award enforceable in a court if necessary.

Because of the emphasis in the New York Convention, the UNCITRAL Model Law, and other state arbitral statutes on the "thin" types of protections, it is tempting to view arbitration as related only to the "thin" rule of law. Certainly, in the after-the-fact

---

[98]   ibid 4.
[99]   Daniels and Trebilcock (n 91) 107.
[100]   ILA Report (n 81) 7.
[101]   Peter Rijpkema, "The Rule of Law Beyond Thick and Thin" (2013) 32 Law and Philosophy 793.
[102]   Tamanaha (n 74) 91.

sense—in the context of review of arbitral awards—that has generally been true. A high threshold must be met in order for a procedural breach to be considered a violation of due process. In addition, both the architecture of the New York Convention and of the Model Law could be considered to exemplify "thin" protections only, as there is no reference to standards of justice or "good law" that would satisfy advocates of "thick" rule-of-law protections.

However, we suggest that at least some states have believed—or at least hoped—that due process would help to ensure that arbitration is consistent with the rule of law in the "thicker" sense as well, given their confidence in the power of process and the safety net of public policy. That view was perhaps always more aspirational than actual, especially given the competing principles of arbitration—party autonomy and efficiency—which sometimes work to temper the power of these rule-of-law concepts. The extent to which it is not borne out in practice might be viewed as illustrated in the investment treaty arbitration arena.

## 4. Intersection of Legitimacy Concerns in ISDS and "Thin" Protections

Procedural protections that are appropriate for international commercial arbitration might be deemed unsuitable, or at least inadequate, for investment treaty arbitration. Thin rule-of-law protections enshrined in due process guarantees can ensure that parties get what they have asked for and that the results meet minimum standards of justice, consistent with the principles of party autonomy as evidenced by their consent to arbitration and in light of the *inter partes* nature of the dispute. The absence of thicker rule-of-law protections to bolster reliance on due process might explain some of the legitimacy critiques levelled against investment treaty arbitration.

Those concerns can be divided into various categories: one possibility is to group them as concerns about intrusions into sovereignty; a lack of consistency in arbitral decision-making; inadequate transparency in the process; and various procedural concerns around arbitral proceedings themselves, including abuse of process and duplication of proceedings.[103]

In commercial arbitration, at least in the idealistic hypothetical arbitration, the goals of the parties are likely to be aligned as evidenced by their agreement to arbitrate any dispute between them. That means the parties have opted to adopt an efficient process that they have designed together to support the outcome they desire in a case whose rough contours they have already envisaged given their pre-existing relationship. The result is to be encapsulated in a decision given by an arbitrator or arbitrators that they have chosen because of their expertise.

This is somewhat idealized; we would not have nearly the number of decisions challenging the validity of the arbitral agreement if the disputing parties' goals were always

---

[103] Bjorklund (n 9).

aligned. Yet there is still general acceptance that due process protections, applied with deference in international commercial arbitration, accord with the "thin" rule of law, and that is sufficient in that context. The procedure and its outcome are usually *inter partes*.[104] The decision is not precedential—it might not even be published—and thus the impact on the "thick" rule of law is minimal.

In the aggregate, of course, commercial arbitration might also pose threats to the "thick" rule of law. One argument is that if so many commercial cases are taken out of the courts that judges are hampered in their ability to develop the law that this might mean commercial arbitration threatens the rule of law in a state if that state cannot develop substantive principles.[105] Yet that concern seems not to have come to pass in that commercial courts in various jurisdictions continue to hear many cases. English courts in particular continue to enjoy their primacy as centres for the adjudication of complex commercial disputes, though other jurisdictions now compete on that front.[106]

Investment arbitration, by contrast, might well be different. Investment treaty arbitration involves the public interest.[107] While cases vary—some are indeed *inter partes* with minimal spillover effects – certain matters go beyond the commercial interests of a few to involve the citizenry of a host state. The disputes managed in investment treaty arbitration often relate to topics that are important for citizens, including natural resources, environment, infrastructure, utilities, challenges to regulations and laws, and human rights, among others.[108] Moreover, the costs of an investor–state arbitration and a potential costly award for compensation are borne by citizens.[109]

Furthermore, the goals of the two disputing parties that were aligned in commercial arbitration are not necessarily aligned—at least at the time of the dispute—in investment treaty arbitration. "Arbitration without privity",[110] as Jan Paulsson so memorably put it, means that the state has offered to arbitrate a type of dispute (an investment dispute) with a certain class of persons (covered investors), but will not necessarily have expected to see the specific dispute that presents itself; depending on the nature of the investment and the regulatory structure of the state, the state might not know of the investment's existence, or of its foreign ownership, prior to the dispute's crystallization. Thus, notwithstanding its standing offer to arbitrate, the state might not want to resolve this particular dispute with this particular investor under this particular treaty. Yet because it has agreed to do so, its ability to refuse to arbitrate is curtailed. The due process protections presume consent to arbitrate (consent is dealt with by other set-aside and annulment provisions). The state, acting on behalf of its citizenry, might have

---

[104] Enuma U Moneke, "The Quest for Transparency in Investor–State Arbitration: Are the Transparency Rules and the Mauritius Convention Effective Instruments of Reform?" (2020) 86 (2) International Journal of Arbitration Mediation and Dispute Management 157, 164.

[105] See Judith Resnik, "Diffusing Disputes: The Public in the Private of Arbitration, the Private in Courts, and the Erasure of Rights" (2015) 124 Yale Law Journal 2680

[106] Lucas Clover Alcolea, "The Rise of the International Commercial Court: A Threat to the Rule of Law?" (2022) 13 (3) Journal of International Dispute Settlement 413.

[107] Daniel Barstow Magraw and Niranjali Manel Amerasinghe, "Transparency and Public Participation in Investor–State Arbitration" (2009) 15 (2) ILSA Journal of International & Comparative Law 337, 339.

[108] ibid 339.

[109] Moneke (n 104) 165.

[110] Jan Paulsson, "Arbitration without Privity" [1995] ICSID Review— Foreign Investment Law Journal 232.

reservations about arbitrating a discrete dispute, even though the principle of consent to arbitration and *that* exercise of party autonomy holds the state to the offer to arbitrate it made in its treaty.

Investment arbitration uses a framework often common in commercial arbitration, though it also can trace its genesis to state–state arbitration.[111] While there is comfort with respect to the procedural safeguards contained in the international commercial arbitration model, those who emphasize the public law elements of treaty-based investment arbitration are unlikely to be satisfied with the protections that thin due process rules afford.[112] The drafters of the ICSID Convention chose to embrace limited grounds of annulment rather than to permit full-fledged appeal. This decision might well have been rational at the time (it is useful to remember that when the Convention was negotiated investment arbitrations were almost all contract based). But if one is concerned about ensuring the validity of a system, or creating a framework that permits the creation of a system, thin protections might be inadequate.

Critics focused on the public element of investment treaty arbitration might stress that the only protections available are that of "thin" nature and thus raise concerns regarding the "substantive correctness" of arbitral tribunals' decisions affecting public interests.[113] They might argue that receiving minimal procedural "thin" protections in exchange for preventing national courts from hearing disputes involving matters of public interest is insufficient. Even worse, opponents could go further and classify investment treaty arbitration as unable to provide private justice that deserves the qualification "justice". Or, to put it another way, some might not be convinced that "thin" rule-of-law aspects are adequate to protect the interests of the populace, yet "thick" rule of law seems foreclosed by the existing legal architecture of arbitration and the competing principles of consent and party autonomy.

Broude and Henckels argue that investor–state arbitration case law suggests that arbitral tribunals perceive investors' rights as endowments and the rights of the host state's population as aspirations.[114] They contend that arbitrators might not even take into account the rights of the host state citizens as those are deemed to be represented by the state.[115] This dichotomy—whether real or perceived—between the citizens and the state that represents them on the international stage also places a strain on the legitimacy of arbitration. This democratic deficit arguably stems from domestic governance and not from investment arbitration, but it manifests itself in investment treaty arbitration in particular. If the state's consent to arbitration is not accepted as having been given on behalf of its citizenry (and moreover in a Westphalian system, arguments that consent was lacking will not be successful), more pressure is placed on the protections that do exist—generally due process requirements affiliated with the thin rule of law.

---

[111] Moneke (n 104) 160. See, also: Taylor St John, *The Rise of Investor-State Arbitration: Politics, Law, and Unintended Consequences* (Oxford University Press 2018).

[112] Bjorklund (n 9) 238.

[113] ibid 237.

[114] Tomer Broude and Caroline Henckels, "Not all Rights are Created Equal: a Loss–Gain Frame of Investor Rights and Human Rights" (2021) 34 Leiden Journal of International Law 93, 101.

[115] ibid 107.

Without "thick" rule-of-law protections, there is no easy avenue for "thick" due process consideration to be used as part of the control mechanism for arbitration.

We might conclude that a tribunal's decision to deny the reception of late submissions during a proceeding, or to enforce an award despite a party's not being able to afford to attend the proceeding, or to deny expansion of due process grounds for set-aside or refuse enforcement of awards, does not violate due process. That might be unquestionable in the realm of international commercial arbitration. However, some might question whether the same outcome should ensue if the party providing late submissions, or unable to afford an arbitral proceeding, or that was denied the expansion of grounds to challenge awards, represents the interests of a population. This concern is exacerbated by the fact that private individuals—the arbitral tribunal—are the ones making decisions affecting the public.[116] David Caron, in his discussion of bounded strategic spaces, discussed the differences between "community-oriented institutions" and "party-originated institutions".[117] International commercial arbitration is fairly clearly the latter; investment treaty arbitration is arguably a bit of both, depending on the dispute. Yet to the extent the public wants it to be, or perceives it to be, a community-oriented institution, protections that are geared primarily towards the parties will seem inadequate.

Another legitimacy concern for ISDS is the lack of consistency and predictability.[118] To the extent that the content of the law itself is unpredictable, disputing parties might well raise concerns about the substantive due process they are accorded—about the "thick" rule-of-law issues aligned with concerns about justice. Decisions are often published, creating a corpus of international law and heightening the sense in which ISDS is creating a "system"—or is perceived to be creating a "system"—that should meet certain rule of law standards: thick as well as thin.

In a slightly odd twist, investment law might be the victim of its own success as it is perceived to be an effective and desirable means of dispute settlement. Building on Professor Shany's "external legitimisation" concept,[119] even if the "thin" procedural protections found in the New York Convention and the ICSID Convention can be viewed as ensuring the effectiveness of arbitration, to the extent that investment treaty arbitration is perceived as illegitimate by outsiders, that effectiveness only increases that perceived illegitimacy.[120] Thus, "thin" due process protections might even be viewed as undermining, or working against, thicker rule-of-law concerns.

Critics of investment treaty arbitration have ample tools to argue that the "thin" protections contained in the New York Convention and the ICSID Convention as grounds to refuse recognition and enforcement or set aside arbitral awards do not suffice to allay legitimacy concerns. To mitigate those concerns, some might propose the inclusion of

---

[116] Bjorklund (n 9) 244.

[117] Caron, "Towards a Political Theory of International Courts and Tribunals" (n 10) 403–04.

[118] Bjorklund (n 9) 245.

[119] Yuval Shany, "Assessing the Effectiveness of International Courts: A Goal-Based Approach" (2012) 106 (2) American Journal of International Law, 225.

[120] Bjorklund (n 9) 240.

"thick" provisions. Nevertheless, if subjective elements such as "good law" and "justice" are included as grounds to challenge awards, the number of claims based on due process grounds would likely increase substantially. Due process paranoia could increase, and the powers of the dispute settlement body—perhaps a multilateral investment court or perhaps an appellate body only—would also increase extraordinarily. This would seem to be something even beyond the appellate review currently under consideration by UNCITRAL Working Group III, but something more akin to "cassation" review. Conferring that kind of power on an international tribunal—even a permanent one—would be unusual.

## 5. Conclusion

Despite the lack of a general definition of due process and rule of law, those principles are protected both domestically and internationally. Due process and particularly the "thin" rule of law play legitimizing roles in arbitration. On the one hand, they contribute to the fulfilment of states' obligation to ensure justice to the citizens through a valid private dispute resolution mechanism. Moreover, they guarantee that any enforceable award is in line with at least minimal procedural protections. The due process protections included in the UNCITRAL Model Law, the New York Convention, and the ICSID Convention are of a "thin" nature.

Due to its flexibility and availability, counsel and parties have often brought challenges based on due process grounds, raising concerns of "due process paranoia" among arbitrators. These concerns appear to be largely unfounded, however, as courts have displayed pro-enforcement behaviour by establishing a high threshold for due process violations.

This can be considered a victory for international commercial arbitration. However, critics of investment treaty arbitration would likely not view this outcome the same way. A due process standard that is undeniably fair in the former might seem unfair in the latter when the situation involves the public interest with decisions that reach beyond the two parties to the dispute. Consequently, critics could argue that "thin" protections are inadequate in a context in which "thick" protections are called for. It is likely only a matter of time until "thick", or at least "thicker", protections are proposed in the context of review of arbitral awards or of first-instance tribunal decisions in the event of a two-tiered multilateral investment court.

## Dedication

*Andrea K Bjorklund*

Writing this chapter in honour of David Caron is bittersweet. I wish he were going to be able to discuss and critique it with me as we did so often about topics of general interest. I first met David when I was an attorney in "L" and he was one of our experts in the

*Loewen* case (The *Loewen Group Inc., et al. v United States*, ICSID Case No ARB(AF)/ 98/3.). When I took a job at the University of California, Davis—just down the road from Berkeley—he generously acted as a mentor but even more wonderfully treated me as a colleague and as a friend. It was a pleasure to spend time with him and Susan in their beautiful home overlooking San Francisco Bay, with the Farallon Islands hovering on the horizon on clear days, and then later to see them in the United Kingdom when he took on the deanship at King's College London. Over the years I have met several of David's students (a few of whom I also taught!); all are unanimous in their praise of him as a supervisor and mentor. Meeting them creates a tangible connection with David, whom I miss. It was a pleasure to write this essay with my former LL.M. student Catalina Turriago, thereby continuing David's tradition of mentoring junior scholars. Catalina was an excellent student and I am honoured now to call her my friend and colleague.

# 15

# By Effective Means

## Cross-Cutting Aspects of Fairness in International Dispute Resolution

*Philippa Webb*

## 1. Introduction

David Caron's career in international dispute resolution spanned roles as judge ad hoc at the International Court of Justice (ICJ), judge at the Iran-US Claims Tribunal, and arbitrator, expert and counsel in multiple fora, including inter-state, investor–state, and commercial arbitrations. An enduring feature of his contributions to peaceful dispute settlement in these roles was his sense of fairness, just as an enduring personal memory of David is how he treated everyone—from a young student to a visiting dignitary—as equals. He seemingly had unlimited time and energy to engage with all of us, with respect, warmth, and grace.

Drawing on David Caron's Expert Opinion in *Chevron Corporation and Texaco Petroleum Company v The Republic of Ecuador*,[1] I explore two aspects of procedural fairness—undue delay and equality of arms—that arise in the consideration of "effective means" in the context of investment claims, in the assessment of the fairness of a criminal trial under international human rights law, and in due process considerations of the ICJ.

The Expert Opinion addressed the meaning of a certain provision of the Treaty between the United States of America and the Republic of Ecuador concerning the Encouragement and Reciprocal Protection of Investment (Treaty).[2] Article II(7) provided that "[e]ach Party shall provide effective means of asserting claims and enforcing rights with respect to investment, investment agreements, and investment authorizations". The Opinion sought to define the standard to be applied by the Tribunal in general and within the context of the claims raised within the arbitration.[3] Applying the

---

[1] *Chevron Corporation and Texaco Petroleum Company v the Republic of Ecuador*, UNCITRAL, PCA Case No 2009-23, Expert Opinion of Professor David D Caron as to Article II(7) of the treaty (3 September 2010) (Expert Opinion). The Expert Opinion was prepared at the request of the claimants. In *Chevron Corporation and Texaco Petroleum Company v Ecuador*, Second partial award on Track II, PCA Case No 2009-23, IIC 1466 (2018), 30 August 2018 (2018 Partial Award), the tribunal refers to a second expert report by David D Caron dated 24 August 2012, but this does not appear to be publicly available.

[2] Treaty between the United States of America and the Republic of Ecuador concerning the Encouragement and Reciprocal Protection of Investment (signed 27 August 1993) Senate Treaty Doc No 103-15.

[3] Expert Opinion (n 1) 4.

Philippa Webb, *By Effective Means* In: *By Peaceful Means*. Edited by: Charles N Brower, Joan E Donoghue, Cian C Murphy, Cymie R Payne and Esmé R Shirlow, Oxford University Press. © Philippa Webb 2024. DOI: 10.1093/oso/9780192848086.003.0015

principles in the Vienna Convention on the Law of Treaties, the Opinion concluded that Article II(7)

> sets forth a positive and mandatory obligation to establish and supply measures that are not only designed to, but are also adequate in practice to, facilitate the investor bringing a cause of action for the possession or enjoyment of a privilege, and for the State's acknowledgment and preservation, as well as execution, of the investor's powers and privileges as pertaining to every kind of investment in the territory of one Party owned or controlled directly or indirectly by nationals or companies of the other Party.[4]

The Expert Opinion drew on a wide range of international law sources, including the jurisprudence of the ICJ, the European Court of Human Rights, and the Inter-American Court of Human Rights.[5] In the same spirit, but without the same focus on a specific provision in a bilateral investment treaty, this chapter will examine "effective means" in terms of the cross-cutting concepts of undue delay and equality of arms in the jurisprudence of international human rights bodies and the ICJ.


## 2. Undue Delay

Undue delay in domestic court proceedings may constitute a violation of the "effective means" standard in an investment arbitration.[6]

In his Expert Opinion, Caron observed that prior arbitral decisions addressing Article II(7) of the Treaty had found that "[f]or any 'means' of asserting claims or enforcing rights to be effective, it must not be subject to indefinite or undue delay. Undue delay in effect amounts to a denial of access to those means."[7] He turned to "several applicable points of guidance offered by the ECHR jurisprudence".[8] In particular, Caron observed that in applying Article 6(1) of the European Convention, the Court "considers allegations of undue delay on a case-by-case basis utilizing the five factors".[9] These factors are: complexity of the issue; the applicant's conduct; the overall conduct of judicial authorities overseeing the trial; what is at stake for the applicant in the

---

[4] ibid 4 and 77, §170.

[5] ibid 121–25. In the context of a different dispute, but addressing the same article of the BIT, a tribunal in *Chevron* had found that the "effective protection" standard to be "*lex specialis* and not a mere restatement of the law on denial of justice"; it considered "effective means" to be "distinct and potentially less-demanding" than the denial of justice standard: *Chevron Corporation (USA) and Texaco Petroleum Company (USA) v The Republic of Ecuador*, Partial Award on the Merits, PCA Case No 34877, 30 March 2010, §§242–244 (2010 Commercial Cases Partial Award).

[6] U Kriebaum, "Investment Arbitration—Rule of Law Demands of the Domestic Judiciary (Denial of Justice, Judicial Expropriation, Effective Means)" (2020) 1 Social Science Research Network 24; M Sattorova, "Denial of Justice Disguised? Investment Arbitration and the Protection of Foreign Investors from Judicial Misconduct" (2012) 61 International & Comparative Law Quarterly 223, 236; AP Karreman and K Dharamananda, "Time to Reassess Remedies for Delays Breaching 'Effective Means'" (2015) 30 ICSID Review 118, 120, 125.

[7] Expert Opinion (n 1) §101, citing 2010 Commercial Cases Partial Award (n 3) §250.

[8] Expert Opinion (n 1) §128.

[9] ibid §164.

proceedings; and state of the hearings, which he described as: "if, for instance, there has been much judicial activity leading up to the point of review, it is possible that a long, but full, delay will not be actionable; while a case that lays stagnant for a significant period of time will likely be actionable".[10]

Caron also pointed to the practice of the Inter-American Court. He explained that the Court considers three factors in assessing whether a delay is "undue": "a) the complexity of the matter; b) the judicial activity of the interested party; and c) the behavior of the judicial authorities. In addition to these factors, the IACHR appears to have codified another factor of 'effectiveness': Judicial action in the dispute must be judged not only by its quantity, but also its quality."[11]

On the basis of his review of the jurisprudence, Caron adopted four factors for determining whether an undue delay had occurred: "complexity of the litigation", "significance of the interests at stake", "the behavior of both the litigants", and "the overall conduct of the relevant authorities", meaning the courts.[12] He observed that:

[b]y undertaking such an analysis, the Tribunal can assess whether, by design or by discretion, the seven years between the commencement of the Lago Agrio litigation and Claimants' assertion of its preliminary jurisdictional objections and today merit the conclusion that the lack of a preliminary decision on Claimants' threshold objections constitutes a breach of Ecuador's obligations of providing effective means of asserting claims and enforcing rights.[13]

The issue of undue delay and its impact on "effective means" was considered in 2010 by a tribunal in the *Chevron* litigation that addressed Article II(7) in the context of a different dispute. In its Partial Award on the merits, the tribunal found a breach of the "effective means" obligation through the undue delay of the Ecuadorian courts in deciding seven cases regarding contractual claims for payment. It explained:

For any "means" of asserting claims or enforcing rights to be effective, it must not be subject to indefinite or undue delay. Undue delay in effect amounts to a denial of access to those means. The Tribunal therefore finds that Article II(7) applies to the Claimants' claims for undue delay in their seven cases in the Ecuadorian courts. The Ecuadorian legal system must thus, according to Article II(7), provide foreign investors with means of enforcing legitimate rights within a reasonable amount of time. The limit of reasonableness is dependent on the circumstances of the case. As with denial of justice under customary international law, some of the factors that may be considered are the complexity of the case, the behavior of the litigants involved, the significance of the interests at stake in the case, and the behavior of the courts themselves.[14]

---

[10] ibid §165.
[11] ibid §§166–167.
[12] ibid §§101, 169.
[13] ibid §169.
[14] 2010 Commercial Cases Partial Award (n 3) §250.

All the cases had been pending in the Ecuadorian legal system for at least thirteen years at the time arbitration commenced. The tribunal considered that the delay was not justified by the complexity of the cases because they were "in essence straightforward contractual disputes".[15] There was "no evidence that any action by the Claimants has actively and significantly contributed to the delays".[16] On the other hand, the courts in Ecuador "failed to act with reasonable dispatch" with "prolonged periods of inactivity".[17] A generalized backlog in the courts could not excuse the delays because

> [t]o the extent that generalized court congestion could alone produce the persistent and long delays of the kind observed here, it would evidence a systemic problem with the design and operation of the Ecuadorian judicial system and would breach Article II(7) according to the systemic standard advocated by the Respondent itself.[18]

For court congestion to be a valid defence, the tribunal considered that it "must be temporary and must be promptly and effectively addressed by the host state".[19] The tribunal held Ecuador liable for damages of US$ 77.74 million plus interest.[20] The 2018 Partial Award in the *Chevron* litigation, by a different tribunal, took note of the other tribunal's interpretation of Article II(7) of the Treaty.[21]

In the context of international human rights law, the right to be tried without undue delay is one of the most litigated aspects of the right to a fair trial. The Human Rights Committee has found violations in cases from every region of the world.[22] More than half the fair trial violations confirmed by the European Court concerned unduly lengthy proceedings.[23] International human rights bodies apply a four-factor test that maps well onto what Caron set out in his Expert Opinion.[24] International human rights bodies consider

(i) the complexity of the case, which is equivalent to what Caron called the "complexity of the litigation";

(ii) the conduct of the defendant, which corresponds to the "the behaviour of both litigants" in civil context;

(iii) the conduct of the authorities, which matches "the overall conduct of the relevant authorities"; and

(iv) the level of prejudice to the defendant as a result of the delay, which relates to "the significant of the interests at stake" in a civil proceeding.

---

[15] ibid §254.
[16] ibid §255.
[17] ibid §256.
[18] ibid §263.
[19] ibid §264.
[20] ibid Decision, ss 2 and 5; 2018 Partial Award (n 1) §4.96.
[21] ibid §4.99; see also §7.17.
[22] M Nowak, *U.N. Covenant on Civil and Political Rights, CCPR Commentary* (2nd rev. edn, N.P. Engel 2005) 334.
[23] Between 1959 and 2017, the figure was 52 per cent. See ECtHR, "Violations by Article and by State 1959–2017", <https://www.echr.coe.int/Documents/Stats_violation_1959_2017_ENG.pdf>.
[24] Expert Opinion (n 1) §§101, 169.

Three observations are worth making when comparing the consideration of undue delay in the context of "effective means" and as a component of the right to a fair trial.

First, Caron and the tribunal considered the practice of the European and Inter-American Courts, but not that of the treaty body that monitors compliance with the International Covenant on Civil and Political Rights (ICCPR) for all States Parties, the Human Rights Committee. The Human Rights Committee explicitly recognises that the first three factors are to be taken into account when assessing undue delay, namely "the complexity of the case, the conduct of the accused, and the manner in which the matter was dealt with by the administrative and judicial authorities".[25] However, in its practice, it has not consistently taken into account the fourth factor of whether the delay resulted in any "prejudice" to the defendant. In its limited case law to date, the African Court of Human and Peoples' Rights appears only to have taken into account three factors (complexity, conduct of the parties, and conduct of the authorities) but not the fourth factor of prejudice.[26] However, the African Commission has explicitly stated in its Principles and Guidelines on the Right to a Fair Trial and Legal Assistance in Africa that among the "[f]actors relevant to what constitutes undue delay" is "whether an accused is detained pending proceedings, and the interest of the person at stake in the proceedings".[27] The international criminal courts have also applied the four factors, including prejudice, to international criminal proceedings.[28]

Second, whereas assessing the complexity of proceedings may in essence be a similar exercise regardless of whether they are civil or criminal, the factor of "prejudice to the defendant" varies in content from "what is at stake for the applicant" in a civil proceeding.[29] Long delays may interact with other fair trial rights and cause prejudice to the defendant's ability to mount a defence. According to the European Court, prejudice may arise if due to the lapse of time "the quality of the evidence available" is damaged.[30]

---

[25] HRC, General Comment No 32 (2007), §35. See also WGAD, *Göksan v Turkey* (Opinion No 53/2019), 16 August 2019, §85; WGAD, *Hussein v Egypt* (Opinion No 83/2017), 22 November 2017, §77. See A Clooney and P Webb, *The Right to a Fair Trial in International Law* (Oxford University Press 2020) 400.

[26] See eg ACtHPR, *Rajabu v Tanzania* (App no 007/2015), 28 November 2019, §64; ACtHPR, *Onyango Nganyi v Tanzania* (App no 006/2013), 18 March 2016, §136; ACtHPR, *Thomas v Tanzania* (App no 005/2013), 20 November 2015, §104. Cf. ACtHPR, *Mallya v Tanzania* (App no 018/2015), 26 September 2019, §§50–53 (mentioning only the three-factor test at §50 but, at §53, also taking into account the state's conduct for the prejudice it bore to the defendant: ie preventing him from exercising his right to appeal). See also ECOWAS CCJ, *Lieutenant Colonel Silas Jock Santoi v Nigeria* (Suit no ECW/CCJ/APP/17/2018), 23 January 2019, §94 (considering, as a fourth factor, "the nature of the dispute [issues for determination, type of consequences on the private or professional life of the people or subjects involved, particularly the significance of the decision for the parties]"); ECOWAS CCJ, *Maseda Industrie SA v Mali* (Suit No ECW/CCJ/APP/10/16), 24 January 2017, §44 (taking into account, as a fourth factor, "l'enjeu du litige pour les parties").

[27] African Commission on Human and Peoples' Rights (ACmHPR) Principles on Fair Trial in Africa Principle N(5)(c). In ACmHPR, *Gabre-Selassie v Ethiopia* (Comm no 301/05), 24 October–7 November 2011, §237, the ACmHPR noted that "even if the Respondent State did not intend to delay the proceedings the African Commission can still review the prejudice the delay has caused the defendants" and ordered compensation.

[28] *Prosecutor v Gbagbo* (Decision) [2013] ICC-02/11-01/11-432, §39; *Prosecutor v Katanga* (Judgment) [2010] ICC-01/04-01/07-2288, §54, n 102; *Prosecutor v Gatete* (Judgment) ICTR-00-61-A (9 October 2012), §18; *Prosecutor v Barayagwiza* (Decision) ICTR-97-19-AR72 (3 November 1999), §§75–77; *Prosecutor v Bizimungu et al.* (Decision) ICTR-99-50-T (27 February 2009), §9; *Prosecutor v Halilović* (Decision) IT-01-48-A (27 October 2006), §§17–20; IRMCT, *Prosecutor v Šešelj* (Judgment) MICT-16-99-A (11 April 2018), §41.

[29] Note, however, that the European Court has described prejudice as "what is at stake" for the defendant: ECtHR (GC), *Frydlender v France* (App no 30979/96), 27 June 2000, §45. See also, *Attorney General's Reference No. 2 of 2001* [2003] UKHL 68, §§16, 146; *Mills v The Queen* [1986] 1 SCR 863, 26 June 1986, §145.

[30] ECtHR, *Massey v United Kingdom* (App no 14399/02), 16 November 2004, §27.

Delay may also lead to witnesses becoming unavailable (due to death or moving away) and the passage of time may affect the memory of witnesses.[31] The Inter-American Court has observed that "[i]f the passage of time has a relevant impact on the judicial situation of the individual, the proceedings should be carried out more promptly so that the case is decided as soon as possible".[32] Moreover, certain types of defendant are more vulnerable and the assessment of prejudice caused by delay requires particular diligence, such as defendants in pre-trial detention, juvenile defendants, and defendants facing the death penalty.[33]

Third, the observations of the *Chevron* tribunal regarding court backlogs are applicable to congestion causing delays in criminal proceedings as well. According to the Human Rights Committee, a state's "difficult economic situation" does not justify undue delay because the rights in the ICCPR "constitute minimum standards which all States Parties have agreed to observe".[34] The Committee, for example, found a violation of the right to be tried without undue delay when there was a delay of eight years caused by "the lack of administrative support available to the judiciary" forcing judges to "write out every word verbatim during the hearings, because of the absence of transcribers".[35] The European Court has also repeatedly pointed out that it is the responsibility of states to "organise their legal systems in such a way that their courts" can comply with the requirements of trial within a reasonable time.[36] The Court has however accepted that "a temporary backlog ... does not involve liability on the part of [states] provided that they take, with the requisite promptness, remedial action to deal with an exceptional situation of this kind".[37]

For its part, the ICJ has addressed the issue of undue delay in diplomatic protection claims in which a party has argued that the exhaustion of local remedies would have been futile. In the International Law Commission (ILC) Draft Articles on Diplomatic Protection, "[l]ocal remedies do not need to be exhausted where: ... there is undue delay in the remedial process which is attributable to the State alleged to be responsible".[38] In the *Interhandel* case, the ICJ considered the claims of Interhandel, a Swiss-based company espoused by Switzerland. The United States argued that Interhandel had not exhausted remedies in US courts.[39] Considering that proceedings initiated by Interhandel were still pending before a US court, the ICJ held that local remedies

---

[31] See eg ICTR Gatete Appeal Judgment of 9 October 2012, §§30, 32.

[32] *Valle Jaramillo v Colombia* (Judgment) Inter-American Court of Human Rights Series C No 192 (27 November 2008), §155.

[33] See Clooney and Webb (n 25) 418.

[34] HRC, *Lubuto v Zambia* (Comm no 390/1990), 31 October 1995, §7.3.

[35] ibid §§5.1, 7.3. The records were later typed out and had to be proofread by the judges.

[36] ECtHR (GC), *Zana v Turkey* (69/1996/688/880), 25 November 1997, §83; ECtHR, *Abdoella v Netherlands* (App no 12728/87), 25 November 1992, §24; ECtHR, *Dobbertin v France* (App no 13089/87), 25 February 1993, §44.

[37] In ECtHR, *Milasi v Italy* (App. No 10527/83), 25 June 1987, §18 and ECtHR, *Baggetta v Italy* (App no 10256/83), 25 June 1987, §§23–25, insufficient efforts were made to improve working conditions in the courts. See also ACmHPR, *Kwoyelo v Uganda* (Comm no 431/12), 12–22 February 2018, §251; ECOWAS CCJ, *Diane v Mali* (Suit no ECW/CCJ/APP/35/17), 21 May 2018, §§41–45.

[38] ILC Draft Articles on Diplomatic Protection (2006), art 15(b).

[39] Interhandel *(Switzerland v United States of America)* (Preliminary Objections, Judgment) [1959] ICJ Rep 6.

had not yet been exhausted; they were also not futile even though the claims had been pursued in US courts for eleven years.[40]

The argument that local remedies had been rendered futile by delay was also rejected by the ICJ in the *Diallo* case, which concerned the treatment of a Guinean businessman and his companies by the government of the Democratic Republic of the Congo (DRC).[41] Exercising diplomatic protection over Mr Diallo, Guinea argued that "[a]fter eight years of proceedings the DRC has shown itself to be incapable of invoking so much as a single real remedy that would have been available to Mr. Diallo" in respect of the violation of his rights as an individual.[42] It emphasized that "excessive delays of the Congolese judicial authorities in the settlement of the cases brought before them and the 'unlawful administrative practices' allegedly inherent in the Congolese legal system".[43] The Court however found that the cases facing delay concerned Mr Diallo's companies and not his direct rights as a shareholder and therefore concluded that the objection as to inadmissibility raised by the DRC on the ground of the failure to exhaust the local remedies against the alleged violations of Mr Diallo's direct rights could not be upheld.[44]

In a case with facts closer to those that arise in investment arbitration, the United States brought proceedings against Italy arising out of a requisition by Italy of the plant and related assets of a company previously known as Elettronica Sicula SpA (ELSI), an Italian company said to have been 100 per cent owned by two US companies.[45] Among various claims, the United States alleged that the time taken (sixteen months) before the Prefect of Palermo ruled on ELSI's administrative appeal against the requisition order was an unreasonable delay that constituted "a denial of the level of procedural justice accorded by international law".[46] The Court rejected this argument, observing that it "must be doubted whether in all the circumstances, the delay in the Prefect's ruling in this case can be regarded as falling below that standard" in general international law.[47] The Court added that United States' "use of so serious a charge as to call it a 'denial of procedural justice' might be thought to be exaggerated".[48]

## 3. Equality of Arms

The "effective means" standard imposes an obligation on states to ensure procedural fairness and effective remedy. It may encompass a consideration of the principle of equality of arms.

---

[40] ibid 27–29.
[41] Ahmadou Sadio Diallo *(Republic of Guinea v Democratic Republic of the Congo)* (Preliminary Objections, Judgment) [2007] ICJ Rep 582.
[42] ibid para 38.
[43] ibid para 73.
[44] ibid paras 74–75.
[45] Elettronica Sicula SpA (ELSI) *(Italy v U.S.)* (Judgment) [1989] Rep 15 para 1.
[46] ibid paras 109–110.
[47] ibid paras. 111.
[48] ibid paras. 111.

In its 2018 Partial Award, the *Chevron* tribunal considered equality in its analysis as to denial of justice rather than "effective means". The tribunal noted that Article 10 of the Universal Declaration of Human Rights and Article 14 of the ICCPR guarantee that all persons shall be equal before courts and tribunals.[49] It also noted that under Ecuador's Constitution, there was the constitutional rights under Articles 75 and 76(7)(k) a right "to the effective, impartial and speedy protection of his or her rights and interests".[50]

As Schill has observed, various guarantees in investment treaties embody the rule of law, and equality before the law is a "prerequisite for fair competition".[51] And Huber has explained that equality of arms is one of the "procedural principles of particular importance, which reflect the cornerstones in a system based on the rule of law in its substantive sense and require, as such, observance in all types of proceedings independently of the subject matter".[52] In practice this means that tribunals must ensure that both parties are in an equal position to present their case, and generally treating states and investors differently would "amount to a violation of this principle".[53]

In his Expert Opinion, Caron concluded with a broader point about fairness in dispute settlement. He observed that the "effective means" obligation is preventative because "it attempts to avoid breaches of treaty and other obligations by ensuring an opportunity at the national level for disputes to be avoided".[54] In this sense, he said, the requirement of "effective means" is "part of a broader trend seen in other treaties supporting the rule of law and access to justice".[55] In his final address at the American Society of International Law, David Caron discussed "the centrality of judging, of ascertaining and applying the substance of the law, and of recognizing its foundational role in dispute settlement".[56] In this regard he made the following observation:

> If one speaks in terms of process, then it is the institution of judging that needs to be particularly valued. In order to strengthen that institution, it is important to acknowledge that it depends on the independence and impartiality of judges, the demand that reasons be given by judges, and the obligation *that the parties be treated both fairly and equally.*[57]

---

[49] 2018 Partial Award (n 1) §8.57.

[50] ibid §8.58.

[51] SW Schill, "International Investment Law and the Rule of Law" in J Jowell and others (eds), *Rule of Law Symposium 2014* (Academy Publishing 2015) 81 90.

[52] Translated extract: S Huber, "Equality of the Parties in Investment Arbitration—Private International Law Aspects", 18 May 2020, <https://conflictoflaws.net/2020/equality-of-the-parties-in-investment-arbitration-priv ate-international-law-aspects/>. Full version: Stefan Huber, "Die Stellung von Unternehmen in der Investition sschiedsgerichtsbarkeit (unter besonderer Berücksichtigung von Korruptionsproblemen)—Unternehmen als gleichberechtigte Verfahrensparteien?" in August Reinisch and others (eds), *Unternehmensverantwortung und Internationales Recht* (C.F. Müller 2020) 303 et seq.

[53] ibid.

[54] Expert Opinion (n 1) §172.

[55] ibid 172.

[56] David D Caron, "Remarks" (2017) 111 Proceedings of the ASIL Annual Meeting 231–240.

[57] ibid 231–40 (emphasis added). See also David D Caron, "Arbitrating with State Parties: The Debate as to the Relative Equality-Inequality of the Parties," presented at "East Meets West: Evolving Issues in International Arbitration in the Asia-Pacific Region", International Chamber of Commerce Conference, San Francisco, 15 March 2010.

In the context of the right to a fair trial, the principle of equality of arms ensures that the same procedural rights are to be provided to all the parties to a case "unless distinctions are based on law and can be justified on objective and reasonable grounds, not entailing actual disadvantage or other unfairness to the defendant".[58] It does not necessarily require identical numbers of counsel or 50:50 division of time for cross-examination.[59] Having said that, it is "one of the features of the wider concept of a fair trial" and gives each party "a reasonable opportunity to present his case under conditions that do not place him at a disadvantage vis-à-vis his opponent".[60]

In a similar way that equality of arms may arise in investment arbitration as an aspect of fair and equitable treatment, denial of justice, or even "effective means", it may take on different guises in international human rights law. Violations of the right to equality of arms have been found on their own, but they have also arisen in relation to a specific component of the right to a fair trial, such as the right to examine witnesses and the right to adequate facilities for the defence.

International human rights bodies have found violations of the right to equality of arms as a standalone right. The Human Rights Committee, for example, found a violation when the defendant did not have the opportunity to cross-examine the victim on his evidence, summon the expert, and call additional witnesses, leading it to conclude that the Russian courts "did not respect the requirement of equality between prosecution and defence in producing evidence and this amounted to a denial of justice".[61] The Committee also found that equality of arms was violated when the defendant was not permitted to present her case in person whereas the Australian government's representative had been able to participate in the oral hearing before the High Court.[62] The European Court has found violations of the principle of equality of arms in several scenarios, including when the prosecutor submitted observations to the appellate court opposing the defendant's appeal which "were not served on the defence".[63] The Inter-American Commission concluded the "doctrine of equality of arms" was violated when medical evidence that the defendant wanted to use to corroborate his claim that he was beaten to elicit a confession was "lost or mislaid" by the state.[64] And the African Commission found the "principle of equality before the law" was violated when the

---

[58] HRC, General Comment No 32 (2007), §13. See Clooney and Webb (n 25) 748.

[59] See eg CCJ, *Gibson v Attorney General* [2010] CCJ 3 (AJ), 16 August 2010, §§33, 34 (equality of arms does not imply perfect parity between the facilities available to the prosecution and the defendant).

[60] ECtHR, *Bulut v Austria* (App no 17358/90), 22 February 1996, §47. See also *Prosecutor v Orić* (Interlocutory Decision on Length of Defence Case) IT-03-68-AR73.2 (20 July 2005), §7; *Prosecutor v Ndayambaje et al* (Decision on Joseph Kanyabashi's Appeal against the Decision of Trial Chamber II of 21 March 2007 concerning the Dismissal of Motions to Vary his Witness List) ICTR-98-42-AR73 (21 August 2007), §26. See further ECOWAS CCJ, *Sory Toure v Guinea* (Suit no ECW/CCJ/APP/22/13), 16 February 2016, §§96–101.

[61] HRC, *Dugin v Russia* (Comm no 815/1998), 5 July 2004, §§9.3.

[62] HRC, *Dudko v Australia* (Comm no 1347/2005), 23 July 2007, §7.4. See also HRC, *Quliyev v Azerbaijan* (Comm no 1972/2010), 16 October 2014, § 9.3; HRC, *Wolf v Panama* (Comm no 289/1988), 26 March 1992, §6.6.

[63] ECtHR, *Bulut v Austria* (App no 17358/90), 22 February 1996, §§44–50. See also ECtHR, *Eftimov v The former Yugoslav Republic of Macedonia* (App. No 59974/08), 2 July 2015, §41 (defendant not permitted to be present at the Supreme Court hearing while the prosecutor did appear); ECtHR, *Zahirović v Croatia* (App. No 58590/11), 25 April 2013, §§44–50 (opinion of the State Attorney's Office never communicated to the defence).

[64] *Vaux v Guyana* (Judgment) Inter-American Commission on Human Rights Case 12.504 (15 October 2007), §§65, 68 (violations of American Declaration arts XVIII, XXV, XXVI).

defendant was denied the same opportunity of presenting his arguments as was given to his opponent before the Supreme Court of the DRC, putting him in a "position of imbalance".[65]

In practice, equality of arms is more often examined in combination with other component fair trial rights. For example, the right to have adequate time and facilities for the preparation of defence and to communicate with counsel of one's own choosing has been considered an "application of the principle of equality of arms" by the Human Rights Committee.[66] Similarly, the Committee considered that the right of the defendant to examine, or have examined, the witnesses against him and to obtain the attendance of his witnesses under the same conditions as the prosecution is "an application of the principle of equality of arms" and guarantees the defendant the "same legal powers of compelling the attendance of witnesses and of examining or cross-examining witnesses as are available to the prosecution".[67] The European Court also discusses the right to equality in relation to other component rights, including the right to call and examine witnesses,[68] the right to prepare a defence,[69] and the right to counsel.[70] And the Inter-American Court has considered equality of arms in relation to the right to defence and the right to call and examine witnesses.[71] The African bodies have also found a violation of equality of arms in the context of having an equal opportunity "to prepare and present ... pleas and indictment during the trial"[72] and when a court relied

---

[65] ACmHPR, *Itundamilamba v Democratic Republic of the Congo* (Comm no 302/05), 9–23 April 2013, §§71, 105 (the right to defence in art 7 was also violated, but with separate reasoning). See also ACmHPR, *Noca v Democratic Republic of the Congo* (Comm no 286/2004), 9–22 October 2012, §§79–81, 201–203; ACmHPR, *Avocats Sans Frontières v Burundi* (Comm no 231/99), 23 October–6 November 2000, §27; ACmHPR, *Dabalorivhuwa Patriotic Front v South Africa* (Comm no 335/2006), 9–23 April 2013, §124.

[66] HRC, General Comment No 32 (2007), §32; HRC, *Robinson v Jamaica* (Comm. No 223/1987), 30 March 1989, §10.4 (violation of arts 14(1), (3)(d)); HRC, *Orkin v Russia* (Comm no 2410/2014), 24 July 2019, §13.6; HRC, *Ismanov v Tajikistan* (Comm no 2356/2014), 5 July 2019, §7.9.

[67] HRC, General Comment No 32 (2007), §39 (but also noting that the right "does not, however, provide an unlimited right to obtain the attendance of any witness requested by the accused or their counsel, but only a right to have witnesses admitted that are relevant for the defence, and to be given a proper opportunity to question and challenge witnesses against them at some stage of the proceedings").

[68] ECtHR (GC), *Schatschaschwili v Germany* (App. No 9154/10), 15 December 2015, §§67, 164–165 (violation of the right to call and examine witnesses and of the "overall fairness of the proceedings").

[69] ECtHR (GC), *Öcalan v Turkey* (App no 46221/99), 12 May 2005, §§140, 173 (violation of art 6(1) taken in conjunction with art 6(3)(b), (c) due to restrictions on the defendant's access to the case file and late disclosure to his lawyers, obliging them to respond hurriedly to a very extensive file); ECtHR, *Gelenidze v Georgia* (App no 72916/10), 7 November 2019, §§31–38 (requalification of the defendant's offence by the appellate court was arbitrary and violated defence rights and equality of arms); ECtHR, *Beraru v Romania* (App no 40107/04), 18 March 2014, §§70, 84 (lack of access to the case file and other documents until a late stage violated art 6(1) taken with art 6(3)(b), (c), (d)); ECtHR, *Matyjek v Poland* (App. No 38184/03), 24 April 2007, §65 (violations of art 6(1), (3) due to limits on access to case file in lustration proceedings).

[70] ECtHR (GC), *Beuze v Belgium* (App no 71409/10), 9 November 2018, §125 (stating that access to counsel at the pre-trial stage contributes to equality of arms); ECtHR (GC), *Salduz v Turkey* (App no 36391/02), 27 November 2008, §§51–53 (the defendant was questioned pre-trial while his right to counsel was denied).

[71] *Norín Catrimán v Chile* (Judgment) Inter-American Court of Human Rights Series C No 279 (29 May 2014), §242 (mentioning the adversarial principle and principle of procedural equality and going on to find violation of the right to defence in art 8(2)(f) as well as arts 9, 8(2), 2(h), 7(1), (3), (5)); *DaCosta Cadogan v Barbados* Inter-American Court of Human Rights Series C No 204 (24 September 2009), §84 (defendant had a right to interrogate witnesses "under the same conditions as the State").

[72] ACmHPR, *Avocats sans Frontières v Burundi* (Comm no 231/99), 23 October–6 November 2000, §§27–31.

on prosecution evidence and "fail[ed] to further its investigations on the alibi defence" raised by the defendant.[73]

Equality of arms has also been a matter of concern before the ICJ. It has considered the principle in the context of the obligation peacefully to settle disputes. In *Timor-Leste v Australia*, the Court observed that

> equality of the parties must be preserved when they are involved ... in the process of settling an international dispute by peaceful means. If a State is engaged in the peaceful settlement of a dispute with another State through arbitration or negotiations, it would expect to undertake these arbitration proceedings or negotiations without interference by the other party in the preparation and conduct of its case.[74]

The Court held that in such a situation, a state

> has a plausible right to the protection of its communications with counsel relating to an arbitration or to negotiations, in particular, to the protection of the correspondence between them, as well as to the protection of confidentiality of any documents and data prepared by counsel to advise that State in such a context.[75]

In an advisory opinion concerning a dispute between a staff member and an international organization, the ICJ pronounced on equality of arms before administrative tribunals. In particular, the Court was "unable to see any such justification for the provision for review of the [International Labour Organization's Administrative Tribunal's (ILOAT)] decisions which favours the employer to the disadvantage of the staff member."[76] In a Declaration, Judge Greenwood took the concept further, commenting on equality of arms in the proceedings before the ICJ itself:

> There are, of course, no parties in the formal sense in advisory proceedings before the Court. Nevertheless, the type of advisory proceeding in which the Court is asked to engage under Article XII of the ILOAT Statute is of a quite different character from those proceedings which result from questions posed by the General Assembly ... If the Court concludes that the ILOAT has exceeded its jurisdiction, or that there has

---

[73] ACtHPR, *Abubakari v Tanzania* (App no 007/2013), 3 June 2016, §193 (violations of arts 7, 14). See also ACtHPR, *Ajavon v Benin* (App no 013/2017), 29 March 2019, §161 (finding the "right to acquire knowledge of the record of proceedings ... related to the right to defence, more particularly the principle of equality of arms between the parties").

[74] Questions Relating to the Seizure and Detention of Certain Documents and Data (*Timor-Leste v Australia*) (Order) [2014] ICJ Rep 147, para 27.

[75] Questions Relating to the Seizure and Detention of Certain Documents and Data (*Timor-Leste v Australia*) (Order) [2014] ICJ Rep 147, para 27.

[76] *Judgment No 2867 of the Administrative Tribunal of the International Labour Organisation upon a Complaint Filed against the International Fund for Agricultural Development* (Advisory Opinion) [2012] ICJ Reports 10, at para 39. See also *Application for Review of Judgment No 273 of the United Nations Administrative Tribunal* (Advisory Opinion) [1982] ICJ Rep 325, paras 29, 31, 41–44; *Application for Review of Judgment No 158 of the United Nations Administrative Tribunal* (Advisory Opinion) [1973] ICJ Rep 166, para 34; *Judgments of the Administrative Tribunal of the ILO upon complaints made against the UNESCO* (Advisory Opinion) [1956] ICJ Rep 1956, 86.

been a fundamental flaw in procedure, the staff member will lose the compensation awarded to her. In substance, therefore, if not in form, the proceedings before the Court are proceedings between the Organization requesting the Opinion and the staff member, and the Court's opinion will determine whether or not the staff member continues to be entitled to the compensation awarded to her. Yet, as the Opinion points out … , the staff member has no direct access to the Court; she can make representations and submit documents to the Court only through the Organization. The resulting disparity is incompatible with modern notions of justice and due process.[77]

The Court did not directly address the critique contained in Judge Greenwood's Declaration, but it has commented on the need for equality of arms for states parties to contentious cases before the Court. In the *Bosnia Genocide* case, the Court decided that a CD-ROM containing exhibits and other documents submitted by Bosnia and Herzegovina should be withdrawn after Serbia and Montenegro raised "serious concerns related to … the principles of fairness and equality of the parties" because of the submission at a late stage of so many documents.[78] And when one party fails to appear, the Court has emphasised that "equality of the parties" is a "basic principle":

> The Court is careful, even where both parties appear, to give each of them the same opportunities and chances to produce their evidence; when the situation is complicated by the non-appearance of one of them, then *a fortiori* the Court regards it as essential to guarantee as perfect equality as possible between the parties.[79]

## 4. Conclusion

The *Chevron* litigation in which David Caron provided an Expert Opinion for the claimants on the meaning of "effective means" ultimately issued an award in favour of the claimants, finding that Ecuador violated its obligations under international treaties, investment agreements and international law. The tribunal unanimously held that a $9.5 billion judgment rendered against Chevron in Lago Agrio in 2011 was procured through fraud, bribery, and corruption. It concluded that the Ecuadorian judgment "violates international public policy" and "should not be recognised or enforced by the courts of other States".[80]

Since the tribunal found that applying the fair and equitable treatment standard under Article II(3)(a) of the Treaty was sufficient, it did not have to address in detail

---

[77] *Judgment No 2867 of the Administrative Tribunal of the International Labour Organisation upon a Complaint Filed against the International Fund for Agricultural Development* (Declaration of Judge Greenwood) [2012] ICJ Rep 10, para 4.

[78] Case Concerning Application of the Convention on the Prevention and Punishment of the Crime of Genocide (*Bosnia and Herzegovina v Serbia and Montenegro*) [2007] ICJ Rep 43, para 54.

[79] Case Concerning Military and Paramilitary Activities in and Against Nicaragua (*Nicaragua v United States of America*) (Merits) [1986] ICJ Rep 14, paras 31, 59.

[80] 2018 Partial Award (n 1) §§10.2–10.10.

the meaning and effect of "effective means" in Article II(7).[81] The tribunal therefore only made passing reference to Caron's Expert Opinion.[82] The Expert Opinion none-theless stands as a masterful analysis of "effective means", illuminated by his analysis of not only arbitral decisions but also the jurisprudence of regional human rights courts. And given David Caron's appointment as judge ad hoc to cases at the ICJ, one cannot help thinking that he would have one day contributed to the evolving jurisprudence of that Court on related concepts, such as equality of arms. He departed too soon. We are instead left with his extensive body of scholarly writings and arbitral decisions, as well as his example as an academic-practitioner of the highest order.

---

[81] ibid §7.20.
[82] ibid §7.18.

# 16

# Early Dismissal of Claims as a Tool to Enhance the Efficiency and Legitimacy of ISDS

*O Thomas Johnson and Elizabeth Sheargold*

## 1. Introduction

Following the first wave of prominent investor–state arbitrations that arose under Chapter 11 of the North American Free Trade Agreement (NAFTA) and other international investment agreements (IIAs) in the late 1990s and early 2000s, one of the first significant procedural reforms of investor–state dispute settlement (ISDS) was the introduction of mechanisms that would allow the early dismissal of unmeritorious cases. The United States included an early-dismissal mechanism in its 2004 Model Bilateral Investment Treaty (BIT),[1] and in bits and free trade agreements (FTAs) it concluded from 2003 onwards, which would allow for the efficient disposal of cases in which "as a matter of law, a claim submitted is not a claim for which an award in favour of the claimant may be made".[2] In 2006 the International Centre for Settlement of Investment Disputes (ICSID) reformed its arbitration rules to add Rule 41(5), which created a new procedure for tribunals to consider a preliminary objection that a claim is "manifestly without legal merit".[3] Subsequently, early-dismissal mechanisms have been

---

[1] US Model BIT (2004), art 28.4. This provision was retained in US Model BIT (2012), art 28.4.
[2] See eg *United States-Chile Free Trade Agreement*, signed 6 June 2003 (entered into force 1 January 2004), art 10.19.4; *Dominican Republic-Central America-United States Free Trade Agreement*, signed 5 August 2004 (entered into force 1 January 2009), art 10.20.4 (hereafter CAFTA-DR; *United States-Peru Trade Promotion Agreement*, signed 12 April 2006 (entered into force 1 February 2009), art 10.20.4 (hereafter US-Peru Trade Promotion Agreement (2006)); *Free Trade Agreement between the United States and Oman*, signed 19 January 2006 (entered into force 1 January 2009), art 10.19.4; *United States-Singapore Free Trade Agreement*, signed 6 May 2003 (entered into force 1 January 2004), art 15.19.4; *Treaty between the Government of the United States of America and the Government of the Republic of Rwanda Concerning Encouragement and Reciprocal Protection of Investment*, signed 19 February 2008 (entered into force 1 December 2012), arts 28.4 and 28.5; *Treaty between the United States of America and the Oriental Republic of Uruguay Concerning the Encouragement and Reciprocal Protection of Investment*, signed 4 November 2005 (entered into force 31 October 2006), arts 28.4 and 28.5.
[3] ICSID Rules of Procedure for Arbitration Proceedings, first adopted 25 September 1967, as amended by the ICSID Administrative Council and in effect as of 10 April 2006, rule 41(5) (hereafter ICSID Arbitration Rules (2006)). See also ICSID Arbitration (Additional Facility) Rules, first adopted 27 September 1978, as amended by the ICSID Administrative Council and in effect as of 10 April 2006, rule 45(6) (hereafter ICSID Arbitration (Additional Facility) Rules (2006)).

included in the IIAs of a range of treaty parties[4] and in the rules of some other arbitration institutions.[5]

Although some commentators expressed concern that the mechanisms may cause delay by adding an extra phase to proceedings or that arbitrators would be unwilling to dismiss claims at an early stage,[6] in general, early-dismissal mechanisms were considered a positive development that would enhance the efficiency and legitimacy of ISDS by allowing unmeritorious cases to be resolved on an expedited basis.[7] In this chapter, we consider whether mechanisms such as ICSID Rule 41(5) and the US treaty provisions are fulfilling their purpose and whether their design could be enhanced, in light of the past fifteen years of arbitral practice applying these procedures. We begin, in Section 2, by examining in greater detail the rationale for including early-dismissal mechanisms in ISDS and their origins in domestic litigation practice, particularly motions to dismiss under the US Federal Rules of Civil Procedure, which provide an avenue for claims which have no chance of success to be dismissed before the parties engage in resource-intensive stages of arbitration such as discovery. In Section 3 we analyse the early-dismissal mechanisms that currently exist in IIAs and arbitral rules, including ICSID 2006 Rule 41(5) (and its successor in Rule 41 of the 2022 ICSID Arbitration Rules), US treaty practice, Articles 8.32 and 8.33 of the recent Comprehensive Economic and Trade Agreement between Canada and the European Union (CETA) and other arbitration rules. Examining the cases in which these procedures have been applied, particularly ICSID Rule 41(5), shows that, while early-dismissal mechanisms have played a useful role in some investor–state arbitrations, many tribunals have been reluctant to decide "novel" or "complex" legal issues through an expedited process, and in some cases the consideration of preliminary objections has delayed or lengthened proceedings.

In Section 4 we suggest two reforms that would enhance early-dismissal mechanisms by redesigning the procedures to promote efficiency—rather than speed—in the management of preliminary objections in investor–state arbitrations. In Section 4.1 we argue that the requirement that a claim be "manifestly" without legal merit should be removed from these rules (or construed less restrictively), as it discourages tribunals from deciding upon

---

[4] See eg *Comprehensive Economic and Trade Agreement between Canada and the European Union*, signed 30 October 2016 (provisionally entered into force in part on 21 September 2017), arts 8.32 and 8.33 (hereafter CETA); *Korea-Australia Free Trade Agreement*, signed 8 April 2014 (entered into force 12 December 2014), art 10.20.6. However, given that most IIAs which are currently in force are older treaties, early-dismissal mechanisms still remain the exception rather than the rule. See Friedrich Rosenfeld, "Early Dismissal of Claims in Investment Arbitration" in Andreas Kulick (ed), *Reassertion of Control Over the Investment Treaty Regime* (Cambridge University Press 2017) 83, 96.

[5] See eg Investment Arbitration Rules of the Singapore International Arbitration Centre, 1st edn, 1 January 2017, rule 26 (hereafter SIAC Investment Rules (2017)).

[6] See Christoph H Schreuer and others, *The ICSID Convention: A Commentary* (2nd edn, Cambridge University Press 2009) 544; Jarrod Wong and Jason Yackee, "The 2006 Procedural and Transparency-Related Amendments to the ICSID Arbitration Rules" in Karl P Sauvant (ed), *Yearbook on International Investment Law & Policy 2009–2010* (Oxford University Press 2010) 233, 238–41.

[7] The importance of being able to resolve these objections on an "expedited basis" was cited by the ICSID Secretariat as a key purpose of the introduction of Rule 41(5). See ICSID Secretariat, *Possible Improvements of the Framework for ICSID Arbitration*, Discussion Paper, 22 October 2004, para 10; ICSID Secretariat, *Suggested Changes to the ICSID Rules and Regulations*, Working Paper, 12 May 2005, 7–8.

legal issues that are novel or difficult. While complex legal issues may require a longer time frame to provide the parties with sufficient opportunity to present their arguments and for the tribunal to decide the question, allowing these issues to be considered before processes such as discovery will increase the efficiency of many arbitrations. In Section 4.2 we argue that early-dismissal mechanisms should generally be focused on objections relating to the merits of the claim. Several cases to date have demonstrated that jurisdictional objections often fail the test applied under ICSID Rule 41(5) and other early-dismissal procedures because they raise issues of fact and/or the interpretation of domestic law. It is therefore usually more efficient for tribunals to manage these objections in a preliminary phase of proceedings on jurisdiction, in which the parties have the opportunity to adduce evidence and call expert witnesses as needed. These reforms would bring early-dismissal mechanisms more in line with the domestic procedures on which their design was based and will ultimately enhance the efficiency and legitimacy of ISDS.

## 2. The Rationale for Including Early-Dismissal Mechanisms in Investment Treaty Arbitration

The United States began to include early-dismissal mechanisms in its IIAS in the early 2000s. The US Model BIT of 2004 included an early-dismissal mechanism,[8] which was mirrored in the investment chapters of several FTAs and in BITs,[9] such as Article 10.20.4 of the US-Peru Trade Promotion Agreement (2006):

> Without prejudice to a tribunal's authority to address other objections as a preliminary question, such as an objection that a dispute is not within the tribunal's competence, a tribunal shall address and decide as a preliminary question any objection by the respondent that, as a matter of law, a claim submitted is not a claim for which an award in favor of the claimant may be made under Article 10.26.1.

The article then goes on to clarify that "[i]n deciding an objection under this paragraph, the tribunal shall assume to be true claimant's factual allegations in support of any claim".[10] The rationale for including this mechanism was to deal efficiently with claims that were "frivolous" or without legal merit, before significant resources were wasted on discovery and other collection of evidence, and before the full development of arguments on the merits of the claims.[11] This innovation in US treaty practice was

---

[8] See US Model BIT (2004), art 28.4. This provision was retained in US Model BIT (2012), art 28.4.
[9] See examples cited in n 2.
[10] US-Peru Trade Promotion Agreement (2006) art 10.20.4(c).
[11] Kenneth J Vandevelde, "A Comparison of the 2004 and 1994 US Model BITs: Rebalancing Investor and Host Country Interests" in Sauvant (ed), *Yearbook on International Investment Law & Policy* (Oxford University Press 2009) 283, 309–10. The Trade Act of 2002, which incorporated the Bipartisan Trade Promotion Authority Act, had explicitly identified "mechanisms to eliminate frivolous claims and to deter the filing of frivolous claims" as a feature which should be included in the investment chapters of future US FTAs, "to secure for investors important

motivated by "bad experiences defending frivolous claims under NAFTA".[12] For example, both the United States and Peru have noted that the origin of Article 10.20.4 of the US-Peru Trade Promotion Agreement (2006) was the finding in *Methanex v US* that the tribunal could not address the US objection that the claims were without any legal merit in a preliminary phase of proceedings.[13] Instead, the *Methanex* dispute proceeded to the merits, where the "tribunal ultimately dismissed all of claimant's claims for lack of jurisdiction, but only after three more years of pleading on jurisdiction and merits and millions of dollars of additional expense".[14]

The early-dismissal mechanism used in US IIAs clearly draws on domestic civil procedure, and in particular on motions to dismiss brought under Rule 12(b)(6) of the US Federal Rules of Civil Procedure. That rule allows a defendant to bring a motion to dismiss on the basis of a "failure to state a claim upon which relief can be granted".[15] A key feature of a Rule 12(b)(6) motion to dismiss is that the facts as pleaded by the plaintiff are to be taken by the court as true. Until 2007, for a motion to dismiss under Rule 12(b)(6) to succeed the court had to find that "the plaintiff could prove no set of facts in support of his claim which would entitle him to relief".[16] This test was refined by the Supreme Court in 2007, and Rule 12(b)(6) is now interpreted as a standard requiring that the claims be "plausible".[17] While there is debate about how to apply this "plausibility" standard in practice,[18] the Court has unequivocally maintained that a motion under Rule 12(b)(6) must be assessed on the assumption that the facts alleged by the plaintiff are true:[19] the "relevant question is whether, assuming the factual allegations are true, the plaintiff has stated a ground for relief that is plausible".[20] As a result, a claim can be dismissed under Rule 12(b)(6) before any discovery or other fact-finding has taken place.[21]

rights comparable to those that would be available under United States legal principles and practice." See 19 USC § 3802(b)(3)(G)(i).

[12] Edward G Kehoe, "Motions to Dismiss in International Treaty Arbitrations" in Arthur W Rovine (ed), *Contemporary Issues in International Arbitration and Mediation: The Fordham Papers 2015* (Brill 2016) 87, 90.

[13] See *Methanex Corporation v United States of America*, Partial Award of 7 August 2002, UNCITRAL Arbitration, paras 109, 126. Both state parties to the US-Peru Trade Promotion Agreement (2006) discussed the origins of Article 10.20.4 in the *Renco v Peru I* dispute. For an overview of the relevance of *Methanex* to the drafting of Article 10.20.4, see *The Renco Group, Inc v Republic of Peru*, Decision as to the Scope of the Respondent's Preliminary Objections under Article 10.20.4, ICSID Case No UNCT/13/1, 18 December 2014, paras 215–218. See also Vandevelde (n 11) 90.

[14] *The Renco Group, Inc v Republic of Peru*, Submission of the United States of America, ICSID Case No UNCT/13/1, 10 September 2014, para 2.

[15] Fed R Civ P 12(b)(6).

[16] *Conley v Gibson*, 355 US 41, 45–46 (1957) (stating the "accepted rule that a complaint should not be dismissed for failure to state a claim unless it appears beyond doubt that the plaintiff can prove no set of facts in support of his claim which would entitle him to relief".)

[17] See *Bell Atlantic Corp. et al v Twombly et al.*, 550 US 544, at 570 (2007) (*Twombly*) (describing the required standard of review as whether the "claim to relief is plausible on its face").

[18] See Suzette M Malveaux, "Front Loading and Heavy Lifting: How Pre-Dismissal Discovery Can Address the Detrimental Effect of Iqbal on Civil Rights Cases" (2010) 14 Lewis & Clark Law Review 65, 80–84; Rakesh N Kilaru, "The New Rule 12 (B)(6): Twombly, Iqbal, and the Paradox of Pleading" (2009) 62 Stanford Law Review 905, 911–13.

[19] *Twombly*, 550 US at 555 (noting that the Rule 12(b)(6) motion is to be considered "on the assumption that all the allegations in the complaint are true" and quoting from *Neitzke v Williams*, 490 US 319, 327 (1989) that "Rule 12(b)(6) does not countenance ... dismissals based on a judge's disbelief of a complaint's factual allegations"). The only exception to this rule is when the facts as pleaded are "sufficiently fantastic to defy reality as we know it: claims about little green men, or the plaintiff's recent trip to Pluto, or experiences in time travel": *Ashcroft, Former Attorney General, et al., v Iqbal et al.*, 556 US 662, 696 (2009) (*Iqbal*).

[20] ibid 696.

[21] Suja A Thomas, "Pondering Iqbal: The New Summary Judgment Motion: The Motion to Dismiss Under Iqbal and Twombly" (2010) 14 Lewis & Clark Law Review 15, 17 (2010).

Similar early-dismissal mechanisms can be found in the civil procedure of other jurisdictions,[22] such as a "motion to strike" in the practice of Canadian courts[23] or an application to strike out pleadings and receive summary judgment on the basis of a failure to state a reasonable cause of action in Australia.[24] The key feature of the US motion to dismiss and similar mechanisms is that they turn on an evaluation of whether—as a matter of law—a claim could possibly succeed even if the facts as stated by the complainant/plaintiff were true.[25] This can be contrasted with other avenues for the early dismissal of claims, such as a motion for summary judgment under Rule 56 of the US Federal Rules of Civil Procedure,[26] which will be granted when "the movant shows that there is no genuine dispute as to any material fact and the movant is entitled to judgment as a matter of law".[27] While a motion to dismiss is assessed on the pleadings and without consideration of whether the plaintiff's allegations of fact can be substantiated,[28] the movant of a motion for summary judgment is "required to point to actual evidence in the record showing an absence of a disputed issue of material fact",[29] such as depositions, documents, affidavits, or interrogatory answers.[30]

The primary purpose of the motion to dismiss in US federal civil procedure is to ensure that "when the allegations in a complaint ... could not raise a claim of entitlement to relief, "this basic deficiency should ... be exposed at the point of minimum expenditure of time and money by the parties and the court".[31] Although a defendant might ultimately be successful in defending an unmeritorious claim, "the threat of discovery expense will push cost-conscious defendants to settle even anemic cases".[32] Thus, the efficiency that can be gained from a motion to dismiss under Rule 12(b)(6) does not rely on the motion being decided within a specific, short period of time but rather on the motion being considered prior to the expenditure of resources on discovery, trial preparation etc.[33] Rule 12(b)(6) and similar early-dismissal mechanisms in domestic court systems provide a means of balancing the plaintiff's right to access justice against

---

[22]  See also Wong and Yackee (n 6) 235 fn 8 (listing similar early-dismissal mechanisms in a range of jurisdictions).

[23]  For example, Rule 21.01(1)(b) of Ontario's Rules of Civil Procedure and Rule 19(24)(a) of the Supreme Court Rules of British Columbia allow a motion to strike where a case has no reasonable prospect of success, assuming the facts as pleaded: *R v Imperial Tobacco Canada Ltd*, [2011] SCJ No 42, [17].

[24]  In Australian practice the party making the strike out application must show "that under no possibility could there be a good cause of action consistently with the pleadings and facts": *Bayne v Baillieu* (1908) 6 CLR 382, 387 (per Griffith CJ). Such an application can be based on the rules of procedure of the relevant jurisdiction, or on the inherent jurisdiction of the court. See *General Steel Industries Inc. v Commissioner for Railways (N.S.W.) and Ors* (1964) 112 CLR 125, 129 (per Barwick CJ); Bernard C Cairns, *Australian Civil Procedure* (11th edn, Thomson Reuters Australia 2016) 538–48 .

[25]  This is also a feature of the equivalent Canadian and Australian early-dismissal mechanisms, discussed at nn 23 and 24. See, respectively, *R v Imperial Tobacco Canada Ltd*, [2011] SCJ No 42, [17] (on Canadian practice) and *Spellson v George* (1992) 26 NSWLR 666, 678–79 (as an example of the Australian practice).

[26]  cf Thomas (n 21) (arguing that the standards for motions to dismiss and summary judgment are converging).

[27]  Fed R Civ P 56(a).

[28]  If on a motion to dismiss under Rule 12(b)(6) the movant presents matters which are outside of the pleadings, then the motion must instead be treated as a motion for summary judgment under Rule 56. See Fed R Civ P 12(d).

[29]  Patricia M Wald, "Summary Judgment at Sixty" (1997) 76 Texas Law Review 1897, 1905.

[30]  See Fed R Civ P 56(c)(1)(a).

[31]  *Twombly*, 550 US, 558 (citations omitted).

[32]  ibid 559.

[33]  In fact a motion to dismiss under Rule 12(b)(6) does not necessarily need to be raised early in proceedings and can be raised at trial itself: Fed R Civ P 12(h)(2)(c). Although at this point in the litigation the gain in efficiency that could be achieved by dismissing a claim on the basis that relief cannot be granted would be minimal at best.

the burden placed on defendants and courts of going through the process of discovery (and potentially trial) for a claim that would be unable to succeed even if the plaintiff obtains the evidence necessary to support its factual allegations.[34]

While the motivation for the United States to include early-dismissal mechanism in its IIAs and their origins in the domestic motion to dismiss can be clearly identified, it is not as easy to impute a single purpose or understanding to the many ICSID contracting states for the amendment of the arbitration rules in 2006 to include Rule 41(5). However, documents prepared by the ICSID Secretariat during the discussion of possible amendments show that Rule 41(5) has some key similarities with US practice. Like a motion to dismiss, Rule 41(5) was intended to focus on the legal basis for the claim, rather than "discussions on the facts of the case at that stage".[35] Those involved in the negotiation and design of Rule 41(5) have described its purpose as allowing for the quick dismissal of "frivolous"[36] or "patently unmeritorious" claims,[37] by "mak[ing it] clear ... that the tribunal may at an early stage of the case be asked on an expedited basis to dismiss all or part of the claim".[38] Such a procedure was considered desirable because the ICSID Secretary General's power to screen claims prior to registration is limited to those which are "manifestly outside the jurisdiction of the Centre",[39] and there was no avenue to quickly review the merits of the claim.[40]

The broader context for the amendment of the ICSID Arbitration Rules in 2006 was the increasing caseload of ICSID, which was accompanied by "new criticisms of process, in particular calls for greater efficiency and transparency—the latter particularly in view of the public importance of issues at stake in many of the new cases".[41] The ability to deal with unmeritorious cases efficiently, without lengthy and costly arbitral proceedings on the merits, was seen as "a useful tool to preserve the integrity and the efficacy of ICSID Arbitration by eliminating one of the key criticisms of the current architecture of investment arbitration".[42] Since 2006, criticisms of ISDS have

---

[34] *Twombly*, 550 US at 558–59. For a critique of the idea that motions to dismiss are the only means available to courts of controlling the discovery process and litigation costs, see Edward D Cavanagh, "The Future of Pleading in the Federal System: Debating the Impact of Bell Atlantic V. Twombly: Twombly, the Federal Rules of Civil Procedure and the Courts" (2008) 82 St John's Law Review 877, 882–89. It is also important to bear in mind that the overuse of motions to dismiss can increase litigation costs, and can potentially be greater than discovery costs in some cases. See Victor Marrero, "Mission to Dismiss: A Dismissal of Rule 12(b)(6) and the Retirement of *Twombly/Iqbal*" (2018) 40 Cardozo Law Review 1, 3–4.

[35] Aurélia Antonietti, "The 2006 Amendments to the ICSID Rules and Regulations and the Additional Facility Rules" (2006) 21 ICSID Review 427, 440.

[36] ibid 440.

[37] AR Parra, "The Development of the Regulations and Rules of the International Centre for Settlement of Investment Disputes" (2007) 22 ICSID Review 55, 65 (2007).

[38] ICSID Secretariat, *Possible Improvements of the Framework for ICSID Arbitration*, Discussion Paper, 22 October 2004, para 10.

[39] See *Convention on the Settlement of Investment Disputes between States and Nationals of Other States*, opened for signature 18 March 1965, 575 UNTS 159 (entered into force 14 October 1966), art 36(3) (hereafter ICSID Convention).

[40] ICSID Secretariat, *Suggested Changes to the ICSID Rules and Regulations*, Working Paper, 12 May 2005, 7–8. See also See ICSID Secretariat, *Possible Improvements of the Framework for ICSID Arbitration*, Discussion Paper, 22 October 2004, paras 9–10.

[41] Parra (n 37) 65; B Ted Howes, Allison Stowell, and William Choi, "The Impact of Summary Disposition on International Arbitration: A Quantitative Analysis of ICSID's Rule 41(5) on Its Tenth Anniversary" (2019) 13 Dispute Resolution International 7, 9.

[42] Eric De Brabandere, "The ICSID Rule on Early Dismissal of Unmeritorious Investment Treaty Claims: Preserving the Integrity of ICSID Arbitration" (2012) 9 Manchester Journal of International Economic Law 23, 25.

intensified, with a mix of both developed and developing nations showing increased caution towards the inclusion of these dispute settlement mechanisms within IIAs.[43] In light of ongoing public debates and criticism regarding ISDS, having efficient procedures to deal with unmeritorious claims remains important for the legitimacy and efficiency of the regime. As we will discuss further in the following section, some changes to the early dismissal mechanism have been made in the 2022 version of the ICSID Arbitration Rules, but these alterations either codified arbitral practice or are procedural amendments which do not significantly alter the early dismissal mechanism.

## 3. The Existing Early-Dismissal Mechanisms in International Investment Law

The following sections outline in greater detail the key early-dismissal mechanisms which currently exist in international investment law, particularly Rule 41(5) from the 2006 ICSID Arbitration Rules and US treaty practice (such as Article 10.20.4 of the Dominican Republic-Central America-United States FTA (CAFTA-DR)), and newer examples such as CETA Articles 8.32 and 8.33. As well as outlining the relevant legal test for when a claim will be dismissed by the tribunal and the procedural requirements for the use of each mechanism, we evaluate how the provisions have been applied in practice.

### 3.1 ICSID Rule 41(5)

As already noted, Rule 41(5) of the 2006 ICSID Arbitration Rules allows for the dismissal of claims that are "manifestly without legal merit". This mechanism is mirrored in ICSID Additional Facility Rule 45(6), although for ease of reference in this chapter we only refer only to ICSID Rule 41(5). The ICSID arbitration rules contain little detail on the procedures and timeframes that should be followed when a preliminary objection is raised under these provisions, although the procedure was intended to deal with objections on an "expedited basis".[44] The objection must be raised within thirty days of the constitution of the tribunal, and "after giving the parties the opportunity to present their observations on the objection", the tribunal should notify the parties of its decision on the objection "at its first session or promptly thereafter".[45] Given that the first session of the tribunal should usually be held "within 60 days after constitution or such other period as the parties may agree",[46] the consideration of a Rule 41(5)

[43] See, generally, O Thomas Johnson and Catherine H Gibson, "The Objections of Developed and Developing States to Investor–State Dispute Settlement, and What They Are Doing about Them" in Rovine (ed) (n 12) 251–69.

[44] See ICSID Secretariat, *Possible Improvements of the Framework for ICSID Arbitration*, Discussion Paper, 22 October 2004, para 10; ICSID Secretariat, *Suggested Changes to the ICSID Rules and Regulations*, Working Paper, 12 May 2005, 7–8.

[45] ICSID Arbitration Rules (2006), rule 41(5); ICSID Arbitration (Additional Facility) Rules (2006), rule 45(6)

[46] ICSID Arbitration Rules (2006), rule 13(1); ICSID Arbitration (Additional Facility) Rules (2006), rule 21(1).

preliminary objection should in theory be resolved relatively quickly. While Rule 41(5) was designed to be an expedited procedure, in practice the length of time required for a tribunal to decide on the preliminary objection has varied considerably. Tribunals have interpreted the phrase "promptly thereafter" flexibly.[47] Among the early cases where Rule 41(5) was invoked, in one dispute the tribunal reached a decision on the objection only forty-five days after it was filed,[48] while in another case the process took 330 days.[49] Rule 41(5) objections have been decided relatively expeditiously in more recent cases. In the twenty arbitrations from 2012–2017 where Rule 41(5) objections were raised, the average period between objection and decision was just over 100 days.[50]

In the 2022 update of the ICSID Arbitration Rules the early dismissal mechanism was expanded upon in the new Rule 41 (ICSID 2022 Rule 41).[51] Like Rule 41(5) from the 2006 Rules, ICSID 2022 Rule 41 provides a mechanism to deal with claims that are "manifestly without legal merit",[52] but the 2022 Rules also clarify that these objections may relate to "the substance of the claim, the jurisdiction of the Centre, or the competence of the Tribunal".[53] ICSID 2022 Rule 41(2)(b) specifies that the written submission raising the objection must "contain a statement of the relevant facts, law and arguments", but does not clarify whether contested issues of fact relevant to the objection can be resolved through the early dismissal process. ICSID 2022 Rule 41 also provides for some modifications to the procedures for the early dismissal mechanism. It extends the time limit for raising the objection to forty-five days after constitution of the Tribunal[54] but removes some of the flexibility Tribunals had under the 2006 Rules to determine how long they need to resolve the objection. Under ICSID 2022 Rule 41 the Tribunal must render its decision or Award within sixty days of the later of: the constitution of the Tribunal or the last submission on the objection.[55] Although the time frame for the Tribunal to issue a decision after receiving the last submission is fixed, the 2022 Rules make clear that the Tribunal can determine the time limits it sees fit for the parties to make submissions.[56] The provision does not stipulate that this could include

---

[47] Chester Brown and Sergio Puig, "The Power of ICSID Tribunals to Dismiss Proceedings Summarily: An Analysis of Rule 41(5) of the ICSID Arbitration Rules" (2011) 10 Law & Practice of International Courts & Tribunals 227, 256.

[48] For the details of this timeline, see *Brandes Investment Partners, LP v Bolivarian Republic of Venezuela*, Award, ICSID Case No ARB/08/3, 2 August 2011, paras 8–13 (hereafter *Brandes v Venezuela*, Award). We note that while the tribunal reached its decision on the preliminary objections within forty-five days, it did not provide more detailed reasoning to the parties for another two months.

[49] For the details of this timeline, see *Global Trading Resource Corp. and Globex International, Inc v Ukraine*, Award, ICSID Case No ARB/09/11, 1 December 2011, paras 16–26 (hereafter *Global Trading v Ukraine*, Award). To date, this arbitration is still the longest time period for the resolution of preliminary objections under Rule 41(5).

[50] Howes, Stowell, and Choi (n 41) 22.

[51] ICSID Rules of Procedure for Arbitration Proceedings, first adopted 25 September 1967, as amended by the ICSID Administrative Council and in effect as of 1 July 2022, rule 41 (hereafter ICSID Arbitration Rules (2022)).

[52] ibid.

[53] ibid. This codifies the approach taken by tribunals under Rule 41(5) of the 2006 ICSID Arbitration Rules: see cases cited at n 64.

[54] ibid rule 41(2)(a). ICSID 2022 Rule 41 also allows for the possibility of the objection being raised before the constitution of the Tribunal, and in such a case the ICSID Secretary-General may fix time limits for written submissions which must then be promptly considered by the Tribunal upon its constitution. See ibid Rule 41(2)(d).

[55] ibid rule 41(2)(e).

[56] ibid rule 41(2)(c).

oral submissions, but it is also not limited to written submissions.[57] Like the 2006 Rules, the 2022 ICSID Rules provide that "a decision that a claim is not manifestly without legal merit" is "without prejudice" to that parties' ability to subsequently raise the same objection through the general process for preliminary objections to jurisdiction under Rule 43.[58]

Throughout this chapter we refer to Rule 41(5) from the 2006 ICSID Arbitration Rules, as this is the provision which has been litigated and debated to date. We expect that many of the cases decided under Rule 41(5) from the 2006 ICSID Arbitration Rules will continue to be relevant when cases are brought under the 2022 Arbitration Rules, because Rule 41 in the 2022 Rules retains core elements of Rule 41(5) from the 2006 Rules—in particular, the limitation of the mechanism to claims which are "manifestly without legal merit" and the allowance for jurisdictional objections raised in the early dismissal process to be raised again through the general preliminary objections process. The most notable difference between the early dismissal mechanisms under the 2006 and 2022 ICSID Arbitration Rules is the time limit for the Tribunal to decide on the claim, which appears to be an effort by ICSID to ensure that early dismissal applications are resolved quickly. However, as we discuss in Section 4.1, fixing timelines for early dismissal processes in the arbitral rules may undermine the potential efficiency of these mechanisms.

To date, there have been at least 42 ICSID arbitrations that have considered preliminary objections under 2006 Rule 41(5) or Additional Facility Rule 45(6).[59] Although these decisions reveal some minor differences in how arbitral tribunals have applied Rule 41(5), there has been a relatively high degree of consistency in the interpretation of the phrase "manifestly without legal merit". As a starting point, consideration under Rule 41(5) is limited to whether there is a legal impediment to a claim succeeding, and "is not concerned, *per se*, with the factual merits" of the claims.[60] Thus, for the purposes of assessing an objection raised under Rule 41(5), a tribunal will "ordinarily presume the facts which found the claim on the merits as alleged by the Claimant to be true".[61] Some tribunals have qualified this by saying that "[t]he tribunal need not accept at face value any factual allegation which the tribunal regards as (manifestly) incredible, frivolous, vexatious or inaccurate or made in bad faith"[62] or which is "plainly without any

[57] In contrast, if the early dismissal claim is raised before the constitution of the Tribunal, the ICSID Secretary-General can fix time limits for written submissions. See ibid rule 41(2)(d).
[58] ibid rule 41(4).
[59] Not all the relevant decisions and awards are publicly available. The ICSID Secretariat maintains a list of cases where the early dismissal mechanism is invoked, which is available at: <https://icsid.worldbank.org/cases/content/tables-of-decisions/manifest-lack-of-legal-merit>.
[60] *Trans-Global Petroleum, Inc v Hashemite Kingdom of Jordan*, Tribunal's Decision on the Respondent's Objection under Rule 41(5) of the ICSID Arbitration Rules, ICSID Case No ARB/07/25, 12 May 2008, para 97 (hereafter *Trans-Global Petroleum v Jordan*, Decision on ICSID Rule 41(5)).
[61] *Emmis International Holding, B.V., Emmis Radio Operating, B.V. and Mem Magyar Electronic Media Kereskedelmi és Szolgáltató Kft. v Hungary*, Decision on Respondent's Objection under ICSID Arbitration Rule 41(5), ICSID Case No ARB/12/2, 11 March 2013, para 26 (hereafter *Emmis v Hungary*, Decision on ICSID Rule 41(5)). See also *Brandes Investment Partners, LP v Bolivarian Republic of Venezuela*, Decision on the Respondent's Objection under Rule 41(5) of the ICSID Arbitration Rules, ICSID Case No ARB/08/3, 2 February 2009, paras 61, 69–70 (hereafter *Brandes v Venezuela*, Decision on ICSID Rule 41(5)).
[62] *Trans-Global Petroleum v Jordan*, Decision on ICSID Rule 41(5), para 105. See also *Rachel S. Grynberg, Stephen M. Grynberg, Miriam Z. Grynberg, and RSM Production Corporation v Grenada*, Award, ICSID Case No ARB/10/

foundation".[63] Tribunals have also agreed that, while Rule 41(5) refers to whether a case has "legal merit", this encompasses jurisdictional objections as well as objections relating to the merits of the claim.[64]

The first tribunal to apply Rule 41(5), in *Trans-Global Petroleum v Jordan*, interpreted "manifestly" as a high threshold which requires that the respondent "establish its objection clearly and obviously, with relative ease and despatch", even if the "exercise may not always be simple".[65] Subsequent tribunals have generally endorsed the standard put forth in *Trans-Global Petroleum v Jordan*,[66] although over time tribunals have become less willing to resolve complex legal issues within the Rule 41(5) process. More recent arbitral awards and decisions have noted that the mechanism should not be used "to address complicated, difficult or unsettled issues of law".[67] Some tribunals have gone so far as to say that Rule 41(5) should only apply to "undisputed or genuinely indisputable rules of law to uncontested facts", and cannot be used to resolve "disputed legal issues".[68] The high threshold for a claim to be dismissed under Rule 41(5) is closely linked to the expedited nature of the procedure, with the *Trans-Global Petroleum* tribunal citing the "severely truncated" time limits as evidence that the procedure should only be able to be used in the most "clear and obvious cases".[69]

In its first five years in effect ICSID Rule 41(5) was only invoked by four respondents. In two of those cases the tribunal upheld the objections and dismissed the entirety of the claims.[70] In another of these early cases, the Rule 41(5) procedure led to the dismissal of one, but not all, claims.[71] In recent years Rule 41(5) has been invoked

6, 10 December 2010, para 6.1.2 (hereafter *RSM Production Company and Ors v Grenada*, Award); *FengZhen Min v Republic of Korea*, Decision on the Respondent's Preliminary Objection Pursuant to Rule 41(5) of the ICSID Arbitration Rules, ICSID Case No ARB/20/26, 18 June 2021, paras 28, 74 (hereafter *Min v Korea*, Decision on ICSID Rule 41(5)).

[63] *Emmis v Hungary*, Decision on ICSID Rule 41(5), para 26.

[64] This was first held in *Brandes v Venezuela*, Decision on ICSID Rule 41(5), para 55, and has been followed by a number of subsequent tribunals. See eg *Global Trading v Ukraine*, Award, para 30; *RSM Production Company and Ors v Grenada*, Award, para 6.1.1; *PNG Sustainable Development Program Ltd v Independent State of Papua New Guinea*, Tribunal's Decision on the Respondent's Objections Under Rule 41(5) of the ICSID Arbitration Rules, ICSID Case No ARB/13/33, 28 October 2014, para 91 (hereafter *PNG Sustainable Development v PNG*, Decision on ICSID Rule 41(5)).

[65] *Trans-Global Petroleum v Jordan*, Decision on ICSID Rule 41(5), para 88.

[66] See eg *Global Trading v Ukraine*, Award, para 35; *Eskosol S.P.A. in Liquidazione v Italian Republic*, Decision on Respondent's Application under Rule 41(5), ICSID Case No ARB/15/50, 20 March 2017, paras 39–41 (hereafter *Eskosol v Italy*, Decision on ICSID Rule 41(5)); *Almasryia for Operating and Maintaining Touristic Construction Co, LLC v State of Kuwait*, Award on the Respondent's Application Under Rule 41(5) of the ICSID Arbitration Rules, ICSID Case No ARB/18/2, 1 November 2019, para 29 (hereafter *Almasryia v Kuwait*, Award).

[67] *Eskosol v Italy*, Decision on ICSID Rule 41(5), para 41.

[68] *Lion Mexico Consolidated L.P. v United Mexican States*, Decision on the Respondent's Preliminary Objection Under Art. 45(6) of the ICSID Arbitration (Additional Facility) Rules, ICSID Case No ARB(AF)/15/2, 12 December 2016, para 66 (hereafter *Lion Mexico v Mexico*, Decision on ICSID AF Rule 45(6)); *PNG Sustainable Development v PNG*, Decision on ICSID Rule 41(5), paras 88–89.

[69] *Trans-Global Petroleum v Jordan*, Decision on ICSID Rule 41(5), para 90.

[70] See *Global Trading v Ukraine*, Award, paras 57–58 and *RSM Production Company and Ors v Grenada*, Award, paras 7.2.1–7.2.25.

[71] *Trans-Global Petroleum v Jordan*, Decision on ICSID Rule 41(5), paras 118–120 (noting that, during the hearing on the Rule 41(5) application, counsel for the Claimant had conceded that one of its claims was "a clear and classic example of where, without any reference whatsoever to facts or without the need to construe facts, this is a claim that is, on further reflection and consideration, manifestly without legal basis" and was therefore withdrawn).

more frequently, with the procedure having been used in at least thirty-eight arbitrations since 2012. However, among these more recent cases the respondent's objections have rarely been upheld, with claims being fully or partially dismissed in only seven cases, leading some commentators to suggest that Rule 41(5) is now being overused.[72] Given the high standard that many tribunals are imposing for a claim to be "manifestly" without legal merit—refusing to decide legal issues that are novel, complex or even disputed—it is unsurprising that few of the preliminary objections raised under Rule 41(5) in recent years have been upheld. A failure to meet such a high standard does not necessarily suggest that the respondent's objection is weak or baseless. As we will argue in Section 4, in our view the construction that tribunals are giving to the requirement that the flaws of a claim be "manifest" undermines the potential for the early-dismissal mechanism to efficiently deal with unmeritorious claims. Moreover, there have been several cases where jurisdictional objections were dismissed when raised under Rule 41(5) but were then upheld in a subsequent phase of proceedings considering those objections under ICSID Rule 41(1), which is not subject to the same expedited timeframe as Rule 41(5) and where the tribunal could engage with disputed issues of fact.[73] These cases may seem to confirm the fears of some commentators that Rule 41(5) would prolong arbitrations through an additional stage of proceedings.[74] As we will discuss in Section 4.2, the ability of respondents to raise the same jurisdictional objection under both Rule 41(5) and Rule 41(1) should be reconsidered.

In total there are ten publicly available decisions under Rule 41(5) in which some or all claims were dismissed. Among these ten decisions, there were three partial dismissals where, after the respondent made its preliminary objection, the claimant conceded that the relevant claim was unsustainable under the terms of the IIA.[75] In another two cases the tribunals dismissed the claims in their entirety because they were contractual claims that could not be properly brought under the relevant IIA.[76] Another three cases—*AFC v Colombia*, *Ansung Housing v China*, and *Almasryia v Kuwait*—saw the tribunals dismiss all claims on the basis that relevant time limits for the initiation of the arbitrations had not been complied with and therefore the tribunal did not have

---

[72] Howes, Stowell, and Choi (n 41) 9.

[73] See eg *PNG Sustainable Development Program Ltd v Independent State of Papua New Guinea*, Award, ICSID Case No ARB/13/33, 5 May 2015, para 379 (hereafter *PNG Sustainable Development v PNG*, Award) (upholding the objection that the tribunal had no jurisdiction because the Claimant did not obtain the Respondent's consent to the jurisdiction of the tribunal in writing, an objection which had been dismissed in the Rule 41(5) procedure because it raised "disputed, and often complex, legal and factual issues": *PNG Sustainable Development v PNG*, Decision on ICSID Rule 41(5), para 99). Similar cases are discussed in Section 4.2.

[74] See Schreuer and others (n 6) 544; Wong and Yackee (n 6) 240; Rosenfeld (n 4) 100–101.

[75] See *Trans-Global Petroleum v Jordan*, Decision on ICSID Rule 41(5), paras 118–120; *Emmis v Hungary*, Decision on ICSID Rule 41(5), paras 17–18 and 71–72; *Accession Mezzanine Capital L.P. and Danubius Kereskedöház Vagyonkezelö Zrt v Hungary*, Decision on Respondent's Objection Under Arbitration Rule 41(5), ICSID Case No ARB/12/3, 16 January 2013, para 64 (hereafter *Accession Mezzanine Capital v Hungary*, Decision on ICSID Rule 41(5)).

[76] See *Global Trading v Ukraine*, Award, paras 56–58 (holding that all claims related solely to contractual rights to payment and that these rights did not qualify as "investments" under the relevant BIT); *Lotus Holding Anonim Şirketi v Republic of Turkmenistan*, Award, ICSID Case No ARB/17/30, 6 April 2020, paras 195–197 (holding that all claims made in the dispute were "properly to be characterized as contract claims relating to contracts entered into by" a subsidiary of the claimant, and that the claimant itself did not have standing to bring these claims) (hereafter *Lotus Holding v Turkmenistan*, Award).

jurisdiction.[77] The *Almasryia* tribunal also dismissed the expropriation claims on their merits, on the basis that the claimant did not hold any property rights which could have been the subject of expropriation.[78] In another case, one of the investor's claims was dismissed under ICSID Rule 41(5) on the basis of a time bar, while other claims were allowed to proceed and remain pending.[79] In the remaining dispute of the ten in which Rule 41(5) objections have been upheld—*RSM Production Company and Ors v Grenada*—all claims were dismissed on the merits, because none could succeed without revisiting questions of fact or law which had already been resolved in a prior contractual arbitration, and the doctrine of collateral estoppel prevented the tribunal from relitigating those questions.[80] The findings of these tribunals demonstrate the utility of the Rule 41(5) procedure in preventing the waste of resources and shortening arbitrations in cases where some or all of the claims raised were fundamentally flawed.

## 3.2 United States Treaty Practice

As already noted in this chapter, US IIAs concluded since the early 2000s have included an early-dismissal mechanism. In this section we refer primarily to Article 10.20.4 of CAFTA-DR as an example of US treaty practice, but we note that an equivalent provision appears in a number of other FTA investment chapters and BITs.[81] CAFTA-DR sub-paragraph 10.20.4(c) requires that, when assessing a preliminary objection made under this provision, the tribunal "shall assume to be true claimant's factual allegations in support of any claim", making the US treaty mechanism very similar to a motion to dismiss under Rule 12(b)(6) of the US Federal Rules of Civil Procedure. However, a tribunal considering the application of Article 10.20.4 was careful to note that there is "no reason to equate" the CAFTA-DR mechanism with US civil procedure, particularly given that the CAFTA-DR provisions were "agreed by Contracting Parties with different legal traditions and national court procedures".[82]

---

[77] See *AFC Investment Solutions S.L. v Republic of Colombia*, Award under ICSID Rule Arbitration Rule 41(5), ICSID Case No ARB/20/16, 24 February 2022, para 231 (Award only published in Spanish; Tribunal held that although notice of the claim was served before the relevant cut-off date, that the arbitration was commenced after the date and was therefore time-barred); *Ansung Housing Co, Ltd v People's Republic of China*, Award, ICSID Case No ARB/14/25, 9 March 2017, paras 122 and 138–141 (noting that the claim was submitted after the lapsing of a three-year limitation period imposed by the BIT, and that this limitation period could not be waived or extended by virtue of the BIT's most-favoured-nation (MFN) clause) (hereafter *Ansung Housing v China*, Award); *Almasryia v Kuwait*, Award, paras 47–48 (noting that the Claimant had failed to comply with a six-month waiting period required under the BIT). cf *Almasryia v Kuwait*, Dissenting Opinion on the Respondent's Application Under Rule 41(5) of the ICSID Arbitration Rules, ICSID Case No ARB/18/2, 1 November 2019 (arguing that the issues raised by the preliminary objections were not appropriate for resolution through the summary process provided) (hereafter *Almasryia v Kuwait*, Dissenting Opinion).

[78] *Almasryia v Kuwait*, Award, para 58. We note that at the time of writing an application for annulment of the award in *Almasryia v Kuwait* was pending.

[79] *Min v Korea*, Decision on ICSID Rule 41(5), para 98.

[80] See *RSM Production Company and Ors v Grenada*, Award, paras 7.1.1–7.2.25.

[81] See treaties cited at n 2.

[82] *Pac Rim Cayman LLC v Republic of El Salvador*, Decision on the Respondent's Preliminary Objections under CAFTA Articles 10.20.4 and 10.20.5, ICSID Case No ARB/09/12, 2 August 2010, para 117 (hereafter *Pac Rim Cayman v El Salvador*, Decision on Preliminary Objections).

A preliminary objection under CAFTA-DR Article 10.20.4 must be raised "as soon as possible after the tribunal is constituted, and in no event later than the date the tribunal fixes for the respondent to submit its counter-memorial". This effectively allows the respondent a much longer time frame in which to raise a preliminary objection, compared to ICSID Rule 41(5), and allows for the possibility that an objection could be raised after the claimant has already advanced written evidence in their memorial. In further contrast to ICSID Rule 41(5), CAFTA-DR Article 10.20.4 does not require that objections be considered within a specific time frame, although the respondent may request expedited consideration under Article 10.20.5. The time frame allowed under the expedited CAFTA-DR procedure is longer than that under ICSID Rule 41(5): ordinarily the tribunal should issue a decision on the objection within 150 days, although this may be extended by thirty days if either party requests a hearing and by up to a further thirty days if the tribunal can show "extraordinary cause".[83] Therefore, where a respondent requests expedited consideration under CAFTA-DR Article 10.20.5, the tribunal should reach a decision on the objection in no more than 210 days, which is roughly twice the average time taken by tribunals to resolve objections raised under ICSID Rule 41(5).

Only a few cases have considered an objection raised under CAFTA-DR Article 10.20.4 or analogous provisions, but the decisions in these cases provide some important insights into how the US treaty provisions vary from ICSID Rule 41(5).[84] Most notably, the legal standard required for a claim to be dismissed under CAFTA-DR Rule 10.20.4 is that a claim cannot succeed as a matter of law; but there is no requirement that the claim be "manifestly" unable to succeed. Consequently, the CAFTA-DR mechanism is not limited to "frivolous" or "legally impossible" claims,[85] and therefore appears to be a broader provision than ICSID Rule 41(5).[86] However, the tribunal in *Pac Rim Cayman v El Salvador*, which was the first to apply CAFTA-DR Article 10.20.4, indicated that perhaps the rule should not be used to resolve difficult questions, noting that "it should not ordinarily be necessary to address at length complex issues of law".[87] Time will tell whether tribunals are prepared to view CAFTA-DR Article 10.20.4 as granting them the same authority to dismiss a claim early as Rule 12(b)(6) of the US Federal Rules of Civil Procedure grants to US federal courts.

A second important contrast to ICSID Rule 41(5) is that CAFTA-DR Article 10.20.4 and its counterparts appear to be limited to objections relating to the merits of a claim, and do not encompass jurisdictional objections.[88] This is clarified in the text of some of

---

[83] See CAFTA DR art 10.20.5.

[84] One tribunal considering objections under CAFTA-DR Article 10.20.4 held that it was "not materially assisted" by comparisons with ICSID Rule 41(5) as the provisions have "different wording and do not share exactly the same object and purpose": *Pac Rim Cayman v El Salvador*, Decision on Preliminary Objections, para 118. See also *The Renco Group, Inc v Republic of Peru I*, Decision as to the Scope of the Respondent's Preliminary Objections under Article 10.20.4, Arbitration under the UNCITRAL Arbitration Rules (2010), ICSID Case No UNCT/13/1, 18 December 2014, para 237 (hereafter *Renco v Peru I*, Decision on Scope of Preliminary Objections).

[85] *Pac Rim Cayman v El Salvador*, Decision on Preliminary Objections, para 108.

[86] Rosenfeld (n 4) 97.

[87] *Pac Rim Cayman v El Salvador*, Decision on Preliminary Objections, paras 110 and 112.

[88] See Kehoe (n 12) 89–90.

the US-style early-dismissal mechanisms, such as Article 10.20.4 of the US-Peru Trade Promotion Agreement (2006).[89] While other provisions such as CAFTA-DR Article 10.20.4 do not explicitly state that jurisdictional objections are outside the scope of the provision, in practice there is no need for respondents to invoke the Article 10.20.4 standard of "not a claim for which an award in favour of the claimant may be made" for objections relating to the competence of the tribunal. Jurisdictional objections can be raised as a preliminary matter and the respondent may request expedited consideration under CAFTA-DR Article 10.20.5, but the relevant provision for assessing whether the objection should be upheld will depend upon the basis for the objection. For example, in *Railroad Development Corporation v Guatemala* the respondent sought expedited consideration of its objection that the tribunal lacked jurisdiction because the notice of arbitration was not accompanied by a waiver of domestic litigation rights required under CAFTA-DR Article 10.18.2(b).[90] Because Article 10.20.4 does not apply there is no need for the tribunal to "assume as true all facts alleged in the notice of arbitration" when assessing jurisdictional objections,[91] although in practice some tribunals considering jurisdictional objections through an expedited process have still proceeded on the basis of that assumption.[92]

## 3.3  Other IIAs and Arbitral Rules

Other IIAs and arbitral rules have begun to incorporate early-dismissal mechanisms which build upon either ICSID Rule 41(5) or US treaty practice, although these newer treaty provisions have not yet been applied in practice. CETA takes an interesting hybrid approach, which incorporates elements of both the ICSID and US models. Article 8.32 of CETA provides that a respondent may "file an objection that a claim is manifestly without legal merit", which the tribunal will assess "assum[ing] the alleged facts to be true".[93] This test closely mirrors ICSID Rule 41(5), with the CETA provision codifying the practice that a tribunal will assume the truth of the facts as alleged by the claimant. Article 8.33 of CETA is based on US treaty practice and provides that a respondent may file an objection that "as a matter of law, a claim ... is not a claim for which an award in favour of the claimant may be made under this Section, even if the facts alleged were assumed to be true".[94] There is very little guidance in the text and preparatory materials to

---

[89] See *Renco v Peru I*, Decision on Scope of Preliminary Objections, para 231.

[90] *Railroad Development Corporation v Republic of Guatemala,* Decision on Objection to Jurisdiction CAFTA Article 10.20.5, ICSID Case No ARB/07/23, 17 November 2008. See also, *Daniel W. Kappes and Kappes, Cassiday & Associates v Republic of Guatemala,* Decision on the Respondent's Preliminary Objections, ICSID Case No ARB/18/43, 13 March 2020, para 55 (hereafter *Kappes v Guatemala,* Decision on Preliminary Objections) (setting out the various objections and relevant treaty provisions, noting that only the one objection relating to the merits was raised under Article 10.20.4, and the remaining objections relating to admissibility and jurisdiction relied upon other treaty provisions).

[91] *Kappes v Guatemala,* Decision on Preliminary Objections, para 220.

[92] See eg *Commerce Group Corp and San Sebastian Gold Mines, Inc v Republic of El Salvador,* Award, ICSID Case No ARB/09/17, 14 March 2011, para 55.

[93] CETA arts 8.32.1 and 8.32.5.

[94] ibid art 8.33.1.

explain why CETA contains two parallel early-dismissal mechanisms.[95] CETA Article 8.32 must be invoked within thirty days of the constitution of the tribunal, and a decision should be rendered "at its first session or promptly thereafter".[96] This adoption of similar timeframes to ICSID Rule 41(5) suggests that Article 8.32 is meant to be a very expedited process, designed to quickly dispose of obviously flawed or unmeritorious claims. In contrast, more generous timeframes are allowed for an Article 8.33 objection, which can be made at any point up to the submission of the respondent's counter-memorial, and there is no fixed time limit in which the tribunal must rule on the objection (although it must be "consistent with any schedule it has established for considering any other preliminary question").[97] The text suggests that the two provisions are intended to be mutually exclusive, with a respondent unable to submit an objection under Article 8.32 if it has raised an objection under Article 8.33.[98] Conversely, if the respondent has already raised an objection under Article 8.32, the tribunal may (but does not have to) decline to consider an objection under Article 8.33.[99]

In 2017 the investment arbitration rules of the Singapore International Arbitration Centre (SIAC) were amended to include a mechanism which allows:

> for the early dismissal of a claim or defence on the basis that:
> a. a claim or defence is manifestly without legal merit;
> b. a claim or defence is manifestly outside the jurisdiction of the Tribunal; or
> c. a claim or defence is manifestly inadmissible.[100]

One immediately notable feature of this provision is that it applies to defences as well as claims and may therefore be invoked by claimants as well as respondent states. Paragraph (a) clearly reflects the language of ICSID Rule 41(5), although the SIAC rule refers separately to a lack of jurisdiction or inadmissibility as grounds for early dismissal. Under the SIAC rule the tribunal has the discretion to decide whether to allow the application for early dismissal to proceed, but if the application does proceed, the tribunal must issue an order or award within 90 days of the filing of the application unless the Registrar extends the time on the basis of exceptional circumstances.[101] Given the short time frame in which an application for early dismissal under these SIAC rules should be resolved, and the requirement that any of the three grounds for early dismissal be "manifestly" apparent, it may be expected that in assessing these objections the tribunal will assume any facts alleged by the claimant to be true. However, this is not required by the text of the SIAC rule, which instead provides that the application for early dismissal "shall state in detail the facts and legal basis supporting the

---

[95] Rosenfeld (n 4) 99.
[96] CETA arts 8.32.1 and 8.32.5.
[97] ibid arts 8.33.2 and 8.33.4.
[98] ibid art 8.32.2.
[99] ibid art 8.33.3.
[100] SIAC Investment Rules (2017), rule 26.1.
[101] ibid rules 26.3 and 26.4.

application".[102] This language suggests the possibility that a claim for early dismissal under the SIAC Investment Rules (2017) may permit a tribunal to consider factual as well as legal disputes, despite the short time frame.

## 4. Enhancing Early-Dismissal Mechanisms in International Investment Law

ICSID Rule 41(5) and the early-dismissal mechanisms found in US IIAs have now been in effect for over fifteen years, and the growing body of arbitral jurisprudence applying these provisions offers insights into how the mechanisms could be improved. These improvements are relevant not just to future reforms of the ICSID Rules or existing US treaties; they also should be considered in the drafting of new IIAs and the updating of other arbitral rules to include early-dismissal mechanisms. The examples of CETA and the SIAC Investment Arbitration Rules (2017) discussed in the previous section show that early-dismissal mechanisms are an increasingly common feature in international investment law, and that their design is heavily influence by ICSID Rule 41(5) and the standard that a claim must be "manifestly without legal merit". In Section 4.1 we argue that the requirement that a claim be "manifestly" unmeritorious should be removed from early-dismissal mechanisms, or construed less restrictively, because it creates too high a threshold and deters tribunals from resolving purely legal questions at an early stage, prior to any factual development. In Section 4.2 we consider the extent to which early-dismissal mechanisms should allow for the consideration of jurisdictional objections, and the potential for unnecessary delay and duplication in proceedings.

### 4.1  Removing the Requirement that Claims Must Be "Manifestly" Flawed

As explained in Section 3.1, the ICSID Rule 41(5) standard that a claim can only be dismissed if it is manifestly without legal merit has been interpreted increasingly stringently by arbitral tribunals to exclude the resolution of novel or complex issues of law. Some tribunals have gone so far as to say that an expedited procedure like ICSID Rule 41(5) should only apply where there is no room for genuine dispute about the relevant legal issue.[103]

---

[102] ibid rule 26.2.

[103] See eg *Lion Mexico v Mexico*, Decision on ICSID AF Rule 45(6), para 66; *PNG Sustainable Development v PNG*, Decision on ICSID Rule 41(5), paras 88–89; *Dominion Minerals v Panama*, Decision on the Respondent's Applications for the Stay of Enforcement of the Award and Under Arbitration Rule 41(5), ICSID Case No ARB/16/13, Annulment Proceeding, 21 July 2022, paras 149–151. Even tribunals applying early-dismissal mechanisms in US treaties—which on their face appear to allow for the dismissal of a broader range of claims as they are not limited to those that are "manifestly" flawed—have held that they should not usually be used "to address at length complex issues of law". *Pac Rim Cayman v El Salvador*, Decision on Preliminary Objections, para 112.

In our view, this standard is unreasonably high and undermines the utility of early-dismissal mechanisms in international investment law. The benefit of early-dismissal mechanisms as they are used in domestic legal systems, such as a motion to dismiss under Rule 12(b)(6) of the US Federal Rules of Civil Procedure, is to allow for the early resolution of legal issues that may be determinative of a claim prior to any factual development occurring, such as discovery or the production of written evidence.[104] The key issue in these domestic procedures is not whether the objection requires the consideration of complex or novel legal issues. Instead, whether a motion to dismiss or similar application in a common-law jurisdiction will succeed depends upon whether the legal issue is determinative of the claim without the need for the court to enter into questions of fact. As put by the Australian High Court in a seminal case on summary dismissal of unmeritorious claims: "[a]rgument, perhaps even of an extensive kind, may be necessary to demonstrate that the case of the plaintiff is so clearly untenable that it cannot possibly proceed".[105] This approach can be contrasted to that currently taken by some investor–state arbitral tribunals, which have drawn a distinction between "a claim by an investor that can be properly rejected out of hand, and one which requires more elaborate argument for its eventual disposition".[106]

Where an objection raised under an early-dismissal mechanism requires the determination of issues of fact or of questions of mixed law and fact,[107] it may well be inappropriate for a tribunal to rule on the substance of the objection at the preliminary stage of proceedings. But where a question of law is isolated from issues of fact,[108] there can be only two justifications for excluding the consideration of complex, novel or disputed issues from early-dismissal mechanisms. One is the requirement of Rule 41(5) that, to be dismissed, a claim be "manifestly without legal merit". The other is that the timeframes for consideration under an expedited procedure are too short to properly resolve the issue and may undermine the claimant's right to due process.[109]

With regard to the first justification, it would hardly be unreasonable to view as "manifestly without legal merit" any claim that cannot succeed even if all of the factual

---

[104] See discussion in Section 2.

[105] *General Steel Industries Inc. v Commissioner for Railways (N.S.W.) and Ors* (1964) 112 CLR 125, 130 (per Barwick CJ).

[106] *MOL Hungarian Oil v Croatia*, Decision on ICSID Rule 41(5), para 45. See also Howes, Stowell, and Choi (n 41) 14–15.

[107] See eg *Pac Rim Cayman v El Salvador*, Decision on Preliminary Objections, para 246.

[108] Purely legal issues have been raised in some ICSID Rule 41(5) proceedings but have gone unresolved. For example, one of the objections raised by the respondent in *PNG Sustainable Development v PNG* related to the interpretation of Article 25(1) of the ICSID Convention. While the tribunal noted that the respondent's legal argument required consideration of "materials extraneous" to the terms of the Convention, there is no indication that the objection required a consideration of issues of fact or of domestic law. See *PNG Sustainable Development v PNG*, Decision on ICSID Rule 41(5), para 97. Similarly, in *MOL Hungarian Oil v Croatia*, one of the objections raised concerned novel and complex issues of treaty interpretation, but in the tribunal's summary of the issue no disputes regarding fact or domestic law were mentioned. See *MOL Hungarian Oil v Croatia*, Decision on ICSID Rule 41(5), para 48.

[109] See eg *PNG Sustainable Development v PNG*, Decision on ICSID Rule 41(5), para 94; *Lion Mexico v Mexico*, Decision on ICSID AF Rule 45(6), para 66; *Trans-Global Petroleum v Jordan*, Decision on ICSID Rule 41(5), para 90; *Almasryia v Kuwait*, Dissenting Opinion, para 89. See also Michele Potestà and Marija Sobald, "Frivolous Claims in International Adjudication: A Study of ICSID Rule 41(5) and of Procedures of Other Courts and Tribunals to Dismiss Claims Summarily" (2012) 3(1) Journal of International Dispute Resolution 137–68.

allegations on which it relies are accepted. Thus far, a uniform view to this effect has not emerged, to say the least. It may be that further amendment of the ICSID Arbitration Rules to remove the "manifestly" requirement will be required if the early dismissal mechanism is to become truly useful. As noted in this chapter, the 2022 version of the ICSID Arbitration Rules retains the "manifestly" requirement for its early dismissal mechanism, suggesting that the current problematic trend in the case law is likely to continue in the next generation of ICSID disputes.[110]

As for the second justification, concerns regarding due process can be mitigated by tribunals using their discretion to order appropriate procedures in light of the complexity of the issues raised in an objection, such as multiple rounds of written submissions and an oral hearing. Currently under ICSID Rule 41(5) tribunals are trusted to determine the appropriate procedures for evaluating the preliminary objection, with some tribunals only requiring one round of written submissions, and others requiring two rounds of written submissions, a hearing and post-hearing briefs.[111] It is notable that hearings were held in all ICSID Rule 41(5) cases where the tribunal dismissed all or some of the claims without the consent of the claimant.[112] The *Global Trading* tribunal held that it was appropriate for it to dispose of claims under ICSID Rule 41(5) because, even at such a preliminary stage of proceedings, it "was unable to see what further materials relevant to the question at issue, be it in the shape of legal argument or authority or in the shape of witness or documentary evidence, either Party might wish to, or be able to, bring forward at a later stage".[113] Where the disputing parties have been given adequate opportunity to put forward argument on the question of law that is at issue, this should provide a sufficient level of due process for a preliminary objection to be resolved.

For this reason, tribunals should be given the discretion to determine appropriate procedures and timeframes for resolving preliminary objections, which can take account of the complexity of the specific issues raised in a given dispute, rather than strict and truncated timeframes being set in the treaty rules themselves. While the 2022 ICSID Arbitration Rules appear to give tribunals discretion as to the appropriate procedures and timeframes for submissions in an early dismissal application,[114] these rules set a limit for the Tribunal to issue its decision of sixty days after the last submission.[115] It is not the period of time in which a decision on an objection is rendered that determines the efficiency of an early-dismissal mechanism. Rather, the potential for significant savings of resources (both time and money) arises when a decision can be made

---

[110] See ICSID Arbitration Rules (2022), rule 41(1).

[111] For a more detailed analysis of the procedures followed in different cases, see Howes, Stowell, and Choi (n 41) 20–21.

[112] See *Trans-Global Petroleum v Jordan*, Decision on ICSID Rule 41(5), para 45; *Global Trading v Ukraine*, Award, para 22; *RSM Production Company and Ors v Grenada*, Award, para 1.3.6; *Accession Mezzanine Capital v Hungary*, Decision on ICSID Rule 41(5), para 77; *Ansung Housing v China*, Award, paras 20–21; *Almasryia v Kuwait*, Award, para 18; *Lotus Holding v Turkmenistan*, Award, para 73. In one dispute some claims were dismissed, with the agreement of the claimant, without a hearing having occurred: *Emmis v Hungary*, Decision on ICSID Rule 41(5), para 22.

[113] *Global Trading v Ukraine*, Award, para 34.

[114] ICSID Arbitration Rules (2022), rule 41(2)(c).

[115] ibid rule 41(2)(e).

on the legal merits of a claim before any factual development takes place. For example, *Global Trading v Ukraine* had the most protracted ICSID Rule 41(5) procedure to date, taking approximately eleven months for the objections to be resolved.[116] However, because that preliminary objection led to the dismissal of all claims in under a year, it was clearly still an efficient means of resolving the dispute, relative to the time it may have taken for the case to be resolved if the tribunal had engaged in more extensive proceedings which included the consideration of evidence. In many cases we imagine that early-dismissal mechanisms will still proceed relatively swiftly, even without strict timeframes being set in the treaty rules. Objections that only require "genuinely indisputable rules of law" to be applied to "uncontested facts"[117] should not require extensive argument to be resolved. Where a question of law is difficult and contested, however, efficiency still often will be served by allowing that question to be resolved through an early-dismissal mechanism, even if the procedure takes several months or longer.

This is demonstrated by the decisions of tribunals that have been able to resolve complex and novel legal issues through the existing early-dismissal mechanisms. The tribunal in *RSM Production Company and Ors v Grenada* had to determine whether the doctrine of collateral estoppel prevented the claimants from succeeding on the merits of any of their claims, because the tribunal constituted under the BIT would be unable to revisit findings of law and fact that had been made in a prior arbitration initiated under a relevant contract. While the *RSM* tribunal noted that the disputing parties agreed on the requirements of the doctrine of collateral estoppel,[118] contentious points of law were debated between the parties and ultimately resolved by the tribunal through the ICSID Rule 41(5) process, including whether the claimants in the BIT arbitration were bound by the findings of the prior contractual arbitration even though they had not been party to it,[119] and the impact of corruption allegations on the finality of the earlier award.[120] The *RSM* tribunal was able to resolve the objection in little more than four months.[121] The *Kappes v Guatemala* tribunal was able to resolve an objection raised under Article 10.20.4 of CAFTA-DR that the treaty language prevented claims for "reflective" losses (losses attributed directly to a shareholder by virtue of its part ownership of an injured corporation). This was a novel legal issue, which no other CAFTA-DR tribunal had yet had to address, and "which required considerable analysis to resolve".[122] After reviewing extensive argument on the interpretation of CAFTA-DR, including consideration of analogous NAFTA cases, the preparatory materials of CAFTA-DR, and the subsequent agreement and practice of the parties, the

---

[116] On the procedural timetable in this case, see *Global Trading v Ukraine*, Award, paras 16–26.

[117] *Lion Mexico v Mexico*, Decision on ICSID AF Rule 45(6), para 66.

[118] *RSM Production Company and Ors v Grenada*, Award, para 7.1.1. We note that the tribunal in *MOL Hungarian Oil v Croatia* described the *RSM v Grenada* case as one involving "straightforward and self-contained questions that suited themselves to summary determination": *MOL Hungarian Oil v Croatia*, Decision on ICSID Rule 41(5), para 51.

[119] *RSM Production Company and Ors v Grenada*, Award, paras 7.1.4–7.1.7.

[120] ibid paras 7.1.15–7.1.30.

[121] See ibid paras 1.2.5–1.3.1 (noting that the objection was filed on 5 August 2010. The award was dispatched on 10 December 2010).

[122] *Kappes v Guatemala*, Decision on Preliminary Objections, para 231.

tribunal denied the preliminary objection and held that there was nothing in the treaty language that barred the claimants from seeking to prove that they had sustained reflective losses.[123] These examples show that it is possible for tribunals to decide difficult or novel questions of law through an early-dismissal mechanism, and that the extent of pleading and time required under these mechanisms can be tailored to reflect the complexity of the legal issue raised in the objection.

## 4.2  Limiting the Ability to Raise Jurisdictional Objections in Early-Dismissal Proceedings

It is uncontroversial that ICSID Rule 41(5) can be used to raise objections relating either to jurisdiction or to the merits of a claim, and this is made clear in the text of Rule 41(1) of the 2022 ICSID Arbitration, although as noted in Section 3.1 there have been several cases where a jurisdictional objection was dismissed under Rule 41(5) but later upheld. The key reason given by the drafters for including jurisdictional objections within the scope of Rule 41(5) was that, while such objections could already be raised as a preliminary matter under Rule 41(1), the latter procedure is not expedited and the tribunal retains the discretion to decide whether the jurisdictional objection would be heard in a separate phase of proceedings or joined to the merits.[124] Thus, although it was "primarily designed to dismiss frivolous claims on the merits", "expedited objections on jurisdiction could not be ruled out of the scope of Rule 41(5)".[125] This can be juxtaposed to the early-dismissal mechanisms found in US treaties, which do not appear to encompass jurisdictional objections (although the US treaties allow objections relating to the merits of a claim or to jurisdiction to be heard on an expedited basis).[126] Some commentators expressed concern that allowing jurisdictional objections to be raised under both ICSID Rules 41(5) and 41(1) would lead to the lengthening of arbitrations,[127] but the US model prevents the respondent having "two bites at the apple".[128] As pointed out by the Tribunal in *Mainstream Renewable Power v Germany*, the 2006 ICSID Arbitration Rules allow three potential avenues for preliminary challenge on jurisdictional grounds: (i) threshold review by the Secretariat under Article 36 of the ICSID Convention; (ii) the early dismissal process under Rule 41(5); and (iii) the general process for raising preliminary objections under Rule 41(1).[129] These three avenues all remain available in the amended 2022 ICSID Rules.

There have been numerous arbitrations in which the respondent has raised a jurisdictional objection under ICSID Rule 41(5), which was dismissed at that stage by the

---

[123]  ibid para 159.
[124]  ICSID Arbitration Rules (2006), rule 41(4).
[125]  Antonietti (n 35) 440.
[126]  See nn 88–92 and accompanying text.
[127]  See Schreuer and others (n 6) 544; Wong and Yackee (n 6) 240; Rosenfeld (n 4) 100–01.
[128]  Kehoe (n 12) 90. See also *Renco v Peru I*, Decision on Scope of Preliminary Objections, para 221.
[129]  *Mainstream Renewable Power v Germany*, Decision on Respondent's Application Under ICSID Arbitration Rule 41(5), ICSID Case No ARB/21/26, 18 January 2022, para 94.

tribunal, and then has been raised again by the respondent under Rule 41(1). In their quantitative study of the use of ICSID Rule 41(5) up to 2017, Howes, Stowell, and Choi found that half of the arbitrations in which Rule 41(5) applications were unsuccessful were later dismissed for lack of jurisdiction.[130] Some tribunals have viewed the raising of unsuccessful jurisdictional objections under Rule 41(5) as contributing additional costs in the proceedings, even though the objections were eventually upheld in a later phase of the arbitration.[131] Conversely, in *PNG Sustainable Development v PNG* the tribunal noted that, while it dismissed the jurisdictional objections under Rule 41(5), that the procedure had helped the tribunal to narrow the scope of the issues which were then to be decided in the subsequent phase of proceedings and thereby streamlined the arbitration.[132]

Rather than demonstrating that respondents have sought to abuse the Rule 41(5) procedure to lengthen or delay proceedings, the cases to date suggest that in many disputes the Rule 41(5) standard was simply not appropriate for resolving the jurisdictional objection. In many cases this is because the Rule 41(5) early-dismissal mechanism proceeds on the assumption that the facts alleged by the claimant are true, while the jurisdictional objections raised by the respondent often rely on questions of fact or mixed issues of fact and law. An illustrative example is *CEAC Holdings v Montenegro*, where the respondent raised a preliminary objection that the claimant was not an "investor" under the relevant BIT because it did not have a corporate seat in Cyprus (its alleged home state).[133] While this objection was not upheld during the Rule 41(5) process, it was upheld in a subsequent phase of proceedings. In that second phase of proceedings the tribunal had had the opportunity to make various findings of fact, including that there was no "conclusive evidence that a registered office exists"[134] and that the alleged registered office did not meet the requirements of the Companies Law of Cyprus, such as being "accessible to the public for purposes of inspecting the company's registers" or being amenable to service.[135] In the hearing on preliminary objections under Rule 41(5), counsel for the Claimant had asserted that it could provide the relevant documents and evidence to show that it did in fact have a registered office in Cyprus, but had not done so at that stage as they did not believe it was "appropriate to have a full-blown ICSID jurisdictional hearing and proceeding" to resolve the Rule 41(5) objections.[136] Both parties had submitted some exhibits in support of their position on the preliminary objections,[137] but the tribunal's decision on the Rule 41(5) objections expressly stated that in the next phase of proceedings the parties were to present

---

[130]  Howes, Stowell, and Choi (n 41) 32.

[131]  See eg *Rizvi v Indonesia*, Award, para 232.

[132]  *PNG Sustainable Development v PNG*, Award, para 410. See also Howes, Stowell, and Choi (n 41) 32–33.

[133]  Although the decision on preliminary objections under ICSID Rule 41(5) in this case is not publicly available, the Award notes that in its decision under Rule 41(5) the Tribunal ordered the parties to prepare for a dedicated phase of proceedings considering this issue, which suggests that it was raised as a preliminary objection at the Rule 41(5) stage. See *CEAC Holdings Ltd v Montenegro*, Award, ICSID Case No ARB/14/8, 26 July 2016, para 182 (hereafter *CEAC Holdings v Montenegro*, Award).

[134]  ibid para 160.

[135]  ibid paras 193, 196.

[136]  ibid para 181.

[137]  These exhibits are mentioned at various points in the award. See eg ibid paras 178–181, 205.

"*all* the evidence and arguments that pertain to the issue of the 'seat'".[138] Thus, *CEAC Holdings v Montenegro* appears to be a clear example of where Rule 41(5) was simply not an appropriate avenue through which to assess the jurisdictional objection as it directly raised issues of fact.

In several of the cases where a jurisdictional objection was dismissed under Rule 41(5) but then upheld in a subsequent phase of proceedings, one of the points at issue was the interpretation of domestic law. Although there is some debate as to whether the interpretation of domestic law should be treated as an issue of fact or law,[139] most tribunals have been unwilling to resolve these questions through an early-dismissal mechanism.[140] In *Rizvi v Indonesia* the respondent argued that the Claimant's alleged investments "did not fall within the scope of Article 2(1) of the [UK-Indonesia BIT]", which states that:

> This Agreement shall only apply to investments by nationals or companies of the United Kingdom in the territory of the Republic of Indonesia which have been granted admission in accordance with the Foreign Capital Investment Law No. 1 of 1967 or any law amending or replacing it.[141]

Although Indonesia's objection was dismissed under Rule 41(5),[142] it then raised objections to jurisdiction under ICSID Rule 41(1), arguing that the investment had not been granted admission in accordance with the requirements of Indonesian law and therefore did not qualify as a covered investment under Article 2(1) of the BIT. To resolve this question the tribunal considered not only issues of treaty interpretation, but also various sources of evidence about the actions of Indonesian regulatory authorities[143] and expert-witness testimony regarding the interpretation of Indonesian law.[144] Having reviewed these additional sources of evidence, the *Rizvi* tribunal concluded that the relevant investment did not meet the requirements of the BIT and that it therefore had no jurisdiction over the claims.[145]

---

[138] ibid paras 182–183 (emphasis added).

[139] See eg *Pac Rim Cayman v El Salvador*, Decision on Preliminary Objections, para 246.

[140] For examples of where the need to interpret domestic law was given by a tribunal as a reason for dismissing a jurisdictional objection under Rule 41(5), see eg *Lion Mexico v Mexico*, Decision on ICSID AF Rule 45(6), para 81; *PNG Sustainable Development v PNG*, Decision on ICSID Rule 41(5), paras 93–96. The interpretation of domestic law has also been at issue in some objections relating to the merits of claims, and which the tribunal held could not be resolved through an early-dismissal mechanism. See eg *Pac Rim Cayman v El Salvador*, Decision on Preliminary Objections, para 246.

[141] *Agreement between the Government of the United Kingdom of Great Britain and Northern Ireland and the Government of the Republic of Indonesia for the Promotion and Protection of Investments*, signed 27 April 1976 (entered into force 24 March 1977), art 2(1).

[142] The decision on preliminary objections made under ICSID Rule 41(5) in this case is not publicly available, but the award which was later issued noted that the objections were "rejected" at that stage of proceedings: *Rafat Ali Rizvi v Republic of Indonesia*, Award on Jurisdiction, ICSID Case No ARB/11/13, 16 July 2013, para 20.

[143] See eg ibid paras 181–198 (where the tribunal assesses the Claimant's evidence that it was granted approval for admission to Indonesia under the relevant legislation).

[144] See eg ibid paras 45–51 (where the tribunal refers to various expert witness statements in its statement of the relevant Indonesian law).

[145] See ibid para 198 and Decision.

In our view, these cases demonstrate that in many instances jurisdictional objections are, by their very nature, not amendable to resolution under early-dismissal mechanisms such as ICSID Rule 41(5) as they will require resolution of disputed issues of fact or the interpretation of domestic law. The first tribunal to consider a jurisdictional objection under ICSID Rule 41(5), in *Brandes v Venezuela*, noted the importance of the tribunal being able to decide the "facts on which the jurisdiction of a tribunal rests", if those facts are contested between the parties.[146]

Although many jurisdictional objections will require examination of disputed facts or issues of domestic law, this does not mean that all jurisdictional objections should be excluded from early-dismissal mechanisms such as ICSID 2006 Rule 41(5) or ICSID 2022 Rule 41. As already discussed, in many of the disputes where claims have been dismissed under ICSID 2006 Rule 41(5) the relevant objections related to the jurisdiction of the tribunal and did not require the tribunal to resolve any contested issues of fact.[147] For this reason, we suggest that respondents be required to elect to bring a preliminary jurisdictional objection under only one preliminary objection procedure—either an early-dismissal mechanism such as ICSID 2022 Rule 41, or as a general jurisdictional objection under a provision such as ICSID 2022 Rule 43. A loss under the early dismissal mechanism would leave a respondent free to pursue a challenge to jurisdiction joined with the merits, but we see no rationale for allowing a respondent to initiate two preliminary-objection procedures concerning the same issue.

## 5. Conclusion

The purpose of any early-dismissal mechanism in arbitration or domestic litigation is to avoid the cost and delay involved in the development and presentation of evidence. Document discovery, the preparation of witness statements and expert reports, and the examination and cross-examination of witnesses and experts at hearings and trials are all time-consuming and expensive. A truly effective early-dismissal mechanism, therefore, will have two characteristics: it will require tribunals to reach a decision on the dismissal application without considering conflicting evidence, and it will require the application to be made before the claimant has had to present evidence. Provisions in treaties such as Article 10.20.4 of CAFTA-DR have the first characteristic in that they explicitly instruct arbitrators to consider the claims before them on the assumption that every factual assertion made by a claimant is true; they lack the second characteristic, however, in that they allow a respondent to apply for early dismissal up to the date fixed for the submission of its counter-memorial, which is to say, after the claimant has submitted its initial memorial and all of the supporting evidence that customarily accompanies that submission. ICSID 2006 Rule 41(5) and ICSID 2022 Rule 41 possess the second characteristic, in that they require that an application be made before the first

---

[146] *Brandes v Venezuela*, Decision on ICSID Rule 41(5), para 68.
[147] See cases cited at nn 75–77.

session of a tribunal; but they *seem* to lack the first characteristic, however, in that they place no express limit on the authority of arbitrators to consider conflicting factual assertions of the parties (none of which, at this stage, would necessarily be supported by any evidence).

The shortcoming of rules such as CAFTA-DR Article 10.20.4 cannot be remedied other than by amendment of the agreements that contain the rules. To be sure, a respondent might well choose to submit its application before seeing the claimant's initial memorial, in which case the interests of efficiency would be well-served. But a respondent also might want to take all the time allowed to prepare its application, in which case the claimant will have expended substantial resources in the preparation and presentation of evidence.

The shortcoming of ICSID 2006 Rule 41(5) and ICSID 2022 Rule 41, on the other hand, can be cured in either of two ways: tribunals can choose to conclude that a claim that will fail even if all the facts alleged by the claimant are true is "a claim [that] is manifestly without legal merit", or these rules can be amended to delete the word "manifestly". The first option strikes us as a reasonable application of the current rules. The premise of either option, however, is that any legal issue, no matter how complex, can be decided fairly and appropriately before the presentation of any evidence in response to a preliminary objection, so long as the parties are given adequate opportunity to present their arguments on those issues. This premise must be correct because courts in many jurisdictions do just this all the time.

# 17

# The Multiplicity of Parallel Procedures
# in International Law

*W Michael Reisman and Mahnoush H Arsanjani*

## 1. Introduction

In international law, the level of actual integration of a great many legal programmes is low. Omnibus treaties, which undertake to prescribe for all the facets of a phenomenon and create mechanisms for interpreting and applying their law to disputes arising under them, such as the 1982 United Nations Convention on the Law of the Sea, are rare. Given the episodic character of formal law-making, more often than not many treaties can only nibble at one part of the problem that initiated the negotiation. Although often envisaged as *part* of a necessarily larger political, social, or environmental programme, individual treaties tend to be narrower in scope, treating only "targets of opportunity", those aspects of a general problem on which political agreement can be reached at that point in time. Thus, an environmental treaty may address only that part of a current problem that is politically ripe for agreement and will incorporate a dispute-resolving procedure confined to that specific problem. Short of even that agreement, the treaty-making may confine itself to "standard setting" and simply ignore an application procedure.

In the aggregate, this inescapable piecemeal approach to treaty-making produces treaties with dispute-resolving mechanisms that are only competent for that part of the general problem the treaty engages.[1] As a result, issues that give rise to disputes often require the remedies of several piecemeal treaties. So it is sometimes necessary, in order to fashion a meaningful remedy in a particular instance, to invoke several different treaties, each with its own provision for the application of its substantive rights and to conduct simultaneous parallel procedures in different forums.[2]

---

[1] According to the latest report of the United Nations Treaty Section, so far 560 multilateral treaties have been deposited with the Secretary-General of the United Nations. See United Nations, *Multilateral Treaties Deposited with the Secretary-General*, <https://treaties.un.org/#:~:text=Depositary%20of%20Treaties-,The%20Secretary%2DGeneral%20of%20the%20United%20Nations%20is%20the%20depositary,and%20protection%20of%20the%20environment>.

There are many other multilateral treaties for which the Secretary-General is not the depository. In addition to multilateral treaties, there are thousands of bilateral treaties, designed to deal with specific issues of concern or interest to their parties and for which the parties agree on rules applicable to those specific issues. Because of multiplicity of so many treaties, some issues or some related features of them have been addressed in more than one treaty.

[2] This pattern of piecemeal codification has led to treaties that contain a so-called without prejudice clause which declares the independence of a treaty from other obligations of states parties under international law or

W Michael Reisman and Mahnoush H Arsanjani, *The Multiplicity of Parallel Procedures in International Law* In: *By Peaceful Means*. Edited by: Charles N Brower, Joan E Donoghue, Cian C Murphy, Cymie R Payne and Esmé R Shirlow, Oxford University Press. © W Michael Reisman and Mahnoush H Arsanjani 2024. DOI: 10.1093/oso/9780192848086.003.0017

Take environmental law: an environmental problem does not always fall neatly within the boundaries of a single treaty. As a consequence, the international lawyer charged with finding a remedy is often compelled to try to shape a bespoke integrated strategy, straddling a number of different treaties and their respective dispute-resolution arrangements. To carry this off, she must either press one of the relevant tribunals to expand its *ratione materiae* jurisdiction on the basis of a theory of "ancillary jurisdiction" and thereby defeat the State Parties' agreement that those matters would not be subject to third-party decision *or* she must initiate proceedings in several forums simultaneously. Both tactics incur international systemic costs. By contrast, these problems do not arise in national courts of general jurisdiction; unlike their international counterparts, they provide "one-stop" forums for the application of the law which has been prescribed by "one-stop" legislatures. In the domestic setting, parallel procedures are resisted.

An expansive theory of ancillary jurisdiction introduces uncertainty about just what is being committed in treaties which were accepted on the expectation that they were confined to one part of a problem or, even short of that, were only standard-setting exercises for which the States Parties were unprepared or unwilling to submit to judicially supervised implementation. Overall, an expansive theory of ancillary jurisdiction may solve the lawyer's problem for a specific case, but it reduces the future willingness of states to accept a jurisdiction which they thought was confined to one treaty by refusing to give effect to the intention of the state-parties to insulate certain issues from third-party decision. The knock-on effects for the legitimacy of the international judicial function, for the willingness of states to refer disputes to adjudication and for the general willingness to participate in the creation of "soft law" arrangements can be systemically costly. Parallel proceedings undertaken to cobble together the partial remedies available in particular treaties increase the costs of adjudication and impose a double burden on the respondent.

In this chapter, we are not concerned with the International Law Commission's study of "fragmentation of international law"[3] and whether such "fragmentation" is a negative or a positive trend. We are concerned only with one of the consequences of the fragmentary character of international law-making, namely multiple parallel proceedings for dispute settlement.

---

other treaties, while keeping alive those other obligations. As a consequence, law-making advances in fits and starts and piece by piece and law-applying is fragmented and not integrated.

[3] For the consolidated final report of the Working Group of the International Law Commission on Fragmentation of International Law Difficulties Arising from the Diversification and Expansion of International Law, see ILC, "Fragmentation of International Law Difficulties Arising from the Diversification and Expansion of International Law, Report of the Study Group of the International Law Commission" (1 May–9 June and 3 July–11 August 2006) UN Doc A/CN.4/L.682 and Corr.1 and Add.1, 2005. For the Report of the Commission see, ILC "Chapter XII, Fragmentation of International Law Difficulties Arising from the Diversification and Expansion of International Law, Report of the Study Group of the International Law Commission" (2006) Yearbook of the International Law Commission Vol. II (Part II) 175.

## 2. Parallel Procedures

Responses to multiple parallel processes vary from sector to sector as a function of the degree to which that sector can provide meaningful remedies for specific problems and the purposes which multiplicity serves in each. The more remedially effective the sector, one would expect the lower the tolerance for multiple parallel procedures. Sectors with a lower degree of remedial effectiveness may also include general prohibitions in their black-letter on parallel procedures, but the actual prohibitions will vary from case to case as a function of a number of variables, including the importance and urgency of the issues at stake to the relevant community. Thus, the apparent inconsistency and legal untidiness of international law's response to the multiplicity of parallel procedures may sometimes be coherent in terms of the animating international policies, if not always in terms of the explicit rules.

The scope of multiple parallel procedures can be defined narrowly and exclusively or broadly and inclusively. For many scholars, procedures are considered to be parallel if they are both (or all) judicial or, at least, judicial and arbitral.[4] This is the legal focus in municipal contexts; there the focus is confined to parallel and contemporaneous judicial procedures, in some instances, parallel arbitral procedures and, in instances in which the New York[5] or Panama Convention[6] is in force, simultaneous judicial and arbitral procedures.

In municipal law, whether its constitutive structure is federal or unitary, this narrow focus is appropriate because of a plethora of courts and tribunals of varying types, endowed with *compulsory* jurisdiction, and distributed horizontally and vertically. In that context, there are many occasions in which disputes may fulfil the jurisdictional and admissibility requisites of two or more forums. Because of variations in procedural and substantive law, some of these forums may seem more favourable to one of the litigants. That possibility can provoke a dash to different court houses, sometimes even by the same litigant. Domestic principles of institutional economy and procedural justice are offended by substantially the same case being pursued simultaneously in two competent, but different and effective forums. Doctrines of *lis alibi pendens* and *forum non conveniens* arrest the multiplication *in limine litis* and in a predictable and orderly way.[7]

---

[4] See Yuval Shany, *The Competing Jurisdictions of International Courts and Tribunals* (Oxford University Press 2008).

[5] Convention on the Recognition and Enforcement of Foreign Arbitral Awards (adopted 10 June 1958, entered into force 7 June 1959) 330 UNTS 38.

[6] Inter-American Convention on international commercial arbitration (adopted 30 January 1975, entered into force 16 June 1976) 1438 UNTS 245.

[7] Sometimes, parties to international disputes intentionally design parallel procedures. Consider the *Taba* case. Article VII(2) of the Egypt/Israel Peace Treaty stated that disputes "shall be resolved by conciliation or submitted to arbitration". When a boundary dispute arose in the course of implementing the treaty, Israel pressed for conciliation, while Egypt insisted on arbitration. The parties, in negotiating their *compromis*, allowed for both positions: the arbitration would commence and then suspend, while the two party-appointed arbitrators on the tribunal proceeded to conduct a conciliation procedure. If the conciliation proved unsuccessful, the arbitration would proceed. In fact, the conciliation effort failed and the arbitration resumed and produced a final award. See *Case concerning the location of boundary markers in Taba (Egypt v Israel)* (1988) XX RIAA 1.

International law's political structure differs in profound ways from domestic legal arrangements. To comprehend the phenomenon of parallel proceedings there, the focus of inquiry may have to be broader and more inclusive. For one thing, the degree of organization and effectiveness of international law varies more widely than it does in advanced domestic legal systems. Normatively, international law asserts that its writ and general principles run to the furthest reaches of its planetary and near-space realms. But when its domain is viewed in terms of degree of organization and predictable remedial effectiveness, international law takes on an archipelagic character in which "islands" of organized and effectively applied law operate alongside "offshore zones" in which the expected effectiveness is considerably lower and, in still others, in which the law simply yields to unilateral political decision.[8] In international law, the level of actual integration of various legal programmes is low. This is not by a deliberate design but by the way in which international law has developed and is developing; a by-product of a system composed of "sovereign" states.

If we shift our attention to the large "offshore" areas in which international law simply expresses normative preferences without providing judicially supervised mechanisms for their implementation, we will encounter another reason for a broader focus for the systemic toleration of multiple simultaneous proceedings. Law, to be meaningful, must be authoritative and controlling. A puzzling feature of international law is that some of the most important norms, for all their authority, are not reliably controlling. To the extent that they become effective, it is due to ad hoc arrangements, "coalitions of the willing", informal alliances of governmental and non-governmental actors, operating simultaneously in different arenas with a common goal. The effectiveness of these arrangements depends, in the end, on their operation in multiple proceedings.

## 3. Environment and Conservation

*Southern Bluefin Tuna* and, especially, *MOX Plant* illustrate one of the reasons we encounter parallel procedures in contemporary international law: the lawyer's search for a competent forum and an adequate remedy for which there is no fixed single treaty and no fixed single jurisdictional arrangement.

In 1947, the United Kingdom opened the Sellafield nuclear site, on the western coast of England, directly across the Irish Sea from the Republic of Ireland.[9] The site included two nuclear reactors and a reprocessing plant to produce plutonium fuel for atomic bombs.[10] The United Kingdom, through the state-owned company British Nuclear Fuels Limited (BNFL), continued to expand Sellafield's facilities through 1994, at which

---

[8] For further elaboration, see W Michael Reisman, *The Quest for World Order and Human Dignity in the Twenty-first Century: Constitutive Process and Individual Commitment: General Course on Public International Law* (Hague Academy of International Law, Martinus Nijhoff Publishers 2012) 31.

[9] *MOX Plant (Ireland v United Kingdom)* (Provisional Measures, Order of 3 December 2001) ITLOS Reports 2001, 95, para 7 (hereafter ITLOS Request for Provisional Measures); Emma Law, "What Is Sellafield?" *Gov.UK* (7 September 2018), <https://nda.blog.gov.uk/2018/09/07/what-is-sellafield/>.

[10] ibid.

point it opened a new reprocessing plant on the site, known as "Thorp",[11] designed to ingest spent oxide fuel, a type of nuclear waste, until then being discarded by the United Kingdom and other countries, and to reprocess up to 97 per cent of it[12] into reusable nuclear fuel.[13] In 1996, BNFL completed construction of another on-site facility, the "MOX Plant".[14] It was designed to transform Thorp's output into a type of nuclear fuel not used by the United Kingdom—mixed-oxide fuel, or MOX. According to the business plan, the MOX would be sold and transported by sea for use by other countries.[15]

On environmental grounds, Ireland opposed the MOX Plant throughout its construction and appealed unsuccessfully multiple times to the United Kingdom Environment Agency (UKEA) to have the project shut down.[16] Finally, shortly before the Plant was due to be commissioned, Ireland filed the first of what would become four parallel international judicial and arbitral proceedings. In these proceedings, Ireland maintained that, from the time of its construction in the 1950s, the Sellafield site had continually emitted nuclear radiation into the surrounding environment and that, as a result, the Irish Sea had become "among the most radioactively polluted seas in the world".[17] Ireland further alleged that the MOX Plant would "requir[e] the transportation of unknown—and potentially very large—quantities of ... hazardous radioactive materials [including plutonium] in close proximity to the territory of Ireland" and would result in "radioactive wastes [being] discharged directly into the Irish Sea".[18]

In 2001, while the UKEA was still considering whether to approve the opening of the MOX Plant for operation, Ireland initiated arbitral proceedings against the UK, at the Permanent Court of Arbitration under the OSPAR Convention.[19] Four months later, just after the UKEA approved the MOX Plant,[20] Ireland initiated another proceeding, this time under Article 287 and Annex VII of UNCLOS, before an ad hoc tribunal at the Permanent Court of Arbitration (PCA). Two weeks later, Ireland, as part of the UNCLOS Annex VII arbitration but before its ad hoc tribunal had been constituted, initiated a third proceeding in ITLOS. The purpose of this proceeding was to

---

[11] BBC News, 'Sellafield Thorp Site to Close in 2018', BBC (7 June 2012), <https://www.bbc.com/news/uk-engl and-cumbria-18353122>; see also Law (n 9).

[12] Martin Leafe, "End in Sight for Reprocessing Nuclear Fuel at Sellafield" Gov.UK (24 January 2017), <https:// nda.blog.gov.uk/2017/01/24/end-in-sight-for-reprocessing-nuclear-fuel-at-sellafield/>.

[13] Law (n 9).

[14] In the Dispute Concerning Access to Information Under Article 9 of the OSPAR Convention and the MOX Plant (Ireland v United Kingdom), PCA Case No 2001-03, Memorial of Ireland (7 March 2002) para 7 (hereafter OSPAR Memorial of Ireland), <https://pcacases.com/web/send Attach/609>.

[15] ibid; Charles de Saillan, "Disposal of Spent Nuclear Fuel in the United States and Europe: A Persistent Environmental Problem" (2010) 34 Harvard Environmental Law Review 461, 485.

[16] In the Dispute Concerning Access to Information Under Article 9 of the OSPAR Convention (Ireland v United Kingdom), PCA Case No 2001-03, Final Award (2 July 2003), 23 RIAA 59, paras 23, 27, 29–30, 32, 34, 36 <https:// pcacases.com/web/sendAttach/121>.

[17] ITLOS Request for Provisional Measures (n 9) paras 9–10; see also OSPAR Memorial of Ireland (n 14), paras 5–7.

[18] OSPAR Memorial of Ireland (n 14), paras 7 and 9; see also ITLOS Request for Provisional Measures (n 9) para 27; Maki Tanaka, "Lessons from the Protracted MOX Plant Dispute: A Proposed Protocol on Marine Environmental Impact Assessment to the United Nations Convention on the Law of the Sea" (2004) 25 Michigan Journal of International Law 337, 340.

[19] Permanent Court of Arbitration, "Ireland v. United Kingdom (OSPAR Arbitration)", <https://pca-cpa.org/en/ cases/34/> (hereinafter PCA OSPAR Arbitration); OSPAR Memorial of Ireland (n 14) paras 51–54.

[20] OSPAR Memorial of Ireland (n 14) para 54.

request provisional measures to suspend the MOX Plant's imminent opening to avert what Ireland claimed would be irreversible environmental injury.

ITLOS accepted the UK's commitment that it would not transport radioactive materials through the Irish Sea until October 2002 at the earliest[21] and concluded that "the urgency of the situation [did not] require … the provisional measures requested by Ireland, in the short period before the constitution of the Annex VII arbitral tribunal".[22]

Ireland's second proceeding had been brought under the Convention for the Protection of the Marine Environment of the North-East Atlantic. Popularly known as the "OSPAR Convention",[23] it held the promise for providing a remedy for a different aspect of the dispute. OSPAR Article 9 requires a State Party to provide, upon request of any other party, "any available information in written, visual, aural or data-base form on the state of the maritime area, on activities or measures adversely affecting or likely to affect it and on activities or measures introduced in accordance with the Convention".[24] The OSPAR tribunal concluded that Ireland had no colourable claims under the Convention,[25] and dismissed the case.[26]

Ireland's Annex VII dispute alleged that the UK had violated UNCLOS by "failing to take the necessary measures to prevent, reduce and control pollution of the marine environment of the Irish Sea".[27] In 2001, the European Commission, in view of the then-pending UNCLOS and OSPAR proceedings, filed a dispute at the European Court of Justice (ECJ), charging that in bringing claims against the United Kingdom under UNCLOS, Ireland had encroached on the ECJ's exclusive jurisdiction.[28] The ECJ held in 2006 that by filing under UNCLOS Annex VII claims that fell under European Community law, including claims expressly arising under the EC Treaty and Euratom Treaty Directives, Ireland had intruded on the ECJ's exclusive jurisdiction.

In the course of multiple rounds of briefing and two weeks of hearings in the Annex VII proceeding, the Annex VII tribunal became aware of the European Community's investigation into whether Ireland had violated European Community law by bringing claims under UNCLOS Annex VII. At Ireland's request, the tribunal issued an order suspending the UNCLOS arbitration pending judgment by the ECJ. When the ECJ found Ireland in violation of European Community law, Ireland withdrew its UNCLOS Annex VII dispute.[29]

Southern Bluefin tuna is a migratory species included in the list of highly migratory species in Annex I of the UNCLOS. Southern Bluefin tuna traverse the high seas of the

---

[21] ibid paras 78–80.

[22] ibid para 81.

[23] Convention for the Protection of the Marine Environment of the North-East Atlantic (adopted 22 September 1992, entered into force 25 March 1998) 2543 UNTS 67 (hereafter OSPAR Convention).

[24] ibid art 9(2).

[25] OSPAR Memorial of Ireland (n 14) para 185(v).

[26] ibid at 59; PCA OSPAR Arbitration (n 19).

[27] ITLOS Request for Provisional Measures (n 9) para 26.

[28] Case C-459/03 *Commission v Ireland* [2006] ECR I-04635 <http://curia.europa.eu/juris/celex.jsf?celex=6200 3CJ0459&lang1=en&type=TXT&ancre=>.

[29] *MOX Plant Case (Ireland v United Kingdom)*, PCA Case No 2002-01, Order No 6 (6 June 2008) <https://pcaca ses.com/web/sendAttach/870>; see also Suzannah Linton and Firew Kebede Tiba, "The International Judge in an Age of Multiple International Courts and Tribunals" (2009) 9 Chicago Journal of International Law 407, 432, 435.

oceans of the Southern Hemisphere, but they also pass through the exclusive economic zones and territorial waters of some States, including Australia and New Zealand. Japan is the main consumer of this fish.

Following the adoption of the 1982 United Nations Convention on the Law of Sea, Japan, Austria, and New Zealand concluded, in 1993, a trilateral treaty on the conservation of southern bluefin tuna.[30] In 1994, a Commission was established by the 1993 Convention to manage the harvesting and conservation of the bluefin tuna. While the 1993 Bluefin Tuna Convention contained provisions for dispute settlement including by arbitration, it required the consent of all parties to the dispute.[31]

Shortly after the establishment of the Commission, Japan pressed the Commission not only for a total allowable catch (TAC) increase, but also for a joint Experimental Fishing Program. In the face of inability of the Commission to agree and the insistence of Japan to commence a unilateral, three-year Experimental Fishing Program (in 1998), Australia and New Zealand, in 1999, each commenced an arbitration against Japan under Annex VII of the UNCLOS concerning the conservation and management of Southern Bluefin tuna. Pending the establishment of the tribunal, Australia and New Zealand filed a request with ITLOS for provisional measures. ITLOS joined the two requests for provisional measures. It also held that there appeared to be a basis of jurisdiction for the arbitral tribunal established under Annex VII of the UNCLOS and the fact that the 1993 Bluefin Tuna Convention applied between the three states, it did not preclude recourse to compulsory dispute settlement under Part XV of the UNCLOS.

The Arbitration Tribunal, established under Annex VII of the UNCLOS, recognized the "archipelagic" character of international law.

> [The Tribunal] recognizes that there is support in international law and in the legal systems of States for the application of a *lex specialis* that governs general provisions of an antecedent treaty or statute. But the Tribunal recognizes as well that *it is a commonplace of international law and State practice for more than one treaty to bear upon a particular dispute. There is no reason why a given act of a State may not violate its obligations under more than one treaty. There is frequently a parallelism of treaties, both in their substantive content and in their provisions for settlement of disputes arising thereunder.* The current range of international legal obligations benefits from a process of accretion and cumulation; in the practice of States, the conclusion of an implementing convention does not necessarily vacate the obligations imposed by the framework convention upon the parties to the implementing convention.[32]

While recognizing the omnibus character of UNCLOS, the Tribunal was conscious of the subsequent treaties concluded among some of its states party dealing with some

---

[30] Convention for the conservation of southern bluefin tuna (with annex) (adopted 10 May 1993, entered into force 20 May 1994) 1819 UNTS 359.

[31] ibid, art 16 and Annex for an Arbitration Tribunal.

[32] *Southern Bluefin Tuna Case between Australia and Japan and between New Zealand and Japan* (Award on Jurisdiction and Admissibility) (4 August 2000) XXIII RIAA 1, para 52 (emphasis added).

aspects of issues addressed also in the UNCLOS. The Tribunal noted that following the conclusion of UNCLOS a number of states concluded other international agreements with maritime elements having different dispute settlement mechanisms and consent requirements. Hence invoking UNCLOS dispute settlement provisions with regard to the disputes arising under these other international agreements would deprive them of the dispute settlement provisions to which parties agreed.[33] The Tribunal, therefore, declined jurisdiction.

## 4. Human Rights

The human rights treaties manifest the piecemeal approach to international law-making. The operative code of internationally protected human rights is expressed in a variety of conventions, each with its own substantive focus and its own application mechanism. Thus, specific human rights are expressed in the Convention on the Elimination of All Forms of Racial Discrimination,[34] the International Covenant on Economic, Social and Cultural Rights,[35] the Convention on the Elimination of All Forms of Discrimination Against Women,[36] the Convention Against Torture and Other Cruel, Inhumane or Degrading Treatment or Punishment,[37] the Convention on the Rights of the Child,[38] the Convention on the Protection of the Rights of All Migrant Workers and Members of Their Families,[39] the Convention on the Rights of Persons with Disabilities,[40] the Convention for the Protection of All Persons from Enforced

---

[33] The Tribunal stated: "The second consideration of a general character that the Tribunal has taken into account is the fact that a significant number of international agreements with maritime elements, entered into after the adoption of UNCLOS, exclude with varying degrees of explicitness unilateral reference of a dispute to compulsory adjudicative or arbitral procedures. Many of these agreements effect such exclusion by expressly requiring disputes to be resolved by mutually agreed procedures, whether by negotiation and consultation or other method acceptable to the parties to the dispute or by arbitration or recourse to the International Court of Justice by common agreement of the parties to the dispute. Other agreements preclude unilateral submission of a dispute to compulsory binding adjudication or arbitration, not only by explicitly requiring disputes to be settled by mutually agreed procedures, but also, as in Article 16 of the 1993 Convention, by requiring the parties to continue to seek to resolve the dispute by any of the various peaceful means of their own choice. The Tribunal is of the view that the existence of such a body of treaty practice—postdating as well as antedating the conclusion of UNCLOS—tends to confirm the conclusion that States Parties to UNCLOS may, by agreement, preclude subjection of their disputes to section 2 procedures in accordance with Article 281(1). To hold that disputes implicating obligations under both UNCLOS and an implementing treaty such as the 1993 Convention—as such disputes typically may—must be brought within the reach of section 2 of Part XV of UNCLOS would be effectively to deprive of substantial effect the dispute settlement provisions of those implementing agreements which prescribe dispute resolution by means of the parties' choice." ibid para 63.

[34] Convention on the Elimination of All Forms of Racial Discrimination (adopted 21 December 1965, entered into force 4 January 1969) 660 UNTS 195.

[35] International Covenant on Economic, Social and Cultural Rights (adopted 16 December 1966, entered into force 3 January 1976) 993 UNTS 3.

[36] Convention on the Elimination of All Forms of Discrimination Against Women (adopted 18 December 1979, entered into force 3 September 1981) 1249 UNTS 13.

[37] Convention Against Torture and Other Cruel, Inhumane or Degrading Treatment or Punishment (adopted 10 December 1984, entered into force 26 June 1987) 1465 UNTS 85.

[38] Convention on the Rights of the Child (adopted 20 November 1989, entered into force 2 September 1990) 1577 UNTS 3.

[39] Convention on the Protection of the Rights of All Migrant Workers and Members of Their Families (adopted 18 December 1990, entered into force 1 July 2003) 2220 UNTS 3.

[40] Convention on the Rights of Persons with Disabilities (adopted 13 December 2006, entered into force 3 May 2008) 2515 UNTS 3.

Disappearance,[41] the American Convention on Human Rights,[42] and the African Charter on Human and Peoples' Rights.[43]

Amidst this Lego-like thicket of cognate treaties, a recurring challenge for practitioners of international human rights law, even the best among us, is finding a willing and effective forum. Consider the following scenario. In state X in North America, an ethnic minority is being subjected to ethnic cleansing by the armed forces of the government. Destruction of villages, widespread murder and rape, the all-too-familiar crimes that accompany ethnic cleansing, are reported. Human rights non-governmental organizations (NGOs), the principal engines for the invocation and application of human rights law, are desperately seeking to arrest the violence. They face the recurring problem of human rights agents: finding an effective and receptive body to apply the law—and, if the remedies are to be meaningful, to do it quickly. Counsel invoke, among others, the Inter-American Commission on Human Rights, the Human Rights Council, the Council of Europe, they arrange to have a cooperating state try to prorogue International Court of Justice (ICJ) jurisdiction or possibly the International Criminal Court, they lobby Congress to condemn the actions and to suspend foreign aid, they initiate actions in US courts under the ever-shrinking Alien Tort Statute,[44] they recruit a celebrity and saturate the air waves with advertisements, and so on and so on.

From the Human Rights advocate's perspective, initiating these multiple parallel processes are a rational tactic and an ethical imperative, as the prospects of even limited success in any one of them are low yet failure in one venue is unlikely to affect the reception in the other possible parallel procedures. Nor is systemic confusion caused by conflicting "decisions" likely to ensue inasmuch as the remedy in each venue or arena is substantially the same and the effect of rejection on jurisdictional grounds is confined to that body.

In principle, the personnel of human rights bodies are sympathetic to the practitioners' efforts and understand the tactical imperatives. There are, however, limitations to institutional tolerance for the specific tactic of pursuing multiple and simultaneous procedures in other human rights bodies.[45] We cannot review trends in all of them. We

[41] Convention for the Protection of All Persons from Enforced Disappearance (adopted 20 December 2006, entered into force 23 December 2010) 2716 UNTS 3.

[42] American Convention on Human Rights (adopted 22 November 1969, entered into force 18 July 1978) 1144 UNTS 123.

[43] African Charter on Human and Peoples' Rights (adopted 27 June 1981, entered into force 21 October 1986) 1520 UNTS 217.

[44] 28 USC § 1350, Alien's action for tort.

[45] For example, Article 33(1) of the Regulations of the Inter-American Human Rights Commission provides: The Commission shall not consider a petition if its subject matter: is pending settlement pursuant to another procedure before an international governmental organization of which the State concerned is a member; or, essentially duplicates a petition pending or already examined and settled by the Commission or by another international governmental organization of which the State concerned is a member.

But paragraph (2) introduces exceptions to the general rule in paragraph (1). However, the Commission shall not refrain from considering petitions referred to in paragraph 1 when: the procedure followed before the other organization is limited to a general examination of the human rights situation in the State in question and there has been no decision on the specific facts that are the subject of the petition before the Commission, or it will not lead to an effective settlement; or, the petitioner before the Commission or a family member is the alleged victim of the violation denounced and the petitioner before the other organization is a third party or a nongovernmental entity having no mandate from the former. Rules and Procedures of the Inter-American Commission on Human Rights <http://www.oas.org/XXXIIGA/english/docs_en/cidh_rules_files/basic16.htm>.

will concentrate on the Human Rights Committee of the International Covenant on Civil and Political Rights, the ICCPR, its First Optional Protocol as well as its Rule 99.

Article 5(2)(a) of the First Optional Protocol of The International Covenant on Civil and Political Rights enjoins the Human Rights Committee from considering individual communications unless, cumulatively, "the same matter is not being examined under another procedure of international investigation or settlement".[46] Rule 99 of the Committee's Rules of Procedure specifies "[t]hat the same matter is not being examined under another procedure of international investigation or settlement". The Committee's practice has been rather liberal with regard to the "same matter". It has defined the "same matter" as "the same claim concerning the same individual, submitted by him or someone else who has standing to act on his behalf before the other international body".[47] In *Althammer*, the Committee determined that the same claim has to involve both the same facts and the same substantive rights. There, a group of retired employees alleged that the discriminatory effects of an Austrian amendment that abolished household benefits while increasing children's entitlements constituted a violation of their right to equality and non-discrimination in Covenant Article 26. Austria argued against the admissibility of the communication, on the ground that the same persons had previously submitted an application involving the same facts to the European Court of Human Rights. The Committee concluded that the two applications differed in terms of the substantive rights, as "the independent right to equality and non-discrimination embedded in Article 26 of the Covenant provides a greater protection than the accessory right to non-discrimination contained in Article 14 of the European Convention".[48]

There has been a similar flexibility with respect to the "same matter". To qualify as the "same matter", the claims must be brought by the same individuals or their representatives. Yet the Committee considered claims of the same matter examined by another procedure when the matter was brought by an unrelated party. In the *Fanali* case, the author of the communication alleged that Italy had violated his right to appeal, under Article 14(5) of the ICCPR following a corruption conviction as part of a larger criminal suit involving several others. Italy objected to the admissibility of the communication

---

[46] Optional Protocol to the International Covenant on Civil and Political Rights (adopted 16 December 1966, entered into force 23 March 1976) 999 UNTS 171, art 5(2)(a).

[47] HRC *Fanali v Italy*, No 75/1980, para 7.2, UN Doc CCPR/C/18/D/75/1980 (31 March 1983) (hereinafter HRC *Fanali*). "[T]he same matter concerns [1]the same authors, [2] the same facts and [3] the same substantive rights." HRC *Althammer v Austria*, No 998/2001, para 8.4, UN Doc CCPR/C/78/D/998/2001 (22 September 2003) (hereinafter HRC *Althammer*).

[48] ibid para 8.4. Similarly, in *Casanovas*, the Committee concluded in part that while the applicant had submitted the same facts to the European Commission of Human Rights, "the rights of the European Convention differed in substance and in regard to their implementation procedures from the rights set forth in the Covenant". HRC *Casanovas v France*, No 441/1990, para 5.1, UN Doc CCPR/C/51/D/441/1990 (26 July 1994). In *Karakurt*, the Committee found the communication admissible despite an earlier procedure, on the ground that the author was advancing "free-standing claims of discrimination and equality before the law, which were not, and indeed could not have been, made before the European organs". HRC *Karakurt v Austria*, No 965/2000, para 7.4, UN Doc CCPR/C/74/D/965/2000 (29 April 2002). But the Committee has deemed communications that allege violations of the same substantive right inadmissible. In *Fernández*, the Committee recalled that the right of association in article 11(a) of the European Convention, as interpreted by the European Court of Human Rights, is "sufficiently proximate" to Article 22(1) of the ICCPR. HRC *Fernández v Spain*, No 1396/2005, para 6.2, UN Doc CCPR/C/85/D/1396/2005 (22 November 2005).

with respect to Article 5(2)(a), as *Fanali*'s co-defendants in the domestic criminal proceedings had submitted the same claim to the European Commission of Human Rights. The Committee, however, rejected Italy's argument, as Fanali had not submitted his specific case to the European Commission.[49] Following *Fanali*, the Committee has repeatedly found that the same claims raised by others before a different international forum did not preclude consideration of an individual communication.[50]

From this practice, two scholars have concluded that in the Committee,

> only individual complaint proceedings before other United Nations human rights treaty bodies, like the Committee Against Torture, or individual proceedings before regional human rights bodies, namely the bodies under the European and American Conventions on Human Rights and the African Charter, will constitute 'procedures of international investigation or settlement for the purposes of [Optional Protocol] Article 5(2)(a).[51]

Dicta from some decisions suggest that in making this determination, the Committee evaluates, on a case-by-case basis, at least three factors: (i) as part of prospective remedial effectiveness, the respondent state's obligation to cooperate with the procedure; (ii) examination of individual cases to conclude a state violation or non-violation of specific rights; and (iii) authoritative determination of the merits of a particular case.[52]

This brief overview of a representative human rights body indicates its openness to allow for the parallel conduct of multiple procedures available in different treaties in spite of the formal legal restraints in place, based on a number of factors, including, we speculate, the gravity and urgency of the violations and their susceptibility to remediation. There may be yet another factor: the ultimate actor in all law is the individual and we would be remiss if we did not take account of the impulse of people in decision-making roles in a constantly evolving international decision-making process to enhance the jurisdiction with which they have been momentarily endowed in order to render justice in cases which they believe call out for it. This sense of responsibility of a court, tribunal, or committee leads it to try to incrementally extend its jurisdiction in circumstances in which a marginal addition will likely be accepted and, even, applauded in some quarters. The subtle process of episodic jurisdictional extension is a factor which should be taken into account.

---

[49] HRC *Fanali* (n 47) para 7.2.

[50] HRC *Blom v Sweden*, No 191/1985, para 7.2, UN Doc CCPR/C/32/D/191/1985 (4 April 1988) ("The Committee noted that consideration by the European Commission of Human Rights of applications submitted by other students at the same school relating to other or similar facts did not, within the meaning of article 5, paragraph 2 (a), of the Optional Protocol, constitute an examination of the same matter."); HRC *Sánchez López v Spain*, No 777/1997, para 6.2, UN Doc CCPR/C/67/D/777/1997 (18 October 1999) ("Since the State party has itself acknowledged that the author of the present communication has not submitted his specific case to the European Court of Human Rights, the Human Rights Committee considers that it is not precluded from considering the communication under article 5, paragraph 2 (a), of the Optional Protocol.").

[51] Sarah Joseph and Melissa Castan, *The International Covenant on Civil and Political Rights: Cases, Materials, and Commentary* (3rd edn, Oxford University Press 2013) 115.

[52] See HRC *Bandajevsky v Belarus*, No 1100/2002, para 5, UN Doc CCPR/C/86/D/1100/2002 (18 April 2006).

## 5.  Investment

The distinctive structure of international investment law makes it especially susceptible to the multiplication of parallel procedures for a single dispute. Here we are speaking of proceedings that have proven themselves, to a remarkable degree, to be remedially effective, thanks to the availability of a large network of national courts for enforcement of their awards. Their susceptibility to the multiplication of proceedings derives from the interplay between the practices of modern global capitalism, corporate law, and principles of contemporary international law. Together, these features endow each corporation with the legal attributes of separate legal personality and nationality.

For financial, business planning, and legal reasons, the vehicles for making direct foreign investments are corporations which are often composed of many other legal entities in intricate horizontal and vertical relationships. Because each component corporation has its own nationality, the overall structure of an investor/claimant may include, like a Matrioshka doll, a variety of legal entities of different nationalities, which can converge in a particular investment. Add to this, the shareholders, with their respective nationalities, and the number of potential nationalities converging in a particular investment may expand.

The many bilateral and multilateral investment treaties and investment law chapters in trade promotion agreements differ in various ways but virtually all afford the qualifying investor substantially the same protections and endow a qualifying investor with the right to initiate arbitration against the state-party which is hosting the investment and has consented *a priori* to the arbitration in the bilateral investment treaty (BIT).

If the host state has concluded BITs with a number of the states of which the investor's components are nationals, which is not unusual, this ensemble of features can allow for situations in which an investor will have the option of having one or more of its corporate components and some of their shareholders initiating, for the same investment dispute, simultaneous arbitrations under different BITs and/or contracts containing international commercial arbitration clauses. Thus, for all intents and purposes, the same investment dispute may proceed in several parallel proceedings.

There are both offensive and defensive reasons for a claimant to try to multiply its BIT arbitration into several parallel proceedings. Defensively, the claimant increases its chances of surviving objections to jurisdiction, on which many arbitral investment initiatives can founder. Offensively, the multiplication of parallel procedures enhances the claimant's chances of ultimately securing a successful outcome.

In theory, the parties to this type of investment dispute can agree to consolidate the multiple procedures. In practice, this is easier said than done for it will generally oblige the respondent state to surrender its potential objections to jurisdiction in return for the claimant yielding its favourable odds for a successful outcome. It may, as a result, prove difficult to reach agreement on consolidation and parallel arbitrations will proceed. Aside from the duplication of costs involved, the most malign outcome of such parallel procedures would be the inconsistency of the legal and factual holdings of the different arbitrations. This has occurred.

Some international investment treaties allow for compulsory consolidation of cases and some try to render a proceeding inadmissible if the claimant does not waive the possibility of pursuing parallel options. For example, Article 1121(1)(b) of the North American Free Trade Agreement (NAFTA)[53] provides in relevant part:

1. A disputing investor may submit a claim under Article 1116 to arbitration only if:

   (a) the investor consents to arbitration in accordance with the procedures set out in this Agreement; and

   (b) the investor and, where the claim is for loss or damage to an interest in an enterprise of another Party that is a juridical person that the investor owns or controls directly or indirectly, the enterprise, waive their right to initiate or continue before any administrative tribunal or court under the law of any Party, or other dispute settlement procedures, any proceedings with respect to the measure of the disputing Party that is alleged to be a breach referred to in Article 1116, except for proceedings for injunctive, declaratory or other extraordinary relief, not involving the payment of damages, before an administrative tribunal or court under the law of the disputing Party.

A similar provision in provided in 2018 United States-Mexico-Canada Agreement (USMCA) (as amended in 2019) Article 14.D.5(1)(e).[54] In sum, a claim that is otherwise well-founded jurisdictionally but in respect of which the investor refuses to waive its right to a parallel proceeding will be inadmissible.

Article 1121 of NAFTA has been interpreted quite strictly. In *Detroit International Bridge Company v Canada*, the tribunal observed that

the last part of Article 1121 (i.e. *"before an administrative tribunal or court under the law of the disputing Party"*) is intended to designate the adjudicative bodies operating under the domestic law of the disputing Party.... It appears highly improbable that NAFTA Parties would accept the initiation of multiple proceedings around the world

---

[53] The corresponding provision in USMCA is Article 14.D.5(1)(e) and (2). Agreement between the United States of America, the United Mexican States, and Canada (adopted 30 August 2018, amended 13 December 2019, entered into force 1 July 2020) <https://ustr.gov/trade-agreements/free-trade-agreements/united-states-mexico-canada-agreement/agreement-between> (hereinafter USMCA).

[54] ibid art 14.D.5(1)(e):

1. No claim shall be submitted to arbitration under this Annex unless:

   ...

   (e) the notice of arbitration is accompanied:
   (i) for claims submitted to arbitration under Article 14.D.3.1(a) (Submission of a Claim to Arbitration), by the claimant's written waiver, and
   (ii) for claims submitted to arbitration under Article 14.D.3.1(b) (Submission of a Claim to Arbitration), by the claimant's and the enterprise's written waivers,
   of any right to initiate or continue before any court or administrative tribunal under the law of an Annex Party, or any other dispute settlement procedures, any proceeding with respect to any measure alleged to constitute a breach referred to in Article 14.D.3 (Submission of a Claim to Arbitration).

discussing the same measures, with the only condition being the application by the court or administrative tribunal of the law of the disputing Party.[55]

There is no reason to believe its replacement by USMCA, Article 14.D.5(1)(e) will be interpreted any differently.

## 6.  International Commercial Arbitration

International commercial arbitration is a girder of the global economy. Like investment arbitration, international commercial arbitration is prone to the challenge of parallel procedures. However, unlike international investment arbitration, which lacks a single constitutive instrument, international commercial arbitration is built on the widely adopted 1958 New York Convention.[56] It establishes a very complex allocation of inter-state jurisdiction that has enabled this form of transnational dispute resolution to flourish despite the numerous opportunities for multiplication of the same proceeding.

International commercial arbitration requires the support of national courts at two critical phases of the process: the initiation of an arbitration by a claimant invoking an arbitral clause and, at the end of the process, control of its integrity and enforcement of its awards. For the front end, Article II(3) of the New York Convention enjoins the court of a State Party

> when seized of an action in a matter and in respect of which the parties have made an agreement within the meaning of this article shall, at the request of one of the parties, refer the parties to arbitration, unless it finds that the set agreement is null and void, inoperative or incapable of being performed.[57]

If all the courts of States Parties faithfully apply this provision, they should reach the same conclusion with respect to the viability of the arbitration commitment; parallel procedures for the same dispute in an arbitral tribunal and a national court should not arise.

With respect to the post-arbitral phase of the process, the New York Convention's Article V anticipates the prospect of multiple parallel procedures for enforcement of an award as the award creditor pursues, worldwide in national courts, the assets of the award debtor. While this allows the multiplication of procedures, Article V controls the potential for abuse by limiting the competence and, consequently, the effect of the decisions of some of those national courts. Only the court of the venue of the arbitration, which the parties or their delegates selected *a priori*, the so-called primary jurisdiction,

---

[55] *Detroit International Bridge Company* (on its own behalf and on behalf of its enterprise, The Canadian Transit Company) *v The Government of Canada*, PCA Case No 2012-25, Award on Jurisdiction, para 317 (2 April 2015).
[56] Convention on the Recognition and Enforcement of Foreign Arbitral Awards (adopted 10 June 1958, entered into force 7 June 1959) 330 UNTS 3 (hereinafter the NY Convention).
[57] ibid art II(3).

is accorded the exclusive competence to annul, with universal effect, an award under one of the grounds of Article V. All other courts of States Parties to the Convention are "secondary jurisdictions" which may only refuse to enforce an award; even if one of them usurps its treaty-assigned role and tries to annul the award, it will not have that effect.

To a remarkable extent, the assignment of function and competence of the New York Convention has worked and has restrained the potential of abusive parallel procedures in international commercial matters. But this effectiveness, too, depends on the faithful application of the Convention. Of late, it has come under challenge in some difficult cases and, on the theoretical level, Article V has been subjected to some by contrary interpretations. The leading exponent of this contrarian view is Professor Emmanuel Gaillard.[58]

## 7.  International Peace and Security

Although we international lawyers study them with devotion, judicial and arbitral decisions are exceptional in the international legal process. The great majority of decisions are shaped in international law's political institutions and by bilateral and unilateral action. Multiple parallel procedures occur at the highest level of those political institutions.

In the area of international peace and security, the United Nations Charter's approach to parallel proceedings is expressed in overlapping jurisdictions and is spelled out in Charter Articles 10 to 12. Article 11(2) provides, in relevant part,

> The General Assembly may discuss any questions relating to the maintenance of international peace and security brought before it by any Member of the United Nations, or by the Security Council, … except as provided in Article 12, may make recommendations with regard to any such questions to the state or states concerned or to the Security Council or to both. Any such question on which action is necessary shall be referred to the Security Council by the General Assembly either before or after discussion.

Article 12(1) decrees

> While the Security Council is exercising in respect of any dispute or situation the functions assigned to it in the present Charter, the General Assembly shall not make any recommendation with regard to that dispute or situation unless the Security Council so requests.

---

[58] Emmanuel Gaillard, *The Legal Theory of International Arbitration* (Martinus Nijhoff Publishers 2010).

According to their text, when the Security Council is seized of a "dispute" or a "situation", the drafters of the Charter did not want the Organization to be speaking in multiple voices. Then only the Security Council was to speak.

Or so it would have seemed.

The ICJ's applications of these Charter provisions have found ways and contingencies in which the Assembly's—and the Court's own—role could be expanded parallel to the Council's primary responsibility.

In the *Certain Expenses*[59] Opinion, the Court effectively ratified the General Assembly's "Uniting for Peace" Resolution, expanding the role of the General Assembly in case of the paralysis of the Security Council. In the *Wall* opinion, the Court held that "[a] request for an advisory opinion is not in itself a 'recommendation' by the General Assembly 'with regard to [a] dispute or situation' ".[60] On the basis of this fine distinction, the Court continued, "while Article 12 may limit the *scope* of the action which the General Assembly may take *subsequent* to its receipt of the Court's Opinion …, it does not in itself limit the authorization to request an advisory opinion".[61]

At the same time, the Court expanded its own role by distinguishing the "legal question" from the "political aspects" of a question, allowing itself, at its discretion, to open yet another parallel procedure. Thus, in the *Wall* Opinion, the Court issued clear dispositives to a non-consenting state with respect to a situation of which the Security Council was seized. The implication of the Court's jurisprudence on this matter seems to be one in which the application of Charter Article 12(1)'s instruction on procedures being pursued in parallel by the two—or three—principal UN organs is one of case-by-case discretion, arguably as a function of the perceived gravity and urgency of the matter at bar.

The Court explicitly ratified these innovations in its *Kosovo* Opinion when it noted, with seeming equanimity, that

> there has been an increasing tendency over time for the General Assembly and the Security Council to deal in parallel with the same matter concerning the maintenance of international peace and security … it is often the case that, while the Security Council has tended to focus on the aspects of such matters related to international peace and security, the General Assembly has taken a broader view, considering also their humanitarian, social and economic aspects.[62]

In this instance, the elevation of the Assembly to a potential parallel proceeding role in security matters was one more step in the demand of the Assembly from the earliest days of the Organization for a more meaningful role than the one assigned it by the

---

[59] *Certain expenses of the United Nations (Article 17, paragraph 2, of the Charter)* (Advisory Opinion) 1962 ICJ Rep 151.

[60] *Legal Consequences of the Construction of a Wall in the Occupied Palestinian Territory* (Advisory Opinion) 2004 ICJ Rep 148, para 25.

[61] ibid para 27.

[62] *Accordance with International Law of the Unilateral Declaration of Independence in Respect to Kosovo* (Advisory Opinion) 2010 ICJ Rep 414, para 41.

Charter. With all due respect, to suggest that the Assembly has been confining itself in these initiatives to "their humanitarian, social and economic aspects" is a small part of the story. Parallel proceedings here are a technique of power sharing.

## 8.  Conclusion

By contrast to the comparative unanimity in a broad, comparative view of domestic law's response to multiple parallel judicial proceedings, no single response for dealing with multiple parallel proceedings emerges in the different islands and offshore zones of international law surveyed here. That should be no surprise. The structure of international law and the decision institutions of its constitutive process differ from their municipal counterparts to the point that attempts to find similarities and to build upon them, whether for scholarly or practical purposes, hold little promise. International law *aspires* on a grand scale, but international *lex scripta* evolves in a "piecemeal" fashion; its jurisdictional creations are not coordinated.

At an even deeper level, the ambivalence manifested in the responses to the phenomenon of multiple parallel proceedings derives from the complementarity and tension in all law between the systemic demand that there be an end to the litigation of an issue, on the one hand, and, on the other, that justice be done no matter how long and how many times are required. And until it is, nothing is final.

Amidst these uncertainties, we cautiously hazard some recommendations to decision-makers. First, where possible, consolidate parallel procedures if an appropriate remedy can be achieved. Second, parallel procedures to secure an urgent remedy for ongoing human rights violations should be tolerated in direct proportion to the reality and gravity of the human rights violations underway and the prospective adequacy of the remedy sought. Third, parallel procedures to enforce a *res judicata* international judgment or award in multiple forums should be permitted. Finally, parallel procedures that are manifestly abusive should be rejected.

## Acknowledgements

This chapter draws on a lecture delivered at the American Society of International Law's Tillar House on 5 December 2019 in the Rosenne Lecture Series. Thanks to Catherine McCarthy, Laith Aqel, Gershon Hasin, and Cina Santos for assistance.

# 18

# Preserving the Judicial Function: Provisional Measures in International Adjudication

*Donald Francis Donovan*

## 1. Introduction

Among David Caron's many contributions to the field of international law, his "political theory of international courts and tribunals" is among the most creative and most enduring.[1] In linking the field of political sociology to international law and in drawing from his own experience as a judge and arbitrator, Caron brought out deep insights into the functions of international courts.

For Caron, international courts played an important role not only in offering a "bounded strategic space" in which State Parties could resolve the dispute between them but also a "social function" related to the parties' broader relationship.[2] He noted the important distinction between the "political decision to create ... an international court or tribunal" and "the task of implementing such a decision"—a task with which he was closely familiar from his participation, early in his career, as a legal assistant at and, late in his career, as a Member of the Iran-United States Claims Tribunal, as well as his close study of that institution.[3] A respected steward of the international judiciary, Caron dedicated his Judge Charles N Brower Lecture at the 2018 Annual Meeting of the American Society of International Law to the "integrity of the foundational judicial task of courts".[4] For Caron, the key was that, "[p]ulled from all sides by constituents with their own priorities, the adjudicator places appropriate limits on his discretion by not losing focus of his judicial task".[5]

---

[1] David D Caron, "Towards a Political Theory of International Courts and Tribunals" (2007) 24 Berkeley Journal of International Law 401, 402.

[2] ibid 402; see also David D Caron, "A Political Theory of International Courts and Tribunals" (2006) Collected Courses of the Hague Academy of International Law.

[3] Caron, Towards a Political Theory of International Courts and Tribunals (n 1) 409; see David D Caron and Matti Pellonpää, *The UNCITRAL Arbitration Rules as Interpreted and Applied: Selected Problems in Light of the Practice of the Iran-United States Claims Tribunal* (Oxford University Press 1994); David D Caron, "The Nature of the Iran-United States Claims Tribunal and the Evolving Structure of International Dispute Resolution" (1990) 84 American Journal of international Law 104.

[4] David D Caron, "Fifth Annual Charles N. Brower Lecture on International Dispute Resolution: The Multiple Functions of International Courts and the Singular Task of the Adjudicator" (2018) Proceedings of the American Society of International Law 231, 239.

[5] ibid 239.

---

Donald Francis Donovan, *Preserving the Judicial Function: Provisional Measures in International Adjudication* In: *By Peaceful Means.*
Edited by: Charles N Brower, Joan E Donoghue, Cian C Murphy, Cymie R Payne and Esmé R Shirlow, Oxford University Press.
© Donald Francis Donovan 2024. DOI: 10.1093/oso/9780192848086.003.0018

I have the honour of paying tribute to Caron's legacy with a modest contribution on the power of international courts and tribunals to award provisional measures, which I hope is consistent with the path that he set out.

In brief, provisional measures are temporary measures that aim to protect the subject matter of a pending dispute by requiring the disputing parties to take, or not to take, some action until the issuance of a final judgment or award. They are akin to preliminary injunctions and other forms of interim measures available in domestic courts.

The basic challenge to which provisional measures respond is that it takes time to hear and resolve a dispute, whether between states, states and private parties, or private parties. There is no omniscient decision-maker who can process all the relevant facts and law and issue an instantaneous decision. At the same time, there will be occasions when one of the disputing parties threatens to take action that might cause a material and irreversible change in the very situation that gives rise to the dispute, in a manner that would effectively deprive the court or tribunal seized of the dispute of the capacity to resolve it—that is, to grant effective relief to one of the parties. Hence, there will be the need, at times, to provide provisional relief, pending final judgment or award, to preserve that capacity. Caron himself wrote in 1986 that provisional measures are "the necessary price of the time-consuming procedural safeguards so deeply embedded in modern litigation and arbitration".[6]

Provisional measures, the need for which may arise in virtually any dispute resolution regime, go to the very core of the adjudicatory function, and the authority to issue them may therefore be understood as a power incidental to the judicial function to decide on the merits. Judge Fitzmaurice noted more than fifty years ago, referring to the International Court of Justice (ICJ), that the power to exercise provisional measures was really a "necessary condition of the Court—or of any court of law—being able to function at all".[7] Put differently, a court without the power to order parties to preserve the dispute until it can give the parties a chance fully to be heard and give itself the chance fully to consider the case is hardly a court at all.

At the same time, a request for provisional measures also puts demands on the international court or tribunal that go to the prudent and responsible exercise of its adjudicatory function—specifically, the need to address the substance of the dispute, even if on a provisional basis, when the international court or tribunal has not yet had the benefit of full evidence, full argument, and full deliberation. As a result, provisional measures are uniformly described, and treated, as an exceptional remedy. That is why, starting with the provisional measures jurisprudence of the ICJ's predecessor, the Permanent Court of International Justice (PCIJ), international courts have exercised discipline and restraint in issuing provisional measures. The Statute of the ICJ, echoing that of the PCIJ, states that the Court can indicate provisional measures only

---

[6] David D Caron, "Interim Measures of Protection: Theory and Practice in Light of the Iran United States Claims Tribunal" (1986) 46 Zeitschrift für Ausländisches Öffenliches Recht und Völkerrecht 465, 516.

[7] *Northern Cameroons (Cameroon v United Kingdom)* (Preliminary Objections) (1963) ICJ Rep 15, 103 (Separate Opinion of Judge Fitzmaurice).

"if it considers that circumstances so require" such measures in order to "preserve the respective rights of either party".[8]

These two basic propositions—first, provisional-measures authority as an essential component of the adjudicatory function, and second, the need to exercise that authority with discipline—drive my remarks in this chapter. I consider these propositions in light of the growth and proliferation in recent decades of international adjudicatory regimes. Specifically, I review the development and elaboration of the criteria by which adjudicators in these regimes assess requests for provisional measures, especially as the need to do so was given impetus by the consensus reached over the last two decades, across various regimes, that provisional measures are binding. I will do so on the conviction that the current treatment of provisional measures reflects the progressive development of the international legal order and the increasing confidence of the international community in international adjudication as an essential component of the rule of law on the international plane.

The chapter proceeds as follows. Section 2 explains how, despite initial disagreement and reticence, the ICJ, the International Tribunal for the Law of the Sea (ITLOS), human rights courts, and arbitral tribunals all found—in my view, necessarily—that provisional measures are binding. Section 3 describes the key criteria that international courts and tribunals have considered before ordering provisional measures, with reference to recent developments in that area. Section 4 concludes.

## 2. Binding Nature of Provisional Measures

Only since the late 1990s has consensus emerged that provisional measures orders create binding international obligations so that a state's violation of the terms of a provisional measures order as such would constitute a freestanding violation of international law. That development is reflected in particular in the law and practice of the ICJ.

Article 41 of the ICJ Statute, which adopts the language of that of the PCIJ Statute, authorized the Court to "indicate ... any provisional measures which ought to be taken to preserve the respective rights of either party".[9] The drafters of the PCIJ Statute deliberately chose the term "indicate" rather than "order" or "prescribe" for the reason that "great care must be exercised in any matter entailing the limitation of sovereign powers".[10] Accordingly, historically, the ICJ abstained from referring to its provisional measures orders as legally binding, instead relying on the parties to implement them in view of the parties' independent obligation to maintain the status quo of their dispute

---

[8] ICJ Statute, art 41.

[9] ICJ Statute, art 41; see also PCIJ Statute, art 41 (authorizing the PCIJ to "indicate ... any provisional measures which ought to be taken to reserve the respective rights of either party").

[10] Karin Oellers-Frahm, "Expanding the Competence to Issue Provisional Measures: Strengthening the International Judicial Function" (2011) 12 German Law Journal 1279, 1284–85 (citing *Procès-Verbaux of the Proceedings of the Advisory Committee of Jurists* 735 (1920)).

pending judicial resolution.[11] Thus, while the ICJ initially expressed disapproval of parties' failure to comply with its provisional measures orders and noted that it was "incumbent on each party to take the Court's indication seriously into account",[12] it did not call such measures binding. At the start of the final decade of the twentieth century, the "preponderant view [wa]s that an indication of interim measures is not binding".[13]

In its first provisional measures order, in *Anglo-Iranian Oil*, the ICJ indicated "provisional measures which will apply on the basis of reciprocal observance" of Iran and the United Kingdom, such as obligations not to prejudice the rights of the other party or not to aggravate the dispute.[14] The question of whether the Court's provisional measures orders were binding arose when the United Kingdom brought a complaint to the Security Council alleging Iran's failure to comply. Before the Security Council could address the complaint, the Court, in 1952, found that it did not have jurisdiction over the dispute.[15]

But the debate about the character of the ICJ's provisional measures authority continued. The first case squarely to put the issue before the Court was the *Vienna Convention on Consular Relations* case, also known as *Breard*.[16] That case put the need for urgent relief in stark terms: Paraguay claimed that criminal proceedings in the US state of Virginia that had led to the conviction and death sentence of its national, Ángel Breard, had violated both his and its rights under the Vienna Convention on Consular Relations (VCCR). On 3 April 1998, eleven days before the scheduled execution, Paraguay filed an Application Instituting Proceedings and a Request for Provisional Measures in the ICJ.[17] On 7 April, the Court held a hearing, and on 9 April, it issued an order directing the United States to take all measures necessary to halt Breard's execution pending the final resolution of the case.[18] Paraguay immediately sought relief from the US Supreme Court on the basis of that order. On behalf of the United States, the Departments of Justice and State advised the Supreme Court that provisional measures indicated by the ICJ were precatory.[19] On 14 April, the Supreme Court declined to order a stay, and Virginia executed Breard the same day.[20]

---

[11] See eg *Anglo-Iranian Oil Co. (United Kingdom v Iran)* (Provisional Measures) (1951) ICJ Rep 89, 93; *Military and Paramilitary Activities in and Against Nicaragua (Nicaragua v United States)* (Merits) (1986) ICJ Rep 14, 144, para 289;

[12] *Military and Paramilitary Activities in and Against Nicaragua (Nicaragua v United States)* (Merits) (1986) ICJ Rep 14, 144, para 289; *Application of the Convention on the Prevention and Punishment of the Crime of Genocide (Bosnia and Herzegovina v Yugoslavia) (Serbia and Montenegro)* (Provisional Measures) (1993) ICJ Rep 325, 349, para 59.

[13] Lawrence Collins, "Provisional and Protective Measures in International Litigation" (1992) 234 Collected Courses of the Hague Academy of International Law 12, 216–20.

[14] *Anglo-Iranian Oil Co. (United Kingdom v Iran)* (Provisional Measures) (1951) ICJ Rep 89, 93.

[15] *Anglo-Iranian Oil Co. (United Kingdom v Iran)* (Jurisdiction) (1951) ICJ Rep 93, 99, 115.

[16] Mr Donovan represented Paraguay, Germany, and Mexico, respectively, and argued before the ICJ in each of the *Breard*, *LaGrand*, and *Avena* cases discussed in this chapter. The views expressed here are his own.

[17] *Vienna Convention on Consular Relations (Paraguay v United States)*, Request for the Indication of Provisional Measures of Protection Submitted by the Government of the Republic of Paraguay (3 April 1998), para 5.

[18] See *Vienna Convention on Consular Relations (Paraguay v United States)* (Provisional Measures) (1998) ICJ Rep 248, 258.

[19] Brief for the United States as *Amicus Curiae* at 49–51, *Breard v Greene*, (1998) 523 US 371 (Nos 97-1390, 97-8214); see also "Agora: *Breard*" (1998) 92 American Journal of International Law 666, 672–73, 684.

[20] *Breard v Greene* (1998) 523 US 371, 378–79 (per curiam); David Stout, "Clemency Denied, Paraguayan Is Executed" (*New York Times*, 15 April 1998).

In its Memorial on the Merits before the ICJ, filed in October 1998, Paraguay contended that the United States had violated not only the VCCR but also its international obligation to abide by the provisional measures order.[21] This was the first time that a state had sought to establish before the ICJ another state's international responsibility based on a failure to comply with provisional measures indicated under Article 41 of the ICJ Statute.[22] Paraguay rested its request squarely on the very function of the Court, arguing that "[b]ecause this Court is a court, and because its job is to apply law, the United States cannot have had the right to act as it did".[23] It continued: "The authority of the Court to indicate provisional measures is thus fundamental to the Court's role as a *judicial* organ'—an organ that resolves disputes by the considered application of law, not the unfettered exercise of power."[24] Paraguay further demonstrated that the notion that provisional measures orders might not be binding had arisen from confusion between "bindingness" and enforceability.[25] The ICJ did not have the chance to answer the question in that case, however, as Paraguay withdrew the case not long after filing its Memorial.[26]

In 2001, in *LaGrand*, the Court definitively resolved the question. That case arose out of virtually identical events as *Breard*, after the US state of Arizona sentenced Walter LaGrand, a German national, to death.[27] After pursuing diplomatic and legal avenues in the United States, Germany requested the ICJ to indicate provisional measures the day before Arizona had scheduled the execution. In language materially identical to that used in the *Breard* order, the Court directed the United States to "take all measures at its disposal to ensure that Walter LaGrand is not executed pending the final decision in these proceedings".[28] The United States again advised the Supreme Court that the ICJ's provisional measures orders were precatory, the Supreme Court declined Germany's request to stay the execution[29] and Arizona carried out the execution later that day.[30]

In its merits judgment, the ICJ held that by executing LaGrand in disregard of the Court's provisional measures order, the United States had breached international law, reasoning much along the lines laid out by Paraguay in *Breard* and echoed by Germany in its pleadings in *LaGrand*.[31] The Court stated for the first time that "orders on

[21] *Vienna Convention on Consular Relations (Paraguay v United States)*, Memorial of the Republic of Paraguay (9 October 1998), Chapter 5(II).

[22] *Vienna Convention on Consular Relations (Paraguay v United States)*, Memorial of the Republic of Paraguay (9 October 1998), paras 1.9–1.10.

[23] ibid para 5.6.

[24] ibid para 5.3; see ibid para 5.61 ("If this Court is to vindicate the role of the rule of law in the quest for peace, it must assert its authority to perform effectively the task the Charter has assigned it").

[25] ibid 228 (citing the *travaux préparatoires* of the Statute of the Permanent Court of International Justice).

[26] See *Vienna Convention on Consular Relations (Paraguay v United States)* (Discontinuance) (1998) ICJ Rep 426, 427.

[27] See *LaGrand (Germany v United States)* (Merits) (2001) ICJ Rep 466, 474–80.

[28] *LaGrand (Germany v United States)* (Provisional Measures) (1999) ICJ Rep 9, 16, para 28.

[29] *Stewart v LaGrand*, (1999) 526 US 115.

[30] See *LaGrand (Germany v United States)* (Merits) (2001) ICJ Rep 466, 479–48, paras 33–34.

[31] Compare *Vienna Convention on Consular Relations (Paraguay v United States)*, Memorial of the Republic of Paraguay (9 October 1998), paras 5.3–5.6, with *LaGrand (Germany v United States)* (Merits) (2001) ICJ Rep 466, 502, para 102 and *LaGrand (Germany v United States)*, Memorial of Germany, paras 4.122–4.123, 4.125.

provisional measures under Article 41 have binding effect".[32] The Court reached this conclusion through an examination of the Statute's object and purpose, which it read to "enable the Court to fulfil the functions provided for therein, and, in particular, the basic function of judicial settlement of international disputes by binding decisions".[33] The Court held that the Statute must be read "to prevent the Court from being hampered in the exercise of its functions because the respective rights of the parties to a dispute before the Court are not preserved".[34] The Court explained that the power to order binding provisional measures "is based on the necessity, when the circumstances call for it, to safeguard, and to avoid prejudice to, the rights of the parties as determined by the final judgment of the Court".[35] The ICJ confirmed that holding in its 2004 judgment under similar facts in *Avena and Other Mexican Nationals*,[36] and its jurisprudence since then has been uniformly in accord.

Other international courts and tribunals have, in turn, concluded that their provisional orders are also binding. The drafters of the United Nations Convention on the Law of the Sea (UNCLOS) made the task straightforward for ITLOS by expressly providing that parties to a dispute before the Tribunal "shall comply promptly with any provisional measures".[37] That provision enabled ITLOS, in March 1998, to issue the first provisional measures order that an international court stated was binding as such.[38]

In 1999, the tribunal in *Maffezini v Spain* became the first investor–state tribunal to decide that provisional measures orders made pursuant to Article 47 of the Convention on the Settlement of Investment Disputes between States and Nationals of Other States (ICSID Convention) are "no less binding" than final awards, though the Convention states only that such orders are "recommended", and its drafters explicitly rejected a proposal that would have expressly made them binding.[39] International commercial tribunals have arrived at similar conclusions in respect of their governing laws and rules.[40]

---

[32] *LaGrand (Germany v United States)* (Merits) (2001) ICJ Rep 466, 506, para 109.

[33] ibid para 102.

[34] ibid para 102.

[35] ibid para 102.

[36] *Avena and Other Mexican Nationals (Mexico v United States)* (2004) ICJ Rep 12, para 21.

[37] UNCLOS, art 290(6); John Norton Moore and others (eds), *United Nations Convention on the Law of the Sea 1982: A Commentary* (2012) 52–59 (citing *travaux préparatoires*).

[38] *M/V "SAIGA" (No 2) (Saint Vincent and the Grenadines v Guinea)* (Provisional Measures) (1998) ITLOS Rep 24, 39, para 48 (noting "the binding force of the measures prescribed and the requirement under article 290, paragraph 6, of the Convention").

[39] *Maffezini v Spain*, ICSID Case No ARB/97/7, Decision on Request for Provisional Measures (28 October 1999), paras 7–9; see also Christoph H Schreuer, *The ICSID Convention: A Commentary* (Cambridge University Press 2001) 761–65 ("Despite the apparently clear restriction to recommendations, [ICSID] tribunals have developed a doctrine under which provisional measures have binding effect on the parties.").

[40] See eg Donald Francis Donovan, "The Allocation of Authority Between Courts and Arbitral Tribunals to Order Interim Measures: A Survey of Jurisdictions, the Work of UNCITRAL and a Model Proposal" (2005) 12 ICCA Congress Series 203; Donald Francis Donovan, "The Scope and Enforceability of Provisional Measures in International Commercial Arbitration: A Survey of Jurisdictions, the Work of UNCITRAL and Proposals for Moving Forward" (2003) 11 ICCA Congress Series 82; Donald Francis Donovan, "Powers of the Arbitrators to Issue Procedural Orders, Including Interim Measures of Protection, and the Obligation of Parties to Abide by Such Orders" (1999) 10 ICC International Court of Arbitration Bulletin 57.

The Inter-American Court of Human Rights followed suit in 2000.[41] With the 2005 ruling of the European Court of Human Rights in *Mamatkulov v Turkey*,[42] the consensus of international courts and tribunals around the binding effect of their provisional measures orders is virtually universal. Scholars have noted the range of adjudicative bodies—spanning human rights, common markets, and inter-state disputes—that have held that their provisional measures are binding since *LaGrand*, reflecting "the mutual influence between international judicial institutions in shaping the regime on provisional measures".[43] But as Judge Abraham pointed out in his separate opinion in the *Pulp Mills* case before the ICJ, if they are binding, it is important that the criteria by which they might be issued be clearly prescribed and consistently applied.[44]

## 3. Criteria for Issuing Provisional Measures

I turn now to the four prerequisites that international courts and tribunals have considered before ordering provisional measures. The first of these—*prima facie* jurisdiction—has long been a feature of provisional measures orders and reflects debates similar to those surrounding their binding effect. The latter three—plausibility of the merits, urgency, and non-aggravation—have largely developed as a result of the consensus that provisional measures are binding.

### 3.1 *Prima Facie* Jurisdiction

A court or tribunal will issue provisional measures only after concluding that it has *prima facie* jurisdiction over the merits of the dispute. Although the linguistic formulations may differ by regime, international adjudicators generally employ the same standard in substance.[45]

---

[41] *Constitutional Court Case (Peru)* (Provisional Measures) (2000) IACtHR Series E No 14, 5–6, para 14 (holding that the American Convention makes it "mandatory for the state to adopt the provisional measures ordered by this Tribunal").

[42] *Mamatkulov et al v Turkey* (Principal Judgment) (2005) ECtHR Nos 46827/99 and 46951/99, 37, paras 128–129.

[43] Armin von Bogdandy and Ingo Venzke, "Beyond Dispute: International Judicial Institutions as Lawmakers" (2011) 12 German Law Journal 979, 1002 (summarizing Professor Oellers-Frahm's contribution in the same volume); see Oellers-Frahm (n 10) 1279.

[44] *Pulp Mills on the River Uruguay (Argentina v Uruguay)* (Provisional Measures) (2006) ICJ Rep 113, 140, para 9 (Separate Opinion of Judge Abraham) ("But, in conducting some review, by nature limited, of the prima facie validity of the requesting party's case, the Court does not overstep the bounds of its mission as a jurisdiction appealed to for interim relief; on the contrary, it is sensibly fulfilling that mission.").

[45] For example, the ICJ has held that "the provisions relied on by the Applicant [must] appear, prima facie, to afford a basis on which its jurisdiction could be founded, but need not satisfy itself in a definitive manner that it has jurisdiction as regards the merits of the case", *Application of the International Convention on the Elimination of All Forms of Racial Discrimination (Armenia v Azerbaijan)*, Order of 7 December 2021 (Provisional Measures), para 15; ICSID tribunals have generally held that the party seeking provisional measures must show a credible claim, namely that its claim is not frivolous or obviously outside the competence of the tribunal, J Commission and R Moloo, "Procedural Issues in International Investment Arbitration", Oxford International Arbitration Series, 2018, para 3.09; and the African Court on Human and Peoples' Rights has held that "before ordering provisional measures, the Court need not satisfy itself that it has jurisdiction on the merits of the case, but simply needs to

Despite some initial disagreement,[46] by the 1970s, the ICJ had adopted the *prima facie* jurisdiction requirement. Starting with the Court's 1951 provisional measures order in *Anglo-Iranian Oil*, the Court indicated provisional measures after concluding that "it cannot be accepted *a priori* that [the] claim … falls completely outside the scope of international jurisdiction".[47] The Court refined the standard for *prima facie* jurisdiction in its 1972 order in *Fisheries Jurisdiction*, clarifying that the Court required "prima facie … a possible basis on which the jurisdiction of the Court might be founded".[48] Whereas the Court "need not, before indicating [provisional measures], finally satisfy itself that it has jurisdiction on the merits of the case, … it ought not to [indicate provisional measures] if the absence of jurisdiction on the merits is *manifest*".[49] Since then, the Court has repeatedly and consistently reaffirmed that while the Court "need not … finally satisfy itself [of] jurisdiction on the merits", it "ought not to indicate such measures unless the provisions invoked by the Applicant appear, prima facie, to afford a basis on which the jurisdiction of the Court might be founded".[50]

Other regimes have adopted much the same requirement. ICSID tribunals, for instance, have accepted that, in order to grant provisional measures pursuant to the Convention and Rules, they must be satisfied that they have *prima facie* jurisdiction to hear the case. In *City Oriente v Ecuador*, the ICSID tribunal found that there needed to be "at least … a *prima facie* basis [for its jurisdiction] without prejudging its decision", namely that "the dispute [wa]s not manifestly outside of the Centre's jurisdiction".[51] Similarly, in the *Paushok v Mongolia* arbitration under the 1976 Arbitration Rules of the United Nations Commission on International Trade Law (UNCITRAL), the tribunal thought it "only need[ed] to decide whether there [wa]s prima facie jurisdiction".[52] Regional human rights systems follow a similar practice.[53] Finally, Article 290 of UNCLOS explicitly imposes the same requirement, in practice requiring only that its

satisfy itself, *prima facie*, that it has jurisdiction", Afr Ct Human & Peoples' Rights, *Matter of African Commission on Human and People's Rights v Kenya* (Provisional Measures) (15 March 2013) para 16.

[46] See Shigeru Oda, "Provisional Measures: The Practice of the International Court of Justice" (1996) Fifty Years of the International Court of Justice 541, 549; Donald W Greig, "The Balancing of Interests and the Granting of Interim Protection by the International Court" (1987) Australian Yearbook of International Law 108, 112; Collins (n 8) 220–22.

[47] *Anglo-Iranian Oil Co. (United Kingdom v Iran)* (Provisional Measures) (1951) ICJ Rep 89, 93.

[48] *Fisheries Jurisdiction (Germany v Iceland)* (Provisional Measures) (1972) ICJ Rep 30, 34, para 18.

[49] ibid para 16 (emphasis added).

[50] See eg *Nuclear Tests (Australia v France)* (Provisional Measures) (1973) ICJ Rep 99, 101, para 13; *Jadhav (India v Pakistan)* (Provisional Measures) (2017) ICJ Rep 231, 236, para 15; *Alleged Violations of the 1955 Treaty of Amity, Economic Relations, and Consular Rights (Iran v United States)* (Provisional Measures) (2018) ICJ Rep 623, 630, para 24; *Application of the International Convention on the Elimination of All Forms of Racial Discrimination (Qatar v United Arab Emirates)* (Provisional Measures Request of Qatar) (2018) ICJ Rep 406, 413, para 14; *Allegations of Genocide under the Convention on the Prevention and Punishment of the Crime of Genocide (Ukraine v Russian Federation)*, Order of 16 March 2022 (Provisional Measures), para 24. cf *Immunities and Criminal Proceedings (Equatorial Guinea v France)* (Provisional Measures) (2016) ICJ Rep 1148, 1179, paras 4–5 (Separate Opinion of Judge Kateka) (querying whether the *prima facie* jurisdiction threshold is stringent enough).

[51] *City Oriente v Ecuador*, ICSID Case No ARB/06/21, Decision on Provisional Measures (19 November 2007) 11, para 50.

[52] *Paushok et al v Mongolia*, Order on Interim Measures (2 September 2008), para 53.

[53] See eg Afr Ct Human & Peoples' Rights, *Matter of African Commission on Human and People's Rights v Kenya* (Provisional Measures) (15 March 2013) para 16; Thomas Buergenthal, "The Inter-American Court of Human Rights" (1982) 76 American Journal of International Law 231, 241.

jurisdiction is "not so 'obviously excluded' " as to make it unlikely that ITLOS will reach the merits.[54]

The evolution of the *prima facie* jurisdiction standard reflects some of the same concerns raised in the debates over the binding nature of provisional measures—namely, the balance between provisional measures authority as a key component of the adjudicatory function and, at the same time, the need to exercise such authority with discipline. While provisional measures are crucial to regulating matters pending a decision on the merits of the dispute itself, international courts and tribunals have at the same time recognized that they should not impose restraints on the parties unless there is some plausible likelihood that it will in fact be in a position to deal with the merits of the dispute.[55] In his separate opinion in the *Armed Activities on the Territory of the Congo* case before the ICJ, for example, Judge Dugard observed that due to their binding character provisional measures "will assume greater importance than before" and that "[i]n these circumstances, the Court should be cautious in making Orders for provisional measures where there are serious doubts about the basis for jurisdiction".[56]

## 3.2  Plausibility on the Merits

A more difficult question in developing provisional measures criteria is to what extent international courts and tribunals may provisionally assess the merits of the dispute as part of a determination whether to issue provisional measures. As a preliminary point, it must be agreed that even where an international court or tribunal makes some assessment of the merits as a consideration in whether to grant provisional measures, it cannot prejudge the case. It remains fully empowered, indeed obligated, to consider the case afresh once it has the full case before it after plenary proceedings.

Traditionally, international courts and investor–state tribunals have shown some reluctance to wade into the merits of a dispute at the provisional measures stage out of fear of prejudging the merits. In his 1991 Hague Academy lecture, Lord Collins observed that "the general practice of the International Court is to treat the underlying merits as, in theory, wholly irrelevant on the application for interim measures".[57] That reluctance was due to a concern that making *any* assessment of a state's compliance or not with an international obligation before having full command of the case was a bridge too far.

---

[54] Thomas A Mensah, "Provisional Measures in the International Tribunal for the Law of the Sea" (2002) 62 Zeitschrift für Ausländisches Öffentliches Recht und Völkerrecht 43, 50 (quoting *Interhandel (Switzerland v United States)* (Provisional Measures) (1957) ICJ Rep 105, 118–19 (Separate Opinion of Judge Lauterpacht)); see also UNCLOS, Art 290 (authorizing provisional measures "[i]f a dispute has been duly submitted to a court or tribunal which considers that *prima facie* it has jurisdiction").

[55] Mensah, "Provisional Measures in the International Tribunal for the Law of the Sea" (n 54) 44.

[56] *Armed Activities on the Territory of the Congo (New Application: 2002) (Democratic Republic of the Congo v Rwanda)* (Provisional Measures) (2002) ICJ Rep 265, 265, para 2 (Separate Opinion of Judge Dugard).

[57] Collins (n 8) 225.

With Judge Abraham's separate opinion to the 2006 order in *Pulp Mills*, which denied respondent Uruguay's application for provisional measures, the ICJ's practice began to change. Referring to Judge Shahabuddeen's separate opinion in the 1991 *Great Belt* case,[58] Judge Abraham observed that before *LaGrand*, the Court had avoided "issues as to the existence and extent of the disputed rights ... before the merits phase"—under the assumption that the provisional measures assessment could be made "without any thought to the merit[s]".[59] But now that the Court had established in *LaGrand* that those measures were binding, Judge Abraham suggested, "the most important point is that the Court must be satisfied that the arguments are sufficiently serious on the merits—failing which it cannot impede the exercise by the respondent to the request for provisional measures of its right to act as it sees fit, within the limits set by international law".[60] His deferential formulation of the standard—that "it might be enough to ascertain that the claimed right is not patently non-existent"—may well have reflected his own view of the novelty of the proposal he had just made.[61]

The ICJ formally adopted the plausibility requirement in its 2009 provisional measures order in *Belgium v Senegal*. There, Belgium argued that Senegal's failure to prosecute or extradite former Chadian president, Hissène Habré, for acts of torture constituted a violation of the Convention against Torture and customary international law. Habré had been granted political asylum by Senegal and was residing there. Belgium filed a provisional measures request asking that Habré be kept under Senegal's control pending final judgment. The Court stated that it could only indicate provisional measures "if it [was] satisfied that the rights asserted by the party requesting such measures [were] at least plausible" and then explained that it need not "establish definitively the existence of the rights claimed by Belgium".[62] It found that those rights were "grounded in a possible interpretation of the Convention" and were thus "plausible".[63] In subsequent cases, the Court continued to assess only the legal basis of the applicant's claim, satisfying itself of the plausibility requirement if the claim asserted an ascertainable right under international law.[64]

ITLOS and regional human rights courts followed suit.[65] So did ICSID tribunals. For instance, in the 2001 *Maffezini v Spain* decision, the ICSID tribunal interpreted the ICSID Rules as requiring that the rights of the applicant party "exist at the time

[58] *Case Concerning Passage Through the Great Belt (Finland v. Denmark), Provisional Measures, Order of 29 July 1991, Separate Opinion of Judge Shahabuddeen*, I.C.J. Reports 1991, p. 28.

[59] *Pulp Mills on the River Uruguay (Argentina v Uruguay)* (Provisional Measures) (2006) ICJ Rep 113, 140, para 5 (Separate Opinion of Judge Abraham).

[60] *Pulp Mills on the River Uruguay (Argentina v Uruguay)* (Provisional Measures) (2006) ICJ Rep 113, 140, para 10 (Separate Opinion of Judge Abraham).

[61] ibid para 10.

[62] *Questions Relating to the Obligation to Prosecute or Extradite (Belgium v Senegal)* (Provisional Measures) (2009) ICJ Rep 139, para 57.

[63] *Questions Relating to the Obligation to Prosecute or Extradite (Belgium v Senegal)* (Provisional Measures) (2009) ICJ Rep 139, para 60.

[64] See eg *Construction of a Road in Costa Rica along the San Juan River (Nicaragua v Costa Rica)* (Provisional Measures) (2013) ICJ Rep 398, paras 17–19.

[65] See eg ITLOS, *M/T "San Padre Pio" (Switzerland v Nigeria)*, Order of 6 July 2019 (Provisional Measures), para 77; ECtHR, *M.S.S. v Belgium & Greece*, App No 30696/09, Judgment (21 January 2011).

of the request" and "not be  hypothetical".[66] Similarly, in 2007, the ICSID tribunal in *Occidental v Ecuador* denied a provisional measures request because the Claimants failed to establish a "theoretically existing right" to the remedy of specific performance they were trying to preserve.[67] Employing a different term but pointing in the same direction, the ICSID tribunal in *PNG v Papua New Guinea* permitted "a consideration of the *prima facie* strength of the parties' respective claims, counter-claims and defenses".[68]

In contrast, the UNCITRAL Model Law, which might be seen to reflect a transnational rule governing provisional measures in international arbitration, calls for a more rigorous inquiry, requiring a "*reasonable possibility* that the requesting party will succeed *on the merits of the claim*".[69] The Model Law also clarifies that this finding will "not affect the discretion of the arbitral tribunal in making any subsequent determination".[70] This appears to more closely resemble the general practice of most domestic jurisdictions, which sometimes require as much as a "likelihood of success on the merits".[71]

Starting in 2016, the ICJ has expanded the bounds of its plausibility analysis. In its provisional measures order in *Equatorial Guinea v France*, the ICJ considered whether the rights asserted by Equatorial Guinea under the Vienna Convention on Diplomatic Relations were plausible as a matter of fact as well as of law. There, Equatorial Guinea sought to ensure that its building in Paris be treated as part of its diplomatic mission. The Court noted that certain services of the Embassy had been transferred to the building such that a plausible right existed.[72]

Then, in its April 2017 order in *Ukraine v Russia*, the Court waded further into an assessment of the merits by requiring the plausible existence of the rights asserted *and* the possibility of the applicant's claims succeeding on the merits. Ukraine had initiated proceedings against Russia with respect to recent events in eastern Ukraine and Crimea, alleging violations of the International Convention on the Elimination of All Forms of Racial Discrimination and the International Convention for the Suppression of the Financing of Terrorism. Although the Court found that some evidence existed to fulfil the plausibility criterion for the racial discrimination claims, it held that Ukraine had not put before it sufficient evidence to find that the terrorism financing claims were plausible.[73]

---

[66] *Maffezini v Spain*, ICSID Case No ARB/97/7, Decision on Request for Provisional Measures (28 October 1999) paras 37–46.

[67] *Occidental v Ecuador*, ICSID Case No ARB/06/11, Decision on Provisional Measures (17 August 2007), paras 64, 79–86 (finding specific performance or restitution legally impossible and disproportionate where a sovereign terminates a foreign investment).

[68] *PNG Sustainable Development Program Ltd v Papua New Guinea*, ICSID Case No ARB/13/33, Decision on the Claimant's Request for Provisional Measures (21 January 2015), para 120.

[69] UNCITRAL Model Law (2006), art 17 A(1)(b) (emphases added).

[70] ibid art 17 A(1)(b).

[71] See UNICTRAL, Settlement of Commercial Disputes: Preparation of Uniform Provisions on Interim Measures of Protection, UN Doc A/CN.9/WG.II/WP 119 (2002) at 4.

[72] *Immunities and Criminal Proceedings (Equatorial Guinea v France)* (Provisional Measures) (2016) ICJ Rep 1148, paras 71–81.

[73] *Application of the International Convention for the Suppression of the Financing of Terrorism and of the International Convention on the Elimination of All Forms of Racial Discrimination (Ukraine v Russian)* (Provisional Measures) (2017) ICJ Rep 104, paras 65–86.

The Court has continued with this broad application of the plausibility analysis in subsequent provisional measures orders.[74] In the *Alleged Violations of the 1955 Treaty of Amity* case between Iran and the United States, for example, the Court considered as part of the plausibility analysis the prospect that the United States would prevail on an affirmative defence on the merits—specifically, whether the United States' re-imposition of sanctions on Iran fell under certain exceptions of the Treaty of Amity, including where measures relate to "fissionable materials" or "essential security interests".[75] The Court concluded that even if some of Iran's asserted rights in its provisional measures request might be affected by such defences, other rights, such as the right to humanitarian supplies, would not.[76]

Likewise, in *Allegations of Genocide under the Convention on the Prevention and Punishment of the Crime of Genocide*, the Court considered both the facts and the law in noting that there was no evidence substantiating the Russian Federation's allegation that genocide had been committed in Ukraine, and that, in any event, it is doubtful that the Genocide Convention authorizes the unilateral use of force in another state's territory for the purpose of preventing or punishing an alleged genocide.[77] On this basis, the Court concluded that Ukraine had "a plausible right not to be subjected to military operations by the Russian Federation for the purpose of preventing and punishing an alleged genocide" in Ukraine.[78]

These developments may very well presage an increasingly robust examination of an applicant's claims and the resisting party's defences. Although international courts and tribunals might formulate different standards for the examination, it seems obvious that a court or tribunal asked to restrain a party on a provisional basis must assure itself that the party seeking the restraint has a reasonable basis for doing so, whether on jurisdiction or the merits. If the rationale for provisional measures is the preservation of the tribunal's capacity to render effective relief in the face of a less-than-full opportunity to examine jurisdiction and the merits, the prospect that it will eventually need to render that relief should be a part of its calculation.

## 3.3  Urgency

Urgency, necessity, and risk of irreparable harm are different formulations of a requirement arising, again, from the fundamental purpose and very rationale of provisional

---

[74] See also *Application of the Convention on the Prevention and Punishment of the Crime of Genocide (The Gambia v Myanmar)*, Order of 23 January 2020 (Provisional Measures), paras 53–56 (finding sufficient evidence of acts committed against the Rohingya group in Myanmar to satisfy itself that rights asserted by The Gambia under the Genocide Convention are plausible).

[75] *Alleged Violations of the 1955 Treaty of Amity, Economic Relations, and Consular Rights (Iran v United States)* (Provisional Measures) (2018) ICJ Rep 623, para 40 (citing Article XX of the Treaty of Amity).

[76] *Alleged Violations of the 1955 Treaty of Amity, Economic Relations, and Consular Rights (Iran v United States)* (Provisional Measures) (2018) ICJ Rep 623, paras 68–70.

[77] *Allegations of Genocide under the Convention on the Prevention and Punishment of the Crime of Genocide (Ukraine v Russian Federation)*, Order of 16 March 2022 (Provisional Measures), para 59.

[78] ibid para 60.

measures. The only reason that an international court or tribunal might intervene in a dispute before it has fully heard the parties is the prospect that one party might take action during the pendency of the dispute that would unacceptably compromise the capacity eventually to render meaningful relief on the merits of the dispute. That is the circumstance these terms are meant to address; that is the "urgency" required.

The traditional formulation captured that need by way of a requirement that the applicant show an imminent risk of "irreparable prejudice". As the ICJ explained in the *Fisheries Jurisdiction* case, such an analysis "presupposes that irreparable prejudice should not be caused to rights which are the subject of dispute in judicial proceedings".[79] To similar effect, the ICJ requires that the acts susceptible of causing irreparable prejudice may "occur at any moment" before the Court rules on the merits.[80] A paradigmatic example can be found in the *Breard*, *LaGrand*, and *Avena* cases. In each case, the applicant state contended that its nationals faced imminent execution that would make it impossible for the Court to order the review of their convictions and sentences as those states sought on the merits. Indeed, in *LaGrand*, the Court, on the eve of the execution, ordered provisional measures *proprio motu* for the first time in its history.

The Court has also found risk of irreparable prejudice in cases regarding continued radioactive fallout,[81] environmental damage,[82] damage to cultural heritage,[83] armed conflict, and the exposures of persons to physical or psychological harm,[84] genocide and torture in particular.[85] Similarly, international human rights courts have indicated provisional measures where applicants have faced risks of torture and cruel, inhuman, or degrading treatment if expelled from the country,[86] deplorable detention conditions,[87] or imminent

[79] *Fisheries Jurisdiction (Germany v Iceland)* (Provisional Measures) (1972) ICJ Rep 30, 34, para 21.

[80] *Application of the International Convention on the Elimination of All Forms of Racial Discrimination (Qatar v United Arab Emirates)* (Provisional Measures) (2018) ICJ Rep 406, para 61.

[81] *Nuclear Tests (Australia v France)* (Provisional Measures) (1973) ICJ Rep 99, 105.

[82] *Certain Activities Carried Out by Nicaragua in the Border Area (Costa Rica v Nicaragua),* (Provisional Measures) (2013) ICJ Rep 398, para 81; *Construction of a Road in Costa Rica along the San Juan River (Nicaragua v Costa Rica)* (Provisional Measures) (2013) ICJ Rep 398, 361–67.

[83] See eg *Application of the International Convention on the Elimination of All Forms of Racial Discrimination (Armenia v Azerbaijan),* Order of 7 December 2021 (Provisional Measures), paras 84, 86; *Request for Interpretation of the Judgment of 15 June 1962 in the Case concerning the Temple of Preah Vihear (Cambodia v Thailand)* (Provisional Measures) (2011) ICJ Rep 537, 552, p 61.

[84] See eg *United States Diplomatic and Consular Staff in Teheran,* Order of 15 December 1979 (Provisional Measures) (1979) ICJ Rep 64, para 42; *Application of the International Convention on the Elimination of All Forms of Racial Discrimination (Qatar v United Arab Emirates)* (Provisional Measures Request of Qatar) (2018) ICJ Rep 406, 431, para 69.

[85] See eg *Questions Relating to the Obligation to Prosecute or Extradite (Belgium v Senegal)* (Provisional Measures) (2009) ICJ Rep 139; *Application of the Convention on the Prevention and Punishment of the Crime of Genocide (The Gambia v Myanmar),* Order of 23 January 2020 (Provisional Measures); *Application of the International Convention on the Elimination of All Forms of Racial Discrimination (Armenia v Azerbaijan),* Order of 7 December 2021 (Provisional Measures), paras 82–83, 85, 87; see also *CEMEX Caracas Investments BV et al v Venezuela,* ICSID Case No ARB/08/15, Decision on the Claimants' Request for Provisional Measures (3 March 2010), para 47.

[86] *Cruz Varas et al v Sweden,* Judgment (Merits and Just Satisfaction), 1991 Eur Ct HR Rep (ser A) (no 201), para 213; Inter-Am Ct HR, *Haitians and Dominicans of Haitian Origin in the Dominican Republic,* Order of 12 November 2000 (Provisional Measures).

[87] See eg ECtHR, *D v United Kingdom,* App No 30240/96, Judgment (1997); ECtHR, *Semenova v Russia,* App No 11788/16, Judgment (Merits and Just Satisfaction) (2017), para 28; Afr Ct Human & Peoples' Rights, *Mugesera v Rwanda,* App No 012/2017, Order for Provisional Measures (28 September 2017), para 4.

execution,[88] and in situations where indigenous communities face a threat to their way of life.[89]

Traditionally, international courts and tribunals have characterized irreparable harm as harm that could not be remedied by monetary compensation.[90] It is doubtful, though, whether that distinction still strictly holds. The UNCITRAL Model Law offers an example. That instrument provides that tribunals may grant preliminary measures if "[h]arm not *adequately* reparable by an award of damages is likely to result".[91] The preparatory materials clarify that the provision was in fact intended to address "the concerns that irreparable harm might present *too high a threshold*".[92] Along these lines, the tribunal in *Paushok v Mongolia* held that international law gave a "flexible meaning" to the requirement of irreparable harm, so that a showing that the injury is not remediable by damages is not always necessary.[93] Echoing the UNCITRAL Model Law and Arbitration Rules, the ICSID tribunal in *Perenco v Ecuador* formulated the question as whether "a party can be adequately compensated by an award of damages if it successfully vindicates its rights when the case is finally decided".[94]

Damage to the economic interests reflected in investment assets might be thought easily to qualify as damage reparable by monetary compensation. Yet ICSID tribunals have not come uniformly to that conclusion. The ICSID tribunal's discussion in *CEMEX Caracas Investments BV et al v Venezuela* highlights this issue of irreparability. In *CEMEX*, an ICSID tribunal presided over by former ICJ President Gilbert Guillaume identified the quintessential forms of irreparable harm, but then reviewed ICSID jurisprudence in order to draw a distinction between, on the one hand, "situations where the alleged prejudice can be readily compensated by awarding damages", and, on the other hand, "those where there is a serious risk of destruction of a going concern that constitutes the investment", which the *CEMEX* tribunal thought could

[88] See eg ECtHR, *Öcalan v Turkey*, App No 46221/99, Judgment (2005); Inter-Am Ct HR, *James et al v Trinidad and Tobago*, Order of 27 May 1999 (Provisional Measures); Inter-Am Ct HR, *"La Nación" Newspaper*, Order of 7 September 2001 (Provisional Measures); Afr Ct Human & Peoples' Rights, *Commission v Libya*, App No 002/2013, Order of 15 March 2013 (Provisional Measures), para 18; Afr Ct Human & Peoples' Rights, *Guehi v Tanzania*, App No 001/2015, Order of 18 March 2016 (Provisional Measures), paras 20–21; Afr Ct Human & Peoples' Rights, *Johnson v Ghana*, App No 016/2017, Order of 28 September 2017 (Provisional Measures), para 18; Afr Ct Human & Peoples' Rights, *Mwita v Tanzania*, App No 021/2019, Ruling on Provisional Measures (9 April 2020) (granting provisional measures to stay execution even though there has been a moratorium on the applicant's death sentence since 1994).

[89] See eg Afr Ct Human & Peoples' Rights, *Indigenous Peoples of the Lower Omo v Ethiopia*, App No 419/2012; Afr Ct Human & Peoples' Rights, *Commission v Libya*, App No 004/2011, Order of 25 March 2011 (Provisional Measures); Inter-Am Ct HR, *Community of Peace of San José of Apartadó v Colombia*, Order of 24 November 2000 (Provisional Measures).

[90] See eg *Aegean Sea Continental Shelf (Greece v Turkey)* (Provisional Measures) (1976) ICJ Rep 3, 11 para 33 (rejecting Greece's provisional measures request on the basis that "the alleged breach by Turkey of the exclusivity of the right claimed by Greece to acquire information concerning the natural resources of the continental shelf... is one that might be capable of reparation by appropriate means").

[91] See UNCITRAL Model Law (2006), Art 17(A)(1)(a); see also UNCITRAL Arbitration Rules (2013), art 26(3)(a).

[92] Report of the Working Group on Arbitration on the work of its fortieth session, UN Doc A/CN.9/547 (16 April 2004), para 89 (emphasis added).

[93] *Paushok et al v Mongolia*, Order on Interim Measures (2 September 2008), paras 68–69.

[94] *Perenco Ecuador Ltd v Ecuador et al*, ICSID Case No. ARB/08/6, Decision on Provisional Measures (8 May 2009), para 43.

qualify as irreparable harm.[95] One reads the opinion not fully convinced of the distinction, and hence wondering whether the tribunal, in a case in which the claim of irreparable harm was weak, was taking the occasion to try to cabin recent jurisprudence that had loosened the requirement.[96]

The urgency analysis under UNCLOS is broader given the object and purpose of that Convention. UNCLOS permits the indication of provisional measures to "preserve the respective rights of the parties to the dispute *or* to prevent serious harm to the marine environment".[97] This has given rise to decisions in which ITLOS has adopted a precautionary approach, establishing an arguably lower threshold for the certainty that the harm will occur. In the *Southern Bluefin Tuna Cases*, the applicants asked ITLOS to indicate provisional measures against Japan to prevent them from increasing tuna fishing in the Southern Ocean. The Tribunal reasoned that, although it "cannot conclusively assess the scientific evidence presented by the parties, it finds that measures should be taken as a matter of urgency to preserve the rights of the parties and to avert further deterioration of the southern bluefin tuna stock".[98]

If recent jurisprudence in the investor–state field has modestly loosened the requirement of irreparable harm, it remains an important discipline to the exercise of provisional measures authority.

## 3.4 Non-Aggravation

The traditional objective of non-aggravation has received increasing attention in provisional measures jurisprudence. The ICJ has consistently held that, although it has "the power to indicate provisional measures with a view to preventing the aggravation or extension of the dispute",[99] non-aggravation cannot, standing alone, provide the basis for provisional measures. If non-aggravation is to be understood as a legal obligation pursuant to Article 41 of the ICJ Statute and not as a limitless diplomatic obligation of states, it becomes clear why this is the case.

By definition, a provisional measures request entails a contention by one party that the adverse party is "aggravating the dispute" in the sense that, in the requesting party's view, the adverse party is taking steps that constitute a violation of its legal obligations. The question must still be whether, applying the criteria surveyed here, the circumstances justify the Court in ordering the adverse party to cease that activity. In the *Pulp Mills* judgment of 2007, the ICJ thus held that in the absence of specific measures meeting the traditional criteria for provisional measures, it could not make a general

---

[95] *CEMEX Caracas Investments BV et al v Venezuela*, ICSID Case No ARB/08/15, Decision on the Claimants' Request for Provisional Measures (3 March 2010), para 55.

[96] See Donald Francis Donovan, "Remarks" (2011) 105 Proceedings of the ASIL Annual Meeting 330.

[97] UNCLOS, art 290(1).

[98] *Southern Bluefin Tuna Cases (Australia/New Zealand v Japan)* (Provisional Measures), (1999) ITLOS Rep 280, paras 70–80.

[99] See eg *Land and Maritime Boundary between Cameroon and Nigeria (Cameroon v Nigeria)* (Provisional Measures) (1996) ICJ Rep 13, para 41.

non-aggravation order. In *Costa Rica v Nicaragua*, the Court reiterated that on every occasion on which it had indicated non-aggravation measures, other specific provisional measures had been indicated.[100]

The criteria by which the Court decides to grant a general non-aggravation order in addition to specific provisional measures, however, is less clear. In *The Gambia v Myanmar*, the Court declined to grant the requested measure of non-aggravation, deeming it unnecessary "in view of the specific provisional measures it ha[d] decided to take".[101] Specifically, the Court had unanimously granted all but two of The Gambia's requested specific measures.[102] It ordered Myanmar to respect its legal obligations under the Genocide Convention, preserve evidence related to The Gambia's allegations, and submit a report to the Court on its measures taken within four months, and thereafter every six months.[103] In *Armenia v Azerbaijan* and *Ukraine v Russia*, however, the Court, after considering all the circumstances, "found it necessary to indicate an additional measure directed to both Parties and aimed at ensuring the non-aggravation of their dispute".[104] Like in *The Gambia v Myanmar*, the Court had granted most of the requested provisional measures in both cases, and the applicants' allegations involved ongoing conduct on the part of the respondent state.[105]

Notwithstanding the ICJ's approach, some arbitral tribunals have appeared to recognize a self-standing right to non-aggravation—at least in circumstances where the procedural integrity of the arbitration is at stake. Whereas in *CEMEX*, the ICSID tribunal adopted the ICJ's position,[106] in *Burlington v Ecuador* and *Quiborax v Bolivia*, the ICSID tribunals held that "the rights to be preserved by provisional measures are not limited to those which form the subject matter of the dispute, but may extend to procedural rights, including the general right to the preservation of the status quo and to the non-aggravation of the dispute".[107] In 2017, the ICSID tribunal in *Nova Group Investments v Romania* interpreted this purportedly standalone right to

---

[100] *Certain Activities Carried Out by Nicaragua in the Border Area (Costa Rica v Nicaragua)* (Provisional Measures) (2011) ICJ Rep 6, para 62.

[101] *Application of the Convention on the Prevention and Punishment of the Crime of Genocide (The Gambia v Myanmar)*, Order of 23 January 2020 (Provisional Measures), para 83.

[102] The Court rejected The Gambia's requests for non-aggravation and for a specific measure requiring Myanmar to provide access to UN investigators. ibid paras 62, 83.

[103] ibid para 86.

[104] *Application of the International Convention on the Elimination of All Forms of Racial Discrimination (Armenia v Azerbaijan)*, Order of 7 December 2021 (Provisional Measures), para 94; *Allegations of Genocide under the Convention on the Prevention and Punishment of the Crime of Genocide (Ukraine v Russian Federation)*, Order of 16 March 2022 (Provisional Measures), para 82.

[105] See *Application of the International Convention on the Elimination of All Forms of Racial Discrimination (Armenia v Azerbaijan)*, Order of 7 December 2021 (Provisional Measures), paras 11, 98; *Allegations of Genocide under the Convention on the Prevention and Punishment of the Crime of Genocide (Ukraine v Russian Federation)*, Order of 16 March 2022 (Provisional Measures), paras 14, 86.

[106] *CEMEX Caracas Investments BV et al v Venezuela*, ICSID Case No ARB/08/15, Decision on the Claimants' Request for Provisional Measures (3 March 2010), paras 64–65.

[107] *Quiborax SA et al v Bolivia*, ICSID Case No ARB/06/2, Decision on Provisional Measures (26 February 2010), paras 117–118; *Burlington v Ecuador*, ICSID Case No ARB/08/5, Procedural Order No 1 (29 June 2009) para 60; see also *Churchill Mining PLC et al v Indonesia*, ICSID Case No ARB/12/14, Procedural Order No 14 (Provisional Measures) (22 December 2014), para 71 (finding it "well settled that provisional measures may be recommended to protect the rights to the *status quo* and to the non-aggravation of the dispute, which are self-standing rights vested in any party to ICSID proceedings").

non-aggravation "narrowly"—"primarily in the same context" as where the "impact on the ongoing ICSID proceeding" implicates the "right to procedural integrity", that is, "only if continuing events in the host State threaten to interfere unduly with the parties' ability to present positions in the arbitration, or the tribunal's ability to fashion meaningful relief at the close of the case".[108] The latter circumstance, of course, is the wellspring of all provisional measures criteria, and nobody would question the inherent authority of an arbitral tribunal to take steps to preserve the procedural integrity of the arbitration itself.

Hence, it remains to be seen whether a right to non-aggravation will extend beyond the right to the procedural integrity of the arbitration and the right, when a party satisfies the settled criteria, to preserve that party's opportunity to obtain effective relief. Observing that "[t]he mere fact of lesser impacts—*i.e.*, that circumstances on the ground in the host State continue to evolve during the course of the ICSID case, possibly increasing the harm about which the investor complains—is not *ipso facto* a violation of the parties' rights",[109] the *Nova Group* tribunal cautioned that if "by the simple step of initiating an ICSID claim, an investor obtains a sweeping right to freeze all circumstances as they then exist (perhaps for a period of years), even where such an overall standstill is otherwise not required to preserve its rights to present its case and obtain meaningful relief", then the doctrine "would take the grant of provisional measures beyond the realm of exceptional circumstances".[110]

## 4. Conclusion

The now-universal recognition of the binding character of provisional measures issued by international courts and tribunals reflects the international community's increased commitment to international adjudication as a means of resolving disputes. If that commitment is to be vindicated, international courts and tribunals will need to continue to develop the governing criteria in a manner that ensures that the provisional measures they issue correspond as precisely as possible to the justification for granting them the authority to do so.

The requirements of establishing *prima facie* jurisdiction and plausibility on the merits, for example, appear to have been developed and refined over the years by various international courts and tribunals to a degree that reflects the tension between the two competing considerations that I mentioned at the outset of this chapter— namely, that the authority to order provisional measures is an essential component of the adjudicatory function, but that at the same time, there is a need to exercise that authority with discipline. International courts and tribunals have come to recognize that the plausibility—in some sense the merits—of the parties' claims and defences as a

---

[108] *Nova Group Investments, BV v Romania*, ICSID Case No ARB/16/19, Procedural Order No 7 Concerning the Claimant's Request for Provisional Measures (29 March 2017), para 236.
[109] ibid para 236.
[110] ibid para 236.

matter of law and fact require consideration on a request for provisional measures. At the same time, they also recognize that that consideration cannot prejudge the outcome of the matter or prejudice the parties' rights.

The requirements of urgency and non-aggravation, on the other hand, appear to require further development. The content of these two criteria might necessarily vary across different regimes that address different subject matters—harm to economic interests, for example, might be more readily reparable than harm to environmental or cultural interests. The apparent lack of clarity with respect to the precise standard of each requirement, and the consequent possible lack of uniformity of application, within each regime, threatens to undermine the legitimacy of provisional measures as a core adjudicatory function. Going forward, international courts and tribunals will continue to refine the interpretation and application of these requirements, including the meaning of "irreparable harm" and the specific circumstances in which orders of non-aggravation may be granted. In doing so, international courts and tribunals should heed Caron's words and ensure that they "place ... appropriate limits on [their] discretion by not losing focus of [their] judicial task".[111]

## Dedication and Acknowledgements

From the time David and I crossed paths as legal assistants at the Iran-United States Claims Tribunal in The Hague in 1984, I treasured him as a friend and admired him as a lawyer, scholar, jurist, and human being. Profuse thanks to Christel Y Tham, Duncan Pickard, Alyssa T Yamamoto, Brooke Davies, and Inesha Premaratne for their assistance in preparing this chapter, an earlier version of which was delivered as the Tang Lecture at the China Arbitration Summit in Beijing on 5 November 2019.

[111] Caron, "Fifth Annual Charles N. Brower Lecture on International Dispute Resolution" (n 4) 239.

# PART IV

# SUBSTANTIVE LAW AND LEGAL PRINCIPLES

# 19

# A Concreteness Requirement in International Adjudication?

## Some Reflections on *Ecuador v United States*

*Lee M Caplan*

## 1. Introduction

The legal standard for determining the existence of a "dispute" between states capable of adjudication by an international court or tribunal has a long and well-known pedigree. Its cornerstone has been the pronouncement by the Permanent Court of International Justice (PCIJ) in the *Mavrommatis Palestine Concessions* case that "[a] dispute is a disagreement on a point of law or fact, a conflict of legal views or of interests between two persons".[1] Building on that definition, the International Court of Justice (ICJ) has established over the years additional requirements for a "dispute", the most significant of which is the presence of positive opposition. In the *South West Africa* case, the ICJ held that a "dispute" only exists if "the claim of one party is positively opposed by the other";[2] that is, there is sufficient evidence that one party has rejected the claim of the other. Later, in the *Land and Maritime Boundary between Cameroon and Nigeria* case, the ICJ elaborated that positive opposition may also be inferred in the absence of an express rejection of a claim "in circumstances where a response is called for".[3] These core criteria have endured for decades, with the ICJ describing them as the "established case law" on the matter.[4]

But does this time-honoured standard contain an implicit requirement that a "dispute" is justiciable only when grounded in a concrete controversy; that is, when it arises out of an underlying allegation by one state that another has breached an international law obligation owed to it?

---

[1] Mavrommatis Palestine Concessions (*Greece v Great Britain*) (Judgment) [1924]. PCIJ Series A, No 2 (hereafter *Greece v Great Britain*).
[2] South West Africa Cases (*Ethiopia v South Africa*; *Liberia v South Africa*) (Preliminary Objections) (Judgment) [1962] ICJ Rep 328.
[3] Land and Maritime Boundary between Cameroon and Nigeria (*Cameroon v Nigeria*) (Preliminary Objections) (Judgment) [1998] ICJ Rep 315.
[4] See eg Application of the International Convention on the Elimination of All Forms of Racial Discrimination (*Georgia v Russian Federation*) (Preliminary Objections) (Judgment) [2011] ICJ Rep 84. The ICJ has also found that the existence of a "dispute" must be decided by "objective determination" rather than the subjective views of the parties. See Interpretation of Peace Treaties Case with Bulgaria, Hungary and Romania, (Advisory Opinion) [1950] ICJ Rep 74.

Lee M Caplan, *A Concreteness Requirement in International Adjudication?* In: *By Peaceful Means*. Edited by: Charles N Brower, Joan E Donoghue, Cian C Murphy, Cymie R Payne and Esmé R Shirlow, Oxford University Press. © Lee M Caplan 2024.
DOI: 10.1093/oso/9780192848086.003.0019

This was a principal question presented in *Ecuador v United States*,[5] a novel case adjudicated under the state–state provisions of the US-Ecuador bilateral investment treaty (BIT). The BIT permitted arbitration of "disputes concerning the interpretation or application of the Treaty".[6] In the arbitration, Ecuador requested an authoritative interpretation of certain provisions of the BIT, divorced from any concrete controversy; it did not allege that the United States had breached the treaty. The United States responded that the resolution of such an abstract matter was beyond the judicial function of the arbitral tribunal. The United States prevailed in the case, but the award, by majority only, left open important questions about whether abstract questions of treaty interpretation are justiciable.

This chapter offers some reflections on a case that to date has received less attention than arguably it should have given the significance of the issues raised.[7] It briefly assesses the approach of international courts and tribunals in handling abstract claims and in interpreting the standard compromissory language—"disputes concerning the interpretation or application of the Treaty"—that permits inter-state dispute resolution under the US-Ecuador BIT and myriad other treaties. It is submitted that the present legal standard for determining the existence of a "dispute" contains insufficient guidance regarding the justiciability of abstract controversies, which could be clarified to include a concreteness requirement, that is, a prerequisite that a "dispute" derive from an underlying claim of breach of international law.[8]

## 2. *Ecuador v United States*

*Ecuador v United States* was an extraordinary case beginning with an extraordinary demand by Ecuador—namely, that the United States agree with Ecuador's preferred interpretation of Article II(7) of the US-Ecuador BIT or, if not, arbitrate the parties' alleged "dispute" over the interpretation of that provision. The impetus for Ecuador's demand was the award in *Chevron v Ecuador*,[9] an investor–state arbitration arising under the

---

[5] *Republic of Ecuador v United States of America*, [2012] PCA Case No 2012-5, <https://pca-cpa.org/en/cases/83/> (hereafter *Ecuador v United States*).

[6] Article VII(1), The Treaty Between the United States of American and the Republic of Ecuador Concerning the Encouragement and Reciprocal Protection of Investment, with Protocol and a Related Exchange of Letters, signed at Washington on 27 August 1993 (hereafter US-Ecuador BIT), <https://2001-2009.state.gov/documents/organization/43558.pdf>. By Ecuador's action, the BIT terminated on 18 May 2018.

[7] The few scholarly works to address the case include Anthea Roberts, "State-to-State Investment Treaty Arbitration: A Hybrid Theory of Interdependent Rights and Shared Interpretive Authority" (2014) 55(1) Harvard International Law Journal 1; Michele Potestà, "State-to-State Dispute Settlement Pursuant to Bilateral Investment Treaties: Is There Potential?" in Nerina Boschiero and others (eds), *International Courts and the Development of International Law: Essays in Honor of Tullio Treves* (Asser Press 2013) 753; Antoine Cottin and Panagiotis Kyriakou, "Revisiting the Dispute Requirement in International Interpretation Proceedings: Deeds, not Words" (2019) 10(2) Journal of International Dispute Settlement 307; Marcin Orecki, "State-to-State Arbitration Pursuant to Bilateral Investment Treaties: The Ecuador-US Dispute" (*Young ICCA Blog*, 14 February 2013), <https://www.youngicca-blog.com/wp-content/uploads/2013/02/State_to_State_Marcin_Orecki_10_02_201.pdf>.

[8] This position is limited to the context of contentious dispute resolution. Although they have rarely done so, states are, of course, always free to consent to the determination of purely abstract questions of treaty interpretation by an international court or tribunal.

[9] *Chevron Corp. and Texaco Petroleum Co. v Republic of Ecuador*, PCA No 34877 (Partial Award on the Merits) (30 March 2011), <https://www.italaw.com/sites/default/files/case-documents/ita0151.pdf>.

BIT, which Ecuador had recently lost. The tribunal found that Ecuador had violated Article II(7) of the BIT when it failed to provide Chevron "effective means" to assert claims and enforce rights in Ecuadorian courts relating to the company's investments.[10] Specifically, the Tribunal ruled that the failure—and seeming unwillingness—of the Ecuadorian courts to rule on the company's multiple contract claims for many years constituted "undue" delays that violated the treaty standard.[11] Ecuador had argued without success that the scope of investment protection under Article II(7) of the BIT did not exceed that which was provided under customary international law.[12]

Ecuador's subsequent diplomatic approach to the United States laid out in detail its criticism of the *Chevron* Tribunal's interpretation of Article II(7) and Ecuador's preferred interpretation of that provision.[13] Ecuador asserted that if the United States disagreed with, or failed to respond to, Ecuador's interpretation, an unresolved "dispute" would exist within the meaning of Article VII of the BIT covering "disputes concerning the interpretation or application of the Treaty".[14] The United States declined to take a position on the merits of Ecuador's proposed interpretation.[15] Ecuador's Request for Arbitration followed, in which it sought "an authoritative determination on the proper interpretation and application of paragraph 7 of Article II of the Treaty".[16] Ecuador argued that a dispute had arisen because the United States had failed to respond "where a response was called for".[17] In its Statement of Defense, the United States strongly criticized Ecuador's "unilateral attempt to secure a new interpretation" of Article II(7) when its demand was "divorced from concrete factual situations over a Party's failure to perform under the Treaty".[18]

In the jurisdictional objection that followed, the United States elaborated on its position. In addition to arguing the absence of positive opposition—asserting that the United States did not and was not obligated to provide a response to Ecuador—it submitted that the tribunal lacked competence to adjudicate an abstract matter. The crux of the US position was that the term "dispute", as used in Article VII of the BIT, had a distinct meaning in international practice, requiring not only positive opposition but also "concreteness". In support of its position, the United States relied on the *Northern Cameroons* case[19] in which the ICJ found that it had jurisdiction "only in connection

---

[10] Treaty between the United States of America and the Republic of Ecuador concerning the Encouragement and Reciprocal Protection of Investment—art II(7) (US-Ecuador BIT); "Each Party shall provide effective means of asserting claims and enforcing rights with respect to investment, investment agreements, and investment authorizations."

[11] Partial Award (n 11) para 262.

[12] ibid paras 225–226.

[13] Letter from Ecuadorian Minister of Foreign Affairs, Trade and Integration Ricardo Patiño Aroca to US Secretary of State Hillary Clinton (8 June 2010) 1 (unofficial translation) (stating, among other things, that the "effective means" obligation be understood as not imposing obligations "greater than those required to implement obligations under the standards of customary international law").

[14] ibid 4.

[15] The events surrounding the US' non-response are set forth in the US Statement of Defense, 7 (noting that Ecuador had withdrawn from ICSID and was in the process of terminating the BIT with the United States).

[16] Request of the Republic of Ecuador to the United States of America, dated 28 June 2011 (hereafter Request for Arbitration), para 14.

[17] ibid.

[18] US Statement of Defense of Respondent United States of America, dated 29 March 2012, 3.

[19] Northern Cameroons (*Cameroon v United Kingdom*) (Preliminary Objections) (Judgment) [1963] ICJ Reports 15.

with *concrete cases* where there exists at the time of the adjudication an actual controversy involving a conflict of legal interests between the parties".[20] Thus, according to the United States, a dispute entails a controversy where "one Party claims that the other Party's act or omission has violated its legal rights, thereby warranting judicial relief capable of affecting the Parties' rights and obligations".[21] Professor Christian Tomuschat, in his role as legal expert on behalf of the United States, supported this position.[22]

The United States also raised concerns that the tribunal's resolution of Ecuador's interpretive question in the abstract would infringe on the United States' sovereign authority to formulate its own interpretations of its investment treaties and could interfere with the enforcement of the *Chevron* award, which Ecuador was at the time of its demand seeking to set aside in Dutch court. With respect to the former concern, the United States cited the *Dual Nationality Cases* in which the Anglo-Italian Commission denied the United Kingdom's request for an authoritative interpretation of the underlying peace treaty in the absence of a concrete controversy.[23] In that case, the Commission held that "[a]n interpretation ... in an abstract and general manner, with obligatory effect for all future cases, would run the risk, because it is abusive, of ending in a judgement blemished by excess of power (it would create rules of law, which is not a jurisdictional function, but a legislative function)".[24] As to the second concern, the United States argued that granting Ecuador the authoritative interpretation it requested would destabilize the system of investor–state arbitration by, among other things, allowing Ecuador to use it collaterally to attack the *Chevron* award.[25]

Ecuador countered the United States' concreteness argument with a two-pronged defence. It began with the plain language of Article VII of the BIT, with an emphasis on the disjunctive construction of the compromissory language: "interpretation or application". Ecuador argued that this formulation established the tribunal's broad competence to decide two distinct categories of disputes: (i) disputes concerning the *interpretation* of the treaty, which involves "the process of determining the meaning of a text"; and (ii) disputes concerning the *application* of the treaty, which involves "the process of determining the consequences which, according to the text, should follow in a given situation".[26] Thus, according to Ecuador, the scope of Article VII was sufficiently broad such that disputes concerning the interpretation and disputes concerning the

---

[20] Memorial of Respondent United States of America on Objections to Jurisdiction, dated 25 April 2012 (hereafter US Memorial) 21.

[21] ibid.

[22] Professor Tomuschat, relying on the *Northern Cameroons* case, opined: "A legal dispute exists only if the parties are opposed [to] one another in respect of a specific claim raised by one party against the other which is rejected in whatever form." Opinion of Dr HC Christian Tomuschat, 24 April 2012 (hereafter "Tomuschat Opinion"), para 7.

[23] US Memorial (n 20) 22–23, 55–59.

[24] ibid 58 (citing *Cases of Dual Nationality*, [2006] XIV RIAA 34).

[25] ibid 59–62.

[26] Counter-Memorial of Claimant Republic of Ecuador on Jurisdiction, dated 23 May 2012 (hereafter Ecuador's Counter-Memorial) para 29 (citing Harvard Law School, "Draft Convention on the Law of Treaties: Article 19. Interpretation", reprinted in [1935] AJIL Supp 937, 938–39 and Oil Platforms (*Islamic Republic of Iran v United States of America*), Preliminary Objection, Separate Opinion of Judge Higgins (12 December 1996), [1996] ICJ Reports 803, para 3).

application of the treaty "can be litigated or arbitrated independently of one another".[27] Otherwise, Ecuador asserted, the distinct category of disputes concerning only the interpretation of the treaty would be rendered a nullity.

Further, Ecuador asserted that the term "dispute", as used in Article VII and as understood in international law, imposed no concreteness requirement. It argued: "just as international law contains no requirement that a breach allegation must exist for a dispute to arise, so too is there no such requirement in relation to whether a dispute is sufficiently concrete".[28] It was therefore enough, in Ecuador's view, that a "dispute" would "have a clear practical consequence in the sense that it can authoritatively determine existing legal rights and obligations of the Contracting Parties, thus removing the existing uncertainty from the legal relations of Ecuador and the United States".[29] Ecuador's position was supported by Professor Alain Pellet who submitted that the only legal requirement was that the resolution of a controversy "affect existing legal rights and obligations of the parties by removing uncertainty from their future legal relations".[30] Professors Stephen McCaffrey and Chittharanjan Amerasinghe, acting as Claimant's experts, concurred in this conclusion.[31]

Ecuador also took aim at the main cases relied on by the United States. It argued that *Northern Cameroons* was mischaracterized. In that case, the UN Trusteeship that the United Kingdom that was alleged to have breached, in fact, terminated two days before Cameroon filed its claim. Thus, rather than concerning the lack of a claim of breach, Ecuador maintained that the absence of concreteness, as recognized by the Court, had to do with ripeness—that is, the Court's inability to render a judgment that "can affect existing legal rights or obligations of the parties".[32] Ecuador also sought to distinguish the *Dual Nationality Claims* case. Ecuador argued that the Conciliation Commission declined to give an opinion not based on a general rule of international law, but rather because the applicable compromissory clause expressly required the existence of a prior concrete claim.[33] Ecuador cited various cases that allegedly resolved an interpretive dispute in the absence of a claim of breach, thus supporting its position that a dispute concerning the interpretation of a treaty need not be predicated on an allegation that the treaty has been breached.[34]

In the absence of any concreteness requirement, the only requirement to demonstrate the existence of a "dispute", according to Ecuador, was positive opposition. To this

---

[27] ibid para 30.
[28] ibid para 58.
[29] ibid para 62.
[30] Pellet Opinion, para 37.
[31] Opinion of Stephen C McCaffrey, 23 May 2012 (McCaffrey Opinion), para 14 (opining that "[b]y refusing to answer a question on a matter of law affecting the legal interests of both states in respect of a bilateral treaty to which they are both parties, the United States put in issue the subject matter of the question. This is especially the case in view of the nature of the question asked by Ecuador, which concerned the *interpretation* of the Treaty. If the United States refused, as it did, to confirm Ecuador's understanding of the authentic interpretation of Article II(7) of the Treaty, where else could Ecuador turn for confirmation but to the dispute settlement mechanism established in Article VII(1) of the Treaty?"); Opinion of Professor CF Amerasinghe, 23 May 2012, para 16 (opinion that "[a] dispute exists when one party expressly opposes the point of view of the other party").
[32] Ecuador's Counter-Memorial (n 26) paras 60–61 (citing *Cameroon v United Kingdom* (n 19) 15).
[33] ibid para 48.
[34] ibid para 46. Pellet Opinion, para 39(2) and (4).

end, Ecuador posited two theories. The first was that the United States had expressly opposed Ecuador's claim when it acknowledged in its submissions that Ecuador's position was "unilateral" and thus opposite that of the United States.[35] The second theory was that the United States' positive opposition could be reasonably inferred because it had failed to provide a response to Ecuador's initial demand for an interpretation when a response was required pursuant to its obligations both under the BIT and international law generally.[36]

A majority of the tribunal comprised of Professor Luiz Olavo Baptista, serving as chair, and Professor Donald McRae, appointed by the United States, rendered an award in favour of the United States, but notably without embracing what it described as the "so-called concreteness requirement".[37] Nor did Professor Raúl Emilio Vinuesa, appointed by Ecuador, in his dissenting opinion.[38] The majority reached its decision, in principal part, by reference to the *Northern Cameroons* case. It began by noting that both parties' reliance on the case was misplaced. According to the tribunal, the case does not stand for the proposition that a "dispute" must be predicated on a claim of breach (the US position) or that its resolution must have "practical consequences" (Ecuador's position). Rather, the majority found that *Northern Cameroons* concerned the effectiveness of a future judgment: namely, a controversy is only justiciable if its settlement can "affect existing legal rights or obligations of the parties, thus removing uncertainty from their legal relations".[39] Parsing the language of the Court, the majority found:

> The use of the plural "parties" is significant, as is the phrase "their legal relations." They clarify that the "practical consequences" must affect and relate to both Parties who are the object of the decision to be rendered in the present case. [40] In other words, they must relate to rights or obligations owed by Ecuador to the United States and vice versa.[41]

For the majority, the key question thus was whether the resolution of the matter before it would have "practical consequences" that affect Ecuador's relationship with the United States by removing any uncertainty in that relationship.[42] It did not, according to the majority, because Ecuador had framed the issues in terms of the scope of its future obligations vis-à-vis US investors, not vis-à-vis the United States: "Such [practical] consequences do not arise in the instant case as it has been pleaded before this Tribunal."[43]

---

[35] Ecuador's Counter-Memorial paras 68–72.

[36] ibid paras 73–101.

[37] *Ecuador v United States of America*, Award, 29 September 2012 (hereafter *Ecuador/United States* Award), para 190.

[38] See Dissenting Opinion of Professor Raul Emilio Vinuesa, 29 September 2012.

[39] *Ecuador/United States* Award, paras 193–195.

[40] ibid para 197.

[41] ibid.

[42] ibid 202.

[43] ibid para 203.

Under the majority's test, the bar for what constitutes a "dispute" was set low. The majority accepted that a claim of breach of treaty by one party against another would easily meet the threshold.[44] However, it found that other less overtly contentious controversies could also qualify as a "dispute". According to the majority, "[t]he outcome [of the instant case] might well have been different", if the United States "had put forward an opinion that differed from that of Ecuador on the proper interpretation of Article II(7), expressed approval for the *Chevron* award's conclusions, or taken issue with Ecuador's actual or proposed implementation of its obligations under Article II(7)".[45] Thus, the majority indicated that, rather than an allegation of breach, the determining factor was whether the United States had ever opposed Ecuador's interpretation. As the United States had never taken a formal position on the meaning of Article II(7), the tribunal's assessment focused on whether positive opposition could be inferred because a response by the United States was called for.[46] The tribunal concluded in the negative since the United States had taken "a principled stance of not wanting to interfere with the decisions of Article VI investor–state tribunals, be they right or wrong".[47] The United States' objection to jurisdiction was thus upheld.

*Ecuador v United States* highlighted the absence of a clear rule on the justiciability of abstract claims. Neither the majority nor the dissenting arbitrator considered themselves bound by a concreteness requirement. This may have contributed to a result driven heavily by the specific facts of the case—namely, the existence of an underlying investor–state arbitration, the *Chevron* arbitration. By virtue of that fact, the majority determined that the controversy was not directly between Ecuador and the United States (thus no "practice consequences" for the bilateral relationship), and the United States had just cause to withhold its interpretation of the meaning of Article II(7) of the BIT (thus no inference of positive opposition). The majority's reasoning is open to criticism, however. BITs are founded on reciprocal obligations between states whereby one state agrees to protect investments in its territory made by investors of the other state. Accordingly, Ecuador's concerns about proper implementation of its BIT obligations arguably affects its relationship with the United States as much as with US investors. The majority therefore arguably placed too much emphasis on how Ecuador framed its claim, and too little on the impact of Ecuador's demand on the bilateral relationship. Further, by the majority's logic, if no underlying arbitration had taken place, a response by the United States would be likely to have been called for under international law and, if not provided, positive opposition could be inferred to determine the existence of a "dispute".

It is submitted that the existence or non-existence of an underlying investor–state arbitration provides no principled basis for determining the justiciability of an abstract

[44] ibid para 204 (discussing the hypothetical that the United States accuse Ecuador of violating Article II(7)).
[45] ibid para 207. Notably, despite the Tribunal's establishment in Procedural Order No 1 of a procedural calendar by which the parties should brief the merits of the case before a jurisdictional ruling, the United States declined to do so on principle to avoid the possibility of creating a "dispute". ibid paras 10, 23–24.
[46] ibid para 215.
[47] ibid para 219.

claim. To be sure, in myriad circumstances, a difference of views between states over the meaning of a treaty could arise outside the context of a related investor–state arbitration or other kind of litigation. Thus, if the majority's low threshold for adjudication were accepted as the general rule, one state could haul another before an international court or tribunal to compel an authoritative interpretation of a treaty with relative ease. While the implications of the majority's approach may be startling, that no international jurisprudence prevented it in the first place is perhaps not surprising in the absence of clear guidance on the treatment of abstract claims in the practice of international courts and tribunals. This practice is discussed in the following section.

## 3. The Approach of International Courts and Tribunals

There have been few occasions in which international courts and tribunals have directly addressed the question of the justiciability of abstract claims.[48] No doubt the significant expenditure of resources and diplomatic capital involved in most inter-state dispute resolution has limited states to the pursuit of only the most essential claims, such as where breaches of international law are involved. The nearly universal presentation of concrete claims before international courts and tribunals is quite likely to have stymied any rigorous consideration of the scope of the judicial function in relation to abstract claims of treaty interpretation. Still, three observations can be made about the existing practice: (i) the legal standard for determining the existence of a "dispute" lacks guidance on the proper treatment of abstract claims; (ii) despite this lack of guidance, the practice of international courts and tribunals suggests the acceptance of a concreteness requirement; and (iii) the lack of guidance in the legal standard requires vigilance on the part of international adjudicators to determine the appropriate division between judicial and sovereign functions.

Regarding the first observation, the definition of "dispute" under existing jurisprudence says very little about how to address abstract controversies. For a "dispute" to exist, there must be "a disagreement on a point of law or fact, a conflict of legal views or of interests between two persons",[49] and positive opposition. The phrases "disagreement on a point of law or fact" and "conflict of legal views or of interests" are objectively broad and could cover a wide range of interactions between states that, in terms of intensity, fall well below a claim of treaty breach. Further, the positive opposition requirement does not alter the nature of the required "disagreement" or "conflict", but rather only the mutuality of its existence. The ICJ's pronouncement in *Northern Cameroons*, even if it were part of the established case law, adds little clarity. The ICJ ruled that it may pass judgment "only in connection with concrete cases where there exists at the time of the adjudication an actual controversy involving a conflict of legal interests between the

---

[48] In fact, before *Ecuador v United States of America*, the next most recent case of this nature was the *Dual Nationality Cases* decided fifty-eight years earlier.
[49] *Greece v Great Britain* (n 1).

parties".[50] The terms "concrete cases" and "actual controversy" are undefined and thus still potentially far-reaching, and the phrase "a conflict of legal interests" (a subset of the *Mavrommatis* formulation) fails to narrow the range of divergences between States that might constitute a "dispute". For decades, no express concreteness requirement has existed in the legal standard.

There has been at best only an undercurrent of support for a requirement of concreteness by a handful of jurists. For example, in his separate opinion in *Northern Cameroons*, Judge Fitzmaurice submitted that

> courts of law are not there to make legal pronouncements *in abstracto*, however great their scientific value as such. They are there to protect existing and current legal rights, to secure compliance with existing and current legal obligations, to afford concrete reparation if a wrong has been committed, or to give rulings in relation to existing and continuing legal situations ....[51]

He added that "a dispute capable of engaging the judicial function of the Court" would at a minimum require that

> the one party should be making, or should have made, a complaint, claim, or protest about an act, omission or course of conduct, present or past, of the other party, which the latter refutes, rejects, or denies the validity of, either expressly, or else implicitly by persisting in the acts, omissions or conduct complained of, or by failing to take the action, or make the reparation, demanded.[52]

In his dissenting opinion in *Alleged Violations of Sovereign Rights and Maritime Spaces in the Caribbean Sea*, Judge ad hoc Caron was perhaps even more direct in support of a concreteness requirement. He observed that, for a "dispute" to exist, "the claim of legal violation by one party must be positively opposed by the other through that party's rejection or denial of the claim of legal violation".[53]

Commentators have offered a range of views on the meaning of "dispute" without providing a clear consensus in favour of a concreteness requirement. Rosenne has noted that a "dispute" is a narrower term than "a "difference" [which is] something broader, and perhaps less concrete, than a dispute".[54] Merrills accepts that a "dispute" may arise from a "claim" or "assertion", observing that what is required is "a specific disagreement concerning a matter of fact, law or policy in which a claim or assertion

[50] *Cameroon v United Kingdom* (n 19).

[51] Separate Opinion of Judge Sir Gerald Fitzmaurice, Northern Cameroons (*Cameroon v United Kingdom*) (Preliminary Objections) [1963] ICJ Rep 97.

[52] ibid 98.

[53] Dissenting Opinion of Judge ad hoc David D Caron, Alleged Violations of Sovereign Rights and Maritime Spaces in the Caribbean Sea (*Nicaragua v Colombia*) (Preliminary Objections) (Judgment) [2016] ICJ Rep 78 (hereafter Caron Dissenting Opinion). See also ibid 79 (emphasis added).

[54] Shabtai Rosenne, *The International Court of Justice: An Essay in Political and Legal Theory* (A.W. Sijthoff's Uitgeversmaatschappij N.V. 1957) 307. See also Shabtai Rosenne, *The Law and Practice of the International Court: 1920–1996 (Volume I) The Court and the United Nations* (3rd edn, Martinus Nijhoff Publishers 1997) 519.

of one party is met with refusal, counter-claim or denial by another".[55] Tomuschat presents an arguably more conservative view, observing that "[t]he Court has consistently proceeded from the assumption that an application must advance a legal claim".[56] According to Collier and Lowe, "[a] dispute is said to be justiciable if ... a specific disagreement ... is of a kind which can be resolved by the application of rules of law by judicial (including arbitral) processes".[57] These views, varied as they are, indicate no clear consensus among commentators about whether the floor of the definition of "dispute" is built on a concreteness requirement.

Despite a longstanding gap in the definition of "dispute", recent developments in the ICJ's practice raise the possibility of a move toward clarification. In *Sovereign Rights and Maritime Spaces*, the ICJ indicated, in the context of establishing positive opposition, that it does not matter which State advances a claim and which one opposes it. Rather, and importantly for present purposes, the Court explained for the first time:

> What matters is that "the two sides hold clearly opposite views concerning the question of the performance or non-performance of certain" international obligations. (*Interpretation of Peace Treaties with Bulgaria, Hungary and Romania*, First Phase, Advisory Opinion, I.C.J. Reports, 1950, p. 74).[58]

The citation to the *Peace Treaties* case in this context is potentially very significant. In that case, the ICJ had observed, merely as a factual matter, that the dispute between the parties concerned questions about "the performance or non-performance of certain treaty obligations".[59] In *Sovereign Rights and Maritime Spaces*, by contrast, this observation appears to have been deliberately elevated to the status of a legal requirement, particularly as the term "treaty obligations" in the earlier opinion has been replaced with the broader and more generalized term "international obligations". This new criterion for what constitutes a "dispute" was included in the same year in the ICJ's opinion in the *Obligations concerning Negotiations relating to Cessation of the Nuclear Arms Race and to Nuclear Disarmament* case.[60] These developments raise the important question: has the Court quietly shored up a longstanding lacuna in the law by introducing an express concreteness requirement?

---

[55] JG Merrills, *International Dispute Settlement* (Cambridge University Press 1993).

[56] Christian Tomuschat, "Article 36" in Andreas Zimmerman and others (eds), *The Statute of the International Court of Justice: A Commentary* (Oxford University Press 2012) 642. See also Tomuschat Opinion (n 22) para 7 ("A legal dispute exists only if the parties are opposed to one another in respect of a specific claim raised by one party against the other which is rejected in whatever form. Divergences about the interpretation of a legal text, which have not led to such a claim, remain at a lower level of differences of opinion for which other modes of settlement may be appropriate.")

[57] John Collier and Vaughan Lowe, *The Settlement of Disputes in International Law: Institutions and Procedures* (Oxford University Press 2000) 10.

[58] Alleged Violations of Sovereign Rights and Maritime Spaces in the Caribbean Sea (*Nicaragua v Colombia*) (Preliminary Objections) (Judgment) [2016] ICJ Rep 26.

[59] Interpretation of Peace Treaties with Bulgaria, Hungary and Romania, First Phase, Advisory Opinion [1950] ICJ Rep 74.

[60] Obligations concerning Negotiations relating to Cessation of the Nuclear Arms Race and to Nuclear Disarmament case (*Marshall Islands v Pakistan*) (Judgment) [2016] ICJ Rep 566.

A second observation to be made is that, whatever the status of a concreteness requirement in the ICJ's jurisprudence, international courts and tribunals, even if rarely confronted with abstract claims, appear to have carefully avoided their adjudication. The PCIJ's opinion in *Certain German Interests in Polish Upper Silesia* is a case in point. In *Polish Upper Silesia*, the PCIJ observed:

> There are numerous clauses giving the Court compulsory jurisdiction in questions of the interpretation and application of a treaty, and these clauses ... appear also to cover interpretations unconnected with concrete cases of application.[61]

The context of this observation is important. The compromissory clause at issue, Article 23 of the German-Polish Convention concerning Upper Silesia, was an early-generation provision that did not refer to "disputes" but rather to "differences of opinion" regarding the construction and application of the treaty. The Court noted that a "difference of opinion" was capable of "exist[ing] as soon as one of the Governments concerned points out that the attitude adopted by the other conflicts with its own views".[62] It made sense then that the Court concluded—and tentatively at that—that a broad compromissory clause, like the one in Article 23, "appear[s] also to cover interpretations unconnected with concrete cases of application".[63] The clear implication is that compromissory language covering "disputes" might be reasonably interpreted as imposing a higher requirement. Interestingly, as already noted, Rosenne drew a similar distinction between a "dispute" and a "difference".

Other pronouncements by the PCIJ in that case about abstract controversies are far less expansive than might appear at first blush. The PCIJ stated: "There seems to be no reason why States should not be able to ask the Court to give an abstract interpretation of a treaty; rather would it appear that this is one of the most important functions which it can fulfil. It has, in fact, already had occasion to do so in Judgment No. 3."[64] Here, the PCIJ was clearly addressing the narrow situation in which states had entered into special agreements, in the absence of a claim of treaty breach, to obtain from the Court an authoritative interpretation of a treaty provision, as was precisely the case in Judgment No 3 in the *Treaty of Neuilly* case referenced by the PCIJ.[65]

Moreover, a careful look at how the PCIJ addressed an abstract issue presented by one of the parties to the case indicates a cautious approach. Germany had presented a series of questions for adjudication, some of which concerned Poland's alleged unlawful expropriation of a factory. They involved a two-part question. The first part, point (a), requested that the Court adjudge whether Poland's expropriation breached the underlying peace treaty. The second part of the question, point (b), was abstract. It stated:

[61] Certain German Interests in Polish Upper Silesia, (Judgment) (Merits), [1926] PCIJ Series A, No 7, 18.
[62] Certain German Interests in Polish Upper Silesia (Preliminary Objections) (Judgment) [25 August 1925] 14.
[63] *Certain German Interests in Polish Upper Silesia*, (Judgment) (Merits) [1926] PCIJ Series A, No 7, 18.
[64] ibid 18–19.
[65] In that case, the parties entered into a special agreement to determine the meaning of the last sentence of the first subparagraph of paragraph 4 of the Annex to Section IV, Part IX, of the Treaty of Neuilly. See *Treaty of Neuilly, Article 179, Annex, Paragraph 4 (Interpretation)* (Judgment) [12 September 1924] PCIJ Series A, No 3.

Should the decision in regard to point (a) be in the affirmative, the Court is requested to state what attitude should have been adopted by the Polish Government in regard to the Companies in question in order to conform with the above-mentioned provisions.[66]

Poland objected to point (b), alleging that it amounted to an unauthorized request for an advisory opinion—something only the League Council or Assembly was authorized to request. The PCIJ dismissed the objection, but not because it believed it could rule on abstract questions. Rather, it preferred to give Germany an opportunity to modify point (b) to make it more concrete. In its judgment on preliminary objections, the Court found:

> It is evident that ... [Germany] could not have intended to obtain an advisory opinion ... [It] asks the Court for a decision, but leaves for its Case on the merits the development of the submission set out under point ... (b), of its application and the exposition of the facts to be laid before the Court at that stage of the proceedings.[67]

In the end, however, because Germany never converted its abstract question into a justiciable claim, the PCIJ declined to consider the question.[68] Accordingly, the PCIJ drew the boundaries of its judicial function at the resolution of Germany's claims of treaty breach.

The *Haya de la Torre* case, decided by the ICJ, is another example of the World Court's aversion to addressing abstract questions.[69] In that case, Colombia sought guidance from the Court on how to implement its prior judgment in the *Asylum* case between Colombia and Peru. In the *Asylum* case, the question presented was whether Colombia's grant of diplomatic asylum to Haya de la Torre, the head of an opposition party in Peru, was in violation of the Havana Convention.[70] The ICJ found that it was. Peru subsequently demanded that Colombia implement the Court's judgment, but Colombia resisted. In the follow-on *Haya de la Torre* case, Colombia petitioned the ICJ "to determine the manner in which effect shall be given to the Judgment of November 20th, 1950 [in the *Asylum* Case]", including, in particular, whether Colombia must surrender Haya de la Torre to Peru.[71] Notably, Colombia alleged no breach of international law.

The ICJ rejected Colombia's request:

---

[66] *Certain German Interests in Polish Upper Silesia* (Preliminary Objections) (Judgment) [25 August 1925] Series A, No 6, 6.

[67] ibid 21.

[68] Finally, the Court recognized that this condition had not been met, and that "the data anticipated by the Court have not been furnished, and the point in question has remained in its purely interrogative form". As a consequence, because Germany never converted its abstract question into a justiciable issue, the Court refused to adjudicate, finding: "In these circumstances, the Court is not in a position to give judgment on this submission; for though it can construe the submissions of the Parties, it cannot substitute itself for them and formulate new submissions simply on the basis of arguments and facts advanced."

[69] Haya de la Torre (*Colombia v Peru*) (Judgment) (hereafter Haya de la Torre) [1951] ICJ Rep 71.

[70] Asylum Case (*Colombia v Peru*) (Judgment) [1950] ICJ Rep 266.

[71] Haya de la Torre (n 69) 73.

Having thus defined [in the *Asylum* case] in accordance with the Havana Convention the legal relations between the Parties with regard to the matters referred to it, the Court has completed its task. It is unable to give any practical advice as to the various courses which might be followed with a view to terminating the asylum, since, by doing so, it would depart from its judicial function.[72]

While the ICJ did not expressly characterize Colombia's request as abstract, it was clearly considered to be non-justiciable on the basis that, contrary to the claims presented in the *Asylum* case, no claim of violation of international law could be decided to establish "the legal relations between the parties".

These examples, although few and far between, suggest that international courts and tribunals eschew the adjudication of abstract questions. Whereas the resolution of concrete questions about whether a party has breached a legal obligation (point (a) in *Upper Silesia* and the question presented in the *Asylum* case) undoubtedly engage the judicial function, abstract questions about what action a state should take to comply with such a legal obligation do not. The latter is left to the states to resolve among themselves within the political or practical spheres of their relationship. Notably, in *Ecuador v United States*, Ecuador sought an authoritative interpretation of Article II(7) of the BIT so it could answer questions such as: "How is Ecuador to organize its court system to avoid violating its obligations under Article II(7)" and "does Ecuador have to double the number of judges".[73] The available international practice suggests that these questions and others like them should be considered abstract and thus non-justiciable because they would require an international court or tribunal to decide how an international law obligation should be implemented, not whether it has been contravened.

A third observation to be made is that a clear delineation of the judicial function in relation to abstract claims is vital to the fair management of inter-state dispute resolution. Judge ad hoc Caron's dissenting opinion in *Sovereign Rights and Maritime Spaces* is an apt reminder. In that case, Colombia raised various objections to the ICJ's jurisdiction. Its second objection alleged the absence of a dispute because Nicaragua had failed to raise claims that Colombia breached international law before Nicaragua filed its application before the Court.[74] Under the third objection, Colombia argued that the Court lacked jurisdiction because Nicaragua failed to satisfy the precondition to negotiate with Colombia in violation of the Bogota Pact.[75]

Judge ad hoc Caron dissented from the Tribunal's dismissal of Colombia's second objection. He observed that, on the facts, Colombia had only ever indicated a reluctance to implement the Court's prior 2012 judgment delimiting the maritime boundary, and that Nicaragua had never formally alleged a violation of its maritime rights until after the proceedings had been initiated. Thus, according to Judge ad hoc Caron,

---

[72] ibid 83.
[73] These questions and others presented by Ecuador are set forth in the US Memorial, 28 (citing Transcript of Preparatory Meeting date 21 March 2012 at 18 (statement of Ecuador's counsel)).
[74] *Nicaragua v Colombia* (n 53) 26 *et seq.*
[75] ibid 34.

Colombia was never afforded the opportunity to positively oppose the claim. On this basis, he reasoned that it may be permissible to infer positive opposition under certain circumstances:

> [i]t is quite another matter for a court, however, to objectively determine the existence of the dispute not from the articulation of a claim by the applicant and response by (including unjustified silence of) the respondent, but rather to infer it from the overall context in which the parties co-exist.[76]

He warned that such an undisciplined approach to ascertaining the existence of positive opposition "could easily shade into an abuse of discretion".[77]

Out of similar concerns, Judge ad hoc Caron also dissented from the Court's rejection of Colombia's third objection. Colombia had argued that Nicaragua never engaged in good faith negotiations with it over the alleged legal violations, a precondition to judicial settlement established under Article II of the Bogota Pact. In response to the Court's conclusion that there was no prospect of settlement, Judge ad hoc Caron opined:

> This conclusion is not supported by the evidence, and is more broadly of concern, for the Court in so doing undermines the centrality of a duty to negotiate both as a part of the peaceful settlement of disputes and specifically as a part of the scheme set out by the Pact of Bogota.[78]

He punctuated his concerns with a citation to *Mavrommatis*, indicating that "before a dispute can be made the subject of an action at law, its subject-matter should have been clearly defined by means of diplomatic negotiations".[79]

One can draw a straight line from the US position in *Ecuador v United States* to Judge ad hoc Caron's dissent. Both raised the dangers of judicial encroachment on sovereign authority to regulate bilateral affairs. In *Ecuador v United States*, the United States opposed Ecuador's broad interpretation of the compromissory language in Article VII of the BIT, asserting it would violate its right to discuss (or choose not to discuss) the meaning of investment treaty provisions with its treaty partners, free from the threat of arbitration. In *Alleged Violations of Sovereign Rights and Maritime Spaces in the Caribbean Sea*, Judge ad hoc Caron warned that disregarding the preconditions for dispute resolution would deprive Colombia of its right to be informed about claims brought against it and to seek their resolution outside of international adjudication. The preservation of these rights and others that guarantee the freedom of sovereign activity outside of a dispute resolution process are not insignificant for the facilitation of inter-state relations. As any determination of judicial competence by an international

---

[76] Caron Dissenting Opinion (n 53) 80.
[77] ibid.
[78] ibid 98.
[79] ibid.

court or tribunal deprives states of the freedom to manage their affairs outside of judicial proceedings, it is incumbent upon international adjudicators to safeguard the
scope of the judicial function, including the meaning of "dispute", carefully with reasonable expectations of states in mind.

## 4. The Compromissory Language

There are hundreds, if not thousands, of treaties that include the phrase (or some close
variation of) "disputes between the Parties concerning the interpretation or application
of the Treaty". Yet surprisingly reasonable and learned minds have long differed about
whether that language permits the adjudication of abstract questions of treaty interpretation. For example, during a 1992 international law conference, two US law professors, Kenneth Vandevelde and José Alvarez, spoke at a panel discussion entitled "The
Development and Expansion of Investment Treaties".[80] They were asked why inter-state
compromissory clauses, like the one in the US-Ecuador BIT, were included in investment treaties and "in what situations do you expect these provisions to be invoked".[81]
Vandevelde answered that state–state arbitration was a vestige of state practice under
Friendship, Commerce, and Navigation (FCN) treaties and should be used as a "back
up" to investor–state arbitration, that is, to resolve claims of treaty violation. By contrast, Professor Alvarez observed that "it is useful to anticipate problems before they
arise" and that "States may disagree on the meaning of certain terms in a BIT".[82] He
submitted therefore that "[i]nterstate dispute settlement provisions should be used by
the United States and its partner states to resolve any such questions", that is, abstract
interpretive questions.[83]

Almost twenty years later, with different leading scholars lining up on each side, the
United States and Ecuador engaged in the same debate about the meaning and purpose of the same compromissory language.[84] Unfortunately, the majority in *Ecuador
v United States* did not address the text of Article VII of the BIT in its award, even in
the face of significant textual arguments by both parties. Ecuador asserted that the disjunctive construction of the compromissory language ("interpretation *or* application")
established a distinct competence for the adjudication of abstract interpretive questions.[85] The United States, by contrast, emphasized that a concreteness requirement in-
heres in the term "dispute", as reinforced by language indicating that justiciable claims
must be "between the Parties" and capable of rendering a "binding decision in accordance with the applicable rules of international law",[86] that is, treaty breach claims. While

[80] Kenneth Vandevelde and José Alvarez, "The Development and Expansion of Bilateral Investment Treaties"
[1992] American Society of International Law Proceedings 532.
[81] ibid 556
[82] ibid.
[83] ibid.
[84] Professors Pellet, McCaffrey, and Amerasinghe, serving as experts for Ecuador, favoured an expansive interpretation of Article VII, whereas Professor Christian Tomuschat, serving as expert for the United States, did not.
[85] Ecuador's Counter-Memorial (n 26) paras 26–30.
[86] US Memorial (n 20) 16–17.

the majority's lack of any interpretive analysis is conspicuous, it is perhaps understandable in light of the unique and inconclusive history of the relevant compromissory language and its varying treatment by international jurists.

The language in Article VII of the BIT likely finds its origins in an early resolution of the Institut de Droit International issued in 1877.[87] That resolution, a reflection of the growing peace movement at the end of the nineteenth century, "[u]rgently recommends that a clause be inserted in future international arbitration treaties, stipulating recourse to arbitration in the event of a dispute over the interpretation and application of these treaties".[88] The Institut's noble goal was to eliminate warfare by promoting international dispute resolution as an alternative.[89]

The Institut's resolution appears to have been inspired by certain proposals in favor of compulsory arbitration at the Hague Peace Conferences. As Professor Hudson recounted:

> In 1899, the Russian delegation at the Peace Conference at The Hague proposed a plan for compulsory arbitration in two classes of cases, in so far as they did not concern vital interests or national honor: [including] disputes relating to the interpretation or application of certain types of treaties... At the Second Peace Conference at the Hague in 1907, the Portuguese delegation proposed exceptions relating to vital interests and independence in engagements to arbitration should not include (i) disputes concerning the interpretation or application of conventions relating to sixteen subjects . . . .[90]

The reason for transforming the compromissory language from the conjunctive in the original Institute resolution ("interpretation and application") to the disjunctive in the Peace Conference discussion ("interpretation or application") is not apparent.[91] What is clear, however, is that Conference delegations were reticent to accept such language in the context of compulsory arbitration, even with broad carve-outs to protect the vital interests and national honour of States. Such proposals failed to gain support at the Conferences and would not enter mainstream treaty practice until decades later.[92]

The United Nations promoted similar compromissory language in 1947, as the world was rebuilding after the Second World War. A resolution entitled "Need for greater

---

[87] "Arbitrage international: clause compromissoire à insérer dans les traités", L'Institut de Droit international, Zurich Session, 1877, <https://www.idi-iil.org/app/uploads/2017/06/1877_zur_01_fr.pdf>.

[88] ibid (stating that it *"[r]ecommande avec instance d'insérer dans les futurs traités internationaux une clause compromissoire, stipulant le recours à la voie de l'arbitrage en cas de contestation sur l'interprétation et l'application de ces traités".*)

[89] For a description of the peace movement from which the Institut's contribution emerged, see David Caron, "War and International Adjudication: Reflections on the 1899 Peace Conference" (2000) 94(1) American Journal of International Law 4, 8–13.

[90] Manley Hudson, *The Permanent Court of International Justice 1920–1942* (The MacMillan Company 1943) 457.

[91] As the negotiating history indicates, conjunctive and disjunctive formulations were proposed throughout the Conference. See James Brown Scott, *The Proceedings of the Hague Peace Conferences: Translation of the Official Texts* (Oxford University Press 1921) 484, 875, 904, 1006.

[92] Note that some treaties concluded in the early 1900s did follow this approach. For a description of such treaties, see Helen May Cory, *Compulsory Arbitration of International Disputes* (Columbia University Press 1932) 8–10.

use by the United Nations and its organs of the International Court of Justice" sought, among other things, to:

> Draw ... the attention of State Members to the advantage of inserting in conventions and treaties arbitration clauses providing, without prejudice to Article 95 of the Charter, for the submission of disputes which may arise from the interpretation or application of such conventions or treaties, preferably and as far as possible to the International Court of Justice.[93]

The discussion of this aspect of the resolution occurred without controversy and without any recorded consideration of the scope of the proposed compromissory language. Notably, however, another aspect of the resolution encouraging the use of the ICJ's advisory function was accompanied by commentary indicating a preference for such use only in concrete cases.[94]

In the period following the UN resolution, at least one nation has been conservative in its interpretation of the scope of the recommended compromissory language. The United States, for example, viewed the compromissory language in its post-war FCN treaties ("disputes between the Parties concerning the interpretation or application of the Treaty") as covering only claims of treaty breach. Specifically, for ratification of its FCNs with Belgium and Vietnam in the context of seeking advice and consent by the US Senate, the US government has explained that "[it] is in the interest of the United States to be able to have recourse to [state-to-state dispute settlement] in case of treaty violation".[95]

Without a more thorough examination, any conclusions to be drawn from this brief history should not be overstated. At the same time, there is likely no overwhelming evidence to be found that the words "interpretation or application" (as opposed to the original "interpretation and application") were expressly intended to cover the adjudication of abstract questions of treaty interpretation. If anything, these historical points, briefly noted, suggest that behind the standard compromissory language lies a general desire to afford international courts and tribunals broad competence to resolve a range of disputes, tempered by a practical reluctance by States to grant adjudicators unbounded jurisdiction, such as by allowing the resolution of abstract claims of treaty interpretation.

---

[93] "Need for greater use by the United Nations and its organs of the International Court of Justice" A/RES/171(II), adopted at the 113th plenary meeting (14 November 1947), <https://digitallibrary.un.org/record/209998?ln=en>.

[94] "It does not ... propose that all points of law should be referred to the Court indiscriminately. There is no question of the Court being flooded with futile and hypothetical questions." See also Yuen-Li Liang, "Notes on Legal Questions Concerning the ICJ" (1948) 42(2) American Journal of International Law 441–42 (noting that the resolution intended that "requests for advisory opinions should not be made in regard to an abstract hypothetical case likely to arise in the future, but on concrete points").

[95] US Senate Report on Commercial Treaties with Belgium and Vietnam (28 August 1961) Appendix, Department of State Memorandum on Provisions in Commercial Treaties Relation to the International Court of Justice, p 7.

The analysis of the standard compromissory language by jurists has also not sharpened an understanding of the outer limits of legal function. To be sure, the words "interpretation" and "application" denote different concepts. An "interpretation" of a treaty involves an examination of what it means, whereas the "application" of a treaty relates to how it is implemented by the parties.[96] Yet the views of eminent jurists have varied considerably about whether a meaningful distinction between the two concepts exists in relation to the judicial function. In the *Headquarters Agreement* case, Judge Shahabuddeen interpreted the standard compromissory language "as a compendious term of art".[97] Suggesting there is little difference between the conjunctive and disjunctive formulations, he stated:

> The phrase in this case happens to be "interpretation or application." Satisfaction of either element will therefore suffice. But, further, since it is not possible to interpret a treaty save with reference to some factual field (even if taken hypothetically) and since it is not possible to apply a treaty except on the basis of some interpretation of it, there is a detectable view that there is little practical, or even theoretical, distinction between the two elements of the formula.[98]

By contrast, in the *Oil Platforms* case, Judge Higgins opined that "the phrase ['interpretation or application'] contains two distinct elements which may form the subject matter of a reference to the Court" and lamented that "[a]ll too frequently, they are treated compendiously".[99]

Judge Shahabuddeen's interpretation arguably presents the more relevant assessment in the context of concrete claims, which underpin the vast majority of inter-state cases. At least where the applicant state alleges a breach of a treaty obligation, that obligation will have to have been *interpreted*, to the extent the content of the obligation is disputed (which is often the case), and *applied* to determine whether the conduct of the respondent state contravenes its obligations. Even where the applicant state does not allege a violation, "interpretation" and "application" are likely still to go hand in hand. Such was the situation, for example in *Case Concerning Rights of Nationals of the United States in Morocco*.[100] There, France requested an interpretation of its obligations under the US-France FCN. France did not assert a breach of the treaty because it was the United States, procedurally the respondent state, that claimed France's lack

[96] See eg UNCTAD, *Dispute Settlement: State–State*, IIA Issue Series, UNCTAD/ITE/IIT/2003/1 (2003) 14; Harvard Law School, "Draft Convention on the Law of Treaties: Article 19. Interpretation" reprinted in [1935] American Journal of International Law Supplement 937, 938–39.

[97] Separate Opinion of Judge Shahabuddeen, *Applicability of the Obligation to Arbitrate under Section 21 of the United Nations Headquarters Agreement of 26 June 1947* (Advisory Opinion) (26 April 1988) ICJ Rep 59.

[98] ibid. See also Frank Berman, "International Treaties and British Statutes" (2005) 26 Statute Law Review 1, 10 (observing "there is a virtually inseparable link between interpretation and application; jurisdictional clauses in treaties invariably cover, as a portmanteau category, 'disputes over the interpretation or application of the present treaty,' in such a way that the competent tribunal is not required to distinguish the one from the other").

[99] Separate Opinion of Judge Higgins, *Oil Platforms (Islamic Republic of Iran v United States of America)* (Judgment) (Preliminary Objection) (12 December 1996) ICJ Rep 847.

[100] *Rights of Nationals of the United States of America in Morocco (France v United States of America)* (Judgment) (27 August 1952) ICJ Rep 176.

of compliance with the terms of the FCN. Thus, the concepts of "interpretation" and "application" were still inextricably intertwined in the case, even though the remedy requested by France was limited to declaratory relief.

The distinction between concepts is more dramatically pronounced if abstract interpretive questions, like the one presented by Ecuador in *Ecuador v United States*, are considered to be justiciable. Outside the process of ascertaining the existence of a treaty breach, the words "dispute … concerning the interpretation of the Treaty" can easily implicate a wide range of low-intensity interactions between states. A "dispute" thus could arise when, for example, states express a difference of view on the meaning of a treaty provision during bilateral discussions on their respective performances under the treaty or seek to amend the terms of the treaty or even, as in the case of *Ecuador v United States*, when one treaty party approaches another with a demand for agreement on a proposed interpretation of the treaty. So long as the view of one state is positively opposed by the other, either expressly or implicitly (where permissible), an international court or tribunal would be competent to determine the meaning of the treaty provision in question. To recognize the existence of such a broad category of justiciable abstract claims would mean that states had intended this coverage based solely on the inclusion of the disjunctive formulation "interpretation or application" in the standard compromissory language.

The history of that language, as briefly explained, and the scant practice of states in presenting abstract claims before international courts and tribunals pursuant to that language, significantly undermine a broad reading of the words "any dispute between the Parties concerning the interpretation or application of the Treaty".

## 5. Conclusion

*Ecuador v United States* revealed a potentially significant lacuna in the legal standard for determining the existence of a "dispute"—that is, the absence of an express concreteness requirement. Ecuador's claim was dismissed, in a split decision, on the ground that positive opposition could not be inferred under the unique circumstances of the case. Particularly, the United States' unwillingness to respond substantively to Ecuador's demand for an interpretation of Article II(7) of the BIT was justified as a means of not interfering with the enforceability of the award rendered in *Chevron v Ecuador*. Had that distinct fact pattern not presented itself or had the United States expressed a view contrary to Ecuador's proposed interpretation, a "dispute" might very well have existed, according to the majority. That possibility should give states pause if they have not contemplated such a broad scope of dispute resolution under their treaties containing the standard compromissory language.

The responsibility for addressing whether abstract claims are justiciable falls first to the states. In *Ecuador v United States*, neither party introduced *travaux préparatoires* of the US-Ecuador BIT to guide the tribunal's interpretive analysis of Article VII of the BIT, presumably because none existed. The brief history of the standard compromissory language, discussed in this chapter, suggests that under many, if not most, treaties the language "any dispute between the Parties concerning the interpretation or application of the Treaty", or some slight variation in terms, is adopted by the treaty partners at face value, without significant negotiation of the meaning of these terms in relation to abstract claims. The practice stands in contrast to other systems of inter-state dispute resolution. For example, the compromissory language of the World Trade Organization's Dispute Settlement Understanding leaves little doubt as to its scope: a "dispute" arises in "situations in which a Member considers that any benefits accruing directly or indirectly under the covered agreements are being impaired by measures taken by another Member".[101] It behooves states to consider whether greater clarity in drafting compromissory language is required and, if so, to pursue the conclusion of future treaties and the amendment and interpretation of existing treaties accordingly.

International courts and tribunals also play a critical role, guided by the ICJ's law and practice. The longstanding formulation of the concept of "dispute" leaves the proper treatment of abstract claims unclear, as evidenced by the staunchly conflicting views on the topic. Certain questions therefore require answers in the interest of ensuring stability and predictability in the relations between states, particularly with regard to the pacific settlement of disputes. First and foremost, does the standard contain a concreteness requirement? The ICJ's incorporation of *Interpretation of Peace Treaties with Bulgaria, Hungary and Romania* into recent recitations of the legal standard suggests the possibility of an affirmative clarification. However, a more comprehensive analysis of the judicial function in relation to abstract claims by the ICJ is called for before its intentions can be fully understood. Second, if the standard lacks a concreteness requirement, what effect does the standard compromissory language have on the possible range of justiciable claims? A deeper assessment of the history of the language, as well as of the state objectives in agreeing on the language, is critical. When formulating answers to these questions in future cases, Judge ad hoc Caron's deep insights provide essential guidance. As he reminds us, a finding of competence by an international court or tribunal reflects a delimitation between the judicial function and sovereign authority to self-regulate international affairs. To overstep that boundary could unduly deprive states of their preferred political and practical dispute resolution options and, in turn, might undermine the legitimacy of the international judicial process as a whole.

## Acknowledgements

The author is grateful for the thoughtful comments on this contribution provided by Charles N Brower and Jeremy K Sharpe.

---

[101] Article 3.3, Understanding on Rules and Procedures Governing the Settlement of Disputes, Annex 2 to Marrakesh Agreement Establishing the World Trade Organization, 15 April 1994, in *World Trade Organization, The Legal Texts: The Results of the Uruguay Round of Multilateral Trade Negotiations* [1999] 354.

# 20

# The Treatment of Relevant Circumstances in Maritime Boundary Delimitation

## Adjudication and Conciliation

*Donald McRae*

## 1. Introduction

The notion of relevant circumstances has been central to maritime boundary delimitation although its origins and articulation are somewhat confused. Parties to maritime delimitation disputes assert their own views of what the relevant circumstances are in their case. Courts and tribunals take account of or disregard what they identify as relevant circumstances, which have ranged from geography, geomorphology, economy, resources, military and security concerns, to historic usage. More recently there has been an attempted systematization of the approach to maritime boundary delimitation in which there is a framework in which relevant circumstances are to be considered.[1] Yet this notwithstanding, arguably the concept of relevant circumstances remains opaque and the ways in which it has been applied by courts and tribunals no less arbitrary than it has ever been.

There may be many reasons for this and perhaps where courts and tribunals are today is the best that can be hoped for. The question, however, is whether the confines of third-party adjudication is at the heart of the difficulty and whether other forms of dispute settlement might offer better opportunities for fulfilling the objectives that resort to "relevant circumstances" is supposed to achieve in maritime delimitation.

In this chapter, I will look at the way that the concept of relevant circumstance has been articulated and applied in maritime delimitation by courts and tribunals. I will then look at international conciliation as exemplified in the recent *Timor Sea Conciliation*, which dealt specifically with the delimitation of a maritime boundary in the Timor Sea between Timor-Leste and Australia.[2] Does the mechanism of conciliation provide a better means for taking account of "relevant circumstances" in maritime delimitation?

---

[1] *Maritime Delimitation in the Black Sea (Romania v Ukraine) (Judgment)* [2009] ICJ Rep 61.
[2] Report and Recommendations of the Compulsory Conciliation Commission between Timor-Leste and Australia in the Timor Sea, 9 May 2018, PCA Case No 2016-10 (hereafter Report). The writer was a member of the Conciliation Commission. The views expressed in this chapter reflect the views of the author only and not the views of the Commission or of other individual members of the Commission.

Donald McRae, *The Treatment of Relevant Circumstances in Maritime Boundary Delimitation* In: *By Peaceful Means.* Edited by: Charles N Brower, Joan E Donoghue, Cian C Murphy, Cymie R Payne and Esmé R Shirlow, Oxford University Press. © Donald McRae 2024.
DOI: 10.1093/oso/9780192848086.003.0020

## 2. Relevant Circumstances in Courts and Tribunals

The role of relevant circumstances in maritime delimitation has been to ensure that the particularities of each maritime area are properly taken into account. In other words, as the Chamber of the International Court of Justice (ICJ) in the *Gulf of Maine Case* said, each case is "monotypic".[3] That idea was behind the International Law Commission (ILC) draft articles that led to the delimitation provisions in the 1958 Conventions. Both Article 12 of the Convention on the Territorial Sea and Contiguous Zone and Article 6 of the Convention on the Continental Shelf provided a method for delimitation, equidistance, but with a qualification to take account of the circumstances of the particular area. In the Territorial Sea Convention, it was "historic title or other special circumstances" and in the Continental Shelf Convention, it was "special circumstances".

The ILC Commentaries on the draft articles that were the basis for the conventions made no reference to "relevant" circumstances. The commentaries on delimitation of the continental shelf referred to "departures necessitated by any exceptional configuration of the coast, as well as the presence of islands or of navigable channels".[4] The Commission was obviously referring to the circumstances that could exist in the particular area being delimited; in other words the "special" circumstances of that area. And that was the language that found its way into the Conventions.

The term "relevant circumstances" emerged in the decision of the ICJ in the *North Sea Continental Shelf Cases*. In articulating a rule for maritime delimitation under customary international law, the Court said, "delimitation is to be effected by agreement in accordance with equitable principles, and taking account of all the relevant circumstances".[5] What is surprising is that the term relevant circumstances can be found only in the *dispositif* of the judgment; it is not found in the reasoning. In their arguments the parties had focused on the circumstances of the North Sea area. Germany argued that the approach of a just and equitable share had to be determined in light of criteria relevant to the particular geographical circumstances of the North Sea.[6] Denmark and the Netherlands argued that the boundary had to be based on equidistance unless there were "juridically relevant" special circumstances.[7]

While not using the term relevant circumstances, the Court used as a surrogate the term "considerations", including the statement that there was no legal limit to the considerations that could be taken into account.[8] The Court also referred to the "geographical circumstances" of the area.[9] The Court then identified the "factors" that were to be taken into account in negotiations that included: the coasts (general configuration,

---

[3] *Delimitation of the Maritime Boundary in the Gulf of Maine Area (Canada/USA) (Judgment)* [1984] ICJ Rep 246, [81]
[4] ILC Draft Articles, Yearbook of the ILC 1956, Vol II, 300.
[5] *North Sea Continental Shelf, (Judgment)* ICJ Rep 1969, 3, [101].
[6] ibid 12.
[7] ibid 21, [14].
[8] ibid 51, [93].
[9] ibid 50, [89].

special or unusual features), the continental shelf (physical, geological, and natural resources) and proportionality between coastal lengths and areas of shelf appertaining to
the coastal state. In a critical statement which presaged its final ruling, the Court said,
"the parties are under an obligation to act in such a way that, in a particular case, and
taking all the circumstances into account, equitable principles are applied".[10] In the operative part, "all the circumstances" became "all the relevant circumstances".

Thus, there was a commonality between delimitation under the treaties and delimitation under customary international law. Both specified a method and a requirement
to adjust in light of the particular circumstances of the area. The Court of Arbitration in
the *Anglo-French Continental Shelf Case* made the point clearly when it said:[11]

> the appropriateness of equidistance or any other method for the purpose of effecting
> an equitable delimitation in any given case is always a function or reflection of the geo-
> graphical and other relevant circumstances of the particular case.

The treaties on the territorial sea and the continental shelf referred to these circumstances as "special" circumstances; the customary international law rule articulated
them in terms of "relevant" circumstances.

The subsequent and lengthy debate over whether "special" circumstances were really
the same thing as "relevant" circumstances always had an air of unreality about it. Both
types of "circumstances" were considerations that were aimed at the same goal: ensuring that the method of delimitation was adapted to the actual circumstances of the
area to be delimited.[12]

The challenge of the concept of relevant circumstances in maritime delimitation has
always been to decide which circumstances of the area to be delimited are relevant and
what impact they are to have in delimitation. In this regard, the statement that special
circumstances and relevant circumstances are essentially the same needs some qualification. Although the same factors that are pertinent to a particular area might readily
be characterized as either "special" or "relevant", the rules under which they function
and the roles they are to play are different.

The equidistance/special circumstances rule of Article 6 of the 1958 Convention on
the Continental Shelf contained both a method—equidistance—and a direction for
how to modify the application of that method if the particular circumstances of the area
to be delimited justified another boundary line. "Special" circumstances could prevent
the unqualified application of the method of delimitation. Equidistance as a method,
strictly applied, might be displaced because of the particular or "special" circumstances

---

[10] ibid 48, [85].

[11] *Case Concerning the Delimitation of the Continental Shelf between the United Kingdom of Great Britain and North Island, and the French Republic*, [1977, 1978] 18 UNRIAA 3, 111 [239].

[12] Malcom Evans, "Relevant Circumstances" in Alex G Oude Elferink, Tore Henricksen, and Signe Veierud Busch, (eds), *Maritime Boundary Delimitation: The Case Law* (Cambridge University Press 2018) 222, 228 argues that even if relevant circumstances and special circumstances were different in the past "today they are not".

of the area. As Malcolm Evans has pointed out, the particular circumstances of the area could affect the manner in which the primary methodology was to be applied.[13]

The role of "relevant" circumstances under the "equitable principles/relevant circumstances" rule was different. "Equitable principles" was not a method of delimitation. It was a direction on how to go about finding the method of delimitation. "Relevant" circumstances under the "equidistance/relevant circumstances" approach thus had a wider role to play. They were not just to oust a particular method of delimitation; they had to be considered in order to establish the method of delimitation. As Evans says, relevant circumstances were invoked as "a means of determining what the primary methodology was to be".[14]

The formula for delimitation adopted in Articles 74 and 83 of the 1982 Convention on the Law of the Sea did not resolve whether the equidistance/special circumstances approach or the equitable principles/relevant circumstances approach to delimitation was to hold sway. By indicating that delimitation had to be on the basis of international law it left open that customary international law might still be the basis for delimiting boundaries, and by making specific mention of "an equitable solution" it left the clear implication that equity was going to be a fundamental objective in maritime boundary delimitation.[15] However, although equity gets a specific mention, equidistance is not referred to and can be brought into Articles 74 and 83 only through the reference to international law.

Notwithstanding this lack of a formal method for delimitation and a focus on equity and not equidistance in the 1982 Convention, courts and tribunals tended to gravitate back to equidistance which provided them with a concrete starting point rather than relying on a direction to determine a method on the basis of equitable principles.

The high point came with the decision of the ICJ in the *Black Sea Case (Romania v Ukraine)*, which established a three-stage process for maritime delimitation. This consisted of drawing a provisional equidistance line, seeing whether the line should be adjusted in light of relevant circumstances and then determining whether the result is proportionate.[16]

The three-stage test has become standard in maritime boundary delimitation and followed not only by the ICJ itself in other cases but also by the International Tribunal for the Law of the Sea (ITLOS) and other ad hoc arbitrations. The one formal variation was stipulated by the Court in *Nicaragua v Honduras*[17] where the unsettled nature of the coastline made it difficult to identify basepoints for the construction of a provisional equidistance line and thus the Court adopted a method other than equidistance

---

[13] ibid 229.

[14] ibid [230].

[15] Thomas Cottier has articulated a framework under which equity in maritime boundary delimitation can be understood and applied. "The model of equitable solution based on international law provides a framework upon which individual boundaries should be agreed to within legal guidelines": Thomas Cottier, *Equitable Principles of Maritime Boundary Delimitation: The Quest for Distributive Justice in International Law* (Cambridge University Press 2015) 227.

[16] *Black Sea*, [116–122].

[17] *Territorial and Maritime Dispute between Nicaragua and Honduras in the Caribbean Sea (Nicaragua v Honduras)* (Judgment) [2007] ICJ Rep 659 [280–281].

to establish a provisional delimitation line. In practice, however, courts and tribunals have usually started with a provisional line drawn on the basis of equidistance.

On its face, the three-stage process provides a clear way for maritime boundary delimitation to be approached, drawing perhaps on what was originally intended in Article 6 of the 1958 Continental Shelf Convention. That is, a method for delimitation is posited and then the particular circumstances of the area have to be considered to see if they would justify a variation from the lines drawn on the basis of equidistance. What is different from the old equidistance-special circumstances rule is that a third stage has been introduced—testing the proportionality of the line to see if the result is equitable.

The three-stage formulation is important, too, because it appears to have indicated clearly the role that "relevant circumstances" are to play in boundary delimitation. They are a corrective to ensure that the line reflects properly the particular circumstances of the delimitation area. It provides no guide as to what circumstances are relevant and what weight they are to be given, but stipulating that the line is in principle an equidistance line, the delimitation approach limits the role of relevant circumstances to deciding whether the provisional line should be remain as provisionally drawn or be adjusted.

The three-stage formula is also an implicit rejection of the equitable principles approach to the construction of a line and as a consequence has an impact of the role of relevant circumstances in deciding on the method for boundary delimitation. As mentioned earlier, equitable principles are not a delimitation method; rather, recourse to equitable principles provides a direction on how the method of delimitation (equidistance, perpendicular, adjusted bisector) is to be determined. And the particular circumstances of the area, the relevant circumstances, play a role in the determination of the delimitation method. Once the method of equidistance has been identified, then there is no role for relevant circumstances in determining a method of delimitation.

The cases have shown that the three-stage approach has the potential for giving equidistance a primacy in maritime delimitation that is at odds with the negotiation of UNCLOS, where equidistance was not even mentioned in Articles 74 and 83, although the need to achieve equity was.[18] Once a provisional equidistance line has been established, the cases show that the line is very infrequently adjusted because of relevant circumstances nor is the line shown to be "significantly disproportionate".

But a closer appreciation of what is happening in maritime delimitation by courts and tribunals suggests that rather than relegating relevant circumstances to a post facto corrective function, the opposite may be true. The three-stage test has not been applied in a way that it can be said that an objective basis on which the relevance of particular circumstances in the area to be delimited can be properly taken into account has been developed. Indeed, it might be argued that the way the three-stage test is being applied has simply reinforced the subjectivity in the appreciation of relevant circumstances that the three-stage test was intended to avoid.

---

[18] Donald McRae, "The Applicable Law" in Elferink, Henricksen, and Busch (eds) (n 12) 92–116.

That this might be so was apparent even before the three-stage approach was articulated and courts and tribunals were proceeding on the basis of a two-stage approach.[19] The first step in the two-stage approach was the drawing of a provisional equidistance line and the second step was determining whether there should be an adjustment of that line in light of relevant circumstances. But, as pointed out, in *Nicaragua v Honduras*, the Court did not draw an equidistance line because of the difficulty of identifying basepoints on the coast. In other words, there, the particular conditions of the coastline in the area to be delimited were taken into account in order to decide what the provisional line should be. In short, in light of the particular circumstances of the area to be delimited, the Court adapted the drawing of the provisional boundary line. It took into account relevant circumstances (a second-stage consideration) in establishing the provisional line (a first-stage task).

Adjustment in the drawing of the provisional equidistance line (taking account of relevant circumstances in the first stage) continued when the approach moved from being a two-stage approach to a three-stage approach. In the *Black Sea Case* the ICJ did not just draw a provisional equidistance line it drew an equidistance line based on a selection of basepoints which disregarded features which would be included by a strict application of equidistance. Thus, by the time it came to assess the line in light of the relevant circumstance, the ICJ had already taken relevant circumstances into account. As a result, there was an air of unreality about the Court's treatment of some of the claims to relevant circumstances. Having disregarded Serpent's Island in the drawing of the provisional equidistance line in *Black Sea*, the Court then asked itself whether Serpent's Island was a relevant circumstance, a matter it had in effect already decided in disregarding it at the first stage of drawing a provisional equidistance line.

This pattern of considering relevant circumstances in the first stage of the three-stage process has continued in other delimitation cases. In *Myanmar v Bangladesh*, ITLOS disregarded St Martin's Island in drawing a provisional equidistance line and then considered whether the island should be considered as a relevant circumstance. It concluded that it should not[20] for precisely the same reasons as it gave for ignoring St Martin's Island as a basepoint.[21] It had already been treated as a relevant circumstance.

Further, although the proportionality, or disproportionality test is carried out at a separate stage from the relevant circumstances stage, it is difficult to distinguish conceptually the test of relevant circumstances to determine whether there is an equitable solution from the test of proportionality. Testing for proportionality involves looking precisely at the particularities of the area to be delimited. A comparison of the ratios of the length of the relevant coasts and ratios of the maritime areas allocated is a comparison based on the particularities of the area being delimited. Nor has the categorization of this as a third stage reduced the subjectivities involved in determining proportion or disproportion.[22]

---

[19] For the development of what became the three-stage approach, see McRae (n 18) 99–105.

[20] *Dispute of the Maritime Boundary in the Bay of Bengal (Bangladesh/Myanmar)*, Judgment, ITLOS Reports, 2012, 4 [317–319].

[21] ibid [265].

[22] Yoshifumi Tanaka, "The Disproportionality Test in the Law of Maritime Delimitation" in Elferink, Henricksen, and Busch (eds) (n 12) 291–318, 314–15.

In light of the above, it is difficult to disagree with Malcolm Evans' conclusion that:[23]

> [e]Even after the introduction of the three-stage approach, they [relevant circum-stances] appear to be as open-textured and as decisive—yet as nebulous—as ever, and continue to operate at all stages of the delimitation process as a means of influencing its outcome, however described or addressed.

In effect, then, courts and tribunals have not been successful in providing a coherent approach to taking account of "relevant circumstances", of the particularities of each delimitation area. The range of factors that might be taken into account in any case are significant. As mentioned earlier, they include geography, geomorphology, economy, resources, military and security concerns, and historic usage, yet there is no real guidance on how these factors are to be assessed. Matters such as natural prolongation, cut-off, or even "catastrophic repercussions" are invoked, but they do not provide sufficient clarity or specificity to qualify as objective standards.

Given the inability of courts and tribunals to develop a regime for maritime de-limitation that takes account of the particularities of each delimitation area and is objective and predictable, the question is whether this is inherent in maritime de-limitation through judicial or arbitral settlement. Would some other form of dispute resolution provide a better means for taking account of the particularities of each boundary area in maritime delimitation? Is there another way of resolving maritime boundary disputes taking account of the relevant circumstances of the area to be de-limited that would achieve the equitable solution that UNCLOS sought to promote? As a measure of this, I will now turn the process of conciliation undertaken in the Timor Sea Conciliation.

## 3. The Timor Sea Conciliation

The Timor Sea Conciliation was the first and, so far, the only conciliation undertaken pursuant to the compulsory conciliation provisions of UNCLOS. Under Article 298 of the Convention, states may exclude certain matters, including the provisions relating to maritime boundary delimitation (Article 15, 74, and 83), from the provisions relating to third-party settlement (Part XV, Section 2) but if it does so the state has to accept submission to conciliation provided for in Annex V, Section 2 of the Convention at the request of any party.

Timor-Leste's invocation of the conciliation provisions of Article 298 was against a background of its concern that attempts to achieve a maritime boundary with Australia were being frustrated. After gaining its independence from Portugal in 1975, the is-land was occupied by Indonesia, which led to many years of guerrilla struggle before

---

[23] Evans (n 12) 243.

Timor-Leste finally gained its independence in 2002, facilitated by the UN. Access to the resources of the seabed off its coast was obviously a matter of high concern to the new state. On the day of its independence, Timor-Leste concluded an agreement with Australia (Timor Sea Treaty) which provided for the formal application of an arrangement that had been entered into between Australia and the United Nations Transitional Authority in East Timor (UNTAET) the previous year, providing for a Joint Petroleum Development Agency (JPDA) in a defined area of the Timor Sea between Timor-Leste and Australia.[24] The arrangement was pending the delimitation of a maritime boundary but no provision was made for a boundary.

The JPDA set out a sharing arrangement between Timor-Leste and Australia for revenues from petroleum activities in the Area on the basis of 90 per cent to Timor-Leste and 10 per cent to Australia and production of liquid natural gas (LNG) commenced in one field (Bayu-Udan)[25] and a number of smaller fields. However, the area of greatest potential was the area known as Greater Sunrise which went beyond the JPDA and was an area that potentially would be divided if there were a maritime boundary between Timor-Leste and Australia.

In 2003 and 2004 discussions were held over the delimitation of maritime boundaries but no agreement was reached. Instead, in 2006, the parties entered into an agreement (Certain Maritime Arrangements in the Timor Sea (CMATS))[26] providing for jurisdiction over the water column of the JPDA to go to Timor-Leste and the parties to share 50:50 in production from the Greater Sunrise field. Article 4 of CMATS provided that there would be a moratorium on maritime delimitation for the period of the Agreement which was to last for fifty years.

Over time Timor-Leste became more and more dissatisfied with the arrangements entered into under CMATS. There was little progress in the development of the Greater Sunrise field which Timor-Leste saw as having the greatest potential for revenue and there were disagreements over the operation of the Timor Sea Treaty. This led to the initiation of two arbitrations by Timor-Leste and a case in the ICJ that called into question the process of the negotiation of the Timor Sea Treaty. The moratorium on maritime boundary delimitation was seen by Timor-Leste as an impediment to gaining full sovereignty over its maritime resources which it considered essential to the completion of its independence as a state.

In April 2016, Timor-Leste invoked the provisions of UNCLOS Article 298 calling on Australia to accept submission of their dispute over the delimitation of maritime boundaries to compulsory conciliation.[27] Australia responded in May 2016 indicating

---

[24] Report (n 2) 11, Map 2. The history of Timor-Leste's gaining of independence and the arrangements regarding the Timor Sea are set out in Report (n 2) [15–35].

[25] Report (n 2) 15, Map 3.

[26] Treaty between Australia and the Democratic Republic of Timor-Leste on certain maritime arrangements in the Timor Sea, 12 January 2006, 2483 UNTS 359.

[27] Notification Instituting Conciliation under Section 2 of Annex 5 of UNCLOS, 11 April 2016, Report, Annex 3.

that it would engage in the process and, in accordance with the terms of Annex V of the Convention, a Conciliation Commission was constituted in June 2016.[28]

This was the first compulsory conciliation commission appointed under UNCLOS and there had been few examples of conciliation on law of the sea matters generally. There had been one maritime delimitation resulting from conciliation, although little was known about the precise process of the conciliation.[29] Thus, the Conciliation Commission had to devise its own Rules of Procedure and determine how it would undertake the process of conciliation. In responding to Timor-Leste's Notification instituting conciliation, Australia had given notice that it intended to challenge the jurisdiction of the Commission, including on the ground that the moratorium on maritime boundary delimitation under CMATS precluded the Commission from entertaining Timor-Leste's request. Thus the Commission had made provision in its Rules of Procedure for a preliminary hearing on this challenge to its competence. After written submissions and a hearing on competence, the Commission rejected the Australian challenge and proceeded with the conciliation.[30]

The request of Timor-Leste was that the Conciliation Commission "assist Timor-Leste and Australia in reaching an amicable settlement of their dispute relating to the delimitation of their permanent maritime boundaries in the Timor Sea". Timor-Leste also made clear that its objective was the conclusion of an agreement that delimits those boundaries.[31]

The Commission thus had to decide how it would approach what was being requested of it. This meant trying to understand the nature of the conciliation process and how it was to be conducted. One of the challenges immediately following a litigation mode, which the challenge to competency had required, was that the parties had to reorient their thinking towards a conciliation approach. In this regard the Commission wrote to the parties emphasizing that it wished "to encourage a flexible and open-minded way forward in which the parties will feel free to explore possible avenues of engagement without fear that such flexibility will later be held against them".[32] The question, then, was how to do this.

The first initiative taken by the Commission was that it would meet with the parties separately in order to encourage them to speak frankly. Indeed, joint meetings between the Commission and both parties occurred only late in the process when the elements of an agreement were being finalized and the terms put into treaty form.

The second initiative was to encourage the parties to take "confidence building measures" that would both recognize and enhance a positive commitment by the parties to

---

[28] The Commission was composed of Judge Abdul Koroma and Judge Rüdiger Wolfrum, appointed by Timor Leste; Dr Rosalie Balkin and Professor Donald McRae, appointed by Australia; and Ambassador Peter Taksoe-Jensen as chair, appointed by agreement of the parties.

[29] *Conciliation Commission on the Continental Shelf between Iceland and Jan Mayen: Report and recommendations to the Governments of Iceland and Norway*, Decision of June 1981, 27 RIIAQ June 1981, 1–34. The Commission had decided not to receive written submissions from the parties.

[30] *Decision on Australia's Objections on Competence*, 19 September 2016, Report, Annex 9.

[31] Notification, Annex 3, paras 7–8.

[32] Report (n 2) [90].

reaching a solution. The measures taken were to remove some of the irritants that had made dealing with delimitation difficult. These measures involved the termination of the CMATS treaty, with its moratorium on boundary delimitation, and the withdrawal of the outstanding litigation between the parties relating to the Timor Sea Treaty.

These actions provided a framework for discussions on delimitation. The parties were, in effect, starting afresh, but afresh still meant that the parties had their longstanding legal positions on the boundaries. At an early stage the parties were invited to submit position papers on the boundary, which they did in December 2016. These papers included an articulation of their legal positions.[33] The Commission engaged in discussions with each party on its position, exploring many of the legal issues that arise in maritime boundary delimitation.[34] However, the Commission made clear that it "would endeavour to shift the Parties' focus away from seeking to reinforce their legal positions and towards a search for a potential settlement".[35]

Nonetheless, the Commission did comment on the parties' legal positions indicating that it was not convinced that either side's legal position was entirely correct and that "there were relevant circumstances that would require the median line to be adjusted to achieve an equitable result".[36]

Indeed, the legal positions of the parties were never far from the surface because they reflected the parties' views on geography, geology, geomorphology, resources, history, fairness, and equity. In short, what the Commission had before it from the parties was a comprehensive account of the "relevant circumstances" of the delimitation area as they were perceived by each party. This provided the basis for the Commission to explore with the parties, through "non-papers" and discussion, options and ideas for moving ahead and possible ways of resolving their differences.

There were two particular considerations that appeared to weigh strongly with the parties. In the background was a third state, Indonesia, which had a part in both the history of the area and a stake in the future. Indonesia and Australia are opposite states and Indonesia is the adjacent state on either side of Timor-Leste.

Australia had already concluded maritime boundary agreements with Indonesia. In 1972 it had concluded an agreement on the delimitation of the continental shelf with Indonesia which followed the southern edge of the Timor Trough, a deep depression in the seabed. Clearly the parties were following a notion of "natural prolongation" which saw the continental shelf of each party as extending as far as the Timor Trough. In 1997, Australia and Indonesia delimited the water column on the basis of a median line between the two states, which runs to the south of the Timor Trough thus differing from the boundary line that applied to the continental shelf. Obviously, Australia did not want its delimitation with Timor-Leste to interfere with its agreements with Indonesia. Timor-Leste still had to delimit its maritime boundaries with Indonesia and by the

---

[33] The parties' positions on boundaries are set out in ibid [230–235].
[34] ibid [236].
[35] ibid [119].
[36] ibid [240].

same token it did not want its delimitation with Australia to affect negatively on its future delimitation with Indonesia.

The other consideration, perhaps the most foundational issue, related to resources. While the location of a boundary line to the west had implication for small actual and potential petroleum fields, a boundary to the east had implications for the Greater Sunrise field, a resource of substantial economic potential. Although the CMATS treaty had provided for the negotiation of an arrangement for Greater Sunrise, including provisions on sharing revenues, no real progress had been made on that front. A large issue between the parties was Timor-Leste's desire to have LNG from Greater Sunrise processed in Timor-Leste rather than in Australia.

The existing gas field in the Timor Sea, Bayu-Undan, was already being exploited on a sharing basis of 90:10 in favour of Timor-Leste. However, the gas from that field was processed by pipeline to the coast of Australia near Darwin and Timor-Leste believed that Australia was getting downstream benefits that were not accounted for in the sharing arrangement. Thus, in the case of Greater Sunrise, Timor-Leste wanted the downstream benefits to go to Timor-Leste through the construction of a processing plant on the south coast of Timor-Leste to be fed by a pipeline from the Greater Sunrise field.

Although the Greater Sunrise field, and indeed the Bayu-Undan field, are geographically closer to Timor-Leste than to Australia, the problem had always been that the Greater Sunrise field lies to the south of the Timor Trough, which had played a role in the 1972 Australia-Indonesia continental shelf delimitation. The Timor Trough is some 2,800 metres in depth. For many years it was believed that given the depth of the Timor Trough a pipeline on the seabed through the Trough was not technically feasible. By the time of the conciliation there was agreement that technically such a pipeline could be built, although the cost of building a pipeline and the risks associated with operating it were disputed.

These factors, past and future relations with Indonesia, access to the resources of Greater Sunrise and how the resources of Greater Sunrise were to be exploited and processed was at the heart of the differences between the parties over the delimitation of their maritime boundaries.

Following the approach to delimitation developed by courts and tribunals, delimitation should proceed by drawing a provisional equidistance line, assessing that line in light of relevant circumstances, and then determining whether the result is disproportionate. The drawing of a provisional equidistance line between Australia and Timor-Leste is not complicated. The two states are opposite states and apart from some islands and reefs off the north-facing coast of Australia[37] and a small island on the south-east tip of Timor-Leste[38] an equidistance line can be readily drawn. The question would then be, how can such a line be assessed in terms of the relevant circumstances?

---

[37] Holothuria Reefs and Troughton Island, ibid 79, Map 4.
[38] Jaco Island, ibid 79, Map 4.

However, the Commission's mandate was not to draw a provisional equidistance line and asses it in light of relevant circumstances and test for proportionality. It was to "assist the parties in reaching an amicable settlement of their differences relating to their dispute over the maritime boundary". This might have led to the delimitation of a boundary or it might have assisted the parties in getting to a point where they would be in a position to settle the boundary themselves. And to get to that point meant that the focus had to be not on the method of maritime boundary delimitation, but on the relevant circumstances. What was of concern to the parties were the particular circumstances of the delimitation area—the exploitation of Greater Sunrise and the potential impact of any delimitation on maritime boundaries with Indonesia.

In January 2017, in a proposal on next steps, the Commission stated that it had a significantly better understanding of the Parties' legal positions and of their "motivations and interests". It further said that "it is time to consider in more detail factors relevant to delimitation as well as options and ideas that might bring the Parties closer together".[39] What the Commission had begun indicating to the Parties was that a boundary that divided the Greater Sunrise area without giving control over the whole of the area to either side had to be contemplated.[40] In short, agreement was unlikely without a regime under which there was shared control over Greater Sunrise.[41]

In March 2017 the Commission provided the parties with "options and ideas for a comprehensive agreement on maritime boundaries in the Timor Sea, including a sketch map of a possible boundary". The Commission also invited the parties to consider "the need for a shared regime for Greater Sunrise and agreement on the development of the resource as part of reaching an agreement on the maritime boundary".[42] In other words, the solution to the parties' differences over a maritime boundary lay in large part in resolving how the Greater Sunrise resource was to be developed.

The parties responded positively to this approach and subsequent discussions focused on governance arrangements for the Greater Sunrise area.[43] At the same time, the Commission sought to focus on areas of the boundary where there were clearly differences and to move the discussion on a development agreement to issues such as revenue sharing.[44] A development plan for Greater Sunrise had implications for the licence holders in that area. With the agreement of the parties, the Commission also engaged with the Greater Sunrise Joint Venture, a consortium of the licence holders that held rights to the Greater Sunrise area.

By the end of the July 2017 session of the Commission with the parties, the Commission was able to identify four "principal issues that continue to separate the Parties".[45] Only one of those issues related to the location of the boundary; the others related to the development regime for Greater Sunrise. By the end of the August meeting

[39] ibid [115].
[40] ibid [240].
[41] ibid [241].
[42] ibid [124].
[43] ibid [136].
[44] ibid [137].
[45] ibid [145].

of the Commission with the parties, agreement had been reached between the parties on the elements of a package for a comprehensive agreement ("The 30 August 2017 Agreement") which provided the basis for further engagement with the Commission towards a resolution of the boundary. The 30 August 2017 Agreement also provided an Action Plan for engaging with the Joint Venture on the development plan for Greater Sunrise.[46] In addition, the 30 August Agreement defined the maritime boundary, which it illustrated on a sketch map.

The Commission process had operated on the basis that it was a package that was being resolved and that nothing was agreed until everything was agreed. However, by the end of August 2017, subject to agreement on all of the elements of the development plan for Greater Sunrise, the maritime boundary had been resolved. The Commission continued to engage with the parties as well as with the Greater Sunrise Joint Venture to resolve the outstanding issues relating to the regime for Greater Sunrise. By this time the parties were engaged in bilateral negotiations on final issues, including the drafting of a treaty. In October 2017 a final draft Treaty was initialled by the parties. Finally, on 6 March 2018 Timor-Leste and Australia signed the treaty establishing their maritime boundaries[47] which came into force on 30 August 2019.

The Treaty both defined the maritime boundary and established a special regime for Greater Sunrise which dealt with the joint development, exploitation and management of the Greater Sunrise field including a revenue sharing arrangement.

The maritime boundary can best be understood in three sections. The southern section is essentially a median line boundary adjusted to take account of particular concerns of the parties. This boundary is an exclusive economic zone (EEZ) boundary covering both the seabed and the water column. The eastern and western boundaries, which are continental shelf boundaries, reflect a response, in the case of the eastern boundary, to the objective of sharing the Greater Sunrise resource and, in the case of both boundaries, of not interfering with past agreements or future negotiations with Indonesia.

The difference in the nature of the boundaries results from the earlier agreements of Australia with Indonesia. The 1972 agreement on the continental shelf between Australia and Indonesia establishes a line that is to the north of the lines establishing water column jurisdiction between the parties. Thus, north of the water column line Australia has only continental shelf jurisdiction and the boundary with Timor-Leste to the east and west of the Timor Sea is a continental shelf boundary. The boundary to the south which relates to areas in which Australia has full EEZ jurisdiction is an EEZ boundary.

What the agreement has done is to recognize that the point of intersection of the boundary line under the Timor-Leste-Australia agreement with the Australia-Indonesia continental shelf boundary should be at the same point as the intersection of

---

[46] ibid [164] and Annex 21.
[47] Treaty Between the Democratic Republic of Timor-Leste and Australia Establishing their Maritime Boundaries in the Timor Sea (hereafter Treaty) Report (n 2) Annex 28.

any future boundary between Timor-Leste and Indonesia with the Australia-Indonesia continental shelf boundary line. Accordingly, the last segment of the boundaries in the west and last three segments of the boundary in the east are "provisional", and subject to adjustment[48] after the entry into force of any agreement between Timor-Leste and Indonesia on their maritime boundaries.[49] This preserves the interest of Australia in its 1972 continental shelf boundary line and the interests of Timor-Leste in its future negotiations with Indonesia.

However, there is a further limitation on the adjustment of the final segments of the boundary. In respect of the eastern boundary, not only must there be an agreement on a boundary between Timor-Leste and Indonesia, there must be "commercial depletion" of the Greater Sunrise Field.[50] In other words, the regime in the Treaty for Greater Sunrise continues until depletion and there is to be no adjustment to segments of the boundary before that time. The same approach is taken with respect to the boundary in the west, where adjustment of the last segment of the boundary can occur only after the depletion of the smaller petroleum fields in the boundary area.[51]

## 4. Relevant Circumstances and Judicial Settlement and Conciliation Processes: An Assessment

How does one compare the treatment of relevant circumstances in the delimitation of the maritime boundary between Timor-Leste and Australia through conciliation with the treatment that relevant circumstances receive through judicial settlement? There is obviously both a difference in method and a difference in process between judicial settlement and conciliation.

In terms of method, a court or tribunal would start with the three-step approach, which involves first drawing a provisional equidistance line. Although the Commission in the Timor Sea Conciliation did not start formally with a provisional equidistance line, equidistance was obviously in the background. Indeed, Timor-Leste had argued for a median line solution to the boundary and Australia had argued that certain segments of the boundary should be based on equidistance.[52] Moreover, in a process that has the objective of achieving an equitable solution, some standard has to be applied to serve as a basis for the assessment of equity. A provisional equidistance line can provide that objective standard. Thus, in terms of having a background standard against which relevant circumstances can be assessed, there is little real difference between a judicial approach and conciliation.

However, when it comes to the identification and application of relevant circumstances real differences do occur. Given the traditional focus of courts and tribunals

---

[48] ibid art 2.
[49] ibid art 3.
[50] ibid art 3.
[51] ibid art 3. Laminaria and Corallina fields.
[52] Report (n 2) [231].

on geographical factors as relevant circumstances, there is little in the geographical relationship of Timor-Leste and Australia that would constitute relevant geographical
circumstances. In many respects it was a classic example of opposite states. Resource
issues are also well recognized as relevant circumstances in maritime delimitation. As
the Court said, in the *North Sea Continental Shelf Cases*, the "unity of any deposits" is
a consideration to be taken into account when delimiting a boundary in accordance
with equitable principles.[53] Economic considerations have also been referred to in
maritime delimitation. But in fact, courts and tribunals have not regarded the location of resources on the continental shelf as a significant factor in delimitation that
would justify adjusting an equidistance line. And although economic considerations
have been raised as relevant circumstances, the standard set in the *Gulf of Maine Case*
of "catastrophic repercussions for the livelihood and well-being of the population of the
countries concerned" limits the circumstances when economic factors will have an influence on the boundary.

In short, it is difficult to see how adjudication could have taken account of the concerns of both parties in the Timor-Leste Conciliation on the basis of the way the law
has been applied in the past. Further, while the factors that were of great concern to the
parties could have been identified as relevant circumstances, what is much less clear is
how they could have been applied to influence the direction of a maritime boundary
and thus warrant an adjustment to a provisional equidistance line.

In fact, as already shown, much of the work of the Commission focused on the particular circumstances and interests of the parties in the Timor Sea. They were not gen-
eric issues of maritime boundary delimitation. The problem in delimitation in the
Timor Sea was that, as the Commission pointed out, the parties would be unable to
delimit their maritime boundaries without first resolving the development and exploitation of Greater Sunrise. This was in many respects at the heart of their dispute.
Achieving an equitable solution in maritime delimitation in the Timor Sea involved
concluding an agreement on a regime for the development, exploitation, and management of the Greater Sunrise field. It was not just a matter of drawing a boundary line.

In terms of process, there is obviously a s ubstantial difference between what a judicial body is able to do and what is open to a conciliation body. A judicial organ dealing
with maritime delimitation must follow rules that have over time narrowed the scope
of what might be considered in drawing maritime boundaries. To some extent this is
inevitable and inherent in the nature of the judicial function. Deciding according to
rules is what distinguishes dispute settlement in accordance with the law from dispute
settlement *ex aequo et bono*.[54]

In other words, the choice for states that have to resolve maritime boundaries is a
choice between a process of judicial settlement which though on its face is objective
and rule-based, in fact permits substantial subjectivity in determining the relevant

[53] *North Sea Continental Shelf Case* (n 5) 51 [94].
[54] Article 38 of the Statute of the ICJ distinguishes between the function of the Court to decide disputes in accordance with international law and to decide disputes *ex aequo et bono*.

396 MARITIME BOUNDARY DELIMITATION

circumstances of the delimitation area and the influence they are going to have on a boundary, or a process that gives a role to a third party to facilitate an agreement that in the parties' views adequately reflects the particular circumstances of the area to be delimited.

At a certain level this may be seen as a simple statement that the settlement of maritime boundaries by agreement is preferable to settlement by judicial settlement. And, indeed, UNCLOS Articles 74 and 83 appear to prioritize agreement as the method for resolving maritime boundaries. But it is more than that. What is being suggested is that the task of ensuring that the delimitation of maritime boundaries takes proper account of the particular circumstances of the area to be delimited may not be dealt with adequately by a process that has a limited ability to consider those circumstances or to get at what in fact divides the parties.

Moreover, it is more than just agreement. There may be a variety of reasons why the parties cannot agree, some related to the characteristics of the boundary and the particularities of the area to be delimited. There may also be non-related political factors that make pursuing an agreement through negotiation difficult. In the case of Timor-Leste and Australia, by the time the parties got to conciliation they were unable to find a way to discuss boundaries. Yet the agreement that was ultimately reached was one that could in principle have been reached by the parties negotiating alone. But that was not possible. The intervention of a third party was the only option. Conciliation was the way in which the parties could indirectly negotiate.

However, the agreement that was reached was not one that could have been reached through judicial settlement. While what was agreed on the actual boundary lines, including the provisional nature of the final segments in the east and west, could have resulted from judicial settlement, a court or tribunal would not have been able to set out the terms of a resource development, exploitation, and management agreement. The most it could have done would have been to send negotiation of an agreement back to the parties. But, in the situation of Timor-Leste and Australia, there could have been no maritime boundary without the conclusion of the agreement on Greater Sunrise.

What this suggests is that, in some circumstances, conciliation provides a better opportunity to resolve maritime boundaries than does judicial settlement, particularly where the relevant circumstances of the area to be delimited are of prime concern to the parties. While accepting in principle the idea that the particular circumstances in the area to be delimited are relevant to delimitation, courts and tribunals in practice have not given such circumstances a significant role in maritime boundaries with the exception of choosing basepoints for the construction of a provisional equidistance line. Moreover, in judicial and arbitral settlement, the impact of the relevant circumstances is limited to an adjustment of the line. Taking account of relevant circumstances cannot lead to any substantive treatment of how the parties deal with the resources of the delimitation area even though at the end of the day the resources are often the real concern of the parties.

Nonetheless, conciliation cannot be seen simply as an alternative to judicial settlement of maritime boundaries. Clearly there will be situations where the parties cannot agree on a boundary but need it settled efficiently and relatively expeditiously. Getting a boundary in place so that resource exploitation can proceed may be the overriding consideration. Judicial settlement or arbitration will produce a result. There is no such guarantee with conciliation. A result was reached in the dispute between Timor-Leste and Australia, but it could have been otherwise.

In its Report, the Commission in the Timor Sea Conciliation reflected on the reasons for success of the process.[55] They included such matters as meeting separately with parties that had lost trust in each other regarding resources and maritime boundaries so that they could speak frankly to the Commission, the use of informal contacts with the parties as well as the meetings that took place between the parties and the Commission, the confidence-building measures that helped rebuild trust between the parties, and the ability to expand the range of issues beyond the actual determination of boundary lines to address the resources that were fundamentally at issue in the delimitation.[56] Critical, too, was the parties' commitment. They entered the process unsure whether it would be helpful or whether it would just exacerbate their differences. But at a certain point it became clear that both parties were invested in reaching a solution. They became committed to the process and thus made it possible for a successful outcome.

Can it be said, then, that the mechanism of conciliation provides a better means for taking account of "relevant circumstances" in maritime delimitation? In some respects, the answer would have to be "yes". In conciliation, the commission and the parties can focus much more directly on the particular circumstances of the delimitation area that the parties wish to be accommodated in delimitation. But that is not to suggest that conciliation is a better way than adjudication to resolve maritime boundaries. The Timor Sea Conciliation was successful due to a variety of factors that were particular to the parties themselves and circumstances that made it possible to find a way to a successful outcome. These factors may not exist in other cases and with other parties. In such cases, judicial settlement, which always guarantees a result, will be a much more suitable option.

## Dedication

David Caron was at the forefront of, and made major contributions to scholarship in, the fields of the law of the sea and international dispute settlement. Indeed, David and I first met in Berkeley 1988 when we both contributed papers to a fisheries symposium. And almost twenty years later we were co-arbitrators in an investment dispute under NAFTA. David was always a generous colleague from whom one learned so much. This chapter in tribute to David links two of his abiding interests, the regulation of the oceans and differing forms of international dispute settlement.

---

[55] Report (n 2) [285–296].
[56] ibid: "For the Commission, however, the ability to calibrate the proceedings to address the elements necessary for an amicable settlement, even where those extend beyond purely legal considerations, is a hallmark advantage of conciliation compared with adjudication" [292].

# 21

# The Public Interest as Part of Legitimate Expectations in Investment Arbitration

## Missing in Action?

*Federico Ortino*

## 1. Introduction

The fair and equitable treatment (FET) standard represents today the most important substantive protection afforded to foreign investments by international investment treaties. While the standard of FET has been interpreted to incorporate various elements such as due process, non-arbitrariness, and proportionality, it is the protection of legitimate expectations which is, in the words of a well-known arbitral tribunal, "the dominant element of that standard".[1]

While investment treaties normally make no express reference to the concept,[2] the invocation of legitimate expectations in the context of investment arbitration has for the most part simply relied on previous awards referring to the concept. Roberts has pertinently noted that such jurisprudence resembles "a house of cards".[3] Nevertheless, in order to delineate the contours of the doctrine of legitimate expectations contained in the treaty standard of FET (and possibly identify the existence of a general principle of law), many scholars have pointed to principles of domestic public law that are common to several different legal systems.[4]

From a quick perusal of domestic public law, one can easily find useful parallels in the way the doctrine has been applied by domestic courts and investment arbitral

---

[1] *Saluka Investments BV v The Czech Republic*, United Nations Commission for International Trade Law (UNCITRAL), Partial Award, para 302.

[2] But see Article 8.10.4 of the 2016 EU-Canada Comprehensive Economic and Trade Agreement (CETA) (provision not in force at time of writing).

[3] Anthea Roberts, "Power and Persuasion in Investment Treaty Interpretation: The Dual Role of States" (2010) 104 American Journal of International Law 179. See similarly Christopher Campbell, "House of Cards: The Relevance of Legitimate Expectations under Fair and Equitable Treatment Provisions in Investment Treaty Law" (2013) 30 Journal of International Arbitration 361, qualifying the construct as "a house of cards on a wobbly table" at 379. See also Josef Ostřanský, "From a Fortuitous Transplant to a Fundamental Principle of Law? The Doctrine of Legitimate Expectations and the Possibilities of a Different Law" in Ingo Venzke and Kevin Jon Heller (eds), *Contingency in International Law: On the Possibility of Different Legal Histories* (Oxford University Press 2021).

[4] Elizabeth Snodgrass "Protecting Investors' Legitimate Expectations: Recognizing and Delimiting a General Principle" (2006) 21(1) ICSID Review 1–58; Chester Brown, "The Protection of Legitimate Expectations As A 'General Principle of Law': Some Preliminary Thoughts" TDM 1 (2009). <www.transnational-dispute-managem ent.com>; <www.transnational-dispute-management.com/article.asp?key=1303>; Patrick Dumberry *A Guide to General Principles of Law in International Investment Arbitration* (Oxford University Press 2020) 328 et seq.

Federico Ortino, *The Public Interest as Part of Legitimate Expectations in Investment Arbitration* In: *By Peaceful Means*. Edited by: Charles N Brower, Joan E Donoghue, Cian C Murphy, Cymie R Payne and Esmé R Shirlow, Oxford University Press. © Federico Ortino 2024. DOI: 10.1093/oso/9780192848086.003.0021

tribunals. For example, domestic courts and investment tribunals have both struggled in identifying under which conditions a legitimate expectation can arise, in particular in the case when a general policy relied upon by an individual or group is replaced by a different policy.

One striking difference, however, between domestic public law and international investment law seems to revolve around the role played by the "public interest" in the application of the doctrine. A common feature that characterizes the doctrine in domestic public law is that a legitimate expectation will not be afforded protection (ie it can lawfully be frustrated) if there exists a public interest that justifies overriding the expectation. For example, under EU law, it is undisputed that "even if the applicant is able to prove a *prima facie* legitimate expectation, this may be defeated if there is an overriding public interest that trumps the expectation".[5] If one moves to the practice of investment tribunals applying the doctrine of legitimate expectations as part of the FET standard, there is disagreement on the role to be played by the public interest, particularly and most surprisingly in recent arbitral awards.[6] For example, the tribunal in *Watkins Holdings v Spain* recently concluded that Spain had failed to accord FET pursuant to Article 10(1) of the Energy Charter Treaty (ECT) because, having provided a stabilization guarantee with regard to the incentive scheme for wind generation applicable to the claimant's investment, Spain had "reneged on these undertakings and this amounts to a frustration of the Claimants' legitimate expectations".[7] Crucially, the tribunal's analysis does not include a discussion of whether an overriding public interest existed that could have justified the frustration of such expectation of regulatory stability.

The aim of this chapter is to explore the extent and possible impact of this apparent anomaly in the application of the doctrine of legitimate expectations in investment treaty arbitration. The chapter focuses on the many recent decisions rendered in the context of the clean energy arbitrations brought in the last ten years in particular against Spain and Italy,[8] where the investors' claims based on FET and legitimate expectations has often been successful.[9] I argue that, in contrast to the way the doctrine has been developed in English and EU law, many (but not all) investment tribunals applying the doctrine of legitimate expectations have attributed little or no relevance to

---

[5] Paul Craig, *EU Administrative Law* (Oxford University Press 2012) 584

[6] There are several earlier decisions where the "public interest" has been expressly acknowledged in the application of the doctrine of legitimate expectations. See *Saluka Investments BV v The Czech Republic*, UNCITRAL, Partial Award, 17 March 2006; para 306; *Total SA v The Argentine Republic*, ICSID Case No ARB/04/01, Award, 8 December 2010, para 123.

[7] *Watkins Holdings v Spain Watkins Holdings Sàrl and others v Kingdom of Spain*, ICSID Case No ARB/15/44, Award, 21 January 2020, paras 526 and 538.

[8] Since 2012, according to the UNCTAD Investment Hub database, there have been fifty-one cases brought against Spain and twelve brought against Italy. There have also been a handful (seven) of similar arbitrations brought against the Czech Republic. On the legal and policy background of these various arbitrations see Fernando Dias Simoes, "When Green Incentives Go Pale: Investment Arbitration and Renewable Energy Policymaking" (2017) 45 Denver Journal of International Law and Policy 251.

[9] For example, at the beginning of 2020, of the nineteen known awards involving Spain, sixteen have found for the claimants often (but not always) based on the conclusion that respondent had frustrated the investor's legitimate expectations. See *PV Investors v Spain*, UNCITRAL PCA Case No 2012-14, Concurring and Dissenting Opinion of Charles N Brower, paras 4–5.

the public interest. This in turn raises significant concerns with regard to the authority and legitimacy of investment treaty law and arbitration.

The chapter starts with a brief analysis of the role that the public interest plays in the protection of legitimate expectations in English and EU public law. This choice is due in part to this author's familiarity with these two legal systems and in part because these two systems have, like the international investment system, extended the relevant notion to cover "substantive" legitimate expectations (ie the expectation of a substantive benefit or advantage) (Section 2). The chapter then analyses the role, if any, of the public interest in the protection of foreign investors' legitimate expectations focusing both on early scholarly commentaries (Section 3) and recent arbitral practice involving claims brought against Spain and Italy following changes to their incentive regimes for the production of solar and wind energy (Section 4). Finally, the paper assesses the implications for investment arbitration of the role played (or not played) by the public interest in the application of the doctrine of legitimate expectations (Section 5).

## 2. The Role of Public Interest in the Protection of Legitimate Expectations in English and EU Law

While the concept of legitimate expectations may be found in many legal systems, its precise content and scope of application varies according to the specific legal system at issue. For example, many of the domestic systems that do recognize and protect legitimate expectations created by public authorities do so only with regard to more "procedural" legitimate expectations (ie an expectation to be consulted or to a fair hearing).[10] This was traditionally also the case in English law,[11] at least until the Court of Appeal in *Coughlan* explicitly expanded the concept to include "substantive" legitimate expectation (ie the expectation of a substantive benefit or advantage).[12] This broader approach has characterized the notion of legitimate expectations in EU law since its beginning, possibly under the influence of the similar broad notion adopted in German law.[13]

Similarly, there is quite a lot of debate among and within domestic legal systems about what the justification for public law's protection of legitimate expectations is (and

---

[10] Aniruddha Rajput and Sarthak Malhotra, "Legitimate Expectations in Investment Arbitration: A Comparative Perspective" in Mahendra Pal Singh and Niraj Kumar (eds) *The Indian Yearbook of Comparative Law 2018* (Springer 2019). This is the case, for example, in Australia, Canada, and, apparently, India. Harry Woolf, Jeffrey Jowell, Catherine Donnelly, and Ivan Hare, *De Smith's Judicial Review* (London, Sweet & Maxwell 2018)699–702; Chintan Chandrachud, "The (Fictitious) Doctrine of Substantive Legitimate Expectations in India" in Matthew Groves and Greg Weeks (eds), *Legitimate Expectations in the Common Law World* (Hart 2017) Chapter 11.

[11] The concept of procedural legitimate expectations includes (i) the expectation that a substantive benefit (enjoyed in the past or promised for the future) will continue until the applicant was otherwise notified and afforded an opportunity to comment and (ii) the expectation (based on an assurance from the public authority) that an opportunity to comment would be given before a benefit is withdrawn. See Woolf and others (n 10) 664 citing *Council of Civil Service Unions v Minister for the Civil Service* [1985] AC 374, 408–09.

[12] Mark Elliott, "From Heresy to Orthodoxy: Substantive Legitimate Expectations in the United Kingdom" in Groves and Weeks (eds) (n 10) ch 10.

[13] Søren Schønberg, *Legitimate Expectations in Administrative Law* (Oxford University Press 2000); Craig (n 5) ch 18.

should be). EU law seems to privilege "legal certainty",[14] despite the fact that in German law, it is the "protection of trust".[15] In English law, according to Forsyth, one can find several answers to the question of why the law protects legitimate expectations:

> The protection of legitimate expectations is often considered to be required by fairness. The advancement of "good administration" is championed by Lord Justice Laws. The abuse of power has been considered the "root concept" justifying the protection of legitimate expectations. And there is also a tendency to create a melange of several of these justifications. It is commonplace for a judge to ask whether the dashing of a legitimate expectation was "so unfair as to amount to an abuse of power."[16]

Another crucial difference is whether the protection of legitimate expectations is limited to promises or representations given by the public administration only, or whether it extends also to those of the legislator. In English law, the doctrine of legitimate expectations only binds the public administration, while in EU law it extends, at least in principle, to the conduct of all of the EU institutions.

Notwithstanding such differences and the evolving nature of the doctrine of legitimate expectations in English and EU law, one can identify two key pillars of the law on legitimate expectations common to both jurisdictions. First, a legitimate expectation can arise from a clear and specific representation made by a public authority, which is reasonably relied on by a person or group (and is subsequently frustrated). Second, a legitimate expectation will receive protection if there is no overriding public interest that justifies the frustration of such expectation. The remainder of this section focuses on the latter, "overriding public interest", pillar.

The role played by the public interest is a well-established component of the doctrine of legitimate expectations in both English and EU law. In English law, "once established, determining whether a legitimate expectation can lawfully be frustrated depends on whether, in all the circumstances, the public interest is sufficient to override the interest in keeping the promise".[17]

For example, in the *Solar Century* case, the applicants complained about the UK government's early termination of a programme for the support of large-scale solar photovoltaic systems. The applicants argued that government's statements leading up to the adoption of the relevant regulation that the programme would not close before 2017 were clear and unequivocal representations, which gave rise to a legitimate expectation. Justice Green eventually found that no legitimate expectation had arisen in that case,[18] but he did clearly recognize that even if it had, the existence of a public

---

[14] ibid 550.

[15] Christopher Forsyth, "The Provenance and Protection of Legitimate Expectations" (1988) 47 Cambridge Law Journal 238, 243.

[16] Christopher Forsyth, "Legitimate Expectations Revisited" (2011) 16 Judicial Review 429, 430 (footnotes omitted).

[17] Yaaser Vanderman, "Substantive Legitimate Expectations" (2016) 21 Judicial Review 174; See also Elliott (n 12).

[18] The Judge noted how all operators must have known and accepted the risk that if uptake for support led to increases in expenditure beyond the agreed treasury limits, the programme could be curtailed in order to bring

policy may have overridden such expectation. Justice Green summarized the overriding public interest step of the analysis in English law as follows:

> And even if a sufficiently certain promise or representation has been made that a policy will continue in force and not be changed until a fixed date there is *always* a balance still to be struck between the retention of that policy and the strength of the (*ex hypothesi*) rational grounds which have arisen and which now are said by the Government to necessitate a frustration of that prior representation or promise.[19]

As noted in this chapter, EU law adopts a similar stance.[20] In *Sofrimport*, for example, the Court of Justice of the European Union found the existence of a general representation creating reasonable expectations.[21] However, the Court did recognize that the Commission could have lawfully frustrated the applicant's legitimate expectations on the basis of "an overriding public interest", although in that case the Court found that the Commission did not demonstrate the existence of any such public interest.[22]

Accordingly, under both English and EU law, the protection of legitimate expectations is subject to a "weighing and balancing" test. As noted by Schønberg, "public authorities must ... consider reasonable expectations and weigh them against the reasons of public policy in favour of a decision which will disappoint such expectations".[23] Two issues remain somewhat disputed with regard to whether or not a *prima facie* legitimate expectation merits protection: the applicable standard of review, and the relationship between legitimate expectations and other grounds of review.

The first issue is the standard by which English and EU courts scrutinize the public authority's decision to disappoint a (*prima facie*) legitimate expectation. In English law, for example, is it a review based on the more deferential "*Wednesbury* unreasonableness" test or is it a review based on the more intrusive "proportionality balancing" test?[24] Similarly, EU courts have been reluctant to assign a discrete legal label to the inquiry into the public interest defence advanced by the defendant in order to defeat the legitimate expectation claim.[25] According to Schømberg, the test in EU law is one

---

expenditure back under control. *Solar Century Holdings Ltd v Secretary of State for Energy and Climate Change* [2016] EWCA Civ 117, para 78.

[19] *Solar Century*, para 73 (emphasis in the original).

[20] Craig (n 5) 629.

[21] Case C-152/88 *Sofrimport Sarl v Commission* [1990] ECR I-2477. In that case, in order to import apples from Chile, the applicant obtained the necessary licence. The Commission took protective measures as permitted by existing regulation suspending all licences for Chilean apples. Applicant's goods were already in transit when the Commission suspended all licences and its apples could not enter the European market. The applicant argued that the regulation giving the Commission the power to adopt protective measures expressly specified, in Article 3(3), that account should be taken of the special position of goods in transit, given the particularly harmful effect of such measures on traders. The Court found in favour of the applicant as the effect of Article 3(3) is "to enable an importer whose goods are in transit to rely on a legitimate expectation that ... no suspensory measures will be applied against him". ibid para 16.

[22] *Sofrimport* paras 16 and 19.

[23] Schønberg (n 13) 128.

[24] See Woolf and others (n 10) 685; AW Bradley, KD Ewing, and CJS Knight, *Constitutional and Administrative Law* (Pearson Education Limited 2018).

[25] Craig (n 5) 637.

of "significant imbalance": EU courts will not allow a policy change to frustrate an applicant's legitimate expectation "if there is a *significant imbalance* between the interests of those affected and the policy consideration in favour of the change".[26] However, it remains unclear whether the "significant imbalance" test is closer to a test of reasonableness or a test of proportionality.

According to one commentator, the key question is not really about identifying what is the standard of review (is it proportionality or reasonableness?) but it is rather about the "intensity of review".[27] In English law, for example, there appears to be a "sliding scale of review, more or less intrusive according to the nature and gravity of what is at stake".[28] As succinctly noted by Vanderman, some of the principles stemming from the English case law with regard to the application of the standard of review to determine whether a substantive legitimate expectation should be protected include the following:

(1) the more the challenged decision lies in the macro-political or macro-economic field, the less intrusive the court's supervision will be (and the less likely the applicant's expectations will be protected);

(2) the more the promise is "pressing and focused" (ie in practice, the number of beneficiaries of such a promise is likely to be small), the more likely it will be upheld;

(3) the method by which the decision is implemented (ie whether notice periods or transitional arrangements were put in place to cushion the impact on recipients of the promise) is relevant to the question of proportionality and fairness;

(4) the burden of evidencing the countervailing public interest is on the public authority.[29]

In addition to identifying the various elements that are relevant in determining the appropriate intensity of review in any particular case (ie "what should *count as adequate review*"), Elliot has also emphasized the related but distinct question of determining "how the court should assess whether what has been proffered by the decision-maker amounts to *adequate justification*".[30] According to Elliot, there may be "institutional" and/or "constitutional" grounds limiting the nature and degree of the court's scrutiny with regard to whether the justificatory burden has been discharged.[31]

---

[26] Schønberg (n 13) 150 (emphasis in the original).

[27] Elliott (n 12) 10: "the difficult question invited by substantive legitimate expectation cases is not the somewhat formalistic one concerning whether a 'proportionality' or 'balancing' or 'reasonableness' test should apply. Rather, the essential question concerns the appropriate intensity of review."

[28] Woolf and others (n 10) 687, citing *R. v Secretary of State for Education and Employment ex p. Begbie* [2001] 1 WLR 1115, para 78.

[29] Vanderman (n 17) 174. See also Woolf and others (n 10) 687. See Daniel Kolinsky, "A Legitimate Expectation of a Successful Challenge?" (2012) 17 Judicial Review 161, 176: "These cases point to the fact that decisions to frustrate legitimate expectations may be upheld by the courts where there is an overriding public interest. In such cases, the more the authority can show it has acted carefully in weighing up its decision to override the expectation (considering the substance of the issue and considerations of fairness) the more likely it is that the court will uphold decisions to override the legitimate expectation."

[30] Elliott (n 12) 229.

[31] ibid.

A second, related issue that remains unclear is the precise relationship between legitimate expectations and other grounds of review.[32] More specifically, if a *prima facie* legitimate expectation will ultimately be protected only in the absence of an overriding public interest based on some form of a proportionality balancing exercise, is there a difference between the protection granted by legitimate expectations, on the one hand, and an autonomous review based on the proportionality principle, on the other?

On this issue, some commentators have suggested that the unsettled status of the doctrine of legitimate expectations (at least in English law) stems from its lack of a sufficiently defined purpose.[33] For some commentators, this may have contributed to the overstretching of the doctrine, in the sense that courts have analysed cases in terms of legitimate expectations, which would have been more appropriately analysed by reference to other review doctrines.[34] For example, if the paradigm case of legitimate expectations is a situation in which "a public authority has provided an unequivocal assurance",[35] the case involving changes in general laws or policies should be subject to other review doctrines (such as reasonableness or proportionality) to the exclusion of an analysis of the legitimate expectations doctrine, unless the applicant can establish an "unequivocal assurance".[36]

Despite these ongoing debates, however, both EU and English law are clear that, in addition to establishing the existence of a clear and specific assurance by a public authority (that could reasonably have been relied on by the applicant),[37] a legitimate expectation will be protected only in the absence of an overriding public interest that outweighs the interest in respecting such assurance.

### 3. Early Recognition of the Role of Public Interest in the Protection of Investor's Legitimate Expectations in Investment Treaty Arbitration

Despite investment treaty tribunals' general unwillingness to provide a robust framework for applying the doctrine of legitimate expectations (beyond general references to the good faith principle and past arbitral practice),[38] early investment tribunals did recognize the role of public interest at least in the application of the doctrine of legitimate expectations in domestic law.

---

[32] Schønberg (n 13) 114.

[33] Forsyth, "Legitimate Expectations Revisited" (n 16) 429. cf Joe Tomlinson, "Do We Need a Theory of Legitimate Expectations?" (2020) 40 Legal Studies 286.

[34] Jason NE Varuhas, "In Search of a Doctrine: Mapping the Law of Legitimate Expectations" in Groves and Weeks (eds) (n 10).

[35] R (Bhatt Murphy) v Independent Assessor [2008] EWCA Civ 755, para 29.

[36] Varuhas (n 34) 20–29.

[37] It has been noted that this appears to be a hurdle that applicants have found difficult to surmount as both English and EU courts will not readily find in the applicants' favour. Craig (n 5) 619.

[38] Michele Potestà, "Legitimate Expectations in Investment Law: Understanding the Roots and the Limits of a Controversial Concept" (2013) 28 ICSID Review 88, 89.

In his separate opinion in *Thunderbird* penned at the end of 2005, Wälde emphasized upfront "the balancing that is, in my view, required between legitimate expectations of a foreign investor and an equally legitimate public interest in preserving a large 'regulatory space' in particular in the field of gambling regulation under Art. 1105 of the NAFTA".[39] In his long (and very much discussed) opinion, which included a comparative analysis, Wälde highlighted the role played by "overriding public interest" in the law on legitimate expectations in both the English and EU legal systems.[40] In his view, the investor's expectation should have received protection as he pointed to some discriminatory elements in the enforcement against the foreign investor that affected, in the foreign investor's favour, the required balancing between the investor's legitimate expectations and the host state's right to regulate.[41]

A few weeks later, the tribunal in *Saluka v Czech Republic*, chaired by the late Sir Arthur Watts, similarly acknowledged that "the determination of a breach of [the FET provision] requires a weighing of the Claimant's legitimate and reasonable expectations on the one hand and the Respondent's legitimate regulatory interests on the other".[42] Even more clearly, though with absolutely no references to domestic law, the *Saluka* tribunal distinguished between (the existence of) legitimate expectations and whether the frustration of such expectations is justified (ie reasonable) in the following terms:

> The Tribunal will assess the legitimacy and reasonableness of these expectations and, if they were legitimate and reasonable, whether they have been frustrated by the Czech Republic without reasonable justification.[43]

In the first issue of the ICSID Review in 2006, Snodgrass authored an extensive analysis of the protection of investors' legitimate expectations, which included an examination of various domestic legal systems.[44] In her working statement of the principle

---

[39] *International Thunderbird Gaming Corporation v Mexico*, Separate Opinion of Thomas Wälde, 1 December 2005, para 2.

[40] ibid para 27 ("European law does not prevent a public authority from reversing its course, but requires a balancing process where the strength of the individual's interest is balanced against the need for flexibility in public policy"); see also ibid paras 30, 48.

[41] ibid para 109.

[42] *Saluka v Czech Republic*, Partial Award, 17 March 2006, para 306. The tribunal had prefaced that statement with the following: "No investor may reasonably expect that the circumstances prevailing at the time the investment is made remain totally unchanged. In order to determine whether frustration of the foreign investor's expectations was justified and reasonable, the host State's legitimate right subsequently to regulate domestic matters in the public interest must be taken into consideration as well." ibid para 305. See also *Suez, Sociedad General de Aguas de Barcelona S.A., and InterAguas Servicios Integrales del Agua S.A. v The Argentine Republic*, ICSID Case No ARB/03/17, Decision on Liability, 30 July 2010, para 216 ("Thus in interpreting the meaning of 'just' or 'fair and equitable treatment' to be accorded to investors, the Tribunal must balance the legitimate and reasonable expectations of the Claimants with Argentina's and particularly the Province's right to regulate the provision of a vital public service."); *Perenco Ecuador Ltd. v The Republic of Ecuador and Empresa Estatal Petróleos del Ecuador (Petroecuador)*, ICSID Case No. ARB/08/6, Decision on Remaining Issues of Jurisdiction and Liability, 12 September 2014, para 560 ("Many cases hold that a central aspect of the analysis of an alleged breach of the fair and equitable treatment standard is the investor's reasonable expectations as to the future treatment of its investment by the host State... The search is for a balanced approach between the investor's reasonable expectations and the exercise of the host State's regulatory and other powers").

[43] *Saluka v Czech Republic*, paras 348 and 350.

[44] Snodgrass (n 4) 1–58.

of legitimate expectations stemming from her comparative survey, Snodgrass clearly emphasized the "public interest" limitation as one of the principle's components: "any individual who, as a result of governmental conduct, holds certain expectations concerning future governmental activity, can require those expectations to be fulfilled *unless there are compelling reasons for not doing so*".[45] While the "public interest" limitation was per se uncontroversial, Snodgrass did focus her analysis on what may constitute "compelling reasons" for not providing protection to an otherwise legitimate expectation. Similarly to the approach put forward in the Separate Opinion in *Thunderbird* and the award in *Saluka*, Snodgrass noted that in the various legal systems that she had analysed, the answer "turns on an explicit or an implicit balancing test that weighs the public interest served by the action that disappoints legitimate expectations against the individual's interest in the fulfilment of his expectations".[46] She then concluded that legitimate expectations "may not be entitled to protection when the public interest served by the act that disappoints the expectations outweighs the individual interest in having his expectations met".[47]

## 4. The Role of Public Interest in the Protection of Investor's Legitimate Expectations in Investment Arbitral Practice

As the "dominant element" of the fair and equitable treatment standard, it is rare to encounter an investment treaty dispute without the doctrine of legitimate expectations being one (if not at the centre) of the claims advanced by the foreign investor. However, while in these disputes the proverbial bone of contention is usually whether a legitimate expectation actually exists, there appears to be very little emphasis placed on the doctrine's other key element, which is, as already described, whether an overriding public interest justifies the frustration of such legitimate expectation. This appears to be true independently of the different approaches or conclusions reached by the many tribunals that have been confronted with a claim based on legitimate expectations. The many decisions in the clean energy saga triggered by the regulatory reforms in the renewable energy sector undertaken in particular in Spain and Italy offer an interesting perspective on the relevance of the "public interest" in the application of the doctrine of legitimate expectations in investment treaty arbitration.[48] In the following section, I identify and describe a prevailing view, according to which investment tribunals accord little or no relevance to the public interest in the application of the doctrine of legitimate expectations, as well as a minority view, which does recognize such relevance, although at times not so clearly.

---

[45] ibid 31 (emphasis added).
[46] ibid 45.
[47] ibid 47.
[48] Since 2016, there have been around twenty decisions on the merits where Spain was the respondent and seven where Italy was the respondent.

## 4.1 The Prevailing View: Little or No Relevance Accorded to the Public Interest

In order to capture the variety of approaches followed in arbitral practice, this section presents three sets of cases supporting what appears to be the prevailing view that the "public interest" has little or no relevance in determining a violation of the FET standard on the basis of the doctrine of legitimate expectations.

The clearest cases showing the lack of any relevance of the public interest in the application of the doctrine of legitimate expectations are undoubtedly those where the arbitral tribunal finds a violation of the FET standard simply by focusing exclusively on whether the investor's alleged legitimate expectations exist and are frustrated.

One such example is *Masdar v Spain*, where the tribunal found that Spain had frustrated the investor's legitimate expectations of regulatory stability in violation of the FET standard in the Energy Charter Treaty (ECT) without considering whether an overriding public interest could justify such frustration. Having identified the key question—"to determine which kind of specific commitments can give rise to protected legitimate expectations"[49]—the *Masdar* tribunal acknowledged two schools of thought: one which considers that such commitments can result from general statements in general laws or regulations, and another which considers that any such commitments have to be specific.[50] In the end, the tribunal did not have to choose between these approaches, as it found that, on the facts of the case, there were specific commitments which created legitimate expectations that the benefits initially granted by the host state to the foreign investor would remain unaltered.[51] Because those benefits were lost through Spain's subsequent regulatory change, a unanimous tribunal found that the respondent was in breach of its FET obligation pursuant to Article 10(1) ECT.[52] The tribunal did not make any reference to whether the frustration of the investor's legitimate expectations could be justified by overriding public interests, even though Spain had contended that the aim of the regulatory changes at issue had been to "guarantee the economic sustainability of the system and to correct over-remuneration".[53]

---

[49] *Masdar v Spain*, Award, 16 May 2018, para 489.
[50] ibid para 490.
[51] ibid para 521.
[52] ibid para 522.
[53] See also *NextEra Energy v Spain*, Decision on Jurisdiction, Liability and Quantum Principles, 12 March 2019, where an unanimous tribunal only focused on determining the existence of a legitimate expectation: "The Tribunal concludes that on the basis of the assurances given to them by the Spanish authorities, in the broader context of the specific terms of Regulatory Framework I, registration in the Pre-assignment Registry and the Ministerial Resolutions of 28 December 2010, Claimants had a legitimate expectation that the regulatory regime in RD 661/ 2007 would not be changed in a way that would undermine the security and viability of their investment... In light of [the] failure by respondent to protect claimants' legitimate expectations, the Tribunal concludes that there has been a denial of fair and equitable treatment and hence a violation of ECT Article 10." ibid paras 596 and 601. See also *Watkins Holdings v Spain Watkins Holdings Sàrl and others v Kingdom of Spain* (ICSID Case No ARB/15/44), Award 21 January 2020, para 538.

Similarly, in finding a breach of the FET standard, the *9Ren Holding v Spain* tribunal quite clearly put the investor's legitimate expectations above the host state's right to regulate in the face of changing circumstances. The tribunal stated as follows:

> 253 This Tribunal does not doubt the constitutional authority of Spain to evolve its regulatory system to keep abreast of changing circumstances. The question is whether under the ECT the cost of such changes should fall on the investors who were attracted to Spain's renewable energy by specific promises of stability rather than fall on Spanish consumers or Spanish taxpayers generally.
>
> 259. While unforeseen events understandably created serious difficulty for the Spanish regulators and the Spanish economy, Spain accepted international obligations under the ECT and the Tribunal's obligation is not to rewrite history but to give effect to the RD 661/2007 embodiment of government policy to the extent RD 661/2007 created legitimate expectations of stability in accordance with its terms.[54]

In other words, in the presence of a promise of stability reasonably relied upon by the foreign investor, any subsequent regulatory change resulting in a loss for such investor will lead to the frustration of such legitimate expectations and a violation of the FET standard, independently of the policy justifications for the change.[55]

There is a second group of cases, which also seems to support the view that the public interest is not relevant in the application of the doctrine of legitimate expectation. While in these cases the arbitral tribunal did not find the existence (and thus frustration) of a legitimate expectation (of stability), the "overriding public interest" prong of legitimate expectation appears to have been completely ignored.

For example, in its analysis of the doctrine of legitimate expectations as one of the essential obligations comprising the FET standard, the majority of the *Stadtwerke München* tribunal made no reference to the possibility, even in principle, for the host state to justify the frustration of an otherwise legitimate expectation on public interest grounds.[56] Moreover, the majority seem to validate, at least implicitly, the proposition that the existence of a specific stabilization commitment assumed by the host state or an expectation reasonably relied upon by an investor would inevitably trump any overriding public interest. The *Stadtwerke* majority stated as follows:

---

[54] *9Ren Holding S.a.r.l. v Kingdom of Spain*, ICSID Case No. ARB/15/15, Award, 31 May 2019, paras 253–259.

[55] *9Ren Holding S.a.r.l. v Kingdom of Spain*, paras 307–310. The tribunal does state that the frustration of legitimate expectation does not necessarily lead to the violation of fair and equitable treatment, but the tribunal seems to simply base this latter step on the existence of an expectation of stability reasonably relied upon by the investor. ibid. See also *Eiser Infrastructure Limited v Spain*, Award, 4 May 2017, paras 362 and 371: "'[T]he fair and equitable treatment standard does not give a right to regulatory stability per se. The state has a right to regulate, and investors must expect that the legislation will change, absent a stabilization clause or other specific assurance giving rise to a legitimate expectation of stability.' ... Respondent faced a legitimate public policy problem with its tariff deficit, and the Tribunal does not question the appropriateness of Spanish authorities adopting reasonable measures to address the situation. However, in doing so, Spain had to act in a way that respected the obligations it assumed under the ECT, including the obligation to accord fair and equitable treatment to investors."

[56] *Stadtwerke München GmbH & Others v Spain*, ICSID Case No. ARB/15/1, Award 2 December 2019.

264. Investor expectations are fundamental to the investment process... Thus, when a State that has created certain investor expectations through its laws, regulations, or other acts that has caused the investor to invest, it is often considered unfair for a State to take subsequent actions that fundamentally deny or frustrate those expectations....

265. The FET standard in the ECT does not, however, protect the investor from any and all changes that a government can introduce into its legislation.... it does not protect it against the changes introduced to safeguard the public interest to address a change of circumstances, nor does it protect the investor who unreasonably and unjustifiably expects that the host government will introduce no amendments to the legislation governing the investment. In the absence of a specific commitment contractually assumed by a State to freeze its legislation in favor of an investor, when an investor argues—as is the case here—that such expectation is rooted, among others, in the host State's legislation, the Tribunal is required to conduct an objective examination of the legislation and the facts surrounding the making of the investment to assess whether a prudent and experienced investor could have reasonably formed a legitimate and justifiable expectation of the immutability of such legislation.

Is the majority's statement that the FET standard does not protect the investor against changes introduced to safeguard the public interest *qualified* by the existence of (i) a specific stabilization commitment as well as (ii) a legitimate and justifiable expectation of stability reasonably relied upon by a prudent and experienced investor? It appears so; otherwise why would the majority carry out its subsequent analysis,[57] eventually finding that "Claimants' asserted expectations were not reasonable or legitimate"?[58]

In a third group of cases, while one does find some reference to the public interest in the tribunal's legitimate expectation analysis, it is far from clear whether such reference represents an implied acceptance of the doctrine's "overriding public interest" prong.[59] The decision of the *Antin v Spain* tribunal, which ultimately found a breach of the FET standard, is a good example of approaches falling within this third group.[60]

The *Antin* tribunal focused its analysis on the "legitimacy" and "frustration" of the claimants' expectations of stability.[61] With regard to the former, the tribunal determined that Spain had indeed represented, through its acts and regulations, that the economic regime applicable to renewable energy projects would remain stable and predictable.[62] With regard to the latter, while the tribunal recognized the host state's right

---

[57] *Stadtwerke München GmbH & Others v Spain*, ICSID Case No. ARB/15/1, Award 2 December 2019, paras 265–307.

[58] *Stadtwerke München*, para 308. See also *Charanne and Construction Investments v Spain*, SCC Case No. V 062/2012, Final Award, 21 January 2016, paras 490 and 503; *RWE Innogy GmbH et al v Spain*, Decision on Jurisdiction, Liability, and Certain Issues of Quantum, 30 December 2019, para 451 (referring to similar statements in *Blusum S.A. v Italy*, ICSID Case No. ARB/14/3, Award, 27 December 2016 and *Eiser v Spain*).

[59] For example, *Antin v Spain*, Award, 15 June 2018 and *OperaFund v Spain*, Award, 6 September 2019.

[60] *Antin v Spain*, Award, 15 June 2018.

[61] ibid paras 535–539: "[The Parties] disagree over the content of the Claimants' expectations and whether those expectations were breached in the present case... Accordingly, the Tribunal will assess the legitimacy of the Claimants' expectations against the existing conditions at the time of the investment, the background of information that the Claimants had or should reasonably have had at the time of the investment and of Spain's conduct prior to, and at the time of, the investment."

[62] *Antin v Spain* (n 59) para 554.

"to exercise its sovereign power to amend its regulations to respond to changing circumstances in the public interest", the tribunal subjected this right to any assurances
given by the host state: "any such changes must be consistent with the assurances on
stability of the regulatory framework provided by the State and required by the ECT".[63]
The tribunal, furthermore, specified that "frustration" would be found "if the host
State eliminates the essential features of the regulatory framework relied upon by the
investor in making a long-term investment".[64] The tribunal then concluded that the
methodology for determining the "reasonable rate of return" under the new regime was
not sufficiently aligned to the representations previously made by Spain regarding the
stability of the legal and economic regime applicable to renewable energy projects.[65]
Thus far the *Antin* tribunal's approach is very similar to the one adopted in *Masdar*
and *9Ren Holding S.a.r.l.*, described in this chapter. However, at the very end of its analysis, the *Antin* tribunal does refer to Spain's argument that the disputed measures had
been adopted to address the so-called tariff deficit (ie the shortfalls of revenues, which
arise when the tariffs for the regulated components of the retail electricity price are set
below the corresponding costs borne by the energy companies)[66] and preserve the sustainability of the electricity system. The tribunal agreed that the tariff deficit posed "a
legitimate public policy problem" for Spain.[67] However, it quickly rejected Spain's argument, noting that the deficit was not caused by the incentives offered under the original
regime (as the deficit "originated before Spain had any significant renewable energy
capacity") and, in any event, finding that those incentives did not play a "significant
role" in the accumulation of such deficit.[68]

Was that the tribunal's attempt to consider whether there existed overriding public
interests that could justify the lawful frustration of an otherwise legitimate expectation?
It is not altogether clear. In any event, the brief reasons adduced by the *Antin* tribunal to
reject the host state's arguments seem to impose a rather strict test for allowing a "legitimate public policy problem" to override the investor's legitimate expectations.

Like the *Antin* tribunal, the majority of the *OperaFund v Spain* tribunal mainly focused its analysis on the existence and legitimacy of the claimants' expectations. Having
concluded that (i) the original host state regulation (RD 661/2007) included a "stability
commitment" and (ii) the claimants had met an "adequate due diligence" requirement
prior to making their investment, the tribunal concluded that Spain had breached the
investor's legitimate expectations and violated its FET obligation by enacting the legislative and regulatory changes between 2010 and 2014.[69] However, just before concluding that the respondent had breached claimants' legitimate expectations and

---

[63] ibid para 555.

[64] Ibid para 556

[65] ibid paras 563–568.

[66] See further Johannesson Linder and others, "Electricity Tariff Deficit: Temporary or Permanent Problem in
the EU?" Economic Papers 534 (October 2014), <https://ec.europa.eu/economy_finance/publications/economic_
paper/2014/pdf/ecp534_en.pdf>)

[67] *Antin v Spain* (n 59) paras 570.

[68] ibid paras 569–572.

[69] *OperaFund v Spain*, Award, 6 September 2019, paras 480–487.

therefore violated the FET standard, the majority added one sentence referring, apparently in agreement, to the *Antin* and *Eiser* tribunals' rejection of Spain's defence based on the tariff deficit.[70] Accordingly, the doubts raised with regard to those two decisions need to be extended to the analysis of the majority in *OperaFund*.


## 4.2  The Minority View: Relevance of the Public Interest

In the clean energy saga cases, there are also a handful of decisions that appear to recognise (more or less clearly) the key role of the public interest in the application of the doctrine of legitimate expectations (as it had been laid out in those early authorities mentioned in the previous section, such as *Saluka*, the *Thunderbird* Separate Opinion, and Snodgrass' journal article).

One of the clearest examples of the orthodox approach is the decision in *CEF Energia BV v Italian Republic*. Having determined that the claimant did enjoy the legitimate expectation (that its photovoltaic investment was to receive certain incentives for a twenty-year period),[71] the *CEF* tribunal asked the question whether such "legitimate expectation had been transgressed in a manner prohibited by the ECT".[72] In order to answer the question, the tribunal emphasised both the importance of the public interest underlying the host state's action under review and the need to balance the claimants' legitimate expectations and the respondent's right to regulate in the public interest. The *CEF* tribunal stated as follows:

> 236. The existence of a breach is not the automatic consequence of a finding that subsequent measures taken by the host state are in contrast with the legal regime and "assurances" of stability on which the foreign investor relied when it made its investment.... the reasons and justification of the state's action must also be evaluated ....
>
> 237. [With regards] "balancing and weighing" the expectations of the Claimant as a foreign investor protected by Article 10(1) ECT, with the right of Respondent as host State to adapt its regulatory framework to changing circumstances, the Tribunal has already duly highlighted ... Claimant's expectation was based on "a clear promise of twenty years of constant currency incentives pursuant to a private law contract".
>
> 238. On the other hand, looking at the actions by Italy which negatively affected the legitimate expectation of Claimant and their reasons, the Tribunal recalls ... [they] resulted in the amount of the tariff obtained by Enersol being less than the one originally granted on which Claimant had relied in making its investment.
>
> 239. As to the reasons for the issuance of the *Spalmaincentivi* the Tribunal has taken note that the Decree Law and accompanying official documents, spell out the reasons for reducing the incentives provided to the PV operators through the various Conto

---

[70]  ibid para 489.
[71]  *CEF Energia BV v Italian Republic*, SC Case No. 158/2015, Award, 16 January 2019, para 234.
[72]  ibid para 235.

Energia. The rationale was that of reducing the burden of electricity bill to the consumers, especially small and medium enterprises, in order to stimulate economic growth and competitiveness. The Tribunal has also taken note that the tariff cut was not the only measure taken to this end as concerns electricity tariffs in the Decree Law 91/2014.

The majority of the *CEF* tribunal concluded that the public policy reasons adduced by the respondent to justify the reduction in the incentives granted to the claimant could not prevail over the claimant's legitimate expectations (according to which, it was entitled to the benefit of the originally granted and agreed incentivized tariff).[73] While the majority emphasized that the host State's measure at issue was not per se "unreasonable", it concluded that the measure failed the balancing test.[74] Interestingly, it appears that the majority adopted a rather strict proportionality balancing test by noting that "the greater the level of engagement as between a sovereign and an investor, … ultimately resulting in legitimate expectations which are clear in both scope and origin, the more rigorous the scrutiny must be of acts which, even if reasonable, cut across those legitimate expectations".[75] While the dissenting arbitrator appeared to agree with the test being put forward by the majority, he eventually disagreed with its application to the facts of the case:

> I believe that the weighing and balancing exercise between the expectations of Claimant in the stability of the 20-year tariff, on the one hand, and the right of Italy to change it in special circumstances in the public interest, as was done through the *Spalma-incentivi*, should lead to the conclusion that Respondent has not thereby breached Article 10(1) ECT.[76]

The adoption of the orthodox approach, however, is not always so clearly set out. In *Greentech v Italy*, for example, the tribunal seems first to exclude any relevance for the public policy justification advanced by Italy, but then carries out a balancing between the investors' legitimate expectations and the host state's right to regulate in the public interest. In that case, faced with similar FET claims as in *CEF Energia BV v Italian Republic*, the respondent had argued that the reasonableness and proportionality of the

---

[73] ibid para 241.

[74] ibid paras 240 and 244.

[75] ibid para 243.

[76] ibid para 247. See *OperaFund v Spain*, Dissenting Opinion, 13 August 2019: "Given the circumstances faced by Spain, the change that occurred did not 'exceed the exercise of the host State's normal regulatory power in the pursuance of a public interest', and it did not 'modify the regulatory framework relied upon by the investor at the time of its investment outside the acceptable margin of change'. The Respondent was faced with a delicate balancing act: it had to reduce public expenditures without imposing excessive burdens on consumers of electricity and citizens, while at the same time continuing to encourage environmental protection and the renewable energy sector, and protecting the legitimate rights of existing investors in the sector… The case-law turns its back on the kind of absolute immutability embraced by the Majority, making clear, that 'the requirements of legitimate expectations and legal stability as manifestations of the FET standard do not affect the State's rights to exercise its sovereign authority to legislate and to adapt its legal system to changing circumstances'. The case-law confirms that Spain was not required to elevate the interests of the investors above all other considerations; the application of the FET standard allows for a balancing exercise by the State."

regulatory change (contained in the *Spalma-incentivi* Decree) were a defence to what would have otherwise constituted a violation of legitimate expectations.[77] Specifically, respondent argued that (i) claimants had profited above the fair remuneration that the system was there to guarantee, (ii) the changes were necessary to re-equilibrate the system and equalize it to reduce its excessive social burden, and (iii) claimants were only affected to a limited extent.[78]

A majority of the *Greentech* tribunal appears initially to reject the respondent's approach, which would have required the tribunal to balance the investor's legitimate expectation with the host state's right to regulate.[79] In the majority's view, by providing repeated and precise assurances that the tariffs would remain fixed for twenty years, Italy had "effectively waived its right to reduce the value of the tariffs".[80] However, the majority then goes on to carry out a balancing exercise between the host State's right to regulate and the investor's legitimate expectations. Focusing on whether there was a "reasonable and valid justification for the changes",[81] the majority nevertheless concluded that respondent's alleged justifications for the *Spalma-incentive* Decree were unpersuasive,[82] and thus found a violation of the FET standard.

There is one last group of decisions that should be mentioned here. These decisions appear to integrate the "public interest" analysis in the determination of whether investors' expectations are indeed "legitimate" and "reasonable". For example, the tribunal in *Charanne v Spain* affirmed that, while an investor cannot have a legitimate expectation that existing rules will not be modified (at least in the absence of a specific commitment to that effect), "an investor has a legitimate expectation that, when modifying the existing regulation based on which the investment was made, the State will not act unreasonably, disproportionately or contrary to the public interest".[83] This position is often linked to the earlier decision in *El Paso v Argentina*, in which the tribunal elaborated on the definition of legitimate expectations as follows:

> legitimate expectations cannot be solely the subjective expectations of the investor, but have to correspond to the objective expectations than can be deduced from the circumstances and with due regard to the rights of the State. In other words, a balance should be established between the legitimate expectation of the foreign investor

---

[77] *Greentech Energy System et al v Italy*, Final Award, 23 December 2018, paras 425–428.

[78] ibid para 429.

[79] "While Italy submitted that its 'right to regulate' must be balanced against the need to protect investors' legitimate expectations, such arguments appear to miss the point in this context." ibid para 450.

[80] ibid.

[81] ibid para 454.

[82] "The primary justification Italy has offered for reducing the tariffs refers to the electricity costs to consumers, including households. However, the decree expressly stated that it was 'intended to reduce electricity rates for customers of medium voltage and low voltage electricity with more than 16.5 kW power available, other than residential customers and public lighting.' Further, Claimants pointed to data showing that electricity costs to consumers have decreased approximately 2-4% as a result of the *Spalma-incentivi* Decree." ibid.

[83] *Charanne and Construction Investments v Spain*, SCC Case No. V 062/2012, Final Award, 21 January 2016, paras 499 and 514.

to make a fair return on its investment and the right of the host State to regulate its economy in the public interest.[84]

It is submitted that this approach is not the most orthodox way to apply the doctrine of legitimate expectations as it mixes the question whether a "legitimate" expectation exists with the question whether a legitimate expectation should be protected in the presence of an overriding public interest.

Moreover, this approach often leads the tribunal to affirm what is (or should be) the investor's legitimate expectation that should be protected independently of a specific promise or representation from the host state.[85] In the best case scenario, like in *Charanne*, the tribunal may be caught in a "circularity" loop: in the critical words of the *Crystallex v Venezuela* tribunal "to state that one has a legitimate expectation under the FET to be treated reasonably or proportionally ... is tantamount to saying that one has a legitimate expectation to be treated 'fairly and equitably' ".[86] In the worst case scenario, this approach may lead the tribunal to overextend the scope of the FET standard to cover measures "outside the acceptable margin of change"[87] or to measures that "drastically and abruptly revise the regime ... in a way that destroyed [the foreign investment's] value".[88]

## 5. The Implications of Disregarding the Public Interest in Applying the Doctrine of Legitimate Expectations

The lack of a clear role for the public interest in the application of the doctrine of legitimate expectations raises at least three concerns.

First, the failure to condition the protection of investors' legitimate expectations on a public interest review in line with the way the relevant doctrine has been defined and applied in domestic law weakens the authority (and legitimacy) of investment tribunals' interpretation of the FET standard. Even if not normally acknowledged by investment tribunals, the success of the legitimate expectations doctrine in the interpretation

[84] *El Paso Energy International Company v The Argentine Republic*, ICSID Case No. ARB/03/15, Award, 31 October 2011, paras 356 and 358. Other often cited decisions are *EDF v Romania*, Award, 8 October 2009, para 219 ("Legitimate expectations cannot be solely the subjective expectations of the investor. They must be examined as the expectations at the time the investment is made, as they may be deduced from all the circumstances of the case, due regard being paid to the host State's power to regulate its economic life in the public interest") and *Parkerings v Lithuania*, Award, 11 September 2007, para 332 ("any businessman or investor knows that laws will evolve over time. What is prohibited however is for a State to act unfairly, unreasonably or inequitably in the exercise of its legislative power").

[85] The Annulment Committee in *MTD v Chile* was the first one to expressly criticize this unorthodox use of the concept of legitimate expectations. See *MTD Equity Sdn. Bhd. and MTD Chile S.A. v Republic of Chile*, ICSID Case No. ARB/01/7, Decision on Annulment, 21 March 2007, para 67.

[86] *Crystallex International Corporation v Bolivarian Republic of Venezuela*, ICSID Case No. ARB(AF)/11/2, Award, 4 April 2016, paras 550–551.

[87] *El Paso Energy International Company v The Argentine Republic*, ICSID Case No. ARB/03/15, Award, 31 October 2011, para 402.

[88] *Eiser v Spain*, para 387. See also *Antin Infrastructure Services Luxembourg S.à.r.l. and Antin Energia Termosolar B.V. v Kingdom of Spain*, ICSID Case No. ARB/13/31, Award, 15 June 2018, para 556.

of the FET standard rests in substantial part on the growing relevance of the doctrine in several domestic public law systems. One should not forget that, as aptly noted in *RWE v Spain* with regard to the Energy Charter Treaty, the concept of legitimate expectations is "a concept which after all is nowhere mentioned in the Treaty language".[89] This is beside the still controversial question of whether or not the doctrine of legitimate expectations is a general principle of law as per Article 38 ICJ Statute.[90] Even assuming that it is not, it is problematic that the application of the doctrine as part of the FET standard in investment treaties does not follow what appears to be one of the core tenets of that doctrine in domestic law (ie the "overriding public interest" prong). At the very least, such departure would need to be properly explained and justified. In other words, is there any reason why a foreign investor's legitimate expectation should be afforded greater protection compared to the expectations created by a public authority at the domestic level? And if one would like to answer that affirmatively, what are the reasons and where are they being spelled out? Interestingly, until recently, there seemed to be a growing consensus in the arbitral practice that the protection of investors' legitimate expectations should be balanced with the host state's right to regulate in the public interest, which included the host state's right to modify the regulatory framework applicable at the time of the investment.[91] However, several more recent decisions rendered in the clean energy arbitrations, already examined, appear to have reversed this trend and once again raise the question about the extent of the protection granted to foreign investors on the basis of investment treaties.

Second, affording protection to legitimate expectations without properly considering the host state's right to regulate in the public interest does not conform with the reasonableness-based nature of the FET standard. While reasonableness is a broad concept (even if one only looks at it as part of public law), a review based on (substantive) reasonableness should be understood to entail, at a minimum, consideration of the policy justification(s) underlying the public conduct at issue, though a variety of other factors may also play a role, including, in our context, the interests of foreign investors and their legitimate expectations.[92] As remarked twenty years ago by Lowe, there is a subtle but important methodological question in defining the FET standard: despite the standard formulation of the underlying treaty provision—"investments shall be accorded fair and equitable treatment"—the key question for the treaty interpreter should

---

[89] *RWE v Spain*, para 455.

[90] See *Obligation to Negotiate Access to the Pacific Ocean (Boliva v Chile)*, Judgment of 1 October 2018, para 162 ("It does not follow from such references that there exists in general international law a principle that would give rise to an obligation on the basis of what could be considered a legitimate expectation. Bolivia's argument based on legitimate expectations thus cannot be sustained.")

[91] See Alex Stone Sweet and Florian Grisel *The Evolution of International Arbitration: Judicialization, Governance and Legitimacy* (Oxford University Press 2017) 203, referring in particular to *Saluka v Czech Republic*, *El Paso v Argentina*, and *Total v Argentina*: "Although there remain important disagreements concerning the content and scope of the LE-FET, it is indisputable that the arbitral process has largely determined its basic parameters, as the dominant argumentation and justification framework in this domain of law". cf Federico Ortino "The Obligation of Regulatory Stability in the Fair and Equitable Treatment Standard: How Far Have We Come?" (2018) 21 Journal of International Economic Law 845.

[92] Federico Ortino *The Origin and Evolution of Investment Treaty Standards: Stability, Value, and Reasonableness* (Oxford University Press 2019) 102–03.

focus on determining whether the host State acted fairly and equitably. Lowe's elaboration is as follows:

> One cannot easily define the content of a right of an investor to be treated fairly and equitably, for example, by examining what the investor does. One can do so very much more easily, however, by focusing not upon what rights the investor has, but upon what the government does, and by asking, not whether any right of the investor has been infringed by government action, but rather whether the government has or has not acted fairly.
>
> The possibility of approaching cases from this broadly "public law" perspective no doubt seems almost platitudinous. There is, I think, a little more in it than that. It suggests, for example, that contrary to the dominant approach in investment arbitrations, there are cases where it is not helpful to try to define an area of watertight rights of investors, into which the State's regulatory authority may not seep. It is more helpful to accept that the State has the right to regulate its economy, and that the real question is, given the nature and extent of any commitments that the State has made to the investor, "is the regulation in question fair or not?"[93]

Accordingly, any "substantive" review of the host State conduct based on the FET standard (whether based on "arbitrariness", "proportionality", or "legitimate expectations") should include consideration of the public interest underlying that very conduct. Taking this argument to its logical conclusion, it is submitted here that even in the presence of a specific and unqualified stabilization promise (whether included in an investment contract or not), a claim for breach of that promise under the FET standard would still need to go through the public interest filter and that promise may not receive protection if, under the particular circumstances at hand, the public interest is found to outweigh the protection of that promise. Of course, this approach would not be applicable if that same claim is brought under either an "umbrella" or "stabilization" clause in the applicable treaty.[94]

Third, the absence of the "overriding public interest" prong in the application of legitimate expectations is particularly problematic in international investment law because of the potentially broad scope of investment treaty standards, generally, and the protection of investor's legitimate expectations, specifically. With regard to the former, in line with well-known principles of attribution in public international law, the conduct of any state organ will in principle be subject to the obligations of international investment treaties "whether the organ exercises legislative, executive, judicial or any other functions, whatever position it holds in the organization of the State, and whatever its character as an organ of the central Government or of a territorial unit of the State".[95] In other words, in the investment treaty system, the doctrine of legitimate

---

[93] Vaughn Lowe 'Regulation or Expropriation?' (2002) 55 Current Legal Problems 447, 459–60.
[94] See Ortino, *The Origin and Evolution of Investment Treaty Standards* (n 91) Chapter 1.
[95] Article 4 ILC Articles on State Responsibility.

expectations affords protection to investors' expectations arising from both administrative and legislative conduct (which, for example, is not the case in English law). With regard to the latter, while in many domestic systems the protection of legitimate expectations is limited to "procedural" expectations (ie an expectation to be consulted or to a fair hearing),[96] investment tribunals have applied the doctrine of legitimate expectations to include the expectation of a "substantive" benefit or advantage (as in English and EU law). Because the latter expectation has the potential to impact directly on what the public authority can and cannot ultimately do, the overriding public interest prong plays in this context a particularly relevant role in the application of the doctrine of legitimate expectations. Accordingly, investment tribunals' failure to consider the public interest underlying the host state's conduct under review becomes even more problematic in the context of extending foreign investors' protection to substantive expectations.

## 6.   Conclusion

In his 2011 Freshfields Lecture, Toby Landau urged the arbitration community to pay more attention to certain core concerns about investment treaty arbitration, particularly after an increase of cases pushing into ever more sensitive areas of sovereign discretion. According to Landau, there was nothing in the existing legal framework to prevent the community from saving investment treaty arbitration from itself.[97] However, the time for investment arbitration to save itself may be running out. Despite arbitral practice gradually bringing some more clarity to the content of investment protection guarantees (ie umbrella clauses, full protection and security, indirect expropriation), there are still serious shortcomings, particularly those revolving around the content of the FET clause. One in particular has been highlighted in this chapter: while investment tribunals now regularly acknowledge host countries' right to regulate in the public interest, many tribunals, and particularly recent ones, still fail to recognize appropriately the legal relevance of the public interest in determining whether a legitimate expectation deserves legal protection. Unsurprisingly, the number of policy makers directly addressing some of these shortcomings is growing (eg India's recent investment policy reforms or the ongoing efforts to "modernize" the ECT). It is hoped that both policy-makers and treaty interpreters of tomorrow will pay greater attention to the insights that can be gained from an analysis of how similar legal doctrines are applied at the domestic level.

---

[96] In English law there are two types of procedural expectations: "If the public authority has distinctly promised to consult those affected or potentially affected, then ordinarily it must consult (the paradigm case of procedural expectation)… If, without any promise, the public authority has established a policy distinctly and substantially affecting a specific person or group who in the circumstances was in reason entitled to rely on its continuance and did so, then ordinarily it must consult before effecting any change (the secondary case of procedural expectation)." *Bhatt Murphy*, Law LJ at paras 22 and 41. See further Kolinsky (n 29) 161.

[97] Alison Ross, "Freshfields Lecture 2011: Saving Investment Arbitration from Itself" (2011) 6 Global Arbitration Review.

# 22

# Conservation and Management of the Living Resources of the Sea

## The Role of Dispute Settlement Procedures

*Bernard H Oxman*

## 1. Introduction

The International Covenant on Economic, Social and Cultural Rights declares: "In no case may a people be deprived of its own means of subsistence."[1] This provision may not ordinarily inform decisions about regulation of fishing, but it is a useful reminder that not only the economic and environmental effects but also the cultural, nutritional, and social consequences of both imposing constraints and failing to impose constraints can be far reaching.[2]

What we would today regard as unreported and unregulated fishing was long the norm in human history. Those who are affected by efforts to restrain fishing speak with the moral clarity of a right to continue to live their lives and pursue their livelihoods as they and their communities have done for generations. That moral clarity is reflected in various instruments and decisions that address access to traditional fishing grounds either in general or in particular contexts such as artisanal fisheries and indigenous peoples.[3]

It is now evident that the vast expansion of fishing effort that we have witnessed is not sustainable. Those who seek to impose legal restraints on fishing speak with the moral clarity of a duty to protect marine life for the benefit of present and future generations. That moral clarity is reflected in various instruments and decisions. Notable among

[1] International Covenant on Economic, Social and Cultural Rights, 19 December 1966, art 1, para 2, 993 UNTS 3.

[2] "From the outset, the IWC [International Whaling Commission] recognised that indigenous or aboriginal subsistence whaling is not the same as commercial whaling. Aboriginal whaling does not seek to maximise catches or profit. It is categorised differently by the IWC and is not subject to the moratorium. The IWC recognises that its regulations have the potential to impact significantly on traditional cultures, and great care must be taken in discharging this responsibility.... [T]he IWC objectives for management of aboriginal subsistence whaling are to ensure that hunted whale populations are maintained at (or brought back to) healthy levels, and to enable native people to hunt whales at levels that are appropriate to cultural and nutritional requirements in the long term." <https://iwc.int/aboriginal>.

[3] See ibid; Treaty between Australia and Papua New Guinea concerning sovereignty and maritime boundaries, 18 December 1978, arts 1(1)(k), 10–12, 1429 UNTS I-24238; Eritrea/Yemen Arbitration (Second Stage, Maritime Delimitation), Award, 9 October 1998, paras 87–112, https://pca-cpa.org/en/cases/81/; *South China Sea Arbitration (Phil. v China)*, Award, 12 July 2016, paras 792–814, 1203(B)(11), <https://pca-cpa.org/en/cases/7/>.

Bernard H Oxman, *Conservation and Management of the Living Resources of the Sea* In: *By Peaceful Means.*
Edited by: Charles N Brower, Joan E Donoghue, Cian C Murphy, Cymie R Payne and Esmé R Shirlow, Oxford University Press.
© Bernard H Oxman 2024. DOI: 10.1093/oso/9780192848086.003.0022

them is the United Nations Convention on the Law of the Sea (UNCLOS) and its 1995 Implementation Agreement on the Conservation and Management of Straddling Fish Stocks and Highly Migratory Fish Stocks (1995 Implementation Agreement).[4]

International law confers on states the right and the duty to conserve living resources. The flag state is competent to prohibit or limit the fishing activities of vessels of its nationality wherever they may be. The main practical question is whether the flag state is willing and able to take effective action to restrict the fishing activities of its vessels where necessary to conserve the targeted stocks or to protect associated or dependent species or ecosystems.

It is plausible to assume that there may be some political and economic costs in doing so. Among the factors that may temper the flag state's willingness to accept those costs are the following:

— if one or more other states whose vessels are engaged in the same fishery do not take similar action, then action by a particular flag state may accomplish little if anything and may put its own vessels at a competitive disadvantage;
— the fishery at issue may be far from the flag state and the protection of that resource may entail little direct benefit for that state;
— the flag state may have little if any interest in protecting foreign nationals and vessels from competition.

Much of the modern international law of fisheries developed to address this problem. Two basic approaches were used. The first seeks to encourage flag states to adopt and enforce stricter measures. The second seeks to expand the regulatory and enforcement role of coastal states. One way to increase the pressure on flag states, minimize the "free rider" problem, and involve coastal states is through arrangements among the states concerned with fishing either for a particular stock or in a particular region or both. But this approach to a solution also poses a new problem. What if agreement cannot be reached among fishing states and coastal states concerned?

## 2. The 1958 Convention on Fishing and Conservation of the Living Resources of the High Seas

In its 1956 report to the UN General Assembly that formed the basis for the 1958 conventions on the law of the sea adopted in Geneva, the International Law Commission (ILC) made the following observations in connection with its draft articles regarding conservation of the living resources of the high seas:

---

[4] United Nations Convention on the Law of the Sea, 10 December 1982, 1833 UNTS 3 (hereinafter UNCLOS); Agreement for the Implementation of the Provisions of the United Nations Convention on the Law of the Sea of 10 December 1982 relating to the Conservation and Management of Straddling Fish Stocks and Highly Migratory Fish Stocks, 4 August 1995, 2167 UNTS 3 (hereinafter 1995 Implementation Agreement).

The articles adopted by the Commission in 1953 were intended to provide the basis for a solution of the difficulties inherent in the existing situation. If the nationals of one State only were engaged in fishing in the areas in question, that State could fully achieve the desired object by adopting appropriate legislation and enforcing its observance. If nationals of several States were engaged in fishing in a given area, the concurrence of those States was essential; article 1 of the Commission's draft provided therefore that the States concerned would prescribe the necessary measures by agreement. Article 3 of the draft was intended to provide effectively for the contingency of the interested States being unable to reach agreement. It provided that States would be under a duty to accept as binding any system of regulation of fisheries in any area of the high seas which an international authority, to be created within the framework of the United Nations, prescribed as being essential for the purpose of protecting the fishing resources of that area against waste or extermination.[5]

The General Assembly then decided to convene an international technical conference at the headquarters of the Food and Agriculture Organization of the UN (FAO) in Rome in 1955 to study the technical and scientific aspects of the matter. In explaining its revision of the text the next year, the ILC observed:

> The nature and scope of the problems involved in the conservation of the living resources of the sea are such that there is a clear necessity that they should be solved primarily on a basis of international cooperation through the concerted action of all States concerned, and the study of the experience of the last fifty years and recognition of the great variety of conditions under which conservation programmes have to be applied clearly indicate that these programmes can be more effectively carried out for separate species or on a regional basis ....
>
> The idea of an international body with legislative powers was dropped and replaced by that of compulsory arbitration in case of dispute.[6]

In the context of the codification and progressive development of international law, this is in effect the origin of the idea that, in cases where the states concerned cannot reach agreement on necessary conservation measures on a sectoral or regional basis, arbitral tribunals with compulsory jurisdiction may serve as what might be styled "conservators of last resort".[7] The 1958 Convention on Fishing and Conservation of the Living Resources of the High Seas (1958 Fishing and Conservation Convention) confers jurisdiction on ad hoc special commissions with the power to render legally binding decisions that may be enforced by the UN Security Council in the same manner as

---

[5] International Law Commission, Articles concerning the Law of the Sea with commentaries, art 49, Commentary, para 4, (1956) II Yearbook of the International Law Commission 286 (hereinafter 1956 ILC Articles).
[6] ibid 287, paras 8, 9.
[7] That phrase was first advanced by me in "Complementary Agreements and Compulsory Jurisdiction" (2001) 95 American Journal of International Law 277, 309.

judgments of the International Court of Justice.[8] This is all the more remarkable because, unlike UNCLOS, the four 1958 law of the sea conventions, which were negotiated on the basis of the ILC articles, did not otherwise include compulsory arbitration or adjudication of disputes.[9]

Arbitrable disputes could arise in at least two different circumstances under the 1958 Fishing and Conservation Convention. One is directed at the recalcitrant flag state. It arises where the states whose nationals are engaged in the fishery in an area of the high seas are unable to reach agreement on conservation measures with each other or with the coastal state.[10] The other is directed either at a recalcitrant flag state or an overly ambitious coastal state. It arises where the coastal state has exercised its right to prescribe urgent unilateral conservation measures that are not accepted by a concerned fishing state.[11]

The fact that arbitration was viewed only as a last resort in the first circumstance is evident in the requirement that twelve months of negotiation elapse before a state may seek constitution of a commission to hear the dispute.[12] No such delay is specified with respect to the second circumstance, perhaps because urgency itself is a substantive prerequisite for coastal state unilateral measures,[13] because those measures might well remain in force during the proceedings,[14] and more generally because of the unilateral nature of the measures. Be that as it may, whether or not a delay is specified before a dispute may be submitted to a special commission, it could take up to six months to constitute the commission following such a request.[15] The commission would then have at least another five months to hear the parties and render its decision.[16] If thereafter "the factual basis of the award of the special commission is altered by substantial changes in the conditions of the stock or stocks of fish or other living marine resources or in methods of fishing", then negotiations resume; the matter could not be submitted to a special commission again until two years have elapsed from the time of the award.[17] And once again, it could then take up to six months to constitute a special commission. Clearly, arbitration is viewed only as a last resort. The primary regulatory mechanism remains political.

---

[8] Convention on Fishing and Conservation of the Living Resources of the High Seas, 29 April 1958, arts 9–11, 559 UNTS 285 (hereinafter 1958 Fishing and Conservation Convention)

[9] The 1958 Conference on the Law of the Sea adopted an optional protocol on settlement of disputes, which was never applied. See Tullio Treves, 1958 Geneva Conventions on the Law of the Sea, UN, 2008 Introductory Note <http://legal.un.org/ avl/ pdf/ ha/ gclos/ gclos_ e.pdf>. Article 73 the 1956 ILC Articles (n 5), which provided for submission to the ICJ of disputes concerning the continental shelf, was not retained in the 1958 Convention on the Continental Shelf (29 April 1958, 449 UNTS 311).

[10] 1958 Fishing and Conservation Convention (n 8) arts 4–6.

[11] ibid art 7. A third circumstance affords access to the commission procedure to any state with a special interest in conservation of living resources in an area of the high seas, even if that area is not off its own coast and its nationals do not fish there. ibid art 8.

[12] ibid arts 4(2), 5(2), 6(5).

[13] ibid art 7(2)(a).

[14] ibid art 7(2),(3).

[15] ibid art 9(2).

[16] ibid art 9(5).

[17] ibid art 12.

The 1958 Fishing and Conservation Convention is the least widely ratified of the four 1958 law of the sea conventions. The close connection between its substantive provisions and compulsory arbitration made this all the more important because express consent is required to confer jurisdiction on an arbitral tribunal. The failure to find a widely accepted solution to the underlying fisheries problem prompted increasingly ambitious coastal state claims to control fishing that destabilized the law of the sea and were a driving force behind the decision to negotiate a new comprehensive convention on the law of the sea.

## 3. The United Nations Convention on the Law of the Sea

The point of departure, as it were, for the approach in UNCLOS to the problem of fishing beyond the territorial sea[18] is not only the 1958 Fishing and Conservation Convention but the 1958 Convention on the Continental Shelf as well. Pursuant to the latter convention, sedentary species are included in the natural resources subject to the sovereign rights of the coastal state with respect to the continental shelf. UNCLOS retains that rule.[19] It also extends the same idea, but with important qualifications, to living resources in the water column pursuant to a newly introduced regime of the exclusive economic zone (EEZ), where coastal states are accorded exclusive sovereign rights with respect to the conservation and management of living resources. It has been estimated that 80 per cent to 90 per cent of world marine fisheries are conducted landward of the 200 nautical-mile limit of the EEZ.

One qualification is that the coastal state has specific duties to conserve living resources in the EEZ at sustainable levels.[20] Another is that the coastal state is required to afford reasonable access to foreign vessels to fish for that portion of the allowable catch in the EEZ that, for the time being, exceeds the harvesting capacity of coastal state vessels.[21] However, while UNCLOS, unlike the 1958 conventions, does in general subject disputes concerning its interpretation or application to arbitration or adjudication,[22] and specifically applies this obligation to disputes "with regard to fisheries",[23] it adds that:

---

[18] By establishing a maximum limit for the territorial sea of 12 nautical miles measured from coastal baselines, repeating and in some respects augmenting the less than geometrically precise requirements for straight baselines articulated in Article 4 of the 1958 Convention on the Territorial Sea and the Contiguous Zone, and permitting independent archipelagic states to draw baselines around archipelagic waters, UNCLOS had the effect of extending the sovereignty of coastal states over larger areas. See UNCLOS (n 4) arts 3, 7, and 47. This was accompanied by new and substantially enhanced provisions regarding passage of ships and aircraft, environmental duties, and compulsory arbitration and adjudication.

[19] ibid art 77. UNCLOS significantly expanded the limits of the continental shelf "to the outer edge of the continental margin, or to a distance of 200 nautical miles from the baselines from which the breadth of the territorial sea is measured where the outer edge of the continental margin does not extend up to that distance". ibid art 76.

[20] ibid art 61.

[21] ibid art 62.

[22] ibid pt XV, s 2.

[23] ibid art 297(3)(a).

424  CONSERVATION AND MANAGEMENT

the coastal State shall not be obliged to accept the submission to such settlement of any dispute relating to its sovereign rights with respect to the living resources in the exclusive economic zone or their exercise, including its discretionary powers for determining the allowable catch, its harvesting capacity, the allocation of surpluses to other States and the terms and conditions established in its conservation and management laws and regulations.[24]

This limitation carries over to other treaties that incorporate the UNCLOS dispute settlement system by reference; this includes the 1995 Implementation Agreement,[25] and the regional fisheries management agreements that also incorporate that system by reference either expressly or by operation of the 1995 Implementation Agreement.[26]

Which disputes regarding living resources are then subject to compulsory arbitration or adjudication? This entails two inquiries. One is geographic, namely: Where? The other is substantive, namely: In what respects?

The first thing one may note in this regard is that the dispute settlement limitation with respect to living resources quoted above applies only to the EEZ. It does not apply either landward[27] or seaward of the EEZ. Moreover because the EEZ regime itself does not apply to sedentary species of the continental shelf,[28] one may reasonably maintain that this dispute settlement limitation does not apply to such species either.[29]

The second thing one may note is that the limitation appears in a sentence that begins with an affirmation of jurisdiction over disputes with regard to fisheries, and in that context specifies that the coastal state "shall not be obliged to accept the submission" of a dispute of a particular type. The limitation could be read to be inapplicable where such a dispute is submitted by the coastal state itself or absent an affirmative objection to jurisdiction in a case.[30]

The third thing one may note is that this dispute settlement limitation is directed to a dispute relating to the sovereign rights of a coastal state regarding the living resources in its own exclusive economic zone, or their exercise. What of its duties with respect to living resources elsewhere, such as the EEZ of another state or the high seas beyond the

[24] ibid. UNCLOS art 298(1)(b) also permits on optional exception for "disputes concerning law enforcement activities in regard to the exercise of sovereign rights or jurisdiction excluded from the jurisdiction of a court or tribunal under article 297, paragraph 2 or 3".

[25] 1995 Implementation Agreement (n 4) art 30(1).

[26] ibid art 30(2).

[27] *South China Sea* Award (n 3) para 759.

[28] UNCLOS (n 4) art 68.

[29] See *Chagos Marine Protected Area (Mauritius v UK)*, Award, 18 March 2015, para 304.

[30] As I previously noted, "[t]he ITLOS provisional measures order in the [*Southern Bluefin Tuna*] case imposed catch limitations on all the parties, even though the applicants' fisheries for southern bluefin tuna are conducted in their respective EEZs. (The order does not discuss the jurisdictional issue this might pose ...)." "Complementary Agreements and Compulsory Jurisdiction" (n 7) 95 American Journal of International Law 294, n 74. The provisional measures requested by the applicants, while specifying a catch limitation only on the respondent, set forth certain general constraints applicable to all the parties, including "that the parties act consistently with the precautionary principle in fishing for SBT pending a final settlement of the dispute". *Southern Bluefin Tuna (New Zealand v Japan; Australia v Japan)*, Provisional Measures Order, ITLOS Case Nos 3 & 4, 1999 ITLOS Rep 280, paras 31–32 (27 August).

EEZ?[31] Might a claim that the coastal state failed to comply with such duties be suffi-ciently narrowly framed, and the requested remedy sufficiently circumscribed, so as to fall outside the jurisdictional limitation?

The authority of the International Tribunal for the Law of the Sea (ITLOS) under Article 292 to order prompt release on bond of fishing vessels and crews arrested in the EEZ appears to be unaffected by the jurisdictional limitation in Article 297, or the optional exception to jurisdiction in Article 298(1)(b) with respect to coastal state en-forcement of its fisheries laws and regulations in the EEZ.[32] The expeditious Article 292 procedure can therefore provide effective enforcement not only of the duty of prompt release on bond but of the prohibition on imprisonment for fisheries violations in the EEZ.[33] This reassurance with respect to both flag state interests and human rights con-cerns regarding liberty and property unquestionably facilitated agreement on coastal state enforcement powers with respect to fishing in the EEZ.

While direct access to ITLOS by a vessel owner (or perhaps a labour union) in this context was not accepted, the text of Article 292 on standing to make an application for prompt release was intended as a compromise unique to this situation: the request may be made either by "or on behalf of" the flag state. While not much of a practical difference between the two was evident in the draft rules proposed by the Preparatory Commission established following adoption of the Convention,[34] and the same might be said of the Rules ultimately adopted by ITLOS, a fair number of applications for prompt release of detained fishing vessels and crews were brought before ITLOS in the early period of its work. The absence of such cases more recently might suggest that the ITLOS opinions facilitated a better understanding by enforcement authorities of the UNCLOS provisions on fisheries enforcement in the EEZ and encouraged compliance.

## 4. The High Seas beyond the EEZ

UNCLOS contains important provisions regarding living resources beyond the EEZ.[35] The freedoms of the high seas enumerated in Article 87 expressly include "freedom

---

[31] See UNCLOS (n 4) arts 63, 64, 66(4), 67(3), 117, 118, 123; 1995 Implementation Agreement (n 4) arts 3(1),(2), 5–8; Request for Advisory Opinion submitted by the Sub-Regional Fisheries Commission, Advisory Opinion, 2 April 2015, ITLOS Rep 2015, p 4.

[32] See UNCLOS (n 4) arts 73(2), 292. France appeared several times as a respondent in prompt release cases brought under Article 292, and did not invoke its declaration under Article 298(1)(b) insofar as the proceedings related to the duty of prompt release under paragraph 2 of Article 73. It did however invoke the declaration in one such case where a French court had confiscated the fishing vessel, which France maintained entailed a wider dispute regarding paragraph 1 of that article. See Bernard H Oxman "Case Report, The 'Grand Prince' (*Belize v France*)" (2002) 96 American Journal of International Law 219, 224. The case was dismissed on other grounds.

[33] See UNCLOS (n 4) art 73(3).

[34] See UN Doc LOS/PCN/152 (Vol I), p 32, arts 49(3), 89(2),(3). (28 April 1995).

[35] As I previously noted: "Specifying the high seas as the object of the inquiry in this context warrants a caveat. Unlike the 1958 Convention on the High Seas, UNCLOS deliberately does not contain a geographic definition of the high seas as such. One can draw a bright line at the two-hundred-mile limit of the exclusive economic zone (EEZ) with respect to coastal state sovereign rights over living resources in the water column. But the freedom of navigation referred to in Article 87 of UNCLOS applies on both sides of that line. So too the regime of the continental shelf where the continental margin extends further." "Book Review: *High Seas Governance: Gaps and Challenges*" (2020) 114 American Journal of International Law 796, 797 (footnotes omitted).

of fishing, subject to the conditions laid down in section 2". Section 2 of Part VII, on "Conservation and Management of the Living Resources of the High Seas", sets forth significant flag state conservation duties comparable to those applicable to the coastal state in the EEZ. This includes certain rights and duties applicable both in the EEZ and beyond.[36] A significant difference is that these are subject to compulsory arbitration or adjudication beyond the EEZ under the UNCLOS dispute settlement system.

UNCLOS expressly addresses the relationship between the International Seabed Authority and the Seabed Disputes Chamber of ITLOS.[37] The relationship between the Commission on the Limits of the Continental Shelf and ITLOS (or other courts and tribunals) was examined in detail in a case involving delimitation of overlapping continental shelf entitlements.[38] There is no comparable guidance to date on the relationship between sectoral and regional fisheries management organizations to which UNCLOS and the 1995 Implementation Agreement entrust significant conservation and management functions, on the one hand, and courts or tribunals exercising compulsory jurisdiction under the UNCLOS dispute settlement system, on the other.

There are however some interesting clues in the language regarding seabed disputes. The text provides that "in no case shall [the Seabed Disputes Chamber] substitute its discretion for that of the Authority" but that it may decide

> claims that the application of any rules, regulations and procedures of the Authority in individual cases would be in conflict with the … obligations of the parties to the dispute … under this Convention, claims concerning excess of jurisdiction or misuse of power, and … claims for damages to be paid or other remedy to be given to the party concerned for the failure of the other party to comply with … its obligations under this Convention.[39]

These provisions are informed by approaches to administrative law questions in national legal systems, and may be of some utility by analogy in the fisheries context as well.

Some aspects of that underlying idea are evident in the advent of a special review procedure in the Convention on the Conservation and Management of High Seas Fishery Resources in the South Pacific Ocean (South Pacific Convention),[40] which was influenced by, and has influenced, other fisheries management agreements.[41] That review procedure is established by Article 17 of the South Pacific Convention on

---

[36] See UNCLOS (n 4) arts 61, 63(2), 64–67, 116(b), 117–120.

[37] ibid art 189.

[38] *Delimitation of the maritime boundary in the Bay of Bengal* (Bangladesh/Myanmar), Judgment, ITLOS Case No 16, 2012 ITLOS Rep 4, paras 369–394, 397, 406–413, 443–446 (14 March).

[39] UNCLOS (n 4) art 189.

[40] Convention on the Conservation and Management of High Seas Fishery Resources in the South Pacific Ocean, 14 November 2009, 2899 UNTS I-50553 (hereinafter South Pacific Convention).

[41] See Convention on the Conservation and Management of Highly Migratory Fish Stocks in the Western and Central Pacific Ocean, 5 September 2000, art 20(6)–(8), Ann II, 2275 UNTS 43 (hereinafter Western and Central Pacific Convention); Convention on Cooperation in the Northwest Atlantic Fisheries, 24 October 1978, as amended 18 May 2017, arts XIV(6)–(12), XV(3)–(7), <https://www.nafo.int/Portals/0/PDFs/key-publications/NAFOConvention-2017.pdf> (hereinafter Northwest Atlantic Convention).

"Implementation of Commission Decisions", not Article 34 on "Settlement of Disputes". It is set into motion if a party to the Convention objects to a decision of the regulatory commission established by the Convention on grounds that it "unjustifiably discriminates in form or in fact against [that party], or is inconsistent with the provisions of this Convention or other relevant international law as reflected in [UNCLOS] or the 1995 [Implementation] Agreement".[42] In that event, within thirty days a review panel of three members is appointed that then must, within another thirty days, hold a hearing, and within forty-five days of its appointment transmit "its findings and recommendations on whether the grounds specified for the objection … are justified and whether the alternative measures adopted [by the objecting party] are equivalent in effect to the decision to which objection has been presented".[43]

This review procedure is an element of a regulatory decision-making procedure that addresses a problem that has plagued international fishery management organizations for decades, namely how to persuade flag states to delegate legally binding regulatory authority to a collective process without a right of veto and without an unqualified right to decline to comply with a particular decision. Among other things, the independent review is presumably designed to protect the objector from the requisite majority, and to protect the majority from the objector's right to substitute alternative measures that the objector alone deems "equivalent in effect" to the challenged decision. Depending on the outcome, the findings and recommendations of the review panel may be implemented or the matter may be submitted to the dispute settlement procedures of the South Pacific Convention, which incorporate by reference the UNCLOS system as elaborated by the 1995 Implementation Agreement.[44]

Another evident feature of this review procedure is its relative speed. The duration of a particular fishing season can be a critical time period from the perspective of conservation as well as the livelihoods of those engaged in the fishery. In the context of ordinary dispute settlement proceedings, the power of a tribunal to prescribe provisional measures may also be a particularly useful tool for addressing urgent problems.

The classic function of provisional measures is "to preserve the respective rights of either party" during the pendency of the litigation.[45] UNCLOS adds "or to prevent serious harm to the marine environment".[46] This of course includes marine life.[47] The 1995 Implementation Agreement makes this explicit. It adds "or to prevent damage to the stocks in question".[48] But that is not all. The 1995 Agreement integrates the right to

---

[42] South Pacific Convention (n 40) art 17(2).
[43] ibid art 17(5), Ann II(5).
[44] Three review panel decisions under the South Pacific Convention can be found at <https://pca-cpa.org/en/cases/33/>, <https://pca-cpa.org/en/cases/156/>, and <https://pca-cpa.org/en/cases/293/>.
[45] Statute of the International Court of Justice, art 41.
[46] UNCLOS (n 4) art 290(1).
[47] See *Southern Bluefin Tuna* Provisional Measures Order (n 30) para 70 ("the conservation of the living resources of the sea is an element in the protection and preservation of the marine environment").
[48] 1995 Implementation Agreement (n 4) art 31. In 1972, prior to the convening of the Third UN Conference on the Law of the Sea, the ICJ, in its provisional measures order in the *Fisheries Jurisdiction* case brought by the United Kingdom against Iceland, noted "the exceptional dependence of the Icelandic nation upon coastal fisheries for its livelihood and economic development" and observed that "from this point of view account must be taken of the need for the conservation of fish stocks in the Iceland area". The order accordingly specifies catch limits for UK fishing vessels in that area. *Fisheries Jurisdiction (United Kingdom v Iceland)*, Interim Protection Order, 1972 ICJ

seek provisional measures into the regulatory system itself. Article 7 provides in pertinent part:

> 2. Conservation and management measures established for the high seas and those adopted for areas under national jurisdiction shall be compatible in order to ensure conservation and management of the straddling fish stocks and highly migratory fish stocks in their entirety. To this end, coastal States and States fishing on the high seas have a duty to cooperate for the purpose of achieving compatible measures in respect of such stocks.
>
> ...
>
> 5. Pending agreement on compatible conservation and management measures, the States concerned, in a spirit of understanding and cooperation, shall make every effort to enter into provisional arrangements of a practical nature. In the event that they are unable to agree on such arrangements, any of the States concerned may, for the purpose of obtaining provisional measures, submit the dispute to a court or tribunal in accordance with the procedures for the settlement of disputes provided for in Part VIII.
>
> 6. Provisional arrangements or measures entered into or prescribed pursuant to paragraph 5 shall take into account the provisions of this Part, shall have due regard to the rights and obligations of all States concerned, shall not jeopardize or hamper the reaching of final agreement on compatible conservation and management measures and shall be without prejudice to the final outcome of any dispute settlement procedure.

Because arbitration under Annex VII is in effect the default procedure for compulsory jurisdiction for most types of disputes under UNCLOS,[49] and accordingly under the 1995 Implementation Agreement and various regional agreements as well, the capacity of an ad hoc arbitral tribunal to act on an urgent request for provisional measures would necessarily depend on the time needed to constitute the tribunal. This alone could take three months.[50] For that reason, UNCLOS accords to ITLOS, a standing tribunal, the power to prescribe provisional measures pending the constitution of an arbitral tribunal to which a dispute has been submitted pursuant to the compulsory jurisdiction articles of UNCLOS.[51] That power was exercised by ITLOS less than a month after receiving the requests for provisional measures in the first fisheries dispute submitted to arbitration under Annex VII.[52] The order required the parties to observe catch limits for southern bluefin tuna at levels last agreed by them.[53] Interestingly, while the arbitral

---

Rep 12, paras 23–24, and *dispositif* para 1(e) (17 August). The provisional measures order in the concurrent case brought by the Federal Republic of Germany is similar.

[49] See UNCLOS (n 4) art 287.
[50] See ibid Ann VII, art 3(d),(e).
[51] ibid art 290(5).
[52] *Southern Bluefin Tuna* Provisional Measures Order (n 30).
[53] ibid para 90(c),(d). In the absence of a prior agreement, the catch limits specified in the ICJ provisional measures order decades earlier were rooted in recent practice. *Fisheries Jurisdiction* (n 48) para 26.

tribunal subsequently dismissed the case for lack of jurisdiction, and accordingly re-
voked the ITLOS provisional measures order, its award stated that "revocation of the
Order prescribing provisional measures does not mean that the Parties may disregard
the effects of that Order or their own decisions made in conformity with it".[54]

## 5. Waters Landward of the EEZ

The waters landward of the EEZ comprise internal waters, archipelagic waters of
archipelagic states, and the territorial sea. All are subject to the sovereignty of the
coastal state.[55]

The sovereignty of the coastal state includes the right to control fishing.[56] The question is whether, and if so in what respects, this right is qualified by concomitant duties
relevant to living resources. Absent such duties there may be little if anything to litigate.

Specific language protecting certain activities of neighbouring states, including
fishing, is included in the text regarding archipelagic waters.[57] No such provisions are
to be found in the UNCLOS text regarding the territorial sea or internal waters. And
no provisions of general applicability specifically addressing conservation of living resources, comparable to those applicable to the EEZ and the high seas, are to be found in
the UNCLOS text regarding waters landward of the EEZ.[58]

There are however specific provisions in Part V (EEZ) from which a duty to conserve
in waters landward of the EEZ might also arise. The most obvious of these are Articles
66 and 67 that respectively address anadromous and catadromous species. Article 64
refers to ensuring conservation of highly migratory species "throughout the region,
both within and beyond the exclusive economic zone".

The 1995 Implementation Agreement sets forth substantial conservation and management obligations with respect to straddling fish stocks and especially highly migratory fish stocks that apply both beyond and within "areas under national jurisdiction".[59]
On its face, the term "areas under national jurisdiction" could be understood to include
not only the EEZ but parts of the sea landward of the EEZ. Such an interpretation is
supported by the object and purpose of the agreement, which is "to ensure the long-
term conservation and sustainable use of straddling fish stocks and highly migratory

---

[54] *Southern Bluefin Tuna Case between Australia and Japan and between New Zealand and Japan*, Award on
Jurisdiction and Admissibility, 4 August 2000, 23 RIAA 1, para 67.
[55] UNCLOS (n 4) arts 2(1), 49(1).
[56] Thus, for example, Article 19(2) regarding the meaning of innocent passage provides: "Passage of a foreign
ship shall be considered to be prejudicial to the peace, good order or security of the coastal State if in the territorial
sea it engages in ... any fishing activities." The provisions regarding innocent passage apply not only to the territorial sea but to internal waters enclosed by a system of straight baselines and to archipelagic waters of archipelagic
states. UNCLOS (n 4) arts 8(2), 17, 52(1). Similarly, with respect to fishing vessels, the coastal state may adopt laws
and regulations relating to transit passage of straits and archipelagic sea lanes passage in respect of the prevention
of fishing, including the stowage of fishing gear. This provision also applies not only to the territorial sea but to
internal waters enclosed by a system of straight baselines and to archipelagic waters of archipelagic states. Arts
35–38, 42(1), 54.
[57] Arts 47(6), 51(1).
[58] The same is true with respect to sedentary species of the continental shelf.
[59] See 1995 Implementation Agreement (n 4) arts 3, 5–7.

fish stocks".⁶⁰ Achievement of that objective can be ensured only if the stock is protected and fishing is properly regulated throughout the stock's migratory range.

While most of UNCLOS is organized by geographic zone, two of its Parts of particular relevance to this chapter apply generally. One is Part XV on settlement of disputes. The other is Part XII on protection and preservation of the marine environment.

Many of the provisions of Part XII address prevention, reduction, and control of marine pollution, which is of course important to protection of marine life. But certain basic provisions at the outset of Part XII are not necessarily limited to the question of pollution, notably including the following:

## *Article 192*

States have the obligation to protect and preserve the marine environment.

## *Article 193*

States have the sovereign right to exploit their natural resources pursuant to their environmental policies and in accordance with their duty to protect and preserve the marine environment.

## *Article 194*

5. The measures taken in accordance with this Part shall include those necessary to protect and preserve rare or fragile ecosystems as well as the habitat of depleted, threatened or endangered species and other forms of marine life.

The foregoing provisions make clear that the coastal state has environmental duties to protect and preserve marine living resources quite apart from the presence, or absence, of specific provisions regarding conservation of living resources.

The "marine environment" is the object of these provisions. The reference to the right of states to exploit "their natural resources" presumably encompasses those within the marine environment. Both terms would ordinarily be understood to include marine areas subject to the sovereignty of the coastal state.⁶¹

The question of the nature and extent of the reach of UNCLOS into internal waters has not been definitively resolved in all respects. But some things are reasonably

---

⁶⁰ Preamble.

⁶¹ Indeed, Part XII contains numerous provisions that expressly refer to the rights and duties of states with respect to ships in their territorial sea and in their ports. And Article 19(2), which expressly applies not only to the territorial sea but to internal waters enclosed by straight baselines and to archipelagic waters of archipelagic states (see n 56), excludes from innocent passage "any act of wilful and serious pollution contrary to this Convention". That reference undoubtedly includes Part XII.

clear. The case for excluding rivers and lakes from provisions of general applicability is relatively strong; such waters are not ordinarily considered to be part of the sea or the marine environment.[62]

UNCLOS hardly ignores marine internal waters. It contains detailed criteria for enclosing bays and other marine areas as internal waters. Those criteria are part of the regime of the sea. They bear little if any resemblance to the rules of international law regarding the acquisition of sovereignty over land territory.

UNCLOS in general, and Part XII in particular, contain numerous references to ports and the rights and duties of port states; international instruments regarding the regulation of fishing are increasingly doing the same.[63] Part XII of UNCLOS expressly addresses port state enforcement with respect to a discharge in violation of international marine pollution standards that occurs in foreign internal waters or that has caused or is likely to cause pollution in the internal waters of the port state.[64] It requires prompt release on bond of foreign vessels detained in port or elsewhere, and Part XV confers jurisdiction on ITLOS to enforce that provision.[65] ITLOS has also exercised its powers to prescribe provisional measures to order release of a visiting foreign warship arrested in port.[66]

The exclusion of marine internal waters from provisions of general applicability would have three effects that are in tension with important functions of UNCLOS:

—It would prejudice the ability to achieve protection and preservation of the marine environment, in particular with respect to both living resources that migrate and pollutants that spread.[67]
—It would exclude important human rights and anti-discrimination limitations set forth in section 7 of Part XII on enforcement powers of port states and coastal states with respect to violations in internal waters.
—It would encourage states to make dubious internal waters claims that prejudice navigational and other rights and freedoms.

The case is particularly strong for including waters enclosed by a system of straight baselines within the reach of provisions of general applicability. The text expressly refers to them as "sea areas".[68] The legal regime in such waters more closely resembles

---

[62] It should be noted nevertheless that UNCLOS reaches into rivers to address the rights and duties of states with respect to anadromous and catadromous species as well as land-based sources of marine pollution. UNCLOS (n 4) arts 66, 67, 207.

[63] See 1995 Implementation Agreement (n 4) arts 21(8), 23, Ann I, art 6(d),

[64] UNCLOS (n 4) art 218(2).

[65] ibid arts 226(1)(b), 292.

[66] "ARA Libertad" (*Arg. v Ghana*), Provisional Measures Order, ITLOS Case No 20, 2012 ITLOS Rep 332 (15 December).

[67] In addition to its general reference to the marine environment, Part XII contains other general references to the areas in which specific provisions apply. Coastal states are required to enforce international pollution control standards with respect to "seabed activities subject to their jurisdiction". UNCLOS, arts 208, 214. Flag states are required to enforce such standards "irrespective of where a violation occurs", arts 211(2), 217(1). Port states may enforce such standards "in respect of any discharge from [a] vessel outside the internal waters, territorial sea or exclusive economic zone of that State", art 218(1).

[68] UNCLOS (n 4) art 7(3).

that of the territorial sea than, say, that of a small bay bordered by a single state. The Convention's provisions on innocent passage and transit passage apply in internal waters enclosed by a system of straight baselines, and its provisions on innocent passage and archipelagic sea lanes passage apply in archipelagic waters.[69] Those provisions require adherence to international safety and pollution rules and standards by both the flag state and the coastal state.[70] Important enforcement powers of port states and straits states in this regard are set forth in Part XII.[71] It would at best be awkward, and at worst unworkable, to exempt the coastal state from compliance with Part XII with respect to its own activities.

Ambitious straight baselines drawn by a fair number of states can be regarded only with difficulty (if at all) as following "the general direction of the coast" and as enclosing waters "closely linked to the land domain".[72] Converting disputes about other matters into baseline disputes may unnecessarily complicate settlement either by the parties or by an international court or tribunal. It may be noted in this regard that the provisional equidistance lines drawn by international courts and tribunals in maritime delimitation cases are often measured from physical features on the coast, without regard to the straight baselines drawn by the parties.[73]

## 6. Jurisdiction with Respect to Environmental Provisions

Disputes concerning the provisions of UNCLOS regarding the protection and preservation of the marine environment are disputes concerning the interpretation or application of the convention. The provisions of section 2 of Part XV regarding compulsory arbitration or adjudication apply to such disputes, subject to sections 1 and 3. Two questions that may arise under section 3 invite particular consideration.

The first is the relevance of the exception to jurisdiction with respect to fisheries in the EEZ that is contained in paragraph 3(a) or Article 297. As previously noted, this exception does not apply to living resources outside the EEZ.[74] The text also makes it reasonably clear that the exception applies only to the coastal state with respect to its own EEZ. Subject to those limitations, the question is: To what extent if any does the exception apply to a dispute with regard to the interpretation or application of provisions regarding the protection and preservation of the marine environment with respect to marine life? There is a spectrum of possible alternative responses, of which three may be highlighted:

---

[69] See n 56. Indeed, UNCLOS specifically permits the enclosure of rivers and bays as internal waters within archipelagic waters. UNCLOS (n 4) art 50.

[70] See arts 21(2),(4), 23, 39(2),(3), 41(3),(4), 42(1)(a),(b), 53(8),(9), 54.

[71] Arts 218, 220(1), 233.

[72] See art 7(3).

[73] See *Maritime Delimitation in the Black Sea (Romania v Ukraine)*, Judgment, 2009 ICJ Rep. 61, paras 127, 131, 136–140, 149 (3 February). This is done notwithstanding the formal position that an equidistance line is measured from the baselines from which the breadth of the territorial sea is measured. See UNCLOS (n 4) art 15.

[74] See nn 27 and 28 and annotated text.

(1) Paragraph 3(a) applies to disputes "with regard to fisheries". This is a reference to the fisheries provisions of the convention, notably those in Parts V and VII. Paragraph 3(a) does not apply to disputes with regard to the environmental provisions of Part XII.

(2) Paragraph 3(a) applies to the sovereign rights of the coastal state with respect the living resources of the EEZ. According to Article 56 these are "sovereign rights for the purpose of exploring and exploiting, conserving and managing the natural resources" of the EEZ. The conservation rights enumerated by Article 61 relate to "harvested species". The enumeration of coastal state rights in paragraph 3(a) of Article 297 has the same focus on harvested species. Jurisdiction with respect to disputes regarding environmental duties under Part XII is not otherwise affected by the exception.

(3) All marine life in the EEZ (except sedentary species) is subject to the sovereign rights of the coastal state with respect to that zone. Any dispute "relating to" such marine life comes within the ambit of the paragraph 3(a) exception.

The second question is the relevance of paragraph 1 of Article 297. That paragraph enumerates three types of cases in which there is jurisdiction over "[d]isputes concerning the interpretation or application of this Convention with regard to the exercise by a coastal State of its sovereign rights or jurisdiction provided for in this Convention". The one identified in paragraph 1(c) applies

> when it is alleged that a coastal State has acted in contravention of specified international rules and standards for the protection and preservation of the marine environment which are applicable to the coastal State and which have been established by this Convention or through a competent international organization or diplomatic conference in accordance with this Convention.

This provision appears in the first paragraph of an article titled "Limitations on applicability of section 2". That article is the first in section 3 titled "Limitations and Exceptions to applicability of section 2". The operative words "Subject to section 3" are the first to appear in section 2 establishing compulsory jurisdiction. Notwithstanding the foregoing considerations, the absence of the word "only" led an arbitral tribunal to conclude that the enumeration in paragraph 1 of Article 297 is not a limitation.[75] It is unclear whether this view will prevail in the future.[76] It has also yet to be definitively determined whether the reference to "sovereign rights or jurisdiction" means that this paragraph is addressed only to the EEZ and continental shelf or also applies to areas subject to the sovereignty of the coastal state.

---

[75] *Chagos Marine Protected Area* Award (n 29) para 317
[76] My views on the matter are elaborated in "Judicial Application of Environmental Standards under the Law of the Sea Convention" in James Crawford and others (eds), *The International Legal Order: Current Needs and Possible Responses* (Brill 2017) 452.

Be that as it may, we might consider what kinds of specific international rules and standards may be contemplated with respect to matters other than marine pollution. This may be important even if Article 297(1) does not pose a jurisdictional problem. Judges and arbitrators are unlikely to feel comfortable fabricating specific standards with only a broad general provision such as UNCLOS Article 192 or a general duty under customary international law to guide them.[77] They are likely to look for more specific guidance, including the prior behaviour of the parties and more detailed instruments whose authority is widely acknowledged or that have been accepted by the parties to the dispute. In its provisional measures order in the Iceland dispute, the ICJ looked to relatively recent annual catch statistics of the United Kingdom (and FRG) to determine the status quo that was to be maintained pending a final judgment.[78] In its provisional measures order in the *Southern Bluefin Tuna* case, ITLOS applied catch limits that had last been agreed by the parties.[79] The award in the South China Sea arbitration looks to UNCLOS Article 194(5) and the Convention on International Trade in Endangered Species of Wild Fauna and Flora (CITES) for guidance in determining the obligation to protect endangered species.[80] Even in the role of conservator of last resort—when faced with a problem of inaction or inadequate action rather than an issue of excess of jurisdiction or misuse of power—an international court or tribunal is likely to be mindful of the admonition in UNCLOS Article 189 to be wary of substituting its discretion for that of the relevant regulatory body.[81]

## 7. Reference to International Law

In addition to the question of the geographic reach of the Convention's provisions of general applicability, there is the question of the role of references to international law. Article 2 of UNCLOS contains one of many references to international law in the text of the convention. It states: "The sovereignty over the territorial sea is exercised subject to this Convention and to other rules of international law."

A reasonable argument may be made that this general reference, whose origin precedes UNCLOS, should be applied only to matters that are not specifically regulated by the convention and in a manner consistent with its provisions. This is suggested not only by the explanation of the reason for such a reference by the ILC[82] but by language

---

[77] Article 30(5) of the 1995 Implementation Agreement refers to "generally accepted standards for the conservation and management of living marine resources" in this context.

[78] See n 48.

[79] *Southern Bluefin Tuna* Provisional Measures Order (n 30) para 90(1)(c).

[80] *South China Sea* Award (n 3) para 956; Convention on international trade in endangered species of wild fauna and flora [CITES], 3 March 1973, 993 UNTS 443.

[81] See text annotated by n 39.

[82] The provision derives from Article 1, paragraph 2, of the 1958 Convention on the Territorial Sea and the Contiguous Zone, which in turn derives from Article 1, paragraph 2 of the ILC articles. The ILC observed in this regard: "Some of the limitations imposed by international law on the exercise of sovereignty in the territorial sea are set forth in the present articles which cannot, however, be regarded as exhaustive. Incidents in the territorial sea raising legal questions are also governed by the general rules of international law, and these cannot be specially codified in the present draft for the purposes of their application to the territorial sea. That is why 'other rules of

addressing the same matter that was formulated specifically for UNCLOS, notably the preamble ("matters not regulated by this Convention continue to be governed by the rules and principles of general international law") and Article 293 ("A court or tribunal having jurisdiction under this section shall apply this Convention and other rules of international law not incompatible with this Convention").

It is also important not to confuse the function of references to international law in the substantive provisions of UNCLOS with the reference in Article 293 quoted above. The jurisdiction of a court or tribunal under section 2 of Part XV of UNCLOS is limited to a dispute concerning the interpretation or application of the convention. That includes a reference to international law in a substantive provision. It does not include international law generally by virtue of Article 293, which, as its text makes clear, is not itself a basis for jurisdiction under that section.

Insofar as protection and conservation of living resources are concerned, in the absence of specific justiciable conservation provisions in the Convention, it would seem to make more sense to resort to the relevant text of Part XII discussed above as the source of the coastal state duty to protect marine living resources than to the general reference to international law in Article 2. Among other things, the Part XII provisions apply to more than just the territorial sea. It is also more difficult to argue that a general reference to international law should be applied to a matter that is regulated by the convention text.

The Article 2 reference to international law may be more helpful where the convention is silent on the issue. While the question of access of foreign fishing vessels to living resources is addressed in detail in the convention with respect to the EEZ, the question is not mentioned with respect to the territorial sea. In a case in which jurisdiction of a court or tribunal derives from an instrument other than section 2 of Part XV of UNCLOS itself, and that instrument refers to international law, there may be no difficulty in applying international law independently of the reference in UNCLOS Article 2. That was the situation in the Eritrea/Yemen arbitration.[83] But if jurisdiction is predicated on section 2 of Part XV of UNCLOS alone, then the reference to international law in Article 2 may become more important in order to establish that the question of access is a question regarding the interpretation or application of UNCLOS. That is what was done in two arbitrations.[84] It is possible to discern a human rights foundation in the articulation of the reasons why international law may require the coastal state to afford reasonable access to artisanal fisheries in the territorial sea in relevant circumstances.[85]

---

international law' are mentioned in addition to the provisions contained in the present articles." 1956 ILC Articles (n 5) 265, art 1, Commentary, para 4.

[83] The arbitration agreement states that the "Tribunal is requested to provide rulings in accordance with international law" and in the context of second (maritime) stage specifies that the "Tribunal shall decide taking into account the opinion that it will have formed on questions of territorial sovereignty, the United Nations Convention on the Law of the Sea, and any other pertinent factor." Eritrea-Yemen Award (n 3) Ann I, art 2. See *South China Sea* Award (n 3) para 259 ("The arbitral tribunal in Eritrea v. Yemen was thus empowered to—and in the Tribunal's view did—go beyond the law on traditional fishing as it would exist under the Convention").

[84] *Chagos Marine Protected Area* Award (n 29) paras 499–517; *South China Sea* Award (n 3) para 808.

[85] Eritrea-Yemen Award (n 3) paras 87, 92, 93–95, 101; *South China Sea Award* (n 3) paras 794, 798, 799, 802, 812. See n 2.

## 8. Conclusion

Arbitration and adjudication are now firmly implanted within the international system for conservation and management of marine living resources as well as the protection and preservation of the marine environment more generally. UNCLOS anchors the system. Its dispute settlement provisions are incorporated by reference (and elaborated upon) in the 1995 Implementation Agreement. Article 30(2) of the 1995 Agreement also applies those provisions to any dispute between parties to the agreement "concerning the interpretation or application of a subregional, regional or global fisheries agreement relating to straddling fish stocks or highly migratory fish stocks to which they are parties, including any dispute concerning the conservation and management of such stocks". A number of fisheries agreements themselves contain provisions for compulsory arbitration or adjudication of disputes modelled on the UNCLOS system.[86] In addition, the environmental provisions of UNCLOS have been applied to protect endangered species, including coral reefs.[87]

In addition to the immediate objective of providing access to justice for the aggrieved and settling disputes that the parties are unable to resolve on their own, and the broader objective of providing authoritative explication of the law and its application in changing circumstances, an important underlying objective of compulsory jurisdiction is to enhance the responsiveness of government agencies to the obligations imposed by treaties and international law. Achieving this objective requires that the influence of international judgments and awards extend well beyond their legal impact on the parties in respect of a particular case. Lawyers throughout the world reflect on the implications of the decisions. They should ensure that governments understand that somehow, someday they too might be haled into court, and that well before that, others may expect them to behave as if that were the case.

As a noted satirist once put it: "Conscience is the inner voice that warns us somebody may be looking."[88]

---

[86] See Western and Central Pacific Convention (n 41) art 31 (incorporating the provisions relating to the settlement of disputes set out in Part VIII of the 1995 Implementation Agreement); South Pacific Convention (n 40) art 34(2) (incorporating the provisions relating to the settlement of disputes set out in Part VIII of the 1995 Implementation Agreement); Northwest Atlantic Convention (n 41) art XV (compulsory proceedings entailing a binding decision pursuant to Part XV, Section 2, of UNCLOS or Part VIII of the 1995 Implementation Agreement); Southern Indian Ocean Fisheries Agreement, 7 July 2006, art 20(1), 2835 UNTS I-49647 (compulsory proceedings entailing a binding decision pursuant to Part XV, Section 2, of UNCLOS or Part VIII of the 1995 Implementation Agreement).

[87] *South China Sea* Award (n 3) paras 950–993.

[88] HL Mencken, *A Mencken Chrestomathy* (1949; republished by Random House USA 1982).

# 23

# Sea Level Rise and Maritime Boundaries

## The Case for Stability, Legal Certainty, and Peaceful Relations

*Nilufer Oral and Bogdan Aurescu*

## 1. Introduction

Thirty years ago, in 1990, David Caron published a pioneering article entitled "When Law Makes Climate Change Worse: Rethinking the Law of Baselines in Light of a Rising Sea Level".[1] Three decades later, this farsighted article has proven to withstand the test of time. When published in 1990, the Intergovernmental Panel on Climate Change (IPCC) had just issued its first report including reference to sea level rise.[2] The 1982 United Nations Convention on the Law of the Sea (UNCLOS) was still four years away from entry into force.[3] At the time, he was among a small group of prescient legal scholars who questioned the possible consequences of sea level rise on baselines and maritime boundaries.[4] Early on he favoured the freezing of either baselines or the outer limits of maritime boundaries in order to promote legal certainty, avoid conflict and prevent unnecessary costs.[5]

This view would, decades later, be influential in the future work on sea level rise and the law of the sea. Beginning in 2008 the Committee on Baselines under the International Law of the Sea of the International Law Association (ILA) undertook a detailed study of maritime baselines and maritime boundaries that included the impacts of sea level rise.[6] Recognizing the complexity of the issue, in 2012, the ILA established the Committee on International Law and Sea Level Rise, of which David Caron

---

[1] David D Caron, "When Law Makes Climate Change Worse: Rethinking the Law of Baselines in Light of a Rising Sea Level" (1990) 17 Ecology Law Quarterly 621. See also David D Caron, "Climate Change, Sea Level Rise and the Coming Uncertainty in Oceanic Boundaries: A Proposal to Avoid Conflict" in Seoung-Yong Hong and Jon M Van Dyke (eds), *Maritime Boundary Disputes, Settlement Processes, and the Law of the Sea* (Brill 2009) 1–17.

[2] Report of United Nations Intergovernmental Panel on Climate Change (25 May 1990).

[3] United Nations Convention on the Law of the Sea (adopted 10 December 1982, entered into force 16 November 1994) 1833 UNTS 397 (UNCLOS).

[4] Their respective articles were published one month apart in 1990. See AHA Soons, "The Effects of a Rising Sea Level on Maritime Limits and Boundaries" (1990) 37 Netherlands International Law Review 207; citing Eric Bird and Victor Prescott, "Rising Global Sea Levels and National Maritime Claims" (1989) 1(1) Marine Policy Reports 177; David Freestone and John Pethick, "International Legal Implications of Coastal Adjustments under Sea Level Rise: Active or Passive Policy Responses?" in J Titus and N Psuty (eds), *Changing Climate and the Coast: Volume 1: Adaptive Options to Sea Level Rise Report to the Intergovernmental Panel on Climate Change from the Miami Conference on Adaptive Responses to Sea Level Rise and Other Impacts of Global Climate Change* (May 1990) 237–56.

[5] Caron, "When Law Makes Climate Change Worse" (n 1) 653.

[6] ILA, "Baselines under the International Law of the Sea, Final Report" (2018).

Nilufer Oral and Bogdan Aurescu, *Sea Level Rise and Maritime Boundaries* In: *By Peaceful Means*.
Edited by: Charles N Brower, Joan E Donoghue, Cian C Murphy, Cymie R Payne and Esmé R Shirlow, Oxford University Press.
© Nilufer Oral and Bogdan Aurescu 2024. DOI: 10.1093/oso/9780192848086.003.0023

was a member.[7] In 2018, responding to a request from states, the International Law Commission placed the topic of sea level rise in relation to international law on its long term work programme and then in 2019 on its current work programme.[8] In the undertakings by the ILA and the ILC, a central issue concerns the status of baselines and maritime boundaries in the face of sea level rise and the consequences for associated maritime entitlements: whether these must change with the ebb and flow of the sea or remain fixed. The issue is also of critical importance to low-lying coastal states and to the many low-lying small island developing states for which their status as islands fully entitled to all maritime zones under UNCLOS could be placed at risk should an island lose its capacity to sustain human habitation and an economic life of its own—in other words, possibly devolve to a "rock" under article 121(3) of the Convention.

Section 2 will provide with a brief overview of the scientific background of climate change and sea level rise. Section 3 will examine the different maritime zones and associated entitlements, followed by an analysis in Section 4 of the possible impacts of sea level rise on maritime baselines, maritime zones, and the associated entitlements. Section 5 will raise questions as to the legal consequences on maritime boundaries established by agreement, judicial adjudication, and customary international law. Section 6 will examine whether baselines are ambulatory and the possibility for fixed baselines and maritime boundaries. Sections 7 and 8 will examine the ambiguity of Article 121 of the 1982 LOS Convention concerning the status of islands entitled to all maritime zones and whether such entitlements could be lost if the island devolves to a rock or low-tide elevation because of sea level rise. Section 9 will examine the need for certainty and stability for maritime boundaries. The chapter will conclude by outlining the different options, noting there need not be one single solution to the pressing challenge of sea level rise and its impact on maritime boundaries and stressing the importance for the international community to cooperate and work together in achieving a solution that will promote certainty, stability, and peaceful relations.

## 2. Scientific Background of Sea Level Rise

The first report of the Intergovernmental Panel on Climate Change (IPCC), published in 1990, foresaw a possible global mean sea-level rise of about 6 centimetres (cm) per decade over the next century (with an uncertainty range of 3–10 cm per decade) under the Business as Usual scenario and 65 cm by the end of the next century (2099) with

[7] ILA, Resolution No 1/2012: "Baselines under the International Law of the Sea" (75th Conference of the International Law Association; Sofia, Bulgaria, 26–30 August 2012); Coalter G Lathrop, J Ashley Roach, and Donald R Rothwell, *Baselines under the International Law of the Sea: Reports of the International Law Association Committee on Baselines under the International Law of the Sea* (Brill 2019) 61–62

[8] At its 3467th meeting, on 21 May 2019, the Commission decided to include the topic in its current programme of work. The Commission also decided to establish an open-ended Study Group on the topic, to be co-chaired, on a rotating basis, by Mr Bogdan Aurescu, Mr Yacouba Cissé, Ms Patrícia Galvão Teles, Ms Nilüfer Oral, and Mr Juan José Ruda Santolaria.

regional variations.[9] The data at that time attributed sea level rise mainly to thermal expansion of the oceans and the melting of some land ice.[10] The IPCC working group estimated that by the year 2100, the sea level would rise two-thirds of a metre, or 2.15 feet.[11] Nearly thirty years later, in 2019, the IPCC published its first Special Report on the Ocean and Cryosphere in a Changing Climate (SROCC).[12] The IPCC concluded with very high certainty that sea levels are rising with accelerations due to ice loss from Greenland and Antarctica ice sheets, which in the 1990 IPCC calculations were listed as possible reasons for acceleration of sea level rise.[13] Moreover, the IPCC projected that extreme sea level events that historically took place just once in a century would occur at least once a year.[14] The SROCC Report also predicted, based on different scenarios, a mean global rise in sea levels up to 1.1 metre by 2100—almost twice the global average predicted in 1990.[15] This significant difference means that the risk to maritime boundaries and to the legal certainty that David Caron first warned about in 1990 is at a significantly higher level today.

The IPCC Fifth Report on Climate Change highlighted the regional variability of sea level rise. For example, sea level rise rates in the Western Pacific would be up to three times larger than the global mean.[16] The Fifth Report also concluded that it was very likely that there would be an increase in the occurrence of future sea level extremes in some regions by 2100.[17] The Report further noted that some 70 per cent of global coastlines are projected to experience a relative sea level change within 20 per cent of the global mean sea level change.[18] The Report projected that

> [g]lobal mean sea level rise will continue during the 21st century, very likely at a faster rate than observed from 1971 to 2010… By the end of the 21st century, it is very likely that sea level will rise in more than about 95% of the ocean area. About 70% of the coastlines worldwide are projected to experience a sea level change within ±20% of the global mean.[19]

The IPCC Sixth Report highlighted that "[g]lobal mean sea level has risen faster since 1900 than over any preceding century in at least the last 3000 years (high confidence)".[20]

---

[9] R Warrick and J Oerlemans, "Sea Level Rise" in JT Houghton, GJ Jenkins, and JJ Ephraums (eds), *Climate Change: The IPCC Scientific Assessment* (IPCC 1990) 261–79. <https://www.ipcc.ch/site/assets/uploads/2018/03/ipcc_far_wg_I_full_report.pdf>.

[10] ibid 266.

[11] Caron, "When Law Makes Climate Change Worse" (n 1) 626.

[12] IPCC, "Special Report on the Ocean and Cryosphere in a Changing Climate" (2019), Summary for Policy Makers ("SROCC Report").

[13] ibid A.3, Observed physical changes, 8.

[14] ibid B.3, Projected physical changes, 18.

[15] ibid. The IPCC in 1990 had estimated up to a global average of 65 cm of sea level rise by the end of the twentieth century. Warrick and Oerlemans (n 9).

[16] ibid.

[17] IPCC, Fifth Report (2013) Executive Summary, Chapter XIII "Sea Level Change" 1140 <http://www.climatechange2013.org/images/report/WG1AR5_Chapter13_FINAL.pdf>.

[18] ibid.

[19] AR5 Climate Change 2014 Synthesis Report Summary for Policymakers, 13.

[20] AR6 Climate Change 2021: The Physical Science Basis, The Summary for Policymakers, para A.24.

These impacts raise existential concerns for the millions of people who live in these vulnerable areas. Coastal areas overall are home to approximately 28 per cent of the global population, including around 11 per cent living on land less than 10 metres above sea level.[21] Sixty-five million people live in Small Island Developing States.[22] Moreover, these are also factors that could render islands uninhabitable, raising questions of international law that will be discussed further on.

## 3. Maritime Zones and Entitlements

The value of maritime zones and boundaries derives from the various rights accorded to the coastal state and third states, including states that are not parties to the delimitation exercise, under international law. Maritime zones, at the same time, have proven to be some of thorniest issues for international law. Reaching agreement on the breadth of the territorial sea was one of the intractable issues for international law, and it took decades to reach the agreement codified in Article 15 of the 1982 Law of the Sea Convention. It took years of negotiations to craft the delicate balance of interests that underlies the suite of maritime zones adopted under the Convention. Each zone brings with it important rights and obligations for the coastal State and third States.[23] Moreover, maritime boundaries are critical for demarcating the limits of associated rights and obligations of coastal and third States.

For example, in the territorial sea, the coastal state, up to 12 nautical miles (NM),[24] exercises sovereignty over the water column, seabed and subsoil, and airspace above. In turn, third states enjoy the customary international law right of unimpeded innocent passage. By contrast, the coastal state has full regulatory authority over foreign-flagged vessels in its internal waters, and foreign-flagged vessels enjoy freedom of navigation in the Exclusive Economic Zone (EEZ), which can extend up to 200 nm from the territorial sea baseline.[25]

In addition to the traditional maritime zones (territorial sea, contiguous zone, continental shelf, and high seas), the 1982 Law of the Sea Convention also created a set of new maritime zones. For example, archipelagic waters for archipelagic states did not exist in the pre-LOS Convention period.[26] In the past, these waters could have been high seas where foreign-flagged vessels enjoyed freedom of the sea rights such as navigation and fishing rights. Under the 1982 LOS Convention, the archipelagic state gained sovereignty rights akin to that of the territorial sea—but not reliant on a

---

[21] SROCC Report (n 12).
[22] ibid.
[23] See in general Robin Churchill, Vaughan Lowe, and Amy Sander, *The Law of the Sea* (4th edn, Melland Schill Studies in International Law 2020)
[24] UNCLOS art 3.
[25] ibid art 57.
[26] ibid art 47 provides: "An archipelagic State may draw straight archipelagic baselines joining the outermost points of the outermost islands and drying reefs of the archipelago provided that within such baselines are included the main islands and an area in which the ratio of the area of the water to the area of the land, including atolls, is between 1 to 1 and 9 to 1." Moreover, paragraphs 2–9 set forth the conditions for establishing such baselines.

distance criteria from the coast.[27] Instead, the archipelagic baseline, which establishes archipelagic waters, relies on outer islands and reefs, which will be discussed further on. Similar to the territorial sea, foreign ships are also granted the right of innocent passage in archipelagic waters, which can only be suspended if necessary for security reasons.[28]

The continental shelf zone, rooted in the famous 1947 Truman Proclamation on the Continental Shelf,[29] was first codified under the 1958 Geneva Convention on the Continental Shelf[30] and then under UNCLOS. The coastal state enjoys sovereignty rights to explore and exploit the natural resources of the continental shelf that includes mineral and other non-living resources of the seabed and subsoil as well as living resources belonging to sedentary species.[31] It is not surprising that many of the maritime delimitation cases involving continental shelf between opposite or adjacent coasts concern access to valuable hydrocarbon resources. One of the important changes made by the 1982 LOS Convention to the 1958 Geneva Convention on the Continental Shelf included the possibility of coastal states to extend their continental shelf beyond 200 nm[32] from the baseline from which the territorial sea is measured, up to 350 nm, if certain conditions are met under Article 76.[33]

Beyond the outer limits of the continental shelf lies the Area—a zone very much the creation of the 1982 LOS Convention, defined as the seabed and ocean floor and subsoil that lies beyond the limits of national jurisdiction.[34] The "Area" and its regime count among the significant innovations of the 1982 LOS Convention. The Area and its resources are exclusively subject to the unique and complex regime of the Common Heritage of Mankind (CHM) in Part XI of the Convention and in the Agreement relating to the Implementation of Part XI of the United Nations Convention on the Law of the Sea.

The EEZ, also a creation of the 1982 LOS Convention, provides the coastal state with exclusive sovereignty rights over a maritime area that can measure up to 200 nm from the baseline from which the territorial sea is measured. The coastal state enjoys exclusive sovereignty rights to explore, exploit, conserve, and manage the natural resources, both living and non-living, of the waters superjacent to the seabed, the seabed, and subsoil; establish and use artificial islands, installations, and structures; protect and

---

[27] ibid art 49(1) and (2).

[28] ibid art 25(3) (territorial sea) and art 52 (archipelagic waters).

[29] Proclamations 2667 and 2668, issued by US President Harry S Truman on 28 September 1945 (10 Fed Reg 12303 and 10 Fed Reg 12304).

[30] Convention on the Continental Shelf (adopted 29 April 1958, entered into force 10 June 1964) 499 UNTS 311 (hereafter CCS).

[31] UNCLOS art 77(4) defines sedentary species as "organisms which, at the harvestable stage, either are immobile on or under the seabed or are unable to move except in constant physical contact with the seabed or the subsoil".

[32] CCS art 1 provides: "For the purpose of these articles, the term 'continental shelf' is used as referring (a) to the seabed and subsoil of the submarine areas adjacent to the coast but outside the area of the territorial sea, to a depth of 200 metres or, beyond that limit, to where the depth of the superjacent waters admits of the exploitation of the natural resources of the said areas; (b) to the seabed and subsoil of similar submarine areas adjacent to the coasts of islands."

[33] UNCLOS art 76(8).

[34] ibid art 1(1).

preserve the marine environment; conduct marine scientific research; and exercise other rights and duties provided under the Convention.[35] In addition, the coastal state has the exclusive competence to determine the total allowable catch of the living resources in accordance with the conditions specified under the Convention.[36] In addition to these exclusive rights, the coastal state also has the obligation to ensure that living resources in the EEZ are not endangered through the taking of proper conservation and management measures based on the best scientific evidence.[37] Third states also enjoy certain rights in the EEZ. These include access to the surplus living resources that the coastal state lacks the capacity to harvest[38] and the right of high seas navigation and overflight, laying submarine cables and pipelines, and to engage in other internationally recognized lawful uses of the sea related to these freedoms as provided under Article 87 and other provisions of the Convention.[39]

The water column beyond the EEZ of a coastal state lies, for purposes of UNCLOS, is governed by the provisions of Part VII for the high seas. It is an area of ocean space which is governed by the longstanding customary international law rule of freedom of the seas as provided for under article 86 of UNCLOS.[40] These include freedom of navigation, overflight, fishing, and the laying of submarine cables and pipelines. In addition, UNCLOS expressly lists the freedom to construct artificial islands and other installations,[41] as well as the freedom to conduct scientific research subject to Parts VI and XIII of the Convention.

The boundaries of these maritime zones rely on the relevant points of the foundational baseline that measures the breadth of the territorial sea. However, these baselines are often constructed upon unstable or tiny features that are vulnerable to disappear, in whole or in part, because of sea level rise. In his article, David Caron rightly highlighted the risks created by the uncertainty concerning the status of maritime boundaries and the potential to disrupt interstate relations. Maritime boundaries are often the result of difficult negotiations, and in those cases where diplomatic negotiations fail, states will seek international adjudication, at significant cost. If the relevant points of the baseline upon which these maritime zones and entitlements depend disappear, what happens to maritime boundaries established by agreement or international adjudication? The pressing question is whether maritime boundaries duly established by agreement or through international adjudication are permanent.

[35] ibid art 56.
[36] ibid art 61.
[37] ibid art 61(2).
[38] ibid art 62(2).
[39] ibid art 58(1).
[40] ibid art 87(2).
[41] ibid art 87(2).

## 4. The Potential Impact of Sea Level Rise on Baselines, Maritime Zones, and Maritime Entitlements

The law of maritime baselines was developed during the first part of the 20th century and codified under the 1958 Geneva Convention on the Territorial Sea and Contiguous Zone[42] and later the 1982 LOS Convention. Reflecting customary international law, both instruments require that under normal circumstances the coastal state is to measure its baseline from the low-water line of the coast as marked on large-scale charts officially recognized by the coastal States.[43] These baselines can be anchored upon unstable points, which in this time of climate change and sea level rise have a higher likelihood of disappearing than in the past. Such points can be small islands, low tide elevations,[44] or fringing reefs.[45] In addition, the coastal configuration of a state may change because of sea level rise and impact the points which were used or are intended to be used for establishing a maritime boundary.

Instead of using the low-water line, states are permitted to draw straight baselines in exceptional circumstances such as where the coastline is deeply indented and cut into, or if there is a fringe of islands along the coast in the immediate vicinity.[46] Article 7 of the 1982 LOS Convention also allows for the use of straight baselines if the presence of a delta or other natural conditions make the coastline highly unstable.[47] An important condition is that the straight baseline cannot "depart to any appreciable extent from the general direction of the coast" and the sea area must have a sufficiently close link to the land to be considered internal waters.[48] These conditions also expose potential vulnerability of the straight baseline to sea level rise, which could inundate some or even all of the fringe of islands, or alter the proximity of the baseline to the coastline should the baseline be moved seaward from their current positions if baselines are not fixed and deemed to be ambulatory. UNCLOS, additionally, provides for the use of straight baselines in the case of rivers that flow directly into the sea[49] and bays that meet specific requirements.[50]

Other features that are vulnerable to sea level rise include low-tide elevations (or "drying rocks"). A low-tide elevation—used for what is familiarly known as 'leap-frogging'—can extend the breadth of the territorial sea of a coastal state significantly. Normally a low-tide elevation has no territorial sea of its own but where it is located wholly or partly at a distance not exceeding the breadth of the territorial sea from the mainland or an island, the low-water line on that elevation may be used as the baseline

---

[42] Convention on the Territorial Sea and the Contiguous Zone (adopted 29 April 1958, entered into force 10 September 1964) 516 UNTS 205 (hereafter TSC).
[43] ibid art 3; UNCLOS (n 3) art 5.
[44] UNCLOS art 13.
[45] ibid art 6
[46] ibid art 7(1); *Fisheries case (United Kingdom v Norway)* (Judgment) [1951] ICJ Rep 116.
[47] UNCLOS art 7(2).
[48] ibid art 7(3).
[49] ibid art 9.
[50] ibid art 10.

for measuring the breadth of the territorial sea.[51] However, as features that emerge only during low tide they are at high risk to become submerged features with sea level rise—unless in the case of use in drawing a straight baseline a permanent feature has been constructed on it, or features have received general international recognition.[52]

What then are the legal consequences to the baseline if the low-tide elevation becomes completely submerged because of sea level rise? Can the coastal state continue to use it for its baseline? If not, this could result in a significant regression of the baseline from which the breadth of the territorial sea is measured.

Other examples of vulnerable features used for baselines include reefs where, in the case of islands situated on atolls or of islands having fringing reefs, the baseline for measuring the breadth of the territorial sea is the seaward low-water line of the reef, as shown by the appropriate symbol on charts officially recognized by the coastal state.[53]

There is also the situation of the archipelagic state, as discussed earlier, which under the 1982 LOS Convention, may draw straight archipelagic baselines joining the outermost points of the outermost islands and drying reefs of the archipelago provided that within such baselines are included the main islands and an area in which the ratio of the area of the water to the area of the land, including atolls, is between 1:1 and 9:1 and additional conditions laid out under Article 47. The loss of an island or drying reef could alter this ratio and call into question the continuing right of the archipelagic state to employ the archipelagic straight base line.

## 5.  Different Sources of Maritime Boundaries

There are different ways in which maritime boundaries are established. The first is through unilateral acts by the state, which may or may not garner international recognition. In the case that the maritime boundaries were established in accordance with international law and have been recognized by the international community could the state rely on the doctrine of historic waters or title? Soons raised this in his 1990 analysis. Recognizing that the traditional doctrine of historic waters applied to internal waters Soons suggested:

> In the case of sea level rise, however, the coastal States would be claiming a certain sea area as its territorial sea or EEZ. It therefore does not concern historic waters in the traditional sense, but it would involve a new category of historic waters. For such cases one could require, mutatis mutandis, that the following conditions be met: the coastal State should, right from the start of the regression of the baseline, continue to exercise in the area concerned, in the same way as it used to do before, sovereignty or sovereign rights, and this should be acquiesced in by the community of States. Acquiescence by

---

[51] ibid art 13(1).
[52] ibid art 7(4).
[53] ibid art 6.

the community of States may be inferred from the absence of protests by interested States.[54]

Caron, however, questioned the application of historic waters or rights. In his assessment in 1990 he opined:

> Yet, although the assertion of historic rights might provide a result similar to that provided by fixing the boundary on the basis of presently accepted baselines, the assertion of such rights must be proved. The assertion is more easily contested than the location of a baseline, and hence carries with it its own uncertainties. If states ultimately intend to assert historic rights, it is better for them to fold that rationale into the justification of fixing such maritime boundaries generally.[55]

The second option for creating maritime boundaries is by means of negotiation and concluding maritime boundary agreements. This in turn raises the question of whether sea level rise could constitute a fundamental change of circumstances (*clausus rebus sic stantibus*) under Article 62 of the Vienna Convention on the Law of Treaties,[56] which is discussed in greater detail further on, but in short, the question being whether maritime boundaries would be included in the exemption from the *clausus rebus sic stantibus* doctrine.

Thirdly, there is the question of the status of maritime boundaries that rest upon the adjudicative process of international courts and tribunals. In 1990, Soons described this situation as being akin to that of boundaries established by agreement which should have the same status of land boundaries and not subject to the rule of fundamental change of circumstances.[57]

Fourth, there is the option of creating a new rule of customary international law that would recognize as permanent those baselines or outer maritime boundaries that were established in accordance with international law and recognized by the international community. In this case, two scenarios are presented. The first is the ambulatory baseline scenario which would require recalculating and drawing a new baseline. Inevitably this would result in a shift landward of the baseline, which in turn might result in the landward movement of all entire outer limits and/or maritime boundaries.

An alternative option is to fix or maintain the baseline or the outer limits of maritime zones. This was the option David Caron advocated in 1990[58] (and later). This option

---

[54] Soons (n 4) 224. For a detailed examination of the application of the doctrine of historic waters to the case of sea level rise see Jenny Grote Stoutenburg, "Implementing a New Regime of Stable Maritime Zones to Ensure the (Economic) Survival of Small Island States Threatened by Sea-Level Rise" (2011) 26 International Journal of Marine & Coastal Law 263, 281–84.

[55] Caron, "When Law Makes Climate Change Worse" (n 1) 651.

[56] Vienna Convention on the Law of Treaties (opened for signature 23 May 1969, entered into force 27 January 1980) 1155 UNTS 331 (hereafter VCLOT).

[57] Soons (n 4) 229.

[58] Soons, in his article published in the same year, struck a more cautious tone concerning the possible option of the creation of a new rule of customary international law for fixed outer boundaries as a less costly option than artificial means of preservation but also less dependable as it requires explicit policy of the coastal states for this. He

would preserve stability in inter-state relations and also save states from expending limited resources on artificial preservation measures, using these for other adaptation purposes.[59] He saw shifting baselines as a

graver risk than waste of resources as it would lead to uncertainty as to the boundaries of some maritime zones during a time when the value of the resources of those zones will be increasing. Uncertainty regarding ownership of a valuable resource is a fertile ground for conflict between states or citizens.[60]

## 6. Weighing the Options: Ambulatory or Fixed?

There are distinct consequences associated with adopting the option of an ambulatory or fixed baseline. Physically, the landward movement of the baseline and outer limits would leave parts of the outer limits of the EEZ to the high seas and the inner limits of the EEZ would become part of what was the territorial sea, and the territorial sea would become part of the internal waters. The practical consequences of applying the ambulatory option could be significant and onerous on the coastal state.

For example, if we take the case of the EEZ, which provides important economic resources to the coastal state, if part of the exclusive economic zone were to become part of the high seas, this would bring about changes to the geographic scope of the sovereign rights and jurisdiction of the coastal state and its nationals. The impact to the coastal state is best exemplified in relation to fisheries activities. For example, under Article 62 of the 1982 LOS Convention, the coastal state is required to determine its capacity to harvest the living resources of the exclusive economic zone. In the case it cannot harvest the entire allowable catch, other states must be given access to the surplus of the allowable catch. Many developing states obtain important revenue from such fisheries access agreements. For example, it is estimated that the independent Pacific Island total access fee payments in 2014 were approximately US$340,285,572.[61] Overall, fisheries exports account for 94.7 per cent of total exports of Micronesia, 81.9 per cent for Cook Islands, 73 per cent for Palau, 61.5 per cent for Samoa, 23.8 per cent for Tonga, and 20 per cent for the Solomon Islands.[62] Likewise, other regions, such as

noted that this would, however, avoid the discrepancy with maritime boundaries that could be fixed permanently by agreement between states. Soons (n 4) 231.

[59] Caron, "When Law Makes Climate Change Worse" (n 1) 638–39. In his article Caron gives the example of Japan in 1988 spending some $240 million in three years to maintain Okinotorishima, described as two rocks just 2 feet above sea level at high tide, from erosion caused by waves. ibid.

[60] Caron, "When Law Makes Climate Change Worse" (n 1) 640–41.

[61] Robert Gillett and Mele Ikatonga Tauati, "Fisheries of the Pacific Islands Regional and National Information", FAO Fisheries and Aquaculture Technical Paper No 625 (2018) 36–37 <http://www.fao.org/3/I9297EN/i929 7en.pdf>.

[62] See ILC, "First Issues Paper by Bogdan Aurescu and Nilüfer Oral, Co-Chairs of the Study Group on Sea-Level Rise in Relation to International Law" (28 February 2020) A/CN.4/740 <https://legal.un.org/docs/?symbol=A/ CN.4/740> para 181 (hereafter ILC, "First Issues Paper"); citing Sustainability Impact Assessment (SIA) of The EU-ACP Economic Partnership Agreements Pacific Region: Fisheries (March 2007).

African coastal states, derive important economic benefits from fisheries access agreements, especially with the European Union. The European Union has concluded fifteen sustainable fisheries partnership agreements with African states.[63]

Conservation efforts by coastal states may also be adversely impacted if baselines were subject to change because of sea level rise. There is an increasing number of marine protected areas that have been established in EEZs. Examples in the South Pacific, an area especially at risk from sea level rise, include the Palau National Marine Sanctuary designated by Palau in 2015 that just took effect on 1 January 2020, covering 80 per cent of Palau's national waters. In 2017, Micronesia placed approximately 10 per cent of its 200-mile EEZ, an area that covers more than 1.3 million square miles, under conservation measures.[64] In 2017, the Cook Islands established Marae Moana—one of the largest marine reserve areas in the world.[65] In 2006, Kiribati established the Phoenix Islands Protected Area (PIPA), which constitutes 11.34 per cent of Kiribati's EEZ and was inscribed on the World Heritage List in 2010.[66] A shift of any part of these areas to the high seas would mean that the coastal state would not be able to maintain the integrity of these marine protected areas and the responsibility to protect the marine environment would fall to the exclusive jurisdiction of flag states.[67]

As noted earlier, rising sea levels could have impact on existing archipelagic waters established by the drawing of archipelagic straight baselines and a complicated calculation of land-to-water ratio measured from the outermost points of the outermost islands and drying reefs, in the extreme case could result in the loss of the archipelagic baseline and consequently the archipelagic water zone.[68] The Maldives has raised this concern in its submission to the International Law Commission, stating that having to redraw archipelagic baselines due to basepoints being submerged could result in a significant decrease in the size of its maritime zones.[69] Kiribati is another example of an archipelagic state at risk. It took some twenty years to construct the limited archipelagic baselines around its capital Tarawa, but sea level rise could inundate drying reefs used

[63] Eric Pichon, "The African Union's Blue Strategy" European Parliamentary Research Service (March 2019) <http://www.europarl.europa.eu/RegData/etudes/ATAG/2019/635574/EPRS_ATA(2019)635574_EN.pdf>.

[64] ILC, "First Issues Paper" (n 62) para 183, citing Federated States of Micronesia, Congressional Act No 19-167 to amend title 24 of the Code of the Federated States of Micronesia (18 April 2017) <http://www.paclii.org/fm/indices/legis/public_laws_19.html>. See also Atlas of Marine Protection <http://www.mpatlas.org/mpa/sites/68808202/>.

[65] ILC, "First issues paper" (n 62) para 183, citing Palau, Marae Moana Act 2017 (No 10 of 2017) <https://www.ecolex.org/details/legislation/marae-moana-act-2017-no-10-of-2017-lex-faoc170527/?q=Marae+Moana+&type=legislation&xdate_min=&xdate_max=>; the exclusive economic zone measures 408,250 square kilometres (km²) (157,630 square miles). See Atlas of Marine Protection <http://mpatlas.org/mpa/sites/7704395/>.

[66] ILC, "First Issues Paper" (n 62) para 183, citing UNESCO World Heritage Committee, "Decision: 35 COM 8B.60" (2010) <https://whc.unesco.org/en/list/1325/>.

[67] Subject to the possibility that states will adopt an internationally legally binding instrument for the conservation and sustainable use of biological diversity in areas beyond national jurisdiction currently under negotiation pursuant to UNGA resolution 72/249.

[68] ILC, "First Issues Paper" (n 62) para 188.

[69] Submission of the Republic of Maldives (31 December 2019) Note Verbale No 2019/UN/N/50, 14 (hereafter Submission of the Republic of Maldives).

in the archipelagic state's calculation.[70] There are some twenty-two states that have claimed such archipelagic status and use archipelagic straight baselines.[71]

## 7. Ambiguities

UNCLOS does not provide for any general rule whether the baseline is ambulatory or fixed. Instead, it only provides for a set of circumstances where the baseline may be ambulatory or permanent. Otherwise, in general, the provisions on baselines entail ambiguities. For example, Article 5 states the general rule that "the normal baseline for measuring the breadth of the territorial sea is the low-water line along the coast as marked on large-scale charts officially recognized by the coastal State". Does the baseline remain the same even if the coastline has receded? The ILA Baseline Committee adopted the view that low-water baseline is ambulatory.[72] The Committee observed that the "preponderance of the scholarship in this area appears to support the view that charts are not determinative of the naturally ambulatory normal baseline, although this view is not universally held".[73] However, the ILA also points to experts who take the opposite view (minority view) that it is the charted line under Article 5 that remains despite physical changes to the baseline.[74] The ILA Baselines Committee adopted the prevailing view for the actual low-water line and not the charted line[75] and that it is ambulatory.[76]

Another provision with ambiguities is Article 7(2). It allows for the use of a straight baseline in the case where a delta or other natural features makes the coastline highly unstable. However, foreseeing where there might be changes in the coastline it also states, "notwithstanding subsequent regression of the low-water line, the straight baseline shall remain effective until changed by the coastal State". Both Soons and Caron saw this as supporting the ambulatory nature of baselines by negative implication.[77] However, does this imply any obligation for the coastal state to make changes? Micronesia formally declared

[70] Stuart Kaye, "The Law of the Sea Convention and sea level rise after the *South China Sea Arbitration*" (2017) 93 International Law Studies Series, US Naval War College 423, 435 (citing Victor Prescott and Clive Schofield, *The Maritime Political Boundaries of the World* (2nd edn, Brill 2004) 176).

[71] For an analysis of some claims (US State Dept) see Kevin Baumert and Brian Melchoir, "A Practice of Archipelagic States: A Study of Studies" (2015) 46 Ocean Development & International Law 60. Indonesia, the Philippines, the Bahamas, the Seychelles, the Maldives, Kiribati, the Federated States of Micronesia, the Marshall Islands, and Tuvalu.

[72] ILA, "Baselines under the International Law of the Sea, Sofia Report" (2012) 28 (hereafter ILA, "Sofia Report"). Based on the recommendation of the ILA Baseline Committee the ILA Committee on International Law and Sea Level Rise was established following a Resolution 1/2012 of the 75th ILA Conference held in Sofia in 2012.

[73] ibid 22.

[74] ibid 23; citing DC Kapoor and Adam J Kerr, *A Guide to Maritime Boundary Delimitation* (Carswell Legal Pubns 1986) 31; Christopher Carleton and Clive Schofield, "Developments in the Technical Determination of Maritime Space: Charts, Datums, Baselines, Maritime Zones and Limits" (2001) 3 (3) Ibru Maritime Briefing 24–25.

[75] The ILA Baseline Committee concluded that the "legal normal baseline is the actual low-water line along the coast at the vertical datum, also known as the chart datum, indicated on charts officially recognized by the coastal State". ILA, "Sofia Report" (n 72) 25.

[76] ibid 31.

[77] Soons (n 4) 634.

its understanding that it is not obliged to keep under review the maritime zones re-flected in the present official deposit of charts and lists of geographical coordinates of points, delineated in accordance with UNCLOS, and that the Federated States of Micronesia intends to maintain these maritime zones in line with that understanding, notwithstanding climate change-induced sea-level rise.[78]

The view that baselines are ambulatory through negative implication also points to provisions concerning continental shelf that expressly provide for the permanency of the outer limits of the continental shelf. Does this mean, *argumentum a contrario*, that in all other cases the rule must be for ambulation? In the case of a submission by a state to the Commission on the Limits of the Continental Shelf, Article 76(8) states "[t]the limits of the shelf established by a coastal State on the basis of these recommendations shall be *final and binding*" (emphasis added). This, presumably, would mean that the outer limits remain regardless of whether the baseline upon which its rests has dis-appeared. This is followed by Article 76(9) which imposes the requirement, similar to Article 16, for the coastal state to deposit with the Secretary General of the United Nations charts and relevant information *permanently* describing the outer limits of the continental shelf. Does this mean that the outer limit of the continental shelf will not change regardless of the fate of the baseline? But then, what is the status of the outer limits of the continental shelf if the coastal state fails to deposit the charts and relevant information, including geodetic data? Ambulatory? Do these two provisions support the interpretation that unless otherwise made express, baselines are ambulatory?

The Convention also includes certain procedural requirements. For example, Article 16 requires the coastal state to give due publicity and deposit a copy of charts or lists of geographical coordinates with the General Secretary of the United Nations for base-lines drawn in accordance with Articles 7, 9, and 10, which are straight baselines, and lines of delimitation drawn in accordance with Article 12 (roadsteads) and Article 15 (delimitation of the territorial sea between opposite or adjacent coasts). If the coastal state fulfils this requirement, does this render the baseline fixed? What if the coastal state does not?

At the time of the negotiations of the 1982 LOS Convention the threat of climate change and sea level rise was unknown. Consequently, the Convention reflects known concerns, such as the case of highly unstable coastlines caused by deltas or other nat-ural features. Moreover, the importance of permanency for the outer limits of the con-tinental shelf is linked to the valuable natural resources and the costs of exploration and exploitation that could be jeopardized should the outer limits be subject to change.[79]

---

[78] Submission of the Federated States of Micronesia (27 December 2019), Note Verbale no FSMUN 058-2019.

[79] Caron, "When Law Makes Climate Change Worse" (n 1) n 79 relaying a conversation with Professor Bernard Oxman (a member of the US Delegation to the Third United Nations Conference on the Law of the Sea) in which he explained that "given the fixed nature of investment in the continental shelf, the inclusion of the word 'per-manent' was intentional. In his view, the inclusion of the word 'permanent,' at least as far as the United States is concerned, likely also reflects earlier recommendations such as that made in an influential 1968 U.S. study which proposed that the outer limit of the continental shelf 'should ... not be subject to change because of subsequent alterations in the coastline or revelations of more detailed surveys.'" (Telephone interview with Professor Bernard

## 8.  Do Islands Devolve into "Rocks"?

Another source of uncertainty created by climate change and sea level rise concerns the physical existence of many islands and low-lying Small Island States. Under the 1982 LOS Convention, islands are entitled to the same maritime zones and entitlements as continental land territory, unless the feature is a rock or a low-tide elevation. Article 121 defines an "island" as a naturally formed area of land, surrounded by water, which is above water at high tide. According to sub-paragraph 2, an island is entitled to the full suite of maritime zones unless it is a rock that "cannot sustain human habitation or economic life of their own", in which case it shall have no EEZ or continental shelf. The famously cryptic language of sub-paragraph 3 has spawned much scholarly debate[80] but, by contrast, evoked little guidance from international courts and tribunals.

The critical difference lies in the vague language whether the feature is "capable of sustaining human habitation or economic life on its own". A full-fledged island gets the full panoply of maritime entitlements, whereas rocks implicitly receive only a territorial sea and possibly a contiguous zone. This difference could be an existential matter, especially for low-lying island States, such as the Maldives, Kiribati, or Tuvalu that are barely above sea level. The risk is not only that the island might become entirely submerged and disappear but could also be rendered uninhabitable because of increased flooding due to elevated tides, infiltration of saltwater in freshwater supplies, loss of agricultural land and food production,[81] and other factors making the island uninhabitable for humans or unable to sustain economic activities.

The consequences of an island disappearing or losing its 'island' status and devolving legally into a rock lacking the capacity to sustain human habitation or an economic life of its own are significant. Would it lose all its maritime zones and entitlements? Maritime zones are anchored to land as expressed in the well-known principle that the *land dominates the sea*,[82] and "is the legal source of the power which a State may exercise

---

H Oxman, University of Miami (28 February 1990), quoting Commission on Marine Science, *Engineering, and Resources, Our Nation and the Sea* (1968) 145.)

[80] For example, Clive Schofield, "The Trouble with Islands: The Definition and Role of Islands and Rocks in Maritime Boundary Delimitation" in Hong and Van Dyke (eds) (n 2) 19, 21; Jon M Van Dyke and Robert A Brooks, "Uninhabited Islands: Their Impact on the Ownership of the Oceans' Resources" (1983) 12 Ocean Development & International Law 265, 271; Jonathan Charney, "Rocks that Cannot Sustain Human Habitation" (1999) 93 American Journal of International Law 863, 870–71. For a detailed overview of islands under international law, see Sean D Murphy, *International Law Relating to Islands*, 386 Recueil des cours (Hague Academy of International Law 2017)

[81] The representative of Fiji during the Sixth Committee meeting stated that "Fijian communities are experiencing the decline of food production due to saltwater intrusion". Fiji Statement at the Sixth Committee UNGA 73rd Session, Specific issues on which comments would be of particular interest to the International Law Commission, 2.

[82] *North Sea Continental Shelf (Federal Republic of Germany v Denmark; Federal Republic of Germany v Netherlands)* [1969] ICJ Rep 3 [96] (hereafter *North Sea Continental Shelf*) . This principle has been restated in subsequent cases. *Delimitation of the Maritime Boundary in the Gulf of Maine Area (Canada v United States of America)* (Merits) [1984] ICJ Rep 246 [157]; *Aegean Sea Continental Shelf (Greece v Turkey)* [1978] ICJ Rep 3 [86] (hereafter *Aegean Sea Continental Shelf*); *Maritime Delimitation and Territorial Questions between Qatar and Bahrain (Qatar v Bahrain)* (Merits) [2001] ICJ Rep 97 [185] (hereafter *Qatar v Bahrain*); *Territorial and Maritime Dispute between Nicaragua and Honduras in the Caribbean Sea (Nicaragua v Honduras)* (Merits) [2007] ICJ Rep

over territorial extensions to seaward" as articulated by the International Court of Justice in its 1969 *North Sea Continental Shelf* cases judgment.[83] Does this mean that an island that was once inhabited and enjoyed the full suite of maritime zones would lose its EEZ and continental shelf—or all maritime zones—if rendered a low-tide elevation?

The 1982 C provides no guidance to these and other related questions. A strict reading of Article 121(3) would lead to the conclusion that an island, which may not have lost territory but has become uninhabitable because sea water infiltration has contaminated its fresh water supplies, might be reclassified as a rock and lose its EEZ and continental shelf entitlements. Such consequences could be economically, socially, and culturally catastrophic. This risk could lead to the economic waste and conflict David Caron warned about in 1990.[84]

International courts and tribunals have proven quite reluctant to bring more substance and clarity to Article 121(3). While there has yet to be a case concerning the possible devolution of a full-fledged *island* to that of a *rock*, there have been a number of international cases seeking the classification of a specific feature as either one or the other.[85] However, the International Court of Justice (ICJ) and tribunals have proven recalcitrant to take on this issue over the years. Nonetheless, according to the Court we know that size alone is not determinative of the island status, as stated in the 2001 *Qatar v Bahrain* maritime delimitation case[86] and later reaffirmed by the Court in the 2012 *Nicaragua v Colombia* case.[87] In a very rare instance, the Court actually expressly classified one feature (Quitasueño) to be a rock under Article 121 (3).[88] Other cases, such as the *Eritrea v Yemen* case[89] and the *Black Sea (Romania v Ukraine)* maritime delimitation case[90] skirted the issue.

The only case to date that has addressed Article 121(3) head on is the 2016 *South China Sea Arbitration between the Republic of the Philippines and the People's Republic of China*.[91] China refused to appear in the case, claiming the Tribunal lacked jurisdiction[92]

---

659 [113], [126] (hereafter *Nicaragua v. Colombia*); *Maritime Delimitation in the Black Sea (Romania v Ukraine)* (Merits) [2009] ICJ Rep 61 [77] (hereafter *Romania v Ukraine*); *The Bay of Bengal Maritime Boundary Arbitration (Bangladesh v India)* (PCA, Award of 7 July 2014) [279] (hereafter *Bay of Bengal Maritime Boundary Arbitration*); *Continental Shelf (Tunisia v Libyan Arab Jamahiriya)* (Merits) [1982] ICJ Rep 18 [73]; *Dispute concerning delimitation of the maritime boundary between Bangladesh and Myanmar in the Bay of Bengal (Bangladesh v Myanmar)* (Judgment) ITLOS Reports 2012, 4 [185].

[83] *North Sea Continental Shelf* (n 82).
[84] Caron, "When Law Makes Climate Change Worse" (n 1) 636–41.
[85] Some examples include the Conciliation Commission on the Continental Shelf area between Iceland and Jan Mayen: Report and recommendations to the governments of Iceland and Norway, decision of June 1981. *Continental Shelf (Libyan Arab Jamahiriya/Malta)* (Application to Intervene) (Judgment) [1984] ICJ Rep 3.
[86] *Qatar v Bahrain* (n 77) [185]; See also *Dubai-Sharjah Border Arbitration* (1981) 91 ILR 543.
[87] *Nicaragua v Colombia* (n 77) [139], [177].
[88] ibid.
[89] Award of the Arbitral Tribunal in the second stage of proceedings between Eritrea and Yemen Arbitration, (Maritime Delimitation), decision of 17 December 1999, United Nations, Reports of International Arbitral Awards, vol. XXII (Sales No E/F.00.V.7) 335, 368 [147]–[148].
[90] *Romania v Ukraine* (n 82) [187].
[91] *In re Arbitration Between the Republic of the Philippines and the People's Republic of China*, PCA Case No 2013-19, Award (12 July 2016) (hereafter *South China Sea Arbitration*); Clive Schofield and David Freestone, "Islands Awash Amidst Rising Seas: Sea Level Rise and Insular Status under the Law of the Sea" (2019) 34 International Journal Marine & Coastal Law 391.
[92] Kate Parlett, "Jurisdiction of the Arbitral Tribunal in Philippines v. China Under UNCLOS and in the Absence of China" (2016) 110 American Journal of International Law Unbound 266–72.

and rejected the validity of the award.[93] Notwithstanding this, the award offers some in-direct clues to answering the question concerning the status of a full-fledged island that becomes uninhabitable due to sea level rise.

The Tribunal was requested to determine the status of a number of features which had been subject to significant human modification. In relation to the possible impact of sea level rise on the future status of islands, the Tribunal made some interesting find-ings concerning paragraph 3 of Article 121.

First, the Tribunal did not require actual habitation to fulfil the criteria of having capacity to sustain human habitation. The Tribunal stated, "the fact that a feature is currently not inhabited does not prove that it is uninhabitable. The fact that it has no economic life does not prove that it cannot sustain an economic life."[94] Second, the Tribunal pointed to the relevance of historical evidence of human habitation and eco-nomic life for establishing a feature's capacity stating:

> If a known feature proximate to a populated land mass was never inhabited and never sustained an economic life, this may be consistent with an explanation that it is unin-habitable. Conversely, positive evidence that humans historically lived on a feature or that the feature was the site of economic activity could constitute relevant evidence of a feature's capacity.[95]

Of particular significance to the present inquiry is the Tribunal's statement in as-sessing historical evidence of past human habitation and economic activities. For example:

> the Tribunal should consider whether there is evidence that human habitation has been prevented or ended by forces that are separate from the intrinsic capacity of the feature. *War, pollution, and environmental harm could all lead to the depopulation, for a prolonged period, of a feature that, in its natural state, was capable of sustaining human habitation.* In the absence of such intervening forces, however, the Tribunal can rea-sonably conclude that a feature that has never historically sustained a human commu-nity lacks the capacity to sustain human habitation.[96]

As observed by one scholar:

> This finding suggests that the original or natural condition—and not human intervention—will determine whether the feature is habitable or not. Arguably, human intervention could include a sea-level rise caused by anthropogenic climate

---

[93] Statement of the Ministry of Foreign Affairs of the People's Republic of China on the Award of 12 July 2016 of the Arbitral Tribunal in the South China Sea Arbitration Established at the Request of the Republic of the Philippines (12 July 2016) <https://www.fmprc.gov.cn/nanhai/eng/snhwtlcwj_1/t1379492.htm>.

[94] *South China Sea Arbitration* (n 91) [483].

[95] ibid [484].

[96] ibid [549] (emphasis added).

change. Accordingly, this change would not alter the 'intrinsic capacity of the feature' and presumably would not affect the feature's status.[97]

## 9. The Need for Stability and Certainty for Maritime Boundaries

One of the questions, as mentioned earlier, concerns the status of maritime boundaries in relation to the possibility of sea level rise being invoked as a fundamental change of circumstance to change agreed upon boundaries—an issue that was flagged by David Caron. He cautioned that it would create uncertainty for the boundaries of some maritime zones and risk conflict.[98] Article 62(2) of the VCLOT specifically excludes the application of the principle of "fundamental change of circumstances" or *clausula rebus sic stantibus* to "boundaries". Likewise, the 1978 Vienna Convention on Succession of States in Respect of Treaties recognizes a special regime for boundaries in Article 11, which provides that succession of a state does not affect "a boundary established by a treaty, or obligations and rights established by a treaty and relating to the regime of a boundary". The question is whether "boundaries" include maritime boundaries.[99]

Scholars have expressed the view that maritime boundaries should have the same status as land boundaries for the purpose of the doctrine of *rebus sic stantibus*.[100] The ILA Sea Level Rise Committee, after conducting an overview of the legal landscape, recommended in the interest of legal certainty and stability that the impact of sea level rise should not be subject to the rule of fundamental change of circumstances for maritime boundaries established by agreements.[101] The ILC First Issues Paper, while in agreement with this view, has expressed the need for greater clarity and definiteness of this important issue.[102] The ILC First Issues Paper also referred to statements by many states expressing the view that the doctrine of fundamental change of circumstances would not apply to maritime boundaries established by treaty.[103] An example provided in the ILC First Issues Paper comes from the Maldives stating:

> sea-level rise does not have any effect on maritime boundaries between two States when they have been fixed by a treaty. Maritime boundary treaties, such as those that Maldives has negotiated, are binding under the rule of *pacta sunt servanda*, and

---

[97]  Kaye (n 70) 431.

[98]  Caron, "Climate Change, Sea Level Rise and the Coming Uncertainty in Oceanic Boundaries" (n 1) 13–14. Soons (n 4) 228.

[99]  The ILA Committee on Sea-Level Rise analysed this issue in detail in its 2016 interim report and also in its 2018 Sydney final report.

[100]  Julia Lisztwan, "Stability of Maritime Boundary Agreements" (2012) 37 Yale Journal of International Law 153; Snjolaug Arnadottir, "Termination of Maritime Boundaries due to a Fundamental Change of Circumstances" (2016) 32 Utrecht Journal of International and European Law 94; ILA, International Law and Sea Level Rise: Sydney Conference (ILA 2018) 19–20 (hereafter ILA, "Sydney Report"); Stoutenburg (n 54) 280–81.

[101]  ILA, "Sydney Report" (n 100) 25; This view was endorsed by the ILA in Resolution 5/2018.

[102]  ILC, "First Issues Paper" (n 62) para 114. See also, ILC "Additional Paper to the First Issues Paper, Bogdan Aurescu and Nilufer Oral (2023)" A/CN.4/761, 47-52.

[103]  ILC, "First Issues Paper" (n 62) para 122.

sea-level rise does not constitute a fundamental change of circumstances that would allow termination or suspension of such treaties.[104]

The ILC First Issues Paper provides numerous other examples of states taking this position.[105]

The ICJ, in the *Aegean Sea Continental Shelf (Greece v Turkey)* judgment, stated quite clearly that maritime boundaries enjoy the same protection as land boundaries. According to the Court, "[w]hether it is a land frontier or a boundary line in the continental shelf that is in question, the process is essentially the same, and inevitably involves the same element of stability and permanence, and is subject to the rule excluding boundary agreements from fundamental change of circumstances".[106] This same position was adopted in the *Bay of Bengal Maritime Boundary Arbitration (Bangladesh v India)* arbitration case. The Tribunal stated, "maritime delimitations, like land boundaries, must be stable and definitive to ensure a peaceful relationship between the States concerned in the long term", as well as in its paragraph 217, which refers specifically to climate change and its effects (among which sea-level rise):

> [i]n the view of the Tribunal, neither the prospect of climate change nor its possible effects can jeopardize the large number of settled maritime boundaries throughout the world. This applies equally to maritime boundaries agreed between States and to those established through international adjudication.[107]

The Tribunal emphasized the

> issue is not whether the coastlines of the Parties will be affected by climate change in the years or centuries to come. It is rather *whether the choice of base points* located on the coastline and reflecting the general direction of the coast *is feasible in the present case and at the present time.*[108]

There is an evident gap in international law on the consequences of sea level rise on maritime boundaries. The risk is not theoretical but actually unfolding in real time. What then are the options available for international law to meet the challenge? In 1990 David Caron took the view that in addition to natural feedback, the law was also part of the feedback mechanism of climate change. He explained: "these legal feedbacks do not alter the amount of climate change, but instead aggravate the suffering that will accompany such change. It is a task of legal scholarship to aid societal adaptation to global climate change by identifying and addressing these legal feedbacks."[109] How then can

---

[104] Submission of the Republic of Maldives (n 69) 9.
[105] ILC, "First Issues Paper" (n 62) paras 123–132.
[106] *Aegean Sea Continental Shelf* (n 82) [85].
[107] *Bay of Bengal Maritime Boundary Arbitration* (n 82) [216]–[217].
[108] ibid [214] (emphasis added).
[109] Caron, "When Law Makes Climate Change Worse" (n 1) 652.

law remedy this legal feedback? Indeed, international law should be seen as part of the tools of adaptation and response measures. In other words, international law should also adapt to the legal consequences of sea level rise by devising legal solutions, such as recognizing the fixed nature of maritime boundaries that have been established in accordance with international law and received international recognition. In which case, the maintaining of existing maritime boundaries, including for islands that become unable to sustain human habitation or an economic life of their own, is an adaptive solution to the problem of sea level rise.[110] The solution that is gaining support is the option of maintaining existing maritime boundaries that have been established in accordance with international law and recognized by the international community. This is the option that is least onerous in terms of costs and importantly serves the strong interest to provide legal certainty and stability.

This was the position expressed in the ILA resolution adopted in 2018 endorsing the ILA Sea Level Rise Committee findings.[111] The need for stability and security was also emphasized in the First Issues Paper prepared by the Co-Chairs of the Study Group of the International Law Commission on Sea-level rise under international law, which also included many statements by UN member states calling in the Sixth Committee for legal certainty and stability, and security.[112] Authors have also written in support of preserving the stability of baselines and maritime boundaries.[113] On 6 August 2021, the Pacific Islands Forum issued the Declaration on Preserving Maritime Zones in the Face of Climate Change-Related Sea-Level Rise.[114] The Declaration supported the preservation of maritime zones declaring that "that once having, in accordance with the Convention, established and notified our maritime zones to the Secretary-General of the United Nations, we intend to maintain these zones without reduction, notwithstanding climate change-related sea-level rise".

---

[110] Nilufer Oral, "International Law as an Adaptation Measure to Sea-Level Rise and its Impacts on Islands and Offshore Features" (2019) 34 International Journal of Marine & Coastal Law 1.

[111] ILA, Resolution No 5/2018 (Sydney, 19–24 August 2018): "ENDORSES the proposal of the Committee that, on the grounds of legal certainty and stability, provided that the baselines and the outer limits of maritime zones of a coastal or an archipelagic State have been properly determined in accordance with the 1982 Law of the Sea Convention, these baselines and limits should not be required to be recalculated should sea level change affect the geographical reality of the coastline."

[112] ILC, "First Issues Paper" (n 62) paras 18, 23, and 27; see also "Additional Paper", (n 102) 11-32.

[113] For example, V Blanchette-Seguin, "Preserving Territorial Status Quo: Grotian Law of Nature, Baselines and Rising Sea Level" (2017) 50 New York University Journal of International Law and Politics 227; Sarra Sefrioui, "Adapting to Sea Level Rise: A Law of the Sea Perspective" in Gemma Andreone (ed), The Future of the Law of the Sea (Springer International 2017) 3–22; Stoutenburg (n 54); Jonathan Lusthaus, "Shifting Sands: Sea Level Rise, Maritime Boundaries and Inter-state Conflict" (2010) 30 Politics 113; Signe Veierud Busch, "Sea Level Rise and Shifting Maritime Limits: Stable Baselines as a Response to Unstable Coastlines" (2018) 9 Arctic Review of Law & Politics 174; Kate Purcell, Geographical Change and the Law of the Sea (Oxford University Press 2019); Christina Hioureas and Alejandra Torres Camprubí, "Legal and Political Considerations on the Disappearance of States Due to Sea Level Rise" in Tomas Heidar (ed), New Knowledge and Changing Circumstances in the Law of the Sea (Brill 2020) 407–26; Massimo Lando, "Stability of Maritime Boundaries and the Challenge of Geographical Change: A Reply to Snjólaug Árnadóttir" (2022) 35 Leiden Journal of International Law 379–95, the author disagrees with the approach of "fluctuating boundaries"; see also Snjólaug Árnadóttir, "Fluctuating Boundaries in a Changing Marine Environment" (2021) 34 Leiden Journal of International Law 471–87.

[114] <https://www.forumsec.org/2021/08/11/declaration-on-preserving-maritime-zones-in-the-face-of-climate-change-related-sea-level-rise/>. The states that joined the Declaration are Australia, the Cook Islands, the Federated States of Micronesia, Fiji, French Polynesia, Kiribati, Nauru, New Caledonia, New Zealand, Niue, Palau, Papua New Guinea, the Republic of the Marshall Islands, Samoa, Solomon Islands, Tonga, Tuvalu, and Vanuatu.

The Declaration was subsequently echoed by the thirty-nine member states of the Alliance of Small Island Developing States (AOSIS) on 22 September 2021, in which AOSIS affirmed that there is "no obligation" under UNCLOS "to keep baselines and outer limits of maritime zones under review nor to update charts or lists of geographical coordinates once deposited with the Secretary-General of the United Nations, and that such maritime zones and the rights and entitlements that flow from them shall continue to apply without reduction, notwithstanding any physical changes connected to climate change-related sea-level rise".[115]

The freezing or maintenance of maritime boundaries also responds to the problem of islands that lose lost their capacity to sustain human habitation or economic life as provided for under Article 121 of the Convention. The principal concern is that states do not lose rights over the valuable maritime zones as a result of climate change induced sea level rise, especially developing states that have contributed the least to the problem. David Caron underlined this in 1990, writing that the proposal for freezing of maritime boundaries is "particularly significant for island states and the peoples of those islands".[116]

## 10. Conclusion

The consequences of sea level rise on baselines and maritime boundaries may have appeared to many as a distant reality in 1990 when David Caron first published his article. However, today, sea level rise is a scientific certainty and many islands and coastal areas are already feeling the impacts. Coastlines are eroding and islands are sinking. International law has not yet resolved the fundamental question – whether maritime boundaries remain fixed or not if baselines disappear or islands become uninhabitable because of sea level rise. The lack of certainty carries the seeds of potential conflict between States taking into account the many maritime delimitation cases adjudicated before the ICJ and international tribunals, and agreements concluded after painstaking and often lengthy negotiations. How many of these would be at risk? Could one party unhappy with the result take advantage of sea level rise and push for a new settlement of otherwise agreed upon maritime boundaries? Would this be contrary to Article 62 of the VCLOT or not? A definitive answer is necessary.

The lack of clarity on this is partly due to the simple fact that climate change was not an issue until after the 1982 LOS Convention had been negotiated and adopted. Clearly, coastal erosion and rising sea levels are not new phenomena. The Netherlands for centuries dealt with rising level of the sea through its system of dykes at great cost. The difference lies in the scale of sea level rise resulting from climate change. Had the risk and scale been known during the Third United Nations Conference on the Law of the Sea

[115] Alliance of Small States, *Alliance of Small Island States Leaders' Declaration* (2021), <https://www.aosis.org/launch-of-the-alliance-of-small-island-states-leaders-declaration/>.
[116] Caron, "When Law Makes Climate Change Worse" (n 1) 653; See also Stoutenburg (n 54).

it is likely that states would have adopted language to preserve stability and certainty of maritime boundaries. After all, the famous preamble of UNCLOS starts: "*Prompted* by the desire to settle, in a spirit of mutual understanding and cooperation, all issues relating to the law of the sea and aware of the historic significance of this Convention as an important contribution to the maintenance of peace, justice and progress for all peoples of the world." It is ultimately in the hands of states to fashion a lasting solution by "peaceful means" to the very immediate threat to baselines and maritime boundaries by sea level rise through good faith and cooperation.

Without doubt, and as clearly reflected in the First Issues Paper of the International Law Commission, many states have expressed the view in favour of legal certainty and stability.[117] These were also the driving features underlying the work of the International Law Association. It can be concluded that on this point, there is broad agreement. The challenge is how to achieve this result through international law-making processes.

The Codification Division of the United Nations, acting as the Secretariat for the International Law Commission, conducted a review of some 250 maritime boundary treaties and found that few included provisions for amendment[118] and none made express reference to the adjustment of a maritime delimitation as a consequence of sea level rise.[119] In practical terms, even if these agreements are open to modification, recalculations, redrawing of baselines, and resetting maritime boundaries can be a lengthy and costly process.

States might also opt for amending UNCLOS or adopting an implementing agreement limited to maritime boundaries and sea level rise. However, this too can be a lengthy and cumbersome route. Moreover, if the objective is legal certainty, stability and security, states would have to arrive at an agreement that was clear and not subject to the same ambiguities that exist in UNCLOS. The most likely option will depend on state practice. Indeed, by undertaking the topic of sea level rise in relation to the international law, the International Law Commission can play the role of catalyst for the development of state practice. The active engagement by states in the Sixth Committee can play an influential role in guiding states to finding solutions. There is emerging state practice, especially from Pacific Island States, which was also assisted by the work of the ILA. Member States of the Pacific Islands Forum (PIF) have declared their commitment to the development of international law to ensure stability of maritime boundaries.[120] An example of this emerging state practice is the shift by member states of PIF from using nautical charts to the use of geographic coordinates.[121]

---

[117] The First Issues Paper observed: "This overview of conventional practice reinforces the general conclusion, which can be drawn after studying the submissions to the Commission and the statements by Member States before the Sixth Committee, that there is a large body of State practice favouring legal stability, security, certainty and predictability of the maritime delimitations effected by agreement or by adjudication." ILC, "First Issues Paper" (n 62) para 138.

[118] ILC, "First Issues Paper" (n 62) paras 133–137.

[119] ibid para 137.

[120] ibid paras 83–86. See also, on emerging state practice, ILA, "Sydney Report" (n 100) 16–18.

[121] ILC, "First Issues Paper" (n 62) para 86.

One other option that could lead to finding a solution that promotes legal certainty, stability, and peaceful relations might be to seek an advisory opinion from the ICJ or the International Tribunal for the Law of the Sea. Practically speaking, the latter option may be preferable, as it does not require action from the General Assembly or Security Council.[122] ITLOS can exercise jurisdiction if an international agreement related to the purposes of the Convention specifically provides for the submission to the Tribunal of a request for an advisory opinion.[123]

There need not be one single solution to the pressing challenge of sea level rise and its impact on maritime boundaries. What matters is that the international community work together in achieving a solution that will promote certainty, stability, and peaceful relations.

---

[122] UN Charter, art 96.
[123] *Request for Advisory Opinion submitted by the Sub-Regional Fisheries Commission* (Advisory Opinion) ITLOS Reports 2015, 4, [60].

# 24

# The Human Right to a Clean Environment and the Jurisprudence of International Courts and Tribunal

*Malgosia Fitzmaurice*

## 1. Introduction

The human right to a clean environment is one of the areas in which international courts and tribunals have developed and to a certain degree shaped international environmental law.[1] In general, they have played an innovative role in its evolution, fleshing out its principles but, as has been observed, their role is restricted by their jurisdiction and applicable law.[2] International courts and tribunals identify the relevant law and apply it to facts.[3]

After many decades of debates and doubts, there is at present a view widely shared by the majority of both scholars and practitioners that a human right to a clean environment exists. This is largely supported by the inclusion of such a right in international conventions. Until very recently, such a right has not had a clearly defined substance, even when it is contained in international conventions, and therefore, it may be said that it had a rather nebulous character.

There is no doubt that through their jurisprudence, international and national courts and tribunals have contributed to development of this right and have given it a more defined content. The most compelling evidence of the existence of such a right was the recent Advisory Opinion of the Inter-American Court of Human Rights,[4] which made a very strong link between general human rights and environmental degradation, including the possibility of the extra-territorial application of environmental human rights in the case of environmental harm. Even if the jurisprudence of international courts and tribunals in relation to consolidating and evolving environmental human

---

[1] "Remarks by Cymie R Payne" (2015) 109 Proceedings of the Annual Meeting (American Society of International Law) 193–95. See also Philippe Gautier, "The Role of International Courts and Tribunals in the Development of Environmental Law" (2015) 109 Proceedings of the Annual Meeting (American Society of International Law) 190–93.

[2] ibid.

[3] "Remarks by Cymie R Payne" (n 1).

[4] Advisory Opinion OC-23/17, 15 November 2017, requested by the Republic of Colombia, <http://www.corteidh.or.cr/docs/opiniones/resumen_seriea_23_eng.pdf>.

Malgosia Fitzmaurice, *The Human Right to a Clean Environment and the Jurisprudence of International Courts and Tribunal*
In: *By Peaceful Means*. Edited by: Charles N Brower, Joan E Donoghue, Cian C Murphy, Cymie R Payne and Esmé R Shirlow,
Oxford University Press. © Malgosia Fitzmaurice 2024. DOI: 10.1093/oso/9780192848086.003.0024

rights is fragmented and mostly confined to a regional context, we can observe very significant and exciting developments, which throw a new light on this issue.

## 2. The Roadmap

This chapter analyses the synergy between human rights and the protection of environment. It takes into account soft law and hard law (international Conventions), which contain an explicit right to a clean environment, and those instruments in which such a right can be derived or presumed from the catalogue of other rights. Traditionally, the debate concerning the link between the environmental degradation and protection and human rights focused on the substantive right to a clean environment. However, in view of the present author, the advent and the wide recognition of the Environmental Impact Assessment (EIA) and the universalization of rights contained in the Aarhus Convention have shifted the focus onto the procedural right to a clean environment. Such a right is in most cases better defined and less nebulous than a substantive right to a clean environment. It states in clear terms the obligations to national organs to implement such a right. A substantive right to a clean environment is frequently formulated in the relevant treaties (applicable by international courts and tribunals) in very general terms (such as the San Salvador Protocol and African Charter), which imposes imprecise obligations on States. This chapter conducts an extensive analysis the relevant case law of international and national courts and tribunals. It may be said that the chapter presents a very varied picture. Some of the decisions are based on a substantive environmental right, some (such as in the case of the European Court of Human Rights (ECtHR)) also invoke a procedural right (eg EIA and the rights included in the Aarhus Convention). The recent developments, such as the Advisory Opinion of the Inter-American Court of Human Rights, has set a very desirable trend of combining both types of human right to a clean environment (substantive and procedural). In general, however, thus far the historical and present case law is a very mixed bag and therefore it is difficult to draw very generalized conclusions. Finally, this chapter deals with communitarian interest in environmental law, including intergenerational equity. In international and national practice, there are examples of such an approach. It may be observed, however, that there no recent international and national law cases are based on the obligations *erga omnes* or *erga omnes partes*. The same applies to the principle of intergenerational equity, which has not been invoked recently before national and international courts and tribunals. It may be hoped that this trend does not signify the stagnation in protection of general interests in environmental law. The synergy between environment and human rights is still developing, but perhaps not as quickly and as smoothly as was expected when the courts first looked at environmental protection through the lens of human rights (such as the initial case law of the ECtHR).

## 3. Soft Law, International Agreements, and United Nations Bodies

The link between the enjoyment of human rights and the environment in which we live was addressed for the first time in 1972 at the UN Conference on the Human Environment. The Declaration of the Conference (Stockholm Declaration) recognizes that "man's environment [is] essential to his well-being and to the enjoyment of basic human rights", such as the right to life. It is clear that:

> [t]he harm caused to individuals and communities by degraded environments—from unsafe drinking water to disappearing wild life—is increasingly seen by many people as a question of "rights" being violated ... Protection of the environment can no longer be seen as simply a policy choice.[5]

There are currently other soft law instruments include both the substantive and the procedural right to a clean environment. Such an example is the Global Pact for the Environment, which in Article 1 (Right to an ecologically sound environment) states as follows: "Every person has the right to live in an ecologically sound environment adequate for their health, well-being, dignity, culture and fulfilment." Articles 9 and 10 embody the procedural human right to a clean environment and include respectively access to information and public participation.[6] The Global Pact for the Environment, text of which was adopted by the United Nations Environmental Assembly in March 2022, has gained a widespread support. It must be mentioned that the most important event in relation to environmental human right took place in July 2022, when UNGA adopted a resolution[7] recognizing the right to a clean, healthy and sustainable environment. This United Nations Political Declaration, in the context of the fiftieth anniversary of the Stockholm Conference, is a recent iteration of the Global Pact for the Environment.

The problems posed by environmental degradation have become a major challenge for the protection of human dignity. Express substantive rights are found in the following international instruments: the African Charter on Human Rights and Peoples' Rights (the African Charter, ACHPR)[8] and the Additional Protocol to the American Convention on Human Rights in the Area of Social and Cultural Rights (San Salvador Protocol).[9]

---

[5] John E Bonine and Svitlana Kravchenko, *Human Rights and the Environment: Cases, Law, and Policy* (Academic Press 2008) 3.

[6] Article 9: "Every person, without being required to state an interest, has a right of access to environmental information held by public authorities. Public authorities shall, within the framework of their national legislations, collect and make available to the public relevant environmental information"; Article 10: "Every person has the right to participate, at an appropriate stage and while options are still open, to the preparation of decisions, measures, plans, programmes, activities, policies and normative instruments of public authorities that may have a significant effect on the environment". <https://globalpactenvironment.org/uploads/EN.pdf>.

[7] United Nations General Assembly Resolution A/76/L.75, signed 26 July 2022

[8] The African Charter, signed 19 May 198 entered into force 21 October 1986. 1520 UNTS 217.

[9] The San Salvador Protocol, signed 8 June 1990, entered into force 16 November 1999, 1144 UNTS 144.

In Article 24, the African Charter, which was the first international treaty to include the right to a clean environment, provides peoples with a right to "a general satisfactory environment favourable to their development". Article 11 of the San Salvador Protocol provides for a right to a healthy environment:

1. Everyone shall have a right to live in a healthy environment and to have access to basic public services.
2. The States Parties shall promote the protection, preservation, and improvement of the environment.

These Conventions include a substantive right to a clean environment. This right is differentiated, however, from a procedural right, which is defined by Principle 10 of the Rio Declaration. It includes three constitutive rights: (i) the right to information; (ii) the right to participate; and (iii) the right to access to justice. These rights are of fundamental importance as they allow the individual and civil society the tools through which they can combat environmental degradation. Such rights have been incorporated in a number of treaties, in particular, the United Nations Economic Commission for Europe (UNECE) Convention on Access to Information, Public Participation in Decision-making and Access to Justice in Environmental Matters (the Aarhus Convention). To some extent, it may be said that such a right is also included in the EIA procedure, which is based on two pillars: the right to information and the right to participation. Such a procedure is contained in the 1991 Convention on Environmental Impact Assessment in a Transboundary Context (the Espoo Convention).[10] This is a global treaty. It defines EIA as "means a national procedure for evaluating the likely impact of a proposed activity on the environment" (Article 1, para vi). This Convention contains the participatory (procedural) rights for the individuals such as, for example, "[t]he Party of origin shall provide, in accordance with the provisions of this Convention, an opportunity to the public in the areas likely to be affected to participate in relevant environmental impact assessment procedures regarding proposed activities and shall ensure that the opportunity provided to the public of the affected Party is equivalent to that provided to the public of the Party of origin" (Article 2, para 6). The view has been also expressed that "due the norm's widespread acceptance means that it has been absorbed into public international law by attaining status as a General Principle of Law",[11] in the meaning of Article 38 of the Statue of the International Court of Justice (ICJ).

At the United Nations level, there was a high degree of recognition of a human right to a clean environment. For example, as early as 1989, in preparation for the Rio Conference, a Special Rapporteur on environment and development was appointed by the Sub-Commission of Prevention of Discrimination and Protection of Minorities.

---

[10] Espoo Convention, entered into force 10 September 1997, 1989 UNTS 309.
[11] Tseming Yang. "Environment Impact Assessment Duty as a Global Legal Norm and General Principle of Law" (2019) 70 Hastings Journal of International Law 549–50.

The Special Rapporteur, Fatma Zohra Ksentini, addressed the link between human rights and environmental degradation in her 1994 final report. She stated that the environment, development, democracy, and human rights are the fundamental building blocks of modern society. Endorsing the view that environmental rights are protected by existing human rights, she reported that there was universal acceptance of the right to a satisfactory environment at national, regional, and international levels. The Special Rapporteur recommended the adoption of the Draft Declaration of Principles on Human Rights and the Environment, which had been drafted by academics and non-governmental organizations (NGOs).[12]

The synergy between human rights and a healthy environment has been recognized by human rights bodies such as the UN Human Rights Committee In its General Comment 36 on the Right to Life, the Committee identified environmental degradation as one of the "the most pressing and serious threats to the ability of present and future generations to enjoy the right to life",[13] where the right to life (International Covenant on Civil and Political Rights (ICCPR), Article 6) is part of the duty of States to protect the environment. However, as it was stated:

> Even though the link between environmental protection and human rights is "undeniable", the scope of the States' duty is not yet sufficiently clear. As is true for many other human rights issues, the Human Rights Committee should use its global coverage to contribute to a coherent and transparent practice that helps establish clear guidelines for States.[14]

It affirms that the protection of the environment is closely linked to the ICCPR.[15]

The UN Human Rights Council (UN HRC, formerly the Commission on Human Rights) has appointed an Independent Expert (Special Rapporteur) on the issue of human rights obligations relating to the enjoyment of a safe, clean, healthy, and sustainable environment. The Special Rapporteur has held that "all human rights are vulnerable to environmental degradation, in that full enjoyment of all human rights depends on a supportive environment".[16] This is supported by a growing view that climate change affects the enjoyment of human rights. This was first recognized by the United Nations General Assembly, which described climate change as "common concern of mankind, since climate is an essential condition which sustains life on earth".[17] More recently, in a 2019 Report, the HRC Special Rapporteur identified several impacts of climate change on human rights, in particular the right to life, adequate food, water and sanitation, and health.[18] Furthermore, human rights bodies' and organizations' concern with climate

---

[12] Report by the Special Rapporteur on environment and development, E/CN.4/Sub.2/1994/9 (6 July 1994).

[13] CCPR/C/GC/36, para 62. Greta Reeh, "Human Rights and the Environment: The UN Human Rights Committee Affirms the Duty to Protect" (EJIL: Talk! 9 September 2019) <https://www.ejiltalk.org/human-rights-and-the-environment-the-un-human-rights-committee-affirms-the-duty-to-protect/>.

[14] ibid.

[15] ibid.

[16] A/HRC/22/43, para 19.

[17] A/RES/43/53, para 1.

[18] A/74/161, part II.

change is becoming more focused. The UN HRC in its 2019 Concluding Observations on the initial report of Capo Verde, for the first time referred to the term "climate change" in concluding observations.[19] It recognized not only its effects on vulnerable small island States but also made detailed recommendations on sustainable development and resilience to climate change.[20] Significantly, the UN HRC recognized that in this process, there should be meaningful and informed participation of all populations. The UN HRC has also dealt with the lawfulness of climate migrants seeking asylum.[21] Whilst the deportation by New Zealand of a Kiribati national claiming climate change asylum was not considered to constitute a violation of Article 6 of the ICCPR,[22] this case highlights the importance of the need to prepare for the human rights ramifications of climate change. The Council of Europe has also recently recognized the need to develop asylum regimes to cater to persons fleeing from long-term climate change.[23]

Other types of environmental degradation, such as the dumping of toxic waste, and the effects it has on the enjoyment of human rights, have also been considered. Since 1996, a Special Rapporteur within the UN HRC has investigated the matter and concluded that toxic waste dumping has a negative impact on the enjoyment of a number of human rights, including the right to self-determination, health, and food.[24] In 2011, the Special Rapporteur's mandate was extended to address all aspects of the management of hazardous substances and wastes.[25] He explicitly recognized that "exposure to hazardous substances, including various pollutants that contaminate food, air and water, infringes on numerous human rights, including the rights to life, health and a life with dignity".[26] Finally, on 8 October 2021, the UN HRC adopted a resolution which "[r]ecognizes the right to a clean, healthy and sustainable environment as human right that is important for the enjoyment of human rights".[27] On 28 July 2022 the UN General Assembly has recognized the right "to a Clean, Healthy and Sustainable Environment".[28]

Another body which has considered the interlinkage between environmental degradation and human rights is the Committee of Economic Social and Cultural Rights Covenant (CESCR) which is a body consisting of eighteen independent experts. Its functions include monitoring implementation of the International Covenant on Economic, Social and Cultural Rights by its States parties. It was established under the UN's Economic and Social Council (ECOSOC) 1985 Resolution in order to carry out the monitoring functions assigned to that Council in Part IV of the Covenant.[29] In its

---

[19] Reeh (n 12).
[20] CCPR/C/CPV/CO/1/Add.1, paras 17 and 18.
[21] CCPR/C/127/D/2728/2016.
[22] CPR/C/127/D/2728/2016, para 9.14.
[23] Resolution 2307/2019.
[24] E/CN.4/1996/17, para 132.
[25] H E/C.12/2000/4, para 25RC/Res/18/11.
[26] United Nations General Assembly A/HRC/18/31, Report of the Special rapporteur on the adverse effects of the movement and dumping of toxic and dangerous products and wastes on the enjoyment of human rights.
[27] HRC: Resolution 48/13. <https://documentny.un.org/doc/UNDOC/GEN/G21/289/50/PDF/G2128950.pdf?OpenElement>.
[28] In favour 161 (zero opposed; eight abstentions), A/76/L75
[29] <https://www.ohchr.org/en/hrbodies/cescr/pages/cescrindex.aspx>.

2000 General Comment[30]14, the CESCR observed that action should be taken to protect the right to health and in particular to "improve all aspects of environmental and industrial hygiene", which required, for example, measures to ensure adequate water supplies.[31]

This strong interlinkage between environmental degradation and the enjoyment of human rights has led to the examination of how human rights can be used as a tool to combat environmental deterioration. In this respect, three approaches have been considered: (i) the application of substantive environmental human rights, that is the right to a clean and healthy environment; (ii) the utilization of procedural environmental rights that require access to information, participation in policy and decision-making, and access to justice; and (iii) the exercise of communitarian rights including intergenerational environmental rights.

## 4. The Human Right to a Clean Environment

This section will critically analyse the application of the rights to a clean environment (substantive and procedural) in case law and advisory opinions of international and national courts.

### 4.1 The African Commission

As it was noted in the discussion of the ACHPR, "[a]ll peoples shall have the right to a general satisfactory environment favourable to their development". In Article 24. In the *Ogoniland* case, the African Commission on Human and Peoples' Rights (African Commission) considered claims that the Nigerian government had adopted oil development practices leading to environmental degradation.[32] The Commission took the view that States must respect the right to health and should refrain from directly threatening the health and environment of their citizens. Furthermore, States were obliged to adopt measures that would prevent environmental degradation. It concluded that Nigeria, whilst enjoying the right to exploit its natural resources, had breached the human rights of people living in the Ogoni region.[33] Significantly, the Commission

---

[30] "General comment is a treaty body's interpretation of human rights treaty provisions, thematic issues or its methods of work. General comments often seek to clarify the reporting duties of State parties with respect to certain provisions and suggest approaches to implementing treaty provisions." Dag Hammarskjold Library, 'What are General Comments of the Human Rights Treaty Bodies?' (15 September 2021) <https://ask.un.org/faq/135547>.

[31] UN Economic and Social Council, Committee on Economic, Social and Cultural Rights, The right to the highest attainable standard of health, E/C.12/2000/4 (2000) <https://tbinternet.ohchr.org/_layouts/15/treatyb odyexternal/Download.aspx?symbolno=E%2fC.12%2f2000%2f4&Lang=en>.

[32] *Social and Economic Rights Action Centre for Economic and Social Rights v Nigeria*, Case no ACHPR/ COMM/A044/1; Communication 115/96 (*The Ogoniland Case*). See also Dinah Shelton, "Decision Regarding Communication 155/96 (Social and Economic Rights Action Center/Center for Economic and Social Rights v. Nigeria). Case No. ACHPR/COMM/A044/1" (2002) 96 American Journal of International Law *937*; F Fons Coomans, "The Ogoni Case before the African Commission on Human and Peoples' Rights" (2003) 52 International and Comparative Law Quarterly 749.

[33] *The Ogoniland Case*, para 67.

concluded that environmental degradation was not only leading to the violation of other rights but also constituted a human rights violation in itself due to its impact on the quality of life.[34] Whilst this decision confirms the justiciable nature of Article 24, the African Commission's restricted regulatory powers and poor record of compliance with its recommendations limited the practical usefulness of its attempts to remedy environmental degradation in Africa.

It should be noted that no express procedural environmental right exists under the African Charter. However, in the *Ogoniland* case, the African Commission recognized such a right based on the ACPHR, Article 24, which grants a substantive environmental right, and gave it meaningful content by supporting the right of the public to information and its participation in environmental matters.[35] The Commission required States when, for example, engaged in the development of EIAs to involve the public in a manner that adopts the three constitutive rights discussed in this chapter.

## 4.2  Inter-American Court of Human Rights

The Inter-American human rights institutions have limited powers in respect of the right to a clean environment. They may only receive reports from States on their observance of this right, and there is no right to individual applications to the Inter-American Commission on Human Rights (IACommHR) or the Inter-American Court of Human Rights (IACtHR) concerning breaches of the San Salvador Protocol. Nevertheless, in a number of cases involving indigenous rights these institutions have recognized the interlinkage between environmental degradation and human rights.[36] In *Mayagna (Sumo) Awas Tigni Community v Nicaragua*,[37] *Maya Indigenous Communities of Toledo District v Belize*,[38] and *Saramaka People v Suriname*[39] cases, it was stressed that economic development should be consistent with environmental obligations.

Article 11 of the San Salvador Protocol has been a basis for environmental cases. *La Oroya* is an unusual case, not relating to indigenous environmental rights, which constitute the majority of cases alleging the breach of human rights on, *inter alia*, environmental grounds. In the *La Oroya* case (*Community of La Oroya v Peru*),[40] The IACommHR, for the first time, considered the responsibility for the breach of human rights of non-indigenous people due to environmental degradation.[41] It was alleged that Peru had violated the rights of La Oroya inhabitants under both the American Convention on Human Rights (ACHR) and the San Salvador Protocol by not

[34] *The Ogoniland Case*, para 51.
[35] Shelton (n 31) 939.
[36] *Yanomami v Brazil*, IACommHR Res 12/85 (5 March 1985).
[37] IACtHR Ser C No 79 (31 August 2001).
[38] IACommHR Report No 40/04 (12 October 2004).
[39] IACtHR Ser C No 172 (28 November 2007).
[40] ACommHR Report No 76/09 (5 August 2009)).
[41] Paula Spieler, 'La Oroya Case: The Relationship Between Environmental Degradation and Human Rights Violations' (2010) Vol. 18, Issue 1, 19.

preventing environmental damage. In considering the case, the IACommHR granted precautionary measures requiring Peru to provide medical treatment to the said inhabitants who had suffered health problems from contamination from a metallurgical complex. Whilst the IACommHR stressed that the alleged violations of the San Salvador Protocol were outside its competence, it felt nonetheless obliged to take the Protocol into account while interpreting the scope and intent of the American Convention.[42]

Without doubt, the important, if not ground-breaking decision in relation to human right to a clean environment is the 2018 Advisory Opinion of Inter-American Court of Human Rights on the Environment and Human Rights.[43] The opinion was issued following a request by Colombia to clarify the extent of State responsibility for environmental harm under the ACHR, in particular the framework of the Convention for the Protection and Development of Marine Environment of the Wider Caribbean Region and customary international law.[44] The Court reaffirmed the existence of "an undeniable relationship" between human rights and the protection of the environment.[45] Furthermore, it reiterated "the independence and indivisibility of the civil and political rights, and economic social, cultural rights, because they should be understood integrally and comprehensively as human rights".[46] On this basis, the Court elevated the right to a healthy environment under Article 11 of the San Salvador Protocol to a justiciable right by interpreting Article 26 of the ACHR to also include such a right.[47] The Court found support for its position in Member States' constitutions and international instruments.[48] Significantly, the Court accepted that in the case of transboundary pollution, there existed an extraterritorial breach of the human right to a clean environment.[49] Thus, these human rights obligations are capable of being invoked by individuals or groups against a foreign State. This recognition allows for cross-border human rights claims due to transboundary environmental damage.[50] The Advisory Opinion

---

[42] La Oroya (n 39) para 54. "Lastly, the Commission is competent *ratione materiae*, because the petition alleges violations of human rights protected under the American Convention. The Commission notes that the petitioners cited Articles 10 and 11 of the Protocol of San Salvador and Articles 2, 3, 6, 16, and 24 of the Convention on the Rights of the Child. While under Article 29 of the American Convention these provisions can be taken into account in interpreting the scope and intent of the American Convention, the Commission reiterates that it is not competent to render decisions on instruments adopted outside the regional purview of the inter-American system ... As for the Protocol of San Salvador, the Commission reiterates that Article 19.6 of that treaty provides a limited competence clause allowing organs of the inter-American system to render judgments on individual petitions related to the rights enshrined in Articles 8.a and 13 ...." <http://www.cidh.oas.org/annualrep/2009eng/peru1473.06eng.htm>.

[43] Advisory Opinion OC-23/17, IACtHR Ser A No 23 (15 November 2017).

[44] Request for Advisory Opinion OC-23, IACtHR (14 March 2016), see further Maria L Banda, "Inter-American Court of Human Rights Advisory Opinion on the Environment and Human Right" (2018) 22(6) American Society of International Law Insights, <https://www.asil.org/insights/volume/22/issue/6/inter-american-court-human-rights-advisory-opinion-environment-and-human>. Camilo Vega-Barbosa and Lorraine Aboagye, "Human Rights and the Protection of the Environment: The Advisory Opinion of the Inter-American Court of Human Rights" (EJIL: Talk! 2018), <https://www.ejiltalk.org/human-rights-and-the-protection-of-the-environment-the-advisory-opinion-of-the-inter-american-court-of-human-rights/>.

[45] Advisory Opinion OC-23/17, paras 47–55.

[46] Advisory Opinion OC-23/17, para 57.

[47] Advisory Opinion OC-23/17, para 57.

[48] Advisory Opinion OC-23/17, para 57–58.

[49] Banda (n 43).

[50] Monica Feria-Tinta and Simon Milnes, "The Rise of Environment Law in International Dispute Resolution: Inter-American Court of Human Rights Issues Landmark Advisory Opinion on Environment and Human Rights" (EJIL: Talk! 26 February 2018), <https://www.ejiltalk.org/the-rise-of-environmen

is instrumental to the IACHR Judgment in the 2020 *Lhaka Honhat v Argentina*.[51] The Court has applied a direct approach to violations of economic, social, cultural, and environmental rights, thus treating environmental rights as autonomous rights. In an indirect approach, the Court establishes State responsibility for violating of these rights only when it constitutes a breach of related civil and political rights. This was the first time that the Court recognized direct justiciability of a right to a clean environment.[52] However, this judgment is quite contentious, and the judges of the Court were divided regarding direct autonomy and justiciability of such a right (eg based on an argument that under the San Salvador Protocol rights which are derived from Article 26 of the Inter-American Convention on Human Rights are not justiciable). Therefore, there is a possibility that the judgment in this case may be reversed in the future.[53]

## 4.3 The Singularity of the European Court of Human Rights and the Right to a Clean Environment

Although the European Convention on Human Rights and Fundamental Freedoms (ECHR) does not contain a direct substantive environmental human right, the ECtHR has determined a right to a clean and healthy environment emerging out of the civil and political human rights embodied in the ECHR and its Protocols. In particular, the ECtHR has interpreted the protection accorded to rights such as the right to life (ECHR, Article 2), the right to respect for private and family life (ECHR, Article 8), the right to freedom from torture (ECHR, Article 3), and the right to property (ECHR Protocol 1, Article 1) as giving effect to environmental rights. The majority of such decisions have concerned the application of ECHR Article 8, which recognizes limitations of the right to respect for private and family life as necessary in a democratic society. This interference must be relevant and sufficient.[54] In *Powell and Rayner v the United Kingdom*[55] and *Flamenbaum and Others v France*,[56] the ECtHR had to balance the violation of inhabitants' quality of life caused by aircraft using Heathrow and Deauville airports respectively, and the right of the community at large including economic stability. In both cases, the Court decided that the disturbance caused to the applicants' quality of life was necessary for the well-being of the community.[57]

---

tal-law-in-international-dispute-resolution-inter-american-court-of-human-rights-issues-landmark-advisory-opinion-on-environment-and-human-rights/>.

[51] *Lhaka Honhat Association Our Land) v Argentina, Merits, Reparations and Costs, Inter-American Court of Human Rights Court*, Series C No 00 (6 February 2020). See on this Diego Mejia-Lemos, "The Right to a Healthy Environment and its Justiciability before the Inter-American Court of Human Rights: A Critical Appraisal of the *Lhaka Honhat v. Argentina* Judgment" (2022) 320, Review of European, Comparative and International Law 317.
[52] ibid 317.
[53] ibid 323.
[54] *Olsson v Sweden* (No 1) App no 10465/83 (Judgment of 24 March 1988), para 64.
[55] Judgment of 21 February 1990.
[56] App nos 3675/04 and 23264/04 (Judgment of 13 December 2012).
[57] *Powell and Rayner v United Kingdom, Judgment, Merits*, App no 9310/81 (A/172), Case No 3/1989/163/219, [1990] ECHR 2, (1990) 12 EHRR 335 Judgment, paras 41–42) or the economic welfare of the region (*Flamenbaum and others v France*, App nos. 3675/04, 23264/0, Judgment, para 154).

More significant progress was made in the landmark judgment in *López Ostra v Spain* case.[58] The applicant in this case claimed that fumes from a tannery waste treatment plant, which was erected 12 metres from her residence, were seriously affecting her own and her family's quality of life. The Court recognized that environmental pollution, even if it did not cause serious health damage, could have a negative effect on the well-being of the applicant and that it hindered the enjoyment of her private and family life. Consequently, the Court decided that Spain had not achieved a proper balance between the applicant's rights and the economic benefits of the plant.[59]

More recently, in *Cordella v Italy*, the ECtHR considered an alleged violation of Article 8 as a result of exposure to air pollution from a steel plant in Taranto.[60] Attempts by national authorities to decontaminate the polluted region were unsuccessful. The State allowed the steelworks to continue for years, despite scientific reports which concluded that such activities were adversely affecting the health of the region's population and environment. Furthermore, inhabitants of the region remained without any information about the progress of proposed clean-up operations. For these reasons, the Court found there to be a violation of Article 8, as Italy did not take all necessary measures to protect the right to respect for private and family life, thus failing to ensure an appropriate balance between the interests of the applicants and the society as a whole.[61]

The *Hatton* cases (2001 and 2003) are an excellent illustration of the ECtHR's ambivalent and conflicting attitude vis-à-vis the human right to clean environment. These cases concerned night flights to and from Heathrow Airport which, it was argued by the applicants, disturbed their sleep. The UK government had introduced the use of noise quotas in order to minimize the disturbance cause by night flights. The case was first heard by a Chamber of the Court in 2001.[62] Referring to the "fair balance" that must be struck between the competing interests of the individual and the community as a whole, the Chamber admitted that the State enjoyed a certain margin of appreciation in determining the steps to be taken to ensure compliance with the ECHR. The Chamber found that despite the margin of appreciation left to the UK government, the implementation of the noise quota scheme failed to strike a fair balance between the country's economic well-being and the applicants' effective enjoyment of their right to respect for their homes and family lives, therefore violating Article 8 ECHR. The UK government requested the referral of the case to the Grand Chamber. The Grand Chamber stated in no uncertain terms that "there is no explicit right under the Convention to a clean and quiet environment" and that only "where the individual is directly and seriously affected by noise or other pollution" may an issue arise under Article 8.[63] Finding that there was no violation of Article 8, the Grand Chamber reiterated the fundamentally subsidiary role of the Court: national authorities have direct democratic legitimacy and

58 *Lopez Ostra v Spain*, App no 16798/90, A/303-C, [1994] ECHR 46, (1995) 20 EHRR 277, para 58.
59 *Ibid*, Judgment para 58.
60 Cordella and Others v Italy, app. nos. 54414/13 and 54264/15, Judgment of 24 January 2019.
61 Cordella and Others v Italy, app. nos. 54414/13 and 54264/15, Judgment of 24 January 2019, para 174.
62 (2002) 34 EHRR 1.
63 *Case of Hatton and Others v the United Kingdom* (App no 36022/97) Grand Chamber, Judgement, 8 July 2003.

are better placed than an international tribunal to assess local needs and conditions. In matters of general policy, which may involve different opinions contained within a democratic society, the actions of domestic policy-makers to ensure compliance with the ECHR should be given a wide margin of appreciation. A minority of judges appended a powerful joint dissenting opinion.[64] The dissenting judges argued that the "evolutive" interpretation of the ECHR leads to the construction of an environmental human right on the basis of Article 8.[65] They asserted that the European Court has confirmed on several occasions, including in *Lopez Ostra*, that Article 8 embraces the right to a healthy environment:

> The Grand Chamber's judgment in the present case, in so far as it concludes, contrary to the Chamber's judgment of 2 October 2001, that there was no violation of Article 8, seems to us to deviate from the developments in the case-law and even to take a step backwards. It gives precedence to economic considerations over basic health conditions in qualifying the applicants' "sensitivity to noise" as that of a small minority of people (see paragraph 118 of the judgment). The trend of playing down such sensitivity—and more specifically concerns about noise and disturbed sleep—runs counter to the growing concern over environmental issues all over Europe and the world. A simple comparison of the above-mentioned cases (Arrondelle, Baggs and Powell and Rayner) with the present judgment seems to show that the Court is turning against the current.[66]

They felt that, unfortunately, the Grand Chamber's judgement in *Hatton* appeared to deviate from these developments, appearing to take a step backwards, and that the UK government had not sufficiently substantiated the economic importance of Heathrow Airport for the country.

The European Court adopted a very restrictive and deferential view towards the State's position regarding environmental human rights and the possibility of redressing environmental degradation through this means in *Hatton*. The Court took into consideration the fact that the UK government had acted in conformity with national laws concerning night flights. By contrast, in *Lopez Ostra* the authorities had failed to comply with domestic law as there was no licence for the tannery. This view was also confirmed by the Court in *Hardy and Maile v the United Kingdom*.[67]

Furthermore, on several occasions, the Court held that not every case of environmental degradation would lead to a violation of Article 8. In *Fadeyeva v Russia*, the applicant complained about air pollution from a steel plant built in the Soviet era that had been subsequently privatized since that time. The Court established a number of

---

[64] *Case of Hatton and Others v the United Kingdom* (App no 36022/97) Grand Chamber, Judgment, 8 July 2003, Joint Dissenting Opinion of Judges Costa, Ress, Türmen, Zupančič, and Steiner.
[65] Joint Dissenting Opinion, para 2.
[66] *Case of Hatton and Others v the United Kingdom* (Application no 36022/97) Grand Chamber, Judgement, 8 July 2003, Joint Dissenting Opinion, para 5.
[67] App no 31965/07 (Judgment of 14 February 2012) (paras 218, 231–232).

requirements for pollution to cause a violation under Article 8. First, it was necessary for the harmful effects of pollution to affect the applicant's home, family, or private life directly. Second, the adverse effects must have reached a certain minimum level, which is not a general level but depends on the relevant circumstances of the case such as intensity and duration of the nuisance. The Court found that the emissions had a detrimental effect on the applicant's health and enjoyment of her home. It stated that the combined negative effects were at a level that was prohibited under Article 8. The failure of the State to provide the applicant with an effective solution constituted a violation of Article 8.[68]

As already mentioned, the ECtHR also considered environmental degradation in the light of the right to life protected under ECHR Article 2. In *Öneryildiz v Turkey*,[69] *Budayeva and Others v Russia*,[70] and *Kolyadenko and Others v Russia*,[71] the Court decided that there was gross negligence attributable to the State resulting in the loss of life from environmental degradation. In all three cases, it concluded that the State had failed to protect the right to life, and held that activities which caused environmental degradation, with potentially lethal effects, should be regulated to ensure the protection of the lives of citizens, including ensuring the public's right to information. Furthermore, the ECtHR required that the States undertake appropriate procedures to identify the level of shortcomings. The Court found that there was an overlap between the positive obligations under Article 2 and those discussed under Article 8 of the ECHR. In *Budayeva*, the State's positive obligations under the Convention were dependent on the origin of the disaster and whether the risks could be mitigated. The Court continued that where the infringement under Article 2 was not caused intentionally, the positive obligation to provide an effective judicial inquiry did not always require criminal action. It may be sufficient to have impartial civil administrative or disciplinary remedies.

In the cases already reviewed, it would appear that despite the omission of environmental rights in the ECHR, the ECtHR has acted in a manner that combats environmental degradation through other human rights protected under the Convention. Nevertheless, in the light of the numerous requirements imposed to satisfy a violation through environmental degradation, it is not unreasonable to state that environmental rights per se are not protected under the Convention unless there is a violation of the rights of individuals.

The ECtHR had also supported in its case law the so-called procedural right to a clean environment. As already stated, the peculiarity of the ECHR is that it does not list the right to a clean environment in its catalogue of protected human rights. However, it has adopted indirect procedural environmental rights based on the ECHR Articles 8 and 10. To a large extent, the jurisprudence of the Court supports the approach taken

---

[68] *Fadeyeva v Russian Federation, Judgment, Merits and Just Satisfaction*, App no 55723/00, ECHR 2005-IV, [2005] ECHR 376, (2007) 45 EHRR 10, para 133 of the Judgment.

[69] App no 48939/99 (Judgment (GC) of 30 November 2004).

[70] App nos 15339/02, 21166/02, 20058/02, 11673/02, and 15343/02 (Judgment of 20 March 2008).

[71] *Kolyadenko and Others v Russia*, App nos 17423/05, 20534/05, 20678/05, 23263/05, 24283/05, and 35673 (Judgment of 28 February 2012).

under the Aarhus Convention.[72] In number of decisions, the Court emphasized the duty of the State to provide access to environmental information as well as environmental procedures which are required to initiate projects, such as EIAs.[73] In the *Guerra* case, for example, the ECtHR held that providing relevant information to the applicants who lived in the vicinity of a factory could have a bearing on the rights protected under Article 8 which includes the protection of private and family life. Furthermore, the Court held that ECHR Article 10, protecting the freedom of expression, prohibits a State from restricting a person from receiving information which others wish to give.[74] It should however be noted that the ECtHR's approach was restricted, and it cannot be construed as imposing on a State a positive obligation to collect and disseminate information on its own accord.

In several cases, the ECtHR has considered that "whilst Article 8 contains no explicit procedural requirements, the decision-making process leading to measures of interference must be fair and such as to afford due respect for the interests of the individual as safeguarded by Article 8".[75] The participation of those affected by environmental issues is necessary in order to comply with ECHR Article 8 and the Aarhus Convention Article 6.[76] The rights of information and participation guaranteed by the Aarhus Convention were explicitly recognized by the ECtHR in *Tătar*. The Court decided that prohibiting interested persons from obtaining information and participating in environmental decision-making would breach such rights. However, it considered this right of participation to be available only to those persons whose rights have been affected and not to the general public.[77]

## 5. Environmental Communitarian Interests Including Intergenerational Rights

The general duty to undertake sustainable development implies recognizing communitarian rights including the rights of future generations. This suggests that the enjoyment of a clean environment should take into account the interests of future generations. As held by the Indian Supreme Court in the 1996 *S. Jagannath v Union of India* judgment, "[s]ome of the salient principles of 'Sustainable Development' ... [include] Inter-Generational Equity".[78] Whilst the environmental rights of future generations continue to attract growing recognition, their effective protection is problematic due to the controversy that surrounds their *locus standi*.

---

[72] For example, in the cases *Affaire Tatar v Roumanie*, Requête no 67021/01 27 January 2009, 67021/01.
[73] *Guerra and Others v Italy*, App no 116/1996/735/932 (Judgment (GC) of 19 February 1998); *Taşkin and Others v Turkey*, App no 46117/99 (Judgment of 10 November 2004); *Giacomelli v Italy*, app. no. 59909/00 (Judgment of 2 November 2006); *Budayeva, Tătar v Romania*, App no 67021/01 (Judgment of 27 January 2009).
[74] *Guerra and Others v Italy*, para 53.
[75] *Taşkin and Others v Turkey*, para 118; *Giacomelli*, details para 82.
[76] Alan Boyle, "Human Rights or Environmental Rights? A Reassessment" (2007) 47 Fordham Environmental Law Review 471, 496.
[77] *Budayeva, Tătar v Romania*, para 97.
[78] *S. Jagannath v Union of India AIR 1997 SC 811* (11 December 1996).

In recent years, the right of standing to protect environmental communitarian interests has been recognized by international and domestic courts. In the *Whaling in the Antarctic (Australia v Japan: New Zealand intervening)* judgment, the ICJ did not elaborate on the community interest standing, however in its pleadings, Australia invoked Japan's responsibility *erga omnes partes*.[79]

The International Tribunal for the Law of the Sea (ITLOS), in its Advisory Opinion on *Responsibilities and Obligations of States Sponsoring Persons and Entities with Respect to Activities in the Area*, examined the communitarian interests in the International Seabed Area (the Area) and its resources, declared under Article 136 of the 1982 United Nations Convention on the Law of the Sea (UNCLOS, the Convention) to be the common heritage of mankind, and which cannot be appropriated or owned by any State or person.[80] The Convention vests all rights in the resources of the Area in humankind as a whole, and authorizes the International Seabed Authority (ISA) to act on behalf of humankind. This doctrine of communitarian interests is relevant in ensuring no damage is done to the Area, its resources, and the maritime environment. The Advisory Opinion held that on the basis of Article 137, the ISA acting on behalf of humankind may be entitled to redress for damage. The Advisory Opinion referred to Article 48 of the International Law Commission Draft Articles on State Responsibility, where every State party may bring a claim for compensation in the light of the *erga omnes* obligation to preserve the environment of the high seas. This opinion augurs well for the protection of communitarian interests, including intergenerational rights. As it was observed in this connection:

> The Chamber's statement may be read as treating all states—whether parties to the LOSC or not—as rights holders under a customary law theory that the marine environment and the Area are the heritage of all humankind. Even if an individualized interest in the resources that might be damaged were necessary, a substantial number of states would be potential rights holders. An argument that is consistent with the position that even non-LOSC parties might be claimants is based on the fact that the LOSC is considered to be a codification of customary international law. Note, however, that some consider both the common heritage element of the Law of the Sea Convention and the ILC Draft Articles' article 48 to be progressive rather than customary law.[81]

---

[79] Whaling in the Antarctic (*Australia v Japan: New Zealand intervening*), Judgment, ICJ Reports 2014, p 226. See James Crawford, "Responsibility for Breaches of Communitarian Norms: An Appraisal of Article 48 of the ILC Articles on State Responsibility for Internationally Wrongful Acts" in Ulirich Fastenrath and others (eds), *From Bilateralism to Community Interest: Essays in Honour of Judge Bruno Simma* (Oxford University Press 2011) 236; James Crawford, *State Responsibility: The General Part* (Cambridge University Press 2013) 373, 362–94.

[80] LOSCC, Article 137.

[81] Cymie Payne, "Collective Responsibility for Sound Resource Management: *Erga Omnes* Obligations and Deep Sea Mining" in *Environmental Rule of Law: Trends from the Americas* (Organization of American States 2015) 116.

Furthermore, although the ECtHR in the majority of cases only grants legal standing to directly injured persons, it is interesting to note that in *Ranstev v Cyprus and Russia* the Court held that

> [a]lthough the primary purpose of the Convention system is to provide individual relief, its mission is also to determine issue on public policy grounds in the common interest, thereby raising the general standards of protection of human rights and extending human rights jurisprudence throughout the community of the Convention States.[82]

The theory of intergenerational equity was introduced by Edith Brown-Weiss in her seminal book, *In Fairness to Future Generations*.[83] In broad brushstrokes, her theory is based on various cultures and philosophical theories such as of John Rawls' theory of intergenerational justice. The main premise of her theory is that each generation holds the planet and its natural and cultural resources on trust for future generations (each generation is both a trustee of the earth for future generations and a beneficiary of the trust settled by previous generations).

However, the lack of consensus on the standing regarding communitarian interests in both national and especially international judicial systems creates problems in the efforts to protect intergenerational rights. A stronger recognition, albeit a patchy one, of intergenerational rights is found in national jurisprudence. Two relevant cases are the *Minors Oposa* and *Farooque* cases, which recognized the standing of communitarian interests and their linkage with intergenerational equity. In the *Minors Oposa* case, a group of children together with an NGO took legal action to halt the destruction of the rainforest. The children claimed that they represented themselves and generations yet unborn. Standing was allowed in so far as "every generation has a responsibility to the next to preserve ... the full enjoyment of a balanced and healthful ecology".[84] The Court stated:

> Needless to say, every generation has a responsibility to the next to preserve that rhythm and harmony for the full enjoyment of a balanced and healthful ecology. Put a little differently, the minors' assertion of their right to a sound environment constitutes, at the same time, the performance of their obligation to ensure the protection of that right for the generations to come ...
>
> While the right to a balanced and healthful ecology is to be found under the Declaration of Principles and State Policies and not under the Bill of Rights, it does not follow that it is less important than any of the civil and political rights enumerated in the latter. Such a right belongs to a different category of rights altogether for

---

[82] *Ranstev v Cyprus and Russia*, App no 25965/04, Judgment 7 January 2010.
[83] Edith Brown-Weiss, *In Fairness to Future Generations: International Law, Common Patrimony, and Intergenerational Equity* (United Nations University 1989).
[84] The Philippines: Supreme Court Decision in *Minors Oposa v Secretary of the Department of Environment and Natural Resources (DENR)*, 39 July 1993, 33 ILM 173, 194.

it concerns nothing less than self-preservation and self-perpetuation—aptly and fittingly stressed by the petitioners—the advancement of which may even be said to predate all governments and constitutions. As a matter of fact, these basic rights need not even be written in the Constitution for they are assumed to exist from the inception of humankind. If they are now explicitly mentioned in the fundamental charter, it is because of the well-founded fear of its framers that unless the rights to a balanced and healthful ecology and to health are mandated as state policies by the Constitution itself, thereby highlighting their continuing importance and imposing upon the state a solemn obligation to preserve the first and protect and advance the second, the day would not be too far when all else would be lost not only for the present generation, but also for those to come—generations which stand to inherit nothing but parched earth incapable of sustaining life.[85]

This recognition is not without critics. Lowe suggests that the *Minors Oposa* judgment enforces not the right of future generations but the duty of present generations.[86] Another question which was raised is the *locus standi* in such cases. Judge Feliciano in his Separate Opinion stated:

The Court explicitly states that petitioners have the *locus standi* necessary to sustain the bringing and, maintenance of this suit (Decision, pp. 11–12). *Locus standi* is not a function of petitioners' claim that their suit is properly regarded as a class suit. I understand *locus standi* to refer to the legal interest which a plaintiff must have in the subject matter of the suit. Because of the very broadness of the concept of "class" here involved—membership in this "class" appears to embrace everyone living in the country whether now or in the future—it appears to me that everyone who may be expected to benefit from the course of action petitioners seek to require public respondents to take, is vested with the necessary locus standi. The Court may be seen therefore to be recognizing a beneficiaries' right of action in the field of environmental protection, as against both the public administrative agency directly concerned and the private persons or entities operating in the field or sector of activity involved. Whether such beneficiaries' right of action may be found under any and all circumstances, or whether some failure to act, in the first instance, on the part of the governmental agency concerned must be shown ("prior exhaustion of administrative remedies"), is not discussed in the decision and presumably is left for future determination in an appropriate case.[87]

In the *Farooque* case, the legal question involved the standing of an NGO to challenge actions which violated the law on environmental protection. In this case, one of the

---

[85] *Minors Oposa*, 295.

[86] Vaughan Lowe, "Sustainable Development and Unsustainable Arguments" in Alan Boyle and David Freestone (eds), *International Law and Sustainable Development: Past Achievements and Future Challenges* (Oxford University Press 1999) 27.

[87] Judge Feliciano, Separate Opinion, *Minors Oposa*, 200–06.

judges stated that although a personal injury is a condition for legal standing, such a principle should not apply in the case of public injuries.[88]

In the *People United for Better Living in Calcutta v State of West Bengal*[89] case, intergenerational equity was taken into account. The Court held that "[t]he present day society has a responsibility towards the posterity ... to breathe normally and live in a cleaner environment".[90] In the *S. Jagannath* case, the Indian Supreme Court had "no hesitation in holding that Sustainable Development ... has been accepted as part of customary international law, thereby recognising the rights of future generations".[91]

In 2018, the Supreme Court of Colombia recognized the legal rights of the Amazon river ecosystem and ordered the creation of a "Intergenerational Pact for the Life of the Colombian Amazon" with the participation of the plaintiffs and NGOs who had complained that the government's failure to control deforestation violated their rights to life, to health, and to enjoy a healthy environment.[92] A similar approach was adopted in New Zealand legislation where the Whanganui River, sacred to the indigenous Maori people, was considered to be legal person, thereby according it the right to sue and be sued by appointed guardians.[93]

It is interesting to note that Maltese legislation specifically protects intergenerational and intragenerational sustainable development in Malta.[94] For this purpose, it established the position of a guardian of future generations, who is given the mandate to, *inter alia*: (i) propose goals and actions to government entities for them to take up in order to contribute towards the goal of sustainable development; (ii) consider requests from the public as to policy matters which can positively contribute to sustainable development; (iii) to request any government entity to provide data or information or to collect data or information about any topic that could have a bearing on sustainable development; and (iv) foster sustainable development principles and actions across Maltese society.

In the 2019 Dutch Supreme Court judgment, *The State of the Netherlands (Ministry of Economic Affairs and Climate Policy) v Stichting Urgenda*,[95] the court held that on the basis of the ECHR, the government had a positive obligation to take measures for the prevention of climate change and that it had to reduce its greenhouse emissions to internationally accepted standards. This judgment, although dealing with the protection of the inhabitants of the Netherlands, reflects the interests of future generations

---

[88] *Dr Mohiuddin Farooque v Government of Bangladesh (Radioactive Milk Case)* 48 BLD (HDC) (1996) 438.

[89] *People United for Better Living in Calcutta v State of West Bengal* AIR 1993 Cal 215, 97 CWN 142.

[90] *People United for Better Living in Calcutta*, para 2.

[91] Te Awa Tupua (Whanganui River Claims Settlement) Act of 2017, Articles 14–15.

[92] Nicholas Bryner, "Colombian Supreme Court Recognizes Rights of the Amazon River Ecosystem", 20 April 2018, International Union for Conservation of Nature.

[93] Te Awa Tupua (Whanganui River Claims Settlement) Bill < https://www.legislation.govt.nz/bill/government/2016/0129/latest/DLM6830851.html?src=qs>.

[94] Sustainable Development Act, Chapter 521 of the Laws of Malta, Article 8; and Sustainable Development Act, Article 8(4).

[95] Supreme Court of the Netherlands, Civil Division, 20 December 2019 No 19/00; see André Nollkaemper and Laura Burgers, "A New Classic in Climate Change Litigation: The Dutch Supreme Court Decision in the Urgenda Case" (EJIL: Talk! 6 January 2020) <https://www.ejiltalk.org/a-new-classic-in-climate-change-litigation-the-dutch-supreme-court-decision-in-the-urgenda-case/>.

in enjoying a healthy climate, and recognizes communitarian interests as the actions of the Netherlands also causes harm beyond its boundaries. A similar approach was taken by the UK Court of Appeal (Civil Division) ruling in *R (Friends of the Earth Ltd) v Secretary of State for Transport*, where it reversed a previous High Court decision which held that a national policy supporting an expansion of Heathrow Airport was lawful.[96] The Appellate Court considered that the policy failed to take into account the impacts of climate change on future generations, as well the UK government's international obligations to reduce carbon emissions under the Paris Agreement.[97] Ultimately, however, this decision was itself overturned by the UK Supreme Court.[98]

There are other numerous contemporary examples of the principle of international equity serving communitarian interests. A very important case was a 2020 decision of Constitutional Court of Hungary which annulled many of the 2017 amendments to the 2009 Hungarian Act on the Forest, Forest Protection and Forest Management, on the grounds that they violated the Fundamental Law of Hungary which refers to the obligation to preserve the country's natural resources and cultural artefacts for the benefit of future generations. The Court observed that the State manages common heritage as the trustee for future generations. This case was brought before the Constitutional Court by the Hungarian Ombudsman for Future Generations.[99] Environmental courts and tribunals, which are separate from standard judicial bodies, fulfil a very significant role in the promotion of intergenerational equity (as of 2016, forty-four countries had 1,200 environmental courts and tribunals).[100] The national position of the Ombudsman for future generations is also instrumental for serving communitarian (intergenerational) interests as they have very often a *locus standi* to bring a case before the courts in the name of future generations and also review draft legislation from the point of view of their interests.[101] Interests of future generations were also proposed to be safeguarded at the forum of United Nations. For example, in 2013, the Secretary-General of the United Nations submitted a report on the need for promoting intergenerational solidarity for the achievement of sustainable development, taking into account the needs of the future generations.[102]

That said, there is as yet no uniform recognition of the direct standing of future (unborn) generations.

---

[96] *R (Friends of the Earth Ltd) v Secretary of State for Transport* [2020] EWCA Civ 214.
[97] *R (Friends of the Earth Ltd) v Secretary of State for Transport* [2020] EWCA Civ 214, paras 222–238 and 242–261.
[98] *R (Friends of the Earth Ltd) v Heathrow Airport Ltd* [2020] UKSC 52.
[99] Edith Brown-Weiss, "Intergenerational Equity", *Max Planck Encyclopaedia of Public International Law*, para 42.
[100] ibid para 47.
[101] Such as the 2014 Constitution of Tunisia created the Authority for Sustainable Development and the Rights of Future Generations, an independent constitutional institution (art 129). Brown-Weiss, "Intergenerational Equity" (n 95) para. 50.
[102] Intergenerational Solidarity and the Needs of Future Generations—Report of the Secretary-General, 68th sess, Agenda Item 19, UN Doc A/68/322 (15 August 2013).

## 6. Evaluation and Trends: Substantive and Procedural Environmental Human Rights to a Clean Environment

The human rights approach to environmental degradation is twofold: (i) substantive and (ii) procedural. With respect to the former, there are some international treaties that refer to substantive rights, such as the African Charter and the San Salvador Protocol. However, their use is limited, and at best regional. The omission of such rights in the ECHR has led the Court to deal with environmental human rights through the lens of protection of other rights which are explicitly established under the Convention. However, the levels imposed by the Court in order to fulfil an "environmental claim" provide a challenge. The ECtHR essentially relies on human rights protected by the ECHR being violated rather than on environmental human rights per se.

Furthermore, there is evidence that when a specific environmental human right is inserted in an instrument it alienates State support, which does not augur well. However, it is debatable in light of present developments evidenced by the 2018 Advisory Opinion of the Inter-American Court of Human Rights whether a negative academic approach to the use of substantive environmental human rights still holds.[103] Some authors believe that the relationship between human rights and environmental protection is far from certain and point towards the *lacunae* or ambiguous language used with respect to a right to a clean environment.[104] Despite certain ambiguities in the case law of the ECtHR, there has been a consistent acknowledgement of the existence of a substantive and procedural right to a clean environment. The relevant provisions of the human rights treaties have been invoked in the proceedings before the international courts and tribunals. The ECtHR merits a separate approach concerning its jurisprudence in the sphere of the synergy between human rights and the environment as it is not based on a specific right to a clean environment in the ECHR (in contrast to the ACHR and the San Salvador Protocol) but is derived from other rights on the basis of evolutionary interpretation of the provisions of the Convention, a process which is notoriously uncertain.

Others argue that there is no intrinsic right of the environment itself for protection.[105] In this area, there has been also marked progress, evidenced by rights accorded to rivers and forests.

That said, it cannot be denied that the right to a clean environment remains largely orientated towards the individual, rather than to States or generations. Despite some significant progress in the utilization of substantive environmental human rights to

---

[103] Gunther Handl, "Human Rights and Protection of the Environment" in Asbjørn Eide and others (eds), *Economic, Social and Cultural Rights* (Kluwer Law International 2001); Gunther Handl, "Human Rights and the Protection of the Environment: A Mildly 'Revisionist' View" in Cançado Trindade (ed), *Human Rights, Sustainable Development and the Environment* (Instituto Interamericano de Derechos 1992); Alan Boyle, "The Role of Human Rights in the Protection of the Environment" in Alan Boyle and Michael Anderson (eds), *Human Rights Approaches to Environmental Protection* (Oxford University Press 1996); Catherine Redgwell, "Life, Universe and Everything: A Critique of Anthropocentric Rights" in Boyle and Anderson (ibid).

[104] Handl, "Human Rights and Protection of the Environment" (n 99) 9.

[105] Boyle, "The Role of Human Rights in the Protection of the Environment" (n 99) 53; Handl, "Human Rights and the Protection of the Environment" (n 99) 138; Redgwell (n 99) 71.

combat environmental degradation, their use has considerable limitations. These difficulties have led to the suggestion that environmental degradation could be better com-
batted through procedural human rights provisions. The three principal rights are: (i)
the right to information; (ii) the right to participate in decision-making; and (iii) the
right of access to justice. These have attracted widespread support and appear to have
had a catalytic role in promoting a better understanding and acceptance of environmental human rights. Nevertheless, it should be recorded that with respect to the right
of access to justice in protecting intergenerational environmental rights, whilst there
are positive developments, particularly in domestic courts, these rights' standing remains problematic.

There is a growing body of case law concerning the so-called participatory human
right to a clean environment.[106] Thus, for example, the right to obtain environmental
information and the participation in environmental decision-taking enjoy widespread
acceptance. In fact, these rights appear to attract growing support, even in organizations that may not have been environmentally sensitive, such as international development banks.[107] The use of procedural environmental rights, however, often meets with
formidable challenges from development and economic interests. Furthermore, such
participatory rights in order to be effective must be accompanied by the right of access
to justice. With regard to procedural environmental human rights, although a number
of such rights can be used to protect communitarian interests, including intergenerational rights, in combatting environmental degradation, it would appear that there is
still much progress to be done with respect to the communitarian right to justice. Such
a right is embodied in the notion of the EIA,[108] which is based on the rights to information and participation. The EIA was a subject of several pronouncements by the ICJ
in the *Pulp Mills*[109] and the *Nicaragua v Costa Rica; Costa Rica v Nicaragua* cases[110],
and the 2011 Advisory Opinion of the ITLOS[111]. In the *Pulp Mills* case,[112] the ICJ established that an EIA now is considered a requirement under general international
law "where there is a risk that the proposed industrial activity may have a significant
adverse impact in a transboundary context, in particular, on a shared resource".[113] In

---

[106] Boyle, "Human Rights or Environmental Rights?" (n 75) 50405.
[107] Alvaro Mendez and David Patrick Houghton, "Sustainable Banking: The Role of Multilateral Development Banks as Norm Entrepreneurs" (2020) 12 Sustainability 1.
[108] See on EIA in general, Stephen Tromans QC, *Environmental Impact Assessment* (2nd edn, Bloomsbury Professional 2012).
[109] *Pulp Mills on the River Uruguay (Argentina v Uruguay)*, Judgment, ICJ Reports 2010, 14
[110] *Certain Activities Carried Out by Nicaragua in the Border Area (Costa Rica v Nicaragua) and Construction of a Road in Costa Rica along the San Juan River (Nicaragua v Costa Rica)*, Judgment, ICJ Reports 2015, 665.
[111] International Tribunal for the Law of the Sea, 'Responsibilities and obligations of States sponsoring persons and entities with respect to activities in the Area', Advisory Opinion of 1 February 2011
[112] See Cymie Payne, "Environmental Impact Assessment as a Duty under International Law: The International Court of Justice Judgment on Pulp Mills on the River Uruguay" (2010) 1 European Journal of Risk Regulation 317–24.
[113] *Pulp Mills* case (n 105), para 204 ("practice, which in recent years has gained so much acceptance among States that it may now be considered a requirement under general international law to undertake an environmental impact assessment where there is a risk that the proposed industrial activity may have a significant adverse impact in a transboundary context, in particular, on a shared resource. Moreover, due diligence, and the duty of vigilance and prevention which it implies, would not be considered to have been exercised, if a party planning works liable to affect the régime of the river or the quality of its waters did not undertake an environmental impact assessment on the potential effects of such works.").

the *Nicaragua/Costa Rica* cases, the ICJ elaborated on the scope and trigger of the ob-ligation to carry out an EIA and noted its link with the obligations of due diligence and to notify and consult; it also stressed the importance of scientific evidence in the settlement of disputes concerning environmental matters.[114] The Court distinguished between the procedural obligations to carry out an EIA, referring to the *Pulp Mills* case, and the obligation to notify and consult. The ICJ has introduced a threefold test. The State alleging a breach had first, to satisfy the Court that there was a risk of significant negative transboundary environmental effects by carrying out a "preliminary assess-ment"; that subject to the existence of such a risk, an EIA had been carried out; and depending on the completion of the second stage in the second, that the affected State be notified and consulted in relation to any potential harm as identified.[115] The ITLOS in its Advisory Opinion has observed that

> [t]he Court's reasoning in a transboundary context may also apply to activities with an impact on the environment in an area beyond the limits of national jurisdiction; and the Court's references to "shared resources" may also apply to resources that are the common heritage of mankind. Thus, in light of the customary rule mentioned by the ICJ, it may be considered that environmental impact assessments should be in-cluded in the system of consultations and prior notifications set out in article 142 of the Convention with respect to "resource deposits in the Area which lie across limits of national jurisdiction".[116]

In the South China Sea Arbitration, the question of the EIA was also raised.[117]

## 7. Conclusion

The great threats to the human person arising out of environmental degradation make it necessary to consider human rights as a tool to protect the individual. Notwithstanding recent very encouraging and exciting developments, it would appear that to some extent there is a lack of global consensus in relation to the content of the substantive and pro-cedural rights to a clean environment. The question may be asked whether the jurispru-dence of international courts and tribunals has contributed to a better understanding of their content and to furthering environment well-being for an individual. As al-ready analysed, the case law in relation to human rights and the environment is based on regional human rights conventions and consequently on the practice of regional human rights courts. Furthermore, in the case of environmental rights that derive from

---

[114] See on this a Special Issue of Questions of International Law (2017) 42.

[115] Simon Marsden, "Determining Significance for EIA in International Environmental Law" (2017) 42 Questions of International Law 5–12.

[116] ITLOS Advisory Opinion, para 148.

[117] Yoshifumi Tanaka, "The South China Sea Arbitration: Environmental Obligations under the Law of the Sea Convention" (2018) 27 Review of European, Comparative and International Law 90.

existing human rights, whilst their application is feasible as demonstrated by the juris-prudence of the ECtHR, these environmental rights are limited to individuals who have suffered direct harm and are restricted by States' a considerable margin of appreciation. Therefore, it may be suggested that the jurisprudence of international courts and tribu-nals in this respect is fragmented. However, the 2018 Advisory Opinion appears to have had a global impact on human rights and the environment, thus evidencing that it is possible that regional case law can acquire a global dimension.

Finally, it may be said that progress has been made by relying on procedural envir-onmental human rights, which now enjoy wider support than in the past. However, the precise legal nature of the EIA as an example of such a procedural human right is still to be fully established. So far, the ICJ has adopted quite a narrow approach to the defining of its content. In the *Pulp Mills* case, it stated that general international law does not "specify the scope and content of an environmental impact assessment".[118] Its judgment in the *Nicaragua/Costa Rica* cases was also criticized for missing the opportunity to analyse in-depth the legal character of the EIA and generally being quite muddled.[119]

That said, it is incontrovertible that international courts and tribunals have continu-ously and progressively contributed to the development of environmental protection of an individual through human rights (substantive and procedural), even if this process is still evolving, and is, in some aspects, still debatable (as evidenced by *Lhaka Honhat v Argetina* case).

---

[118] ITLOS Advisory Opinion (n 110) para 205.
[119] Marsden (n 109) 7–9.

# 25

# From Delegation to Prescription

## Interpretive Authority in International Investment Agreements

*Jeremy K Sharpe*

## 1. Introduction

International investment agreements (IIAs) traditionally have delegated broad authority to arbitral tribunals to interpret and apply open-textured provisions. In recent decades, arbitrators have helped transform amorphous treaty provisions into concrete rules through adjudication of hundreds of investment treaty disputes. Arbitrating parties and tribunals routinely invoke such "precedents", solidifying their legal status over time.

In some quarters this was precisely the idea. When IIAs were first developed, international investment law was uncertain and contested. The mechanisms for resolving international investment disputes—primarily diplomatic protection—were considered inadequate and ineffective. Many capital-exporting states hoped that IIAs would strengthen the customary international law of foreign investment and, for some perhaps, promote an international common law of investment protection.[1] The rapid growth of investment treaty arbitration in recent years has spurred this development. Today, there truly is an emerging common law of international investment, increasingly based on arbitration awards, decisions, and procedural orders.

But have states delegated too much authority to arbitral tribunals? For many states, the answer is clear. Virtually all new IIAs reflect state efforts to assert greater control over international investment law and arbitration.[2] States are defining key treaty protections, clarifying their meaning and scope. States are preserving greater regulatory discretion, including by exempting from arbitration certain core government activities such as tax or monetary policy. And states are promoting greater coherence in investment treaty arbitration, including by expressly authorizing non-disputing party submissions and binding interpretations by treaty parties. Such reforms—aimed at

---

[1] See eg Committee on Foreign Relations, Convention on the Settlement of Investment Disputes, S. Exec. Rep't No 2 (2d Sess. 1966), reprinted in (1966) 5 ILM 646, 657 (discussing with State Department legal adviser the ICSID Convention as "a step in the direction really of building up the common law of international law, which is so sorely needed in the whole field of international law"); RY Jennings, "State Contracts in International Law" (1961) 37 British Yearbook of International Law 156 (arguing that the "great need of elaboration" of the international law of state contracts could "best be accomplished by its application to concrete cases by arbitral tribunals").

[2] For convenience, the term "states" here includes other actors engaged in treaty-making, such as the European Union.

Jeremy K Sharpe, *From Delegation to Prescription* In: *By Peaceful Means*. Edited by: Charles N Brower, Joan E Donoghue, Cian C Murphy, Cymie R Payne and Esmé R Shirlow, Oxford University Press. © Jeremy K Sharpe 2024. DOI: 10.1093/oso/9780192848086.003.0025

improving consistency, correctness, and legitimacy in investment treaty arbitration[3]—invariably constrain arbitral authority.

A further development is less noted but no less significant. States are using drafting techniques to provide guidance for the interpretation of their treaties. These include:

- Interpretive guidelines, which tell tribunals how to interpret important treaty provisions, such as indirect expropriation, national treatment, and fair and equitable treatment (FET);
- Interpretive clarifications, which provide "greater certainty" on the meaning of investment protections in new treaties and interpretive gloss on existing treaties;
- Interpretive indicators, which may tilt the interpretive balance toward the drafting states' policy preferences, such as environmental protection; and
- Interpretive markers, which record in the *travaux préparatoires* states' preferred treaty interpretations, such as the scope of most-favoured-nation (MFN) treatment.

This chapter explores the emergence, development, and increasing importance of these four techniques in contemporary IIAs, showing how they may curtail arbitrators' interpretive discretion, influence the interpretation of prior investment treaties, and even alter the outcome of arbitral cases. These techniques starkly illustrate the move from a traditional "delegation" model of IIAs to a more "prescriptive" model. Given their increasing use, these techniques are likely to significantly affect the development of international investment law and arbitration for years to come.

## 2. Drafting Techniques for Guiding the Interpretation of IIAs

### 2.1 Interpretive Guidelines

Many newer IIAs contain interpretive guidelines. Guidelines promote the correct interpretation of a rule rather than change its content. The United States was an early adopter of such guidelines, and many other states followed suit. In the early 2000s, the US government began introducing guidelines in IIAs in response to claims against the United States under the investment chapter of the North American Free Trade Agreement (NAFTA).[4] In 2002, the US Congress instructed US trade negotiators to

---

[3] See eg United Nations Commission on International Trade Law, Note by Secretariat, *Possible reform of investor–State (ISDS): Interpretation of investment treaties by treaty Parties* (17 January 2020).

[4] Earlier examples may be found in the Energy Charter Treaty, which the United States helped negotiate but did not sign. The ECT contains, for instance, an "understanding" to help interpreters determine whether an investment is "controlled" by a covered investor. The ECT's understanding has guided tribunals' interpretation of "control" not only in relation to the definition in of "investment", in Article 1(6), but also to other provisions of the treaty. Indeed, the understanding has influenced the interpretation of control in other treaties not containing the understanding. See eg *International Thunderbird Gaming Corp. v United Mexican States*, Award (26 January

conclude free trade agreements (FTAs) that accord no greater substantive rights to foreign investors than are accorded to US investors under US law.[5] Acknowledging the difficulty of defining fixed rules, Congress requested the development of guidelines for use by arbitral tribunals. Such guidelines were to be "consistent with United States legal principles and practice"[6] and draw on "U.S. case law interpreting the relevant legal principles".[7] The guidelines formulated by US negotiators and developed by other states have significantly contributed to the development of international investment law and arbitration. The importance of such guidelines is evident in three bedrock investment treaty protections: expropriation, non-discrimination, and FET.

## 2.1.1 Expropriation

Most IIAs require contracting states to pay compensation when expropriating investments, including through measures equivalent to a direct expropriation. States, however, ordinarily are not required to compensate foreign investors for financial harm caused by non-discriminatory regulatory measures of general application. In practice, it often can be difficult to distinguish an indirect expropriation from a non-compensable regulatory measure. In recent years US IIAs have provided guidance to help draw that line. In particular, US negotiators have borrowed from the US Supreme Court's decision in *Penn Central v New York City*, which identified three factors of particular significance for determining a "regulatory taking" under the US Constitution:

(1) The economic impact of the regulation on the claimant;
(2) The extent of interference with the claimant's reasonable investment-backed expectations; and
(3) The character of the government action.[8]

The *Penn Central* factors have since found their way, wholly or partly, into scores of treaties and model treaties, including many not involving the United States.[9] Arbitrating parties and tribunals, moreover, routinely invoke the *Penn Central* factors,[10] including in cases decided under treaties not containing the clarifying language.[11]

---

2006) para 106, note 3 (citing ECT understanding for the proposition that "a showing of effective or 'de facto' control is ... sufficient for the purpose of Article 1117 of the NAFTA").

  [5] The US government applies these same directives when negotiating bilateral investment treaties (BITs), "ensuring greater consistency with US FTAs and broad congressional support for the US BIT programme". Lee M Caplan and Jeremy K Sharpe, 'United States' in Chester Brown (ed), *Commentaries on Selected Model Investment Treaties* (Oxford University Press 2013) 755, 756.
  [6] Trade Act of 2002, Pub L 107–210 (107th Cong, 2d Sess) s 2102(b)(3).
  [7] S Rep 107–139 (107th Cong, 2d Sess) (2002).
  [8] *Penn Central Transportation Co. v New York City*, [1978] 438 US 104, 124.
  [9] See UNCTAD International Investment Agreements Navigator, <https://investmentpolicy.unctad.org/international-investment-agreements> (hereafter UNCTAD IIA Navigator).
  [10] See eg *Railroad Development Corp. v Republic of Guatemala*, ICSID Case No ARB/07/23, Award (29 June 2012) paras 79–155 (applying *Penn Central* factors to interpret the Dominican Republic-Central America-United States FTA (DR-CAFTA).
  [11] See eg *Glamis Gold, Ltd. v United States*, Award (8 June 2009) para 356 (noting both disputing parties' reliance on *Penn Central* factors to interpret NAFTA).

Some IIAs modify or supplement the *Penn Central* factors.[12] For example:

- The New Zealand-Korea FTA modifies the first factor to clarify that the economic impact "must be so severe in the light of its purpose that it cannot be reasonably viewed as having been adopted and applied in good faith".[13]
- The Australia-Hong Kong investment agreement modifies the second factor, clarifying that "whether an investor's investment-backed expectations are reasonable depends, to the extent relevant, on factors such as whether the government provided the investor with binding written assurances and the nature and extent of governmental regulation or the potential for government regulation in the relevant sector".[14]
- The China-Japan-Korea investment agreement modifies the third factor, inviting scrutiny of the "character and objectives of the action or series of actions, including whether such action is proportionate to its objectives".[15]

Still other IIAs have reformulated and repackaged the *Penn Central* factors. The China-New Zealand FTA, for instance, looks to whether the state's deprivation of the investor's property is (i) either severe or for an indefinite period, and (ii) disproportionate to the public purpose.[16] Such deprivation is "particularly likely" to constitute an indirect expropriation when it is (i) discriminatory in its effect, either as against the particular investor or against a class of which the investor forms part, or (ii) in breach of the state's prior binding written commitment to the investor, whether by contract, licence, or other legal document.[17]

Finally, some IIAs have developed guidelines for specific types of government measures, such as tax measures. The Republic of Korea's recent IIAs, for example, identify four considerations beyond the *Penn Central* factors, including whether a measure reflects "internationally recognised tax policies, principles, and practices".[18] Other states are following suit.[19]

Many newer IIAs also provide guidance on when governmental measures are *not* expropriatory. The 2012 US Model BIT, for instance, provides:

---

[12] See eg EU-Canada Comprehensive Economic and Trade Agreement (CETA) (adding, as a fourth element, "the duration of the measure or series of measures by a Party"); 2019 Belgium-Luxembourg Model Bilateral Investment Treaty (BIT), art 8.2 (same).

[13] See also CETA, annex 8-A, para 2(a) (calling for consideration of "the economic impact of the measure or series of measures, although the sole fact that a measure or series of measures of a Party has an adverse effect on the economic value of an investment does not establish that an indirect expropriation has occurred").

[14] Australia-Hong Kong Special Administrative Region (SAR) Investment Agreement, Annex II (Expropriation) note 42 (2019). See also ASEAN-Australia-New Zealand FTA, Annex on Expropriation and Compensation, art 3(C) (2009) (clarifying that a claimant's expectations depend on whether the impugned measure "breaches the government's prior binding written commitment to the investor whether by contract, licence or other legal document").

[15] Protocol to the China-Japan-Korea Investment Agreement, art 2(b)(iii) (2012). See also CETA, Annex 8-A, para 2(d) (examining "the character of the measure or series of measures, notably their object, context and intent").

[16] China-New Zealand FTA, Annex 13 (2008).

[17] ibid.

[18] Australia-Korea FTA, Annex 11-I (2014); Korea-New Zealand FTA, Annex 10(E) (2015).

[19] See eg Kazakhstan-Singapore BIT, art 21(3) (2018).

Except in rare circumstances, non-discriminatory regulatory actions by a Party that are designed and applied to protect legitimate public welfare objectives, such as public health, safety, and the environment, do not constitute indirect expropriations.[20]

This observation was first included in the 2004 US Model BIT and has been echoed in later agreements, including those not involving the United States.[21]

Other states employ similar language in their IIAs. Canada, for instance, puts the focus on the severity of the measures in light of their purpose:

Except in rare circumstances, such as when a measure or series of measures are so severe in the light of their purpose that they cannot be reasonably viewed as having been adopted and applied in good faith, non-discriminatory measures of a Party that are designed and applied to protect legitimate public welfare objectives, such as health, safety and the environment, do not constitute indirect expropriation.[22]

Many states have adopted such provisions, including in agreements not involving Canada.[23]

Other states highlight factors such as reasonableness, legitimacy, and proportionality. Newer Chinese IIAs, for instance, provide:

Except in rare circumstances, such as where the measures adopted substantially exceed the measures necessary for maintaining reasonable public welfare, legitimate regulatory measures adopted by one Contracting Party for the purpose of protecting public health, safety and the environment, and that are for the public welfare and are non-discriminatory, do not constitute indirect expropriation.[24]

Still other states employ similar language to emphasize their right to regulate in such matters as public morals,[25] consumer protection,[26] human rights,[27] resource management,[28] and real estate price stabilization.[29]

---

[20] 2012 US Model BIT, Annex B, para 4(b). Some tribunals interpret such language as reflecting the police power exception under customary international law. See eg *Philip Morris Brands SARL et al. v Oriental Republic of Uruguay*, ICSID Case No ARB/10/7, Award (8 July 2016) para 301.

[21] States as diverse as Australia, Burkina Faso, Iceland, India, Latvia, Nicaragua, Singapore, and Turkey have adopted such language. See UNCTAD IIA database.

[22] 2004 Canada Model BIT 2004, Annex B.13(1)(c).

[23] States as diverse as Austria, Belgium, Brunei Darussalam, Colombia, Hong Kong SAR, India, Iran, Japan, Korea, Kosovo, Kyrgyzstan, Luxembourg, Nigeria, Singapore, Slovakia, Tajikistan, and Vietnam have employed this formulation in their BITs. See UNCTAD IIA database.

[24] See eg China-Tanzania BIT, art 6(3) (2013).

[25] China-Hong Kong SAR Investment Agreement, Annex 3, para 3 (2017).

[26] India-Uruguay BIT, Annex 1, para 4(b) (2008).

[27] 2015 Norway Model BIT, art 6(8) (stating that paragraphs 1–6 of the expropriation provision "do not in any circumstances apply to a measure or a series of measures, other than nationalizing or expropriating, by a Party that are designed and applied to safeguard public interests, such as measures to meet health, human rights, resource management, safety or environmental concerns").

[28] ibid.

[29] India-Korea CEPA, Annex 10-A, para 3(b) (2009). For a formulation addressing judicial measures, see China-India BIT, Protocol, Ad art 5(3) (2006, terminated 2018) ("Except in rare circumstances, non-discriminatory

Recent IIAs thus reflect tremendous experimentation with guidelines for determining an indirect expropriation.[30] Such guidelines help tribunals demarcate the line between a state's right to regulate and its duty to respect treaty commitments. Absent such guidance, tribunals may, wittingly or not, substitute their own policy preferences for those of the treaty parties.

### 2.1.2 Non-discrimination

A second example of interpretive guidelines concerns the non-discrimination obligations of national and MFN treatment. As relative standards, they invite a comparison of treatment accorded to other investors or investments in "like circumstances" or "like situations". Identifying proper comparators thus is essential. Yet arbitral tribunals often assess likeness differently.[31] The tribunal in *Methanex v United States* recognized the need to compare entities in the "most" like circumstances.[32] But what are the most like circumstances? Who bears the burden of establishing likeness? And is a claimant truly in like circumstances with an alleged comparator if the state had valid grounds for treating investors or investments differently?

The Comprehensive and Progressive Agreement for Trans-Pacific Partnership (CPTPP) seeks to answer these questions through interpretive guidance. Appended to the treaty is a "drafters' note" on the interpretation of the phrase "in like circumstances".[33] The purpose of the note is to "ensure that tribunals follow" the treaty parties' "shared intent" concerning like circumstances.[34] To that end, the note provides three clarifications. First, the phrase "like circumstances" is meant to "ensure that comparisons are made only with respect to relevant characteristics". This is a "fact-specific inquiry" that considers the "totality of the circumstances", including "competition in the relevant business or economic sectors" and the "legal and regulatory frameworks" applicable to the comparators.[35]

Second, the claimant "bears the burden to prove that the respondent failed to accord to the claimant or the claimant's covered investment treatment no less favorable than it

---

regulatory measures adopted by a Contracting Party in pursuit of public interest, including measures pursuant to awards of general application rendered by judicial bodies do not constitute indirect expropriation or nationalization.").

[30] Such guidance may even be used for the quantification of damages. See eg 2018 EAC Model Investment Treaty, art 7.2 (identifying relevant circumstances for quantifying the fair market value of expropriated investments, including duration of the investment and history of profits, mitigation, contributory fault by the investor, and harm to the environment or local community).

[31] *Occidental Exploration & Prod. Co. v Ecuador*, LCIA Case No UN 3467, Final Award (1 July 2004) para 175 (comparing the claimant, an oil exporter, to exporters of flowers, seafood, and mining products); *The Loewen Group, Inc. and Raymond L. Loewen v United States of America*, ICSID Case No. ARB(AF)/98/3, Award, (26 June 2003), para 140 (declining to recognize any other investor in like circumstances, thus precluding a national treatment violation).

[32] *Methanex Corp. v United States*, Final Award of the Tribunal on Jurisdiction and Merits (3 August 2005) Part IV, Chap B, para 19 (internal quotation marks omitted).

[33] CPTPP, "Drafters' Note on Interpretation of 'In Like Circumstances' Under Article 9.4 (National Treatment) and Article 9.5 (Most-Favoured-Nation Treatment)".

[34] ibid para 3.

[35] ibid.

accords, in like circumstances", to another investor or investment. This clarification requires the claimant to establish both like circumstances and less favourable treatment.

Third, the "like circumstances" analysis includes determining "whether the treatment distinguishes between investors and investments based on legitimate public welfare objectives".[36] That is, legitimacy of the state's public welfare objectives is distinct factor that may allow a tribunal to find that an investor or investment was not in like circumstances before inquiring into whether the treatment received was or was not less favourable.

The most distinguishing feature of the drafters' note arguably is its attempt to flesh out the "relevant characteristics" of like circumstances by reference to arbitral awards interpreting similar language in NAFTA's investment chapter.[37] By instructing tribunals to "follow" certain decisions when interpreting a specific treaty provision, the treaty parties implicitly invite tribunals not to follow other, inconsistent decisions. The CPTPP parties might periodically update the note, addressing further developments in arbitral case law. Such guidance provides states with potentially important means of controlling arbitral "precedent".

### 2.1.3 Fair and equitable treatment

A third example of interpretive guidance concerns FET. Most IIAs require the treaty parties to provide "fair and equitable treatment" without further elaborating its meaning or scope. In recent years, FET has become the most frequently invoked and relied upon standard in investment treaty arbitration. The elements often considered at the "core" of FET, such as transparency, stability, and legitimate expectations, have been developed primarily through arbitral decisions interpreting the terms fair and equitable treatment.[38]

States have responded differently to FET's rapid evolution. Some states have begun eliminating FET from their newer IIAs.[39] This approach risks depriving investors of protection against harmful government measures not captured by the treaty's other substantive standards. Other states have sought to specify the elements of FET, such as denial of justice, manifest arbitrariness, or targeted discrimination.[40] This approach similarly risks failing to protect investors against harmful government measures not contained in an exhaustive list of proscribed treatment. Still other states have linked FET to the minimum standard of treatment under customary international law (CIL). This approach carries the risk that arbitral tribunals will interpret the CIL standard no differently than an "autonomous" FET treaty standard, negating the treaty parties' efforts to circumscribe the rule. The tribunal in *Merrill & Ring v Canada*, for instance, opined:

---

[36] ibid.

[37] ibid paras 4–5 (citing cases).

[38] *See Crystallex International Corp. v Bolivarian Republic of Venezuela*, ICSID Case No ARB(AF)/11/12, Award (4 April 2016) para 539.

[39] See eg 2017 India Model BIT.

[40] See eg CETA, art 8.10. Article 8.10(f) recognizes that the treaty parties may subsequently adopt further elements of FET through a joint committee of the treaty parties.

[I]n the end, the name assigned to the standard does not really matter. What matters is that the standard protects against all such acts or behavior that might infringe a sense of fairness, equity and reasonableness.[41]

The tribunal in *Saur v Argentina* similarly dismissed the distinction between the treaty standard and the customary standard as "dogmatic and conceptualist".[42]

Many newer IIAs make clear that the name assigned to the standard really does matter and that distinctions between customary and conventional standards are far from conceptual.[43] The CPTPP makes this clear through guidelines containing four clarifications.

First, the CPTPP clarifies that FET is not an autonomous treaty standard. It is part of the "minimum standard of treatment" under "customary international law".[44]

Second, the CPTPP clarifies the contours of FET, indicating what falls inside and outside of the standard. It specifies that FET "includes the obligation not to deny justice in criminal, civil or administrative adjudicatory proceedings in accordance with the principles of due process embodied in the principal legal systems of the world", but it does not "create additional substantive rights" or extend beyond the minimum standard of treatment under CIL.[45] The "mere fact" that a measure upsets an investor's expectations, moreover, is not a breach of FET.[46]

Third, the CPTPP clarifies how tribunals should interpret the FET standard—that is, by reference to "a general and consistent practice of states that they follow from a sense of legal obligation".[47] The CPTPP thus confirms that the method for ascertaining and applying CIL is different from the method for ascertaining and applying an autonomous treaty standard. The former looks to state practice and *opinio juris*, while the latter starts with the ordinary meaning of the terms in context and in light of the treaty's object and purpose.[48]

Fourth, the CPTPP affirms the claimant's burden to establish all elements of its claims, "consistent with general principles of international law applicable to international arbitration".[49] This clarification expressly applies to any claim alleging a breach of the minimum standard of treatment.

These three examples—indirect expropriation, non-discrimination, and FET—show how states may use interpretive guidelines to promote the proper interpretation of amorphous treaty provisions. Interpretive guidelines facilitate proper treaty

---

[41] *Merrill & Ring Forestry L.P. v Government of Canada*, Award (31 March 2010) para 210.
[42] *SAUR International S.A. v Republic of Argentina*, ICSID Case No ARB/04/4, Award (22 May 2014) para 491 (translation).
[43] See Martins Paparinskis, *The International Minimum Standard and Fair and Equitable Treatment* (Oxford University Press 2014) preface.
[44] CPTPP, art 9.6(1).
[45] CPTPP, art 9.6(2).
[46] Further, CPTPP Article 9.6(5) provides: "the mere fact that a subsidy or grant has not been issued, renewed or maintained, or has been modified or reduced, by a Party, does not constitute a breach of this Article, even if there is loss or damage to the covered investment as a result".
[47] CPTPP, Annex 9-A.
[48] See Vienna Convention on the Law of Treaties, art 31(1).
[49] CPTPP, art 9.23(7).

interpretation by highlighting, clarifying, and amplifying the ordinary meaning of treaty terms in their context and in the light of the treaty's object and purpose.[50] This practice may well become routine, as protocols are added and updated to address an ever-growing body of international investment awards, decisions, and orders.

## 2.2 Interpretive Clarifications

Interpretive clarifications are the second main form of interpretive guidance in IIAs.[51] Like guidelines, interpretive clarifications promote the correct interpretation of treaty provisions, but they are included for "greater certainty", "greater clarity", or "the avoidance of doubt". A key proponent of their use, the US government, argues that such terms are not intended "to create or limit a right or obligation but to reflect an understanding that the scope of a particular right or obligation is already implied in other provisions of the text".[52] Such terms are "not strictly necessary", and the same interpretation should apply "even in the absence of such clarification".[53]

Interpretive clarifications in IIAs serve at least four purposes, beyond their general goal of highlighting, clarifying, and amplifying the ordinary meaning of treaty terms in their context and in the light of the treaty's object and purpose.[54] First, they help elucidate, and restate, the scope of common treaty provisions. The definition of "investment" provides a typical example. The Israel-Myanmar BIT, for instance, contains a common asset-based definition of investment, which may be interpreted broadly. The agreement clarifies, however: "[F]or the avoidance of doubt, investment does *not* include" (i) public debt operations, or (ii) claims to money arising solely from commercial contracts for the sale of goods and services or credits granted in relation to a commercial transaction.[55] Use of the phrase "for the avoidance of doubt" suggests that these are not new limitations employed solely for this agreement.[56]

Second, interpretive clarifications provide a gloss on *prior* treaties. As the United States argues, such provisions "serve to spell out more explicitly the proper interpretation of similar provisions *mutatis mutandis* [in] other agreements or in the same

---

[50] See Vienna Convention on the Law of Treaties, art 31(1).

[51] See Vienna Convention on the Law of Treaties, art 31(3) ("There shall be taken into account, together with the context: (a) any subsequent agreement between the parties regarding the interpretation of the treaty or the application of its provisions; (b) any subsequent practice in the application of the treaty which establishes the agreement of the parties regarding its interpretation ....").

[52] *Pope & Talbot Inc. v Government of Canada*, Second Submission of the United States (25 May 2000) para 6.

[53] *Spence International Investments, LLC, Berkowitz et al. v Costa Rica*, ICSID Case No UNCT/13/2, Submission of the United States (17 April 2017) para 2 ("The introductory phrase '[f]or greater certainty' confirms that Article 10.1.3 is not strictly necessary because the CAFTA-DR would not apply retroactively even in the absence of such clarification.").

[54] See Vienna Convention on the Law of Treaties, art 31(1).

[55] Israel-Myanmar BIT, art 1(1)(6) (2014) (emphasis added).

[56] But see Israel-Japan BIT, art 1(a) (2017): "For the avoidance of doubt *in this Article*, an investment does not include ...", suggesting that no such limitation should be read into other Japanese agreements. Indeed, Japan's subsequent IIAs to date do not contain the "greater certainty" language, suggesting that Japan truly intended to limit the application of the clarification in the Japan-Israel BIT to that treaty alone. See eg Japan-UAE BIT (2018); Japan-Argentina BIT (2018); Japan-Armenia BIT (2018).

agreement".[57] Interpretative clarifications, in other words, do not "change the nature of the substantive obligations that existed under ... prior agreements; instead, they merely elucidate, for the benefit of tribunals charged with interpreting the treaty, the Parties' intent in agreeing to those obligations".[58] This understanding is crucial, as new treaty language can impact the interpretation of previous treaties using the same or similar language.[59]

Third, interpretive clarifications may confirm, and restate, a rule of customary international law. Many IIAs, for example, clarify the CIL rule on the non-retroactivity of treaties. The DR-CAFTA, for instance, provides, "for greater certainty", that the investment chapter "does not bind any Party in relation to any act or fact that took place or any situation that ceased to exist before the date of entry into force of this Agreement".[60] Such language, the *Berkowitz v Costa Rica* tribunal recognized, merely affirms "the customary international law rule on the non-retroactivity of treaties".[61]

Fourth, interpretive clarifications may respond to issues raised in specific arbitration cases. The many examples include:

- *"Market share" as investment.* The tribunal in *SD Myers v Canada* appeared to accept that a claimant's "market share" in Canada qualified as an "investment" under NAFTA Chapter Eleven.[62] Agreements such as Pacer Plus clarify: "For greater certainty, market share, market access, expected gains and opportunities for profit-making are not, by themselves, investments."[63]
- *Trade-related damages.* The tribunal in *Cargill v Mexico* appeared to award the claimant both trade- and investment-related damages.[64] Agreements such as CPTPP clarify: "For greater certainty, if an investor of a Party submits a claim to arbitration ... it may recover only for loss or damage that it has incurred in its capacity as an investor of a Party."[65]
- *An investor that "seeks to make" an investment.* The claimant in *Mesa v Canada*, claimed to qualify as an investor that "seeks to make an investment", because it had

---

[57] *Alberto Carrizosa Gelziz et al. v Republic of Colombia*, PCA Case No 2018-56, Transcript of Hearing on Jurisdiction (15 December 2000) pp 217–18. *See also Omega Engineering LLC et al. v Republic of Panama*, ICSID Case No ARB/16/42, Submission of the United States of America (3 February 2020) footnote 24.

[58] *Windstream Energy LLC v Government of Canada*, Respondent's Rejoinder (6 November 2015) para 92 (quoting Andrea J Menaker, "Benefiting From Experience: Developments in the United States' Most Recent Investment Agreements" (2006) 12 (1) University of California Davis Journal of International Law and Policy 122).

[59] Kenneth J Vandevelde, *US International Investment Agreements* (Oxford University Press 2009) 111–12 (noting that "redundancies originally inserted simply to remove any doubt about the meaning of a BIT provision could complicate negotiations because of a fear that their deletion would appear to be a weakening, rather than a stylistic pruning, of the BIT provision").

[60] DR-CAFTA, art 10.1.3 (2004). See also 2017 Colombia Model BIT, 'Scope of Application' (same).

[61] *Berkowitz et al. v Costa Rica*, ICSID Case No UNCT/13/2, Interim Award (25 October 2016) para 222.

[62] *SD Myers Inc. v Government of Canada*, Partial Award (13 November 2000) para 232.

[63] Pacific Agreement on Closer Economic Relations Plus, ch 9, note 1 (2017). See also New Zealand-Korea FTA, ch 11, note 4 (2015).

[64] *Cargill, Inc. v United Mexican States*, ICSID Case No ARB(AF)/05/2, Award (18 September 2009) para 523 (concluding that the profits generated by Cargill's sales to its Mexican subsidiary "for marketing, distribution and re-sale ... were so associated with the claimed investment ... as to be compensable under the NAFTA").

[65] CPTPP, art 9.29.2.

already begun "due diligence and transaction work" in Canada.[66] Agreements such as the Canada-Colombia FTA provide, for greater certainty, that an investor "seeks to make an investment" only when it has taken "concrete steps" required for the investment (eg applying for a permit and obtaining financing for the investment).[67]

- *Denial of benefits.* The tribunal in *Plama v Bulgaria* determined that the respondent could not deny benefits of the Energy Charter Treaty after the claimant had already initiated arbitration.[68] Many IIAs clarify, for greater certainty, the contracting parties' right to deny such benefits "at any time, including after the institution of arbitration proceedings".[69]
- *Overlapping breaches.* The tribunal in *SD Myers v Canada* determined that a breach of the national treatment obligation "essentially establish[es]" a breach of the minimum standard of treatment obligation.[70] Many IIAs clarify, for greater certainty, that a breach of one treaty provision (or a provision of a different treaty) does not itself constitute a breach of FET or the minimum standard of treatment.[71]
- *MFN and dispute resolution.* The tribunal in *Maffezini v Spain* interpreted the MFN provision of the Argentina-Spain BIT to encompass international dispute resolution procedures.[72] Many IIAs clarify, for greater certainty, that the MFN provision does not extend to such procedures.[73]
- *Compensation for an "unlawful expropriation".* The tribunal in *ADC v Hungary* awarded the claimant the value of its expropriated investment as of the date of the award (rather than the lower value as of the date of expropriation), based on the CIL standard for an "unlawful" expropriation.[74] The 2018 Netherlands Model BIT clarifies:

The compensation referred to in paragraph 1 of this Article shall amount to the fair market value of the investment at the time immediately before the expropriation or the impending expropriation became known, whichever is earlier. *For greater*

---

[66] *Mesa Power Group LLC v Government of Canada*, PCA Case No 2012-17, Award (24 March 2016) para 321 (stating Claimant's position).

[67] Canada-Colombia FTA, ch 8, note 12 (2008). *See also* Canada-Jordan BIT, art 1(t) (2009); Canada-Panama FTA, art 9.01.

[68] *Plama Consortium Ltd. v Republic of Bulgaria*, ICSID Case No. ARB/03/24, Decision on Jurisdiction (8 February 2005) para 165.

[69] See eg East African Community Model Investment Treaty, art 19.3 (2016). See also Australia-Indonesia CEPA, art 14.3, note 20 (2020) ("For greater certainty, the benefits of this Chapter may be denied at any time before or after an investment is made, including after an investor has submitted a claim to arbitration.").

[70] *SD Myers Inc. v Government of Canada*, Partial Award (13 November 2000) para 266.

[71] See eg CPTPP, art 9.6.3. The NAFTA Parties initially made such a clarification through a joint interpretation. NAFTA Free Trade Commission, Notes of Interpretation of Certain Chapter 11 Provisions (31 July 2001) para B.3.

[72] *Emilio Augustín Maffezini v Kingdom of Spain*, ICSID Case No ARB/97/7, Decision on Jurisdiction (25 January 2000) paras 38–64.

[73] See eg ASEAN-China Investment Agreement, art 5(4) (2009); 2016 Czech Republic Model BIT, art 3(3); Azerbaijan-San Marino BIT, art 4(3) (2015).

[74] *ADC Affiliate Ltd. et al. v Republic of Hungary*, ICSID Case No ARB/03/16, Award (27 September 2006) paras 476–499.

*certainty*, this method to evaluate the compensation also applies in case of unlawful expropriation.[75]

Such interpretive clarifications have become routine in newer IIAs. The CPTPP, for instance, uses such terms forty-five times in the investment chapter alone. States likely will continue to use them, including to help control the development of arbitral "precedent".


## 2.3  Interpretive Indicators

Interpretive indicators are the third main form of interpretive guidance in IIAs. Interpretive indicators can tilt the interpretive balance towards the treaty parties' policy preferences. In addition to preambular language, states often express such preferences through "right to regulate" and "non-regression" clauses.

### 2.3.1  Right to regulate

IIAs increasingly affirm the treaty parties' implied right to regulate. Norway's 2015 model BIT is illustrative:

> Nothing in this Agreement shall be construed to prevent a Party from adopting, maintaining or enforcing any measure otherwise consistent with this Agreement that it considers appropriate to ensure that investment activity is undertaken in a manner sensitive to health, safety, human rights, labour rights, resource management or environmental concerns.[76]

Such provisions may appear superfluous. States clearly have the right to regulate in the public interest, and arbitral tribunals routinely acknowledge that right. Such provisions may also appear tautological. If a state's right to adopt, maintain, or enforce any measure must be "otherwise consistent" with the state's investment obligations, what protection does a right-to-regulate clause really add?

In practice, such provisions serve as interpretive indicators, pointing tribunals towards the treaty parties' policy preferences as an expression of the treaty's object and purpose.[77] The case *Al-Tamimi v Oman* illustrates their potential use.[78] The claimant had alleged that the respondent unlawfully blocked the development and operation of a limestone quarry, in breach of the Oman-US FTA. The claimant argued that the respondent's right to enforce its environmental laws did not give it "*carte blanche* to violate basic principles of fair and equitable treatment".[79] The tribunal sought to balance the host state's right to enforce its environmental laws against the investor's right to fair

---

[75] 2019 Netherlands Model BIT, art 12(5) (emphasis added).

[76] 2015 Norway Model BIT, art 12 (draft dated 13 May 2015). The model's preamble further "[r]ecognises that the provisions of this agreement and provisions of international agreements relating to the environment shall be interpreted in a mutually supportive manner".

[77] See Vienna Convention on the Law of Treaties, art 31(1).

[78] *Adel A. Hamadi Al Tamimi v Sultanate of Oman*, ICSID Case No ARB/11/33, Award (3 November 2015).

[79] ibid para 186.

and equitable treatment. The tribunal first turned to Article 10.10 of the FTA, which provides:

> Nothing in this Chapter shall be construed to prevent a Party from adopting, maintaining, or enforcing any measure otherwise consistent with this Chapter that it considers appropriate to ensure that investment activity in its territory is undertaken in a manner sensitive to environmental concerns.

The tribunal recognized that, by these terms, the treaty "places a high premium on environmental protection", adding:

> The wording of Article 10.10 provides a forceful protection of the right of either state Party to adopt, maintain or enforce any measure to ensure that investment is "undertaken in a manner sensitive to environmental concerns", provided it is not otherwise inconsistent with the express provisions of [the investment chapter].[80]

As relevant context for interpreting Article 10.10, the tribunal looked to the agreement's environment chapter, which affirmed that neither party should "fail to effectively enforce its environmental laws, through a sustained or recurring course of action or inaction, in a manner affecting trade between the Parties, after the date of entry into force of this Agreement".[81]

The text of Article 10.10, read in context, informed the standard by which the tribunal reviewed the state's environmental enforcement measures. The tribunal found it "clear that the state Parties intended to reserve a significant margin of discretion to themselves in the application and enforcement of their respective environmental laws".[82] Investment tribunals, it recalled, "do not have an open-ended mandate to second-guess government decision-making", particularly "in light of the express terms of the present Treaty relating to environmental enforcement".[83]

The tribunal further determined that the text, read in context, "qualifies the construction" of the treaty's substantive obligations: "When it comes to determining any breach of the minimum standard of treatment under Article 10.5, the Tribunal must be guided by the forceful defence of environmental regulation and protection provided in the express language of the Treaty."[84] The tribunal concluded:

> [T]o establish a breach of the minimum standard of treatment under Article 10.5, the Claimant must show that Oman has acted with a gross or flagrant disregard for the basic principles of fairness, consistency, even-handedness, due process, or natural justice expected by and of all States under customary international law .... It will

---

[80] ibid para 387.
[81] ibid para 388 (quoting art 17.2.1 of the US-Oman FTA).
[82] ibid para 389.
[83] ibid.
[84] ibid para 390.

certainly not be the case that every minor misapplication of a State's laws or regulations will meet that high standard. That is particularly so, in a context such as the US–Oman FTA, where the impugned conduct concerns the good-faith application or enforcement of a State's laws or regulations relating to the protection of its environment.[85]

The *Al-Tamimi* award thus shows the powerful influence that interpretive indicators may have on a tribunal's interpretation and application of key substantive obligations, such as FET.

The case *Aven v Costa Rica* further illustrates the influence of interpretive indicators, albeit through a somewhat different approach.[86] That claimant alleged that unlawful administrative and judicial action had destroyed the value of its tourism development project on the coast of Costa Rica, in breach of the respondent's obligations under the DR-CAFTA. In its defence, the respondent highlighted the important public purpose served by environmental protection.[87]

Such defences have fared poorly in the past. The tribunal in *Santa Elena v Costa Rica*, for instance, concluded two decades ago:

> Expropriatory environmental measures—no matter how laudable and beneficial to society as a whole—are, in this respect, similar to any other expropriatory measures that a state may take in order to implement its policies: where property is expropriated, even for environmental purposes, whether domestic or international, the state's obligation to pay compensation remains.[88]

The *Aven* tribunal, for its part, could however point to treaty language embodying the value the contracting parties placed on environmental protection. Article 10.11 of the DR-CAFTA, the tribunal observed, "recognised that nothing prevents the Treaty Parties 'from adopting, maintaining, or enforcing any measure otherwise consistent with this Chapter that it considers appropriate to ensure that investment activity in its territory is undertaken in a manner sensitive to environmental concerns.'"[89] For the tribunal, this language had consequences:

> Although the express terms of Article 10.11 essentially subordinate the rights to investors under Chapter Ten to the right of Costa Rica to ensure that the investments are carried out "in a matter sensitive to environmental concerns", this subordination is not absolute in the view of the Tribunal. It requires that the actions to be taken by the States Parties to DR-CAFTA [are] in line with principles of international law, which require acting in good faith.[90]

---

[85] ibid.

[86] *David Aven et al. v Republic of Costa Rica*, Case No UNCT/15/3, Final Award (18 September 2018).

[87] ibid para 8.

[88] *Compañía del Desarrollo de Santa Elena, S.A. v Republic of Costa Rica*, ICSID Case No ARB/96/1, Award (17 February 2000) para 15 (addressing solely the quantum of damage for an admitted expropriation).

[89] *David Aven et al. v Republic of Costa Rica*, Case No UNCT/15/3, Final Award (18 September 2018) para 412.

[90] ibid.

The issue, the tribunal recognized, was not a question of "not applying" the treaty's investment protections.[91] Instead, the treaty parties were "giving *preference* to the standards of environmental protection that were stated to be of interest to the Treaty Parties at the time it was signed".[92] Giving preference to expressed policy considerations arguably is what the treaty parties envisaged when drafting such provisions.

### 2.3.2 Non-regression clauses

A second type of interpretive indicator is found in non-regression clauses. Such clauses seek to avoid a "race to the bottom"—for example, encouraging investment by reducing protections for the environment and labour. The 2012 Model BIT, for example, provides in Article 12(2):

> The Parties recognize that it is inappropriate to encourage investment by weakening or reducing the protections afforded in domestic environmental laws. Accordingly, each Party shall ensure that it does not waive or otherwise derogate from or offer to waive or otherwise derogate from its environmental laws in a manner that weakens or reduces the protections afforded in those laws, or fail to effectively enforce those laws through a sustained or recurring course of action or inaction, as an encouragement for the establishment, acquisition, expansion, or retention of an investment in its territory.

Such clauses have become commonplace in IIAs. For environmental protection alone, more than 130 states reportedly have concluded non-regression clauses in their more recent IIAs.[93] Tribunals have begun looking to such clauses to guide their interpretation of substantive standards.[94]

Other states have included non-regression clauses in IIAs to safeguard other important policy goals. France's model BIT, for instance, highlights cultural and linguistic diversity.[95] The United States' model BIT highlights the treaty parties' "obligations as members of the International Labor Organization (ILO) and their commitments under the ILO Declaration on Fundamental Principles and Rights at Work and its Follow-Up".[96] Arbitrating parties and tribunals may rely on such non-regression clauses to better align their interpretations with the parties' policy preferences, including by

---

[91] ibid.

[92] ibid (emphasis added).

[93] See Andrew D Mitchell and James Munro, "No Retreat: An Emerging Principle of Non-Regression from Environmental Protection in International Investment Law" (2019) 50 Georgetown Journal of International Law 625, 629.

[94] As already noted, the *Al Tamimi* tribunal relied on the non-regression clause in the US-Oman FTA as relevant context for interpreting the respondent's obligations under that treaty.

[95] See 2006 France Model BIT, art 1(5) ("No provision in this Agreement shall be interpreted as preventing one of the Contracting Parties from taking any measure aimed at governing investments made by foreign investors and the conditions for the activities of such investors in the context of measures designed to preserve and encourage cultural and linguistic diversity.") (translation).

[96] 2012 US Model BIT, art 13(1). States may also express policy preferences in preambular language. See eg 2015 Norway Model BIT, Preamble (reaffirming the parties' commitment to democracy, the rule of law, human rights and fundamental freedoms, sustainable development, anti-corruption, and corporate social responsibility).

applying soft-law sources referred to by the contracting parties. Given their ubiquity in contemporary IIAs, such provisions may play an important role in future arbitral cases.

## 2.3  Interpretive Markers

Interpretive markers are the fourth main form of interpretive guidance in IIAs. States may lay markers in the *travaux préparatoires* to guide subsequent interpretation. These markers, in other words, are "suppressed from the treaty text", but are nonetheless "recognise[d] as part of the agreement's negotiating history and expressive of [the parties'] understanding of the scope of the standard".[97]

There are at least two kinds of interpretive markers. First, states may conclude a "negotiated understanding" of the treaty that is not included or referred to in the text. The negotiating history of the Colombia-UK BIT, for instance, clarifies the parties' intention concerning FET:

> Both States confirm that, without wishing to narrow the meaning of the concept of "fair and equitable treatment" as it is interpreted in accordance with international law, they do not understand this term to incorporate a stabilization clause. Thus a Contracting Party is not prohibited from exercising regulatory powers, whenever introduced, that impact on investments of the investor of the other Contracting Party, so long as these powers are exercised in a fair and equitable manner.[98]

The treaty parties record that these "understandings are to be preserved as part of the negotiating history of the Agreement to provide clarity on the intention of the Contracting Parties when including the provisions already referred to".[99]

Second, one or more states may include a "disappearing footnote" in a draft of the treaty. A draft of what became the DR-CAFTA, for instance, contains a footnote proposed by one delegation to reflect the treaty parties' "understanding and intent" that the MFN clause does not encompass dispute resolution procedures and "therefore could not reasonably lead to a conclusion similar to that of the *Maffezini* case".[100] The proposed footnote was to "be included in the negotiating history as a reflection of the Parties' shared understanding" but "deleted in the final text of the Agreement".[101] Parties

---

[97] Catharine Titi, "The Evolution of Substantive Investment Protections in Recent Trade and Investment Treaties" (2018) RTA Exchange, ICTSD/IDB 8.

[98] Understanding with Regard to Fair and Equitable Treatment in the Bilateral Investment Agreement Between the United Kingdom of Great Britain and Northern Ireland and the Republic of Colombia dated 19 May 2009, <https://investmentpolicyhub.unctad.org/Download/TreatyFile/3255>.

[99] ibid.

[100] Free Trade Area of the Americas, Third Draft Agreement (21 November 2003) note 13, <http://www.ftaa-alca.org/FTAADraft03/ChapterXVII_e.asp>.

[101] ibid.

may cite, and tribunals may rely upon, such disappearing footnotes when adjudicating cases,[102] as "supplementary means" of interpretation.[103]

Negotiated understandings and disappearing footnotes raise fairness concerns.[104] IIAs serve not only the contracting parties but also third parties, including actual or prospective investors who may rely on IIA commitments when investing.[105] These parties may have difficulty accessing the *travaux préparatoires* or other material arising from the negotiation, conclusion, or implementation of an agreement, even if such material is publicly available.[106] It may be burdensome for investors or their counsel to look beyond the terms of IIAs to understand their content. Even if considered fair, negotiated understandings and disappearing footnotes also may prove ineffective. Arbitral tribunals may discount, or even disregard, such draft or extra-textual language. Any negotiated understandings or clarifying footnotes thus should be part of the treaty itself, for reasons of fairness and efficacy.[107]

## 3. Conclusion

States increasingly provide greater interpretive guidance in their IIAs as part of their broader efforts to rebalance rights and obligations and recalibrate investment protections. The techniques developed to guide the interpretation of IIAs exemplify the modern prescriptive model for IIAs.

Interpretive guidance naturally has its limits. States cannot foresee or legislate for every problem that may arise in the increasingly complex and fast-changing regime governing foreign investment. Nor can states ensure fair and just dispute resolution without giving adjudicators sufficient interpretive discretion to account for uncertainty, complexity, and change.

In practice, interpretive guidance and arbitral discretion are complementary. Their relationship is dynamic. States will increasingly provide interpretive guidance in their

[102] See eg *ICS Inspection and Control Services Ltd. v Argentine Republic*, PCA Case No 2010-9, Award on Jurisdiction (10 February 2012) para 302 (citing DR-CAFTA's disappearing footnote on MFN).
[103] See Vienna Convention on the Law of Treaties, art 32.
[104] See generally Esmé Shirlow and Michael Waibal, "A Sliding Scale Approach to *Travaux* in Treaty Interpretation: The Case of Investment Treaties" (2021) 89 British Yearbook of International Law, (addressing fairness concerns with tribunals' use of *travaux préparatoires* in international investment arbitration).
[105] See eg Mahnoush H Arsanjani and W Michael Reisman, "Interpreting Treaties for the Benefit of Third Parties: The 'Salvors' Doctrine' and the Use of Legislative History in Investment Treaties" (2010) 104 American Journal of International Law 597, 604 ("When treaties are designed to induce private parties that did not participate in the negotiations to rely upon their terms and to do specific things, fundamental principles of legality argue, even more, for fidelity to a method based on the text and on those post-text events that are available to the parties and are expressive of their agreement.").
[106] See eg *HICEE B.V. v Slovak Republic*, PCA Case No 2009-11, Dissenting Opinion of Judge Charles N Brower (23 May 2011) para 33 (criticizing as unfair the tribunal's reliance on "Explanatory Notes" prepared by the Netherlands government during negotiation of the Netherlands-Czechoslovak BIT, "[g]iven the substantial difficulties encountered by both Claimant and Respondent in obtaining *any* documents from the Dutch Government regarding the BIT, and the lack of reference to the Notes on the Dutch Foreign Ministry website, where the BIT at issue was posted").
[107] The United States-Peru Trade Promotion Agreement, for instance, now includes the DR-CAFTA's "disappearing footnote" in footnote 2 to the investment chapter.

IIAs, restricting arbitral discretion in certain respects. Arbitrators will adjudicate under that guidance, further developing law and practice. And states will refine their guidance in future treaties, building on or rejecting those decisions. The process should give states more control over the development of international investment law and practice; prevent tribunals from substituting their policy judgments for those of the treaty parties; and provide greater clarity to arbitrators and investors alike. Over time, this dialogue between states and tribunals should bring greater consistency, predictability, and legitimacy to international investment arbitration. Interpretive guidance thus may be considered indispensable to states' broader reform of the investor–state dispute settlement regime.

## Acknowledgements

I am grateful to Lee M Caplan and Martins Paparinskis for comments on a draft of this chapter.

# 26

# Delegation Run Amok

*George A Bermann*

## 1. Introduction

The proper allocation of authority between courts and arbitral tribunals over the enforceability of agreements to arbitrate has long occupied a central place in US arbitration law, domestic and international alike. From US Supreme Court case law over the years, there has emerged a reasonably well-understood distinction between those issues of enforceability that a court will address if asked by a party to do so and those that it will not. Fundamental to the Court's jurisprudence is a recognition that some enforceability issues—"gateway issues"—so seriously implicate the consent of parties to arbitrate their disputes that a party contesting the enforceability of an arbitration agreement on those grounds is entitled to a judicial determination of the matter, while others—"non-gateway issues"—do not.[1] The Supreme Court has adopted the convention of also referring to gateway issues as issues of "arbitrability", even though that is not how the term arbitrability is understood throughout most of the world.[2]

Classic gateway issues include whether an agreement to arbitrate was ever validly formed,[3] whether a non-signatory is bound by it,[4] and whether it encompasses the dispute at hand.[5] What these issues all have in common is the perception that they directly implicate the consent of the parties to submit a dispute to an arbitral rather than a judicial forum.[6] By contrast, classic non-gateway issues include the timeliness of requests to compel arbitration of a dispute[7] and the satisfaction, or not, of conditions precedent to arbitration.[8] These issues do not question the consent of the parties to arbitrate but whether the claim for one reason or another should not be entertained. Parties are free to

---

[1] See *Lamps Plus, Inc. v Varela*, 587 US ___ (2019), 139 S Ct 1407, 1415, 1419 (2019); *Granite Rock Co. v Int'l Brotherhood of Teamsters*, 561 US 287, 299 (2010); *Stolt-Nielsen S.A. v Animalfeeds Int'l Corp.*, 559 US, 662, 684 (2010); *Mastrobuono v Shearson Lehman Hutton, Inc.*, 514 US 52, 57 (1995); *Volt Info. Scis., Inc. v Bd. of Trs. of Leland Stanford Junior Univ.*, 489 US 468, 479 (1989); *Mitsubishi Motors Corp. v Soler Chrysler-Plymouth, Inc.*, 473 US 614, 626 (1985).

[2] The general understanding of arbitrability internationally is the legal capacity of a category of claims to be arbitrated. See George A Bermann, "Arbitration Trouble" (2012) 23 American Review of International Arbitration 367, 369.

[3] See eg *Painewebber v Elahi*, 87 F.3d 589 (1st Cir 1996).

[4] See eg *GE Energy Power Conversion Fr. SAS, Corp. v Outokumpu Stainless USA, LLC*, 140 SCt 1637 (2020).

[5] See eg *Tracer Rsch. Corp. v Nat'l Env't Servs. Co.*, 42 F.3d 1292 (9th Cir 1994).

[6] *See* George A Bermann, "The 'Gateway' Problem in International Commercial Arbitration" (2012) 37 Yale Journal of International Law 1.

[7] See eg *Howsam v Dean Witter Reynolds, Inc.*, 537 US 77 (2002).

[8] See eg *BG Grp., PLC v Republic of Argentina*, 572 US 25, 34 (2014).

George A Bermann, *Delegation Run Amok* In: *By Peaceful Means*. Edited by: Charles N Brower, Joan E Donoghue, Cian C Murphy, Cymie R Payne and Esmé R Shirlow, Oxford University Press. © George A Bermann 2024. DOI: 10.1093/oso/9780192848086.003.0026

raise their arbitrability objections for the first time before an arbitral tribunal itself for decision, but US law also allows parties to raise them for the first time before a court if they so prefer. By contrast, non-gateway issues are in principle reserved to the arbitrators.

## 2. *First Options* and Delegation

Complicating the gateway/non-gateway distinction is the Supreme Court's recognition that parties are free, in an exercise of party autonomy, to reserve the determination of gateway issues exclusively for arbitral determination, thereby foregoing athe ccess to a court on those matters to which they are otherwise entitled. In the Court's terminology, parties thereby "delegate" to a tribunal exclusive authority to determine issues over which a party would ordinarily be entitled to a judicial determination.

In the leading decision, *First Options of Chicago, Inc. v Kaplan*, the Court unanimously affirmed a ruling by the appeals court annulling an award rendered against a married couple, the Kaplans, on the basis of that court's independent finding that only the couple's wholly owned company, not the couple themselves, were parties to and bound by the agreement to arbitrate and were liable to payment of an award rendered against them pursuant to that agreement.[9] The Court there squarely stated:

> Courts should not assume that the parties agreed to arbitrate arbitrability unless there is "clea[r] and unmistakabl[e]" evidence that they did so... [T]he "who (primarily) should decide arbitrability" question ... is rather arcane. A party often might not focus upon that question or upon the significance of having arbitrators decide the scope of their own powers. And, given the principle that a party can be forced to arbitrate only those issues it specifically has agreed to submit to arbitration, one can understand why courts might hesitate to interpret silence or ambiguity on the "who should decide arbitrability" point as giving the arbitrators that power, for doing so might too often force unwilling parties to arbitrate a matter they reasonably would have thought a judge, not an arbitrator, would decide.[10]

The Supreme Court has thereafter reaffirmed on several occasions that "[t]he question whether the parties have submitted a particular dispute to arbitration, i.e., the 'question of arbitrability' is 'an issue for judicial determination [u]nless the parties clearly and unmistakably provide otherwise.'"[11]

In sum, the Court in *First Options* took as its point of departure the conviction that, due to the fundamental importance of consent to arbitrate, issues of arbitrability warrant independent judicial determination if sought. At the same time, it left open

---

[9] *First Options of Chi., Inc. v Kaplan*, 514 US 938 (1995).
[10] ibid 944–45 (citations omitted). The Court cited in support of this proposition its prior rulings in *AT & T Techs., Inc. v Commc'ns Workers of Am.*, 475 US 643, 649 (1986); *United Steelworkers of Am. v Warrior and Gulf Navigation Co.*, 363 US 574, 583 n 7 (1960).
[11] *Howsam*, 537 US at 83. *See also BG Grp.*, 572 US at 34.

the possibility that the parties could agree to forego access to a court on issues of arbitrability, including whether the parties agreed to arbitrate, whether their agreement was valid, whether a non-signatory could invoke the agreement or be bound by it, and whether the dispute at hand fell within the agreement's scope of application.

In *First Options*, the Kaplans chose to challenge enforcement of the arbitration agreement before the arbitral tribunal, rather than a court, as was their privilege.[12] Having failed to persuade the tribunal that they were not bound to arbitrate, the Kaplans participated in the arbitration under protest, and lost.[13] The question whether they were bound to arbitrate came before a court only on a post-award basis, viz. in an action by the Kaplans to annul the resulting award.[14] However, in most of the decided cases, the question whether a party ever agreed to arbitrate is raised in the context of a motion to compel arbitration, in other words, prior to arbitration even getting underway.

## 3. *Kompetenz-Kompetenz* in Institutional Rules

Central to *First Options* is the notion of "clear and unmistakable" evidence of a delegation. In the great majority of delegation cases, respondents have argued that, when parties adopt in their arbitration agreement a set of institutional rules containing a *Kompetenz-Kompetenz* provision, they "clearly and unmistakably" manifest an intention to "delegate" the determination of gateway issues to an arbitral tribunal.[15] According to the doctrine of *Kompetenz-Kompetenz*, an arbitral tribunal has authority to determine its own jurisdiction.[16]

Every US Court of Appeals to address the matter has taken the view that the parties' incorporation by reference in their arbitration agreement of procedural rules containing a *Kompetenz-Kompetenz* provision clearly and unmistakably signifies an intention on their part to vest exclusive authority over the arbitrability of a dispute in an arbitral tribunal.[17] However, no Court of Appeals has offered serious reasoning in support of that position, as typified by the early Eighth Circuit ruling in *FSC Sec. Corp. v Freel*, in which the Court had only this to say:

---

[12] *First Options*, 514 US at 941.

[13] ibid.

[14] ibid.

[15] See Jack M Graves and Yelena Davydan, "Competence-Competence and Separability-American Style" in Stefan Kröll and others (eds), *International Arbitration and International Commercial Law: Synergy, Convergence and Evolution: Liber Amicorum Eric Bergsten* (Kluwer Law International 2011) 162; Joseph L Franco, "Note, Casually Finding the Clear and Unmistakable: A Re-Evaluation of First Options in Light of Recent Lower Court Decisions" (2006) 10 Lewis & Clark Law Review 442, 469–70.

[16] See generally, C Ryan Reetz, "The Limits of the Competence-Competence Doctrine in United States Courts" (2011) 5 Dispute Resolution International 5.

[17] *Blanton v Domino's Pizza Franchising LLC, 2020 US App.* LEXIS 18975 (6th Cir 2020) ("[C]onsider that every one of our sister circuits to address the question—eleven out of twelve by our count—has found that the incorporation of the AAA Rules (or similarly worded arbitral rules) provides 'clear and unmistakable' evidence that the parties agreed to arbitrate 'arbitrability.' ").

> [T]he parties expressly agreed to have their dispute governed by the NASD Code of Arbitration Procedure.... [W]e hold that the parties' adoption of this provision *is* a "clear and unmistakable" expression of their intent to leave the question of arbitrability to the arbitrators.[18]

Other Courts of Appeals have decided the matter in a similarly perfunctory fashion.[19] They all make the same unexplained assumption that, if arbitrators *have* authority to determine arbitral jurisdiction, then the courts necessarily *do not*.

Worse yet, the majority of Court of Appeals decisions that followed do not even purport to address the issue, but instead simply "join" the views that other Courts of Appeal had previously taken. For example, the Fifth Circuit in *Petrofac, Inc. v DynMcDermott Petroleum Operations Co.* confined itself to the following: "We agree with most of our sister circuits that the express adoption of these rules presents clear and unmistakable evidence that the parties agreed to arbitrate arbitrability."[20] Notwithstanding the high stakes associated with delegations of authority to determine arbitrability, the Courts of Appeals have evidently failed to give them any serious consideration.

For reasons set out in what follows, the position taken by the Courts of Appeals in these cases is fundamentally misguided. First, the way to make a delegation clear and unmistakable is *not* to bury it in appended rules of arbitral procedure but rather to state it plainly in the arbitration agreement itself. Second, even if incorporation by reference were a sufficient delegation vehicle, the language of the *Kompetenz-Kompetenz* provisions in these cases fails to support an inference that if tribunals may determine their arbitral jurisdiction, courts by definition may not. Third, it is well established that *Kompetenz-Kompetenz* in US law signifies only that tribunals may determine their authority; it does not make that authority exclusive. Fourth, treating a standard *Kompetenz-Kompetenz* clause as sufficient to establish clear and unmistakable evidence of a delegation effectively reverses *First Options'* strong presumption that parties are entitled to an independent judicial determination of arbitrability if that is what they seek.

### 4.  *Schein, Inc. v Archer & White Sales, Inc.*

The question whether the incorporation by reference of institutional rules containing a *Kompetenz-Kompetenz* provision constitutes clear and unmistakable evidence, within the meaning of *First Options*, first drew the Court's attention in the case of *Henry Schein, Inc. v Archer and White Sales, Inc.* The issue before the Court there was not whether a

---

[18]  *FSC Sec. Corp. v Freel*, 14 F.3d 1310, 1312–13 (8th Cir 1994).

[19]  See eg *Oracle Am., Inc. v Myriad Grp. A.G.*, 724 F.3d 1069, 1074–75 (9th Cir 2013) ("We see no reason to deviate from the prevailing view that incorporation of the UNCITRAL arbitration rules is clear and unmistakable evidence that the parties agreed the arbitrator would decide arbitrability"); *Qualcomm Inc. v Nokia Corp.*, 466 F.3d 1366 (Fed Cir 2006) ("We agree with the Second Circuit's analysis ... and likewise conclude that the 2001 Agreement, which incorporates the AAA Rules ... clearly and unmistakably shows the parties' intent to delegate the issue of determining arbitrability to an arbitrator.").

[20]  *Petrofac, Inc. v DynMcDermott Petroleum Operations Co.*, 687 F.3d 671, 675 (5th Cir 2012).

*Kompetenz-Kompetenz* provision in a set of incorporated rules constitutes clear and unmistakable evidence of a delegation but rather whether, assuming a valid delegation has been made, a court could avoid referring the case to arbitration on the ground that the particular challenge to arbitrability being advanced was "wholly groundless".[21] The Court in *Schein* ruled unanimously that no such "wholly groundless" exception exists.[22]

However, during oral argument in *Schein*, several members of the Court expressed some doubt whether the incorporation of institutional rules containing a *Kompetenz-Kompetenz* clause did in itself amount to a delegation within the meaning of *First Options* in the first place. The arbitration clause in *Schein* had stated:

> Any dispute arising under or related to this Agreement (except for actions seeking injunctive relief and disputes related to ... intellectual property of Pelton & Crane), shall be resolved by binding arbitration in accordance with the arbitration rules of the American Arbitration Association.[23]

This clause contained no language whatsoever suggestive of a delegation.

At the very outset of oral argument, Justice Ginsburg queried counsel as to why the above-quoted arbitration agreement divested courts of authority to determine arbitrability:

> But clear and unmistakable delegation, why can't it be both; that is, that the arbitrator has this authority to decide questions of arbitrability, but it is not exclusive of the court? We have one brief saying that that is indeed the position that the Restatement has taken.
>
> ....
>
> When ... the model case is this Court's [*Rent-A-Center*] decision, and there the clause said the arbitrator, not the court, has exclusive authority. And here we're missing both the arbitrator, to the exclusion of the court, and the arbitrator has exclusive authority.[24]

Similarly, Justice Kagan inquired:

> *First Options* is a case where we said we're not going to treat these delegation clauses in exactly the same way as we treat other clauses. And there was an idea that people don't really think about the question of who decides, and so we're going to hold parties to this higher standard, the clear and unmistakable intent standard.[25]

Justice Breyer observed:

---

[21] *Henry Schein, Inc. v Archer and White Sales, Inc.*, 576 US, 139 S. Ct. 524, 527–28 (2019).
[22] ibid.
[23] ibid 528.
[24] Transcript of Oral Argument at 7, 18, *Schein*, 139 S. Ct. 524 (2019) (No 17-1272) [hereinafter OA Tr].
[25] ibid 17.

[S]o you say step 1. Is there clear and unmistakable evidence that an arbitrator is to decide whether a particular matter X is arbitrable? Is that right?

. . . .

Step 1 is we have to decide … whether there is a clear and unmistakable commitment to have this kind of matter decided in arbitration.[26]

Justice Gorsuch in turn asked:

[T]here's just maybe a really good argument that clear and unmistakable proof doesn't exist in this case of—of a desire to go to arbitration and have the arbitrator decide arbitrability?[27]

Significantly, in its directions on remand in *Schein*, the Court specifically invited the Fifth Circuit to address the question whether *First Options'* clear and unmistakable evidence requirement had been met:

We express no view about whether the contract at issue in this case in fact delegated the arbitrability question to an arbitrator. The Court of Appeals did not decide that issue. Under our cases, courts "should not assume that the parties agreed to arbitrate arbitrability unless there is clear and unmistakable evidence that they did so." On remand, the Court of Appeals may address that issue in the first instance. … [28]

It is a sign of the importance of this predicate question that members of the Court raised the issue, despite not having granted certiorari on it and the parties not having focused on it in their briefs.

However, the Fifth Circuit failed on remand to make the determination that the Court requested. Instead, it simply followed its prior decision in *Petrofac, Inc. v DynMcDermott Petroleum Operations Co.* to the effect that "an arbitration agreement that incorporates the AAA Rules 'presents clear and unmistakable evidence that the parties agreed to arbitrate arbitrability'".[29] The Court then declined to refer the parties to arbitration on the ground that the claim being brought fell within a "carve-out" to the arbitration agreement.[30] The Supreme Court granted certiorari on the "carve-out" question while denying a cross-motion or grant of certiorari on the question whether the parties had made a sufficiently clear and unmistakable delegation. It then heard oral argument, but subsequently dismissed the case on the ground that certiorari had been improvidently granted.[31] The

---

[26] ibid 20, 24.
[27] ibid 42.
[28] *Schein*, 139 S Ct at 531 (citations omitted).
[29] *Archer and White Sales, Inc. v Henry Schein, Inc.*, 935 F.3d 274, 279 (5th Cir 2019) (citing *Petrofac, Inc. v DynMcDermott Petroleum Operations Co.*, 687 F.3d 671, 675 (5th Cir 2012)).
[30] *Archer and White Sales*, 935 F.3d at 281–82.
[31] Writ of Certiorari, *Schein*, 141 SCt 107 (2021) (No 19-963) (per curiam). See also Brief for Petitioner, *Schein*, No 19-963, 2020 WL 5074342, at *14–15 (5th Cir Aug 2020).

Court therefore ultimately addressed neither the "carve-out" nor the delegation question.[32]

## 5. Incorporation by Reference

It is questionable at the very outset that evidence of a delegation should be considered clear and unmistakable when it is relegated to a separate document that is only incorporated by reference in an arbitration agreement to arbitrate, rather than set out in an arbitration agreement itself. By definition, a provision as consequential as a delegation of authority to determine gateway issues cannot be deemed clear and unmistakable when it is buried in a referenced set of procedural rules. Parties can reasonably be expected to read a contractual arbitration clause carefully before agreeing to it. An arbitration clause is where a party entertaining any doubts over whether it was jeopardizing its right of access to a court on the question whether it consented to arbitrate is likely to look. By contrast, a party cannot realistically be expected to scrutinize lengthy and detailed rules of arbitral procedure incorporated by reference in an arbitration clause in search of enlightenment on that matter. Practically speaking, for most parties, rules of arbitral procedure assume importance only once arbitration is initiated. Why, more particularly, would a party look to an instrument outside the arbitration agreement and denominated *rules of arbitral procedure* to find principles that address the relationship between *arbitral* and *judicial jurisdiction*, which is not a procedural matter?

In the only case in which the Supreme Court has faced a delegation clause—*Rent-A-Center, West, Inc. v Jackson*—the parties did what anyone intent on making evidence of a delegation clear and unmistakable would do.[33] They placed the delegation of authority directly in their arbitration agreement itself.[34] No party seeking to make a delegation genuinely conspicuous would choose to place it anywhere else, including a set of referenced procedural rules.

But even if incorporation by reference were good enough, which it is not, the presence of a *Kompetenz-Kompetenz* clause in a set of incorporated rules in itself falls far short of clearly and unmistakably manifesting an intention to delegate, and for several reasons.

## 6. The Meaning of *Kompetenz-Kompetenz*

A *Kompetenz-Kompetenz* clause unquestionably vests authority in an arbitral tribunal to determine its own jurisdiction.[35] The relevant procedural rule in the *Schein*

---

[32] The Supreme Court also denied certiorari in another case, raising directly the question whether a *Kompetenz-Kompetenz* clause in incorporated rules of procedure constitutes a clear and unmistakable indication of an intention to make a delegation. Denial of Writ of Certiorari, *Piersing v Domino's Pizza*, No 20-695 (US 25 January 2021).

[33] *Rent-A-Center, W., Inc. v Jackson*, 561 US 63 (2010).

[34] ibid at 66.

[35] Gary B. Born, International Commercial Arbitration 1141 (3rd edn, Wolters Kluwer 2021).

case—Rule 7 of the AAA Commercial Arbitration Rules—states directly as follows: "The arbitrator shall have the power to rule on his or her own jurisdiction, including any objections with respect to the existence, scope or validity of the arbitration agreement(s)."[36] By its plain meaning, Rule 7 gives tribunals authority that they arguably would not otherwise have. This is significant. Absent such a provision, a tribunal whose jurisdiction is challenged on arbitrability grounds could be stopped in its tracks if and when a party challenging arbitrability has recourse to a court for a determination of the matter. The tribunal is likely to suspend proceedings pending a judicial determination, resulting in delay and expense, and compromising two of arbitration's strongest selling points: speed and economy. Conferring authority on a tribunal to determine its own competence is thus neither negligible nor to be taken for granted. It contributes importantly to arbitration's efficacy as a dispute resolution mechanism.

But it does not follow from the fact that arbitrators *have* authority to determine arbitrability that courts *do not*. In order for *Kompetenz-Kompetenz* to achieve its important purpose, it need not be understood as divesting courts of authority to make that jurisdictional determination if asked to do so. In order to reach the result it did in the *Schein* case, the Fifth Circuit, like the Courts of Appeals in the other cases, was required to read into the *Kompetenz-Kompetenz* clause in the AAA Rules the word "exclusive" which is not there.[37] That is a big and very serious leap, and by no means a necessary one, as the above-cited remarks by members of the Supreme Court at the oral argument in *Schein* reveal.

The way in which parties properly dispel doubt over whether they have delegated to a tribunal sole authority to determine matters of arbitrability is through the simple device of making arbitral authority over gateway issues expressly exclusive. That is precisely what the parties did in the *Rent-A-Center* case. Their arbitration agreement stated:

[t]he Arbitrator, *and not* any federal, state, or local court or agency, shall have *exclusive* authority to resolve any dispute relating to the interpretation, applicability, enforceability or formation of this [Arbitration] Agreement including, but not limited to any claim that all or any part of this [Arbitration] Agreement is void or voidable.[38]

In other words, the parties in *Rent-A-Center* took two simple steps to make their intent to delegate authority to determine arbitrability clear and unmistakable. As already noted,[39] they placed the delegation clause in the arbitration agreement itself, not in rules incorporated by reference—and they expressly declared that authority to be "exclusive". Significantly, the question whether there was a valid delegation in *Rent-A-Center* was never even raised.

---

[36] American Arbitration Association (AAA), Commercial Arbitration Rules R-7 (1 Oct 2013).
[37] *Archer and White Sales, Inc. v Henry Schein, Inc.*, 935 F.3d 274, 280 (5th Cir 2019).
[38] *Rent-A-Center, W., Inc. v Jackson*, 561 US 63, 66 (2010).
[39] See Denial of Writ of Certiorari, *Piersing v Domino's Pizza*, No 20-695 (US 25 January 2021) and text accompanying note 24.

Certain lower federal courts, both before and after the trend among the Courts of Appeal had emerged, have properly understood the difference between granting authority to tribunals and depriving courts of that authority, and could not bring themselves to describe reference to *Kompetenz-Kompetenz* in incorporated procedural rules as clear and unmistakable evidence of a delegation. One federal district court, in a circuit that has not yet ruled on the issue, bucked the trend among the Courts of Appeals:

> It is hard to see how an agreement's bare incorporation by reference of a completely separate set of rules that includes a statement that an arbitrator has authority to decide validity and arbitrability amounts to "clear and unmistakable" evidence that the contracting parties agreed to ... preclude a court from answering them. To the contrary, that seems anything but "clear." And the AAA rule itself does not make the purported delegation of authority any more "clear" or "unmistakable." The AAA rule simply says that the arbitrator has the authority to decide these questions. It does not say that the arbitrator has the sole authority, the exclusive authority, or anything like that. The language of the rule does not suggest a *delegation* of authority; at most it indicates that the arbitrator possesses authority, which is not the same as an agreement by the parties to give him sole authority to decide those issues.[40]

Another federal district court felt obliged to follow the prevailing view, but not without strongly condemning it as "incongruous", "ridiculous", and "bordering on the absurd".[41] It added: "[h]ow this could be considered clear and unmistakable can only be explained if the true meaning of 'clear' and 'unmistakable' are [sic] ignored".[42] The court nevertheless felt obliged to follow the trend.[43]

The meaning of *First Options* also arises regularly in state courts since the Federal Arbitration Act (FAA) does not create federal subject-matter jurisdiction, much less exclusive jurisdiction. Some of these courts, like certain federal district courts, have rightly rejected the facile assumption that a grant to arbitrators of authority to determine arbitrability necessarily divests courts of that authority. A Florida appellate court recently stated:

> [W]e find something missing. This [institutional] rule confers an adjudicative power upon the arbitrator, but it does not purport to make that power exclusive. Nor does it purport to contractually remove that adjudicative power from a court of competent jurisdiction.
>
> ....
>
> We respectfully disagree with [holdings finding otherwise] because we do not believe they comport with what *First Options* requires .... [N]one of these cases have ever examined how or why the mere "incorporation" of an arbitration rule such as

---

[40] *Taylor v Samsung Elecs. Am., Inc.*, No 19 C 4526, 2020 WL 1248655, at *4 (ND Ill 16 Mar 2020).
[41] *Ashworth v Five Guys Operations, LLC*, No 3:16-06646, 2016 WL 7422679, at *3 (SD WVa 22 Dec 2016).
[42] ibid.
[43] ibid.

the one before us … satisfies the heightened standard the Supreme Court set in *First Options*, nor how it overcomes the "strong pro-court presumption" that is supposed to attend this inquiry. Most of the opinions have simply stated the proposition as having been established with citations to prior decisions that did the same.[44]

The Florida court is not alone.[45]

The only reason any US Court of Appeals has advanced in support of its position that a *Kompetenz-Kompetenz* provision in incorporated procedural rules constitutes clear and unmistakable evidence of a delegation is that the AAA, the institution whose rules were invoked in that case, had amended the language of the rules precisely in order to meet the *First Options* clear and unmistakable evidence test.[46] That may well be the case, but is of little import. It does not matter what the AAA thought it was doing. What matters is what parties signing an arbitration agreement think they are doing. That the AAA thinks its amended clause constitutes clear and unmistakable evidence does not mean that it does. It does not.

## 7. *Kompetenz-Kompetenz* in US Law

In fact, *Kompetenz-Kompetenz* has been consistently understood in the United States to authorize an arbitral tribunal to determine its jurisdiction if challenged, and nothing more.[47] In point of fact, there has never been any inconsistency in US law between *Kompetenz-Kompetenz*, on the one hand, and access to a court on issues of arbitrability, on the other. Decades before arbitral institutions were putting *Kompetenz-Kompetenz* provisions in their procedural rules, courts and tribunals were already practising *Kompetenz-Kompetenz*,[48] without any supposition that it barred courts from making an independent judicial determination of arbitrability prior to arbitration if so requested.

---

[44] *Doe v Natt*, No 2D19-1383, 2020 WL 1486926, at *7–9 (Fla Dist Ct App 25 Mar 2020) (citations omitted).

[45] See *Ajamian v CantorCO2e, LP*, 137 Cal Rptr 3d 773, 782–83 (Cal Ct App 2012) (citations omitted):

> "The 'clear and unmistakable' test reflects a 'heightened standard' of proof. That is because the question of who would decide the unconscionability of an arbitration provision is not one that the parties would likely focus upon in contracting, and the default expectancy is that the court would decide the matter. Thus … a contract's silence or ambiguity about the arbitrator's power in this regard cannot satisfy the clear and unmistakable evidence standard.
>
> ….
>
> Appellants … point … primarily to … the arbitration provision['s] … proviso that arbitration may be conducted according to the rules of the AAA (under which an arbitrator has the power to determine the validity of an arbitration agreement). [Appellee] disagrees with appellants' arguments… [Appellee]—and the trial court—have it right."

[46] *Blanton v Domino's Pizza Franchising LLC*, 962 F.3d 842, 8495050 (6th Cir 2020).

[47] Ashley Cook, "Kompetenz-Kompetenz: Varying Approaches and a Proposal for a Limited Form of Negative Kompetenz-Kompetenz" (2014) 2014(1) Pepperdine Law Review 17, 25 (explaining that US law does not "even contemplate[e] negative kompetenz-kompetenz"); William Park, "Challenging Arbitral Jurisdiction: The Role of Institutional Rules" (2105) 16 Boston University School of Law, Public Law and Legal Theory Paper no 15-40, ("[C]ourts will provide early decisions on the validity of a dispute resolution clause alleged to be void *ab initio* because, for instance, the person signing the contract lacked authority to commit the company sought to be bound.").

[48] James Crawford, "Continuity and Discontinuity in International Dispute Settlement: An Inaugural Lecture" (2010) 1 Journal of International Dispute Settlement 3, 15–20.

The fact that *Kompetenz-Kompetenz* does not preclude access to a court on arbitrability issues is actually built into the key instruments of domestic and international arbitration law in the US. The Federal Arbitration Act specifically calls upon courts to compel arbitration only if they are "*satisfied that the making of the agreement for arbitration … [was] not in issue*".[49] Similarly, under Article II of the New York Convention, courts do not refer parties to arbitration if they find the arbitration agreement to be "*null and void, inoperative or incapable of being performed*".[50] Courts could not possibly perform their obligations under the FAA or the New York Convention if *Kompetenz-Kompetenz* operated to negate judicial authority to make arbitrability determinations. In sum, the *Kompetenz-Kompetenz* principle in US law has never entailed the corollary that, if arbitrators *may* decide arbitrability, courts *may not*.

The understanding of *Kompetenz-Kompetenz* in US law contrasts sharply with the understanding that prevails in certain other countries, which view the doctrine as *both* vesting tribunals with authority to determine arbitrability *and* divesting courts of that authority. The jurisdiction that most resolutely adheres to this approach (but not the only one to adopt it) is France. Under settled French law, *Kompetenz-Kompetenz* has *both* a "positive" *and* a "negative" dimension.[51] The former affirmatively confers on tribunals authority to determine their jurisdiction, while the latter deprives courts, prior to arbitration, of that authority.[52] Significantly, however, even under French law, negative *Kompetenz-Kompetenz* is not entirely unreviewable. The Civil Procedure Code expressly authorizes courts to decline to enforce an arbitration agreement if they find it "manifestly void or manifestly not applicable".[53] The sharp difference between the US version of *Kompetenz-Kompetenz* ("positive" only) and the French version (both "positive" and "negative") pervades the international arbitration literature. The fact that *Kompetenz-Kompetenz* in US law has a positive dimension is simply uncontested.[54]

In short, whether incorporated in institutional rules or not, *Kompetenz-Kompetenz*, as indisputably understood in US law, does not deprive courts of the authority, when asked, to determine the arbitrability of a dispute prior to arbitration—much less deprive them of that authority "clearly and unmistakably". There is no justification for altering the established meaning of *Kompetenz-Kompetenz* merely because it has made its way into a set of incorporated procedural rules.

---

[49] Federal Arbitration Act, 9 USC § 4 (emphasis added).

[50] Convention on the Recognition and Enforcement of Foreign Arbitral Awards art II(3), June 10, 1968, 21 UST 2517, 330 UNTS 38 (emphasis added). See also Federal Arbitration Act § 201.

[51] See generally Emmanuel Gaillard and Yas Banifatemi, "Negative Effect of Competence-Competence: The Rule of Priority in Favor of the Arbitrators" in Emmanuel Gaillard and Domenico Di Pietro (eds), Enforcement of Arbitration Agreements and International Arbitral Awards: The New York Convention in Practice, (Cameron May 2008).

[52] Born (n 35) 1161.

[53] Code de Procédure Civile [CPC] [Civil Procedure Code] art 1448 (Fr.).

[54] See eg Graves and Davydan (n 15) 157.

## 8. A Reversal of Presumptions

The Supreme Court in *First Options* deliberately made judicial authority to determine arbitrability the rule, and deprivation of that authority the exception, doing so out of a commitment to the principle of party consent lying at the heart of US arbitration law. By its own account, the Court in that decision prescribed a "heightened standard" for finding a delegation.[55] In a word, parties must decidedly "go out of their way" to withdraw from courts the authority to decide issues of arbitrability that they ordinarily enjoy. The "clear and unmistakable" standard cannot be understood any other way.

The Supreme Court's purpose in *First Options* would be frustrated if the mere inclusion of a *Kompetenz-Kompetenz* clause in procedural rules referenced in an arbitration agreement were treated, *per se*, as clear and unmistakable evidence of a delegation under *First Options*. There is nothing in the language of a standard garden-variety *Kompetenz-Kompetenz* clause, wherever it may be found, that puts a party on sufficient notice of a delegation. A party reading that language would have no idea that, by signing the agreement, it was relinquishing its fundamental right of access to a court to demonstrate that it never consented to arbitration, that is, that the agreement was never formed, is not binding on it, is invalid, or has no application to the dispute. As the Court stated in *First Options* itself, treating as a valid delegation a clause that is less than clear and unmistakable "might too often force unwilling parties to arbitrate a matter they reasonably would have thought a judge, not an arbitrator, would decide".[56] The Court considered *Kompetenz-Kompetenz* far too "arcane" to be given that effect.[57]

The inescapable conclusion from all that precedes is that a *Kompetenz-Kompetenz* provision, wherever placed, is altogether too oblique a means of informing parties of a matter as momentous as loss of the right of access to a court on matters of arbitrability—a right of access that they have every reason to believe they enjoy. It is worth recalling here the concern voiced by Justice Kagan in *Schein*:

> [I]f you look at *First Options*, *First Options* is a case where we said we're not going to treat these delegation clauses in exactly the same way as we treat other clauses. And there was an idea that people don't really think about the question of who decides, and so we're going to hold parties to this higher standard, the clear and unmistakable intent standard.[58]

Moreover, today *Kompetenz-Kompetenz* provisions are ubiquitous. They are found in virtually every modern set of institutional rules; the AAA Rules are by no means

---

[55] *Rent-A-Center, W., Inc. v Jackson*, 561 US 63, 69 n.1 (2010).
[56] *First Options of Chi., Inc. v Kaplan*, 514 US 938, 945 (1995).
[57] ibid.
[58] OA Tr (n 24) 17.

exceptional.[59] They are also found in virtually every modern arbitration law that States enact to regulate international arbitral activity conducted on their territory. Under the leading model law of international arbitration, widely adopted around the world and even by a good number of US states: "[t]he arbitral tribunal may rule on its own jurisdiction, including any objections with respect to the existence or validity of the arbitration agreement".[60] It is consequently the rare international arbitration indeed that is conducted in the absence of a *Kompetenz-Kompetenz* provision. In other words, such provisions have become, for all practical purposes, "boiler-plate". Parties do not need to "go out of their way" to subject their arbitrations to *Kompetenz-Kompetenz.* All modern arbitration laws and rules do that for them.

In short, treating a standard *Kompetenz-Kompetenz* provision as *per se* clear and unmistakable evidence within the meaning of *First Options* effectively reverses the presumption that the Supreme Court so emphatically established in that case in favour of a party's right of access to a court on the basic issue of consent to arbitrate. It comports neither with the letter nor the spirit of *First Options* to treat a *Kompetenz-Kompetenz* provision in a set of incorporated institutional rules as clear and unmistakable evidence of an intention to deprive parties of access to an independent judicial determination of arbitrability. That simply cannot be the result that the Supreme Court had in mind in rendering the *First Options* decision.

It would also be a great mistake to assume that if US courts lose their authority to ensure the arbitrability of a dispute prior to arbitration, they will recover it at the end of the process. Under US law, once a proper delegation is made, courts are sidelined, not only pre-arbitration but also in post-award review. The case law holds that, under a proper delegation, courts also cannot, in a vacatur or confirmation action, meaningfully ensure that the award debtor consented to arbitration. They owe extreme deference to a tribunal's determination whether an arbitration agreement exists, is valid, is applicable to a non-signatory and encompasses the dispute at hand.[61] According to the Restatement, in order to be overturned, a tribunal's finding of arbitrability on the basis of a delegation must be "baseless",[62] resting this conclusion on the Supreme Court's ruling in the case of *Oxford Health Plans LLC v Sutter.*[63]

Thus, under a delegation, *at no point* in the arbitration life cycle will parties have the benefit of an independent judicial determination whether they indeed consented to arbitrate. That is too drastic a result to follow from the mere presence of a standard *Kompetenz-Kompetenz* provision only found in the rules of procedure referenced in an agreement to arbitrate.

[59] Thus, Article 23(1) of the UNCITRAL Arbitration Rules (2013) similarly provides that "[t]he arbitral tribunal shall have the power to rule on its own jurisdiction, including any objections with respect to the existence or validity of the arbitration agreement".

[60] United Nations Commission for International Trade Law (UNCITRAL), Model Law on International Commercial Arbitration, art 16(1) (2006).

[61] See *Schneider v Kingdom of Thailand*, 688 F.3d 68, 71 (2d Cir 2012); *Chevron Corp. v Republic of Ecuador*, 949 F Supp 2d 57, 65–67 (DDC 2013).

[62] Restatement of the Law, the US law of International Commerce and Investor–State Arbitration, § 4.12, reporters' note e (American Law Institute, Proposed Final Draft No 623, 2019) [hereinafter Restatement].

[63] *Oxford Health Plans LLC v Sutter*, 569 US 564, 569 (2013).

A comparison with French law in this regard is here too highly illuminating. As noted, under French law, courts have virtually no role in ensuring that a dispute is arbitrable before compelling parties to arbitrate.[64] For all practical purposes, a dispute will proceed to arbitration on the merits if a tribunal, in its exercise of *Kompetenz-Kompetenz*, finds a dispute to be arbitrable. The involvement of a court at this stage is negligible.

However, French law justifies this result precisely on the ground that *after* an arbitration comes to a close and an award is rendered, a party that failed to convince the tribunal to dismiss a case on arbitrability grounds has access to a court to have the resulting award annulled or denied enforcement on those same grounds. Moreover, the inquiry into arbitrability that a French court performs on that occasion is completely *de novo*.[65] In other words, courts fully regain at the end of the process the role they were denied at the outset. Under a delegation clause, US courts do not.

## 9. The Restatement and Academic Commentary

The delegation question received sustained attention at the time the recently adopted the American Law Institute's (ALI) Restatement of the US Law of International Commercial and Investment Arbitration was prepared. The Reporters, the ALI Council, and the ALI membership at large faced directly the question whether the incorporation of *Kompetenz-Kompetenz* language from a set of arbitral rules constituted clear and unmistakable evidence of an intention to withdraw from courts their authority to determine arbitrability.

In its lengthy deliberations, the ALI closely examined the proposition that the presence of *Kompetenz-Kompetenz* provisions in incorporated institutional rules satisfies the *First Options* test. It looked at the proposition from every angle, carefully weighing both the strengths and weaknesses of the proposition. The Reporters concluded with confidence that the proposition was unsustainable,[66] and their position was unanimously adopted by both the ALI Council and the ALI membership when the entire Restatement was approved in May 2019.[67]

---

[64] Section 7.

[65] Ina C Popova and others, "France" (2020) European Arbitration Review 28, 34.

[66] Restatement (n 62) § 2.8, art b, reporter's note b(iii).

[67] Petitioner may, as it did previously in its submission during the certiorari process, attempt to undermine the relevance of the ALI Restatement by suggesting that the final version of the Restatement retreated from a stronger position on the point taken in an earlier draft. Petitioner observed that the final draft of the Restatement did not state that it "reject[s] the majority line of cases ... as based on a misinterpretation of the institutional rules being applied". This observation is disingenuous. First, it is the Comments, not the Reporters' notes, that state the official position of the ALI, and Comment *b* to the relevant section in the draft of the Restatement as approved states unequivocally that "the rules ... do not expressly give the tribunal exclusive authority over these issues". Restatement, note 62, § 2.8, art B, reporter's note b(iii) As for the Reporters' notes, note b(iii) examines at length the relevant language of a large number of institutional rules similar to the AAA's and observes that not a single one constitutes "clear and unmistakable" evidence within the meaning of *First Options*. There was no need to state a global summary of that finding. As Chief Reporter of the Restatement, I can affirm that this amicus brief accurately reports the ALI's position.

Commentators similarly recognize the anomaly, in light of what the Court meant to achieve in *First Options*, of treating a *Kompetenz-Kompetenz* provision in incorporated rules as clear and unmistakable evidence of a delegation:

> A ... conclusion from *First Options* is that absent rebuttal of the anti-arbitration presumption—and any such rebuttal will surely be very rare—existence and validity questions will not be subject to a negative competence-competence doctrine in the United States. This conclusion is not affected by whether one party has initiated arbitral proceedings or whether arbitrators have been seized of the matter. Court jurisdiction to decide arbitrability [prior to arbitration] will also be full and not limited by a prima facie standard.[68]

That author elsewhere described the courts' position as "startling" and "misguided".[69] He notes that parties include in their arbitration agreement institutional rules containing a *Kompetenz-Kompetenz* clause "almost as a matter of course".[70] Treating such a clause as barring independent judicial review, he writes, "seems unwise and unlikely to have been intended by parties when they opt for institutional arbitration".[71] Significantly, he concludes: "It will fall to the [Supreme] Court itself to correct this error in a future decision."[72]

## 10.  Conclusion

The US Courts of Appeal have seriously erred in treating the incorporation by reference in an arbitration agreement of procedural rules containing a *Kompetenz-Kompetenz* clause as "clear and unmistakable" evidence of an intention to withdraw from parties the right to a judicial determination of the question whether they validly agreed to arbitrate a given dispute. In order to be clear and unmistakable, a delegation should be placed directly in the parties' agreement to arbitrate, not relegated to a set of procedural rules that parties will almost certainly read, much less with care, upon signing the underlying contract.

The Courts are also deeply mistaken in assuming that if arbitrators have authority to determine the arbitrability of a claim, courts necessarily do not. US arbitration law distinguishes itself from French arbitration law by, among other things, embracing "positive", while rejecting "negative", *Kompetenz-Kompetenz*. That tribunals may determine

---

[68] John J Barceló III, "Who Decides the Arbitrators' Jurisdiction? Separability and Competence-Competence in Transnational Perspective" (2003) 36 Vanderbilt Journal of Transnational Law 1115, 1133. See generally Stavros Brekoulakis, "The Negative Effect of Compétence-Compétence: The Verdict has to be Negative" (2009) Austrian Arbitration Yearbook on International Arbitration 237.

[69] John James Barcelo, "Kompetenz-Kompetenz and Its Negative Effect—A Comparative View" (2017) 23 Cornell Law School, Legal Studies Research Paper No 17-40.

[70] ibid.

[71] ibid.

[72] ibid.

arbitral jurisdiction does not mean that courts may not. The meaning of *Kompetenz-Kompetenz* in US law does not change merely because rules of arbitral procedure contain that term.

Nor is there any indication to the contrary in *First Options*. US courts, including the Supreme Court, are well aware of the fact that, *Kompetenz-Kompetenz* notwithstanding, they have not only the right but also the obligation to determine the arbitrability of a claim if they are asked to do so. Both the FAA and the New York Convention plainly so state. In demanding clear and unmistakable evidence of a delegation, the Supreme Court in *First Options* must necessarily have been demanding a good deal more than that, as the very phrase "clear and unmistakable" itself proves.

*Kompetenz-Kompetenz* provisions are found everywhere on the arbitration landscape, domestic and international alike. Even if parties do not inscribe it directly in their arbitration agreement, virtually all modern arbitration laws and rules expressly embrace it. If the mere presence of what has become standard boiler-plate language suffices to establish clear and unmistakable evidence of a delegation, the presumption that the Supreme Court carefully and emphatically established in *First Options* will, for all practical purposes, be reversed.

This makes it all the more important that the very high bar set by the Court for a valid delegation in *First Options* be maintained, something the US Courts of Appeal have utterly failed to do. Without any serious reasoning whatsoever, they have taken a position that is inimical to the fundamental principles that (i) parties are not required to submit their claims to arbitration without their consent and that (ii) they are presumptively entitled, upon request, to an independent judicial determination of that matter. At stake is something even more basic than the principle of consent itself, namely the legitimacy of arbitration itself. It is not news that arbitration is increasingly under attack.[73] US courts should do nothing to place that legitimacy at risk. In insisting that the mere presence of a *Kompetenz-Kompetenz* provision in incorporated institutional rules of arbitral procedure by definition meets *First Options*' requirement of clear and unmistakable evidence of a delegation, they have done just that.

---

[73] See generally, James H Carter, "The Culture of Arbitration and the Defence of Arbitral Legitimacy" in David D Caron and others (eds), *Practising Virtue: Inside International Arbitration* (Oxford University Press 2016) 97, 97.

# PART V

# LOOKING TO THE FUTURE

# 27

# International Law and Democratic Backsliding

*Tom Ginsburg*

## 1. Introduction

In 2017, David Caron gave the Charles N Brower Lecture on International Dispute Resolution at the Annual Meeting of the American Society of International Law, and focused on the role of the adjudicator.[1] Drawing on ideas associated with his former colleague (and my own PhD advisor) Martin Shapiro, Caron noted a fundamental distinction between the *functions* of courts—which include law-making, social control, legitimation, and regime construction, among many others—and the *task* of adjudicators, which he viewed as resolving the dispute before them on the basis of the relevant law.[2] Caron urged adjudicators to focus on the *task* rather than the *functions*, arguing that only by doing so could they preserve the integrity of the institutions they inhabit.

Caron inhabited the classical world of interstate dispute resolution, beginning and ending his career at the Iran-United States Claims Tribunal (IUSCTR). It was a body for which the task and the function were fairly aligned. The audience for the IUSCTR was primarily the two states that had set it up to resolve issues between them, as well as the private claimants who were seeking recompense, primarily from Iran, for expropriations and other wrongs. Caron's own analysis of the IUSCTR focused heavily on the intentions of the parties, and he used this angle to cut through various arguments about the Tribunal's "nature".[3] The Tribunal's legal personality depended exclusively on the will of the two parties, as well as that of the Government of the Netherlands which agreed to host it. The task of the Tribunal was dispute resolution. In terms of Shapiro's "functions", the Tribunal engaged in some law-making in the course of deciding principles of international investment law, but this was incidental to its main mission.[4]

The jurisprudential implication of a focus on the intentions of the parties is that courts should restrict their pronouncements only to those necessary to resolve the dispute at hand. In the Brower lecture, Caron critiqued dicta in which the International Court of Justice (ICJ) expressed its sympathy for human rights victims, and urged the

---

[1] David D Caron, "Remarks by David D Caron" (2018) 111 American Society of International Law Processings 231.

[2] Martin Shapiro, *Courts* (University of Chicago Press 1981).

[3] See his notable analysis in David D Caron, "The Nature of the Iran-United States Claims Tribunal and the Evolving Structure of International Dispute Resolution" (1990) 84 American Journal of International Law 104.

[4] On the impact of the IUSCTR, see Charles N Brower and Jason Brueschke, *The Iran-United States Claims Tribunal* (Martinus Nijhoff Publishers 1998); George H Aldrich, *The Jurisprudence of the Iran- United States Claims Tribunal* (Oxford University Press 1996).

Tom Ginsburg, *International Law and Democratic Backsliding* In: *By Peaceful Means*.
Edited by: Charles N Brower, Joan E Donoghue, Cian C Murphy, Cymie R Payne and Esmé R Shirlow, Oxford University Press.
© Tom Ginsburg 2024. DOI: 10.1093/oso/9780192848086.003.0027

judges to focus on the immediate legal task at hand.[5] Reviewing some discussion in the case of *Armed Activities on the Territory of the Congo*, he agreed with the view of Judge Thomas Buergenthal, who wrote in a separate opinion that the ICJ's expression of sympathy for victims dealt "with matters the Court has no jurisdiction to address once it has ruled that it lacks prima facie jurisdiction to issue the requested provisional measures".[6] Caron contrasted this with the view of Judge Koroma, who found that the ICJ had effectively discharged the responsibilities of the Court in this part of its opinion.[7]

Caron's minimalism emphasizes a dispute resolution perspective. Even from the narrow perspective of adjudicating between two private parties, one might take issue with it, since in many contexts the language of a judicial opinion can soften the blow to the loser, and help legitimate the court's answer. Dicta are there for a reason. Another of Caron's former colleagues, the psychologist Tom Tyler, has emphasized the importance of procedure and the feeling of being heard to the legitimacy of law (though to be fair, his ideas of procedural justice may not fit easily in the context of inter-state dispute resolution, since the relevant psychological research has been conducted on individuals).[8] But to Caron, the graver risk was the distortion of the judicial task in the service of various social functions. This is an expression of professional caution.

From my perspective, we must recognize that in some fields, the "task" of judges is not adjudicating between sovereign equals or private parties but rather explicitly developing the law or enforcing certain deeper values. Human rights law is one such area in which the law itself is open-ended and often vague. The job of judges is not just to adjudicate between an aggrieved individual and a state but rather to expand the law and to make sure it tracks evolving understandings of rights. Some of these rights concern the very functioning of democracy itself. Furthermore there has been a series of democracy charters adopted by regional organizations, which judges are tasked with enforcing.[9] In such cases, I argue, the task of judges cannot be separated from their social function. They must be purposive and not formalist, considering the broader systemic effects of their decisions.

In this chapter I examine one specific function of international courts, namely the promotion, support, and disciplining of democracy. It might seem odd to consider this as a kind of core function of international law, which, as classically defined, does not inquire into the internal political or governance arrangements of states.[10] Yet it is also the case that the expansion of international institutions, including courts, has typically

---

[5] Caron, "Remarks" (n 1) 237; *Armed Activities on the Territory of the Congo (Democratic Republic of the Congo v Rwanda)* (Provisional Measures) [2002] ICJ Rep 219, 257 (Declaration by Judge Buergenthal).

[6] Caron, "Remarks" (n 1) 257.

[7] *Armed Activities on the Territory of the Congo* (Provisional Measures) (n 5) 254 (Declaration by Judge Koroma).

[8] Tom Tyler, *Why People Obey the Law* (Princeton University Press 1990).

[9] Inter-American Democratic Charter (adopted 11 September 2001) 40 ILM 1289; African Charter on Democracy, Elections and Governance (adopted 30 January 2007, entered into force 15 February 2012) (ACDEG); Economic Community of West African States (ECOWAS) Protocol A/SP1/12/01 on Democracy and Good Governance Supplementary to the Protocol relating to the Mechanism for Conflict Prevention, Management, Resolution, Peacekeeping and Security (adopted 21 December 2001) A/SP1/12/01.

[10] See eg UN Charter (adopted 26 June 1945, entered into force 24 October 1945) 1 UNTS XVI, art 2(4) ("[a]ll Members shall refrain in their international relations from the threat or use of force against the territorial integrity or political independence of any state").

occurred at moments of global democratization, namely after the Second World War and the Cold War. While not all international institutions are committed to democracy by any means, it is a longstanding view among international relations scholars that democracies are more likely than non-democracies to cooperate across borders. And a rich institutional architecture of democracy has developed since the Cold War. In a 2017 report, the Secretary-General of the United Nations notes that his organization has provided electoral assistance to one-third of its member states.[11] I have already mentioned regional democracy charters, which began with the Organization of American States (OAS) and expanded to Africa, requiring democratic governance as an international matter. The European Convention of Human Rights also has an architecture in this regard, as does the European Union. As international institutions devote lip service to promoting democracy, courts have had to confront issues related to this function.

Such confrontations have become more common in our era of democratic backsliding, which has meant that courts are now called on to play a role in enforcing democracy charters. Indeed, as I write, democracy is viewed as being in a full-scale "retreat" around the world, with fewer democracies each year.[12] This has pushed courts to address a new function. In doing so, a dispute resolution perspective is insufficient. In Caron's sense, I am suggesting that for some courts, the *task* of resolving cases should align with the function of preserving democracy, and they should engage in it.

## 2. Coup and Response

On the 18 August 2020 a number of soldiers from a military base in Kati, Mali departed from their camp, drove to the capital of Bamako, and arrested the country's President, Ibrahim Boubacar Keïta, and Prime Minister Boubou Cissé.[13] Their operation was swiftly followed by the formation of the *Conseil National du Salut de Peuple* (CNSP), a quintet of five military colonels who promised to restore peace and order to Mali. Naturally, this raised concerns among international observers.[14]

Regional response was swift. The African Union condemned the coup, and the fifteen-member Economic Community of West African States (ECOWAS) met immediately to impose sanctions.[15] The regional organization is no stranger to Malian politics, having played a central role in the aftermath of the 2012 Malian coup as well

---

[11] United Nations General Assembly, "Strengthening the Role of the United Nations in Enhancing the Effectiveness of the Principle of Periodic and Genuine Elections and the Promotion of Democratization: Report of the Secretary-General", 79th Session, Item 73(b) of the provisional agenda, UN Doc A/72/260 (1 August 2017).

[12] Nate Schenkkan and Sarah Repucci, "The Freedom House Survey for 2018: Democracy in Retreat" (2019) 30(2) Journal of Democracy 100.

[13] Cyril Bensimon, "Au Mali, un colonel major à la retraite pour succéder aux colonels de la junte" (*Le Monde Afrique*, 22 September 2020) <http://www.lemonde.fr/afrique/article/2020/09/22/au-mali-un-colonel-major-a-la-retraite-pour-succeder-aux-colonels-de-la-junte_6053140_3212.html>.

[14] ibid.

[15] "[Vos réactions] Mali: embargo de la Cédéao, les Maliens s'impatientent" (*RFI*, 5 October 2020) <Http://www.rfi.fr/fr/podcasts/20201005-vos-r%C3%A9actions-mali-embargo-la-c%C3%A9d%C3%A9ao-les-maliens-s-impatientent> (audio).

as intervening militarily, alongside French forces, in the 2013 Malian Civil War.[16] ECOWAS issued an ultimatum, threatening to increase the already severe sanctions to a full embargo if a civilian government was not put in place by 22 September.[17] Mali depends on imports for a substantial portion of their food supply, which had already greatly suffered from the closing of borders caused by COVID-19.[18] It seemed that ECOWAS was in a position of relative strength.

What followed, however, was a rather strained negotiation between the CNSP and ECOWAS. Initially, the *Conseil* rejected any calls for a civilian government. In response, ECOWAS slightly softened its demands during a summit with the CNSP at Accra, agreeing "that the President of the transitions could either be a civilian, or a retired member of the military".[19] Their gambit seemed to pay off. The CNSP appointed Bah N'Daw, who formerly ran the Malian air force and worked as the Minister of Defense, to serve as the President of the transition. However, the leader of the CNSP, Assimi Goïta, was appointed to be Vice President alongside N'Daw.[20] A civilian prime minister was also appointed and on 5 October, a twenty-five-person cabinet was formed with just four members of the military.[21] Sanctions were lifted soon thereafter. The next year, Goïta pushed aside N'Daw in a second coup and is now Interim President.

Why would an economic community mobilize itself to be concerned with the formation of a cabinet? The answer lies in a document adopted by ECOWAS member states in 2001 called the Protocol on Democracy and Good Governance, encapsulating many of the norms then in ascendance such as the separation of powers, independent judiciary, and free and fair elections.[22] This has led to a number of interventions, including in Sierra Leone and Liberia, as well as suspensions of several other member states. In 2016, Operation Restore Democracy in the Gambia persuaded dictator Yahya Jammeh to leave office peacefully after he ignored an electoral loss. ECOWAS has effectively articulated and enforced a regional democracy norm.

Such activity is a far cry from the limitation in the United Nations Charter that prohibited the UN from intervening in any matters "essentially within the domestic jurisdiction".[23] That an international organization created to facilitate economic integration could intervene to "restore democracy" reflects normative developments in the

---

[16] "Mali Conflict: West African Troops to Arrive 'In Days'" (*BBC News*, 15 January 2013) <http://www.bbc.com/news/world-africa-21029916>.

[17] Bensimon (n 13).

[18] Yenizié Koné, "How is COVID-19 Worsening Food Insecurity in Mali? COVID-19 Poses Threats on Food Security in Mali" (*Michigan State University*, 11 September 2020) <http://www.canr.msu.edu/news/how-is-covid-19-worsening-food-insecurity-in-mali>.

[19] Bensimon (n 13) (translation is my own).

[20] "Mali: le président de la transition, Bah N'Daw, a prêté serment" (*RFI*, 25 September 2020) <http://www.rfi.fr/fr/afrique/20200925-mali-le-pr%C3%A9sident-la-transition-bah-n-daw-a-pr%C3%AAt%C3%A9-serment>. Funnily enough, Goïta proposed that he retire from the military in order to become President. His offer was refused by ECOWAS. As vice president, he remains in charge of "the questions of defense and security".

[21] Admittedly, they all hold key posts. "Mali: le nouveau gouvernement de transition nommé, des militaires aux postes stratégiques" (*RFI*, 5 October 2020) <http://www.rfi.fr/fr/afrique/20201005-mali-nouveau-gouvernement-transition-militaires-postes-strat%C3%A9giques>.

[22] ECOWAS Protocol (n 9); See Olabisi D Akinkugbe, "Towards an Analyses of the Mega-Political Jurisprudence of the ECOWAS Community Court of Justice" in James Thuo Gathii (ed), *The Performance of Africa's International Courts: Using International Litigation for Political, Legal, and Social Change* (Oxford University Press 2020).

[23] UN Charter (n 10) art 2(7).

1990s in international law and regional organizations. In the case of ECOWAS, bloody civil wars with regional spillover in the 1990s pushed states to realize that they had a common interest in regional stability. Similarly the AU adopted the African Charter on Democracy, Elections, and Governance (ACDEG) in 2007, which condemns and defines an unconstitutional change of government, a category that now includes coups, intervention by mercenaries or rebels to replace a democratically elected government, a refusal of an incumbent to yield office after losing an election, and "any amendment or revision of the constitution or legal instruments, which is an infringement on the principles of democratic change of government".[24]

To be sure, the democracy charters and their institutional accoutrements have not always been effective. And it is not the case that they are vindicating a global "right" to democracy as proposed by Thomas Franck in the early 1990s.[25] That project was highly contingent and generally rejected.[26] Instead of a universal set of global protections for democracy, as Franck imagined, what we observe is a contingent set of interventions. To paraphrase Louis Henkin, some countries in some regions of the world have joined together to enforce some democratic norms some of the time.[27] But this is still an important and significant development.

## 3. Democracy Charters: The Normative Framework

Democracy charters as international legal documents have gained prominence in recent years, and their roots lie in regional human rights law. The Council of Europe, and its central accomplishment, the European Convention on Human Rights, were created in the aftermath of the Second World War and designed as a defence of democracy.[28] The Convention declares in its preamble that rights and freedoms are best maintained by effective political democracy.[29] As Sir David Maxwell-Fyfe wrote, it was to be "a beacon to those at the moment in totalitarian darkness and ... give them hope of return to freedom".[30] Eventually the States Parties created an adjudicative body, the European Court of Human Rights (ECtHR), which went on to construct an elaborate, effective,

---

[24] African Charter on Democracy (n 9).

[25] Thomas M Franck, "The Emerging Right to Democratic Governance" (1992) 86 American Journal of International Law 46; see Gregory H Fox and Brad R Roth, "Democracy and International Law: A (Re-) Introduction" in Gregory H Fox and Brad R Roth (eds), *Democracy and International Law* (Edward Elgar 2020).

[26] Gregory H Fox and Brad Roth (eds), *Democratic Governance and International Law* (Cambridge University Press 2000); Susan Marks, *The Riddle of All Constitutions: International Law, Democracy and the Critique of Ideology* (Oxford University Press 2000) 75; Susan Marks, "What Has Become of the Emerging Right to Democratic Governance?' (2011) 22(2) European Journal of International Law 507; Dobrochna Bach-Golecka, "The Emerging Right to Good Governance" (2018) 112 American Journal of International Law Unbound 89; see Alexandru Grigorescu and Emily Komp, "The "Broadening" of International Human Rights: The Cases of the Right to Development and Right to Democracy" (2017) 54(2) International Politics 238.

[27] Louis Henkin, *How Nations Behave* (2nd edn, Columbia University Press 1990) 47.

[28] Ed Bates, *The Evolution of the European Convention on Human Rights: From Its Inception to the Creation of a Permanent Court of Human Rights* (Oxford University Press 2010) 5.

[29] European Convention for the Protection of Human Rights and Fundamental Freedoms as Amended by Protocols Nos 11 and 14 (adopted 4 November 1950, entered into force 3 September 1953) 213 UNTS 222, Preamble.

[30] ibid.

and influential regime of rights protection.[31] In determining when rights violations occurred, the Court did more than indirectly police democratic institutions; it also played
a critical role in *defining* the space of democratic deliberation in the negative, namely
through its jurisprudence on limitations of rights. Five core articles of the European
Convention, namely those on the right to a fair trial; private and family life; freedom of
thought, conscience and religion; freedom of expression; and freedom of association,
are explicitly subject to restrictions imposed by the state, to the extent the restrictions
can be justified as necessary in a democratic society.[32] Democracies cannot torture or
deny anyone the right to fair trial, but other rights are subject to a kind of balancing between the rights of the individual and those of the society as a whole. Such balancing
inherently involves lawmaking, albeit in an incremental case-by-case fashion.

In Africa too, democracy has been enshrined in particular instruments. The African
Union has played a major role in the articulation of norms focused on democratic
preservation. A major first step was Article 30 of the Constitutive Act of the Union,
adopted in 2000 at Lomé, which prohibits unconstitutional changes in government.[33]
The categories of unconstitutional changes included coups, intervention by mercenaries, replacement of government by rebels, and the refusal of an incumbent to step
down after free and fair elections. We have already mentioned the 2007 ACDEG, which
added "any amendment or revision of the constitution or legal instruments, which is
an infringement on the principles of democratic change of government".[34] These and
other AU norms are enforced in several ways. These include monitoring by the African
Commission on Human and People's Rights, the African Peer Review Mechanism, and
the Peace and Security Council (PSC), an organ of the Union, which can impose sanctions, including suspension, for failure to abide by the policies. And of course adjudication before the African Court of Human and Peoples' Rights (African Court) is also
a possibility.

Beyond this continent-wide framework, the sub-regional communities in East and
West Africa have something to say about democracy. The East African Community
is a regional intergovernmental organization comprised of six member states whose
founding treaty includes democracy as a guiding principle. Its Court of Justice can hear
cases in this regard. In West Africa, the fifteen-member Economic Community of West
African States (ECOWAS) is a regional economic union. In 2001, the member states
adopted a Protocol on Democracy and Good Governance, encapsulating many of the
norms then in ascendance such as the separation of powers, independent judiciary, and
free and fair elections.[35] This has led to a number of successful interventions, including
arguably that in Mali described above. It too has a court, the Community Court of

---

[31] See generally Alec Stone Sweet and Clare Ryan, *A Cosmopolitan Legal Order: Kant, Constitutional Justice and
the European Convention on Human Rights* (Oxford University Press 2018).
[32] European Convention on Human Rights (n 27) arts 6, 8, 9, 10, and 11.
[33] See also Constitutive Act of the African Union (adopted 11 July 2000, entered into force 26 May 2001) 2158
UNTS 3 art 4(p).
[34] African Charter on Democracy (n 9) art 23.
[35] ECOWAS Protocol (n 9); see Akinkugbe (n 22).

Justice (CCJ), which has been very active and has a mandate to adjudicate human rights issues, even though it has no specific instrument it is meant to enforce in this regard.

The Organization of American States (OAS) was founded in 1948, during a period of relatively stable democratic governance in the region, and had as its primary concern the preservation of democracy. To this end, Article 9 of the OAS Charter allows suspension, by a two-thirds vote of member states, of any country whose "democratically constituted government has been overthrown by force". In addition, the OAS adopted the American Declaration of Human Rights in 1948, and later the American Convention of Human Rights in 1969. These documents led to the creation of the Inter-American Commission and eventually the Inter-American Court of Human Rights (IACtHR). In 2001, the member states of the OAS adopted the Inter-American Democratic Charter, providing that "(t)he peoples of the Americas have a right to democracy and their governments have an obligation to promote and defend it", as robust an affirmation of Franck's right to democratic governance as can be found.[36] Article 7 of that document asserts that "[d]emocracy is indispensable for the effective exercise of fundamental freedoms and human rights in their universality, indivisibility and interdependence, embodied in the respective constitutions of states and in inter-American and international human rights instruments". Article 20 provides mechanisms to respond to any "unconstitutional alteration of the constitutional regime that impairs the democratic order".

In short, even if there is little at the global level, there is now a thick set of norms at the regional and subregional level for much of the world that articulate democratic governance as a norm. Around two-thirds of the world's governments are subject to some such instrument. These instruments generally do not treat democracy as a "right" in Franck's sense, but of course the adjudication of individual human rights issues such as rights to speech and assembly obviously has implications for democratic governance.

# 4.  Courts

Our main topic is courts. What role have they played in protecting democracy? By virtue of their general role in enforcing regimes of trade integration or human rights protection, they have been granted responsibility for hearing complaints that arise under the democracy charters, as well as other instruments with a collateral relationship with democratic governance.

## 4.1  Europe

In Europe, the key norm comes from Protocol 1 of the European Convention on Human Rights, which entered into force in 1954. Article 3 states that "[t]he High Contracting

---

[36] Inter-American Democratic Charter (n 9) art 1.

Parties undertake to hold free elections at reasonable intervals by secret ballot, under conditions which will ensure the free expression of the opinion of the people in the choice of the legislature".[37] In its jurisprudence on these political rights, the ECtHR has distinguished between the right to vote ("passive" electoral rights) and the right to run for office ("active" electoral rights).[38] Relying on this provision, it has insisted on the extension of the franchise to prisoners,[39] those placed under guardianship for psychiatric care,[40] and those in the midst of bankruptcy proceedings.[41] It also held, in response to a complaint by a Turkish Cypriot who had been denied voter registration under a constitutional provision in Cyprus, that Cyprus had to allow Turks to vote after nearly forty years of disenfranchisement.[42] But the Court has not found a violation in limitations on expatriate or non-resident voting.[43]

Several of the provisions of the European Convention allow states to restrict rights as necessary in democratic society, which invites courts to gradually articulate regional norms as a minimum European floor. The doctrine of margin of appreciation, in which states have some flexibility in implementing particular rights, is one in which the court must look beyond the particular parties at hand, to determine the existence or lack of a Europe-wide consensus. This is a law-making function, which the narrow framework of dispute resolution does not capture. The "task" of the Court under the instrument is one demanding a look beyond the issues between the parties.

## 4.2   Africa

Africa's regional and continental courts have been very active in helping to articulate regional democracy norms in a part of the world with a poor democratic history. In doing so, they have been very creative, reaching beyond the texts in many cases to spell out concretely what constitutional norms require. They are in fact creating a regional definition of an unconstitutional change in government, blending international and national constitutional norms. One close observer has called this the "Africanization of Constitutional Law".[44]

For example, in one case the African Court found a national constitutional provision to be a violation of the African Charter.[45] The legal hook for this was a provision of the Court protocol to issue "appropriate orders", a very expansive formulation of remedial

---

[37] Protocol European Convention for the Protection of Human Rights and Fundamental Freedoms (adopted 20 March 1952, entered into force 18 May 1954) ETS 9 art 3.

[38] 'Right to Vote' (*European Court of Human Rights*, October 2016) <http://www.echr.coe.int/Documents/FS_Vote_ENG.pdf>.

[39] *Hirst v United Kingdom* (No 2) (2006) ECHR 681.

[40] *Alajos Kiss v Hungary* (2010) ECHR 692.

[41] *Albanese v Italy* App no 77924/01 (ECtHR 23 March 2006).

[42] *Aziz v Cyprus* (2004) ECHR 271.

[43] *Oran v Turkey* (2014) ECHR 396.

[44] Micha Weibusch, "Africanisation of Constitutional Law" in Adem K Abebe and others (eds), *Comparative Constitutional Law in Africa* (Edward Elgar Press 2021).

[45] *Christopher R. Mtikila v United Republic of Tanzania*, No 009/2011 and No 011/2011, Judgment, African Court of Human and Peoples' Rights (14 June 2013).

power.[46] Tanzania's parliament had amended the constitution to prohibit non-party in-dependent candidates from running for electoral office, but the African Court ruled that this violated individual rights to freedom of association and political participation, as well as other provisions of the African Charter. The idea is that freedom of associ-ation includes freedom not to associate with a party. It then ordered the country to take constitutional steps to remedy the situation.[47] This ruling thus elaborated an internal rule governing party competition, surely something that would traditionally have been considered to be "essentially within the domestic jurisdiction" of a state.

In other cases, the Court found that the Côte d'Ivoire's electoral rules, which allowed the ruling party and president to appoint the majority of members of the electoral com-mission, were incompatible with the ACDEG as well as the African Charter, and the ECOWAS Protocol on Democracy and Good Governance.[48] The African Court is em-powered to interpret not just its own Charter but also "any other relevant human rights instrument" that the state party has ratified.[49] The Court relied on these sources to find, in essence, that an independent electoral commission was a human right of sorts.[50] This is obviously an institutional intervention into the constitutional structure of a govern-ment. In other cases, the Court has found that criminal sanctions for defamation are incompatible with the freedom of expression.[51] In these cases, the Court has been ex-pansive, using its broad power of "appropriate" orders to require structural changes in the relevant laws.

One instance in which the African Court was called on directly to maintain the in-tegrity of democratic institutions came when President Kagame of Rwanda proposed a referendum on allowing him another term in office.[52] Opponents appealed to the African Court, alleging a violation of the ACDEG, and asking for interim measures blocking the referendum.[53] The referendum was held before the case could be heard, illustrating that sometimes individual adjudication is too little too late. But the very fact the case arose shows the power courts are wielding. It may also illustrate the polit-ical limits of adjudication: Rwanda subsequently withdrew from the protocol allowing individuals and non-governmental organizations (NGOs) access to the Court, and the number of states parties to that document has declined to six from a high of ten.[54]

---

[46] ibid para 124.

[47] ibid para 126.

[48] *Actions Pour la Protection des Droits de l'Homme (APDH) v The Republic of Cote d'Ivoire*, No 001/2014, Judgment, African Court of Human and Peoples' Rights (18 November 2016).

[49] African Court on Human and Peoples' Rights, 'Rules of Court' (1 September 2020) Rule 29(1)(a) <http://ww.african-court.org/en/images/Basic%20Documents/Rules_of_Court_-_25_September_2020.pdf> accessed 12 November 2020.

[50] See *APDH v The Republic of Cote d'Ivoire* (n 46) (interpreting a number of instruments in its decisions).

[51] Adem K Abebe, "Taming Regressive Constitutional Amendments: The African Court as a Continental (Super) Constitutional Court" (2019) 17 ICON 89, 14.

[52] Christina Murray, Eric Alston, and Micha Wiebusch, "Presidential Term Limits and the International Community" (September 2018) Institute of Development Policy University of Antwerp Working Paper/2018.09, 12–13 <http://www.uantwerpen.be/images/uantwerpen/container2673/files/Publications/WP/2018/wp-201809.pdf> accessed 12 November 2020.

[53] ibid.

[54] The current list is Benin, Burkina Faso, Côte d'Ivoire, the Gambia, Ghana, Malawi, Mali, Tanzania, and Tunisia. Four states (Benin, Côte d'Ivoire, Rwanda, and Tanzania) made such a declaration and withdrew. Abebe (n 51).

## 4.3  Latin America

The IACtHR and national courts applying the American Convention on Human Rights have been especially important in adjudicating cases involving Article 23, which provides for the right to political participation. Article 23(1) grants every citizen the rights

> to take part in the conduct of public affairs, directly or through freely chosen representatives; to vote and to be elected in genuine periodic elections, which shall be by universal and equal suffrage and by secret ballot that guarantees the free expression of the will of the voters; and to have access, under general conditions of equality, to the public service of his country.[55]

There has been a jurisprudence articulating these rights, with a notable set of cases deploying the third prong in the context of judicial employment decisions after attempts to purge or pack courts.

But courts have at times strayed too far in the direction of focusing on individual rights at the expense of systemic or structural considerations. In what we might call an abuse of human rights law, national courts that are partial to incumbents have used these rights to upend term limits,[56] and have held that term limits interfere with the international rights to political participation and to be elected.[57] An early mover in this regard was Nicaragua, which prohibited consecutive terms and allowed only two terms total for a president during his or her lifetime. In 2009, Sandinista leader Daniel Ortega was nearing the end of his second five-year term in office, having served in the 1980s. But Ortega lacked sufficient support in the legislature to amend the constitution. Instead he turned to the Supreme Court, which struck the provisions that prohibited re-election because they interfered with the higher principle of constitutional equality by limiting Ortega's own right to run on an equal basis. This was a crucial juncture in Nicaragua's slide from being a weak democracy to authoritarianism and laid the basis for further creative argument.

The 1982 Constitution of Honduras allowed only a single-term presidency. Not only was the term limit unamendable, but there was a kind of "poison pill" provision whereby anyone who even *proposed* changing the term limit would be punished with immediate removal from office.[58] In 2009, incumbent president Manuel Zelaya called

---

[55] American Convention on Human Rights, "Pact of San Jose, Costa Rica" (adopted 22 November 1969, entered into force 18 July 1978) OASTS No 36 art 23.

[56] Mila Versteeg and others, "The Law and Politics of Presidential Term Limit Evasion" (2020) 120 Columbia Law Review 173, 232.

[57] See eg Decision of 22 April 2015, Supreme Court of Justice, Constitutional Chamber (Honduras).

[58] Constitution of Honduras art 239: "A citizen who has previously served as President cannot be President or Vice President of the Republic. Whoever breaks this provision or proposes its reform, as well as those who support him directly or indirectly, will immediately cease in the performance of their respective offices and will be barred for ten years from the exercise of any public function." This provision was retained from Honduras' constitution of 1957, and similar provisions were found in the constitutions of Peru 1933 and Guatemala 1945 (art 133). As Rosalind Dixon, David Landau, and Yaniv Roznai note, this was accompanied by two others that made sure proposing term limit extensions was to be treated as a most serious infraction: Article 42(5) threatens those who support re-election of the president could lose their citizenship, and article 4 calls any infringement of alternation in

for a non-binding referendum on changing the limit, provoking a claim that he had violated the constitutional provision.[59] After the country's Supreme Court ruled that Zelaya was in violation of the Constitution and enjoined the plebiscite, the military implemented an order to arrest Zelaya, and he was forcibly spirited out of the country. The Organization of American States quickly turned the issue into an international one, labelling it a coup d'état. This illustrates the regional architecture to defend democracy.

A few years later, Zelaya's successor Juan Orlando Hernandez sought to serve a second term in defiance of the constitution. In a 2015 decision, the Supreme Court found the constitutional provisions limiting the discussion of presidential term limits to be a violation of fundamental individual rights of freedom of expression.[60] Importantly, it sourced these rights not only in the domestic constitution which it was reviewing but in international human rights instruments. The Court noted that since the American Convention preceded the Honduran Constitution, the country was bound to observe the Convention in its formulation of all national law, and thus struck a constitutional provision on the basis of international human rights law.[61] In doing so, it acted consistently with IACtHR doctrine of "conventionality control" which holds that all State Parties to the American Convention on Human Rights are obligated to interpret all national law to conform with the Convention, as interpreted by the IACHR.[62] Hernandez remains in office today.

A similar decision striking constitutional term limits on the basis of the regional right has been adopted in Bolivia.[63] Perhaps even more bizarrely, in Bolivia, the Plurinational Constitutional Tribunal went to the original draft of the Constitution and rejected term limits on the grounds that they had only been agreed to as a political compromise.[64] The political context here was even more troubling than in Honduras. First elected in 2006 as the country's first indigenous president, Evo Morales headed a leftist party, the Movement for Socialism (MAS) which sought transformative social and political change. In 2009, the movement succeeded in its project of promulgating an innovative constitution, including several novel institutional structures and an extensive set of rights. The Constitution had a limit of two terms for the presidency and this led to a challenge to Morales' attempt to stand for re-election in 2014. The country's Supreme

the presidency to be "treason". See David Landau, Rosalind Dixon, and Yaniv Roznai, "From an Unconstitutional Constitutional Amendment to an Unconstitutional Constitution? Lessons from Honduras" (2019) 8 Global Constitutionalism 40, 45.

[59] See Noah Feldman and others, "Report to the Commission on Truth and Reconciliation of Honduras: Constitutional Issues" (March 2011) FSU College of Law Public Law Research Paper No 536, 10–11 <https://papers.ssrn.com/sol3/papers.cfm?abstract_id=1915214>.
[60] Decision of 22 April 2015 (Honduras) (n 54) cited in Landau and others (n 58) 52 n 47.
[61] See "The President of Honduras Starts His Second Term under a Cloud" (*Economist*, 27 January 2018) <http://www.economist.com/the-americas/2018/01/27/the-president-of-honduras-starts-his-second-term-under-a-cloud> accessed 12 November 2020.
[62] Eduardo Ferrer Mac-Gregor, "Conventionality Control the New Doctrine of the Inter-American Court of Human Rights" (2015) 109 American Journal of International Law Unbound 93; see also *Barrios Altos v Peru*, Merits, Judgment, Inter-American Court Human Rights Series C No 75 (14 March 2001) para 44.
[63] Sentencia Constitucional Plurinacional No 0084/2017, Tribunal Constitucional Plurinacional (28 November 2017) 3 (Bolivia). See Versteeg and others (n 56) 233.
[64] ibid.

Court ruled that, since he had been initially elected under a prior constitution, his first term would not count against his total number of terms. In 2016, with his second term under the new constitution coming to a close, Morales' supporters sought a constitutional amendment that would allow him to run for a third term. However, to their surprise, the proposal failed in a public referendum. Not to be deterred, Morales turned to his Constitutional Tribunal, reliably filled with his appointees. In 2017, the Tribunal issued a decision finding that the term limit provision was itself unconstitutional.

The Tribunal again relied heavily on international law and the fact that the Constitution integrated these principles in Article 256.[65] It invoked Article 23(1) of the American Convention, quoted earlier in this chapter. The Court noted that under the Pact of San Jose, the only limitations on these rights were for age, nationality, residence, language, capacity, or criminal activity; since prior service was not in this list, it could not be used to exclude a candidate from exercising their political rights to run again.[66] Under this view, term limits would seem to be a per se violation of the American Convention.

These decisions, while sounding in the preservation of democracy, in fact pose a threat to it as they are being used to facilitate executive entrenchment by particular individuals. In both cases, they reflect the culmination of efforts by an incumbent in changing the composition of the relevant court. They are not simply the result of a misunderstanding of the relevant law or threats to democracy but instead a strategic deployment of international law to upend local democracy.

This view, as Landau and his colleagues note, takes a very broad view of the role of international law, displacing in many respects the ideas of a sovereign people exercising constituent power. It illustrates the anti-democratic potential of traditional arguments about monism in international law: if we assume that international law is always on a higher plane, then we risk its abuse by antidemocratic forces.

As a normative matter of international law, it seems particularly odd to assert that term limits violate the personal rights of the leader to run for repeated re-election. When a person assumes the office of president, they will typically, by law, enter into a position of special status. In many systems they cannot be sued and they have immunities for professional actions. They may also, by law, lose the right to manage their own financial affairs, as well as to speak in a personal capacity. It is no surprise then, that the special status means that one's political rights are limited as well.

Yet in each of these term limit decisions, courts approached the issue as a bilateral one, framing the issue as a dispute pitting the rights of a particular individual against the state. Treating the adjudication as a task to be completed, rather than a part of a more functional conception of democratic preservation, required the tribunals to read the founding human rights documents and democracy charters at a particular level of

---

[65] Political Constitution of the Republic of Honduras (18 January 1982) art 256.I ("The international treaties and instruments in matters of human rights that have been signed and/or ratified, or those that have been joined by the State, which declare rights more favorable than those contained in the Constitution, shall have preferential application over those in this Constitution.").

[66] Tribunal Constitucional Plurinational (n 63) 74.

abstraction, in which individual provisions trumped a broader purposive reading of the Charter.

## 5. Conclusion

It is in the nature of courts that they tend to hear one case at a time and to have trouble dealing with large structural issues. The case-by-case nature of the judicial process has been celebrated for many reasons. It tends to facilitate incremental rather than radical change.[67] It also allows strategic litigators to advance claims for rights and justice across time. But the fact that cases involve discrete, individuated disputes also means that agents of democratic erosion can act strategically to exploit holes in the jurisprudence to accomplish their ends. A narrow focus on particular rights might lead courts toward systemic errors, in which the individual litigants' rights might actually contribute to structural weakening of democratic constraints. A focus on judging as a narrow task, to be completed without a sense of the broader function, exacerbates this concern.

My argument regarding the Latin American term limits cases is that in order to play their *function* properly in enforcing a democracy charter, judges should focus on higher level purposes that animates the rights they serve. This involves paying some attention to the consequences of the decision beyond the two parties before the judge. As Shapiro pointed out, judging as a social practice relies heavily on the idea that disputes are bilateral in character, and dichotomous in outcome.[68] But decisions have consequences beyond the parties themselves. Particularly in the context of broad mandates that go to higher level principles, such as democracy charters, an overly narrow conception of the task can undermine these principles.

Caron's concern was that the functions of judges are myriad, and that paying too much attention to them might distort the core effort of resolving disputes. Drifting too far from this core task, he implies, leads to indeterminacy. The argument echoes one made in the US context made by Justice Scalia in favour of originalism as a mode of constitutional interpretation. Scalia argued that other theories of interpretation are so indeterminant as to invite judges to impose their own policy views on litigants.[69] He also was fond of pointing out that judges are not well equipped to look at consequences of their decisions outside the four corners of the law; that is the task of legislators, not judges. These are powerful arguments, and many forests have died in rebuttal of them.

One way to square the circle is to move up the level of abstraction as to what the judicial task involves. In the case of democracy charters, one can ask judges to see their task not as resolving disputes about the scope particular rights but as enforcing broader principles of democratic governance, towards which those rights are oriented. This

---

[67] David Strauss, "Common Law Constitutional Interpretation" (1996) 63 University of Chicago Law Review 877.

[68] Shapiro (n 2).

[69] Antonin Scalia, "Originalism: The Lesser Evil" (1989) 57 University of Cincinnati Law Review 849.

might be easier in places like Africa, which has a richer and more precise set of democratic norms, than in Latin America.

Given the propensity of non-democratic governments to ignore the pronouncements of regional courts, there is an element of self-interest here. If regional courts do not play a role in preserving democracy when it is under threat, they may find that they have fewer cases and less impact. Ensuring their own effectiveness is not a "task" of the judicial process but, on the international plane at least, a precondition of judging.

## Author's Note

This chapter draws loosely on my article "International Courts and Democratic Backsliding" (2019) 46 Ecology Law Quarterly 111; (2019) 37 Berkeley Journal of International Law 265.

# 28

# The High-Water Mark of International Judicialization?

*Karen J Alter*

## 1. Introduction

We are living in a moment that political scientists would call a critical juncture. Many elements of the current order are being challenged, among them democracy, the international liberal order, and globalization. Given that international law depends in important ways on these contested elements, and given that the rule of law is also under threat in many parts of the world, it is easy to extrapolate that international law and international courts are also under threat. But here is what we know about critical junctures. By destabilizing the existing institutional order, critical junctures create new openings and possibilities that make significant and even radical change possible. But critical junctures do not necessarily lead to change.[1] Looking backwards, there is a strong association between major change and critical junctures, yet this coincidence is misleading. When there is a revolution of some kind, analysts search for the causes and the result is usually a finding that the existing order was eroding, and that politics and society had reached a critical juncture. Yet if the focus is on critical junctures and not when fundamental change occurs, then it becomes clear that critical junctures create new possibilities but the outcome is quite underdetermined. We can expect political entrepreneurs to arise; we can expect long-standing complaints to be resurrected; we can expect turmoil and flux. What then happens, however, is much harder to predict.

It is with this in mind that I ask the question of whether we have reached a high water mark of international judicialization? This book is a tribute to the life and work of David Caron so in some ways I am asking whether the work of David Caron is also being undone? I also have a stake in this question. In 2014, I published a book titled *The New Terrain of International Law: Courts, Politics, Rights*, which boldly heralded a growing influence of international law and international courts in international relations and a new reality of compromised state sovereignty.[2] I was careful to state the permissive condition of the trend: that legality remained politically valuable. So long as legal behaviour was considered more legitimate, international courts (ICs) would be

[1] Giovanni Capoccia and R Daniel Kelemen, "The Study of Critical Junctures in Historical Institutionalism" (2007) 59 World Politics 341–69.
[2] Karen J. Alter, *The New Terrain of International Law: Courts, Politics, Rights* (Princeton University Press 2014).

Karen J Alter, *The High-Water Mark of International Judicialization?* In: *By Peaceful Means*. Edited by: Charles N Brower, Joan E Donoghue, Cian C Murphy, Cymie R Payne and Esmé R Shirlow, Oxford University Press. © Karen J Alter 2024. DOI: 10.1093/oso/9780192848086.003.0028

brought in as adjudicators of international legality. This chapter examines the legality permissive condition alongside a second permissive condition, that states continue to permit access and jurisdiction for the adjudication of disputes involving international law, and thus that international dejudicialization does not happen.

The question this chapter investigates is whether 2014 was perhaps the high-water mark of the changes I was documenting. The high-water mark claim requires that the trends actually reverse. If the trends do not reverse, then our current turmoil may not be the high-water mark for the changes my book described. Arguing from the world of practice, David Caron would probably expect the continued judicialization of international politics. I will agree, doing so through the lens of mechanisms and theory. To be clear, the issue at stake is *not* whether the rapid acceleration of international laws in courts in the post-Second World War and especially the post-Cold War period continues. There was a big bang of international law and institution creation, but at this point any increase in judicialization will be slower and more incremental.[3] Rather, on the table is the question of whether the judicialization of international politics actually reverses.

Section 2 defines the judicialization of politics and summarizes the causal forces that led me to declare the new terrain of international law, exploring whether these forces have eroded. Section 3 explores what we know about the counter-trend of dejudicialization. Dejudicialization is not the only way that judicialization might reverse. ICs could find their authority diminished, or the permissive condition of valuing legality could erode. Section 2 explores these options too. Section 4 takes seriously the notion that we are in a transitional moment, considering two likely scenarios. The 'Sleeping Beauty mode' possibility has the institutions remain in repose, ready to awake when kissed by a prince. A second possibility is that the magic is gone, and Sleeping Beauty's institutional body decays through de facto dejudicialization, a loss of authority, or the decreased salience of international law in international relations. The argument for repose is based on the reality that international institutions evolve, but they rarely die. The argument for decay is based on a claim of backlash, that the current order is being rejected and we are indeed returning to the prior international condition of nationalism, balance of power politics, and a decline of Western power. Both of these may be interim outcomes, should the permissive conditions that legality is valuable remain.

## 2. What Provoked the Judicialization of International Relations?

Judicialization is the name for when stakeholders transfer policy-making debates and politics into the legal domain so that courts and judges increasingly dominate politics and policy-making.[4] International judicialization occurs when domestic

---

[3] Karen J Alter, "The Future of International Law" in Diana Ayton-Shenker (ed), *The New Global Agenda* (Rowman & Littlefield 2018) 25–42..

[4] Neal C Tate and Torbjörn Vallinder, *The Global Expansion of Judicial Power*. New York University Press 1995) 28.

and international disputes are transferred into the international legal arena, so that courts and judges interpret the international legality of behaviours and actions that occur within or outside of national borders. Insofar as sovereignty confers on governments a right to pursue whatever domestic or international policy they see fit, judicializing international relations compromises sovereignty. Because international relations scholars expect international law not to be very influential, the international judicialization claim is not that litigation and judges dominate but rather that appeals to legal adjudicators become regular parts of international relations in sovereignty-compromising ways.

Scholars who write about international judicialization often discuss the proliferation of international courts, the rising rates of adjudication in front of these courts, and the salience of issues and disputes that are being adjudicated. The end of the Cold War generated an historic proliferation of international courts and international adjudication. In 1989 there were six operational permanent international courts plus the General Agreement on Tariffs and Trade (GATT) dispute settlement system, but only Europe's Court of Justice (CJEU) and its Court of Human Rights (ECtHR), and to a much lesser extent the BENELUX court, were regularly used. The other international adjudicatory bodies—the International Court of Justice (ICJ), the Inter-American Court of Human Rights, the Andean Tribunal of Justice, and the GATT dispute settlement system had collectively issued fewer than 200 binding international legal rulings despite their many years of existence.[5] Then, between 1990 and 2005, eighteen new permanent international courts were created. Most of these new international courts emulated the design of Europe's international courts.[6] This creation and emulation spread judicialization beyond the exceptional situation of Europe.

The judicialization of European politics is a phenomenon unto itself, and many consider Europe's Court of Justice and its Human Rights Court to be exceptions that define the European Union as sui generis. Excluding Europe's supranational courts, international adjudication exploded so that by the end of 2015, well over 10,000 binding legal rulings have been issued by permanent international courts with membership that reaches beyond Europe.[7] This means that between 1945 and 1989, permanent ICs with membership that reached beyond Europe issued fewer than 200 binding legal rulings. In the next fifteen years, a much larger number of these ICs issued over 10,000 binding legal rulings.[8] Rising adjudication levels were because not only the number of international courts grew but also the new international courts had the 'new style' features of compulsory jurisdiction and access for a range of non-state actors to initiate litigation.[9]

[5] Alter, *The New Terrain of International Law* (n 2) 72.
[6] Karen J Alter, "The Global Spread of European Style International Courts" (2012) 35(1) West European Politics 135–54.
[7] Europe's supranational ICs only have European states as members. They include the CJEU, ECtHR, the European Free Trade Area (EFTA) and BENELUX courts. Non-European ICs may be physically located in Europe, but their judges and members extend beyond Europe.
[8] *The New Terrain of International Law* drew on data through 2011. I periodically updated the data. My last update was in 2017, including data through 2015.
[9] Alter, *The New Terrain of International Law* (n 2) 84.

One should see my IC-focused data as a sampling of what was occurring more generally; ad hoc and quasi-judicial bodies also experienced an increase in international adjudication, and domestic enforcement of international law also grew.[10] New aspects of international politics were also internationally judicialized. The outbreak of war in the former Yugoslavia started a process of strengthening international criminal law and its enforcement, including creating the ad hoc international criminal courts for the former Yugoslavia, Rwanda, and Sierra Leone, a new adjudicatory body to investigate Khmer Rouge atrocities in Cambodia, and the creation of a permanent and jurisdictionally far-reaching International Criminal Court.

These evolutions occurred in tandem, but this does not mean that they are necessary conditions for international judicialization. Rather, Alter, Helfer, and Hafner-Burton argue that international rights claiming and the application of international law by judicial and quasi-judicial bodies are the two necessary conditions to judicialize international relations. These conditions are also fulfilled if domestic adjudicators enforce international law, and if international bodies use law and existing legal interpretations to inform their decisions and actions.[11]

Even if not necessary conditions, one can plausibly imagine that if the forces that drove and sustained international adjudication were to erode then the phenomenon of international judicialization might also diminish. The forces driving international judicialization were historically contingent. The high-water mark question arises precisely because the larger set of normative, ideational, and social enabling conditions may well be ending. I will be overly brief in recapping what I have argued elsewhere, but we must remember that dejudicialization is not judicialization played backwards. The two phenomena are different.

Undoubtably, international judicialization fits within the post-Second World War global zeitgeist, even if this zeitgeist did not pre-ordain international judicialization. One factor driving both domestic and international judicialization was the Cold War, which generated a competition wherein Western countries emphasized human rights, democracy, and economic success through the expansion and openness of national markets. At the domestic level, this competition contributed to a rapid spread of constitutionalism and judicialization in the democratic world, and much later a formalist mimicry of these trends in the non-democratic world.[12] These domestic developments embedded international legal norms, including human rights and economic openness, into national laws and national institutions,[13] which in turn generated the compliance partners and compliance supporters that international judicialization relies upon.

---

[10] Kathryn Sikkink, *The Justice Cascade: How Human Rights Prosecutions Are Changing World Politics* (Norton 2011).

[11] Karen J Alter, Laurence R Helfer, and Emile Hafner Burton, "Theorizing the Judicialization of International Relations" (2019) 63(3) International Studies Quarterly 449–63, 451–53.

[12] Alec Stone Sweet, "Judicialization and the Construction of Governance" (1999) 32(4) Comparative Political Studies 147–84, Tom Ginsburg, "The Global Spread of Constitutional Review" in Keith Whittington, Daniel Keleman and Gregory A Caldeira (eds), *The Oxford Handbook on Law and Politics*(Oxford University Press 2008) 81–98.

[13] Zachary Elkins, Tom Ginsburg, and Beth Simmons, "Getting to Rights: Treaty Ratification, Constitutional Convergence, and Human Rights Practice" (2013) 54(1) Harvard International Law Journal 61–95.

When international adjudicators then worked to reinforce norms and practices that were also part of domestic law, they found domestic support for their efforts.[14]

An additional ideational factor arose in the 1980s, with the finding of democratic peace theory. This finding emerged when Michael Doyle reanalysed the *Correlates of War* data and made a startling discovery: democracies do not fight war against each other.[15] Today the conversation and findings of a democratic peace theory are significantly more qualified, but the idea that democracies were more peaceful seized the imagination of Western leaders and international institutional actors, contributing to a renewed drive to spread democracy and the rule of law around the world.[16] Neoliberalism, with its penchant for protecting private property, was an additional ideational factor promoting robust and enforceable international law.[17]

Elsewhere I identified a number of institutional factors driving these trends.[18] The end of the Cold War led to a rush of previously Soviet-aligned and non-aligned countries entering Western institutions. In Europe, the European Union extended to twenty-seven countries and the Council of Europe to forty-seven members. Central and Eastern European polities readily paid the price of entry to these two institutions, committing to robust international judicial oversight by the CJEU and/or ECtHR.[19] Outside Europe, membership in a reconfigured World Trade Organization (WTO) grew (today 164 countries are part of the WTO). The price of admission to the WTO was a commitment to Western intellectual property rules and a compulsory dispute settlement system. Alongside the growth of WTO membership came a reinvigoration of regional integration systems.[20] I see these two developments as related. WTO membership contributed to acceleration of the legalization and judicialization of regional integration systems, in part because Member States needed to commit and implement WTO rules but also because the WTO allowed regional institutions to extend preferential trade benefits to their members. The neoliberal zeitgeist was also a factor. Regional integration systems added and/or enhanced their dispute settlement systems as part of institutional reform updates.[21]

Developments in the United States and Europe also contributed to international judicialization. American aggressive free trade promotion presented US trade partners with a choice of letting the United States Trade Representative or the GATT's dispute settlement system determine whether or not a state was complying with GATT trade rules. Given this choice, and given the resentment US unilateralism engendered, a compulsory WTO dispute settlement system became newly attractive.[22] As a separate

---

[14] Alter, *The New Terrain of International Law* (n 2) 53–58, 159–60.
[15] Michael Doyle, "Liberalism and World Politics" (1986) 80(4) American Political Science Review 1151.
[16] Thomas Carothers, "The Rule of Law Revival" (1998) 77(2) Foreign Affairs 95–106.
[17] Quinn Slobodian, *Globalists: The End of Empire and the Birth of Neoliberalism* (Harvard University Press 2018).
[18] Karen J Alter, "The Evolving International Judiciary" (2011) 7 Annual Review of Law and Social Science 387–415.
[19] Andrew Moravcsik, "Explaining International Human Rights Regimes: Liberal Theory and Western Europe" (1995) 1(2) European Journal of International Relations 157–89.
[20] Tanja A Börzel and Thomas Risse-Kappen, *The Oxford Handbook of Comparative Regionalism* (1st edn, Oxford University Press 2016).
[21] Karen J Alter and Liesbet Hooghe, "Regional Dispute Settlement" in ibid 538–58.
[22] John H Barton and others, *The Evolution of the Trade Regime* (Princeton University Press 2006) Chapter 3.

yet contemporaneous matter, European judges and governments started to experiment with expansive understandings of universal jurisdiction with the result that Western courts started to prosecute gross violations of human rights committed by non-nationals outside their territory.[23] This idea of universally applied international criminal law became legally ensconced as states joined the Rome Statute of the International Criminal Court and then passed domestic war crimes legislation and in some cases authorized a universal jurisdiction enforcement of international criminal law. As with the WTO story, the larger dynamic of preferring local to international, and international to American or European international law enforcement made creating and using ICs more attractive.

Meanwhile the forces that contributed to national courts increasingly applying international law—such as the activation of the Alien Tort Statute in the United States, European courts adjudicating human rights violations committed abroad, and national judges applying the New York Convention on the enforcement of arbitral awards—have their own origin stories. The quasi-judicial bodies such as UN Treaty bodies reviewing human rights complaints, and specialized claims commissions or international institutional inspection panels also have their own origin and activation stories. Because domestic and quasi-judicial bodies also contribute to the judicialization of international politics, Alter, Helfer, and Hafner-Burton argued that "states do not fully determine the content, scope, or impact of delegation or adjudication and that legal processes can diminish the role of executives and legislatures".[24]

Now for the permissive conditions that facilitated these trends. The overarching permissive condition is that international legality is valuable. We must then ask is why is international legality—having a government's actions seen as legal under international law—valuable? Part of the answer has to do with Western power. Because American and European governments were so avowedly (if at times hypocritically) committed to international law, invoking international law became a useful way to push back against Western governments.[25] States, non-governmental and private actors around the world met law with law and weaker countries also learned that they could use law and adjudication to push back on the assertions of powerful states.

Since their creation, international institutions have also actively encouraged countries around the world to follow international law. International institutions embrace international legality at least in part because international law is the primary basis for their own authority. In the post-Cold War era, international institutions embraced a liberal version of the rule of law, arguing that the rule of law would contribute to economic development and government legitimacy.[26] A cottage industry of rule of law indicators emerged to advise foreign investors and international actors about the quality

---

[23] Naomi Roht-Arriaza, *The Pinochet Effect: Transnational Justice in the Age of Human Rights, Pennsylvania Studies in Human Rights* (University of Pennsylvania Press 2005).

[24] Alter, Helfer, and Hafner Burton (n 11) 450.

[25] Ian Hurd, "The Strategic Use of Liberal Internationalism: Libya and the UN Sanctions, 1993–2003" (2005) 59(Spring) International Organization 495–526.

[26] Stephen Haggard, Andrew Macintyre, and Lydia Tiede, "The Rule of Law and Economic Development" (2008) 11 Annual Review of Political Science 205.

of national legal systems.[27] Adopting rule of law reforms thus became a way to appease the International Monetary Fund and the World Bank, and it opened the financial tap of the European Union, the United States, and foreign investors and creditors. The active political support of Western countries and international institutional actors was an important accelerant of states accepting IC authority and international legal review.

But more fundamentally, a rule of law only works insofar as powerful governments will submit to law and independent judiciaries. On the flip side, powerful governments submit because publics and investors believe that legality is an important condition of legitimate governance and legal certainty. If the social expectation that governments follow the law, both national and international, erodes, or if law and legal interpretation is rendered politically subordinate to the will of political powers, then governments will be able to submit selectively to international law.

The combination of ideational, institutional, and Western support drove the judicialization of international relations, and it made legality the legitimating language of international relations. It is too soon to say that US and European support are over, but US President Donald Trump's contempt for international law, international institutions, and the rule of law more generally, suggested that Western support for international law and multilateralism might be waning. China and Russia have also signalled their expectation that international law and international adjudication should respect state sovereignty better.[28] Political scientists also find that support for democracy, globalization, and the rule of law has fractured, creating a new political cleavage (the so-called GAL-TAN (Green-Alternative-Libertarian and Traditional-Authoritarian-Nationalist) cleavage) that has politics organized around politicians who support globalization and the liberal international order and those who promote more traditional, authoritarian, and national objectives.[29] Meanwhile, authoritarian leaders have learned how to flip the Western version of the rule of law on its head, using constitutionalism and legal formalism to subvert the rule of law at home.[30] Brexit in combination with Hungary and Poland's willingness to test European leaders has challenged the European Union's broad commitment to the rule of law. These developments were in reaction to the globalization and international judicialization just described. Do they portend a reversal that would substantiate a high-water mark assessment?

Before moving on, let me reiterate that only necessary conditions for international judicialization are rights claiming (actors who frame their arguments in international law and/or who press claims based in international law in court), and domestic and

---

[27] Mila Versteeg and Tom Ginsburg, "Measuring the Rule of Law: A Comparison of Indicators" (2017) 42(1) Law & Social Inquiry 100–37.

[28] See ASIL Insight Russia and China Issue Joint Declaration on Promotion and Principles of International Law (25 June 2016), <https://www.asil.org/blogs/russia-and-china-issue-joint-declaration-promotion-and-pri nciples-international-law-june-25>. For a discussion of this statement, see Lauri Mälksoo "Russia and China Challenge the Western Hegemony in the Interpretation of International Law", <https://www.ejiltalk.org/russia-and-china-challenge-the-western-hegemony-in-the-interpretation-of-international-law/>.

[29] Liesbet Hooghe and Gary Marks, "Cleavage Theory Meets Europe's Crises: Lipset, Rokkan, and the Transnational Cleavage" (2008) 25(1) Journal of European Public Policy 109–135. For more on GAL-TAN, see Pippa Norris and Ronald Inglehart, *Cultural Backlash: Trump, Brexit, and the Rise of Authoritarian-Populism* (Cambridge University Press 2018).

[30] Kim Lane Scheppele, "Autocratic Legalism" (2018) 85(2) University of Chicago Law Review 545–83.

international adjudicatory bodies with jurisdiction and authority to render an inter-national legal determination.[31] So long as these two conditions hold, and as long as powerful actors respond to legal arguments, we are likely to find litigants turning to international law to counter questionable and patently illegal behaviours of governments.

## 3. Factors Driving the Dejudicialization of International Relations

If rights claiming and willing judges are the only two necessary conditions for inter-national judicialization, then the best way for nationalists and sovereignty-jealous governments to reverse international judicialization may be to eliminate international adjudication or remove contested international legal issues from the purview of judges. Removing legal oversight from the remit of courts is called "dejudicialization". If we care about democratic choice and judicial review as part of a system of checks and bal-ances then both democracy and sovereignty require that states be allowed to retreat where international law becomes intrusive to the point of limiting national choice.[32] Normative objectives may still mean that we want the withdrawal choice to be legis-latively validated, and we might reject the validity of states trying to opt out of vio-lations of *jus cogens*, but beyond these caveats, dejudicialization should be seen as a valid choice. The question, therefore, is what are the conditions that contribute to inter-national dejudicialization?

The international dejudicialization question has been asked by Daniel Abebe and Tom Ginsburg, who first consider formal dejudicialization. States can withdraw from the jurisdiction of an international adjudicatory body, or states can collectively rewrite the mandates of international courts, limiting access or removing jurisdiction to adju-dicate a body of disputes. Let me add two additional dejudicialization strategies. State actors or Supreme courts can create a national constitutional block on the authority of international legal rulings in the domestic realm, either through national constitu-tional change or a legal interpretive evolution.[33] By creating new institutions or chan-ging policy, state actors remove a set of cases or legal issues from the purview of courts. All four modes of dejudicialization are about state actors choosing to dejudicialize, at least with respect to the interpretation and application of international law.

---

[31] Alter, Helfer, and Hafner Burton (n 11) 451–52. Alec Stone Sweet might also add economic exchange to this list, since he believes that trade and commerce naturally produce transnational litigation: Stone Sweet (n 12) 147–84.

[32] Laurence R Helfer, "Overlegalizing Human Rights: International Relations Theory and the Commonwealth Caribbean Backlash Against Human Rights Regimes" (2002) 102(7) Columbia Law Review 1832–911.

[33] For more on this third strategy, see David Sloss, *The Death of Treaty Supremacy: An Invisible Constitutional Change* (Oxford University Press 2016); Jens David Ohlin, *The Assault On International Law* (Oxford University Press 2015); Jeffrey Kahn, "The Relationship between the European Court of Human Rights and the Constitutional Court of the Russian Federation: Conflicting Conceptions of Sovereignty in Strasbourg and St Petersburg" (2019) 30(3) European Journal of International Law 933–59.

| Actors | Causes | Mechanisms | | |
|--------|--------|------------|---|---|
| | | *Less severe* | | *More severe* |
| States (political branches) | Agency problems; failure of anticipated benefits to materialize; changes in government/preferences | Defund; court-packing; ignore decisions; restrict; narrow jurisdiction; criticize | Exit–withdraw from protocols as individual states | Cooperate with other states to *dejudicialize* the regime entirely |
| National courts | Institutional or reputational rivalry | Limit standing; narrowly interpret substantive law or remedies | Restrict/narrow jurisdiction | Render international decisions domestically inapplicable |
| Public | Unpopular decisions | Engage/petition court | Domestic protest | Lobby governments to withdraw from regime |
| Litigants | Failure of courts to provide anticipated benefits | Engage/petition court | Forum shopping | Avoid system: fail to file cases so as to de facto *dejudicialize* |

**Figure 28.1**  Unwinding judicialization: Mechanisms of backlash[*]
[*]Reprinted with permission from Abebe and Ginsburg, ibid 526.

Drawing on the literature of comparative judicial politics, Abebe and Ginsburg theorized about when international dejudicialization might be a rational choice. The authors reject relying on theories that predict judicialization—namely functionalism, and rights-oriented theories—to theorize dejudicialization. To be sure, states can respond in extreme ways, seeking to eliminate entirely an international court.[34] But Abebe and Ginsburg argue that this type of response is unlikely insofar as it requires universal assent, and because alongside those actors who see international judicial intervention as a loss are actors who gain from international adjudication.[35] In their view,

> full dejudicialization by states is a costly response that will take significant political effort to effectuate. Still it may be an option worth taking for states if either (a) the court decisions are producing net losses on a regular basis that exceed political costs of dejudicialization or (b) collateral costs and benefits, outside the control of judges, make it undesirable to retain the system.

The counter-forces that discourage the more extreme form of dejudicialization are: (i) if the legal regime itself is not all that important, states may choose non-compliance or over the work of dejudicialization; (ii) if the legal regime is part of an institutional system where the benefits of membership outweigh the costs of inconvenient compliance; (iii) if states are willing to bear short-term costs to lock in what they perceive to be a long-term benefit; or (iv) if calculating costs and benefits is impossible, states might choose a strategy other than dejudicialization to achieve their goal. In Figure 28.1 I replicate their table that theorizes how different actors may choose to engage in dejudicialization in less and more severe ways:

---

[34]  Karen J Alter, James T Gathii, and Laurence R Helfer, "Backlash against International Courts in West, East and Southern Africa: Causes and Consequences" (2016) 27(2) European Journal of International Law 293–328.
[35]  Daniel Abebe and Tom Ginsburg, "The Dejudicialization of International Politics?" (2019) 63(3) International Studies Quarterly 521–30.

Because they are drawing from the comparative judicial politics literature, and given their focus on diminishing the jurisdiction of international adjudicators, Abebe and Ginsburg's framework is missing a few additional means to the same dejudicialization end. International relations scholars would add the possibility that hegemonic actors could create alternative venues (aka contested multilateralism)[36] or enact a payback tit-for-tat response that dissuades other countries, firms, and peoples from drawing international legal avenues that, as a formal matter, remain legal and political options. Also possible is that hegemonic actors use their power to repatriate specific policies and issues back to international political bodies or to the domain of national choice.

Abebe and Ginsburg theorize about the more extreme and permanent forms of dejudicialization, but they argue that it is more likely that the mechanism of dejudicialization will be a feedback reaction where the court stays intact but participants vote with their feet—they stop bringing cases, they stop participating in legal processes, and they stop paying attention to legal rulings. Looking beyond state choices and formal jurisdictions, Alter, Helfer, and Madsen theorize about how the choices and practices of a broader set of legal, sub-state, and political actors build and diminish IC legal authority.[37] They provide a metric for assessing IC authority that involves different audiences accepting an IC ruling as binding and taking meaningful action to realize respect for international legal rulings.[38] Alter et al. discuss four different IC audiences: (i) the parties to the dispute (narrow authority); (ii) similarly situated litigants, including potential state-level defendants, that might extrapolate what a legal ruling means for them (intermediate authority); (iii) the larger legal field (extensive authority); (iv) and the public more generally (popular authority). These audiences correspond to the categories Abebe and Ginsburg discuss, except the focus is not on decisions to dejudicialize. What Alter et al. add is that the political influence and power of ICs grows both as the jurisdictional reach of ICs grow *and* as more audiences accept IC authority. The opposite is also true. Dejudicialization can shrink ICs' de jure jurisdiction and authority, but IC authority will also be undermined if fewer audiences accept the binding nature of IC rulings in general or for certain issues, and as IC audiences stop endeavouring or expecting that states respect IC rulings.[39] Overall, Alter et al. theorize that a decision to dejudicialization is only one way IC authority decreases. IC authority also diminishes via backlash by key constituencies and by irrelevance.

If we think about this broader way through which international judicialization may reverse, then it is clear that multiple factors may contribute to de facto dejudicialization of international relations. This points to additional limitations of Abebe and Ginsburg's rationalist framework. Abebe and Ginsburg presume that rational states will remain committed to international cooperation writ large and to the rule of law, so that the

---

[36] Julia Morse and Robert Keohane, "Contested Multilateralism" (2014) 9(4) The Review of International Organizations 385–412.

[37] Karen J Alter, Laurence R Helfer, and Mikael Rask Madsen, *International Court Authority* (Oxford University Press 2018).

[38] The metric is meant to be a way to assess how factors external to the IC impact IC authority.

[39] ibid 453–59.

primary question becomes how and why states might choose to dejudicialize or otherwise limit the domestic impact of international judicial rulings. But should a state enter the throes of backlash politics, these countervailing concerns may become less important. In other words, a more scorched-earth strategy would be to erode the permissive conditions discussed in Section 1—the value of legality in politics more generally, and/or in international politics more specifically. This strategy could also influence the audiences who are in a position to grow or diminish IC authority.

This brings me to the question of backlash. Like Abebe and Ginsburg, most scholars equate dejudicialization and backlash. I have been generally dissatisfied with existing conversations about dejudicialization and backlash because they do not help us understand how IC audiences come to reject IC authority or how the permissive conditions enabling IC authority are eroded.[40] I set out to rethink entirely what backlash politics is about, joining with Michael Zürn and engaging a broad set of social scientists. The Alter and Zürn definition of backlash politics has three jointly necessary and co-constitutive elements, meaning that one element alone is insufficient and does not on its own portend a politically consequential backlash politics. The definition also includes "frequent companions" that are caused by the necessary elements, and that when present serve as accelerants of backlash politics.

The first necessary element is that backlash politics involve retrograde imaginaries that seek to return to a prior social condition, one that may be real or imagined. Retrograde is not the same thing as regressive. Indeed for backlash advocates, the return is usually cast in progressive terms as recovering a better world that has been lost.[41] The retrograde imaginary generates frequent companion of emotional appeals and nostalgia. A second required element is that backlash proponents have extraordinary goals and tactics that reject dominant scripts. These goals and tactics generate the frequent companions of a willingness to break taboos and break from well-accepted norms and practices so as to challenge dominant scripts. The scripts being rejected can vary.[42] For the topic at hand, the rejection of liberalism, democracy, globalization, and the international liberal order is the dominant script, the rejection of which could contribute to the erosion of IC authority and with it the willingness of political supporters and states to submit to international adjudication and contested legal rulings that apply international law. This idea fits with debates about democratic decline, discussed in Section 3. For the topic at hand, this idea is channelled in Michael Madsen, Pola Cebula, and Micha Wiebush's discussion of ordinary and extraordinary ways that states push back

---

[40] Dejudicialization conversations tend to be formal and institutional, and I have long pointed out the challenges associated with formal dejudicialization (Karen Alter, "Delegation to International Courts and the Limits of Recontracting Power," in Darrell Hawkins et al (eds), *Delegation and Agency in International Organizations* (Cambridge University Press 2006). Meanwhile legal backlash conversations tend to presume that poor IC judicial function explains a loss of IC legitimacy. Instead, I think that de facto dejudicialization really emerges by mobilizing a counter-politics that then enables political leaders to renegotiate formal rules or to walk away from expectations that they comply with international law.

[41] Karen J Alter and Michael Zürn, "Conceptualizing Backlash Politics: Introduction to a Special Issue on Backlash Politics in Comparison" (2020) 22(4) British Journal of Politics and International Relations 563–84, 566; Karen J Alter and Michael Zürn, "Theorising Backlash Politics: Conclusion to a Special Issue on Backlash Politics In Comparison" (2020) 22(4) British Journal of Politics and International Relations 739–52, 742–43.

[42] Alter and Zürn, "Conceptualizing Backlash Politics" (n 42) 566–67, 571.

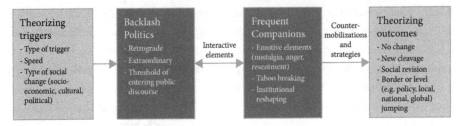

**Figure 28.2**  Backlash politics—a framework*
*Reprinted with permission from ibid 576.

or backlash against international courts.[43] The third jointly necessary condition is a threshold criterion that backlash politics must enter popular discourses and thus become elements of national politics.[44] This threshold criterion differentiates groups who simply want to return to their way of life from those who want their polity and the larger society to return to their retrograde imaginary. Its frequent companion is an institutional reshaping designed to lock in political advances. The threshold criterion also helps us think about when and how the permissive conditions for judicialized international relations may erode.

Conceived of this way, backlash politics do not stay within the rational realm of political leaders making cost-benefit analysis. Instead, backlash politics may seek a full-throttled return to absolute national sovereignty and majoritarian politics with fewer legal checks and balances. Supporters of populist backlash politics may also be willing to destroy sacred cows, like the idea that international law or democratic norms are a standard of legitimate behaviour. The framework is captured in Figure 28.2.

As Figure 28.2 implies, whether backlash politics succeeds in its full agenda is a separate question. The outcome of backlash politics depends on the counter-strategies that are employed.[45] Opponents can buy time, waiting for backlash leaders to leave office. The Sleeping Beauty and decay strategies—both of which are discussed in the next section—are interim strategies that either buy time or that reshape institutions so as to implement the extraordinary objective of social reversion. An additional countering strategy may involve judicial retreat from the most hotly contested issues[46] so as to peel away support for the backlash movement. For example, one might imagine (and even welcome) a proposal to return the issue of safeguards and countervailing duties to a less judicialized committee oversight and deliberation structure within the WTO. Such a decision would not amount to a formal decision to dejudicialize or to change the WTO's dispute settlement system, but it would remove this hotly contested issue from the dispute settlement system. Backlash opponents can also co-opt backlash language

[43] Mikael Rask Madsen, Pola Cebulak, and Micha Wiebush, "Backlash against International Courts: Explaining the Forms and Patterns of Resistance to International Courts" (2018) 14(2) International Journal of Law in Context 197–220.
[44] Alter and Zürn, "Conceptualizing Backlash Politics" (n 42) 567–68.
[45] ibid 739–52.
[46] Laurence R Helfer and Erik Voeten, "Walking Back Human Rights in Europe?" (2020) 31(3) European Journal of International Law 797–827.

and strategies, instigating an institutional reform that addresses some of the popular complaints while avoiding a larger social revolution. For example, strategists might work to make ICs more accountable or to protect national sovereignty so as to address some popular concerns. These strategies may or may not involve dejudicialization, and the result may be change in kind but not in whole. In other words, the case load and international judicial politics and practices may change, but the water level might stay roughly the same, or even rise.

The larger point of this section is that dejudicialization should be theorized as feedback politics that is neither illegitimate nor catastrophic. The United States has withdrawn from various compulsory jurisdiction clauses regarding the ICJ,[47] and it is far from alone.[48] International legal systems have also been redesigned.[49] In other words, formal dejudicialization and IC reform occurs, but it is significantly less prevalent and less likely than the harder to measure informal or de facto dejudicialization.

De facto judicialization occurs when issues are removed as a subject of national or international legal contestation because cases are diverted to a political form or because litigants stop raising cases, states stop respecting legal rulings, or national judges and legal advocates also stop seeing international legal rulings as binding. De facto dejudicialization can occur piecemeal, issue by issue, country by country, and audience by audience. Abebe and Ginsburg would agree that this piecemeal process is far more likely compared to a wholesale rewriting of international law and the mandates of international courts. De facto dejudicialization could reach a tipping point of decay, where resurrection no longer becomes likely or possible. Or de facto dejudicialization might be a temporary repose. Section 3 considers these possibilities.

Meanwhile, a backlash politics that seeks to erode the permissive conditions of valuing legality or expecting governments to submit to the rule of law involves a more fundamental social change. ICs would sometimes be a direct target, but mostly de facto international dejudicialization is collateral damage of the larger backlash objective, which is a return of populist-authoritarian nationalism. While piecemeal dejudicialization may be a fully valid choice, the larger object challenging liberalism, democracy, globalization, and the international liberal order could erode David Caron's life's work.

## 4. Where We Are Headed: Sleeping Beauty Mode or Decay?

The reality is that institutions seldom die but they often evolve or are superseded. A reason why change is more likely than dissolution is because change takes effort.

---

[47] The United States withdrew from ICJ's optional protocol, and from the provisions of the Vienna Convention on Consular Affairs that conferred compulsory ICJ jurisdiction for disputes involving that treaty. For more, see: https://www.lawfareblog.com/walking-away-world-court

[48] Laurence Helfer, "Exiting Treaties" (2005) 91 Virginia Law Review 1579–648; Emilie Hafner-Burton and Laurence Helfer, "Emergency and Escape: Explaining Derogations from Human Rights Treaties" (2011) 76(4) International Organization 673–707.

[49] Alter, Gathii, and Helfer (n 34) 293–328.

Why invest in destruction when transformation can subsume the contested elements of the status quo, while locking in a preferable alternative? The caveat to this statement is that building takes collaboration and effort, whereas a single man can mobilize a mob that serves as a wrecking ball of destruction. The wrecking ball driver may imagine that he is engaged in creative destruction, but when the subject is social change, those who have experienced war and social tumult are understandably reluctant to embrace the nihilism of destroy first and build support later.

With this in mind, and recognizing that we are in the midst of a critical juncture, the prognosticating question is where are we most likely to be headed? I see two medium-term possibilities, both of which reject the idea that nothing at all will change. The first potentiality—Sleeping Beauty Mode—involves change in the form of stasis with nothing fundamentally altered. The second possibility—decay—erodes without destroying, forcing the construction of something different or new. What happens in the long run, and what the construction of something new looks like depends on the strategies and choices of the various stakeholders.

## 4.1 Sleeping Beauty Mode: Repose Until Political Conditions Become More Favourable

In the version of the Sleeping Beauty fairy tale that I know, the parents do something that leads an evil fairy to curse their baby to lie dormant for 100 years. The curse is enacted when the young adult Sleeping Beauty pricks her finger on an enchanted needle. This means that the die is cast, but the princess does something that contributes to her slumber. The cursed magic is lifted when a handsome prince arrives to bestow a kiss. It is unclear how long Sleeping Beauty was asleep, but she wakes well before the hundred years, and she is as attractive and fresh as the day she pricked her finger.[50] In the IC version of the parable, backlash politics cast the die so that the contested ruling is mostly the needle prick that activates the curse.

The medium-term Sleeping Beauty prognostication involves a return to the international judicial practices of the 1960s. Back then, international adjudicatory bodies (the ICJ, CJEU, ECtHR, the GATT) were sporadically activated by states choosing international judicial resolution and by lawyers who wanted to see what might happen if they raised a case or who wanted to help build international law.[51] Once activated, the international adjudicators issued careful rulings that legal scholars often lauded as

---

[50] My discussion is gendered. I implied that men drive wrecking balls, and the title of 'Sleeping Beauty Mode' renders women victims but not agents. I think gender plays a significant role in backlash politics. While female backlashers do exist (e.g. Phyllis Schlafly and Marie Le Pen), men tend to be especially attracted to wrecking balls and nationalist backlash politics.

[51] Guillaume Sacriste and Antoine Vauchez, "The Force of International Law: Lawyer's Diplomacy on the International Scene in the 1920s" (2007) 32(1) *Law & Social Inquiry* 83–107; Antonin Cohen and Michael Rask Madsen, "Cold War Law: Legal Entrepreneurs and the Emergence of a European Legal Field (1946–1965)" in Volkmar Gessner and David Nelken (eds), *European Ways of Law* (Hart 2007) 175–200; Karen J Alter, "Jurist Advocacy Movements in Europe: The Role of Euro-Law Associations in European Integration (1953–1975)" in Karen J Alter (ed), *The European Court's Political Power* (Oxford University Press 2009) 63–91.

visionary and impactful. Yet the rulings typically garnered little public or international political attention, in large part because they asked so little of states. This was an intentional strategy. International judges were playing off the different time horizons of politicians, who mainly cared if a ruling disrupted something important and immediate. So long as international adjudicators made their rulings substantively palatable, the aura of benign neglect was maintained.[52]

In the short term, Sleeping Beauty mode would return to this world where international adjudicators proceed with great care. International judges might choose to stick to the letter of the law, applying extant law to clear violations in ways that uphold the judicial mandate to apply the law. They might also actively try to avoid political pushback by limiting novelty in their legal claims and circumscribing the remedial demands associated with their rulings. To some extent what I am suggesting is not very different from what now occurs, except that there may be even fewer headline-making international legal rulings. So long as international judges are clearly staying within their mandate and powers, the onus shifts to states to change laws that they no longer support.

This would be a change insofar as the more conservative and the less helpful international judges are, the less likely litigants are to use litigation to try to push the boundaries of the law. The positive feedback loop of legal expansion might revert to a negative feedback loop that contributes to decreased claiming of legal rights.[53] The legal system would still matter in that governments would be more likely to settle out-of-court cases where a clear violation of the law exists. Indeed, even authoritarian leaders generally compensate and settle cases to avoid bad publicity. Less clear-cut cases will also proceed so long as both parties are willing to live with a judicial resolution of the dispute. This means that international adjudication will still operate, but far fewer disputes will be transferred from the political realm to the legal ream because international judges are likely to be timid in the face of political controversy.

Whether we can really return to the 1960s is an open question. International law and international jurisprudence have developed far beyond what they were in the 1960s and 1970s. Also, in the 1960s, citizens expected and demanded less of their leaders and of international judges, and international legal rules were not as embedded in national systems. For example, in the 1960s the prohibition on torture might have been seen as a soft law provision of the Universal Declaration of Human Rights. Today, there is an international convention prohibiting torture that has been ratified by with 170 state parties, a quasi-judicial international oversight body associated with this convention, 167 national constitutions include provisions regarding torture,[54] and there may be domestic legislation that prohibits torture. These many legal and institutional anchors

---

[52] Karen J Alter, "Who Are the Masters of the Treaty? European Governments and the European Court of Justice" (1998) 52(1) International Organization 125–52, 130–33.

[53] Karen J Alter, "The European Legal System and Domestic Policy: Spillover or Backlash" (2000) 54(3) International Organization 489–518, 512.

[54] This figure is generated in a search of the Constitute Project which allows one to search the world's constitutions. See https://www.constituteproject.org/constitutions?lang=en.

make it much harder to unwind or dejudicialize certain legal issues. It is also often difficult to turn the clock entirely back because parents, siblings, and lovers who have already lost what matters most to them tend to be dogged in their pursuit of justice. The memory of those who have lost something they value will be the prince of this parable. They will lie in wait until political conditions improve, awakening Sleeping Beauty should the political climate once again become propitious.

## 4.2  Decay: Formal Institutions on a Bed of Eroded Norms

The normative/ideational decay prognostication would involve democracy and the rule of law decaying, in which case the norm of valuing legality will also erode. Those who study democratic decline increasingly focus on the often unstated and usually extra-legal norms that sustain a political system. For example, Steven Levinsky and Daniel Ziblatt argue that even well-designed constitutions cannot guarantee democracy. Instead, key to the system's continuance is an unrelenting commitment to the values and norms of the system. The system also depends on forbearance, forgoing options including ceding some legal rights that might generate short-term wins at the cost of eroding the norms and values needed to sustain democracy.[55] The opposite of forbearance is to break the norm of mutual tolerance and coexistence, resorting to all-out war by antagonists through both traditional and non-traditional means. This opposite fits with Alter and Zürn's discussion of extraordinary goals and tactics. Applied to the international legal context, these insights suggests that decay would occur through the backlash politics discussed in Section 2, and thus through a public sphere normative war on the international legal and political system. Norms could also erode if stakeholders eschew forbearance, pursuing legal strategies that are bound to ostracize core constituencies and undermine faith in the rule of law.

So far, I have focused on norms and litigation strategies, but governments also have resources to further an agenda of decaying the international liberal order while keeping the formal trappings of a significantly pared down international law. The institutional decay choice is outlined by Kim Scheppele's analysis of autocratic legalism and Tom Ginsburg's analysis of authoritarian international law. Scheppele describes an authoritarian toolkit to eliminate checks and balances, including but not limited to judicial checks.[56] The authoritarian strategy is subtle because the goal is neither destruction nor dejudicialization but rather institutional conversion. The authoritarian leader leaves intact the formal institutional trappings of the legitimated constitutional order while filling the institutions with staff who will be loyal and subservient. The leaders can then gain the legitimacy benefits of legality without the risk of losing in cases that truly matter to them. The outcome may resemble Sleeping Beauty mode but autocratic legalism involves purging, threats of coercion, and displays of loyalty. In all likelihood,

---

[55] Steven Levitsky and Daniel Ziblatt, *How Democracies Die* (1st edn, Crown 2018) Chapter 5.
[56] Scheppele (n 30)

subservient bodies would be asked to avow patently self-serving legal interpretations of political leaders. Should ICs comply with the autocrat's request, the Sleeping Beauty that remained would thereby be disfigured.

The longer decay proceeds, the more likely a fundamental resetting will follow. Tom Ginsburg identifies the outlines of what this resetting might look like in the international realm.[57] As with Scheppele, the autocrat's goal is to ensure the survival of the regime in power. The desired retrograde condition is one of near-absolute sovereignty, which does not mean that authoritarian leaders seek to return to imperialism or rule by coercion. Behaviour that shocks the conscience is hard to defend; actions that are seen as legitimate are much more attractive. An authoritarian international law therefore *needs* international law to protect national sovereignty and to validate the practices that help domestic regimes stay in office.

For some, the reset of decay and authoritarian international law would be a return to the more minimalistic ideal of using international adjudication to further the peaceful settlement of inter-state disputes, but not the rights of individuals or weak powers. The worst abuses would still give rise to legal condemnation, if only to uphold the appearance of the rule of law and the political stability of the United Nations system. Meanwhile, the institutions would be stacked with loyalists who mostly tow the government's line.

As with the Sleeping Beauty mode, whether this type of revision is possible remains an open question. I recently investigated how the advent of multilateralism changed the operation of international law.[58] That analysis considered how long-distance traders and global firms would seek the Sovereign's support yet also engage in behaviour that the Sovereign disliked, using distance and the regime complex of existing laws to escape Sovereign control. The analysis also included a discussion of Susan Pedersen's book analysing League of Nations debates regarding the Mandate System.[59] In Pedersen's telling, colonial powers intended to use the Mandates to expand their colonial rule, but Germany—which had been dispossessed of its colonies—refused to play along. For interwar Germany, the League of Nations became a place where it could invoke the textual international rules to embarrass its European competitors. The upshot is that controlling what multilateral actors and people living or working beyond the Sovereign's reach can be quite difficult. We may therefore find that decay ends up creating an awakened Sleeping Beauty that has undergone minor plastic surgery and a personality transplant. The retrograde objective of returning to the prior condition of significantly less international judicialization may or may not be accomplished and international judicialization will be reshaped but not eliminated.

[57] Tom Ginsburg, "Authoritarian International Law?" (2020) 114(2) American Journal of International Law 221–60.

[58] Karen J Alter, "From Colonial to Multilateral International Law: A Global Capitalism and Law Investigation" (2021) 19(3) International Journal of Constitutional Law 798–864.

[59] Susan Pedersen, *The Guardians: The League of Nations and the Crisis of Empire* (Oxford University Press 2015).

### 4.3  Fasten Your Seatbelts. It's Going to Be a Bumpy Ride

This discussion suggested a binary choice, alongside reasons to believe that neither choice is actually tenable. Not only is international dejudicialization politically difficult to orchestrate but the embedding of international legal norms in multiple international institutions, in multiple national systems, in private contracts, and in the expectations of people around the world, means that dejudicialization in one venue may not actually unwind the judicialization of international politics.

Prognosticating is difficult because the future depends on the agentic decisions of a range of actors, and even the most powerful governments cannot control these decisions. The two first-mover actors are those who fulfil the necessary conditions of international judicialization. Potential litigants can choose to litigate cases they can legally win, or they can choose forbearance—avoiding cases that might provoke a counter-response. Once a case is raised, judges get to choose what then happens. Will international judges validate suspect government actions? Will international judges use legal technicalities to dodge controversial cases? Will they become legal formalists, following the letter of the law even if doing so upsets governments? Or will international judges "go big or go home", promoting legal justice where and when they can. A separate question is what will national judges, international institutional actors, and state-level bureaucracies decide to do should violations of international law be brought into their purview?

There is no one-size-fits-all answer because litigants and adjudicators vary in temperament, because so many litigants and adjudicators get to decide on a case-by-case basis. This means that the most likely outcome is a continued mix of prudent reluctance, necessary confrontation, and transformational ambition. Insofar as there will be clear violations of international law, insofar as there will be political leaders who prefer provocation to a quiet out of court settlement of valid claims, and insofar as there will be genuinely grey and complex issues, we are likely to see stakeholders muddling through. This time we won't have David Caron to help navigate the waters, but we will have many others who follow his stead.

## 5.  Conclusion: So Have We Reached the High-Water Mark of International Judicialization?

Even if the measure of international judicialization is the number of permanent international courts, I still don't think we have reached the high-water mark of international judicialization. The reason is that part of the proliferation of international courts involved a counter-hegemonic strategy of creating closer to home international legal venues that would either be more controllable or that would better reflect the values, goals, and people of the region. This means that one answer to international judicialization run amok is *more* international judicialization that hopefully will not run amok. We therefore see the European Union proposing an international investment court, China creating a Belt and Road court,[60] and scholars like Maya Steinitz making a reasoned case for an International Civil Court of Justice.[61]

More importantly, the measure of international judicialization *is not* the number or the activity of international courts. Judicialization is about transferring disputes from the political to the legal arena. There are now hundreds of venues where adjudicators will apply pre-existing international legal rules to disputes that arise. Also transferring private and inter-state disputes to these legal and quasi-legal venues is a tremendously useful governance strategy. As Dan Kelemen argues, adversarial legalism provides a fire-alarm system of oversight that lets private actors flag egregious violations that might otherwise erode the public trust. Fire-alarm oversight is also an attractive way that small and resource-constrained bureaucracies can provide oversight.[62] Indeed relying on citizen monitors may be a far more effective way for governments to remain small, to keep their agents alert, and (as Martin Shapiro suggested) to control their people and the countryside.[63]

I am thus suggesting that my caveats in the discussion of both Sleeping Beauty mode and decay prognostication will stop de facto dejudicialization. If I am right, then we have not reached the high-water mark of international judicialization. Let me end by repeated what I wrote while President Trump's assault on international law was ongoing.

> In some ways writing about the future of international law is a bit like writing about the future of breathing: we can safely predict that every living person will continue to breathe. This is because international law is an essential language and medium of international relations; it is the mode through which countries interact with each other ... Since few, if any, states are likely to trend toward a survivalist autarky, and international law is how states communicate and understand the rules of international relations, the fundamental role-of international law, and the vast majority of specific international laws is unlikely to change. But just as some people will be born and others will die, aspects of international law will change.[64]

This chapter has added that the judicialization of international relations is also likely to continue, with more litigants, courts, and national leaders getting involved in influencing the international adjudication game. If David were still with us, he would have both plenty of material to work with and deep wells of support in every corner of the world for a peaceful and lawful dispute settlement agenda.

[60] To be sure, the Belt Road Court is a Chinese domestic institution. Because international judicialization involves the transferring of international disputes into the legal arena, special bodies created to deal with transnational disputes fit the definition. For more, see Alter, Helfer, and Hafner Burton (n 11) 453.
[61] Maya Steinitz, *The Case for an International Court of Civil Justice* (Cambridge University Press 2018).
[62] R Daniel Kelemen, *Eurolegalism: The Transformation of Law and Regulation in the European Union* (Harvard University Press 2011).
[63] Martin Shapiro, *Courts: A Comparative Political Analysis* (University of Chicago Press 1981).
[64] Alter, "The Future of International Law" (n 3) 25.

# Index

*For the benefit of digital users, indexed terms that span two pages (e.g., 52–53) may, on occasion, appear on only one of those pages.*